THE UNITED STATES AND IRAN:

A Documentary History

THE

UNITED STATES

AND

IRAN

A DOCUMENTARY HISTORY

Yonah Alexander and Allan Nanes, Editors

Prepared in Association with the
World Power Studies Program, the
Center for Strategic and International Studies,
Georgetown University

ALETHEIA BOOKS

UNIVERSITY PUBLICATIONS OF AMERICA

ISBN: 0-89093-378-2

Library of Congress Catalog Card Number: 80-53318

Manufactured in the United States of America

Contents

Introduction

The dramatic downfall of Shahanshah (King of Kings) Mohammed Reza Pahlavi in January 1979, after a 37-year rule, marked the end of an era in which the United States had pursued a basically benign policy toward Iran, a country of enormous strategic and economic importance in the Middle East. Less than a year later, in November 1979, the seizure of the U.S. Embassy in Tehran and of some 60 American hostages by Iranian revolutionaries brought home to all Americans, in the most brutal fashion, the fact that there had indeed been a radical transformation in the relations between the United States and Iran, and that the new relationship between these two powers would be different from any in the annals of U.S. history.

The plight of the hostages and the strategy and tactics for winning their release dominated U.S. policy toward Iran—and some would say it dominated U.S. foreign policy generally—at least until the abortive military mission to rescue them some six months later. Regardless of how the current difficult and frustrating crisis of the hostages will ultimately be resolved, it is clear—with the United States depicted as the "great Satan" of Ayatollah Ruhollah Khomeini's rhetoric—that much has changed since the early days of American-Iranian contact.

The very entry of the United States into diplomatic relations of any significance with Iran came about because the Iranians judged the United States to be a truly disinterested party. It was this perception that underlay Iran's first request for American advisers in 1911. Impressed with the noninterventionist attitude of the United States, Iran began looking to the United States to offset the British and Russian power in Iran. The first opportunity for any substantial U.S. involvement in Iran came during World War II, when Great Britain invited Iran to assist in the struggle against the Axis, and when to this end American noncombat forces were stationed in Iran. American policy toward Iran developed cautiously, however, because the United States recognized that Iran was primarily within the British-Soviet sphere of influence.

It was not until the Azerbaijan crisis of August 1945-December 1946 that the United States played an active role in Iranian affairs. The support that the United States gave at this critical period, which resulted in the withdrawal of Soviet troops from northwestern Iran, persuaded Iranians that the United States provided the counterweight which they were seeking. Yet the period of growing friendship between the two nations did not endure for very long before it was briefly interrupted.

The failure of the United States to grant Iran considerable aid to finance her plans for rapid economic development brought a wave of anti-American feelings in 1950. This development also contributed to some extent to the growth of Iranian nationalism, which culminated in the nationalization of the British-owned oil industry by Dr. Mohammed Mossadeq in March 1951. Following the rather unsatisfactory resolution of the Anglo-Iranian oil dispute, and fearful of an immediate or potential Soviet takeover, the United States allegedly intervened in Iranian internal affairs in mid-August 1953. With the ouster of Dr. Mossadeq and the return of the Shah to power, the British predominance was replaced with significant American influence in Iran.

Economic development was, of course, a key component in the late Shah's drive to make Iran a modern state. Until the current revolutionary turmoil set in, that development had made significant progress, giving Iran one of the world's highest sustained growth rates. Public investment was directed primarily toward building up governmental infrastructure and basic industry. Land reform was pushed through under the auspices of the Shah, but agricultural development lagged behind projections.

After the OPEC-engendered increase in oil prices in 1973—an increase in which Iran played a leading role—Iran's revenues from oil exports increased dramatically. The increased revenues were used not only for development, but also for massive arms purchases from the United States as Iran pursued, with the support of the United States, a policy aimed at regional dominance. That support originated in the Nixon Doctrine, which proclaimed that the United States would participate in the defense and development of allies and friends, but would not shoulder the entire burden; instead, those friends and allies, especially in the Third World, would be primarily responsible for their own security.

The increasing militarization of Iran may well have exacerbated the strains already present in the society. The pressures of modernization, resentment at the repression practiced by the Shah's regime, the distance between the ruling class and the nation as a whole, and widespread economic problems all contributed to a revolutionary upheaval that could not be contained. However, even the commentators who had long predicted the Shah's fall did not forecast the advent to power of the Ayatollah Khomeini and his Islamic Republic, free of foreign influences. From that point forward Iran's relations with the United States deteriorated rapidly, culminating in the seizure of the hostages.

The rush of events in Iran touched off a flurry of introspection in the United States concerning the policies which successive administrations had pursued in Iran. What had gone wrong? Why had the United States failed to assess correctly the strength of the elements which brought down the Shah? Why had the United States linked its fortunes so closely to those of the Shah in the first place? What did the national interests of the United States truly consist of as applied to Iran? And what are the full implications of the transformation of Iran from a friendly ally to a hostile adversary of the United States?

Clearly, these are some of the pertinent questions which require serious examination. In an attempt to deal with these issues we became aware of certain facts in connection with the availability of material on the complex and controversial relationship between the United States and Iran. First, while some documents are familiar to the scholar and the general reader, many more sources remain virtually unknown or forgotten. Second, the overwhelming proliferation of published and unpublished material requires some guidance for the specialist and the nonspecialist alike. Third, an exhaustive documentary history formed from all of the accessible sources would be far too great to fit within a single volume. And fourth, since there exists no single collection which brings together in a compact yet comprehensive fashion the entire documentary history of United States-Iranian relations, the need for such a work is obvious.

It is out of these realizations that this volume grew. We hope that it will serve as a reference work of lasting value by offering everyone interested in and concerned with United States-Iranian relations a convenient opportunity to find the information necessary for study and further research.

A Note on the Text

In typesetting hundreds of documents from a wide range of sources, we have found a number of instances of variations in the spelling of places and personal names. Except where we have corrected obvious typographical errors which were present in the original documents, we have retained the original spelling and punctuation of the documents.

The Editors*
September 1, 1980

---

* All of the opinions expressed in the commentaries are those of the editors and not of the institutions with which they are affiliated.

The editors wish to thank Randolph Boehm, research editor, for his untiring assistance in locating the documents for this book.

1

A Peripheral Relationship: 1856 - World War II

Throughout the nineteenth century and in the early years of the twentieth, Iran (or Persia as it was then known) was a country remote from American diplomatic concerns. There was no crisis of any kind involving the two countries. The Treaty of Commerce and Navigation, which was signed in 1856, was the main point of reference for relations between the two countries until the 1930s.

This very lack of interest in Iranian affairs became a diplomatic asset for the United States when Iran sought advisers to administer its finances in 1911. An American, Morgan Shuster, was picked, largely because he came from a country that was not suspected of attempting to aggrandize itself at the expense of Iran. Unfortunately, the Shuster Mission accomplished little, falling victim to both Russian intrigue and Persian inertia. But the reputation of the United States as a trustworthy outsider did not suffer.

In the years immediately following the first World War, as the documentation shows, the United States began to take a more active interest in the future of Iran, to the extent of opposing perceived threats to its integrity and independence. This concern may have been a factor in Iran's decision to seek U.S. help once again in straightening out its tangled finances. But the mission headed by Arthur Millspaugh was opposed by powerful vested interests and eventually it was withdrawn with its task uncompleted.

Following Millspaugh's departure, there was no special U.S. concern with Iran or any unusual U.S. presence there until the United States became a belligerent in World War II. Until that time, Iran was a backwater for American diplomacy, a Middle Eastern kingdom at the outer edges of U.S. consciousness. Few Americans were aware of the efforts of Reza Shah (father of the late Shah) to modernize his country, and perhaps fewer cared.

The distance between the two governments in the 1930s is illustrated in the documents from that era. In what might otherwise be seen in a somewhat humorous vein, there were Iranian protests at the arrest of their ambassador for speeding, and at newspaper stories concerning Reza Shah's background, which the latter sought vainly to suppress. When he could not get his way, he withdrew his diplomatic representatives. Iran thus displayed a rather superficial understanding of the meaning of democracy and the functioning of the American government. The United States, on the other hand, was apparently little disturbed by this action, thus illustrating the relatively low value it placed on Iran's friendship. Indeed, throughout the rest of the 1930s, Iran remained a minor factor in U.S. diplomacy.

TREATY OF FRIENDSHIP AND COMMERCE

December 13, 1856	*Treaty signed at Constantinople.*
January 16, 1857	*Ratified by Persia.*
March 10, 1857	*Senate advice and consent to ratification.*
March 12, 1857	*Ratified by the President of the United States.*
June 13, 1857	*Ratifications exchanged at Constantinople.*
June 13, 1857	*Entered into force.*
August 18, 1857	*Proclaimed by the President of the United States.*
May 10, 1928	*Terminated.*

In the name of God the Clement and the Merciful.

The President of the United States of North America, and his Majesty as exalted as the Planet Saturn; the Sovereign to whom the Sun serves as a standard; whose splendor and magnificence are equal to that of the Skies; the Sublime Sovereign, the Monarch whose armies are as numerous as the Stars; whose greatness calls to mind that of Jeinshid; whose magnificence equals that of Darius; the Heir of the Crown and Throne of the Kayanians; the Sublime Emperor of all Persia, being both equally and sincerely desirous of establishing relations of Friendship between the two Governments, which they wish to strengthen by a

Treaty of Friendship and Commerce, reciprocally advantageous and useful to the Citizens and subjects of the two High contracting parties, have for this purpose named for their Plenipotentiaries,

The President of the United States of North America, Carroll Spence, Minister Resident of the United States near the Sublime Porte; and His Majesty the Emperor of all Persia, His Excellency Emin ul Molk Farrukh Khan, Ambassador of His Imperial Majesty the Shah, decorated with the portrait of the Shah, with the great cordon blue and bearer of the girdle of Diamonds, &c, &c, &c, &c.

And the said Plenipotentiaries having exchanged their full powers, which were found to be in proper and due form, have agreed upon the following articles.

ARTICLE I

There shall be hereafter a sincere and constant good understanding between the Government and citizens of the United States of North America and the Persian Empire and all Persian subjects.

ARTICLE II

The Ambassadors or Diplomatic agents, whom it may please either of the two high contracting parties to send and maintain near the other, shall be received and treated, they and all those composing their Missions, as the Ambassadors and Diplomatic agents of the most favored nations are received and treated in the two respective countries; and they shall enjoy there, in all respects, the same prerogatives and immunities.

ARTICLE III

The citizens and subjects of the two high contracting parties, travellers, merchants, manufacturers and others, who may reside in the Territory of either Country, shall be respected and efficiently protected by the authorities of the Country and their agents, and treated in all respects as the subjects and citizens of the most favored Nation are treated.

They may reciprocally bring by land or by sea into either Country, and export from it all kinds of merchandise and products, and sell, exchange or buy, and transport them to all places in the Territories of either of the high contracting parties. It being however understood that the merchants of either nation, who shall engage in the internal commerce of either country, shall be governed, in respect to such commerce by the laws of the country in which such commerce is carried on; and in case either of the High contracting powers shall hereafter grant other privileges concerning such internal commerce to the citizens or subjects of other Governments the same shall be equally granted to the merchants of either nation engaged in such internal commerce within the territories of the other.

ARTICLE IV

The merchandise imported or exported by the respective citizens or subjects of the two high contracting parties shall not pay in either country on their arrival or departure, other duties than those which are charged in either of the countries on the merchandise or products imported or exported by the merchants and subjects of the most favored Nation, and no exceptional tax under any name or pretext whatever shall be collected on them in either of the two Countries.

ARTICLE V

All suits and disputes arising in Persia between Persian subjects and citizens of the United States shall be carried before the Persian tribunal to which such matters are usually referred at the place where a Consul or agent of the United States may reside, and shall be discussed and decided according to Equity, in the presence of an employeé of the Consul or agent of the United States.

All suits and disputes which may arise in the Empire of Persia between citizens of the United States, shall be referred entirely for trial and for adjudication to the Consul or agent of the United States residing in the Province wherein such suits and disputes may have arisen, or in the Province nearest to it, who shall decide them according to the laws of the United States.

All suits and disputes occurring in Persia between the citizens of the United States and the subjects of other foreign Powers shall be tried and adjudicated by the intermediation of their respective Consuls or agents.

In the United States Persian subjects in all disputes arising between themselves, or between them and citizens of the United States or Foreigners shall be judged according to the rules adopted in the United States respecting the subjects of the most favored nation.

Persian subjects residing in the United States, and citizens of the United States residing in Persia shall when charged with criminal offences be tried and judged in Persia and the United States in the same manner as are the subjects and citizens of the most favored nation residing in either of the above-mentioned countries.

ARTICLE VI

In case of a citizen or subject of either of the contracting parties dying within the Territories of the other, his effects shall be delivered up integrally to the family or partners in business of the Deceased, and in case he has no relations or partners, his effects in either Country shall be delivered up to the Consul or agent of the Nation of which the Deceased was a subject or citizen, so that he may dispose of them in accordance with the laws of his country.

ARTICLE VII

For the protection of their citizens or subjects and their commerce respectively, and in order to facilitate good and equitable relations between the citizens and subjects of the two countries, the two high contracting parties reserve the right to maintain a Diplomatic Agent at either seat of Government, and to name each three Consuls in either Country, those of the United States shall reside at Teheran, Bender Bushir, and Tauris; those of Persia at Washington, New York and New Orleans.

The Consuls of the high contracting parties shall reciprocally enjoy in the territories of the other, where their residences shall be established, the respect, privileges and immunities granted in either country to the Consuls of the most favored Nation. The Diplomatic Agent or Consuls of the United States shall not protect secretly or publicly the subjects of the Persian Government, and they shall never suffer a departure from the principles here laid down and agreed to by mutual consent.

And it is further understood, that if any of those Consuls shall engage in trade, they shall be subjected to the same laws and usages to which private individuals of their Nation engaged in commercial pursuits in the same place are subjected.

And it is also understood by the High contracting parties, that the Diplomatic and Consular Agents of the United States shall not employ a greater number of domestics than is allowed by Treaty to those of Russia residing in Persia.

ARTICLE VIII

And the high contracting parties agree that the present Treaty of Friendship and Commerce cemented by the sincere good feeling, and confidence which exists between the Governments of the United States and Persia, shall be in force for the term of ten years from the exchange of its ratification, and if before the expiration of the first ten years neither of the high contracting parties shall have announced, by official notification to the other, its intention to arrest the operation of said Treaty, it shall remain binding for one year beyond that time, and so on until the expiration of twelve months, which will follow a similar notification, whatever the time may be at which it may take place; and the Plenipotentiaries of the two high contracting parties further agree to exchange the ratifications of their respective Governments at Constantinople in the space of six months or earlier if practicable.

In faith of which, the respective Plenipotentiaries of the two high contracting parties have signed the present Treaty and have attached their seals to it.

Done in duplicate in Persian and English, the thirteenth day of December one thousand eight hundred and fifty six, and of the Hijéreh the fifteenth day of the moon of Rebiul Sany one thousand two hundred and seventy three of Constantinople.

CARROLL SPENCE
EMIN UL MOLK FARRUKH KHAN

EARLY DIPLOMATIC COMMUNICATIONS

Condolences on President McKinley's Assassination

Mr. Tyler to Mr. Hay

No. 67

Legation of the United States
Teheran, September 16, 1901

SIR: On Saturday, the 14th instant, about half past 4 in the afternoon, I received your telegram announcing that the President died at a quarter past 2 on the night of the 14th.

I immediately wrote out a notification and sent a copy to the foreign minister with a request that he would lay it before His Majesty the Shah. . . . The Shah sent one of his sons-in-law, a personage of high distinction, and whom I have known some years. He was instructed to say that His Majesty was greatly affected at the receipt of this sad intelligence, and that he considered the grief and loss of the American Government and people was his own, and that they had his truest and most-genuine sympathy. . . .

I have, [etc.,]

JOHN TYLER
Vice Consul-General, in Charge.

Congratulations of the Shah on the Accession of President Roosevelt

The Shah of Persia to President Roosevelt

No. 70

Teheran, September 20, 1901

On the occasion of the accession of your excellency to the Presidency I sincerely congratulate you, and express the best wishes that I make for your happiness and the prosperity of the United States.

MOZAFFER ED DINE

President Roosevelt to the Shah of Persia

Executive Mansion
Washington, September 23, 1901

I reciprocate your friendly greeting with cordial wishes for your welfare and the prosperity of Persia.

THEODORE ROOSEVELT

Congratulations on the Anniversary of the Shah's Birthday

Mr. Tyler to Mr. Hay

Legation of the United States
No. 70   *Teheran, September 28, 1901*

SIR: I have the honor to inform you that in accordance with general custom I attended this morning the diplomatic reception held by His Majesty the Shah, at the palace in Teheran, to celebrate his birthday. This is an annual function, and is made the occasion of some pleasant courtesies between the Shah and the representatives of foreign countries.

He made inquiries about the President's health, and told me that he had been given to understand that he was a personage of great ability and force of character. I replied that such was the general opinion.

In consequence of the legation being in mourning for the late President, I did not attend the banquet given in the evening by the prime minister, and on this account I was kindly excused.

I inclose a copy and translation of the usual note sent to the minister for foreign affairs on the morning of the Shah's birthday.

I have, [etc.,]   JOHN TYLER
Vice Consul-General in Charge

THE SHUSTER MISSION

The Persian Chargé d'Affaires to the Secretary of State

Imperial Legation of Persia
No. 21   *Washington, December 28, 1910*

EXCELLENCY: I have the honor to transmit to your excellency an exact copy of a cablegram which I have received from our minister of foreign affairs, for your kind consideration and attention.

Accept, [etc.,]   MIRZA ALI KULI KAHN

[INCLOSURE]

The Minister for Foreign Affairs to the Persian Minister at Washington

Teheran, December 25, 1910

Request immediately Secretary of State put you in communication with impartial American financial people and arrange preliminary employment for three years subject to ratification by Parliament of distinterested American experts as treasurer general to organize and conduct collection and disbursement revenues, assisted by one expert accountant and one inspector to superintend actual collection in provinces; secondly, one director to organize and conduct direct taxation assisted by one expert inspector similar to above. American minister informs us Secretary of State ready and willing. Avoid other methods of proceeding and irresponsible persons who may offer advice and services. Give exact copy to Secretary of State and do whatever he may suggest. Wire reports briefly. No. 9876.

HUSSEIN KULI

The Secretary of State to the Persian Chargé d'Affaires

Department of State

No. 34   *Washington, January 5, 1911*

SIR: I have the honor to acknowledge the receipt of your note No. 21 of the 28th instant, transmitting a copy of a cablegram received by your legation from the ministry of foreign affairs at Teheran requesting the assistance of this department in placing you in communication with American financial experts with a view to the ultimate employment by the Persian Government of five American financial assistants.

In reply I have the honor to inform you that this matter is receiving the kindly consideration of this Department, with a view to effecting, if possible, a compliance with the wishes of your Government.

Accept, [etc.,]   P.C. KNOX

The Persian Chargé d'Affaires to the Secretary of State

Imperial Persian Legation
Washington, February 17, 1911

SIR: I have the honor to acknowledge the receipt of your communications of January 19 and February 14, in which the State Department transmitted to this legation two lists of names suggested, at my Government's request, as being financial experts suitable to undertake the work of reorganizing the finances of the Persian Empire.

As the department is aware, the men selected are as follows: Mr. W. Morgan Shuster, of Washington, D.C.; Mr. F.S. Cairns, of Iloilo, P.I.; Mr. C.S. McCaskey, of the New York customhouse; Mr. R.W. Hills, of Washington, D.C.; Mr. Bruce G. Dickey, of Pine Island, Minn.

Of the three names submitted on the Department's list of January 19, I talked first with Mr. W. Morgan Shuster, who was at the head of the list.

In view of the Department's considerate suggestion to the effect that when the two more important posts had been filled, the selection of the other three assistants should be made in consultation with those two men, and that the Department would approve this course, I have the honor to inform you that Mr. C.S. McCaskey, acting deputy surveyor in the New York customhouse, was recommended by Mr. Shuster to the Department and myself as his immediate assistant. I understand that the War Department is familiar with Mr. McCaskey's previous services and record, and that the State Department is likewise aware of them.

On January 30, after making tentative arrangements as to terms and conditions with these gentlemen, I cabled my Government submitting these terms for approval, and February 8 I received a cable dispatch approving the terms and conditions in the form in which they were recommended by me.

An accurate but not strictly literal translation of said cablegram is as follows:

Teheran, February 8, 1911

Persian Legation, *Washington:* Cablegram regarding financial assistants received. Compensation approved. Minimum period engagement three years. Cable traveling expenses for five. Determine remaining conditions in favor of Government. Important conditions are:

(1) Being obedient to orders of ministers of finance;

(2) Option of Government to annul contracts with payment of six months' compensation;

(3) In case sickness lasts more than three months Government shall have right to annul contract;

(4) In case of nonfulfillment of duty Government shall have right to annul contract without payment of any advance compensation or traveling expenses;

(5) From day of arrival in Teheran salaries shall be paid at end of every three months;

(6) In case assistants shall resign of their own accord, compensation shall be paid for period of actual services rendered without return traveling expenses;

(7) Assistants shall not interfere with religious or political matters nor engage in commerce.

No. 87   Mohtachemos-Saltaneh

In the name of my Government I have the honor to express sincere thanks for the kindly interest and good offices of your Department in assisting me to bring these negotiations to a successful termination.

I have, [etc.,]   Mirza Ali Kuli Kahn

The Secretary of State to the Persian Chargé d'Affaires

Department of State No. 36   *Washington, February 24, 1911*

Sir: I have the honor to acknowledge the receipt of your note of the 17th instant, in further reference to the matter of employment by your Government of five American financial assistants, stating that arrangements have now been practically concluded with Mr. W. Morgan Shuster, Mr. F.S. Cairns, Mr. R.S. McCaskey, Mr. R.W. Hills, and Mr. Bruce G. Dickey, for service with the ministry of finance.

It is a source of gratification to this Department that it has been able, as you so kindly intimate in your note, to be of assistance to your Government in this matter; and it is my earnest hope that the services rendered by the American advisers will be of material assistance in the development of satisfactory financial and economic conditions in the Persian Empire.

Accept, [etc.,]   For Mr. Knox: HUNTINGTON WILSON

The American Minister to the Secretary of State

American Legation
No. 128   *Teheran, May 24, 1911*

SIR: Mr. Shuster, Mr. McCaskey, and Mr. Dickey arrived here a few days ago and have been installed for the present in the Attarbek Park, the finest place in Teheran as a residence. They have made a good impression on the Persians, are working already with the finance minister, Mamtaz Ed Dowleh. Mr. Hills, I understand, has arrived at Engeli. The three I have met seem to be admirably chosen.

I am, [etc.,]   CHARLES W. RUSSELL

American Legation
No. 182   *Teheran, June 13, 1911*

SIR: I inclose a translation of an act of the Medjles passed today, giving full powers in financial matters or Treasury business to Mr. Shuster. This was passed by an almost unanimous vote. Little overt opposition.

I am, [etc.,]   CHARLES W. RUSSELL

The Acting Secretary of State to the American Minister

Department of State
Washington, July 31, 1911

In view of alarmist press telegrams, report concisely by telegraph concerning the political situation, with particular reference to the return of the deposed Shah and the attitude of the British and Russian Governments toward the internal situation and toward the American financial advisers.

ADEE

The American Minister to the Secretary of State

American Legation
Teheran, August 1, 1911

Renewal of effort by Russian minister to prevent Shuster controlling expenditures of customs receipts and have Belgian director of customs pay Russian loan coupons and other fixed charges without Shuster's authorization as required by recent Persian law. No question except as to which of them shall direct bank custodian of customs to pay, as Shuster, in writing, long since affirmed his intention to do so. Russian minister and now other legations, including German Legation, claim contracts call for payment by customs administration.

Today minister for foreign affairs complained to Berlin claiming Shuster is paying officer of customs administration. German minister and Italian chargé d'affaires are partly influenced by Shuster's omission to call upon anyone. Russian minister seeking, I have reason to believe to prevent Shuster's success. Russian minister of finance, Russian bank, British bank and, after a struggle, Belgian customs director, had acquiesced in Shuster's views vigorously asserted.

RUSSELL

The Persian Chargé d'Affaires to the Secretary of State

Imperial Persian Legation
No. 64   *Washington, November 25, 1911*

EXCELLENCY: I have the honor to inclose for your excellency's consideration the translation of a cipher cable received this afternoon from the minister of foreign affairs at Teheran. As the inclosed cable explains, I am advised to communicate with my Government by cable as soon as I may have the pleasure of receiving a reply from your excellency.

Accept, [etc.,]   MIRZA ALI KULI KHAN

[INCLOSURE]

The Minister for Foreign Affairs to the Persian Legation at Washington

Teheran, November 25, 1911

Through the cables Nos. 968 and 967 you have been advised of the attitude of the Russians, of interrupting the relations, of ordering troops, and finally of compliance with their demands; and you know that all these (Russian) steps are directed toward (forcing) the dismissal of Mr. Shuster. For they consider Mr. Shuster's activities such as the "opposition to the Belgians, the engaging of Maj. Stokes, and the appointing of Englishmen for the north, and especially the publication of communications and correspondence against Russia in the English papers"—as opposed to their policy and interest. They are therefore exerting themselves to destroy Mr. Shuster's work and to subject this Government to such threats and pressure which would destroy the very independence of this country. Some (?) days ago (?) Mr. Shuster sent a long letter, either (?) against Russia and England and especially against Russia, to the (London) Times, and he afterwards published and spread that letter in Teheran.

Yesterday, when I went to the Russian legation for apology, and I supposed that the compliance with the demand made in reference to the Garden of Shoaes Salteneh will remove their pretext for the sending of troops, I found that the Russian minister brought up the subject of the letter (i.e., Mr. Shuster's to the Times), claiming it to be a "great insult to the Russian Government," and wishing to use it as a pretext against withdrawing the troops. I am certain that the proposal which they (Russians) will make to us would be the dismissal of Mr. Shuster, and on this matter the affair of Persia and Russia will reach the point of extreme difficulty, in such a manner that we might either consent to Mr. Shuster's removal or to the actual, immediate destruction of the country.

You must do your best to call on the minister of foreign affairs and discuss this matter and immediately learn the view of the United States Government. In any event immediately cable the view of the United States foreign office as to the policy of action which the Persian Government must adopt in this instance. Third of Zi-haja. No. 889

VOSSOUGH-ED DOUVLEH

The Department of State to the Persian Legation at Washington

[AIDE MÉMOIRE]

Department of State
Washington, November 27, 1911

On November 26 the Department of State received from the Imperial Legation of Persia a copy of a telegram to the general effect that various activities of Mr. W. Morgan Shuster, treasurer general of Persia, including press propaganda critical of the attitude of certain foreign powers, are complained of by the Imperial Russian Government and have thus involved the Government of Persia in difficulties.

The Persian chargé d'affaires having been instructed to discuss the situation with the Secretary of State and to seek the views and advice of the American Government in the premises, the Secretary of State desires to express his appreciation of the considerate motive of this communication.

In view of the circumstances under which the Persian Government selected and engaged Mr. Shuster, an American citizen, to fill an important post as an official of Persia, the Government of the United States recognizes that the difficulties indicated present for the decision of the Government of Persia political questions in regard to which the Secretary of State does not find it appropriate to offer any suggestion.

The American Minister to the Secretary of State

American Legation
Teheran, November 30, 1911

Have shown Shuster paraphrase your telegram November 28, 5 p.m. Persian Government apparently were not informed of your statement by Persian chargé d'affaires. At his request I transmit the following from Shuster:

> In reference to my contract with Persian Government on file Department of State, I have faithfully performed same, executing duties of treasurer general under greatest difficulties to the satisfaction of Persian Legislature, Government, and people. At noon yesterday Russia presented 48-hour ultimatum to Persia demanding my dismissal and that my assistants should be subjected to the approval of Russia and England. Six other Americans serving here with contracts similar to mine and eight others en route to sign contracts, all authorized by Persian Legislature. Russia evidently intends making it impossible for Americans to serve Persian Government. Russian semiofficial press has long been waging campaign of abuse against me, calling me Jew. Apparently no prospect of Persian Parliament revoking my contract. Request prompt information as to protection to which American citizens having contracts made with friendly sovereign nation are entitled under these peculiar circumstances. I am personally indifferent to result, but feel heavy responsibility for 14 other Americans brought here largely through my influence. It is probable that the failure of Parliament revoke my contract will be followed by actual interference by Russia with my duties, powers, and rights thereunder. I am asking this information not as Persian official but as American citizen.

RUSSELL

The Secretary of State to the American Minister at Teheran

Department of State
Washington, December 1, 1911

Your telegram of November 30, 10 p.m. In response to an appeal for the influence of the United States in the present crisis the Persian chargé d'affaires has today been informed that under all the circumstances this Government has nothing to add at this time to what was indicated in the aide mémoire handed him on the 27th ultimo, the pertinent part of which was telegraphed you on November 28, 5 p.m. This indisposition to interfere or advise as to the present decisions and political questions of paramount importance to Persia and directly affecting other powers must be clearly understood by the Persian Government.

Turning to the status of Mr. Shuster and his assistants in their capacity as American citizens you will impress upon the Government of Persia the expectation of this Government that all proper measures be taken to insure their personal safety and well-being.

In conversation with your British and Russian colleagues you will assure yourself that their Governments will not fail, either now or in case a changing situation should throw upon them heavier responsibilities, to insure to Shuster and his associates the personal security consideration and justice due them as American citizens.

The legation will, of course, afford these American citizens all proper protection in case of jeopardy and will safeguard any rights growing out of the terms of their contracts with the Persian Government.

KNOX

The American Ambassador to Russia to the Secretary of State

American Embassy
No. 129   St. Petersburg, December 15, 1911

SIR: I have the honor to report that I called today upon M. Sazonoff, the minister of foreign affairs.

In connection with Persian matters he confirmed the statement telegraphed to you on December 8, 1911, to the effect that complete personal protection would be given to Mr. Shuster, including, if necessary, an armed escort out of Persia.

He added that Mr. Shuster's selection was particularly disagreeable to Russia, not only on account of his action, but because he is a Jew. I ventured to say that in this at least I thought he was mistaken, but he insisted upon it with great emphasis and ascribed Shuster's interests to this alleged fact. Nevertheless he assured me that Shuster's personal protection by Russia could be absolutely relied upon.

I have, [etc.,]   CURTIS GUILD

The Secretary of State to the American Minister at Teheran

Department of State
Washington, December 27, 1911

No telegram received from you between your December 22, 6 p.m., and your December 26, 11 a.m., which has been acted upon. Has Mr. Shuster resigned or been dismissed from his official Persian position, and when does he plan to depart from Teheran? Do his associates also leave, and how many American citizens in the party?

KNOX

The American Minister to the Secretary of State

American Legation
Teheran, December 28, 1911

Your telegram December 27, 2 p.m. Have sent no telegram between dates mentioned.

The Cabinet notified Shuster in writing that the Cabinet and the commission mentioned in my telegram of December 22, 6 p.m., yielding to the ultimatum were compelled to recall him from the Persian service, employing expression similar to language of the ultimatum. He answered acquiescing and expressing willingness to turn over to successor who might be designated. Polite oral messages accompanied the

Cabinet communication and Shuster's response. He hopes to depart from Teheran within a week or two. Date not fixed yet. His party will consist only wife, two small daughters, nurse, secretary, and one or two American men.

RUSSELL

UNITED STATES ATTITUDE TOWARD PERSIAN NATIONAL ASPIRATIONS

The Persian Minister (Mehdi Khan) to the Secretary of State

Washington, December 17, 1917

DEAR MR. SECRETARY: The war aims and noble sentiments of the United States Government, so eloquently set forth by His Excellency, President Wilson, in his message to Congress on December 3 [4], wherein a permanent peace is defined as one based upon international justice and guaranteeing the sovereignty and independence of every nation, have encouraged and actuated the Imperial Persian Government to appeal to the Government of the United States to assist Persia to share in the benefits of these great blessings.

The Persian Government has therefore advised this Legation by cable to officially seek the assistance of the United States Government in securing for Persia representation in the peace conference which will convene at the termination of this great war. It is the ardent desire of Persia to place her sovereignty and independence upon a firm foundation without in any way infringing upon the rights of others.

It is a regrettable fact that in spite of her efforts from the beginning of the war to protect her neutrality, both of the belligerent groups have time and again violated Persian neutrality, and her territory has not been free from the forces of both sides. These forces have repeatedly inflicted severe losses upon the subjects of Persia in the north and in the south, as is well known by Your Excellency and by the United States Government.

Besides the heavy losses resulting from actual battles between hostile troops, who have burned and destroyed towns and villages, the Russian troops of both the former and recent *régimes* have perpetrated great intentional wrongs upon the people of Persia, and have levied large sums upon various communities, not to mention large supplies of food which they have requisitioned and extorted from the people. A detailed list of these losses will be submitted for the information of the

United States Government.

Persia feels that these losses and wrongs necessitate and justify her to have representation at the peace conference, in order that the obstacles interposed through foreign interference with her internal affairs, which have threatened her independence and retarded her progress and development, may be wholly removed. These include certain treaties and conditions which foreign powers have forcibly imposed upon Persia. Another obstacle which has resulted in internal disorder and a violation of Persia's sovereignty is the illegal activities of the military forces of the neighboring powers on Persian territory. The Legation therefore feels impelled to request the United States Government to use its good offices to the end that the forces of foreign powers who have wrought such illegal acts should evacuate the territories of Persia. The Legation, likewise, in view of recent developments in the Near East, requests the United States Government to make a declaration which will guarantee the sovereignty and independence of Persia. The granting of such help to Persia at this time will not only confirm and establish the principles of humanity and justice, which the United States so nobly advocates for all nations, but it will secure the foundations of that lasting peace which constitutes the chief aim for which America entered the war.

Furthermore, it is my personal belief that, in view of the recent important events in Russia and the Near East, a favorable answer by the United States Government to the request from Persia will produce an immediate good effect in Persia and yield useful results for all concerned.

The Legation begs to submit herewith a memorandum containing the several requests made by Persia of the United States Government.

Please accept [etc.]   MEHDI KHAN

The Persian Legation to the Department of State

[MEMORANDUM]

. . . The just aims for the attaining of which Persia seeks the help and good offices of the United States are expressed in the seven following paragraphs:

1. Persian participation in the peace conference.
2. To guarantee Persia's independence and sovereignty.
3. The evacuation of Persian territory by foreign troops.
4. To indemnify Persia for the losses inflicted upon her.
5. To eliminate foreign influence from the north and the south.
6. To respect the neutrality of Persia.
7. To revise the treaty of Turkomanchai (1828) and to abolish all other arrangements and agreements which have been forcibly imposed upon Persia, especially the forcible impositions of recent times.

*The Secretary of State to the British Ambassador on
Special Mission (Reading)*

Washington, February 14, 1918

My Dear Mr. Ambassador: I have received your Embassy's note of
January 30, No. 138, stating that His Majesty's Secretary of State for
Foreign Affairs recently addressed a note to the Persian Minister in
London giving him the assurance that the British Government was
genuinely anxious to assist the Persian Government to maintain the
independence and integrity of Persia and that the British Minister at
Teheran would be instructed to discuss with the Persian authorities the
manner in which this object could be carried out in such a manner as to
be acceptable to Persian public opinion; and enquiring whether the
United States Government would be willing to instruct the American
representative at Teheran to associate himself with the British and
French Ministers in making a joint declaration to the Persian Government to the effect that it was the "desire and determination of the three
Governments to respect the integrity of Persia and to promote the
development of the country on independent and self-determined lines as
soon as the abnormal conditions created by the present war have been
removed."

In reply I beg to state that it does not seem advisable for the United
States Government to instruct the American Minister at Teheran to
associate himself with the British Minister in making the proposed
declaration to the Persian Government. As I have already indicated to
the British Government, this Government is genuinely desirous of
assisting in the restoration of a normal condition of affairs in Persia on
account of its friendship both for Great Britain and for Persia, but in
view of the very different positions which Great Britain and the United
States occupy towards Persia, I cannot but feel that a joint declaration by
Great Britain and the United States would not be the wisest procedure at
this time. Moreover, I feel that a declaration to the effect that the British,
French and American Governments were ready to promote the development of Persia on self-determined lines "as soon as the abnormal conditions created by the present war have been removed" might be
misinterpreted in Persia.

On January 19 the Department was advised by the American Minister at Teheran that he had received a protest from the Persian Government against an alleged violation of Persian sovereignty and
independence through the organization of Persia of military forces
financed by the United States and the Entente. On January 23 [24] this
Government instructed the American Minister at Teheran to deny
emphatically that the United States was financing any military forces
being organized in Persia and at the same time to inform the Persian
Government that the United States strongly sympathized with the desire

of Persia to maintain its freedom and sovereignty and would not be a party to any act which would infringe such freedom and sovereignty. Inasmuch, therefore, as the United States has already indicated to Persia its attitude toward Persian sovereignty and independence, I feel it would be perhaps superfluous at the present time for the United States to make any further declaration in this respect.

The note which His Majesty's Secretary of State for Foreign Affairs has addressed to the Persian Minister in London gives an assurance that His Majesty's Government are anxious to assist the Persian Government to maintain the independence and integrity of Persia, and it seems to me, therefore, that the first important step will have been taken when the instruction mentioned in Mr. Barclay's note under acknowledgment is sent to the British Minister at Teheran.

If you will be good enough to let me know when this instruction is sent, I shall be happy to instruct the American Minister at Teheran to keep in touch with his British colleague and advise me of the results of the discussions between the British Minister and the Persian authorities.

May I repeat once more that I shall also be glad to receive any further views which you may have on the Persian situation, more especially if, in your opinion, this Government can help in any way, with the exception of the joint declaration above referred to, towards preserving the independence of Persia and improving the relations between Persia and the Entente Powers.

I am [etc.]   ROBERT LANSING

The Minister in Persia (Caldwell) to the Secretary of State

Teheran, August 31, 1918, 5 p.m.

Treaties of seven powers besides Russia contain provisions for extraterritorial rights as reported in civil cases, which privileges accrue to the United States by reason of most favored nation treatment. The Russian commercial treaty of Turkomanchai is the only one, however, which provides for criminal jurisdiction of foreigners and this privilege would seem to be lost to all countries by the abrogation of all Russian treaties. In view of the very unsatisfactory system of justice in Persia I consider it essential for safeguarding our rights that Americans should not be brought before a Persian criminal court.

Present Cabinet inclined to approve action of late Cabinet but will not attempt to interfere with treaties of other nations.

Russian concession contracts were very onerous to Persia and in view of this and the friendly attitude of Persians of all classes [garbled passage] it would not seem expedient to protest against this part of the abolition. As regards treaties, criminal jurisdiction is only important matter modified as far as America is concerned, and if Department does not think we can continue to claim this by right of present and immemorial use, a *modus vivendi*, by an exchange of notes or other means, could doubtless be arrived at. British Legation has informed Persian Government that matter has been referred to London but in meantime has signified its refusal to acquiesce in any unilateral abrogation by Persia of her treaties. Should the Department adopt similar views I should suggest reserving criminal jurisdiction privileges of Russian treaty to American citizens. German Legation has agreed to suspend article 13 of her treaty of 1873 giving her extraterritorial rights in civil cases; it is likely that such offer is merely to gain popular sentiment here during the war.

CALDWELL

The Persian Chargé (Ali-Kuli Khan) to the Secretary of State

No. 177   *Washington, October 5, 1918*

EXCELLENCY: I have the honor to submit for the information of your Government translations of recent communications received from the Persian Government, pertaining to the occupation of Persian territory by the troops of the belligerent powers, which, in violating the neutrality of Persia, has resulted in offending the public feeling and provoking a desperate situation, of which the ravaging famine is but one aspect. In presenting the enclosed data, I beg to state that Persia looks to America to insure her, after the war, against a recurrence of such hopeless conditions, which have afflicted the people of that ancient land. We have full confidence that the great principles of humanity and justice enunciated by your Government will in the day of peace extend their blessings towards Persia, as one of the countries which has endured long years of manifold trials with patience and long suffering.

Accept [etc.]   MIRZA ALI-KULI KHAN, N.D.

POSTWAR RELIEF TO PERSIA

The Minister in Persia (Caldwell) to the Secretary of State

Teheran, December 10, 1917, 9 a.m.

Unmitigated famine conditions continue throughout Persia as a result of crop failure and war, many starve daily. Food extremely scarce and prices unbelievable. Local relief inadequate and committees unable to relieve situation.

If American Red Cross or other organizations could assist local authorities and American Presbyterian Mission, such would be desirable and worthy and besides have a good political effect. See my telegram of October 22, 9 a.m., and dispatch No. 330 of October 4.

Caldwell

The Secretary of State to the Minister in Persia (Caldwell)

Washington, January 10, 1918, 6 p.m.

23. Your December 10, 9 a.m. If American Red Cross undertakes to furnish relief for famine how could relief supplies best be purchased and distributed?

Lansing

The Minister in Persia (Caldwell) to the Secretary of State

Teheran, January 22, 1918

Repetition [of my] January 14, 5 p.m. Your cipher telegram January 10, 6 p.m. Relief needs urgent for different cities. Report several deaths daily. Limited amount of wheat, rice, foodstuffs could be purchased throughout the provinces through the Persian Government, which fixes prices. Medical supplies would be most difficult. Importation of foodstuffs and supplies impracticable if not impossible. Prices exorbitant, wheat $15 to $20 per bushel. Distribution could be made through local American missionaries and existing committees. Persian citizens and authorities cooperating but task too great for them alone. One local organization spends $20,000 monthly in Teheran but cares for only 10 percent of city's needy. Conditions are similar in all the provinces.

Caldwell

The Secretary of State to the Vice Chairman of the American Red Cross (Wadsworth)

Washington, January 25, 1918

Sir: There is herewith enclosed to you a paraphrase of a telegram dated January 22, from the American Minister at Teheran, relative to the famine conditions in Persia.

Believing that a practical expression of American good will towards Persia, at the present time, would be very beneficial, the Department feels that if the American Red Cross is able to take any steps towards the alleviation of the famine conditions in Persia, such action, under present conditions, would be especially desirable.

I am [etc.]   For the Secretary of State: William Phillips
Assistant Secretary

The Acting Secretary of State to the Minister in Persia (Caldwell)

Washington, March 5, 1918, 7 p.m.

29. Your March 1. What is status Persian Cossacks referred to? Are they in service of Persian Government or under Russian control? Send detailed report of your information relative to conflict. Does Persian Government approve Turkish treatment of Armenians? It is of great interest to the United States that there should be no conflict between Persians and Armenians and German propaganda undoubtedly aims at producing such conflict. Have you no suggestions as to what can be done in this matter? Call attention of Persian Government to appropriation by American Committee for Armenian and Syrian Relief for distressed inhabitants of Persia, and also inform Persian Government that American Red Cross has appropriated a relief fund of $200,000 a month for two months, to be divided between distress in Turkey, Caucasus, and Persia. Red Cross states appropriation will probably continue for four additional months.

POLK

The Secretary of State to the Minister in Persia (Caldwell)

Washington, April 22, 1918.

44. Deliver following message to Persian Government and also Crown Prince at Tabriz:

The American Committee for Armenian and Syrian Relief working under the auspices of the Red Cross has for the past two years and a half sent over $1,880,000 for the relief of Moslems and Christians alike, irrespective of race, creed, or locality. Of the above sum, during the last few months more than $265,000 has been sent to Teheran for distribution to relieve Moslems there and at Meshed and other Persian towns, to purchase food, clothing, and medicines.

American diplomatic agents and American missionaries have distributed our money freely. The disinterested character of the missionaries, their educational, philanthropic work, their medical schools, have been known to Your Royal Highness, and they have had no political motives of any kind.

A cloud we understand has broken whereby some of those who have received our aid are at conflict with each other at Salmas and vicinity. In the name of humanity and for the love of freedom of which your great poets have sung, and for the sake of your great country, we appeal to Your Royal Highness to use your kind and great influence and the forces at your command to make peace among those at conflict irrespective of religion and nationality. May your country be a harbour for the oppressed ones until this bloody war is ended. We are ready for any service that Your Royal Highness may demand for the benefit of your nation and subjects. Signed The American Relief Committee.

LANSING

The Secretary of State to the Minister in Persia (Caldwell)

Washington, May 10, 1918, 6 p.m.

53. Report situation of Jews throughout all Persia.

LANSING

The Minister in Persia (Caldwell) to the Secretary of State

Teheran, May 13, 1918, 11 a.m.

Your telegram 53, May 10, 6 p.m. Needy Jews in Persia estimated thirty to forty thousand of which probably 25 per cent are starving and in dire need.

CALDWELL

The Secretary of State to the Minister in Persia (Caldwell)

Washington, May 29, 1918

60. Draw on Secretary of State $15,000 deposited by Joint Distribution Committee by method most advantageous to save exchange, consult Committee Bienfaisance Israelite, Teheran, Alliance Israelite, Hamadan, and British Consul, Ispahan, and other leaders, Jewish community especially, and distribute money relieving Jewish distress. Send detailed reports from local committees for Joint Distribution Committee at earliest opportunity.

LANSING

The Persian Minister of Foreign Affairs (Moshaver-ol-Mamalek) to the Secretary of State

Teheran [undated]
[Received November 21, 1918, 12:55 a.m.]

YOUR EXCELLENCY: At the time when Persia greets in her Capital the American Relief Mission headed by the Honorable Professor Judson, I hasten to beg Your Excellency kindly to convey to the noble nation of the United States the heartfelt thanks of the Persian Government and people for that charitable and benevolent action. I am convinced that this further mark of friendship and good will given to Persia by the United States will draw still closer the ties of good harmony existing between our two countries and will enhance the Persian people's friendship for the American nation and the growing esteem they profess for its Government, which in the days of trial always gives evidence of its true sympathy with Persia.

MOSHAVER-OL-MAMALEK

UNITED STATES PROTESTS BRITISH POSTWAR
ANGLO-PERSIAN AGREEMENT

The Secretary of State to the Ambassador in Great Britain (Davis)

Washington, August 20, 1919

5844. Your urgent 2831, August 18, 7 p.m. The Anglo-Persian agreement has caused a very unfavorable impression upon both the President and me and we are not disposed to ask our Minister at Teheran to assist the British Government or to ask him to preserve a friendly attitude toward this agreement. At Paris I asked of Mr. Balfour three times that the Persians have an opportunity to be heard before the Council of Foreign Ministers because of their claims and boundaries and because their territory had been a battle ground. Mr. Balfour was rather abrupt in refusing to permit them to have a hearing. It now appears that at the time I made these requests Great Britain was engaged in a secret negotiation to gain at least economic control of Persia. The secrecy employed and the silence observed seem contrary to the open and frank methods which ought to have prevailed and may well impair the bases of a peace inspired by friendliness. We cannot and will not do anything to encourage such secret negotiations or to assist in allaying the suspicion and dissatisfaction which we share as to an agreement negotiated in this manner.

You will respond to Lord Curzon's request in this general sense.

LANSING

The Secretary of State to the Minister in Persia (Caldwell)

Washington, September 4, 1919

Your 169, August 28. You are instructed to deny both to Persian officials, and to any one else interested in this matter, that America has refused to aid Persia. You will also state that the United States has constantly and consistently showed its interest in the welfare of Persia and that the American Mission at Paris several times endeavored earnestly to secure a hearing for the Persian Mission before the Peace Conference. The American Mission was surprised that it did not receive more support in this matter but the announcement of the new Anglo-Persian Treaty probably explains why the American Mission was unable to secure such hearing. It would appear also that the Persian Government at Teheran did not strongly support the efforts of its Mission at Paris.

The Government of the United States has learned with surprise of the recent Anglo-Persian Treaty which would seem to indicate that Persia does not desire American support and cooperation in the future, in spite of the fact that the Persian delegates in Paris strongly and openly sought our assistance.

LANSING

The Ambassador in Great Britain (Davis) to the Secretary of State

London, September 13, 1919, 2 p.m.

3039. Following letter received September 12th from Lord Curzon.

". . . I shall of course communicate the sense of your letter to my Government without delay as I did the request which you have made at our interview of the 18th. Prior to that meeting, my only knowledge touching the Anglo-Persian agreement had been gathered from the public announcement of its conclusion made some three days earlier, and it is perhaps unfortunate therefore that you gathered from our conversation any impression as to the attitude of my Government, of which I was then unaware. But I should tell you that upon communicating with Washington, I learned that neither the President nor the Secretary of State were favorably impressed by what they conceived to be the secrecy with which the agreement was negotiated, and felt that there had been some lack of frankness in the matter more especially as the presence of the Persian delegation in Paris seemed to offer numerous occasions for a full statement of the intentions and purposes of the British Government in the premises, and that they were therefore indisposed to take the responsibility of any steps which would indicate their approval of the treaty thus negotiated.

Upon receipt of this information I put myself in touch with Colonel House, repeating to him the conversation at Paris between him and yourself as you had detailed it to me. His recollection confirms your own as to the fact that you presented to him the inadvisability of receiving before the Conference the Persian delegation, representing that the subject of Persia should be otherwise dealt with,—all of which he repeated to the President. But unfortunately he cannot recall any allusion to the contents or character of the instant treaty or to the intention to negotiate an engagement of this sort and is thus unable to dispel the feeling of surprise which the President and Secretary entertain.

I welcome Your Lordship's letter, therefore, as affording an opportunity to clarify the situation and remove any misunderstanding which may exist."

Before transmitting this reply I submitted it to Colonel House, who confirms the accuracy of that portion relating to himself. Have also discussed subject with Lord Gray, who tells me he has advised Foreign Office to give out explanatory statement specifically announcing, among other things, intention to submit any customs changes to nations affected for their criticism.

DAVIS

The Secretary of State to the Ambassador in Great Britain (Davis)

Washington, October 4, 1919, 1 p.m.

6049. Your 3039 and 3098. It is noted that Lord Curzon in view of his conversation with Colonel House states that he was under the impression that the Government of the United States was aware of the character of the negotiations which he was conducting with the Persian Government and that he believed that the United States would give the agreement cordial approval. Colonel House recalls indeed a casual conversation with Lord Curzon regarding Persian affairs but it did not occur to him that he was being formally approached as the official channel of communication with the United States Government in this instance.

Lord Curzon's letter takes exception to a *communiqué* issued by the American Minister in Teheran on September 7 which was published in the local press of Teheran and which his Lordship states was of a nature to be regarded as a challenge to the Anglo-Persian agreement of an unfriendly and almost hostile character. He points out what he conceives to be a striking resemblance between the British Agreement with Persia and that which the American Government has under consideration with the Liberian Government. In conclusion his Lordship requests this Government, without delay, to inform the Persian Government and the Persian press that the *communiqué* above referred to was not intended to cast any aspersions on the Anglo-Persian agreement but only to refute any misapprehensions caused by an article in the Persian *Raad*.

You may advise Lord Curzon that the Government of the United States was not aware until formal announcement that an agreement was being negotiated by the British and Persian Governments; that the *Communiqué* above referred to sets forth the facts of the situation as viewed by this Government, and which it does not seem necessary to repeat herein.

On August 23 this Government was advised of the following article appearing in the *Raad*, the official cabinet organ in Teheran: "America, the only government able to assist Persia, abandoned her; the four great powers at Paris decided that Persia should be under protection and that it is a part of Great Britain's portion. Persia has been deceived by President Wilson's good workers [fine words?] and Persia is in the same position as Egypt." This was followed by other telegrams from the American Legation in Teheran indicating that the highest Persian officials openly stated that America had refused to aid Persia. In this connection you may remind his Lordship that the people of the United States have always been deeply interested in the welfare of Persia and during the recent terrible famine American philanthropy on a generous scale, came to the relief of suffering Persians and did what it could to mitigate the unhappy conditions then existing.

It was deemed essential therefore, by this Government in view of the statements of the Persian officials and press to authorize the American Minister at Teheran to deny that the United States had refused to aid Persia and it is not surprising that the Minister's denial soon became publicly known in Teheran. This Government may be pardoned in pointing out that the source of such action arose solely from the act of His Majesty's Government in concluding, without the preliminary knowledge and acquiescence of this Government, an agreement with the Government of the Shah which promises so materially to affect the relations of the United States with Persia.

Lord Curzon takes occasion to dwell upon the alleged similarity of the Liberian and Persian problems and of the relationships of the United States and Great Britain to those respective countries under the prospective agreements. It may not be amiss, therefore, to point out once more the underlying circumstances concerning the relations of the United States and Liberia.

The Republic of Liberia was founded one hundred years ago through agencies of the United States Government in conjunction with the American Colonization Society, a private enterprise.

Ever since its foundation, this Government has taken a deep interest in the welfare of Liberia and has repeatedly aided her in boundary troubles arising from the extensive encroachments of foreign powers. Latterly the assistance of this Government, as a completely disinterested friend of the Republic, has been especially necessary in view of the threatened attempt of foreign nations, to infringe the sovereignty of Liberia, for their own ends, either through direct means, such as the control of Liberian frontier forces, or indirectly, through the acquisition, by their nationals, of concessions granting extensive control over the industrial, commercial, and financial life of Liberia. The traditional attitude of historical responsibility toward Liberia which the United States has always held, was stated by Secretary of State Bayard in 1886 to France: "We exercise no protectorate over Liberia but the circumstances that the Republic of Liberia originated through the colonization of American citizens and was established under the fostering sanction of this Government, gives us the right as the next friend of Liberia to aid her in preventing any encroachment of foreign powers." This statement has been ever since the keynote of the American policy in Liberia.

It should be especially noted that the Government of the United States, whenever it has interested itself in Liberian affairs has done so at the express request of the Government of the Republic and with the fullest approval of the Liberian people. In fact, Liberia throughout her history has evinced the fullest confidence in the disinterested attitude of this country and has repeatedly expressed the desire that the United States interest itself most closely in Liberian affairs. Indeed an arrangement similar to that now contemplated was formally and spontaneously suggested by the Liberian Government as long ago as 1908 and the plan of reorganization now proposed has received the widest approbation of the Liberian Government and people.

Whatever may be the apparent similarity of the contemplated agreement between the United States and Liberia to that consummated between Great Britain and Persia, you should point out with all earnestness that, in addition to the underlying dissimilarity of the two problems, as indicated above, the character of the negotiations leading up to the agreements were of an entirely different nature. On the one hand, in the case of Persia an agreement was entered into by His Majesty's Government with the Shah which affected the relations of Persia to the United States without obtaining the views of the Government of the United States; on the other hand, in the case of Liberia the American Government has been scrupulously careful not to enter upon direct negotiations with Liberia upon a matter which even touched upon the relations of Liberia with Great Britain until a preliminary understanding with His Majesty's Government had been reached. To this end, by a memorandum to the British Embassy in Washington of November, 1918, the British Government was made aware of the vital needs of Liberia and of the desire of the United States Government to come to its assistance. It was not, however, until September, 1919, and after protracted negotiations that the approval of His Majesty's Government to the contemplated arrangement with Liberia has been obtained—thus causing a delay of ten months in extending the contemplated assistance to Liberia.

In conclusion you may point out that this Government is glad of the opportunity afforded by Lord Curzon frankly to express its views in this matter and to say that it is not in a position at the present time to give approval to the Anglo-Persian agreement until and unless it is clear that the Government and people of Persia are united in their approval and support of this undertaking.

The passage regarding Colonel House should be shown to him before communication to Foreign Office.

Last paragraph your 3098 American Minister Teheran has received no further instruction since authorization to issue public statement which he did approximately in the form quoted by Lord Curzon.

LANSING

The Ambassador in Great Britain (Davis) to the Secretary of State

London, October 8, 1919, 4 p.m.

3205. Your 6049 and 6060. Have transmitted today to Foreign Office note embodying your 6049. It being no longer possible to reach Colonel House I have substituted for the last five lines of your first paragraph referring to him the following.

"I am permitted to quote a recent letter from Colonel House to the effect that 'I have no reason to doubt that Lord Curzon's memory as to what occurred between us is correct, nevertheless, the fact remains that there was no discussion of details and I was left with no impression as to what the agreement with Persia was to be. It was all so casual that I am sure it made no impression upon the President either.'"

Remainder of note follows despatch with slight paraphrasing. Copy forwarded by mail.

DAVIS

RENEWED PERSIAN OVERTURES FOR AMERICAN ADVISERS

The Minister in Persia (Caldwell) to the Acting Secretary of State

Teheran, January 6, 1921, 10 a.m.

3. Situation in the Middle East undoubtedly approaching grave turning point. With the withdrawal of the British forces from north Persia, Anglo-Persian agreement becomes impossible of execution and the British Legation here admits that it means sacrifice of British interests throughout Persia except extreme south. British Minister states that even if Medjlis were to meet at once and ratify the agreement it would be too late as his Government had apparently decided not to assume any responsibility which might involve it in protecting Persia against possible Bolshevik invasion.

In view of the fact that the American people seem to take lively interest in the possibilities of certain natural resources of Persia I venture to suggest that the present moment furnishes unparalleled opportunity to establish this interest in practical form.

Immediate and most pressing need of the Persian Government is a number of military officers to take the place of the Russians recently dismissed. They are determined not to employ British and the latter claim even were they now asked they would not accept. If the Persian Government could at once contract privately for the services of at least 30 experienced American officers to reorganize and command the Persian forces it may yet be possible to prevent disturbances locally and above all to prevent Persia from being driven into the arms of Soviet Russia. They should arrive here not later than April, that is to say just before British complete their evacuation. Moral effect of announcing such a step, which need not of course involve the American Government, would be enormous as Persians of all classes still have unbounded confidence in America and would probably rally to the support of American officers with sufficient enthusiasm to bring new life into the body politic and act as deterrent to any designs the Bolsheviki may have. And with the ever-present danger of Bolshevism the world can hardly afford to allow such moral values to remain unused. Furthermore, as the Persian Government is about to conclude a convention with Soviet Russia the presence of Americans would be that [the] test of the latter's sincerity as regards promise of nonintervention provided the British leave the country. The Persian Government would of course also ask for American financial and other technical experts but the most urgent demand is giving [getting?] military officers to maintain discipline during the critical stage of transition.

Unless some such measures be adopted it is difficult to see how utter collapse of the Government can be avoided. The decisions of the next few weeks will determine the fate of this part of the world for a generation and if we intend to participate in its economic development no more favorable moment will ever present itself to lay the foundation.

As it is probable that the Persian Government will approach the Legation on the subject the Department's views would be greatly appreciated. It is also respectfully suggested that in the meantime the British Government be sounded as to its attitude in the event of Persian request for American advisers. The Legation understands from the British Minister that there might be no objection as Great Britain had virtually decided to abandon Persia to her fate.

CALDWELL

The Chargé in Persia (Engert) to the Secretary of State

Teheran, June 21, 1921, 4 p.m.

35. During a recent audience with the Shah and conversations with the Minister of Foreign Affairs both expressed the hope that relations between the United States and Persia will become more intimate and that it will be possible to find American agricultural advisers as well as a financial expert to head a Persian bank. They also intimated readiness to grant liberal concessions for oil, railroads, mines, et cetera in return for loans and they invite American experts to explore the country and to negotiate regarding terms.

As the Persian Medjlis will be opened tomorrow and that body will presumably be favorably disposed toward American interests no time should be lost if we intend to participate in the economic development of Persia. I have so far always answered evasively but with a little encouragement it should be possible to accomplish a great deal.

The British appear to be reconciled to the fact that they cannot now hope for exclusive privileges in north Persia but in the interest of civilization it would be regrettable if the Persians gained the impression that we were particularly anxious to thwart British plan on general principles, an impression which the attitude of this Legation during the last few years has done much to create and perpetuate and which undoubtedly contributed towards *rapprochement* between Persia and Soviet Russia. For purely geographic reasons the British will always have a certain legitimate influence here which generally speaking is wholesome and serves as an antidote to Bolshevikism. If therefore American capital desires to invest in north Persia it might perhaps be advisable to sound London and possibly invite cooperation as otherwise the Persians are certain to try the time-honored Oriental practice of playing one against the other.

I understand the Persian Minister to Spain now in London will soon proceed to Washington to negotiate for American advisers and it is intended that he remain there as Minister.

ENGERT

Memorandum by the Assistant Secretary of State (Dearing)

[Washington,] November 10, 1921

The Persian Minister called upon me today to say that he had received urgent telegrams from his Government and that he would be obliged if we could name a financial adviser as soon as possible. It was requested that he be named without specific statement as to his powers because he was needed at once. The Minister indicated that his Government would accept any suggestion the Department might make with regard to salary and added that the functions, powers, etc., of the adviser could easily be arranged with the Persian Government as soon as he could be appointed. The Minister referred to the fact that his Government needed financial assistance at once and seemed to feel that it was chiefly on account of the need of paying the Persian Army. Later telegrams which he has left at the Department indicate a fear of the Government at present in power that they may lose control unless the Army is paid. The Minister indicated that while he had approached various bankers and oil men he had not been able to get very far with them.

He told me that the British had asked for the Khostaria oil concession for the Anglo-Persian but that his Government had replied with absolute finality that the concession could not be given to the Anglo-Persian Company and that it had reverted absolutely to the Persian Government. The Minister said that his Government had appealed to the British to help them in their financial situation but that the British had said they could do nothing and had practically invited them to seek assistance elsewhere. This would seem to indicate that there need not necessarily be much danger of treading on British toes if financing is arranged in America.

D[EARING]

Memorandum by the Under Secretary of State (Fletcher)

[Washington,] November 29, 1921

After dinner at the Persian Legation last night, I had a conversation with the Minister on the subject of the appointment of an American financial adviser to Persia. The Minister informed me that his Government was very anxious to appoint an American financial adviser, and that he had been told by the State Department in conversations with Mr. Dearing, Mr. Robbins and others that a list was being prepared and would be submitted to him. I told him that I had understood that the matter had been discussed with him, but that on mature reflection, the Department felt that it would be inadvisable to have a financial adviser appointed before the arrival of the American Minister in Persia. I told him that Mr. Kornfeld* enjoyed the confidence of the President; that in view of our previous experience in Persia I felt that we should proceed with the utmost caution so that whatever was done would be to the permanent benefit of both countries. The Minister seemed very disappointed, and said that he felt, because he had already telegraphed his Government that an adviser would be suggested by the State Department, that his Government would not understand and would criticize him. I told him I would be very glad to explain through our Chargé at Teheran any difficulty arising on this score.

He then asked if it would be possible that an adviser would be selected who might accompany our new Minister to Persia. I told him that I was not inclined to approve of this course either, as I wished to have the new Minister make a thorough investigation of conditions there, so that the State Department could act intelligently in its dealings with Persia. I pointed out to him that any loan which might be floated in this country would need to be approved by the State Department, and that our approval would necessarily be contingent upon the reports of the new Minister, and that I did not see that any time would be gained by the appointment of an adviser at this time. The Minister asked whether it would be necessary to have the Government's approval of a loan made by private companies. I replied that if private companies wished to make a loan or advance from their own resources the approval of this Department would not be necessary. The Minister said that he had already employed Mr. Shuster, who was helping him with his negotiations with the oil companies and others who might be interested in Persian concessions and Persian finance.

I promised the Minister that he would have an opportunity to

---

* Joseph Saul Kornfeld, appointed Minister to Persia November 9, 1921.

confer with Dr. Kornfeld, who is expected in Washington within the next week.

H[ENRY] P. F[LETCHER]

1st MILLSPAUGH MISSION, 1922-1927

The Secretary of State to the Persian Minister (Alaï)

Washington, June 22, 1922

SIR: In reply to your note of June 16, 1922, communicating the desire of your Government to employ American citizens as advisers in various branches of the Persian Administration and indicating that the appointment of a Chief Financial Adviser was particularly pressing, I have the honor to state that after careful consideration the Department suggests the name of Dr. A.C. Millspaugh, Economic Adviser of this Department as a person with whom you might desire to communicate in regard to this matter.

In case, before making a choice, your Government should desire that further names of persons available for such employment should be submitted, the Department is prepared to do so.

As it seems probable that the person whom you may select as financial adviser will desire to be consulted in regard to his subordinates I have refrained from suggesting further names for such positions.

In the event that your Government should decide to communicate with Dr. Millspaugh and that an agreement should subsequently be reached with him to assume the duties of Financial Adviser to Persia, I desire that it be made quite clear that Dr. Millspaugh undertakes this work in a purely private capacity, and that all connection with the Department of State will cease immediately upon his entering the employ of the Persian Government. In acceding to the request of the Persian Government for the suggestion of an American citizen as Chief Financial Adviser to Persia my Government assumes no responsibility for any action which the Financial Adviser may take as an official in the employ of the Persian Government.

Accept [etc.]

CHARLES E. HUGHES

The Administrator General of the Finances of Persia (Millspaugh)
to the Secretary of State

Teheran [undated]
[*Received July 26, 1924, 3:27 a.m.*]

American Financial Mission have asked settlement in view of violation of contracts.

MILLSPAUGH

The Minister in Persia (Kornfeld) to the Secretary of State

Teheran, July 28, 1924, 10 a.m.

67. Department's telegram 36, July 24, 6 p.m. Millspaugh advised me July 24 that he sent protest July 17. He alleges following violations of contract: Governmental expenditures of public funds without his approval, taking decisions on financial questions without consulting him, failure to give him opportunity of attending meetings of Council of Ministers when discussing financial questions, ignoring his recommendations regarding financial personnel over which he claims complete power, interference with his administration, et cetera.

Millspaugh maintains "when the Administrator General of Finances holds that an order on [or] an instruction of Government or of Minister of Finance is unlawful or contrary to his contract or the contracts of the other American administrators he will not obey. Within the limits of the jurisdiction prescribed in his contract he has full right to use his judgment to make any decision which he considers correct." Millspaugh demands that he be permitted to do work without interference or obstruction, direct or indirect, not to be pressed to take action for special, personal, or political advantage of anyone, be permitted to exercise powers clearly given to them in their contracts and all violations shall immediately cease. If the Government does not accept these views mission requests to be advised immediately in order to discuss settlement of their contracts.

KORNFELD

The Acting Secretary of State to the Minister in Persia (Kornfeld)

Washington, July 30, 1924, 7 p.m.

48. Your 67, July 28, 10 a.m.; 68, July 28, 5 p.m.

1. It is regarded by the Department as unfortunate that circumstances have disposed Millspaugh to demand termination of contracts of Financial Advisers. Department has no complete knowledge of the views of the Persian Ministry and of the course it has taken, or of the attitude and wishes of the Administrator General, but Department views with regret the present crisis. It will be clear to you that for the United States and for the Legation it is of paramount importance that adjustment regarding murder of Vice Consul Imbrie* should be reached without delay. It is not the wish of the Department that the raising of

---

* Robert Imbrie, American vice consul at Teheran, murdered July 18, 1924.

any other question should become an obstacle to that adjustment.

2. It is clearly understood here that members of Financial Mission are in the service of Persian Government, and that if stipulations of their contracts are respected there is no proper ground for diplomatic interference. But if the Persian Government has not given pledges for the future as was asked by the American Mission, or if it is about to adopt a course which may cause resignation of American officials, the Department believes that, should you approve and after you have consulted the Administrator General, you may with propriety, in fairness and candor to the Persian Government, make informal representations that if Americans should relinquish posts in consequence of evident intentions of Persian Government, the effect upon sentiment in the United States would be unfortunate, and coming so soon after the murder of Imbrie it might unhappily be regarded in America as evidence of Persia's intentions toward the United States and its citizens.

Cable report.

GREW

The Chargé in Persia (Murray) to the Secretary of State

No. 637   *Teheran, September 7, 1924*

SIR: Referring to the Department's telegrams Nos. 36 and 48, dated July 24 and July 30, respectively, the Legations telegrams Nos. 67, 68, and 84 of July 28, 10 a.m., July 28, 5 p.m., and August 6, respectively, the Consulate's telegram No. 10 of July 31, and the Legation's despatches, Nos. 604 and 623, dated July 30 and August 26, respectively, all referring to the difficulties which have recently arisen in the position of the American Financial Mission in Persia, and which have culminated in a demand, on the part of the members of the mission, for a cancellation of their contracts, I have the honor to inform the Department that I have had two conferences with Dr. Millspaugh on July 31 and September 5, respectively, and one with Zoka-ol-Molk, the present Minister of Finance on September 6, during which the entire matter and the advisers' demands and the attitude of the Persian Government was fully discussed.

In my talk with Dr. Millspaugh on July 30, he discussed freely the contents of what has been called the advisers' "ultimata" addressed to the Persian Government on 26 Saratan (July 17) and 2 Asad (July 24) and transmitted to the Department in the Legation's despatch No. 604 of July 30. Dr. Millspaugh seemed profoundly discouraged over what he considers the systematic opposition during the past six months of the Persian Government to all his efforts to put Persia's financial house in order. Both the Council of Ministers and the Medjliss had evinced an unwillingness to cooperate with him either in the approval or the passage of his financial projects so that he viewed with the utmost pessimism any chance of success for his financial mission in Persia unless their present contracts were cancelled on the basis of repeated violation on the part of the Persian Government and new contracts were submitted to and passed by the Medjliss granting the Administrator General practically dictatorial powers in questions concerning the budget and an absolute guarantee of military support in the collection of the taxes. He felt that any other solution would be merely begging the question and sure to lead eventually to failure.

It may be added that the attitude of the other members of the financial mission was even more uncompromising than that of Dr. Millspaugh, and that they were averse to withdrawing in any degree, however small, from the original demands on the Persian Government that their contracts be terminated.

In the succeeding fortnight the Prime Minister addressed a conciliatory communication to Dr. Millspaugh, dated 15 Asad (August 6) containing rather vague promises of complete cooperation with the American advisers and requesting fuller specifications from the Administrator General as to exact violations of his contract. The latter was at the same time verbally informed by the Persian Government that a commission of Persian notables was to be formed for the consideration of the advisers' complaints and to effect if possible a solution of their difficulties.

I was informed on August 9 by Colonel MacCormack that the commission appointed by the Prime Minister which contained, among others, such prominent men as Moshir-ed-Dowleh and Mostowfi-ol-Mamalek, was doing little to get at the root of the trouble, and that even Moshir-ed-Dowleh had frankly expressed the idea that the Persians in general were averse to the plans of the advisers to reorganize completely the financial system and impose new taxation in order to balance the budget, but that they desired rather to have a mission of "advisers" in the true sense of the word who would "advise" the Persian functionaries as to the proper steps to be taken and back them up in the execution thereof. Colonel MacCormack informed Moshir-ed-Dowleh that if such was their understanding as to the function of the American advisers they had employed the wrong men.

Again on September 5, in a conference with Dr. Millspaugh, he expatiated on the impossibility of continuing further his activity as Administrator General of Finances unless a radical change . . . meanwhile intervened. . . .

. . . In the opinion of the Administrator General, if Persia is to be rescued from her present desperate financial straits, it will be necessary to reduce the budget for the War Ministry one million tomans each year until it has reached the sum of six million tomans which he considers a reasonable sum for the maintenance of an army of 30,000 to 40,000 men.

. . . I was interested to note that the advice of the best friends of the American advisers, namely that of Zoka-ol-Molk, the present Minister of Finance, and Sardar Moazzam Khorassani, the present Minister of Public Works, had not failed to have effect on Dr. Millspaugh's rather inexorable demand that a cancellation and settlement of his contract should precede any discussion of his further remaining in Persia. He now appears more willing to present his "irreductible minimum" to the Persian Government and to negotiate on a basis thereof. I may state at this point, for the information of the Department, that in my opinion, based on a close observation of the present critical situation, this decision on the part of Dr. Millspaugh is a wise one inasmuch as there are several fundamental reasons, which will be pointed out below, why a persistence on the part of Dr. Millspaugh in his original unbending demands would be unfortunate at the present time.

On the following day, September 6, I requested a conference with the Minister of Finance, Zoka-ol-Molk, which he granted me at six o'clock in the evening. After prefacing his remarks with numerous declarations of friendship and goodwill to the advisers which I believe are borne out by fact, he expressed the hope that Dr. Millspaugh could be made to see the wisdom of a more conciliatory attitude to the Persian Government in the present crisis and pointed out two fundamental principles which must not be lost sight of if this crisis is to be allayed. In the first place he felt that while Dr. Millspaugh is in some degree right in his contentions with regard to the violation of his contract, there was something to be said for the other side; sight must not be lost of the fact that Persia is an oriental country that has been for decades in a mire of financial distress and that too vigorous a remedy for the invalid might prove fatal.

The one absolute necessity at the present time was that Dr. Millspaugh should withdraw from his position that the budget of the War Ministry should be reduced. Unless he could see the wisdom of this concession, all would be lost. While frankly admitting that most fair-minded Persians would agree that the expenditures of the Ministry of War were excessive, and a great burden upon the finances of Persia absorbing as it did almost one-half of her revenues, Persians nevertheless realized the great advantages that had accrued to Persia thru the organization by Sardar Sepah* of the present army and the inestimable advantage which this force had been to the financial advisers in backing up their reforms.

He further referred to the difficulties which Shuster had encountered in this regard and the necessity with which he was faced of organizing a Treasury *Gendarmerie* in the country, an act which more than anything else had aroused the antagonism of the Russians which led to his expulsion.

---

* Reza Khan.

He believed that the present armed force in Persia, while it was insufficient to defend the country from invasion, had to its credit remarkable accomplishments in subduing tribes rebellious to the central authorities and in making it possible for a financial mission to function. Without Sardar Sepah, he said, any idea of an American mission in Persia would have been out of the question. . . .

With regard to Dr. Millspaugh's original demand that, before the complete cancellation and settlement of his contract, he could not discuss the matter with the Persian Government, the Minister of Finance made what I consider is a very just observation. In the first place, such an action could not but be regarded as a rather humiliating and high-handed action toward the Persian Government with whom Dr. Millspaugh had voluntarily entered into contractual obligations, and would arouse the suspicion that after such cancellation he would show himself so inflexible that the mission would depart with the entire money settlement for five years in their possession, and secondly, that, given the open opposition of the Russians, the covert opposition of the British, and the general unfriendliness of the Belgians and the French, the concerted action on the part of these Legations, once the contracts had been cancelled, would make any passage by the Medjliss of new contracts an absolute impossibility. In my former conference with Dr. Millspaugh I was gratified to see that he accepted the soundness of the Finance Minister's reasoning.

The second essential point which he emphasized was that Dr. Millspaugh should carefully guard himself from giving any impression to the Medjliss of a desire to dictate the terms of any new rights in his contract which might be agreed upon between the Government and the Financial Mission. This would be a fatal step on the part of the Administrator General. Unusual powers had been granted to Mr. Shuster during his activity in Persia, but these powers had all been voluntarily granted by the Medjliss which was an ardent supporter of Shuster. . . .

I have [etc.]   W[ALLACE] SMITH MURRAY

The Chargé in Persia (Murray) to the Secretary of State

No. 669   *Teheran, October 6, 1924*

. . . In the last conference, namely on September 24 [25?], at which Dr. Millspaugh persistently stood out for a reduction of the budgets of all Ministries as the only way out of the present financial impasse, the Prime Minister unexpectedly offered to reduce his own budget 200,000 tomans a year which, together with the proportional cut on all other Ministries, will enable Dr. Millspaugh to balance the budget for the present fiscal year.

It may be noted that certain concessions on both sides were made in the question of budget reductions inasmuch as the Administrator General desired to cover the entire million toman deficit, as estimated for the present year, by deducting in *in toto* from the War Minister's budget.

After coming to this agreement, the Administrator General impressed upon the Prime Minister the necessity that the latter sponsor personally the agreement arrived at with regard to ministerial reductions in order to avoid obstructions and delays on the part of these Ministries. This the Prime Minister promised to do and on the next day in a meeting of the Council of Ministers announced the reductions to the various Ministers as a *fait accompli*.

A further important obligation assumed by the Prime Minister at this conference was the guarantee of unlimited support of the Persian army to be afforded the American financial advisers in the collection of taxes. The withdrawal of this support has at various times been used by the Prime Minister in order to bring pressure upon the Administrator General to accede to certain demands of the Government.

The solution of a third important and difficult question was that of the control of the Ministry of Posts and Telegraphs. Inasmuch as this Ministry has, in the last years, had a surplus of 508,000 tomans over its expenses, it has been a hotbed of corruption and intrigue in order to prevent, at all costs, this surplus from reaching the hands of the American advisers. There had been constant friction and disputes between the Administrator General and all Ministers of Posts and Telegraphs appointed since his arrival over the control of that Ministry's finances. . . .

In the latter mentioned conference between Dr. Millspaugh and the Prime Minister this question was frankly discussed, and Dr. Millspaugh stated frankly that he could no longer tolerate the insubordination of the Ministry in question and, in order to alter the situation prevailing therein, the permanent Under-Secretary, Mokber-ed-Dowleh, must be dismissed. He presented a demand at the same time that the Belgian Acting Director of Posts, Mr. Emil Pire, who has always been in close league with Mokber-ed-Dowleh in opposing the American advisers, should not be permitted to return to Persia from Stockholm where he has been attending the conference of the International Postal Union. The Prime Minister concurred in this demand and promised to take action.

With regard to the settlement of the questions raised by the Financial Mission as to the violation of their contracts, Dr. Millspaugh requested the dismissal of the unwieldly commission of fourteen which has been considering the matter but has accomplished nothing, and the appointment of a Commission of three, composed of the present Minister of Finance, Zoka-ol-Molk, the President of the Medjliss, Motamen-ol-Molk, and one deputy.

As the Department was informed in the above-mentioned telegram,

Dr. Millspaugh made a substantial concession at this time with regard to the contracts of the advisers, namely, that they would not insist upon an immediate cancellation and settlement before they consented to consider the continuation of their services. This concession on his part was unquestionably a wise one.

It is obvious that the above solution of the advisers' difficulties represents a signal victory for Dr. Millspaugh, and one which will no doubt add much to his prestige in the future. . . .

I have [etc.]   W[ALLACE] SMITH MURRAY

The Secretary of State to the Minister in Persia (Philip)

Washington, December 18, 1926, 6 p.m.

52. The Persian Minister called today on the Secretary of State and as directed by his Government asked that influence of Department be exerted to persuade Millspaugh to give up his endeavors (1) to regulate finances of Ministry of War and (2) to hinder railway projects in Persia.

In commenting on the former matter, the Persian Minister pointed out that present ruler of Persia when still Minister of War had caused resignation of foreign military experts; and he represented that if the American Administrator now successfully forced his claims to regulate war budget, ground might be given for revival of subject of military missions by other governments. The Persian Minister's attention was called to the difference between purely fiscal character of supervision of army budget by the American Administrator and a military expert's concern with the army itself. It was made clear to Persian Minister that although the United States is of course anxious to have the American Adviser accomplish his mission, yet the Department feels some delicacy in attempting to make suggestions to him on a strictly professional aspect of his duties growing out of his powers as Administrator General. Assurances were given to the Persian Minister, however, that you would be informed of his request in order that you might employ your unofficial influence to allay misunderstandings between his Government and the Administrator General.

The Department expressed its surprise over the second point brought up by the Minister and offered the suggestion that the American Administrator's manifest diligence in engaging an American engineer and assistants appeared to contradict the supposition that he was opposed to the aspirations of Persia to develop her transportation system.

You will please review the above with Doctor Millspaugh and report by cable the outcome of your conference with him, giving also your own views on the meaning and importance of the Persian Minister's representations and stating what measures for improving the adviser's position you would recommend.

KELLOGG

The Minister in Persia (Philip) to the Secretary of State

No. 231   *Teheran, December 30, 1926*

. . . Mostowfi-ol-Mamalek then spoke at length of his interest in the Mission and his desire to see its work, "which has only begun," crowned with success. He reverted to the necessity for great tact, patience and carefulness on Millspaugh's part in the application of his reforms to a country such as Persia. In this connection he said that, when Prime Minister several years since, he had impressed upon Millspaugh, at the outset, the absolute necessity for slow and persuasive measures rather than those of an abrupt and didactic nature if success were to be attained. He still considers the work but at its commencement, though he acknowledges that great and surprising advances have been accomplished, and he sincerely hopes that every means will be adopted by Millspaugh and his associates to conform their work rather to the understanding and the character of the people than to drastic rules and regulations suitable, perhaps, to a western nation with a very different past and very different problems from those of Persia, etc. The Prime Minister concluded by assuring me that his best efforts both with the Shah and his Cabinet would be given toward the assurance of the retention of the American Financial Mission and the success of its efforts.

I have [etc.]   HOFFMAN PHILIP

The Minister in Persia (Philip) to the Secretary of State

No. 275   *Teheran, February 22, 1927*

. . . The crux of this question of course is to be found in the eventual decision of the Persian Government as to the retention of Millspaugh.

Of this, I feel it is possible to say, a very large majority of the public opinion in Persia is in favor. I would go further and surmise that the Shah also is in favor of this, although he may feel that he would prefer a more complaisant and personally sympathetic chief of the American Mission. I am also of the opinion that the actual enemies of the Mission feel that they are hardly strong enough to bring about the defeat of a proposal to renew Millspaugh's contract.

Therefore, I judge that the point upon which the future of the Millspaugh Mission will turn is that of the powers to be vested in the Administrator General of Finances in a new contract.

This feature is one of vital importance to the future work of the Mission. It is that in regard to which the attitude of the Shah is uncertain as yet. It is that upon which the enemies of the Mission probably will focus all their energies.

It is that question of powers which doubtless forms the chief topic of innuendo and suggestion on the part of various foreign interests who seek to discredit and weaken the position of the American Advisers.

Doctor Millspaugh has emphatically stated to me that he would not remain should any material curtail[ment] of his authority be decided upon, but that he is prepared to continue his work should he be offered a contract of the same nature as that now held by him. In this eventuality, I understand he has several propositions to make in regard to minor changes in his contract as well as in the composition of the Mission. . . .

Much interest has centered upon the advent of Prince Firouz (Nosrat-ed-Dowleh) into the Ministry of Finance. . . .

The new Minister already has displayed insistent determination to assert his authority in matters pertaining to the Mission and to seek out matters which may be open to criticism. In certain respects he has given the impression that he believes his predecessors have been entirely too subservient to the will of Doctor Millspaugh and that they have in this connection failed to exercise many of the powers to which they have been entitled. I have counseled Millspaugh to meet this attitude with entire equanimity and to cheerfully afford Prince Firouz every opportunity of familiarizing himself with the real aims and difficulties of his work. The result of such a course should be to render the more obvious and public any attempt on the part of the Minister to bring unjust criticism to bear upon the efforts of the Mission.

Millspaugh now seems inclined to believe that Prince Firouz will recognize both the advantage to his official career in supporting a work so palpably beneficial to the public weal, as well as the futility of openly attacking the Mission in the face of existing popular opinion in its favor. The Minister recently informed one of Millspaugh's assistants that he intends soon to see the Shah and to recommend the retention of the Millspaugh Mission. No allusion was made however to the probable attitude he would assume with the Shah respecting the powers to be vested in the Administrator General under a new contract.

I have [etc.]   HOFFMAN PHILIP

Memorandum of an Audience Given to the American Minister (Philip) by Reza Shah Pahlavi

April 14, 1927

Alluding to the object of the audience the Minister said to the Shah that before His Majesty's departure from Teheran when the Minister had asked for an audience he had heard certain rumors to the effect that His Majesty was not satisfied with the services of the American Mission. He had therefore wished to go directly to His Majesty and try to find out whether they were true and if so what was wrong and whether he (Minister) could assist in solving a possible misunderstanding, etc. He had heard that conditions had since improved.

The Shah replied it was true that he had expressed dissatisfaction with the American Mission. This has not been caused by any personal matters, and his Majesty had no motives. He was thinking exclusively of the interests of the country. He had from the beginning been one of the strongest supporters of the American Mission for he realized the country was in need of the services of this Mission. He had praised and commended those members of the mission who had served satisfactorily, and he had criticized those whose services were not satisfactory. He believed those who had served well should be asked to continue their services and those whose services were not satisfactory should be replaced either by some of the present members of the Mission or by some new ones.

Dr. Millspaugh's methods of action were not satisfactory to the government and if he failed to improve in this respect the government would be compelled to replace him either by one of the members of the present mission or by engaging a new man.

Upon the Minister expressing a desire to know what actions of Dr. Millspaugh were unsatisfactory the Shah said he violated the laws. He wrote provoking letters to the government. Instead of presenting a quarterly report of his activities, as had been provided in his contract, he published pamphlets in which he wrote things which were provoking to the government and which created bad impressions against the country in the eyes of foreigners as well as Persians.

The Minister said he would appreciate it if the Shah would confide in him the case in which Dr. Millspaugh had violated the laws, for that was exactly what he wished very much to know. He said personally he had a great admiration for Dr. Millspaugh and that his government and the American people believed the American mission had made much success and that it[s] success was chiefly due to the leadership of Dr. Millspaugh. The Minister had spoken to every member except, possibly, one of the Mission and he had been told by all of them that Dr. Millspaugh was the spirit of the Mission and without him it would have been unable to accomplish what already had been done. He believed that no member of the present Mission would be able to replace Dr. Millspaugh as successfully. The Minister could probably suggest several men in America who might be highly qualified to replace Dr. Millspaugh, but it is doubtful if any of them would be available and if so it is probable that their service would command as much as seventy-five to one hundred thousand dollars annually.

Dr. Millspaugh might have his own weaknesses, but his value should be judged from a comparison of his defects with his good qualities. Somebody had said to the Minister Dr. Millspaugh might have twenty undesirable qualities, but he also had sixty (60) good qualities. He would therefore be better than another who might be found to have 50 good qualities and 50 bad qualities. He had good motives. He was sincerely devoted to his duty which was to serve Persia as well as he could, etc.

The Shah said he had written documents which proved that Dr. Millspaugh had violated the laws. According to his contract, which was a law, he was to do things with the concurrence of the Minister of Finance. He had failed to do this. He would say Dr. Millspaugh had 99 good qualities and but one undesirable: that was his disregard for the dignity of government. This was a very grave thing. It was enough to obliterate all his advantages. Unless he changed in this respect the government would be obliged to terminate his contract even if that might result in difficulties for the government. The government preferred to be in difficulties and be independent, rather than be comfortable and be deprived of that independence.

He could not see why it would be difficult to find a new man who could take the place of Dr. Millspaugh, or to replace him by one of the present members of the Mission.

The Minister said he had heard rumors of agitations against the Mission created by elements which were inspired from selfish motives. Of course he was not in a position to judge of the truth of these rumors, but he could see that if anybody had the desire to weaken the Mission the best method of going about it would be to attack the position of Dr. Millspaugh. He admitted Dr. Millspaugh was a student and a man of the desk rather than a courtier or a diplomat, and that in the cultivation of relations with men rather than facts he was at a certain disadvantage. It was a fact, however, that those who were in charge of finances and the control of expenditures throughout the world were not generally popular with those who were affected by their rulings. This is the same in the United States as elsewhere. But there it is generally accepted and appreciated as an effort to benefit the country as a whole.

He added that the members of the Mission were in a state of uncertainty in regard to whether or not their contracts would be renewed and it would be useful if a decision in regard to this subject could be taken at an early date.

The Shah said he was prepared to support the work of Dr. Millspaugh with his sword, even if he reduced his own salary or that of his son. He paid no attention to intrigues for he was convinced that the American Mission was very useful to Persia. The government would surely renew the contracts of the members of the Mission. He believed, and he said to Dr. Millspaugh, that in the future the government will benefit more from the services of the Mission than in the past. For in the past the members of the Mission had been acquiring experience and in the future they would be in a position to use that experience. If Dr. Millspaugh's contract was to be renewed the government should be assured that he would improve his methods of dealing with it. If he did not undertake to improve those methods the government would have to amend his contract so that he would be in a position wherein he would not be able to exercise them. If none of these things could be done the government would have to replace him.

He agreed with the Minister that Dr. Millspaugh had much improved his methods during the past few months, and he expressed the hope that he would remain that way.

The Minister offered his services in case it was ever felt that he could assist in improving conditions. The United States Government was only interested in the successful accomplishment of the task which the American Financial Mission had undertaken. His government and the American people admired His Majesty for the great work that he had up to the present done for his country and they sincerely hoped that he would be able to do more in the future.

The Shah appreciated the cordial sentiments that the President of the United States had expressed in regard to him on various occasions, to Persians as well as to others who had visited the United States. America was young but her people were full of energy. They naturally liked energetic men.

The Minister in Persia (Philip) to the Secretary of State

Teheran, July 30, 1927, 5 p.m.

50. Department's 36, July 28, 5 p.m., delivered on 30th instant. My telegram No. 49, July 22, 11 a.m. Millspaugh refused and will leave August 3rd or 4th.

PHILIP

NEGOTIATIONS FOR OIL CONCESSIONS IN PERSIA

The Persian Minister (Alaï) to the Secretary of State

Washington, February 21, 1924

SIR: Your Excellency has doubtless been informed that, in connection with the contract signed in December last by the Persian Government and the representative of the Sinclair Consolidated Oil Corporation in Teheran for the exploitation of petroleum in four of the five northern provinces of Persia, the Standard Oil Company of New Jersey have let it be known in a letter addressed by them to Mr. A.G. Berger on January 18th, referred to by the *New York Times* of February 4th last, as about to appear in the current number of *The Lamp* (a copy of the advance sheets of which is enclosed) that they hold jointly with the Anglo-Persian Oil Company, Ltd., a British corporation, a one-half interest in the so-called Khoshtharia grants covering approximately three and one-quarter provinces in north Persia, and that they will take the proper steps to protect their rights and to develop a petroleum production.

In view of this attitude on the part of the Standard Oil Company of New Jersey, I deemed it advisable to publish, on my own initiative, a letter in the *New York Times* of the 8th instant, reciting briefly the various phases of my Government's negotiations with the Standard Oil and the Sinclair interests. That letter has, I understand, been brought to Your Excellency's attention, but nevertheless I enclose herewith a copy to complete the record.

Having kept my Government informed of recent developments, I have just been instructed by the Minister for Foreign Affairs to submit the following points for Your Excellency's consideration.

In the first place, my Government reiterate the sentiments expressed in a memorandum which I had the honour of handing you shortly after my arrival in Washington on September 15, 1921, namely, that the Persian Government and people have always recognized the altruism and impartiality which distinguish the American Government and people. They particularly appreciate the concern of the United States for fair play, for the respect of the independence of the smaller nations and for the maintenance of the economic open door.

It was because of their implicit faith in the lofty ideals and trusted friendship of America that my Government, over a year ago, confided the reorganization of their finances to American advisers and have consistently courted the technical and financial cooperation of this country in the industrial and economic development of Persia.

In harmony with this desire for America's friendly cooperation my Government and the Madjless have consistently acted during the negotiations for an oil concession in the five northern provinces of Persia, as the following brief outline of the negotiations will demonstrate.

Early in November, 1921, the Standard Oil Company of New Jersey were approached by Mr. W. Morgan Shuster, as Fiscal Agent of the Persian Government, with a view to enlisting their interest in the development of the north Persian oil fields. As a result of these negotiations, I was able to submit by cable to my Government a draft agreement for a concession in the five northern provinces of Persia and for a five million dollar loan. Upon the receipt of this agreement, the matter was discussed in the Committees on Foreign Affairs and Public Works of the Madjless. After consideration in the Committee of the Whole, the Madjless passed a resolution approving the granting of a concession for the north Persian oil fields to the Standard Oil Company of New Jersey, and laid down certain conditions intended to safeguard the public interest, among which may be mentioned the condition that the Standard Oil Company of New Jersey should not, in any circumstances, assign or transfer this concession or enter into partnership without the approval of the Madjless. This condition was merely the enunciation of the fundamental policy of my Government that the capital employed must be entirely American. The resolution, of which a copy is enclosed, was communicated to the Standard Oil Company of New Jersey by Mr. Shuster, with a view to ascertaining whether it was prepared, as my Government hoped would be the case, to enter into an agreement in conformity with the conditions laid down therein.

Some months of negotiation ensued, during which representatives of the Anglo-Persian Company, Ltd., approached the Standard Oil Company and informed it of the exclusive rights which the former claimed in the north Persian oil fields under the supposed Khoshtharia concession. Thereupon, in February, 1922, the Standard Oil Company signified a desire to associate itself in the development of the Persian Oil fields on a fifty-fifty basis with the Anglo-Persian Company. Although I repeatedly requested it, I was never able to obtain from the Standard Oil Company a copy of its agreement with the Anglo-Persian Company, or any information as to its scope. Nevertheless, I was certain that an association of this kind would be distasteful to my Government and the Standard Oil Company was so advised by me. That Company, however, was insistent that this was the only plan upon which it would enter into the proposed concession and a new draft agreement was drawn up on this basis in February, 1922, and forwarded to my Government for consideration. This February proposal was rejected because of the association with the Anglo-Persian Company. On account of this association between the Standard and Anglo-Persian Companies and in order to give the Government more latitude in carrying on the negotiations, the Madjless on June 11, 1922, voted an amendment to its previous resolution, empowering the Government to negotiate a petroleum concession in North Persia with any independent and responsible American Company. With these broad powers, my Government extended the scope of its negotiations and sought proposals from not only the Standard Oil Company of New Jersey but from the Sinclair Consolidated Oil Corporation.

At the end of June, the Standard Oil Company indicated its willingness to conform to the resolution of the Madjless and to take and operate the concession entirely on its own account without entering into partnership with any other company so far as the carrying out of the concession was concerned. This new attitude of the Standard Oil Company, which, it will be observed, left out of consideration entirely any partnership alliance with the Anglo-Persian Company, was set forth in an initialed memorandum of June 30, 1922, a copy of which is herewith enclosed. At the same time, my Government was receiving proposals from the Sinclair Consolidated Oil Corporation through its representative in Teheran. Also after the receipt of the June memorandum, my Government sought more definite terms, in conformity therewith, from the Standard Oil Company, and a draft concession was forwarded to Teheran in the following August. With the Standard and the Sinclair proposals in hand, my Government, in view of the great importance of the concession and the vital interests involved, sought the views of the Madjless by laying both proposals before a special committee of that body.

After a thorough examination by this Committee and by my Government, the Standard declining to make any substantial modifications in their proposal or to send a representative to Teheran to discuss the matter directly with the Government, both sets of proposals were rejected because they did not seem to safeguard sufficiently the interests of Persia. In view of this, the Madjless deemed it best to pass a law laying down in greater detail the basis of a concession which my Government was authorized to grant to any independent and reputable American concern that might show interest in the matter. The Standard Oil Company of New Jersey did not show any inclination to meet the requirements of the law and made no proposals, but the Sinclair Consolidated Oil Corporation submitted terms following closely the conditions laid down in the Oil Law. The Standard manifesting no further interest in the concession, an agreement was consequently signed last December by the Government and the Sinclair representative in Teheran subject to the ratification of the Madjless, as the Sinclair Company was the only applicant in the field.

Now that there is at last a prospect of the northern oil fields of Persia being developed under purely American auspices, the Standard Oil Company of New Jersey advances certain claims on the basis of association with the Anglo-Persian Oil Company, Ltd., in the so-called Khoshtharia concession.

I need not repeat the arguments laid in detail before Your Excellency in my note of January 3, 1922, which to your judicial mind will, I am sure, carry conviction that these so-called concessions are null and void. If the Standard Oil Company believed it had acquired any valid rights under these alleged concessions by virtue of association with the Anglo-Persian Company, why did it continue for two years to negotiate for a new concession with the Persian Government? The negotiation indicates the doubtful sincerity of the claims now advanced by the Standard Oil Company.

I cannot, therefore, but express surprise that a large American corporation should in these circumstances ally itself with a policy known by it to be repugnant to the Persian nation and openly declare that it maintains its so-called rights under the Khoshtharia concessions and that it proposes to enforce them in defiance of the Persian Government.

The Standard Oil made the mistake of yielding to the unwarranted contentions of the Anglo-Persian Oil Company. They were repeatedly warned by Mr. Shuster and myself of the strong feeling of suspicion inevitably entertained in Teheran, in view of past experiences, as to British motives and aims, and of the decision of the Persian Government to stand on the firm ground of the invalidity of the alleged Khoshtharia concessions. In spite of this warning, the Standard Oil Company made their proposal of February, 1922, to exploit the five northern provinces in association with the Anglo-Persian Oil Company on a fifty-fifty basis.

In view of the facts of the case and the known policies of my Government, Your Excellency will appreciate that the announced determination of the Standard Oil Company in association with the Anglo-Persian Company to enforce its rights under concessions which my Government regard as invalid, cannot be carried out within Persian territory with my Government's approval. Should, however, the Standard Oil Company of New Jersey, as an American concern, seek the assistance of the United States Government with a view to asserting its alleged rights in the North Persia oil fields, I, acting under instructions from my Government, beg you to take into consideration the history of this whole transaction as I have outlined it above:—the association of the Standard Oil Company with a British concern, in which the British Government has a predominant influence,—an association peculiarly distasteful to my Government, my Government's well-founded view that the concessions, on which these companies base their rights, are null and void, and also the earnest desire of Persia for American aid, free from foreign influences, in the development of her natural resources.

In conclusion, I am instructed to express again the gratitude of the Government and people of Persia for the friendly and valuable assistance already given them by Your Excellency and to formulate the hope that your Government will continue the policy of encouraging unalloyed American enterprise in Persia.

Pray accept [etc.]   HUSSEIN ALAÏ

The Chargé in Persia (Murray) to the Secretary of State

No. 647   *Teheran, September 19, 1924*

. . . Before I could proceed to a discussion of the only asset remaining from the wreckage, the American financial mission, whose existence hangs now by a thread, the Prime Minister launched at once into the question of the oil concession and expressed his deep personal disappointment that, after three years effort, and an expenditure by the Persian Government of more than 300,000 tomans on telegrams alone, and the passage by the Medjliss of all but two of the articles of this concession, the Sinclair company now appeared to have lost interest in the fate of the concession and was willing to let it lapse. Despite repeated efforts on the part of the Persian Government to ascertain the intentions of the company since Mr. Soper's departure, no answer to its inquiries had been received.

I thereupon requested the Prime Minister to inform me exactly of the present prospects for the passage of the oil concession and promised him I would do what was possible under the circumstances to obtain, through the Department, information from the Sinclair company as to its intentions. He then assured me that the concession could and would pass the Medjliss if that body were sure of its acceptance by the Sinclair company, and that he personally would see that the loan clause was eliminated. It was desirable that Persia find money, it was true, but in view of the urgent necessity of resuscitating her economic life, the question of an immediate loan could be disregarded.

As the circumstances attending the passage, up to the last important article of this concession, despite America's disinterest and the bitterest opposition of the British, are so remarkable, the Legation would find it very helpful if the Department were inclined to instruct it as to the best policy to follow in the circumstances.

Since my arrival in Teheran in April 1922, I have watched closely the evolution of this exceedingly complicated question so that I trust the Department will not take it amiss if I venture to offer the following observations based on my personal acquaintance with the issue from this angle.

1. It is unquestionable that the Standard Oil Company could, in November 1921, after the decision of the Medjliss to negotiate with that company for the award of the oil concession in the northern provinces, have had it for the asking. This was never done.

2. It is equally as unquestionable that, after the alliance between the Standard Oil Company and the Anglo-Persian Oil Company and the subsequent incredible offer to the Persian Government to exploit these provinces on a basis of 50-50 participation with the Anglo-Persian Oil Company, the Standard Oil Company could have obtained the concession by no means short of a miracle. A most casual knowledge of the state of Persian sentiment (right or wrong) towards the British since the ill-fated Anglo-Persian Agreement, and of Soviet Russian sentiment since the collapse of Britain's attempt to seize Baku in 1919 should suffice to prove the truth of this statement.

3. Any company, American or otherwise, that obtains the concession to exploit these provinces must, of necessity, have made its peace, at least economic, with Soviet Russia. It is obvious from a glance at the geographical lay of these fields that, barring unexpected events in Russia, the Soviets have, and will continue to have, the last say as to the development of these resources in North Persia. The key of these resources is the Caucasus, and that key is in Russia's possession.

4. It is exceedingly unlikely that, even granting the recent Anglo-Soviet Russian reconciliation, such as it is, and the possibility that an agreement will be reached on a mutual policy and plan of action elsewhere, such a cooperation could easily be arrived at with regard to the Asiatic policy of these Powers. Hence, were American economic intervention in North Persia for the moment blocked or even definitely defeated, it is inconceivable that Great Britain will be able to obtain what she may have prevented America from obtaining.

The advantage to Britain of such a "negative victory" is, however, by no means to be underestimated. Great Britain's interest in Persia dates from the seventeenth century, and her policy may be said to be geared to centuries, whereas ours is scarcely geared to years. She can wait.

It is furthermore the conviction of the Prime Minister, as of most enlightened Persians, that the policy of the Standard-Anglo-Persian combination in seeking to acquire these fields was purely that of the dog-in-the-manger awaiting a new turn in Russia and an absorption on world markets of a greater oil supply without menacing present prices.

5. If American participation in the development of Persia is to be regarded as desirable, the circumstances attend[ing] the competition of these two American companies for the concession may be regarded as unfortunate, and this for the following reason, namely:

Whereas the British Government would appear to have regarded the Standard Oil Company, by virtue of its alliance with the Anglo-Persian Oil Company, a company in which 50% of the stock is owned by that Government, as entitled to the mobilization of the last ounce of influence available to the British Legation at Teheran in order to acquire, in the American company's name, a concession that doubtlessly would have passed eventually into the complete possession of the British shareholders, the American Government, justly, of course, was obliged to regard both of the American companies as equally entitled to the support, or rather to the neutrality, of the American Legation in Teheran. Hence the anomalous situation of one American company competing without the assistance of its Government's representative against another American company enjoying the fullest protection and support of a foreign Legation. It may therefore be safely stated that, had the American Government been in a position under the circumstances, to have lent its open assistance in the matter, the concession would doubtlessly have been granted two years ago. . . .

I have [etc.]   W. SMITH MURRAY

CONSULTATIONS ON RESTRICTION
OF THE OPIUM TRADE

The Secretary of State to the Chargé in Persia (Murray)

Washington, September 15, 1924, 5 p.m.

83. 1. The Department hopes that the Government of Persia will be represented at the forthcoming opium conference at Geneva in November next. The question of production of raw opium is one of prime importance and without the cooperation of the producing countries it will be difficult to reach a satisfactory conclusion. The Department suggests, therefore, that you communicate the views of this Government to the Government of Persia through appropriate channels in substantially the following form:

"As the Government of Persia is undoubtedly aware, a conference to consider measures to restrict the traffic in opium and other dangerous drugs will be held in Geneva in November of this year. This is a humanitarian question of world-wide importance in which the Government of the United States has always been deeply interested, and it is hoped that the Persian Government will find it possible to participate in the work of the conference.

One of the principal questions to be considered is the production of raw opium and its transportation in international commerce. It is the earnest hope of this Government that the Government of Persia will cooperate in an international effort to terminate the production and transportation of raw opium in quantities over and above those needed for medicinal purposes, thereby attacking the problem at its source.

The Government of the United States would be glad to have the views of the Government of Persia in this regard, and hopes that the delegates at the conference will be prepared to discuss sympathetically this fundamental point, with a view to accepting the principle."

2. In addition to the above communication to the Persian Government the Department desires that you should make certain oral representations as well. See Department's telegram No. 65, August 12 [13], 4 p.m. On August 22 the Department addressed to you a written communication enclosing a copy of a note dated July 10 received from the British Ambassador at Washington, referring to certain instructions to British consular officers in the Persian Gulf concerning the illicit trade in opium, and a copy of the Department's reply. The note also inquired whether this Government would be disposed to instruct you to inform the Persian Government of the interest of the United States in the adoption of measures tending to suppress illicit traffic in opium. In replying to this note the Department stated that action would be taken by you only if a satisfactory settlement by the Persian Government of the questions arising in the killing in Teheran of Vice-Consul Imbrie had

been reached. While the Department does not consider that at the present time entire satisfaction has been secured in the Imbrie case, nevertheless, in view of the expressed acquiescence of the Persian Government in certain of the demands of this Government and in view of the importance which this Government attaches to the control of illicit traffic in opium, the Department considers it advisable for you to proceed with the suggested representations at once.

The Department believes that it would be entirely appropriate for you to bring the matter to the attention of the Persian Government and to state that it is this Government's hope that the Persian Government will be in a position to enforce regulations which would result in bringing the illicit opium trade to an end. You may state that any action which may be taken by the Persian Government to suppress the illegal opium traffic would be helpful to the United States in making more effective its own very stringent regulations in that connection.

[3.] Before making such representations you may confer with your British colleague in order that your representations may, as nearly as possible, coincide in time with those to be made by him. Department assumes that your British colleague will be pleased to furnish you detailed information as to the attitude of the British Government in this matter and to show you a draft copy of the King's Regulations relating to the control of the traffic in opium between the Persian Gulf and the Far East which the Department understands are to be issued on January 1, 1925.

The Department, in reply to an inquiry in the British note, stated that it refrains from making suggestions to the American financial adviser otherwise than through the regular channels of the competent Persian authorities. The Department assumes, however, that Dr. Millspaugh already appreciates the interest of this Government in the effective control of the traffic in opium.

HUGHES

The Secretary of State to the British Ambassador (Howard)

Washington, August 21, 1924

EXCELLENCY: I have the honor to acknowledge the receipt of Your Excellency's note No. 624 of July 10, 1924, with regard to the illicit trade in opium from ports in the Persian Gulf to China and other far eastern countries. In this communication you indicate that the British Government has decided to issue regulations to its consular officers in the Persian Gulf setting forth the procedure to be observed in granting clearance to British vessels carrying cargoes of opium. You further state that before the regulations in question are issued the British Government proposes to invite the Persian Government to cooperate in the control of the opium traffic in the Persian Gulf, in view of the very considerable financial and economic interests of the latter government. You also inquire, under instructions from your Government, whether the Government of the United States, in view of the interest it has taken in the regulation of the traffic in opium, would be inclined to instruct the American Minister at Teheran to support the representations which His Majesty's Chargé d'Affaires has been instructed to make.

In reply I have the honor to state that subject to the reservation in the concluding paragraph of this note, the Department is instructing the American Minister at Teheran to inform the appropriate Persian authorities that the Government of the United States trusts that the Persian Government will take the necessary steps to obtain a more effective control of the traffic in opium with a view to the elimination of the illicit traffic in that drug.

The American Minister is being instructed also to inform the Persian authorities that this Government has taken stringent measures to regulate the traffic in opium so far as the United States and its possessions are concerned, and that any action which may be taken by the Persian Government to suppress the illegal opium traffic in south Persia would be helpful to the United States in making more effective its own regulations.

With regard to your suggestion that the Department intimate to the Administrator General of the Finances of Persia the desirability of inducing the Persian Government to cooperate in this matter, I would add that while the Department is following with interest the work of the Financial Adviser it refrains from making suggestions to him otherwise than through the regular channels of the competent Persian authorities. The third, fourth and fifth quarterly reports of the Administrator General indicate, however, that plans have already been made which, if carried out, will result in a closer supervision of the domestic consumption as well as of the international trade in opium. These reports also show that some progress has been made in the extension of the control of this trade.

In conclusion I desire, however, to add that pending a satisfactory settlement by the Persian Government of the questions arising from the killing in Teheran of Vice Consul Imbrie, this Government would not be disposed to make the representations outlined above, and the American Minister has been so advised.

Accept [etc.]   CHARLES E. HUGHES

The Secretary of State to the Minister in Persia (Kornfeld)

No. 330   Washington, August 22, 1924

SIR: The Department has received a note dated July 10, 1924, from the British Ambassador at Washington, of which a copy is enclosed, which refers to certain instructions to British Consular Officers in the Persian Gulf, concerning the illicit trade in opium. The note also inquires whether this Government would be disposed to instruct you to inform the Persian Government of the interest of the United States in the adoption of measures tending to suppress the illegal traffic in opium.

In the light of reports received by the Department which indicate that there is a substantial illicit trade in opium in Persian Gulf ports, the Department considers that it would be entirely appropriate for you to bring this matter to the attention of the Persian Government, and to state that it is this Government's hope that the Persian Government will be in a position to enforce regulations which would result in bringing the illicit opium trade to an end.

You may further refer to the fact that this Government is much interested in the suppression of the illicit traffic in opium, that it has taken stringent measures to regulate this trade as far as the United States and its possessions are concerned, and any action which may be taken by the Persian Government to suppress the illegal opium traffic would be helpful to the United States in making more effective its own regulations.

Before making such representations you may confer with your British colleague in order that the representations which you may make may, as nearly as possible, coincide in time with those to be made by the British representative.

You will observe the statement in the Department's communication to the British Government with respect to the suggested representations to Doctor Millspaugh on this subject. Having noted the plans outlined in the third, fourth and fifth quarterly reports of the Administrator General of the Finances of Persia for the control of the opium traffic, the Department assumes that Dr. Millspaugh already appreciates the interest of this Government in the effective control of the traffic in opium.

As indicated in the last paragraph of the note to the British Embassy and in the Department's telegram No. 65 of August 13, 4 p.m., the above instruction is only to be acted upon if a satisfactory settlement by the Persian Government of the questions arising from the killing in Teheran of Vice Consul Imbrie has been reached. Otherwise the Government would not be disposed to make representations in other matters not of immediate urgency.

I am [etc.]   CHARLES E. HUGHES

The Persian Minister for Foreign Affairs (Moshar-ol-Molk) to the American Chargé (Murray)

[INCLOSURE-TRANSLATION]

No. 11339   [Teheran,] September 30, 1924/Mizan 8, 1303

MR. CHARGÉ D'AFFAIRES: I beg to acknowledge the receipt of your letter of September 16, 1924, No. 16, concerning the commission that will be formed in Geneva in the month of November in order to adopt a decision with regard to placing restriction on the commerce and production of opium.

As you are well aware the Imperial Government of Persia has signed the 1912 Opium Agreement of The Hague, with a reservation regarding Chapter III, and that it has, up to the present, made every effort to assure the success of this enterprise. You will, however, agree with me in the fact that the particular circumstances existing in Persia make it impossible to take final measures in this connection without having first studied and considered those circumstances.

The Imperial Persian Government, despite its sincere desire to restrict the production and commerce of opium, finds it, unfortunately, impracticable suddenly to place a prohibition on it without having taken certain particular points into consideration, such as the substitution of other products for the production of opium, and the adoption of an appropriate decision whereby the domestic consumption of opium could gradually be stopped.

This view of the Persian Government has duly been stated to the special branch of the League which is attended by the representatives of the United States Government, and it is reported that the American representatives have realized the difficulties confronting the Persian Government and concur with the Persian representatives in that, in order to bring about the complete enforcement in Persia of the Hague Agreement, it is necessary that practical methods of so doing should be resorted to.

I beg to reiterate the statement that my Government is exceedingly desirous of being able, with the concurrence of your Government and the other Governments, to remove the existing difficulties and gradually to fulfill the provisions of The Hague Convention and the decisions adopted by the League of Nations. Definite instructions have been given to the Persian representatives who will attend the commission that is to meet in Geneva in the coming month of November, and I am hopeful that the views of the Persian Government in the matter of the method of placing restriction on the production and trade of opium will be accepted.

In the meantime I beg to request you to use the good offices of your Honorable Legation in assuring your Government of the good-will of the Persian Government in this matter, and to request it to lend its assistance and cooperation to the representatives of the Persian Government in their just representations in order to find a practical means of settling this affair.

I avail [etc.]

MOSHAR-OL-MOLK

The Secretary of State to the Chargé in Persia (Murray)

Washington, January 19, 1925, noon

2. Department's 83, September 15, 5 p.m., point 2, and written instruction 330, August 22, 1924.

Further communication has been received from British Embassy inquiring whether this Government would now be prepared to approach the Persian Government with respect to latter's exercising a more effective control of illicit traffic in opium from ports in Persian Gulf to Far Eastern countries.

Cable promptly action, if any, which you have taken other than as reported in your written despatches 652 September 23 and 671 October 8. Department notes you have consulted with British Chargé d'Affaires but record does not indicate that you have made either written or oral representations relative to particular phase of the matter mentioned in British note. Report whether you see any objection to such action at this time.

HUGHES

The Chargé in Persia (Murray) to the Secretary of State

Teheran, January 21, 1925, 9 a.m.

5. Department's No. 2, January 19, noon. I have not made any representations on opium question to Persian Government after those which I reported to Department in my despatches Nos. 652, of September 23, and 671, of October 8. Reasons are as follows: (1) Until complete liquidation of Imbrie incident I regarded such discussions as inappropriate. (2) In view of Persia's contribution to solution of opium problem in form of Colonel MacCormack's memorandum on Persian opium,* it was my feeling that representations to Persian Government in my note of September 16 were sufficient reminder.

I venture to make following observations with regard to further representations on particular phase of matter mentioned in British note: (1) Between 60 and 70 tons of Indian opium have been sent in bond, in the past 10 months, to Bushire tax-free transshipment. In order to put an end to this traffic, the Council of Ministers issued an order a month ago prohibiting entirely importation of opium into Persia. (2) Colonel MacCormack is of opinion that pending report of opium investigation commission, whose despatch to Persia the League of Nations has suggested (so I am informed) and to which the Persian Government has agreed, further representations are not necessary. . . .

MURRAY

---

* Memorandum on Persian opium prepared by Col. D.W. MacCormack of the American Financial Mission in Persia and presented by the Persian delegation at the Second Opium Conference. Printed in League of Nations, *Records of the Second Opium Conference, Geneva, November 17th, 1924—February 19th, 1925*, vol. II, p. 194.

The Secretary of State to the Chargé in Persia (Murray)
Washington, February 7, 1925, 3 p.m.

4. Your 5, January 21, 9 a.m. In view of the definite statement in the Department's note of August 21, 1924, to the British Embassy, copy of which was enclosed with Department's written instruction to you of August 22, it is desired that you address a further communication to the Persian Government in regard to the traffic in opium embodying the substance of the second and third paragraphs of Department's note of August 21. In your communication you may also in your discretion refer to relevant facts set forth in annex 4 to MacCormack memorandum, and you may state that the Government of the United States has been pleased to note action already taken by Government of Persia toward suppressing illicit traffic from ports of Persian Gulf, adding that it is the earnest hope of the Government of the United States that this action will be pressed to a successful conclusion.

You may use your discretion on consulting further with your British colleague before sending note.

Telegraph briefly action taken.

HUGHES

UNITED STATES RECOGNITION OF CHANGE IN PERSIAN DYNASTY

The Secretary of State to the Chargé in Persia (Amory)

Washington, November 3, 1925, 1 p.m.

53. Referring your 78 of November 1, and 79 of November 2, Department sanctions acknowledgement, in manner you have suggested, of circular from Foreign Office. You may also carry on, at your discretion, the business of the Legation with the Provisional Government, following, when expedient, the procedure of representatives of other powers.

The Foreign Office circular alludes to the government of Reza Khan as provisional, and anticipates that a definitive form of government will be later set up by Constituent Assembly. It is, therefore, assumed by the Department that there is not at present any question of formal recognition, and that before that question arises there will be an opportunity to consider further the legal status of the new government and its attitude toward international agreements made under the Kajar dynasty.

Advise Department of steps taken.

KELLOGG

The Secretary of State to the Chargé in Persia (Amory)

Washington, November 4, 1925, 7 p.m.

55. (1) Should Department's 53, November 3, not entirely meet exigency as set forth in your 80, November 3, cable your suggestions.

(2) You may intimate to Persian officials that this Government does not wish to delay its expression of friendliness toward Persia in the present situation. But since, according to your report, the present Provisional Government looks to a Constituent Assembly for eventual confirmation of its authority, the Department judged that confirmation might fittingly precede formal recognition by this Government. Any recommendation which you may feel disposed to make will, however, receive the Department's careful consideration.

KELLOGG

The Secretary of State to the Chargé in Persia (Amory)

Washington, November 5, 1925, 6 p.m.

56. Your 81, November 5, 4 p.m.

(1) You are authorized to deliver to Persian Government a communication stating that this Government accords recognition to the provisional regime inaugurated in Persia pursuant to the recent decision of the Persian National Assembly pending the final decision to be taken by the Constituent Assembly. You should add that this recognition is accorded on the understanding that all international agreements between the United States and Persia will be scrupulously observed by the new regime.

(2) [Paraphrase.] The form "recognition of the provisional regime" seems at once more exact and more in keeping with the general policy of the United States than the form "provisional recognition" used by British. . . . [End paraphrase.]

(3) Persian Chargé today inquired of Department whether you had been authorized to call on the Chief of State. Department sees no objection to such action if you consider it desirable. At that time you could impress upon Reza Khan that the United States desires to maintain with the new provisional regime in Persia relations of cordial understanding.

Having determined upon the action outlined above the Department leaves it to your discretion to take such further action of a ceremonial or other character as may be necessary in view of the recognition accorded the provisional regime.

KELLOGG

The Secretary of State to the Persian Chargé (Kazemi)

Washington, December 21, 1925

SIR: I beg to acknowledge the receipt of your communication of December 13, 1925 in which you have informed me that, on December 12th, the Constituent Assembly at Teheran, convoked for the purpose of deciding upon the permanent form of government in Persia and the person of the Chief of State, decided in favor of a Constitutional Monarchy in which the ruling dynasty shall be his Imperial Majesty Reza Shah Pahlevi and his male descendants.

I am pleased to be able to inform you that, on December 15 [16], the American Chargé d'Affaires at Teheran was instructed to address a communication to the Persian Government stating that the Government of the United States, having noted the action of the Constituent Assembly of Persia in investing the Constitutional Monarchy of Persia in His Imperial Majesty Reza Shah Pahlevi, and being informed that the latter has taken the oath, extends recognition to the Government of Persia. This recognition has been accorded on the understanding that all international treaties and agreements between the United States and Persia shall be scrupulously observed. This communication was delivered on December 17th.

On December 16th, the President of the United States cabled the following message to His Imperial Majesty Reza Shah Pahlevi:

"It affords me great pleasure to express my sincere congratulations on this occasion of Your Majesty's accession and my best wishes for Your Majesty's good health and happiness. It is my earnest hope that during Your Majesty's reign the friendly relations now existing between Persia and the United States of America and between the peoples of our two countries will be still further strengthened. I shall make it my pleasant duty to cooperate with Your Majesty to that end, and I am certain that Your Majesty will find in Mr. Hoffman Philip, newly appointed Minister of the United States to Persia and now en route to Your Majesty's capital, a diplomatic representative eminently fitted to further that cooperation."

Accept [etc.]

FRANK B. KELLOGG

TREATY REGULATING COMMERCIAL RELATIONS BETWEEN THE UNITED STATES AND PERSIA

May 14, 1928   Exchange of notes at Tehran.
May 14, 1928   Entered into force; operative with respect to certain
                provisions from May 10, 1928.
July 11, 1928   Supplemented by agreement.
June 16, 1957   Replaced by treaty of August 15, 1955.

The American Minister to the Acting Minister of Foreign Affairs (Pakrevan)

Legation of the United States of America
Teheran, Persia, May 14, 1928

EXCELLENCY: I have the honor to inform you that my Government, animated by the sincere desire to terminate as soon as possible the negotiations now in progress with the Imperial Government of Persia in regard to the conclusion of a Treaty of Friendship, as well as Establishment, Consular, Commercial and Tariff Conventions between the United States of America and Persia, has instructed me to communicate to the Imperial Government of Persia in its name the following provisional stipulations:

1) After May 10, 1928, the diplomatic representation of Persia in the United States, its territories and possessions, shall enjoy, on a basis of complete reciprocity, the privileges and immunities derived from generally recognized international law.

The Consular representatives of Persia, duly provided with exequatur, will be permitted to reside in the United States, its territories and possessions, in the districts where they have been formerly admitted.

They shall, on a basis of complete reciprocity, enjoy the honorary privileges and personal immunities in regard to jurisdiction and fiscal matters secured to them by generally recognized international law.

2) After May 10, 1928, Persian nationals in the United States, its territories and possessions, shall, on a basis of complete reciprocity, be received and treated in accordance with the requirements and practices of generally recognized international law.

In respect to their persons and possessions, rights and interests, they shall enjoy the fullest protection of the laws and authorities of the Country, and they shall not be treated, in regard to the above mentioned subjects, in a manner less favorable than the nationals of any other foreign country.

In general, they shall enjoy in every respect the same treatment as the nationals of the Country, without, however, being entitled to the treatment reserved alone to nationals to the exclusion of all foreigners.

Matters of personal status and family law will be dealt with in separate notes to be concluded and exchanged at the earliest possible date.

3) After May 10, 1928, and as long as the present stipulations remain in force, and on a basis of complete reciprocity, the United States will accord to merchandise produced or manufactured in Persia upon entry into the United States, its territories and possessions, the benefits of the tariff accorded to the most favored nation; from which it follows that the treatment extended to the products of Persia should not be less favorable than that granted to a third country.

In respect to the regime to be applied to the Commerce of Persia in the matter of import, export, and other duties and charges affecting commerce as well as in respect to transit warehousing and the facilities accorded commercial travelers' samples; and also as regards commodities, tariffs and quantities in connection with the licensing or prohibitions of imports and exports, the United States shall accord to Persia, on a basis of complete reciprocity, a treatment not less advantageous than that accorded to the commerce of any other country.

It is understood that no higher or other duties shall be imposed on the importation into or disposition in the United States, its territories or possessions, of any article, the product or manufacture of Persia, than are or shall be payable on like articles, the product or manufacture of any foreign country; similarly, and on a basis of complete reciprocity, no higher or other duties shall be imposed in the United States, its territories or possessions, on the exportation of any articles to Persia than are payable on the exportation of like articles to any foreign country.

On a basis of complete reciprocity, any lowering of duty of any kind that may be accorded by the United States in favor of the merchandise of any other country will become immediately applicable without request and without compensation to the commerce of Persia with the United States, its territories and possessions.

Providing that this understanding does not relate to:

1) The treatment which the United States accords or may hereafter accord to the commerce of Cuba, or any of the territories or possessions of the United States, or the Panama Canal Zone, or to the treatment which is or may hereafter be accorded to the commerce of the United States with any of its territories or possessions, or to the commerce of its territories or possessions with one another;

2) Prohibitions or restrictions authorized by the laws and regulations in force in the United States, its territories or possessions, aiming at the protection of the food supply, sanitary administration in regard to human, animal or vegetable life, and the enforcement of police and revenue laws.

The present stipulations shall become operative on the day of signature, and shall remain respectively in effect until the entry in force of the Treaty and Conventions referred to in the first paragraph of this note, or until thirty days after notice of their termination shall have been given by the Government of the United States to the Imperial Government of Persia, but should the Government of the United States be prevented by future action of its legislature from carrying out the terms of these stipulations the obligations thereof shall thereupon lapse.

I shall be glad to have your confirmation of the understanding thus reached.

I avail myself of this opportunity to renew to Your Excellency the assurances of my highest consideration.

HOFFMAN PHILIP

The American Minister to the Acting Minister of Foreign Affairs (Pakrevan)

Legation of the United States of America
Teheran, Persia, May 14, 1928

EXCELLENCY: I have the honor to inform you, in the name of my Government, that I have received and taken note of the contents of your note of today's date setting forth provisional stipulations in regard to Diplomatic, Consular, tariff and other relations between the United States and Persia.

I avail myself of this opportunity to renew to Your Excellency the assurance of my highest consideration.

HOFFMAN PHILIP

The American Minister to the Acting Minister of Foreign Affairs (Pakrevan)

[TRANSLATION]

Legation of the United States of America
Teheran, May 14, 1928

MR. ACTING MINISTER: I would be very glad to receive from Your Excellency an assurance on the part of the Imperial Government that American missionaries in Persia will be authorized, as in the past, to carry on their charitable and educational work.

I take this occasion to renew to you, Mr. Acting Minister, the assurances of my high consideration.

HOFFMAN PHILIP

The Acting Minister of Foreign Affairs to the American Minister (Philip)

[TRANSLATION]

Teheran, May 14, 1928

MR. MINISTER: In reply to your request relative to American missionaries, I have the honor to inform you that they will be authorized to carry on their charitable and educational work on the condition that it contravenes neither the public order nor the laws and regulations of Persia.

Please accept, Mr. Minister, the assurance of my high consideration.

F. PAKREVAN

IRAN* PROTESTS AMERICAN PRESS TREATMENT: WITHDRAWS REPRESENTATIVES

Memorandum by the Under Secretary of State (Phillips)

[*Washington,*] *March 14, 1936*

The Chargé d'Affaires of Iran handed me this morning a translation and copy of a message which he had just received from his Government with regard to a recent publication in the New York *Mirror* referring to the Shah as formerly a stable hand; the Chargé admitted that the instruction came directly from the Shah himself. After reading it I expressed astonishment at its terms, saying that it was scarcely the kind of message which passed between two friendly governments; I did not wish, therefore, to discuss it, but would prefer to discuss the unfortunate publication of the *Mirror*. I thereupon laid the Shah's message aside and took up the accompanying message left by the Chargé, which dealt only with the *Mirror's* publication; I said that this Government naturally regretted any indignity against the head of a friendly state which had been committed in this country, either by the press or otherwise; I pointed out that, in this particular incident, the *Mirror* was a very unimportant publication, with a limited circulation and, in consequence, that this particular reference to the Shah would be noticed by very few people and even by them promptly forgotten; I explained the lack of control which this Government had over the American press, which I felt sure he fully understood; if, for example, the Department

---

* On March 22, 1935, the name "Iran" came into official use for the country known to that time as "Persia."

should communicate in writing with the *Mirror* or make any protest with regard to this particular incident, the *Mirror* would, in all probability publicize this fact and the objectionable reference to the Shah would consequently be broadcast throughout the country and the incident, which is now unnoticed, could very easily become known throughout the nation because of what might be interpreted by the American press as governmental restraint exercised upon an independent American journal. Furthermore, I added that I was doubtful whether our laws, which guaranteed freedom of the press, would operate in this particular case; I would, of course, be very glad to study our laws to see whether they might apply in such a way that this Government could properly make representations to the *Mirror*.

The Chargé d'Affaires expressed gratification at my reply, intimated, nevertheless, that he would like to see some action taken by the Department vis-à-vis the *Mirror* and expressed the hope that I could give him some answer to his instructions on Monday next.

(The Shah's message, to which I did not refer except at the opening of the conversation, threatened to break off diplomatic relations with the United States unless the Department took certain specified steps vis-à-vis the *Mirror's* statement.)

WILLIAM PHILLIPS

Memorandum by the Chief of the Division of Near Eastern Affairs (Murray)

[*Washington*,] March 17, 1936

I went to see the Iranian Chargé d'Affaires on Sunday morning, March 15, to discuss the message which he left with the Under Secretary on March 14 in which the Iranian Government threatened that it will "revise their political relations with the United States" unless this Government takes immediate steps, "even making an exception in this case," to cause the New York *Daily Mirror* to retract the statement made in its issue of February 8, 1936 to the effect that the Shah "was formerly employed in the stables of the British Legation in Teheran."

In reply to my inquiry of Mr. Ghods as to his explanation for this extraordinary communication, he reiterated the old story about the Shah's extreme sensitiveness to foreign criticism and said he felt sure that the Iranian Foreign Minister who signed the telegram was carrying out the exact instructions of the Shah. He confirmed my impression that the Shah would have little hesitation in going through with his threat unless something could be done at this end to appease the Shah's wrath. He furthermore confirmed a suspicion I had had that the reception scheduled for last Saturday evening at the Iranian Legation in honor of the Shah's birthday had been called off by specific order of His Majesty and that the motivation for this action was undoubtedly the story in the New York *Daily Mirror*.

Mr. Ghods then recounted his conversation with the Under Secretary, which he described as "extremely helpful." He said he had immediately wired his Government and pointed out that Mr. Phillips, in view of his great friendliness to Iran, did not wish to consider that an unfriendly communication had been delivered to him; that Mr. Phillips had, however, assured him that he would examine carefully into the situation and if it were possible under American law he would see to it that punishment was meted out for the offending article. In other words, Mr. Ghods was very happy that Mr. Phillips had not turned him down at once, since a communication in that sense to his Government would, he felt, have resulted in immediate and drastic action in Teheran. He said he intended to call at the Department the following day, when he hoped to receive further word as to the action which the Department was prepared to take under the circumstances.

I pointed out to Mr. Ghods the unusual character of his Government's demands and emphasized again to him that the freedom of the press in this country is not merely an empty phrase but is a very actual reality. He said he realized this fully but that unfortunately the Shah of Iran did not and was unwilling to accept any such excuses where criticism of his person was concerned. Mr. Ghods told me that he had written twice to the Editor of the New York *Daily Mirror* requesting him to correct the false statement but that his requests had been ignored. He therefore felt that he had no other alternative than to appeal to the Department for help.

I questioned Mr. Ghods closely as to whether, in the event the Department, as an entirely exceptional measure, endeavored to bring about a retraction of the offensive statement, the Iranian Government would consider such action as a precedent and would consider itself justified in demanding that we follow the same procedure in all future instances where something unpleasant or untrue might be said regarding the Shah. The Chargé said he thought the present case could be handled in such a manner that his Government would be given to understand that a precedent was not being established and that our action in this instance was entirely exceptional and a gesture of goodwill to the Shah. I emphasized to Mr. Ghods the absolute necessity of making this point clear to his Government since any misunderstanding in the matter could only create further difficulties.

I asked the Chargé whether he thought it desirable to bring our Legation in Teheran into the picture in any manner. He said he thought it would be better to leave the matter for the time being entirely in his hands since everything depended on the exact wording of any communications delivered to the Iranian Government on this subject. I think his suggestion is a wise one, everything considered.

After discussing this question with Mr. McDermott* yesterday morning, it was decided that any direct communication between the Department and the Editor of the New York *Daily Mirror* would be ill-advised. It was suggested that I endeavor to get in communication with Mr. James T. Williams, personal representative of Mr. Hearst in Washington, and discuss the situation with him in complete confidence. I explained the matter fully and in confidence to Mr. Williams this morning, who seemed to appreciate fully the difficulty in which the Department is placed and, while pointing out that he had no authority whatsoever over the Editor of the New York *Daily Mirror*, said he would be glad to communicate directly by long distance telephone with Mr. Hearst and put the matter up to him. He reminded me that no assurances could be given that the Editor of the *Mirror* could be brought to take the action desired by the Iranian Government but assured me that he (Mr. Williams) would do his best.

There the matter stands for the time being. Mr. Williams is coming to see me this afternoon to discuss further phases of the matter before he takes it up with Mr. Hearst.

WALLACE MURRAY

Memorandum by the Under Secretary of State (Phillips)

[*Washington,*] *March 17, 1936*

I sent for the Iranian Chargé d'Affaires this afternoon and referred to my last conversation with him on Saturday morning when I told him that I would look into the matter which he had presented to me and would advise him whether any action could be taken by the Government against the New York *Daily Mirror*. I said that I was now satisfied, although I regretted this fact very much, that there was nothing in our laws that permitted the Government to take any step vis-à-vis the *Mirror*; however, as we were anxious to show the Shah every consideration in this case, we had not abandoned hope that something could be done to elicit some expression of regret or correction by the *Mirror* itself; we had today asked a third person, who was in a position to approach the *Mirror* independently to see what could be done in the circumstances; I wished it understood, however, that this action on our part was not to be taken as a precedent; as the Chargé d'Affaires well understood, some of our papers had been guilty of indignities against the chiefs of other states, viz., Japan, the King of Rumania, the Queen Mother of Rumania, Hitler, Mussolini; unfortunately, they had all been caricatured at one time or another, and it was even possible that something might be said in the future which would not be pleasant reading to the Shah himself; we could guarantee nothing, but in order to show

---

* Michael J. McDermott, Chief of the Division of Current Information.

our friendly feelings toward Iran and the Iranian people we were making this special effort in this particular case.

The Chargé d'Affaires expressed much appreciation of our efforts in his Government's behalf; he expressed the hope that the *Mirror* would not publish the letter which he himself had written to the *Mirror* two or three days after the incident; the incident having progressed as far as it had, the publication of his letter now would probably not be considered sufficient by the Shah; he hoped, therefore, that some expression by the *Mirror* itself would be given.

WILLIAM PHILLIPS

The Acting Secretary of State to the Chargé in Iran (Merriam)

Washington, March 19, 1936, 4 p.m.

11. Your 21, March 15, 9 a.m. On March 14 the Iranian Chargé d'Affaires called upon me to protest against the article which appeared in the New York *Mirror*. He handed me a message which he had been instructed to deliver, one section of which contained a threat to sever relations unless immediate steps were taken by this Government, even as an exceptional measure, to have the article amended. I told him that in view of the friendly relations existing between Iran and the United States I preferred not to discuss the message but rather the unfortunate *Mirror* article.

I said that this Government naturally regretted any indignity against the head of a friendly state, explained that the *Mirror* was an unimportant journal with limited circulation, and that the reference to the Shah would be noticed by few and promptly forgotten even by them. I also pointed out the lack of control which this Government had over the American press and expressed doubt whether, in view of the constitutional provisions concerning freedom of the press, there was any law which would apply in such a case as that presented. I agreed, however, to study the situation with the utmost goodwill.

After careful consideration the Department is left in no doubt that this Government is entirely without means to take any legal action in this matter. However, in order to demonstrate clearly our sincere desire to liquidate this incident to the satisfaction of the Iranian Government we are approaching the publishers and urging them, as a matter of cooperation and in the interest of our continued friendly relations with Iran, to publish a suitable correction.

On March 17 I conveyed to the Iranian Chargé d'Affaires the information contained in the preceding paragraph.

The foregoing is for your information. In view of the delicate character of the question you should refrain from taking it up in Teheran. However, if the subject is broached to you, you should be guided by the above considerations, in which connection you should stress these obvious facts: (1) that this Government, under its constitution, is prohibited from interfering in any manner with the freedom of the press and (2) that the action it is taking with a view to obtaining a correction by the New York *Mirror* is altogether unique and is being taken only because of its sincere desire to cultivate friendly relations with Iran. It must not be regarded as constituting a precedent and you should lay particular emphasis on that point in any conversations into which you are drawn.

PHILLIPS

Memorandum by the Chief of the Division of Near Eastern Affairs (Murray)

[*Washington,*] *March 26, 1936*

After learning from the Secretary of Mr. James T. Williams that the text of the correction agreed upon with the Iranian Chargé d'Affaires was published in the first edition of the New York *Daily Mirror* today, March 26, I immediately informed Mr. Ghods, who said he had seen the correction and immediately informed his Government by telegraph that the correction had been published.

Mr. Ghods expressed deep appreciation for the assistance which the Department has rendered him in this matter.

WALLACE MURRAY

The Secretary of State to the Chargé in Iran (Merriam)

Washington, March 26, 1936, 6 p.m.

12. Department's 10 [11], March 19, 4 p.m. *Daily Mirror* today printed following under heading "Correction":

"It has been brought to the attention of the *Mirror* that a statement contained in its issue of February 8, 1936, to the effect that His Majesty, the Shah of Iran, was formerly in the hire of the British Legation at Teheran, is wholly without foundation, and that His Majesty has since his earliest youth served his country in the army.

"The *Mirror* regrets the publication in its columns of such an erroneous statement and is happy to make this correction."

HULL

Memorandum by the Chief of the Division of Near Eastern Affairs (Murray)

[*Washington,*] *March 31, 1936*

In conversation yesterday afternoon with the Iranian Chargé d'Affaires he took great pains to emphasize to me that the decision of his

Government to withdraw all Iranian representatives in this country and to close the Iranian Legation in Washington would not in any way affect the status of our Legation in Teheran. He explained that in withdrawing Iranian representation in this country the Shah had desired to indicate his displeasure over the attitude of the American press towards himself personally and towards Iran in general. Since the Shah was not in any way displeased with the American Legation in Teheran, the Iranian Government would continue, as in the past, to have most friendly relations with that Legation and to conduct business with it as usual. I inferred, in fact, from the Iranian Chargé's remarks that his Government would be displeased if we took any steps to reduce the present status of our representation in Iran.

It is clear from the above that the present action of the Iranian Government cannot in any way be regarded as a severance of diplomatic relations between the two countries. It is solely a unilateral act on the part of the Iranian Government to give emphasis to the Shah's displeasure over the attitude of the American press.

WALLACE MURRAY

The Secretary of State to the Chargé in Iran (Merriam)

Washington, April 30, 1936, 7 p.m.

22. Your 31, April 16, noon. Mr. Hornibrook has returned and has informed the Department of the conversation which he had on March 15th with Mr. Kazemi, then Minister for Foreign Affairs. In that conversation Mr. Kazemi thought fit to urge that this Government take steps to amend the Constitution so as to restrict the freedom of the press. The absolute impossibility of any such steps must be clear to anyone who is familiar with American institutions and the American form of government.

Under the circumstances it is apparent that no useful purpose could be served by sending a special envoy to Teheran and the proposed mission has therefore been definitely abandoned.

Please bring the foregoing to the attention of the Minister for Foreign Affairs, leaving with him an *aide-mémoire* of your conversation.

HULL

The Secretary of State to the Chargé in Iran (Merriam)

Washington, May 15, 1936, 5 p.m.

24. Your 33, May 9, 5 p.m. You should seek an early occasion to impress upon Soheily that there was no misunderstanding whatever of the representations which Kazemi made to Mr. Hornibrook on March 15. Mr. Hornibrook's report on this matter confirmed by your despatch

743, March 17, makes it perfectly clear that Kazemi envisaged an amendment of the American Constitution with a view to restricting the freedom of the press. It should be unnecessary to remind the Iranian
authorities that this Government cannot even discuss with any foreign
government such a wholly unwarranted suggestion.

You should also impress upon Soheily that the Department's decision that no useful purpose would be served by following your suggestion regarding the sending of a special envoy to Teheran was not based
upon any pretext but upon the nature of Kazemi's representations
referred to above. . . .

For your confidential information and general guidance, the Department is not inclined to view with any particular concern the mere
withdrawal of Iranian representation in Washington provided the Iranian Government continues normal relations with our Legation at
Teheran. That Government's intention to continue such relations was
reported in your telegram No. 26, March 29, 5 p.m. Your relations with
the Iranians could therefore be cordial and scrupulously correct and you
should carefully avoid giving any impression that you fear that any
developments such as press comments in this country might alter the
status quo. You will of course report promptly any contrary disposition
on the part of the Iranian authorities.

HULL

The Chargé in Iran (Merriam) to the Secretary of State

No. 860   *Teheran, July 25, 1936*

SIR: I have the honor to inform the Department that at the request
of His Excellency A. Soheily, Under Secretary of State for Foreign
Affairs, I called upon him at the Foreign Office on July 23, 1936,
accompanied by the Legation Interpreter.

Somewhat wearily, and with a smile which appeared to me to
indicate that his heart was not in it, Mr. Soheily produced a clipping
from the *Brooklyn Eagle* of June 13, 1936 which, under the caption
"Stranger than Fiction," reproduced a sketch of the Shah, with the
legend: "The present Shah of Persia descends from no long line of
royalty—he himself was a stable boy originally."

His Excellency said that he had had the clipping on his desk for
some time and had been undecided whether to bring it to my notice, but
he had eventually concluded that it would be best to do so. He said that
he realized my Government had no control over the press, but asked me
to request the Department of State to make an investigation with a view
to determining what lay behind the publication of such derogatory
remarks in the American press which, as I could observe, kept
recurring. . . .

Considering the opportunity a good one, as Soheily seemed to be carrying out his duty without real zest and with some boredom, although conscientiously, I remarked that although the American press had given a good deal of annoyance to the Iranian Government, it could be turned to good account. I hoped that when a new Iranian Minister should be appointed to Washington, he would approach the press directly and in the right way; he would find that it was conducted by friendly, decent and capable men who would willingly learn the truth about Iran, and print material that would be pleasing both to Iran and to ourselves.

Soheily observed that it did not look as though the appointment of a new Minister would take place in the near future.

I said that naturally I did not presume to assume that a new Minister would be appointed soon, though of course I hoped one would be. I was merely trying to state the problem he would be up against, and to indicate some of the methods of dealing with it based on my personal knowledge of American conditions.

Soheily then said that huge appropriations would be needed to use with the foreign press for the purposes which I mentioned, which were not available.

I said that an appropriation was unnecessary, that I did not have paid propaganda in mind—that, as a matter of fact, it was impossible to buy news space in American journals. What I had in mind was that the new Minister would best meet the press problem by cultivating friendly personal relations with journalists and editors, and by informing them of what was going on in Iran. These men were friendly disposed and on the lookout for new and unusual material, and there was certainly an enormous amount of interest attaching to this country of which they were now largely in ignorance.

I added that American newspaper men hated nothing more than to see a foreign Minister running to the Department of State with complaints about the press. They liked a direct approach, and if an Iranian Minister who should be displeased about the press went directly to the editor and asked: "Why do you print such things about us?" he would be likely to get satisfactory results.

Soheily was unwilling to be led too far astray, and merely repeated his original request, to which I again assented. In reply to a question intended to bring out how much urgency he attached to the matter, he said that he did not think there was any necessity for using the telegraph, but that he did wish to have a definite reply, because he was keenly interested in establishing who or what, in Iran, the United States or elsewhere, was responsible for attaching to the Shah, in the American press, descriptions of an untrue and offensive nature. He thought that it would be better to explain the matter fully to the Department of State in writing, and not to use the telegraph. . . .

I am under the impression, however, that the suspicion of the

Foreign Office that some person is in back of exceptionable articles in the American press, is quite sincere.

Respectfully yours,   GORDON P. MERRIAM

Mr. William H. Hornibrook to the Chargé in Iran (Merriam)

[*Salt Lake City,*] *July 29, 1936*

DEAR MR. MERRIAM: Your letter under date of June 24th, was received today and I hasten to correct what appears to be a misapprehension as to representations which were made by the Legation to the Iranian Government in connection with the attacks of the American press against the Shah.

In your letter you state: "According to my recollection, it was the Legation which on the 14th or the 15th of March suggested that you would do what you could about securing legal protection for foreign sovereigns from the American press when you reached home."

No such representations were at any time made by me, nor by any member of the Legation staff. The only representations authorized, and the only representations made as far as my knowledge goes, were in the form of a definite promise that I would be very glad indeed to present in their entirety, the views of the Iranian Government pertaining to a change in our Constitution immediately upon the date of my arrival in Washington. It was also rather broadly hinted to Soheily, that it would perhaps be unwise for the Foreign Office to take any further action in connection with its complaint as to unfriendly newspaper publicity in the American Press prior to the date of my arrival in Washington and the submission of my personal report on American-Iranian relations. This was done in the hope that a "cooling time" would thus be provided during the period that I was in transit. It was hinted that at such conference there might be a possibility of working out informally, some plan with the American Press Association which would be helpful, but at no time was an express or implied promise given that such an objective could be obtained, that I proposed to recommend a change in the organic laws of the United States or that I would do more than to present the views of the Iranian Foreign Office as to such proposed change. . . .

Kazemi was in no frame of mind to listen to explanations. His reply was in the form of a question and an answer and was as follows: "Is not France like the United States, a Republican form of Government? France only recently changed its laws so that unpleasant comments about sovereigns of friendly states are now prohibited. What France did I am sure that your Country could do even tho a change in your laws would be necessary in order to accomplish this purpose."

I then explained to the Minister the long series of delays that would of necessity ensue under our form of Government in the event that a proposal of this character should be formally submitted to Congress. I ventured the opinion that perhaps the best that could be hoped for would be informal representations to the press by the Department of State but that I was not authorized to give any assurance as to the Department's position on that subject. I did agree, however, to submit his views to Washington as soon as I arrived, and, if, after the matter had been discussed I could find a way to be helpful, I would, of course, do what I could to work out some informal solution of the difficulty. This angle of the situation was thoroughly explored while I was in Washington with the result that Department officials agreed the time was not opportune to take the matter up officially with the American Press Association.

The final words of the Minister were: "We are depending upon your Government to make the necessary changes in your laws and we are depending upon you to present our views to Washington.". . .

WILLIAM H. HORNIBROOK

The Secretary of State to the Chargé in Iran (Merriam)

No. 255   *Washington, September 14, 1936*

SIR: The Department acknowledges the receipt of your despatch No. 860 of July 25, 1936, reporting your conversation with the Iranian Under Secretary of State for Foreign Affairs with reference to an item which appeared in the *Brooklyn Eagle* of June 13, 1936, concerning the Shah. Your observations to Mr. Soheily, as reported in your despatch under reference, meet with the Department's approval.

With reference to the request of Mr. Soheily that the Department "make an investigation with a view to determining what lay behind the publication of such derogatory remarks in the American press," it is clear from the Department's inquiries and from its general knowledge of the subject that no agencies are working in this country with a view to weakening the long established ties of friendship between Iran and the United States. As you explained to the Under Secretary at the time of your interview, statements regarding the Shah such as that which appeared in the *Brooklyn Eagle*, even when they are erroneous, are in no wise intended to be derogatory to His Imperial Majesty. On the contrary, the people of this country from the earliest days have cherished the highest admiration for persons who have risen to positions of eminence as a result of their own ability and force of character. In this connection it is perhaps needless to recall that President Lincoln, who is admittedly an outstanding American statesman and an international figure, is even to this day commonly referred to as "The Rail-splitter" from the fact that in his youth he earned his living by splitting trees for fence rails. That President Lincoln started life in such humble labors only adds to the admiration in which he is held by the people of this country.

Therefore, when the American press refers to the vigorous and manly background of the Shah, such references, even though historically inaccurate in certain instances, can be interpreted only as an effort, possibly misguided but nevertheless sincere, to honor His Imperial Majesty and raise him even higher in the estimation of the American people. Moreover, that the American press and the American people are animated by the most friendly sentiments towards Iran and towards its eminent ruler are clearly indicated by the numerous articles which appear in the daily papers and in periodicals commenting upon the rapid progress which Iran has made under the guidance of His Imperial Majesty.

The Department is therefore entirely persuaded that no agencies are working in this country with a view to beclouding American-Iranian relations. Indeed, even if inimical agencies should attempt to promote unfriendly feelings between the United States and Iran, it is difficult to understand how they could hope to succeed in the face of the obvious fact that the two countries have no conflicting interests.

You may bring the foregoing orally to the attention of Mr. Soheily and assure him in the most express terms that not only is this Government convinced that there are no factors seeking to weaken the ties of friendship between the two countries, but also that in the view of the Department no real basis exists upon which such a movement could be founded.

Very truly yours,   CORDELL HULL

2

The Impact of World War II

In the war years, the United States and Iran experienced greatly increased contact, but it was, in a sense, fortuitous rather than planned. Winning the war was the clear U.S. priority, and a vital means to this end was to assure the steady and voluminous flow of U.S. supplies to the Soviet Union, which was engaging the greatest number of German troops on the broadest front. Thus some 30,000 U.S. troops were dispatched to Iran, with the primary job of keeping supplies on the move to Russia via the Iranian railroads.

The presence of the troops gave an early indication of that clash of cultures which was to become such a sore point in later years. But if Iranians were sometimes disturbed by the behavior of the soldiers, there were also times when the Iranians were won over by the good humor and generosity of the GIs. Certainly the friction that occasionally surfaced between Iranians and American troops was not serious enough to destroy the Iranian government's perception of the United States as a relatively benign power.

Thus the United States was again favored as a source of advisers. Dr. Millspaugh returned to Iran a second time to head another economic advisory team. In this instance, however, the friction that arose did prove to be serious because many of the well-educated Iranian professionals believed that the Millspaugh appointment challenged their competence. Although Millspaugh was given broad powers, he was unable to make much headway against the opposition he encountered, and he eventually left Iran.

Despite Millspaugh's lack of success, Iran and the United States signed an agreement whereby the U.S. would train Iran's national police force (gendarmerie). That mission was to remain in Iran into the postwar years, and the force it molded was to play a significant role in Iranian affairs for some time to come.

On the world stage, the United States signed the Tehran Declaration in 1943, pledging itself to uphold Iran's independence and integrity. This instrument was probably a true reflection of U.S. policy, given the idealism of the war years. Support for Iran's nationhood was supplemented by the recognition of increasing mutual interest of the two countries in the economic sphere. In this vein, agreements were reached between the two countries relative to reciprocal trade and air transport. Additionally, at the Moscow Conference of 1945, the United States informed the Soviet Union that it expected Soviet troops to be withdrawn from Iran as agreed at Tehran. The Soviet Union balked at this admonition, and the United States apparently pressed it no further at that time.

UNITED STATES' ATTITUDE TOWARD THE TRIPARTITE AGREEMENT BETWEEN GREAT BRITAIN, THE SOVIET UNION, AND IRAN

Memorandum of Conversation, by the Secretary of State

[Washington,] August 22, 1941

The Minister of Iran called at his request. He handed to me the attached memorandum relative to serious differences between his Government and the Government of Great Britain. The Minister then proceded orally to refer to this threatened invasion by the British and requested my views as to what the attitude of this Government would be in the event of such invasion. He dwelt at length upon the principles governing normal peaceful international relations which I and other officials of this Government often refer to and proclaim, and he concluded his statement with an inquiry as to what this Government would be disposed to do in the way of preventing the threatened British invasion.

I replied that the British military authorities, of course, plan all of their strategy without any consultation or discussion with any official of this Government, that there seems to be a possibility of invasion of that general area of the world by the Germans and of the necessity of defensive activities to be taken against them by the British. I then said that no one could tell when or just where such invasion would finally develop if it should develop, and that of course, this Government could not define any new policy, if it should have in mind any such policy in a contingent way, upon a purely theoretical military situation to which the Minister referred. I said that our two countries are on thoroughly friendly relations and we feel most kindly towards the people of Iran, but that I think the Minister must realize that I am not in a position to discuss contingent or theoretical cases in advance. I added that while Iran is neutral, as the Minister states, the Germans have no respect whatever for neutrality, but counsel a neutral nation to remain perfectly quiet and neutral until Hitler gets well ready to invade and conquer it in short order and throw it into a state of serfdom or semi-slavery; and that the British aided by us and others are struggling desperately to prevent the Hitler conquest from reaching Great Britain and thereby most seriously endangering the Western Hemisphere.

The Minister repeatedly talked as though his country would fight if the British undertake by force to occupy it for any purpose. I indicated that the British, of course, have nothing against Iran, but on the contrary have extensive trading relations with them. They are only striving to defend themselves successfully against German invasion. The Minister did not press further for a promise on the part of this Government to interfere, except to say that if this Government would say but one word to the British, he believed that they would not invade Iran.

C[ORDELL] H[ULL]

The Shah of Iran (Reza Shah Pahlavi) to President Roosevelt

[TRANSLATION]

Tehran, [August 25, 1941, 10 p.m.?]

Your Excellency has surely been informed that the Russian and British forces have crossed brusquely and without previous notice the boundaries of this country occupying certain localities and bombarding a considerable number of cities which were open and without defense. The old pretext which the Russian and English Governments raised consisted in the concern which those countries claimed to feel because of the sojourn of certain Germans in Iran, despite the assurances given by my Government that those Germans will soon leave Iran. No subject for concern could longer exist and I no longer can see for what reason they have proceeded to those acts of aggression and to bombarding without reason our cities. I consider it my duty, on the basis of the declarations which Your Excellency has made several times regarding the necessity of defending principles of international justice and the right of peoples to liberty, to request Your Excellency to be good enough to interest yourself in this incident, which brings into war a neutral and pacific country which has had no other care than the safeguarding of tranquility and the reform of the country. I beg Your Excellency to take efficacious and urgent humanitarian steps to put an end to these acts of aggression. Being assured of the sentiments of good will of Your Excellency, I renew to you the assurance of my sincere friendship.

REZA PAHLAVI

Memorandum by the Chief of the Division of Near Eastern Affairs (Murray)

[Washington,] August 26, 1941

At the conference in the Secretary's office this morning, the rush telegram no. 106 of August 25, 6 p.m. from Teheran was discussed. This telegram contains the official request of the Iranian Government that "the President of the United States use his good offices with the British and Russian Governments to bring about the immediate cessation of hostilities, looking to an amicable settlement of the present dispute."

There was a diversity of opinions as to the best procedure to follow in this matter in the realization, as the Secretary put it, that we are handling "a red-hot iron." I strongly advanced the viewpoint that even at this late hour we should make every endeavor to induce the British to negotiate with the Iranians with a view to obtaining their friendly collaboration and, if possible, to make an alliance with them for the common defense of their territory. I emphasized that it would be far better for the British in a situation of this kind to be surrounded by a friendly, cooperative Iranian people than to have to face dogged opposition, sabotage and, perhaps, guerrilla warfare.

Mr. Welles took what was perhaps the most extreme view, that we should avoid at all costs using our good offices in this matter and that we should confine ourselves to informing the British Government of the present Iranian request, and inquiring of the British Government whether we could be helpful in any way to the British in this matter.

After considerable further discussion it seemed to be agreed upon that it might be well to do three things,

(1) to reply to the Iranian Government suggesting that they make every effort to come to an amicable settlement with the British Government in this matter, and adding that we on our part would keep in close touch with the British with a view to being as helpful as possible to the Iranians;

(2) to notify the British Government at once without comment in a

separate telegram that we have received the present request from the Iranian Government; and

(3) to take up separately with the British Government the larger aspects of this question. In this telegram we would point out that the present Anglo-Soviet invasion of Iran has aroused nation-wide attention and discussion in this country; that the situation is a delicate one politically; and that we desire to be informed by the British Government without delay along the following lines:

(a) The Iranian Government has complained bitterly that the British and Soviet demands upon that Government were based entirely on the alleged presence in Iran of subversive German agents. The Iranian Government furthermore maintains that at no time has the British Government approached the Iranian Government with a view to obtaining its friendly collaboration in this matter or to suggest an Anglo-Iranian alliance in the common cause. This Government desires to be informed at once as to the accuracy of the Iranian claims in this matter.

(b) While this Government is informed that the British Government has given the Iranian Government assurances as to the safeguarding of its integrity and sovereignty, we are not informed of the precise measures envisaged by the British Government in order to give effect to these assurances. What guarantees, for instance, are the British preparing to give the Iranians in order to protect Iran against Nazi aggression that may result from the present Anglo-Soviet invasion? What assurances furthermore have been given the Iranians as to indemnification for damages and losses that may be suffered as a result of this occupation?

(c) What are the intentions of the British and Soviet Governments with regard to the extent of occupation of Iranian territory?

(d) What assurances are the British in a position to give the Iranians that in the territory occupied by the Soviets there may not be widespread oppression, persecution and purge of upper-class Iranians, and confiscation of their property?

(e) In case the Iranians show the disposition to meet all the demands of the British and are willing even to negotiate an alliance with Britain, would the British be in a position to take over such occupation of the country as may be necessary for their purposes and to bring about a withdrawal of Soviet forces?

The British will doubtless bear in mind in replying to these questions the importance of our being able to reassure American public opinion as to all phases of the present operation.

President Roosevelt to the Shah of Iran (Reza Shah Pahlavi)

Washington, September 2, 1941

I have received Your Imperial Majesty's communication regarding the recent entry of British and Russian forces into Iran. I have been following the course of events in Iran with close attention and have taken careful note of Your Majesty's remarks.

I am persuaded that this situation is entitled to the serious consideration of all free nations including my own, and Your Majesty may rest assured that we are giving it such consideration and are maintaining our traditional attitude with respect to the basic principles involved.

At the same time I hope Your Majesty will concur with me in believing that we must view the situation in its full perspective of present world events and developments. Viewing the question in its entirety involves not only vital questions to which Your Imperial Majesty refers, but other basic considerations arising from Hitler's ambition of world conquest. It is certain that movements of conquest by Germany will continue and will extend beyond Europe to Asia, Africa, and even to the Americas, unless they are stopped by military force. It is equally certain that those countries which desire to maintain their independence must engage in a great common effort if they are not to be engulfed one by one as has already happened to a large number of countries in Europe. In recognition of these truths, the Government and people of the United States of America, as is well known, are not only building up the defenses of this country with all possible speed, but they have also entered upon a very extensive program of material assistance to those countries which are actively engaged in resisting German ambition for world domination.

Your Imperial Majesty's Minister at Washington is fully informed of this Government's views on the international situation, and of the great effort on which this country is engaged, and I am certain that he has transmitted this information, based on his discussions here, to Your Majesty's Government.

My Government has noted the statements to the Iranian Government by the British and Soviet Governments that they have no designs on the independence or territorial integrity of Iran. In view of the long-standing friendship between our two countries, my Government has already sought information from the British and Soviet Governments as to their immediate as well as long-range plans and intentions in Iran, and has suggested to them the advisability of a public statement to all free peoples of the world reiterating the assurances already given to Your Majesty's Government.

I desire to assure Your Imperial Majesty of my good will and to renew to you the assurance of my sincere friendship.

FRANKLIN D. ROOSEVELT

The Minister in Iran (Dreyfus) to the Secretary of State

Tehran, December 19, 1941, 11 a.m.

260. The Foreign Minister informs me the Iranian Government

would like to have the United States adhere after signature to the Iranian-Russo-British treaty which has been initialed and which will be presented to Majlis in a few days. American adherence would, he says, increase the value of the treaty in Iranian eyes by tenfold. He added that he has not considered it opportune to broach the matter to the Allied representatives. I will forward a copy of the final draft by air mail.

DREYFUS

The Minister in Iran (Dreyfus) to the Secretary of State

Tehran, December 20, 1941, 1 p.m.

261. Reference my No. 260. Prime Minister reiterated to me today desire of Iran Government to have United States adhere to treaty. He explained that the Government's situation is precarious because of wide-spread dissatisfaction created by Russian occupation. He stated that Soviet propaganda, political activity and interference continue and that Russians seem to feel they have a sphere of influence in Iran as I note [apparent omission]. He expressed opinion that Iran's position vis-à-vis the Allies might be improved were United States to adhere to the treaty.

DREYFUS

The Secretary of State to the Minister in Iran (Dreyfus)

Washington, December 29, 1941, 10 p.m.

165. Your 260, December 19, and 261, December 20. Although it is unlikely that the Department would be able to fall in with this suggestion in its present form, we shall be glad to study the matter, with a view to making such helpful suggestions as may be possible, as soon as the text of the treaty is received.

In your discretion you may so inform the Iranian Government.

HULL

The Shahanshah of Iran to President Roosevelt

Tehran, January 31, 1942

Knowing that Your Excellency follows the course of events in Iran with close attention I have pleasure in informing you that my Government taking into consideration the principles of the Atlantic Charter with which we are in complete agreement and of which we desire to benefit on a footing of equality with the other nations of the world have signed a treaty of alliance with Great Britain and the USSR. In appending our signature to this document we rely upon the goodwill and the friendship which binds the United States to Iran and feel confident that your traditional attitude towards the basic principles involved will ensure the fulfillment of the pledges given and reserving for my country and people a brighter future of peaceful development within our borders.

MOHAMMAD REZA PAHLAVI

President Roosevelt to the Shahanshah of Iran

Washington, February 6, 1942

I have received Your Imperial Majesty's communication informing me that the Imperial Iranian Government has entered into a treaty of alliance with the Governments of Great Britain and the Union of Soviet Socialist Republics. I have taken note of this treaty and am gratified to observe among its provisions an undertaking by the Allied Powers to respect the territorial integrity, the sovereignty and the political independence of Iran, as well as certain undertakings of Your Imperial Majesty to cooperate with the Allied Powers in their struggle against cruel aggressors who seek to deny the right of free peoples to exist. In keeping with the traditional friendship which has existed for so long between our countries, it is my hope that the conclusion of this treaty will foster the peaceful development of Iran and ensure the prosperity of Your Imperial Majesty's people.

FRANKLIN D. ROOSEVELT

Memorandum of Conversation, by the Chief of the Division of Near Eastern Affairs (Alling)

[Washington,] March 20, 1942

Participants: Mr. Schayesteh, Minister of Iran; Mr. Murray,* Mr. Alling.

The Iranian Minister called today and said that he had received a telegram from his Government directing him to discuss with the Secretary of State the situation in Iran along the following lines:

Mr. Schayesteh was to point out that the Tripartite Treaty which Iran had signed with Great Britain and Soviet Russia had been based on the principles of the Atlantic Charter. The Iranian Government considered the principles enunciated in that Charter of great importance to its national welfare. In view of developments during the past few months the Iranian Government was beginning to fear that under the present circumstances Great Britain might be willing or might be obliged, to concur in and approve of certain designs which the Soviet Government might have on Iranian territory. Accordingly, the Iranian Government

---

* Wallace Murray, appointed Adviser on Political Relations for the Division of Near Eastern Affairs, March 13, 1942.

believed that the situation could be clarified if the United States Government would make some declaration regarding Iran in accordance with the principles of the Atlantic Charter.

Mr. Schayesteh went on to say it was no secret that his countrymen had a strong dislike for the Russians and, although they did not dislike the British to the same extent, there was nevertheless a feeling of mistrust in Iran toward Great Britain. He pointed out that he was aware from visas which he had issued and from stories which he had read in the American press of the part which the United States and its armed forces were playing in Iran. He assumed that the part which the United States played would increase and become of greater importance. He felt, therefore, that it would be altogether desirable for this Government, which was fully trusted by his Government and by the Iranian people, to make some gesture which would reassure his Government and people regarding their future status. As things were, he said, the Iranians had no great incentive to resist aggression if their country was to become the subject of Soviet Russian designs. He stressed the fact that action such as he had indicated on the part of this Government would, he felt, induce the Iranians to play a more active part and to cooperate more wholeheartedly with the occupying forces. He emphasized the fact that such action as was proposed by his Government should be taken without delay, since otherwise it would be too late, as had been the case in other Asiatic countries. In this connection he pointed out that the Burmese had given no assistance to the British and had in fact helped Britain's enemies. This was because, in his opinion, the Burmese felt that if they fought for the British there was no assurance of freedom or independence. He stated that in the case of Java the Javanese had given somewhat more assistance to the Dutch because in the past they had been given somewhat greater freedom. In the case of Australia, he said that obviously the Australians would fight to the finish because they were defending their own liberty and independence.

Mr. Murray told the Minister that he thought it was quite appropriate to explain to the Acting Secretary* at the time of his coming interview the views which he had just presented, and that there was no impropriety in so doing. The question was raised whether the Minister envisaged a declaration regarding Iran solely by the United States or whether he contemplated a more extensive declaration, say by Soviet Russia, the United States, the United Kingdom and China. He said that he had not given this matter great thought, but he was inclined to believe that a declaration by the United States alone would make a greater impression upon his people. He was also asked whether it was envisaged that the proposed declaration apply to Iran alone or whether he contemplated that it would apply to other countries in the Near East which were seeking complete independence. Here again he said he had

---

* Sumner Welles.

no definite or final thought, but he felt that Iran was of such importance to the Allied Powers that perhaps it would be best to confine the declaration to that country. . . .

Memorandum of Conversation, by the Acting Secretary of State

[Washington,] March 23, 1942

The Minister of Iran called to see me this morning.

The Minister made a very long exposition of the subject matter contained in full detail in Mr. Murray's [Alling's] memorandum of his conversation with the Minister on March 20.

At the end of the Minister's statement, he asked me what the opinion of this Government might be.

I replied to the Minister that I greatly appreciated the expression of friendship for the Government and people of the United States which he had made in behalf of his Government and told him that his Government and he personally might be assured that this friendship was fully reciprocated. I said it was our desire here to do everything we could to cooperate with the Government of Iran in lending assistance which might be desired, including the services of technicians and experts.

I said that with regard to the specific question he had raised, the Soviet Government had made no communication to the Government of the United States of any character whatsoever with regard to its aspirations and desires concerning new frontiers or new spheres of influence as an outgrowth of the present war.

I stated that the British Government had kept the United States Government informed of the conversations which had been held between the Soviet and British Governments concerning various matters of this character, but that this Government had not been informed by the British Government of any discussion between the Soviet and British Governments which affected Iran.

I stated that, for these reasons, it seemed to me that it would not only be inappropriate, but positively prejudicial, for this Government—out of a clear sky insofar as it was concerned—to make any public declarations concerning the independence and integrity of Iran.

I stated that the general position of this Government was fully set forth in the provisions of the Atlantic Charter as signed by the President of the United States and that the principles there enumerated constituted the determined policy which this Government intended to pursue.

The Minister thanked me very effusively and said that he fully agreed that in the light of the circumstances which I had mentioned there would be no appropriate occasion for the United States, at this juncture, to make any public declaration of the kind he had discussed with Mr. Murray. He emphasized the fact that this suggestion on his part had been an individual and informal suggestion and had not been made under instructions of his Government.

I stated at the conclusion of our interview that I would be very glad to keep in touch with the Minister so that if any matters affecting Iran came to my attention, I would have the opportunity of talking them over with him for the information of his Government.

S[UMNER] W[ELLES]

UNITED STATES CONCERN OVER IRANIAN FOOD SHORTAGES

The Chief of the Iranian Trade and Economic Commission (Saleh) to the Chief of the Division of Near Eastern Affairs (Murray)

1181   *New York, N.Y., February 24, 1942*

MY DEAR MR. MURRAY: You may be already informed that as a result of shortage in the supply of wheat my Government has been having difficulties in assuring the supply of bread in many cities of Iran.

The United Kingdom Commercial Corporation which had promised to supply the needed amount of wheat has been unable to do so as a result of transportation difficulties.

Due to these circumstances the Minister of Finance in Tehran discussed the matter with the Honorable William Bullitt, United States Special Envoy to the Middle East, and Mr. Bullitt was good enough to promise that upon his return to Washington he would try to make arrangements for the shipment to Iran of certain quantities of wheat which might be sent on board steamers bound for the ports of the Persian Gulf.

I have now received a cable from the Minister of Finance, stating that the question of bread supply in many towns of Iran is becoming extremely acute and asking whether any decision has been taken on the subject of wheat shipment as discussed with Mr. Bullitt.

I had in mind to go to Washington, in order to discuss this matter with you personally but, as you know, it is nearly impossible to make reservations at any hotel in Washington, and the matter being of an urgent nature I decided that I should write to you while awaiting for hotel arrangements.

No person realizes better than yourself the importance of this question in the situation in Iran. Bread being the chief food of the country, a shortage of it would naturally result in famine and I am confident that your Government would like to take any steps that are possible to prevent such a forthcoming condition.

May I, therefore, request you to be good enough to see what can be done on this subject before it is too late and to inform me of your decision so that I can send a telegram to the Minister of Finance. With my best wishes, very sincerely yours,   ALLAH YAR SALEH

The Minister in Iran (Dreyfus) to the Secretary of State

Tehran, April 6, 1942, 4 p.m.

97. Following answers to numbered paragraphs of Department's No. 80, April 1.

(1) British Minister assumes the 17,000 tons referred to by Department consists of 8,000 tons and 8,800 flour (half of latter for Polish army in Iran) to be delivered in April only. None has arrived but first consignment expected shortly.

(2) Iranians allege that British promises of 8,000 tons monthly not being fulfilled, only about 6,000 being received. British express annoyance that Iranians would prefer Allied seamen to risk lives to bring wheat rather than make local hoarders disgorge.

(3) All of above wheat for Iranian Government which is responsible for distribution.

(4) British state they have furnished Iran 40,000 tons since August mostly from India. They are now sending 3,000 tons monthly to East Iran from India. Iranian Government has purchased some 6,000 or 7,000 tons from Soviets and 10,000 tons bought in United States by Saleh.

(5) British and Iranians do not agree on minimum needs. Latter place minimum needs up to end of July at 60,000 tons of which 20,000 immediately. They further estimate they will need to import 100,000 tons from July 1942 (harvest time) to July 1943. British believe that promised April deliveries plus whatever they can send in May plus other Iranian purchases should tide Iran over until new crop comes in. British Minister informs me confidentially that in his opinion very little wheat need be imported after new crop comes in and that small amount needed might be obtained in Iraq where there should be surplus.

(6) Although Iranian estimate of 60,000 tons needed up to July seems high it may be that British estimate is too low and that some wheat from United States will be required. No estimate of needs after July can properly be made until new crop comes in. Iran although normally self-sufficient in wheat may have to continue importing as sowings this year were subnormal due to disturbed conditions.

This matter of economic assistance for Iran must be approached carefully since it involves not only our relations with Iran but also the British and hence our war effort. British as Department knows have had great difficulty with Iranians and have had to use question of supply of essential goods as a weapon to obtain some degree of cooperation.

British relations with Iran have arrived at a critical stage as result of present dispute over issue of currency and exchange control (see Department's No. 55 and my 82, 83, 87 and 93). Iranians finally increased note issue by 700 million rials but refused to issue currency against sterling holdings because of lack of confidence in both British and sterling. Instead new issue is backed by gold and crown jewels.

[Here follows further report on exchange situation.]

I have consistently recommended avoidance of undue pressure on Iranians and advised against joining British in representations to Iran Government unless such action essential to war effort. I feel that present Iranian intransigence toward British is potentially harmful to war effort and I recommend we work in close harmony with British in question of supplies for Iran. While British themselves are somewhat responsible for their bad relations with Iran we cannot escape fact that Iranians by refusal to cooperate with our Allies are creating potentially harmful situation. Our economic policy with regard to Iran should dovetail with that of British in order to avoid placing our Allies in disadvantageous position and to prevent appearance of backing Iran against British.

DREYFUS

The Minister in Iran (Dreyfus) to the Secretary of State

Tehran, October 17, 1942, 10 p.m.

327. The political situation in Iran has suddenly deteriorated and position of Qavam Cabinet is precarious. The situation derives from strong calling for issue of 2 billion additional rials coupled with widespread dissatisfaction at British refusal to furnish wheat and general discontent at treatment accorded Iran as Allies [ally]. These matters were brought to fore by statement made to press by Sheridan,* pertinent passages of which follow:

"I would like to emphasize that before leaving my country I was assured that the United Nations will not permit Iran to suffer through no fault of our [your?] own. Unfortunately Iran occupies a geographical position which makes it necessary for the United Nations to use your roads and railroads for your [our?] transport of war supplies to Russia. This has caused a complete disruption of your transport services and this as I said above is all due to absolutely no fault of the Iranian people. Every freedom loving individual in the world, yourselves included, must do everything they can to aid the destruction of the German menace.

Rest assured therefore that both the United States and Great Britain have a sincere desire to help you in every way possible but you must help yourselves up to the maximum limit of your own resources. As the months progress if we find that your own resources are insufficient then I assure you that you will have a sympathetic and helping hand from both Britain and America."

---

* J.P. Sheridan, Food and Supply Adviser to the Iranian Government.

British took exception to Sheridan's statement since they felt he had no right to bind them to furnish wheat to Iran. Sheridan has assured me he will make no further statements of political nature without consulting me. . . .

Crux of situation is wheat. British maintain there is sufficient wheat in hoarding to take care Iran's needs. I have consistently . . . advised an open mind on wheat shipments until we can determine whether measures being taken will bring sufficient wheat to light. I recommend we await Sheridan's judgment after he has had more time to study food situation. Iranians are at present one jump ahead bread shortage which here is tantamount to starvation. Sheridan has been able keep no more than 2 days' supply wheat on hand in Tehran and is working desperately to bring in stocks from provinces; he is confident can obtain 35,000 tons in Azerbaijan and 15,000 tons in Khorassan if only he can obtain cooperation of Soviet railway and military authorities. My opinion is there will be wheat shortage within few months and we should keep in mind possible necessity of shipping some 50,000 tons.

Iranians seek promise from Allies their essential needs especially in wheat will be met before they commit themselves to further cooperation or issue of currency. If Qavam Cabinet resigns bill for additional currency must necessarily be tabled in which event Allies will be placed in difficult position of suspending war work or taking matters in own hands. I would recommend we give Iran Government guarantee we will undertake, on Sheridan's statement that he is unable to uncover enough wheat to last till next harvest, to furnish deficit or at least much as we are able. This would I realize run counter to British policy in Iran. I have impression that British Legation is playing again game of divide and rule and may be endeavoring force out Qavam and obtain more suitable Quisling. It is rumored they favor Tadayyan for Prime Minister. At any rate British policy here seems to me to lack comprehension and vision.

DREYFUS

The Secretary of State to the Secretariat of the Joint Chiefs of Staff

Washington, November 19, 1942

SIRS: As you may be aware, there has arisen in Iran during the past few weeks an acute political and economic situation, largely caused by a serious shortage of grain. Because of the food shortage, and generally unsatisfactory economic conditions, the Iranian Majlis (parliament) has been reluctant to make available Iranian currency needed for the operations of United Nations troops, and even more serious difficulties have appeared to threaten the Anglo-American position in Iran.

The Department of State, the British Foreign Office at London, and the British and American Ministers at Tehran have been endeavoring to work out a solution to this problem, and it has now been agreed that the

American and British Governments shall undertake, under certain conditions, to make up any deficit in the domestic Iranian grain supplies which may be found to exist prior to the gathering of the 1943 harvest. These Governments will also undertake to provide transport for the movement of grain from surplus areas in Iran to deficit areas in that country. A copy of the agreement, which it is hoped will be signed and made public within a few days, is attached herewith.

Apart from the undertaking contained in the agreement, the British Government is endeavoring to arrange for the early shipment to Iran of 20,000 tons of wheat as a replacement for an equivalent quantity of Iranian grain reported to have been purchased by the Soviet Government. The Department of State has given its approval to this shipment, which is expected to be made as follows: 5,000 tons during the month of November, 5,000 tons during the month of December, and the remaining 10,000 tons as soon as possible thereafter.

In this connection, the Foreign Office has stated that the despatch to Iran at this time of 20,000 tons of wheat will necessitate a corresponding reduction in other commodities programmed for shipment to the Persian Gulf and forwarding overland through Iran. Mr. Eden has informed the Soviet Ambassador at London that shipments to Russia via Iran will necessarily be reduced, and the appropriate British authorities are also being advised of the situation. The Foreign Office has requested that the Department do likewise in Washington. Accordingly, it would be appreciated if you would take the matter under consideration and inform all interested agencies in this country, such as the Office of Lend-Lease Administration and the War Shipping Administration.

I should like to emphasize that, in all probability, additional wheat shipments to Iran will be necessary during the coming year, if famine conditions in that country are to be avoided. I assume that such later shipments will also necessitate a revision of shipping programs for other commodities, in the light of available shipping space and the capacity of Persian Gulf ports and the Iranian transport system. Consequently, it is hoped that the Joint Chiefs of Staff and other interested agencies will keep this factor in mind.

By way of background, I should explain that grain, wheat and barley, is the staple foodstuff of the Iranian people. For this reason, an adequate supply of grain for the people has always been the touchstone of success for any Iranian Government. It is significant that upon his recent accession to power, the present Prime Minister publicly declared that if he could assure the provision of bread to the public, all his other problems would solve themselves. His relative lack of success in this undertaking, which has been signalized by recent bread riots in Iran, has resulted in weakening the position of his cabinet to a point at which its fall is threatened.

The Department of State feels that the United Nations should do everything possible, consistent with their urgent military needs, to see that the minimum food requirements of the Iranian people during the current crop year are fulfilled. The considerations which have led the Department to adopt this position may be summarized as follows:

(1) This Government has proclaimed that a power which is in occcupation of the territory of another is responsible for the well-being of the population of the occupied country. We are, therefore, morally bound to apply this principle to those countries which we or our associates have been forced to occupy as well as to the territories occupied by the enemy.

(2) This Government, and all of the United Nations, are vitally interested in the maintenance of the supply route to Russia through Iran and in the possible future use of Iran as a base for defensive or offensive operations against the enemy in the Middle East. It has seemed to this Department, and officers of the War Department have concurred, that the achievement of these objectives would be immensely complicated, if not entirely defeated, if our technical and combat forces in Iran should be confronted with a starving and rebellious population. This consideration, in our view, gains added force from the fact that about one-fourth of the population of Iran is composed of nomadic tribes whose preferred occupation until a few years ago consisted in preying upon transport routes and settled communities. Many of the tribes have recently resumed these activities, with the result that already some highways have become unsafe, or even temporarily closed from time to time.

(3) It is highly probable that a real failure of the bread supply would result in the collapse of the Iranian Government, and that the United Nations would then be forced to proceed to military occupation of the entire country and establishment of a puppet Government at Tehran. It is superfluous to point out that this would necessitate diversion of troops from the fighting fronts. It would also have unfortunate repercussions in the other Moslem nations and territories.

Very truly yours,   /s/ CORDELL HULL

UNITED STATES EXTENSION OF
LEND-LEASE AID TO IRAN

[A proposed lend-lease agreement and collateral exchange of notes were presented to the Iranian Minister at Washington on August 13, 1943. Negotiations in 1944 and 1945 were terminated by the ending of the war, and no formal agreement was concluded.]

President Roosevelt to the Lend-Lease Administrator (Stettinius)

Washington, March 10, 1942

MY DEAR MR. STETTINIUS: For purposes of implementing the authority conferred upon you as Lend-Lease Administrator by Executive Order No. 8926, dated October 28, 1941, and in order to enable you to arrange for Lend-Lease aid to the Government of Iran, I hereby find that the defense of the Government of Iran is vital to the defense of the United States.

Very truly yours,   FRANKLIN D. ROOSEVELT

The Acting Secretary of State to the Minister in Iran (Dreyfus)

Washington, March 13, 1942, 6 p.m.

66. On March 11 [10] the President found the defense of Iran vital to the defense of the United States, thereby making Iran eligible to receive Lend-Lease assistance. For the present it is considered advisable to keep this development secret, except for the Iranian officials immediately concerned, and you are requested to see that no announcement on the subject is made in Iran. Iranian Minister in Washington has been informed.

With reference to your 61, March 11, you should take the first opportunity to emphasize to the Prime Minister that this action represents definite evidence of this Government's intention to help Iran. You may further state that arrangements are going forward with all possible speed to send wheat to Iran under Lend-Lease authority on a cash reimbursement basis. Action is being taken on a requisition for 20,000 tons, which it is proposed to ship at the minimum rate of 2,000 tons monthly or in greater quantities if the shipping situation permits. It should be noted that no effective action in this regard could have been taken by this Government prior to the designation of Iran as eligible for Lend-Lease, since no other Governmental machinery exists for such operations. . . .

WELLES

The Minister in Iran (Dreyfus) to the Secretary of State

Tehran, May 4, 1942, 11 a.m.

140. Prime Minister's announcement yesterday of extension of lend-lease aid to Iran made in a speech to Majlis was extremely well received by Deputies and public. He began his speech by saying that

United States long in cordial relations with Iran has once again given practical demonstration of its good intentions toward this country. American advisers, he said, have rendered brilliant services to Iran, mentioning specifically those in fields of education and health. Iranians have responded to taxes [these?] high and disinterested services with similar feelings toward United States and have tried to follow American example in order to improve internal organization of their country. He ended by saying he was sure the Deputies and all persons interested in Iran's welfare will welcome this good news which is sure to have important repercussions in economic affairs of Iran interrupted by frequent and enthusiastic cheers from Deputies.

Extension of lease-lend aid should serve to strengthen our already cordial relations with Iran. However, actual harm may result if there is much delay in supplying Iran with much needed goods.

DREYFUS

The Secretary of State to the Secretary of War (Stimson)

Washington, October 19, 1942

MY DEAR MR. SECRETARY: As you are aware, the Government of Iran has presented to this Government requests for certain military supplies which it desires to obtain under the Lend-Lease procedure for the use of the Iranian Army and rural police force. I understand that these requests have been submitted to the International Division, Services of Supply, War Department, which has presented them for consideration by the appropriate allocation bodies.

In this connection, and for guidance in the future handling of similar cases, an officer of the War Department has asked that the Department of State set forth its views with regard to the procedure to be followed in the requisitioning and consignment of Lend-Lease supplies of a military character which may be allocated for the use of the Iranian forces.

Iran became eligible for Lend-Lease aid on March 11 [10], 1942, the President having declared its defense vital to that of the United States and the Iranian Government having made the formal representations required by the terms of the Act of March 11, 1941. There is, therefore, full legal authority to furnish Lend-Lease assistance direct to the Iranian Government. Accordingly, this Department believes that requisitions for supplies to be used by the Iranian military and rural police forces should be made out and presented by the authorized Iranian representatives in the United States and that the supplies should be consigned for overseas shipment to the Iranian Government or an agency in Iran designated by that Government.

In making this decision, the Department has been guided by the following considerations:

1) Since supplies of the type in question will be intended solely for the official use of the Iranian Government, it is not necessary for this Government to retain control of them in order to ensure that they do not reach an undesirable ultimate consumer.

2) Major General Clarence S. Ridley, Army of the United States, has been designated adviser to the Iranian Army on matters pertaining to the service of supply and will be in a position to supervise the receipt and use of articles supplied to the army.

3) Colonel H. Norman Schwarzkopf, Army of the United States, is now serving as adviser to the Iranian rural police force and will be in a position to supervise the receipt and use of articles supplied to that force.

4) The Iranian Government has repeatedly expressed its strong desire to receive Lend-Lease aid direct from the American Government, without the intermediation of any third party. It is believed that any other procedure would offend the Iranian Government and would dissipate the good effect which our assistance may be expected to produce.

The Department has, of course, no thought that the indicated procedure should be applied to the furnishing of supplies needed by the military forces of the United Nations stationed in Iran.

Sincerely yours,   For the Secretary of State:
DEAN G. ACHESON
Assistant Secretary

WARTIME POLITICS

The Acting Secretary of State to the Minister in Iran (Dreyfus)

No. 202   *Washington, March 13, 1943*

SIR: There is enclosed herewith a copy of a memorandum which represents the view of the Department on the general policy to be followed by this Government with respect to Iran and which you may, accordingly, take for your guidance in this connection. The Department would be glad to have any observations you may care to make, in the light of your knowledge of conditions on the spot, regarding the practicability of putting into effect the line of policy laid down in this memorandum. You are also requested to suggest, from time to time, whatever measures may seem to you likely to be effective in attaining the objective set forth, namely, the development, with American assistance, of a stable Iranian Government and a strong Iranian economy.

In working toward this objective, the Department considers it essential to avoid any appearance of conflict with Great Britain or the Soviet Union, and it is believed the safeguarding of legitimate British and Russian economic interests in Iran is a requisite for the success of our efforts.

Very truly yours,   SUMNER WELLES

Memorandum by John D. Jernegan of the Division of Near Eastern Affairs: American Policy in Iran

[ANNEX]

[*Washington,*] *January 23, 1943*

This Government has come during the past year or more to play a relatively active part in Iranian affairs. In the past, the United States has had no important political interests in Iran and has been seriously concerned with events in that country only from time to time. Our recent activity, therefore, is rather a new departure and has arisen primarily out of our participation in the war and natural concern that political matters in all theaters of war operations should develop favorably with respect to the United Nations. Iran has been, and is, important in this connection because of its value as a supply route to Russia, its strategic location and its vast production of petroleum products. When occasion has arisen to set forth our policy, we have based it upon the foregoing considerations, and I feel that they constitute ample justification for the attitude we have adopted.

I believe, however, that it is worthwhile at this time to put down on paper certain much broader considerations which, it seems to me, should likewise impel us to follow a positive policy in Iran, not only while the prosecution of the war is still foremost in our minds but also in the period when victory is in our grasp and we come to the conclusion of the peace.

I should like to suggest that Iran constitutes a test case for the good faith of the United Nations and their ability to work out among themselves an adjustment of ambitions, rights and interests which will be fair not only to the Great Powers of our coalition but also to the small nations associated with us or brought into our sphere by circumstances. Certainly, nowhere else in the Middle East is there to be found so clearcut a conflict of interests between two of the United Nations, so ancient a tradition of rivalry, and so great a temptation for the Great Powers concerned to give precedence to their own selfish interests over the high principles enunciated in the Atlantic Charter.

For considerably more than one hundred years, Russia has been pressing down upon Iran from the north, repeatedly threatening new annexations of territory, repeatedly attempting in one way or another to dominate Iran. Three times in the present century alone Russian troops had entered Iranian territory against the will of the Iranian people.

For the same period of time, Great Britain has opposed the Russian movement southward, fearing for her position in the Persian Gulf and Indian Ocean and especially fearful of the potential threat to India. British troops have been on Iranian soil at least twice since the turn of the century and British influence has been exerted over and over again to counter the Russian expansion.

Although Russian policy has been fundamentally aggressive and British policy fundamentally defensive in character, the result in both cases has been interference with the internal affairs of Iran, amounting at times to a virtually complete negation of Iranian sovereignty and independence. It is superfluous to point out that this has created an ingrained distrust of both powers in the Iranian people and has not been without effect upon the attitude of the other weak peoples of the Middle East.

If this were merely history, it would be of no importance. Unfortunately, there are signs that history may be in the process of repeating itself. The basic factors are unchanged: Russia is still without a warm-water port; Britain still clings to her predominant position in the Middle East and east of Suez. Even if we assume the eventual independence of India and Burma and a British withdrawal from Iraq, Palestine and Egypt, there is every reason to suppose that Britain would not welcome an advance into that area by Russia.

Once again Russian and British troops are in Iran, the former in the north, the latter in the south and center. It is true that their presence is made necessary by imperative considerations of military expediency and that their withdrawal at the conclusion of the war has been solemnly promised, but I need not recall the hundreds of instances in which the forces of a Great Power have entered the territory of a weaker nation for one purpose and have remained, indefinitely, for other purposes.

Largely because of this occupation of Iranian territory, the governmental machinery of Iran, and its economic structure, have been seriously weakened. This has become both a reason and an excuse for direct intervention by the Russian and British authorities in Iranian political matters. At the present moment, no Iranian Cabinet can survive without the direct support of the Allied powers. While it is obvious that the United Nations could not permit a hostile government to function at Tehran, it is equally obvious that the Iranian political and economic organization must be strengthened to a point at which it will be able to function efficiently by itself, if Iran is to survive as an independent nation. It is unnecessary to point out that a political vacuum is as impossible as a physical vacuum; if Iran falls into a state of anarchy, some power must assume responsibility for its government, and it may be assumed that the first to offer themselves for this task would be one or both of the present occupying powers.

Apart from the general situation in Iran, I believe we should be fully alive to the character of the present Russian occupation of the northern provinces. In Azerbaijan, the Soviet authorities have greatly restricted the operations of the Iranian civil authorities and have virtually immobilized the small Iranian military forces which they reluctantly permitted to return to the area. They have alternately encouraged and discouraged the restive Kurds, always a thorn in the flesh of the local government. More important still, they have been so successful in propagandizing the population that our Consul at Tabriz has reported that a soviet could be established overnight in Azerbaijan if the Russians gave the word. In this connection, it is well to remember that Azerbaijan is inhabited largely by a Turkish-speaking population whose cultural ties with Soviet Transcaucasia and Turkish Kurdistan are almost as strong as those with the rest of Iran. It is also the most important grain-producing area of Iran and would be a welcome addition to the food resources of Transcaucasia.

There are other items which might be mentioned: the strained relations between the Russian and British authorities in Iran; the suspicion with which the Russians appear to view every move made by the British or Americans, for example their obvious hesitancy in agreeing to our operation of the southern section of the Trans-Iranian railroad; the apparent attempt by the Russian government to weaken British influence by leaving the British to bear the brunt of Iran's economic problems; the continued refusal of the Soviet authorities in Iran to permit transportation of grain from Azerbaijan to meet the urgent needs of Tehran; the impending move by the Russians to take over control of Iranian arms plants.

On the British side, the blunt, uncompromising attitude which has characterized British policy towards Iran does not augur well for a future amicable adjustment of Anglo-Iranian relations. Nor is it reassuring to recall the recent British proposal to arrogate to the Allies power to modify the Iranian cabinet at will.

It may be that the situation outlined above represents nothing more than the inevitable result of the stress and strain of coalition warfare and that once the victory is won all parties will be glad to revert to their former positions, leaving Iranian sovereignty as intact as it was before the Anglo-Russian occupation. Both Britain and Russia have repeatedly promised to do so, and both powers, and Iran as well, have adhered to the principles of the Atlantic Charter.

I should like to submit, however, that the United States has a vital interest in seeing to it that the United Nations *do* live up to the Atlantic Charter and, consequently, in making it as easy as possible for them to do so.

What I have in mind is the situation which will arise when the war is won, or nearly won, and the time comes to think of British and

Russian withdrawal from Iran, with consequent full rehabilitation of Iranian self-government. Have we not some reason to anticipate that the respective British and Russian forces may remain suspiciously eyeing each other, each proclaiming its entire willingness to withdraw as soon as the other has done so? Is it not possible that one or both powers will allege, perhaps with reason, that Iran is in such a state of confusion that she must be "protected" for a time? And is it probable that either would withdraw and allow the other to carry out this "protection"?

Carrying this thought one step further, if Russia should really harbor ambitions for expansion in Iran, is it not all too likely that she would insist upon Iran's need for Soviet guidance, and that she would violently oppose the interposition of another interested power in the role of tutor? And if Great Britain should give way on this, would not Britain all the more cling to her position in Iraq and other parts of the Middle East, as protection against a future Russian thrust toward Suez, thus checking the progress which we hope to see in the direction of independence for all Near Eastern peoples?

I think we may assume that the Iranian Government has long since thought of all the foregoing considerations and that its ever-stronger appeal for American assistance is largely based upon them. So far, we have rested our response to this appeal primarily upon our interest in winning the war. I wonder if we should not also begin, privately, to base our response upon our interest in winning the peace? The United States, alone, is in a position to build up Iran to the point at which it will stand in need of neither British nor Russian assistance to maintain order in its own house. If we go at this task whole-heartedly, we can hope to remove any excuse for a post-war occupation, partition, or tutelage of Iran. We can work to make Iran self-reliant and prosperous, open to the trade of all nations and a threat to none. In the meantime, we can so firmly establish disinterested American advisers in Iran that no peace conference could even consider a proposal to institute a Russian or British protectorate or to "recognize the predominance" of Russian or British interests. If Iran needs special assistance of a material character, we can provide it and so remove any cause for claims for compensation by other powers. We can forestall loans carrying with them control of the customs or other servitudes upon the Iranian Government. If railroads, ports, highways, public utilities, industries, are to be built, we can build them and turn them over to the Iranian people free of any strings.

I realize that objections can be raised to such a policy. Some which occur to me at the moment are: (a) it is unprecedented in our relations with the Middle East; (b) it impinges on a "sphere of influence" hitherto considered exclusively British and Russian; (c) there is no guarantee that it will succeed; (d) it might involve expenditure and loss of money; (e) if it came into public notice, it might arouse domestic criticism on the part of isolationists.

To answer these seriatim:

(a) The present war and the problems of future peace for the United States are likewise unprecedented. We have now realized, and publicly stated over and over again, that we cannot be indifferent to the welfare of any part of the world, no matter how remote, because sooner or later it will affect our own peace.

(b) The very fact that Iran has been a "sphere of influence" in dispute between two Great Powers, makes it all the more desirable that a third, disinterested, power should be called in to eliminate the dispute. Both Britain and Russia would be relieved of an anxiety and constant source of friction if each could be assured that the other would have no special position in the area, and it is not inconceivable that both would regard this assurance as worth whatever ambitions might be given up. In this connection, it seems hardly possible that either could suspect the United States of having imperialistic designs in a country so far removed from us and where we could never hope to employ military force against an adjacent Great Power.

(c) If war cannot be waged without taking risks, I submit that the same is true of the making of peace. In any case, if we try and fail, we shall have lost nothing more than if we do not make the attempt. If the ambitions of Britian and Russia, their mutual distrust, or their established interests, are so strong that they would override a purely disinterested effort on our part to improve conditions in Iran, then we may assume that peace, in that part of the world, was doomed from the beginning.

(d) The expenditures involved, even if all of them should be a total loss would be insignificant by contrast with the cost of the present war, and infinitesimal beside the material and human cost of a failure to make a satisfactory peace throughout the world.

(e) This objection will be met with in connection with any effort by the United States to participate in a cooperative post-war settlement, and we must be prepared to accept it. In the case of Iran, it could be countered by emphasis on the humanitarian aspects and should appeal to the normal American sympathy with anything savoring of assistance to the underdog. If properly presented, a policy of help for Iran might, indeed, receive the same sort of popular approval as has been accorded to our support of China.

Finally, I should like to reiterate the conviction previously expressed that if the principles of unselfish fair-dealing enunciated by the Atlantic Charter are ignored when it comes to Iran, or any other country in similar circumstances, the foundations of our peace will begin to crumble immediately. In my opinion, this is the overriding argument which should lead us to seize every opportunity to direct events in such a way that there will be no occasion for power politics or conflict of interests among the United Nations in their relations with Iran.

If this conclusion is sound, I believe that we should not only comply to the best of our ability with Iranian requests for advisers and supplies but should also take the initiative in suggesting the employment of American specialists and application of American methods in various fields; further, we should not be content merely to support or oppose British or Russian policies and demands in Iran, but should put forward positive suggestions of our own for the improvement of conditions. To this end, we should regard ourselves as at least equally responsible with the British and Russians for the solution of Iranian problems and need not, in any way, leave the initiative to them merely because they happen to be the occupying powers. Moreover, here in Washington we should actively enlist the cooperation of all appropriate agencies of the Federal Government in support of this policy, and we should not confine ourselves solely to steps whose close connection with the war effort can be clearly demonstrated. If necessary, we should make it clear to the other agencies that we regard measures to promote a satisfactory ultimate settlement in Iran as being only slightly less important than those immediately directed towards the winning of the war, and that we consider it most unwise to defer all such measures until the war is over.

The Minister in Iran (Dreyfus) to the Secretary of State

[EXTRACT]

No. 480   *Tehran, March 9, 1943*

SIR: I have the honor to submit the following discussion of current American-Iranian relations.

The Department is well aware of the friendly attitude toward the United States which has been shown during the last year or so by the Iranian people and press. The purpose of this despatch is to consider how these cordial relations have been affected by our increased activity in Iran and by the deteriorated internal situation of the country.

I suggested in despatch No. 363 of October 26, 1942, that there is a growing tendency on the part of the Iranians to classify the United States with the British and Russians and, at least by inference, to blame us increasingly for Iran's woes. While this tendency is still noticeable and has even increased to a certain extent, the press and public continue on the whole to treat the United States in a friendly and favorable manner. It would seem not unlikely, however, that Iranian criticism of the United States will grow as our complex problems in Iran multiply, as the Iranians feel more and more the inevitable pinch of the war, as some of the more difficult Iranian problems continue unsolved, and as Iranians begin to find that American advisers are human beings capable of error. . . .

There is an increasing tendency on the part of the Iranians to think of the United States as one of the allies when they heap abuse and blame on the allies for Iran's unfortunate food situation. I greatly regret the delays which took place in getting the 25,000 tons of wheat from the United States under way since it is arriving too late to meet the winter famine. However, it certainly was no fault of this Legation or of the Department of State, both of which moved heaven and earth to see that Iran's wheat shortage was met. I am constrained to repeat that the fault must rest on the shoulders of the British who, even if well-intentioned, delayed the matter consistently because they were of the opinion that wheat hoards existed in the country and could be brought to light if sufficient pressure were put on the Iranians. The press takes the view that Iran has been pillaged by the allies, who now look blandly on while Iran starves. British propaganda in this matter of food has, in true style, tripped itself up and smashed its nose on the curb stone. . . .

There are those who believe the existence of undercover efforts on the part of the British and Russians to discredit our advisers and American efforts in Iran. I see no evidence that the British are indulging in any kind of propaganda or whispering campaign to discredit us. They are undoubtedly aware that, considering their own low repute, any such program would fall on sterile ground and operate only to their own harm. As the Department knows, the British have in some cases requested that American advisers be sent to Iran. However, I have a feeling that the British agreed readily to our adviser program in the hopes that American prestige in this country, which they know has been at a peak, will fall considerably when the Iranians discover advisers are ordinary human beings and not supermen. The British know from bitter experience how difficult the Iranians are to deal with and perhaps take secret delight in letting the Americans have their round. As to the Russians, I have received several indications that they are beginning to resent the American adviser program. The Russian Ambassador has let drop a number of remarks which would indicate he is not entirely pleased. The Foreign Minister told me, for example, that the Ambassador had in conversation with him inquired pointedly as to why the Iranians are employing American advisers when it is well known that the Russians are the best administrators in the world. While these are only straws in the wind future Russian reaction to our program should be carefully observed.

I have given above some of the less favorable aspects of Iranian reaction to our efforts. It should be emphasized that they are definitely minority views covering exceptional cases. The press, public, and Majlis continue to treat us, on the whole, in a most friendly and flattering manner. Scores of press items monthly deal with America, principally with our war effort. They give stories of leading American personalities, reproduce pictures of planes and ships, print facts regarding American war production and generally deal with the American war effort in a favorable light. . . .

Respectfully yours,   LOUIS G. DREYFUS, JR.

The Minister in Iran (Dreyfus) to the Secretary of State

[EXTRACT]

No. 517   Tehran, April 14, 1943

. . . Some of the obstacles in the way of the attainment of our Iranian objectives were discussed in my despatch No. 480, March 9th. They may, it occurs to me, be divided roughly in the four sources from which they may possibly spring—(1) the Soviets (2) the Iranians themselves (3) the British and (4) the Americans. While I have discussed these possible obstacles in various recent despatches and telegrams, it may be useful to recapitulate them briefly in this despatch.

(1) The Soviets. I have reported in a series of telegrams and despatches in the last month the effort which is being made by the Russians to ensconce themselves securely in Iran, by means of astute propaganda, by socialist indoctrination, by good example of their forces and by a policy consisting of a strange mixture of kindness and strong arm methods. Soviet policy in Iran continues to be, as recorded in the Department's memorandum, positive and aggressive. . . .

(2) The Iranians themselves are perhaps the greatest possible source of danger to our position in Iran. . . .

As indicated in my telegram No. 355 dated April 6, there is evidence of a concerted and deeprooted campaign against our advisers. This springs undoubtedly from corrupt and selfish political elements in the Majlis who stand to lose personally with the institution of the kind of a regime our advisers contemplate. This campaign may well be, as is commonly thought here, abetted by the Russians. I have suggested to the Department the necessity of adopting a strong line in dealing with the Iranians in this matter. Unless we can require that our advisers be supported and given powers, their efforts will fail and the whole program will fall to the ground. The result of such failure would be not only to let down the Iranians but as well to cripple our own prestige. Our policy should be firm but kind, forceful but friendly, insistent but considerate. The Prime Minister, a few days ago in a conversation concerning the delay in granting Millspaugh's powers, remarked smilingly that foreigners are apt to forget that Iran is an oriental country and that things here are not done in a day. This is a statement of fact which is too often overlooked by foreigners who think of Iranians as westerners simply because they have adopted western clothing and strive to emulate us in things material.

(3) The British. There is no evidence that the British have offered any great degree of obstruction to our adviser program or the development of our influence in Iran. On the contrary, they have encouraged and sometimes suggested the appointment of Americans. However, at the risk of seeming to be an alarmist who sees a burglar behind every tree, I venture the opinion that the British have had two factors in mind in supporting our program—first, that if given enough rope we might hang ourselves in Iran by making a failure of the adviser program and second, to use us, as do the Iranians, as a buffer to counter the growing menace of Soviet domination of the country. I have not the slightest doubt that British enthusiasm for our program will wane if the Russians withdraw or if their influence becomes sufficiently reduced.

(4) The Americans. We must, finally, be sure that our own house is in order. We should, first, select competent and well balanced advisers and, second give them the advice and support they require. On the whole, as I have reported in a series of despatches dealing with the work of the various missions, our choices have been good. The Millspaugh, Ridley, and Schwarzkopf missions are composed of able and sensible men. . . .

In conclusion, it seems to me imperative that we should continue on our way with patience and balance, with our objective ever in view. We must not be discouraged. The Iranians oscillate politically between dictatorship, democracy and chaos in almost perfect keeping with Plato's theory. They have remarkable resiliency, powers of recovery and ability to throw off foreign invasion, conditions which are apt to keep them going when States considered stronger and more modern have succumbed.

Respectfully yours,   LOUIS G. DREYFUS, JR.

The Minister in Iran (Dreyfus) to the Secretary of State

Tehran, April 21, 1943, 3 p.m.

409. Iran appears to be on verge of another political crisis. Large part of bazaars closed yesterday afternoon and there is some uneasiness in city although no riots have occurred. Closing of bazaars is widely regarded as protest of merchants and politicians against passage of Millspaugh Powers Bill (my 385 [386], April 14) which was to be considered yesterday by Majlis and which had already been approved by Majlis Finance Committee. This gesture is a most damning indictment of present Iranian political system. It protests the passage of legislation which represents only hope of country in order that vested interests of merchant profiteers and corrupt political elements may prevail over common welfare. Suffering of the masses because of high prices has reached an unbearable pitch. Meat if it can be found costs several dollars a pound; pound sugar in black market costs $2. This suffering is a result

of unbridled greed and cannot be corrected until Government takes strongest of measures. General Ahmadi, who by decree of Council of Ministers of April 17 became Military Governor, has published proclamation asking commerce to reopen, calling attention to provisions of existing military law, ordering curfew at 9:00 and warning public that strong measures to protect public interests will be taken.

I am convinced Iran is headed for disaster unless a government strong enough to cope with entrenched classes can be instituted. Such a government might consist of a trinity of power—Millspaugh to make necessary regulations—a strong Prime Minister to put them into effect and a War Minister like General Ahmadi to enforce them on pain of summary and capital punishment.

DREYFUS

The Secretary of State to President Roosevelt

Washington, August 16, 1943

MY DEAR MR. PRESIDENT: I enclose herewith, for your consideration, a summary statement of policy which has, in general, served as the basis of the Department's attitude towards Iran during the past eight or nine months. I believe that you will agree with the fundamental principles expressed therein. . . .

Faithfully yours,   CORDELL HULL

[ENCLOSURE]

American Policy in Iran

The historic ambitions of Great Britain and Russia in Iran have made that country a diplomatic battleground for more than a century. The geographical, political and economic bases of those ambitions remain unchanged, and the present attitudes of the British and Soviet Governments and their representatives in Iran give strong reason to fear that their rivalry will break out again as soon as the military situation permits. This danger is greatly increased by the existing economic and political weakness of the Iranian Government and the presence on Iranian soil of British and Soviet armed forces.

If events are allowed to run their course unchecked, it seems likely that either Russia or Great Britain, or both, will be led to take action which will seriously abridge, if not destroy, effective Iranian independence. That such action would be contrary to the principles of the Atlantic Charter is obvious. Its effect upon other peoples of the Near East, and elsewhere, might well be disastrous to our hopes for an equitable and lasting post-war settlement.

The best hope of avoiding such action lies in strengthening Iran to a point at which she will be able to stand on her own feet, without foreign control or "protection," and in calling upon our associates, when necessary, to respect their general commitments under the Atlantic Charter and their specific commitments to Iran under the Treaty of Alliance of 1942, the provisions of which were noted by the President in a communication to the Shah of Iran.

The United States is the only nation in a position to render effective aid to

Iran, specifically through providing American advisers and technicians and financial and other material support. We are also the only nation in a position to exercise a restraining influence upon the two great powers directly concerned.

Since this country has a vital interest in the fulfillment of the principles of the Atlantic Charter and the establishment of foundations for a lasting peace throughout the world, it is to the advantage of the United States to exert itself to see that Iran's integrity and independence are maintained and that she becomes prosperous and stable. Likewise, from a more directly selfish point of view, it is to our interest that no great power be established on the Persian Gulf opposite the important American petroleum development in Saudi Arabia.

Therefore, the United States should adopt a policy of positive action in Iran, with a view to facilitating not only the war operations of the United Nations in that country but also a sound post-war development. We should take the lead wherever possible, in remedying internal difficulties, working as much as possible through American administrators freely employed by the Iranian Government. We should further endeavor to lend timely diplomatic support to Iran, to prevent the development of a situation in which an open threat to Iranian integrity might be presented. In carrying out this policy, we should enlist the support of all branches of the American Government.

The success of the proposed course of action is favored by the exceptionally high regard in which this country is held by the Iranian people. There is also reason to believe that the British Government would acquiesce, or even lend its active support. The attitude of the Soviet Government is doubtful, but this Government should be in a position to exert considerable influence if occasion should arise. It goes without saying that the safeguarding of legitimate British and Soviet economic interests in Iran should be a basic principle of American action.

Memorandum of Conversation, by the Third Secretary of Legation in Iran (Jernegan)

[*Tehran,*] *September 21, 1943*

Subject: American Policy toward Iran; Attitude of Persian Gulf Service Command.

I called on General Connolly to pay my respects and to present a letter of introduction from Colonel Douglas V. Johnson, Chief, Central African-Middle Eastern Theater, Theater Group, Operations Division, War Department. The conversation, during which General Connolly took the initiative and did most of the talking, lasted for more than an hour and a half and covered a wide field. It may be roughly summarized as follows:

(1) *Relation of PGSC to American Foreign Policy:* General Connolly led off by saying that he thought there should be closer coordination between American political and military activity throughout the world. Both the War Department and the State Department were "on the same team" and should each be fully aware of what the other was doing and wanted to accomplish. In this connection, he cited the teamwork of

British diplomatic and military officials, which was the result of centuries of British military and political activity in all parts of the world. Prior to the present war, the State Department had not needed to consider the American military organization in carrying out its policies, because our Army had been confined to the United States. Now, however, we had troops abroad in large numbers and in many places, and it was essential that their commanders be informed regarding the objectives of our foreign policy. Otherwise, they might unintentionally handicap our diplomatic operations or miss opportunities to further our policies. American military forces were frequently in a position to take concrete, positive action, whereas the State Department and its representatives abroad could only persuade.

With respect to his own position, General Connolly said that his orders were solely to expedite the movement of goods to the Soviet Union, under the direction of the War Department. He was not informed regarding American political objectives in Iran and had not been able to ascertain that the United States had any definite policy toward this country. Consequently, he had felt that the only course open to him was to avoid scrupulously any action of any kind which might involve his command in political matters. As he put it, he was "walking a tight rope" between the intricate maneuverings of the Soviets, British and Iranians. However, if he were fully informed regarding American policy, assuming that we had any real interests in Iran, it might be possible for his command "to give the ball a push in the right direction" from time to time.

I remarked that Colonel Stetson had called at the State Department during his recent visit to Washington and had asked whether the Department did, in fact, have any definite policy toward Iran. We had shown him a memorandum on this subject. I said I was somewhat surprised that General Connolly had not long-since received a copy, or at least a summary, of that memorandum from the War Department, because copies had been furnished General Handy, chief of the Operations Division, and General Wedemeyer, chief of the Strategy Group of that Division.

(2) *American Interests in Iran:* General Connolly said that he was doubtful as to whether the United States really had any justifiable interest in Iran. The only important, concrete American interest in this part of the world seemed to lie in our oil concessions, which were down around Bahrein Island and not in Iran at all.

I said that in the opinion of the State Department we had two interests, one practical and one which might be called idealistic. The first General Connolly had already mentioned, the oil fields of Arabia. In strict confidence, I could say that these were taking on great importance in the eyes of the United States Government, notably the War and Navy Departments. A large immediate development of those fields was,

I believed, being initiated, and they were also regarded as most important from the standpoint of future reserves. Iran came into this picture because a great power established on the Iranian side of the Persian Gulf would be in a position to deny us the use of the Arabian fields. In this respect, our position was becoming similar to that of the British, whose oil fields in southern Iran would be jeopardized if another great power controlled Iran.

Our other interest in Iran, I said, was less immediately practical and selfish. The State Department felt that if Iran should lose its independence, whether in name or in fact, as a result of the war, it would be negation of the principles of the Atlantic Charter, the principles to which all the United Nations were pledged and for which we had repeatedly announced we were fighting. Such a negation would destroy the confidence of the world in the good faith of the United Nations and would begin the disintegration of the peace structure which we hoped to set up. The same thought would, of course, apply to an encroachment upon the rights of a small nation in any part of the world, but Iran was of particular interest in this connection because circumstances seemed to single it out as being in special danger.

I went on to say that Iran's danger, in the view of the State Department, might be lessened if it could be rehabilitated and enabled to stand on its own feet. There would be less temptation for an interested great power to step in and establish a protectorate, or annex all or part of the country, if Iran were a going concern. A state of chaos in the country would provide at one and the same time an excuse and an opportunity for foreign intervention. The State Department's policy, therefore, was to lend such assistance as might be practicable to improve conditions in Iran.

General Connolly appeared to feel that this statement of American interests might be logical, but he doubted whether the policy it envisaged could be or should be carried out. . . .

The Chargé in Iran (Ford) to the Secretary of State

No. 717   *Tehran, November 10, 1943*

SIR: I have the honor to transmit herewith a memorandum of a conversation with the Shah of Iran which may be of interest to the Department. Points which seem of some significance are:

1) The Shah's recognition that Iran must set its house in order if it is to avoid foreign intervention.

2) His emphasis on the necessity for social reform in Iran.

3) His relative (apparent) lack of concern regarding the intentions of the occupying powers, and his statement that the Soviet attitude toward Iran had shown marked improvement in the past two months.

4) His expressed desire for continued American interests in Iran,

obviously as a counterbalance to the Soviets and British.

The thought was suggested to me by the trend of his remarks, that the Shah may not desire the withdrawal of the foreign troops now in Iran at too early a date. If this interpretation is correct, (and it is not in accord with the expressed wishes of the Foreign Minister, who says he is anxious to see the troops depart as soon as possible) it may indicate a fear on the Shah's part that there would be danger of revolution if Iran were left to its own devices at this moment. He may well feel that the maintenance of this throne depends upon effecting an improvement of conditions before the dissatisfaction of the people has a chance to express itself freely in action as well as in words.

Respectfully yours,   RICHARD FORD

The Chargé in Iran (Ford) to the Secretary of State

No. 771   *Tehran, December 29, 1943*

SIR: I have the honor to refer to the Department's instruction No. 293 of December 2, 1943 transmitting two memoranda of conversations regarding the desire of the Iranian Government to have foreign troops withdrawn from Iran at an early date. It is noted that the Iranian Minister has put forward the view of his Government that conditions have radically changed since the conclusion of the Tripartite Treaty of January 29, 1943 [1942] and that the evacuation of the Allied troops should not be postponed until after the end of the war, for the following reasons:

(a) All Axis agents have been eliminated from Iran.

(b) There is no longer any threat of an enemy invasion of Iran.

(c) Iran has joined the United Nations.

I assume that the Iranian Government really has in mind only the withdrawal of British and Soviet combat·troops, since there are no American combat forces in Iran and the presence of American, British or Soviet technical units for operating purposes will obviously be necessary so long as this country continues to be used as a major route for the transport of supplies to the U.S.S.R.

The Legation has informally and confidentially consulted on this subject General Ridley,* Colonel Schwarzkopf* and General Scott (chief of staff to General Connolly, who is away). Their views, which they do not wish attributed to them in any way, and those of Colonel Baker, the Legation's Military Attaché, are, in composite summary:

(1) It is highly improbable that all dangerous Axis agents have been eliminated from Iran.

(2) The tribes continue to constitute a threat to the security of the supply line, and the presence of foreign troops undoubtedly exercises a deterrent effect upon them.

---

* American advisers heading the Military and *Gendarmerie* Missions, respectively.

(3) The Iranian Army and *Gendarmerie* are not yet in a position to cope with the tribes unassisted and probably will not be able to do so for some time to come.

(4) The Persian Gulf Command and the American advisers to the Iranian Army and *Gendarmerie* prefer to have the existing arrangement maintained, whereby the British Army is responsible for security in the south and the Soviet Army in the north.

I do not think that one need be a military expert to agree with the foregoing. It is quite clear that the Iranian military forces are for the time being incapable of dealing with restive tribes, such as the Qashqai and the Kurds, and I think the same may be said of the police forces vis-à-vis individual Axis agents. One cannot, of course, say definitely that hostile activities of the tribes and agents would increase if foreign troops were not on hand, but it seems probable. In any case, the danger exists. There is a further, more remote, possibility that the withdrawal of Allied forces would open the way to general disturbances in the nature of revolution, expressing the widespread dissatisfaction of the Iranian people with the present government and social system.

Respectfully yours,   RICHARD FORD

UNITED STATES WARTIME MISSIONS TO IRAN

*Memorandum of Conversation, by John D. Jernegan
of the Division of Near Eastern Affairs*

[*Washington,*] *May 8, 1942*

Participants: The Iranian Minister, Mr. Alling, Mr. Jernegan.

The Iranian Minister called to explain the desires of his Government with respect to assistance from the United States in the form of advisers. In addition to the quartermaster general and the two agricultural experts already requested, the Iranian Government now asks for a military aviation officer, a military engineer officer, and a civilian financial adviser. It is likewise anxious to obtain two police organizers, one for the city police of the country and one for the rural *gendarmerie*. The Minister explained that there appeared to have been a misunderstanding regarding the request made in January of this year for a police officer. The Department had understood that this man would reorganize the *gendarmerie*, whereas in fact, a man for the city police had been desired. However, as men for both types of work were now requested, it would appear that no harm had been done.

The Minister was informed of the Department's efforts to obtain the services of Colonel H. Norman Schwarzkopf, and he was given a copy of the biographical sketch of Colonel Schwarzkopf which has been furnished by the War Department. He expressed the opinion that Colonel Schwarzkopf would seem to be well qualified for the post in charge of the *gendarmerie*, but he requested such further information as the Department might be able to obtain regarding his experience with the New Jersey State Police.

With respect to the request for a financial adviser, the Minister emphasized that the type of man needed is one of high qualifications both as a financier and as a practical executive in the field of government finance and taxation. He said that neither a theoretical economist nor a man with purely banking experience would be satisfactory. What is needed, according to the Minister, is a man capable not only of advising but of drawing up and executing practical programs of taxation, currency control, et cetera.

Mr. Alling mentioned, in connection with the military advisers requested, that certain technical difficulties might be encountered if the officers selected should be required to become officers in the Iranian Army, since we understood that American Army officers would be forced to resign from our Army in order to enter any foreign army. This they would be reluctant to do in view of the possible loss of retirement status, eligibility for promotion and matters of that sort. Although he said that military advisers of this kind would normally be expected to become officers in the Iranian Army and would find the work simplified by so doing, the Minister indicated that he thought it would not be unduly difficult to arrive at some arrangement in this respect if our own army regulations should prove inflexible.

Memorandum by the Adviser on Political Relations (Murray)

[*Washington,*] *August 3, 1942*

It seems to me that the present political crisis in Iran which has resulted in the fall of the Soheily Cabinet is of such vital concern to us that we cannot ignore it.

The obvious fact is that we shall soon be in the position of actually "running" Iran through an impressive body of American advisers eagerly sought by the Iranian Government and urgently recommended by the British Government.

We have had in Iran, as you will recall, General Greely, acting as Quartermaster General of the Iranian Army, and the British are pressing us to send a military mission to take entire control of the training and functioning of the Army. Two first-class Army officers have already proceeded to Iran to organize and run the *gendarmerie* of the country which will guarantee internal security. A competent police official in this country is about to be engaged to reorganize the police forces of

Iran. The Public Health Service is finding us an official to head that service in Iran. A Director of Supply and Transportation is about to be engaged and has already agreed to accept the offer of the Iranian Government. And, finally, a full-fledged Financial Mission, more ambitious even than the Millspaugh Mission of 1922-1927, is about to be assembled here and sent to Iran.

In the light of these developments it seems to me odd indeed that the British and Soviet Ambassadors in Tehran should be picking over the lot of Iranian politicians and deciding "whose man" should be put in power without prior consultation with our Legation.

I had occasion to discuss this situation briefly and informally with the Iranian Minister on Saturday, and I told him quite frankly that from my experience in the past in Iran I would not be prepared to recommend to the Department that we proceed with this impressive group of American advisers for Iran unless it was clear beyond any doubt that the various members of any Government that might be formed in the country were competent and willing to cooperate fully with our people there. I said it was simply a waste of time and services of valuable people to send them to Iran and spend most of their time overcoming the hurdles and obstacles placed in their way by intriguing Government officials who gave public lip service to the efforts being made by our people but secretly worked to nullify their accomplishments.

The Minister, who is fully aware of the almost constant intrigues against the Millspaugh Mission when it was in Iran, said he entirely agreed with me that we should not let that situation occur again, and that he wished to think the matter over and discuss with me again the ways and means to facilitate, and not obstruct, the efforts of these first-rate American advisers who are being employed in this country to help Iran in these desperate days.

WALLACE MURRAY

The Under Secretary of State (Welles) to President Roosevelt

Washington, October 20, 1942

MY DEAR MR. PRESIDENT: In your memorandum of October 15 you ask me to speak to you with regard to Mr. Willkie's suggestion that the Persian Prime Minister would be made very happy if you could send four or five high ranking officers to Iran to train their army.

Last May the Department of State informed the War Department that the type of mission suggested would be desirable and recommended favorable action. Since that time there has been a good deal of discussion of the matter with the War Department which has taken the position that it would be difficult to spare the necessary personnel. Finally, last month however, the War Department informed the Department of State that it was designating Major General Clarence S. Ridley as adviser to the Iranian Army and that General Ridley would be instructed to make a thorough survey of the situation and report to the War Department his views as to the advisability of despatching an American military mission. General Ridley is now en route to Tehran.

You may be interested to know that in addition to the mission of General Ridley, American assistance to Iran has taken the form of several non-military missions in different fields. The most important are:

(a) A mission headed by Colonel Schwarzkopf, to reorganize and administer the Rural Police.

(b) An American expert to reorganize and administer the National City Police.

(c) An American Food and Supply Adviser.

(d) A financial mission, which would probably be headed by Dr. Arthur Millspaugh, who was Administrator General of Finances of Iran from 1922 to 1927.

(e) A permanent Director General of Public Health who is yet to be selected.

I believe that the work of these various missions will be of great benefit since the officers and experts we have sent to Iran will not only be able to exert considerable personal influence upon Iranian opinion in a sense favorable to the general cause of the United Nations, but they will also be able to assist in the rehabilitation of the country which would seem to be a fundamental requisite for the ultimate conversion of Iran into an active and willing partner on our side. I feel now more than ever that the United States Army mission to work with the Iranian Army could in fact play an extremely important role in this work.

I shall see that you are informed as soon as General Ridley's recommendations are received.

Believe me [etc.]   SUMNER WELLES

The Minister in Iran (Dreyfus) to the Secretary of State

No. 489   *Tehran, March 18, 1943*

SIR: I have the honor to enclose a copy of Dr. Millspaugh's first monthly report to the Iranian Government dated Bahman 1321 (February 19, 1943). This draft, Dr. Millspaugh explained to me in a confidential covering note, will be slightly revised for publication. I thought it wise to forward the draft without waiting for its revision or publication, because it contains information which will be of great interest to the Department.

Dr. Millspaugh's factual and interesting report reveals how quickly and thoroughly he has taken up again the thread of Iranian life. Its frank recognition of Iran's ills, its promises of reforms and benefits to come and, above all, its note of compassion and understanding for the

Iranian people should insure it a sympathetic reception by the Iranians. Dr. Millspaugh's plans for correction of this country's many problems are still, he reports, in the nebulous stage of study. Among the more important are increased taxation to counteract inflation and tap excess profits, rent and price control, reduction of the budget, salary increases accompanied by radical reduction in the number of unnecessary government employees, sale of gold and silver in the open market as a means of combatting inflation, rationing of essential products, and an internal treasury loan. . . .

Respectfully yours,   LOUIS G. DREYFUS, JR.

The Minister in Iran (Dreyfus) to the Secretary of State

Tehran, April 6, 1943, 3 p.m.

355. Department's 149, March 29. Sheridan informs me Minister of Food now states that notification of employment of Sheridan's assistants cannot be telegraphed to Iranian Legation Washington until contracts approved by Majlis. This about face by Iranian Government is an indication not only of lack of cooperation but also of bad faith. I recommend Department make no further endeavor to hold these men. I have made it clear to Iran Government that this Legation and Department will support no further requests for American advisers until convincing truth [proof?] given that Iran Legation at Washington is authorized to negotiate.

This brings up the more important general question of position of our advisers in Iran. I am sorry to report there is widespread and impetuous obstruction of our advisers amounting almost to sabotage. Millspaugh is meeting serious obstacles in efforts to put reforms into effect and his necessary bill for full powers has been hanging fire in Majlis a month; he reports opposition is even coming from Minister of Finance Saleh. Millspaugh is of opinion that Iran is hovering on brink of a financial precipice. Present financial undertakings would require spending this year of 2 billion rials beyond revenue and Allied expenditures make it necessary to find an additional amount of 2½ billions. Although Iran is not in a position to meet these expenditures all efforts to effect economy especially in War Ministry meets with stiff opposition. Schwarzkopf and Timmerman* contracts continue to be delayed for political reasons. It is generally stated Majlis will not approve employment of any more Americans.

There is mounting evidence this campaign against advisers is concerted and deeprooted. Campaign is widely attributed to Russians but I have obtained no evidence this is true. Whether or not Russians are to some extent responsible the deeper responsibility must rest on shoulders of Iranian political elements who in their predatory search for

---

* L. Stephen Timmerman, City Police Adviser to the Iranian Government.

power and graft show no appreciation of country's welfare. Saleh, that erstwhile friend of America* in conversation yesterday with member of staff bitterly criticized United States policy stating that American prestige is rapidly sinking because of (1) hostile attitude of people toward Allied occupation forces (2) failure of our advisers to effect reforms (3) limited shipments of goods to Iran under Lease Lend (4) delay in shipping wheat and (5) failure of Americans to deter Russians in their use of pressure on Iran. Saleh stated many Iranians feel American advisers are not qualified to correct country's ills and declared Majlis members feel America is interested merely in using Iran as a highway to Russia and will put Iranians off with vague promises of future assistance. Saleh's opinion is typical of evergrowing group of Iranians who close their eyes to substantial aid already given Iran in wheat, trucks, tires, etc., and fail to recognize that reason our advisers are unable to accomplish more is because their efforts meet with complete lack of cooperation.

I have come to opinion that strong line with Iranians is now essential, a view with which Millspaugh is in full accord. He is making firm but restrained demand that his full powers will be passed and that certain other measures necessary for country's financial salvation be put into effect. In absence of some earnest Iranian good will he is prepared if necessary to withdraw from Iran. Other American advisers are of similar persuasion. All of us agree that supreme effort should be made to make a success of our adviser program and every effort will be bent toward achievement of this goal. If, however, present bad will, lack of appreciation of true American position and political obstruction continue I believe that only dignified solution would be withdrawal of all (repeat all) our advisers. Iranians unfortunately cannot be made to realize seriousness of their financial situation which is driving them inevitably toward disastrous inflation nor do they appreciate fact that American presence in Iran is perhaps only guarantee against worst fear of Iranian upper classes—Russian domination. I will keep Department informed.

DREYFUS

The Minister in Iran (Dreyfus) to the Secretary of State

[EXTRACTS]

Tehran, April 14, 1943, 4 p.m.

. . . As a result of my frank conversations with Prime and Foreign Ministers and Shah I already perceive some improvement in situation outlined my 355. Prime Minister informs me that in special Cabinet meeting Ministers unanimously agreed that Iran's only hope lies in the

---

* Mr. Saleh had formerly been head of the Iranian Economic Mission to the United States.

American advisers and that the Cabinet will cooperate with them. Shah called me on Monday to discuss the situation and reiterated in the warmest terms his approval of the adviser program. He declared he personally would like to go beyond signing the United Nations Declaration, make an alliance with the United States and enter the war with Iranian troops. I have heard on good authority, however, that the Shah is averse to Millspaugh's curtailment of army budget because this threatens his control of army on which his hopes of maintaining himself in power are based.

On whole I do not believe there has developed any strong or widespread feeling against Americans here. I have always foreseen development of present kind of selfish opposition and am hopeful it can be controlled or removed by use of firm but kindly pressure.

DREYFUS

The Minister in Iran (Dreyfus) to the Secretary of State

Tehran, April 14, 1943, 5 p.m.

386. Department's 176, April 10 and my 385, April 14.

1. Full Powers Bill gives Millspaugh *inter alia* powers for period up to 6 months after war over the price, purchase, importation, distribution etc. of non-food commodities including raw and finished goods.

2. Control rents, wages, and charges for other services.

3. Assume where necessary the powers granted Government and certain Ministries under anti-hoarding and other specified laws.

4. Inventory stocks, license dealers and manufacturers, seize stocks, issue coupons, maintain Government store, and take other reasonable and necessary action for stabilization of prices and distribution of goods.

5. Within scope of bill to issue regulations having force of law and

6. Employ nine American citizen assistants for work in Ministry of Finance, especially in price control.

Millspaugh is facing an important test not only in Full Powers Bill but also in his economy struggle with army. War Ministry is demanding increased appropriation of 500,000,000 rials which Millspaugh cannot conscientiously approve. However, in order not to lose support of army and in spirit of conciliation, he proposed following solution to Prime Minister:

He would grant half the increase if Prime Minister agrees to support Full Powers Bill and certain other necessary measures of economy and internal administration. Prime Minister seemed favorably disposed. However, subsequently when Millspaugh found out that without his knowledge Government introduced into Majlis and enacted a law appropriating 60,000,000 rials for additional units in army, he considered this a breach of faith and conveyed to Prime Minister his disapproval of the appropriation and withdrew his proposal for increase in War Ministry Budget.

DREYFUS

The Minister in Iran (Dreyfus) to the Secretary of State

No. 602   *Tehran, July 4, 1943*

. . . Dr. Millspaugh, the Department will probably already have observed, is a power to be reckoned with in Iran. He is gradually assuming control over the entire financial and economic structure of Iran and is laying elaborate and far reaching plans to correct many of the country's ills. He is perhaps the only man in Iran at present who can obtain passage of legislation by the Majlis when he desires to put on the necessary pressure. Frankly, politicians are afraid of him even though they may obstruct, delay, grumble and criticize. For example, there was bitter opposition in the Majlis on Thursday, in discussing the bill for the employment of six assistants for the Millspaugh mission, to that section which provided for exemption of the American advisers from income tax payments. In spite of this, the full bill was passed quickly and by a comfortable majority.

Dr. Millspaugh's test of strength, however, is still to come. This will be when he actually puts into effect and enforces such unpopular measures as the income tax law and a contemplated plan for the requisition of certain private motor cars. When he begins to tread on the toes of the entrenched classes, who consider themselves as "untouchables," the day of his supreme test will have come. He is ready for the fray.

Respectfully yours,   LOUIS G. DREYFUS, JR.

The Minister in Iran (Dreyfus) to the Secretary of State

Tehran, November 1, 1943, 2 p.m.

1037. The Financial Laws Commission of the Majlis met with Millspaugh on Saturday and after a long session approved an agreed draft of the income tax bill. Since the Majlis continues unnecessarily to delay passage of this essential bill Millspaugh and his staff of Americans will cease work on November 3. There is every indication that this action will insure and hasten the passage of the tax bill after which Millspaugh and his staff are prepared to withdraw their resignations and return to work. It is necessary to proceed in this manner since the Majlis has little desire to pass an income tax bill and because the session ends on November 22.

While I have every hope that the bill will pass and Millspaugh will remain I have decided to postpone my departure for the United States until the question is finally settled. I will not therefore proceed with the Secretary's party.

DREYFUS

The Chargé in Iran (Ford) to the Secretary of State   ᵛ

Tehran, November 11, 1943, 3 p.m.

1056. Medjliss today passed income tax project in its entirety and while a few minor changes were made Millspaugh states that on the whole it is acceptable. He said [asked?] that departure of Shields, Hurst and Breitenbach be expedited.

FORD

The Chargé in Iran (Ford) to the Secretary of State

No. 922   *Tehran, April 25, 1944*

SIR: I have the honor to refer to my telegrams number 246 dated April 10 and number 249 dated April 11, 1944 concerning the Majlis debate on the program submitted by the New Prime Minister, Mr. Saed, and the violent attacks it produced on the American Financial Mission. Reference is also made to the Legation's despatch number 920 dated April 18, 1944 covering the recent press campaign against Dr. Arthur C. Millspaugh and his mission.

The attacks on Dr. Millspaugh in the Majlis were not entirely unexpected, but the number of deputies desirous of voicing anti-Millspaugh sentiments, the violence of the attacks and the complete lack of any adequate defense of the mission have come as something of a surprise. The prestige of certain of the attacking deputies, moreover, especially Dr. Mossadegh, bodes no good for the future of the mission. Dr. Mossadegh's speech in opposition to the Financial Mission was devoted primarily to criticism of the Mission's handling of the food supply, price control and distribution, the phases of his work concerning which Millspaugh meets the most criticism and opposition. Mossadegh also flayed the Government for the type of men selected for the Mission, maintaining that all American advisers should be recommended and their performance guaranteed by the United States Government. This argument is, of course, completely ridiculous since all men coming to Iran for service with the Iranian Government come under strong Departmental recommendations and for the most part, all have been extremely capable men. Unfortunately as stated above, Dr. Mossadegh, despite his recent defeat at the hands of Seyid Zia ed-Din, is a very popular man in Iran, and his words carry a great deal of weight. His speech for the most part was from start to finish rather absurd and showed an amazing lack of knowledge for a man of his experience and reputation. . . .

The opposition to Millspaugh seems to come from three distinct groups: (1) the extreme nationalists led by Mossadegh; (2) the profiteers; and (3) the Russians. Of the three groups the second is by far the most vocal and the most irrational in its criticism and the third the most quiet but potentially the most dangerous. The Tudeh party vote mentioned above undoubtedly reflects the Soviet view on the American program since there is no reason to assume that the Russians are in any way hostile to Saed with whom they have usually been on good terms. Despite these trends and despite the furor of the past few weeks, I do not believe that the Iranian Government has any intention of dropping the adviser program although they would undoubtedly be delighted with the withdrawal of Millspaugh himself. It is possible, of course, that the Majlis may enact legislation limiting the powers of the Americans so that they will become literally "advisers."

While Dr. Millspaugh is having a stormy passage and may not himself be able to weather the storm, I believe that there will be no serious attempt on the part of the Iranians to get rid of the whole financial mission. The air has been cleared now and Millspaugh now has a chance to answer specific complaints which I believe he will be able to do satisfactorily. The deputies have had their say and for the most part will probably let the matter drop at least for a while although certain members of the Majlis who are irreconcilably hostile to Millspaugh, such as Mossadegh, will keep up the attacks for some time to come. The situation is serious but not at the moment critical and it demands the utmost in tact, perserverance, and tolerance from every American in the employ of the Iranian Government. I shall not fail to keep the Department informed regularly of the position of the Financial and other missions in Iran.

Respectfully yours,   RICHARD FORD

The Secretary of State to the Chargé in Iran (Ford)

Washington, May 17, 1944, 4 p.m.

303. The following is the proposed note to the Prime Minister, referred to in the Department's preceding instruction:

"The American Government has observed with growing anxiety the increasing intensity and frequency of the attacks being made against the American advisers in the Iranian Majlis and press. The failure of the Iranian authorities to give the persons attacked the support which they have the right to expect not only as foreign advisers but also as high officials of the Iranian Government has been observed in Washington with especial surprise and concern.

It should be recalled that the American advisers were sent to Iran at the repeated and insistent request of the Iranian Government. The Department of State has done its utmost to cooperate, by selecting men of ability and integrity to staff the various missions and to expedite their departure in spite of war restrictions on travel. The Iranian authorities were confidently expected to be no less cooperative in return.

The Legation endeavored to make clear to the Iranian Government from the outset that it was worse than useless to send advisers to Iran unless they were given full support and sympathy by all persons concerned and that the American Government would hardly feel justified in continuing its efforts to furnish advisers unless the Iranian Government shared this attitude. This viewpoint was expressed to Prime Minister Qavam on August 11, 1942, by Minister Dreyfus acting under the Department's instructions. It is only after receiving the Prime Minister's warm assurances of support for the advisers that the Department agreed to lend its assistance.

The Department deprecates any suggestion that American advisers were sent to Iran to act as mere political buffers. They were sent to Iran to assist the Iranian Government to rebuild its financial and economic structure which had suffered so severely because of the war, and for no other purpose. The American Government would welcome assurances that the Iranian Government concurs in our view of the purpose of the adviser program.

Moreover, it is sincerely hoped, for the ultimate benefit of Iran and in the interests of the cordial relations existing between our two countries, that the Iranian Government may be able to bring about an atmosphere of harmony in which the advisers will be able to accomplish the task which they have undertaken and which the Department ardently desires be carried to a successful conclusion.

President Roosevelt, in sponsoring and signing the Declaration on Iran of December 1, 1943, manifested his sincere desire to devote the influence of the United States and its available resources to the assistance of Iran. The American adviser program is a prominent implementation of this policy. If the Iranian Government and people do not desire this help, the American Government has no intention of pressing them to continue to accept it."

HULL

The Chargé in Iran (Ford) to the Secretary of State

Tehran, June 2, 1944, 6 p.m.

393. Department's 325, May 25 and my 37 [372], May 26. Foreign Minister has sent me lengthy note dated June 1 in reply to our note delivered May 27. Summary follows:

1. Foreign Minister regrets Washington believes Iranian Government "has been subject to influence and looks upon American advisers in the unfavorable light in which they are regarded by the people and the Majlis." Iranian Government is entirely favorable to advisers; has supported them in the past and intends to continue its support in the future. It confirms assurances given by former Prime Minister Qavam in this regard. It will defend its American employees against obstructions placed in way of their useful economic and financial measures.

2. Iranian Government is most grateful that, notwithstanding pressing war needs for manpower, American Government has been willing to allow a number of efficient Americans to accept employment with Iranian Government. Saed is very glad that American Government wishes to devote its influence and available resources to assist Iran and that it considers adviser program as means of implementing this policy.

Iranian Government and people look to United States for help and hope to take full advantage of such assistance.

3. Saed is surprised Department has conceived idea that Iranian Government brought advisers to Iran in order to use them as political buffers. Iranian Government has always intended to employ these Americans for purely financial and economic reforms.

4. Iran's desires, which are happily in agreement with those of the United States, are, first, that through the American advisers Iranian financial and economic conditions shall be improved; and, second, that friendship between two Governments should be made stronger than ever. Iranian Government is most pleased with existing good relations and Saed will not fail to take any action necessary to maintain those relations.

5. Legation has been informed of "well-grounded reasons" for public agitation and for press criticism directed at person of Millspaugh. This criticism should not be interpreted as attack against all American advisers. Reflection of this agitation in Majlis made it necessary to find some means of relieving popular concern, and, after consultation with Deputies it was proposed to Iranian Government that Millspaugh should confine himself to his original financial duties, being relieved of his recently added economic powers, which have nothing to do with his contract. There has been no action whatsoever against American advisers, but present situation must be studied amicably and existing defects in operations removed in spirit of goodwill.

Note concludes by expressing hope that friendly solution will be found.

Full text by air mail.

FORD

The Acting Secretary of State to the Ambassador in Iran (Morris)

Washington, October 25, 1944, 8 p.m.

634. Iranian Minister acting on instructions has formally requested Dept to endeavor to obtain War consent to the continuing of the Ridley Mission contract for additional year. Minister states that there are many projects which will not be finished by March 1, 1945, while on the other hand the need of Iran for a well organized armed force justifies and necessitates the continuance of the mission.

Dept is impressed with the Iranian Government's views and desires to reopen the question of the termination of the Ridley Mission on March 1, 1945. As stated in Dept's 462, July 31, a primary consideration in our policy toward Iran is a desire to strengthen that country so that it can maintain internal security and avoid the dissensions and weaknesses which breed interference and aggression. A cornerstone of this policy should be the building up of Iran's security forces. In view of these considerations Dept is requesting War to reconsider its decision to terminate the Mission on March 1. . . .

. . . You might say that while the limited objectives of the mission as originally conceived may be largely accomplished by March 1, the more important objective of building up Iran's security forces to the point where they can maintain internal security after the withdrawal of foreign forces has only been begun. In addition to these practical considerations the withdrawal of the mission against Iranian desires at the very time when the Iranian Army will have to meet its crucial test might have unfortunate psychological and political repercussions. While Dept hopes that General Ridley himself would be willing to continue as head of the mission, a replacement could be considered if he should insist on coming home.

STETTINIUS

Office of Strategic Services Research and Analysis Branch: The Present Situation in Iran with Regard to the Millspaugh Mission (May-October 1944)

. . . IX. CONCLUSIONS

As his agreed period of grace was drawing to a close, Millspaugh published a letter to the Prime Minister reviewing the work of the past few months, calling attention to the following accomplishments: (1) sufficient imported goods are now on hand for all the needs of the country; (2) prices are lower; (3) monopoly goods are being actively distributed; (4) stored local productes are now being exported; (5) government transport is now adequate and continuous; (6) larger stores of grain are now in government hands than at any time in history; (7) no agreement or trade with a foreign country causing a loss to Iran has been sanctioned; (8) revenues have notably increased and there is hope of a balanced budget; and (9) in cooperation with the cabinet, post-war plans have been adopted. Millspaugh further expressed satisfaction that all misunderstanding between himself and the government had disappeared. Realizing that there would still be some who would continue to oppose his mission, Millspaugh stated that he had given much thought to the suggestion that it was unconstitutional for him to have broad special powers without being answerable directly to the Majlis, as are cabinet ministers, and that he had come to the conclusion that he should surrender, step by step, his economic powers.

This letter met with considerable criticism in the press, some portions of which tried to belittle the achievements of the mission as reviewed by Millspaugh; on the whole, however, the statement seems to have made a fairly good general impression, especially by the proposal for voluntary relinquishment of special economic powers. The validity of Millspaugh's claims may be judged by the above analysis. Had the

Soviet request for oil concessions and the subsequent crisis in Soviet-Iranian relations not come to occupy major attention, it is certain that the future of Millspaugh and his mission would have secured serious consideration by the end of October; especially since Millspaugh himself precipitated a minor crisis by his dismissal of Ebtehaj. Even though delayed, the question is sure to be discussed soon.

Most would agree that the Financial and Economic Mission will continue in Iran, at least for some time. The chief matter in doubt is the continuance of Millspaugh as the head of the mission and Administrator General of Finances. For the present the anomalous situation has developed wherein Millspaugh is supported by the British and Seyyid Zia-ed-Din, along with those Iranian political groups that are determined to resist further Soviet encroachments; while responsible U.S. officials, deprecating the anti-Soviet reputation acquired by Millspaugh, have withdrawn from him their support and would prefer to see him leave his post. It would appear that for the long-term success of this and other advisory missions in building up a strong and independent Iran, some more general and particular agreement concerning such an advisory program might be sought among the three major interested powers.

When that debate comes it will probably take the form of a struggle between Millspaugh and Ebtehaj. Each will have much to say against the other. Extreme nationalists, leftists and labor unions, many disgruntled business groups, and those that are pro-Soviet or in favor of appeasing Russia, will range behind Ebtehaj in an effort to oust Millspaugh. In their favor will be (a) the failure of Millspaugh to secure clear-cut economic and financial gains; (b) Iranian resentment of Millspaugh's personnel policies; (c) the alleged anti-Soviet and pro-British policies of Millspaugh throwing Iranian foreign relations off balance; (d) the poor legal case Millspaugh had for his dismissal of Ebtehaj; and possibly (e) the withdrawal of U.S. support from Millspaugh. In Millspaugh's favor could be listed (a) the strong support by Zia-ed-Din who now wields considerable influence in the Majlis; (b) the support of the British and those who may—temporarily, at least—back any force in government which will oppose the Soviets in their most recent pressure; (c) his own voluntary suggestion for the gradual surrender of his economic powers; and (d) the possible difficulty of changing the head of the mission.

The Ambassador in Iran (Morris) to the Secretary of State

Tehran, January 8, 1945, 5 p.m.

18. Medjliss today passed bill canceling as of this date the special economic powers granted Millspaugh by the law of 13 Ordibehesht. Council of Ministers is authorized to dissolve or reallocate the economic

organizations which were under Millspaugh administration by virtue
of that law and to annul change or retain all regulations issued thereunder. . . .*

MORRIS

Agreement Establishing a United States Military
Mission with Iranian Gendarmerie

November 27, 1943: Agreement signed at Tehran.
November 27, 1943: Entered into force; operative from October 2, 1942.
September 11, 13, 1948: Article 20 amended.
August 4, September 6, 1944; September 27, 29, 1945; July 25, August 8,
1946; September 11, 13, 1948; August 16, 22, 1950; April 18, 1954; March
15, 19, 1955; February 13, 1956; April 10, June 14, November 12, 1961;
February 7, March 19, 1962; June 10, 29, 1968; June 29, July 23, 1969;
September 2, October 8, 1970: Extended.

In conformity with the request of the Government of Iran to the
Government of the United States of America, by authority of the law for
the employment of American officers for the Gendarmerie voted on
October 21, 1943, the President of the United States of America has
authorized the assignment of a mission of officers, non-commissioned
officers and experts of the United States Army, the number of officers of
which shall not exceed eight, with a view to reforming the affairs of the
Gendarmerie, according to the following articles.

TITLE I

Purpose and Duration

ARTICLE 1: The purpose of this Mission is to advise and assist the
Ministry of Interior of Iran in the reorganization of the Imperial Iranian
Gendarmerie.

ARTICLE 2: This Mission shall be effective as of October 2, 1942 and
shall continue for a minimum of two years and any extension mutually
agreed upon between the interested parties unless previously terminated
as hereinafter provided; and provided further that the authority granted
the President of the United States for the detail of such officers remains
in effect for such period. Any member of the Mission may be recalled at
any time upon the request of the Government of the United States of
America provided a replacement with equal qualifications is furnished.

ARTICLE 3: This Agreement may be terminated before the expiration of the period prescribed in Article 2 in the following manner:

a. By either of the Governments, subject to three months' written
notice to the other Government.

b. By the recall of the entire personnel of the Mission by the
Government of the United States of America in the public interest of the
United States of America.

---

* This action by the Majlis effectively terminated the Millspaugh Mission.

ARTICLE 4: This Agreement is subject to cancellation upon the initiative of either the Government of the United States of America or the Government of Iran at any time during a period when either Government is involved in foreign hostilities. In case of cancellation, all provisions hereinafter set forth concerning termination shall apply.

TITLE II

Composition and Personnel

ARTICLE 5: This Mission shall consist at all times of such personnel of the United States Army as may be agreed upon by the Government of Iran through its authorized representative in Washington and by the War Department of the United States of America.

TITLE III

Duties, Rank, and Precedence

ARTICLE 6: The personnel of the Mission shall perform such duties as may be proposed by the Chief of the Mission and approved by the Minister of the Interior of Iran.

ARTICLE 7: The members of the Mission shall be responsible solely to the Minister of Interior of Iran through the Chief of the Mission.

ARTICLE 8: Each member of the Mission shall serve on the Mission with the rank he holds in the United States Army or such simulated rank as may be bestowed upon him by the Iranian Government. The members of the Mission shall wear either the uniform of the United States Army or of the Imperial Iranian Gendarmerie to which they shall be entitled, at the discretion of the Chief of the Mission, but shall have precedence over all Iranian Gendarmerie officers of the same rank.

ARTICLE 9: Each member of the Mission shall be entitled to all benefits and privileges which the Regulations of the Iranian Army and the Iranian Gendarmerie provide for officers of corresponding rank of the Imperial Iranian Gendarmerie.

ARTICLE 10: The personnel of the Mission shall be governed by the disciplinary regulations of the Iranian Gendarmerie except insofar as such regulations are contrary to the regulations of the United States Army.

TITLE IV

Compensation and Perquisites

ARTICLE 11: Members of the Mission shall receive from the Government of Iran such net annual compensation in United States currency as may be agreed upon between the Government of the United States of America and the Government of Iran for each member. This compensation shall be paid in twelve (12) equal monthly installments, each due and payable on the last day of the month. The compensation shall be net after deduction of any tax, now or hereafter in effect, of the Government of Iran or of any of its political or administrative subdivisions. Should there, however, at present or while this Agreement is in effect, be any taxes that might affect this compensation, such taxes shall be borne by the Ministry of Interior of Iran in order to comply with the provision of this Article that the compensation agreed upon shall be net.

Article 12: The compensation agreed upon as indicated in the preceding article shall commence upon October 2, 1942, or upon the date of departure of each Mission member if the latter date is subsequent to October 2, 1942, and except as otherwise expressly provided in this agreement shall be paid following the termination of duty with the Mission before his departure for the United States, for the period of any accumulated leave which may be due.

Article 13: The compensation due for the period of accumulated leave shall be paid to a detached member of the Mission before his departure from Iran.

Article 14: Each member of the Mission and his family shall be furnished by the Government of Iran, except in the case where each member is replaced under the provisions of Article 2 of this Agreement, with first class accommodations for travel, via the shortest usually traveled route, required and performed under this Agreement, between the port of embarkation in the United States of America and his official residence in Iran, both for the outward and for the return trip. The Government of Iran shall also pay all expenses of shipment of household effects, baggage and automobile of each member of the Mission between the port of embarkation in the United States of America and his official residence in Iran as well as all expenses incidental to the transportation of such household effects, baggage and automobile from his official residence in Iran to the port of entry in the United States of America. Transportation of such household effects, baggage, and automobile shall be effected in one shipment, and all subsequent shipments shall be at the expense of the respective members of the Mission except as otherwise provided in this Agreement, or when such shipments are necessitated by circumstances beyond their control. Payment of expenses for the transportation of families, household effects and automobiles, in the case of personnel who may join the Mission for temporary duty at the request of the Minister of Iran, shall not be required under this Agreement, but shall be determined by negotiations between the War Department of the United States of America and the authorized representative of the Government of Iran in Washington at such time as the detail of personnel for such temporary duty may be agreed upon.

Article 15: The Government of Iran shall grant, upon request of the Chief of the Mission, exemption from customs duties or other imposts in articles imported by the members of the Mission for their personal use and for the use of members of their families.

Article 16: Compensation for transportation and traveling expenses in Iran on official business of the Government of Iran shall be provided by the Government of Iran in accordance with the provisions of Article 9.

ARTICLE 17: The Government of Iran shall provide the Chief of the Mission with a suitable automobile with chauffeur, for use on official business. Suitable motor transportation, with chauffeur on call, shall be made available by the Government of Iran for use of the members of the Mission for the conduct of the official business of the Mission.

ARTICLE 18: The Government of Iran shall provide suitable office space and facilities for the use of the members of the Mission.

ARTICLE 19: By authority of the last paragraph of item (c) of the Law of October 21, 1943, if any member of the Mission, or any of his family should die in Iran, the Government of Iran shall have the body transported to such place in the United States of America as the surviving members of the family may decide, but the cost to the Government of Iran shall not exceed the cost of transporting the remains from the place of decease to New York City. Should the deceased be a member of the Mission, his services with the Mission shall be considered to have terminated fifteen (15) days after his death. Return transportation to New York City for the family of the deceased member and for their baggage, household effects and automobile shall be provided as prescribed in Article 14. All compensation due the deceased member, including salary for fifteen (15) days subsequent to his death, and reimbursement for expenses and transportation due the deceased member for travel performed on official business of Iran, shall be paid to the widow of the deceased member or to any other person who may have been designated in writing by the deceased while serving under the terms of this Agreement; but such widow or other person shall not be compensated for accrued leave due and not taken by the deceased. All compensations due the widow, or other person designated by the deceased, under the provisions of this Article, shall be paid within fifteen (15) days of the decease of the said member.

TITLE V

Requisites and Conditions

ARTICLE 20: The Minister of Interior of Iran will appoint the Chief of the Mission Advisor to the Ministry of Interior in charge of Gendarmerie affairs as head of the Imperial Organization of the Iranian Gendarmerie for the duration of this contract and he shall have precedence over all officers of the Imperial Iranian Gendarmerie. He will have immediate charge of the entire administration and control of the Gendarmerie and he will have the right to recommend to the Ministry of Interior and in accordance with regulations the appointment, promotion, demotion, or dismissal of any employee of the Gendarmerie and to put this into effect with the approval of the Ministry of the Interior and no other authority shall have the right to interfere, and he will have the right with the approval of the Minister of the Interior to transfer and reassign any officer, gendarme, or employee of the Gendarmerie.

Article 21: The Government of Iran agrees that, while this agreement is in effect, it will not engage officers of other foreign armies or personnel from any other country to serve in the Imperial Iranian Gendarmerie or branches in which the members of the United States Military Mission are serving.

Article 22: Each member of the Mission shall agree not to divulge or in any way disclose to any foreign government or to any person whatsoever any secret or confidential matter of which he may become cognizant in his capacity as a member of the Mission. This requirement shall continue in force after the termination of service with the Mission and after the expiration or cancellation of this Agreement.

Article 23: Throughout this agreement the term "family" is limited to mean wife and dependent children.

Article 24: Each member of the Mission shall be entitled to one month's annual leave with pay, or to a proportional part thereof with pay for any fractional part of a year. Unused portions of said leave shall be cumulative from year to year during service as a member of the Mission.

Article 25: The leave specified in the preceding Article may be spent in Iran, in the United States of America, or in other countries, but the expense of travel and transportation not otherwise provided for in this Agreement shall be borne by the member of the Mission taking such leave. All travel time shall count as leave and shall not be in addition to the time authorized as leave.

Article 26: The Government of Iran agrees to grant the leave specified in Article 24 upon receipt of written application, approved by the Chief of the Mission with due consideration for the interests of the Government of Iran.

Article 27: Members of the Mission that may be replaced shall terminate their services on the Mission only upon the arrival of their replacements except when otherwise mutually agreed upon in advance by the respective Governments.

Article 28: The Government of Iran shall provide suitable medical attention to members of the Mission and their families. In case a member of the Mission becomes ill or suffers injury, he shall, at the discretion of the Chief of the Mission, be placed in such hospital as the Chief of the Mission deems suitable, with concurrence of the Minister of Interior of Iran, and all expenses incurred as the result of such illness or injury while the patient is a member of the Mission and remains in Iran shall be paid by the Government of Iran. If the hospitalized member is a commissioned officer he shall pay his cost of subsistence. Families shall enjoy the same privileges agreed upon in this Article for members of the Mission, except that a member of the Mission shall in all cases pay the cost of subsistence incident to hospitalization of a member of his family, except as may be provided under Article 9.

ARTICLE 29: Any member of the Mission unable to perform his duties with the Mission by reason of long continued physical disability shall be replaced.

ARTICLE 30: The Council of Ministers will have the right to cancel such provisions of this Agreement as refer to any member of the Mission, duly and competently proved to be guilty of interference in the political affairs of the country or of violation of the laws of the land.

IN WITNESS WHEREOF, the undersigned, Mohamed Saed, Minister of Foreign Affairs of Iran, and Louis G. Dreyfus, Jr., Envoy Extraordinary and Minister Plenipotentiary of the United States of America, have signed this Agreement in duplicate in the English and Persian languages, at Tehran, this 27th day of November, one thousand nine hundred and forty-three.

M. SAED   [SEAL]

LOUIS G. DREYFUS JR.   [SEAL]

UNITED STATES WARTIME PRESENCE IN IRAN

Stationing of United States Noncombat Troops in Iran

The Minister in Iran (Dreyfus) to the Secretary of State

Tehran, December 13, 1942, 2 p.m.

435. Subject of Department's 341 discussed with Foreign Minister who has given consent of Iran Government to American operation southern section Trans-Iranian Railway subject to approval British and Russian Governments as required by Tripartite Pact. British approval given and Soviet Ambassador has requested authority from his Government for similar approval.

After stressing pleasure of Iranians to have railroad operated by Americans, Prime Minister suggested since operation necessitated presence of American Armed Forces in Iran their presence should be regularized by signing agreement between our two Governments. Department's instructions in this regard would be appreciated.

General Andrews now in Tehran urged the advisability of arranging with Iran Government that jurisdiction over infractions of law by members of United States Forces should remain with United States authorities.

DREYFUS

The Secretary of State to the Minister in Iran (Dreyfus)

Washington, December 23, 1942, 4 p.m.

390. Your 435, December 13. Department would prefer not to conclude any general, over-all agreement covering presence of American armed forces in Iran but rather to conclude individual *ad hoc* agreements to cover specific problems as they arise. This is the policy which has been followed in other foreign territories, such as Egypt, where American troops are stationed.

Consideration is being given to preparation of draft agreement to take care of question of jurisdiction over offenses which may be committed by members of American armed forces.

HULL

*Memorandum of Conversation, by the Chief of the
Division of Near Eastern Affairs (Alling)*

[Washington,] December 24, 1942

The Minister called at his request and brought up the subject of the operation by the American Army of the Trans-Iranian Railroad. He said that according to his understanding, the United States army was to operate the southern section of the railroad, that is, the part between Bandar Shahpur and Tehran, while the Russians were to continue to operate the northern part beyond Tehran. I told him that that was also my understanding. He said that this division of responsibility was bound to bring unsatisfactory results and that, in his opinion, it would be to the advantage of all concerned—Americans, Russians and Iranians—to have the American Army operate the entire line. I told him that I could appreciate his point of view, but that I had no information as to the local considerations which had brought about the decision to have the American Army operate only a portion of the line. The Minister was most insistent that his point of view be taken into consideration. I gathered the impression that he felt that the Russians would be likely to let the portion of the line that they are operating deteriorate and that after the war, the Iranians would find themselves with a sadly inferior section of railroad.

The Minister then went on to bring up another question in regard to the railroad. He said that we would recall that under the Tripartite Agreement, Iran had granted the Russians and the British the right to operate the Trans-Iranian Railroad. He was somewhat concerned that since part of the line was now about to be operated by the American Army, the Russians and British might later insist that this was not a complete fulfillment of the terms of the Tripartite Agreement. Subsequently, upon reviewing the matter, it was ascertained that the British had already informed the Iranians that they had no objection to American operation of the line. According to the same telegram from Tehran, the Soviet Ambassador was seeking authority from his Government to give similar assurance to the Iranians. The Minister was informed of this information, but he did not seem to be convinced that British and Russian approval had, in fact, been given. It might be desirable to check on this point with our Legation at Tehran.

Memorandum by the Chief of the Division of Near Eastern Affairs (Alling)

[Washington,] January 26, 1943

The Iranian Government has asserted that the presence on Iranian territory of American troops constitutes an infringement of Iranian sovereignty and has suggested that this matter be adjusted through the adherence of the United States to the Anglo-Russian-Iranian Treaty of Alliance of January 29, 1942. Under this treaty, Great Britain and Russia have the right to maintain troops in Iran and to operate and control any or all means of communication in Iran.

NE does not consider it politically feasible to propose adherence of this Government to a Treaty of Alliance with Iran, and we have intimated as much to the Iranian Minister here. However, in view of the insistence of the Iranian Government upon the necessity for "legalizing" the status of American troops in Iran, it is believed that some form of executive agreement on this subject should be concluded.

There is attached a rough draft of a suggested agreement, modeled closely upon the appropriate sections of the Treaty of Alliance. It will be noted that provision is made to avoid conflict with the Treaty but that the agreement is not itself based upon the Treaty. It will also be noted that the United States assumes no obligation, except that of interfering as little as possible with the internal affairs of Iran. This may seem to make the bargain rather one-sided, but it should be borne in mind that we are merely asking for ourselves rights already possessed by the British and Russians, and that the Iranians, in fact, welcome our presence in Iran as a possible offset to British and Russian influence. . . .

PAUL H. ALLING

The Ambassador in Iran (Morris) to the Secretary of State

Tehran, January 24, 1945, 11 a.m.

49. During interview with Foreign Minister he discussed pending question of agreement regularizing status of our troops in Iran and suggested that since troops may shortly be leaving Iran matter might be adjusted by having Majlis pass a resolution approving action of Government in originally admitting troops to Iran and otherwise legalizing their status in this country for the duration of the war. In advancing his

suggestion Entezam professed he was motivated by sincere desire to settle this question as simply and expeditiously as possible.

I gave no opinion as to what reception this proposal might receive from my Government but suggested that Entezam submit matter through his Minister in Washington to Department to which he agreed.

This initial telegram is for Department's information. I shall follow it up with further comments after I have had an opportunity to discuss question with PGC.*

MORRIS

Iranian Charges Concerning Misconduct of American Troops in Iran

The Minister in Iran (Dreyfus) to the Secretary of State

No. 579   Tehran, June 10, 1943

SIR: I have the honor to enclose a list of incidents in which members of the American armed forces in Iran have been involved and which have called for rather voluminous exchange of notes between the Legation and the Foreign Office.

These incidents cover a period of more than a year. They have not been brought to the Department's attention prior to this date because they have reached serious proportions only within the last few months. Many of these accidents and incidents are trivial and in a number investigation has shown that no blame could be attributed to the Americans involved. However, the growing volume of complaints from the

---

* In despatch 203, February 13, 1945, the Ambassador expressed his opposition to the Iranian suggestion that the status of American military forces in Iran be regularized by an act of the Majlis. He pointed out that although this course of action would provide legality for the presence of the troops from the viewpoint of Iranian domestic law, it might fail to give the United States adequate protection against possible Iranian claims for damages, taxes, customs duties, etc. The Ambassador concluded that he and Brig. Gen. Donald P. Booth, Commanding General of the Persian Gulf Command, believed it advisable to negotiate a formal treaty or agreement to handle the matter.

No further action on the question of regularizing the status of American troops in Iran occurred until March 1945 when the Iranian Minister informed the Department of State that the Iranian Government no longer deemed an agreement necessary and considered the matter closed. No correspondence concerning this action by the Iranian Minister has been found in Department files. However, on September 29, 1945, the American Embassy in Iran issued a statement in reply to critical articles in certain Tehran newspapers about the presence of American troops in Iran and other matters. The statement noted the abrupt suspension by the Iranian Government of negotiations for an agreement governing the presence of American troops in Iran in December 1943, and stressed that the United States Government had repeatedly expressed willingness thereafter to reopen negotiations until the matter was closed by the action of the Iranian Minister in March 1945. The text of this statement was transmitted to the Department in telegram 789, October 2, 1945, 5 p.m.

Foreign Office about the conduct of the American troops and the frequency of automobile accidents have made it necessary to report the matter in detail. I would prefer, of course, to send the Department copies of all correspondence upon the subject but regret that it is much too bulky for my staff to cope with. The enclosure will give the Department a general picture of the nature and frequency of the incidents which have tended to make each successive note from the Foreign Office sharper in tone.

I realize that when a great body of troops are moved into a foreign country, there are bound to be a number of incidents offensive to the nation playing host no matter how sincerely the guests may endeavor to prevent them. However, their volume in Iran is alarming and I fear that if there is no improvement in this situation, our position in Iran may deteriorate. The incidents of drunkenness are particularly offensive to a Mohammedan people. The automobile accidents cannot be prevented entirely since fast driving is often necessary in the all-important job of moving war material to the Soviet Union. It must be remembered, too, that Iranian pedestrians are extremely careless and are often responsible for accident. Many of the accidents have been caused by Iranian chauffeurs rather than by American personnel.

There is no doubt that the numerous accidents and the rather frequent incidents of drunkenness and rowdyism have had an adverse effect on American prestige in Iran. However, as I pointed out before our forces came to this country and have remarked subsequently, this was to a certain extent unavoidable. I am not yet prepared to state that the conduct of our forces is much worse than the average of occupying forces. . . . I suggest that for the moment we keep an open mind on the subject, meanwhile making every endeavor to bring about an improvement. I will keep the Department fully informed of developments.

Respectfully yours,   LOUIS G. DREYFUS, JR.

The Minister in Iran (Dreyfus) to the Secretary of State

Tehran, June 15, 1943, 10 a.m.

. . . Foreign Minister has expressed to me informally his dissatisfaction with large number of incidents especially traffic accidents involving members of PGSC.* I must admit that volume is alarming. See despatch 579, June 10. However, the operations involving transport of war supplies to Russia are important and urgent and a certain number of incidents is inevitable. I do not observe any widespread disregard of Iranian rights by American Army nor any gross carelessness by American drivers. I was pleased at friendly and conciliatory tone of Connolly's reply in present case. This and my personal explanation to

---

* Persian Gulf Service Command.

Foreign Minister seem to have disposed satisfactorily of this particular case.

DREYFUS

The Minister in Iran (Dreyfus) to the Secretary of State

No. 591   Tehran, June 24, 1943

SIR: With reference to my Despatch No. 579 dated June 10, 1943 concerning traffic accidents and incidents of misconduct involving personnel of the United States Army in Iran, I have the honor to enclose another list of such occurrences which have come to the attention of the Legation since the list enclosed in my previous despatch was prepared.

There are also enclosed two copies of notes from the Foreign Office as typical examples of the sort of communications the Legation is receiving daily. One of these is very representative of the accident type of note and it will be noted from it and from the enclosed list that the great majority of the accidents involve pedestrians. In a great many cases the investigations conducted by the appropriate authorities of the Persian Gulf Service Command show that no fault could be attached to the American drivers involved. By American standards this is undoubtedly true, and the drivers would, without question, be absolved of all blame in any traffic court in the United States. It is impossible, however, to expect the oriental Iranian pedestrian to behave when alarmed by an approaching automobile in the same manner that a similar person would in the United States. The reflexes of the Iranians, to whom the automobile is still a comparatively recent innovation, are relatively slow, and by the time the pedestrian endeavors to get out of danger it is apt to be too late.

General Connolly in a letter to me dated June 14, stated his serious concern over the number of automobile accidents and listed the steps he was taking to reduce them, consisting of the institution of traffic patrols and orders to his command to adhere to fixed speed limits. No improvement has been noticeable to date, however.

The question of misconduct and drunkenness is becoming increasingly serious and I am asking General Connolly to give the matter serious consideration. I will report more fully on the subject in a separate despatch.

There are many more disgraceful incidents that have come to the notice of the Foreign Office and the reputation of the American soldier in Tehran is at about the lowest ebb possible.

Needless to say the Iranians are getting thoroughly tired of these incidents, and the tone of the notes from the Foreign Office is becoming increasingly strong. The Foreign Minister has personally expressed to me his concern over the growing number of these cases, and it is clear that if nothing is done to correct the situation in the near future our prestige in Iran will suffer serious damage.

Respectfully yours,   LOUIS G. DREYFUS, JR.

EXPANSION OF UNITED STATES-IRANIAN
TRADE RELATIONS

Treaty on Reciprocal Trade between
United States and Iran

April 8, 1943	*Agreement and exchange of notes signed at Washington.*
October 24, 1943	*Ratified by Iran.*
March 31, 1944	*Proclaimed by the President of the United States.*
May 29, 1944	*Ratification and proclamation exchanged at Washington.*
May 29, 1944	*Supplementary proclamation by the President of the United States.*
June 28, 1944	*Entered into force.*
April 12, 1960	*Amended.*
July 27, 1960	*Terminated August 25, 1960.*

AGREEMENT

The President of the United States of America and His Imperial Majesty the Shah-in-Shah of Iran, being desirous of strengthening the traditional bonds of friendship between the two countries by maintaining as heretofore the principle of equality of treatment as the basis of commercial relations and by granting mutual and reciprocal concessions and advantages for the promotion and extension of trade, have decided to conclude a Trade Agreement and for that purpose have appointed their Plenipotentiaries, as follows:

The President of the United States of America:

Cordell Hull, Secretary of State of the United States of America; and His Imperial Majesty the Shah-in-Shah of Iran:

Mohammed Shayesteh, Envoy Extraordinary and Minister Plenipotentiary at Washington;

who, after communicating to each other their respective full powers, found to be in good and due form, have agreed upon the following Articles:

ARTICLE I

1. The United States of America and Iran will grant each other unconditional and unrestricted most-favored-nation treatment in all matters concerning customs duties and subsidiary charges of every kind

and in the method of levying duties, and, further, in all matters concerning the rules, formalities and charges imposed in connection with the clearing of goods through the customs, and with respect to all laws or regulations affecting the sale, taxation or use of imported goods within the country.

2. Accordingly, articles the growth, produce or manufacture of either country imported into the other shall in no case be subject, in regard to the matters referred to above, to any duties, taxes or charges other or higher, or to any rules or formalities other or more burdensome, than those to which the like articles the growth, produce or manufacture of any third country are or may hereafter be subject.

3. Similarly, articles exported from the territory of the United States of America or Iran and consigned to the territory of the other country shall in no case be subject with respect to exportation and in regard to the above-mentioned matters, to any duties, taxes or charges other or higher, or to any rules or formalities other or more burdensome, than those to which the like articles when consigned to the territory of any third country are or may hereafter be subject.

4. Any advantage, favor, privilege or immunity which has been or may hereafter be granted by the United States of America or Iran in regard to the above-mentioned matters, to any article orginating in any third country or consigned to the territory of any third country shall be accorded immediately and without compensation to the like article originating in or consigned to the territory of Iran or the United States of America, respectively.

ARTICLE II

Articles the growth, produce or manufacture of the United States of America or Iran, shall, after importation into the other country, be exempt from all internal taxes, fees, charges or exactions other or higher than those imposed on like articles of national origin or of any other foreign origin.

ARTICLE III

1. No prohibition or restriction of any kind shall be imposed by the Government of either country on the importation of any article the growth, produce or manufacture of the other country or upon the exportation of any article destined for the other country, unless the importation of the like article the growth, produce or manufacture of all third countries, or the exportation of the like article to all third countries, respectively, is similarly prohibited or restricted.

2. No restriction of any kind shall be imposed by the Government of either country on the importation from the other country of any article in which that country has an interest, whether by means of import licenses or permits or otherwise, unless the total quantity or value of such article permitted to be imported during a specified period,

or any change in such quantity or value, shall have been established and made public. If the Government of either country allots a share of such total quantity or value to any third country, it shall allot to the other country, unless it is mutually agreed to dispense with such allotment, a share based upon the proportion of the total imports of such article supplied by that country in a previous representative period, account being taken in so far as practicable of any special factors which may have affected or may be affecting the trade in that article, and shall make such share available so as to facilitate its full utilization. No limitation or restriction of any kind other than such an allotment shall be imposed, by means of import licenses or permits or otherwise, on the share of such total quantity or value which may be imported from the other country.

3. The provisions of this Article shall apply in respect of the quantity or value of any article permitted to be imported at a specified rate of duty.

ARTICLE IV

1. If the Government of either country establishes or maintains any form of control of the means of international payment, it shall accord unconditional most-favored-nation treatment to the commerce of the other country with respect to all aspects of such control.

2. The Government establishing or maintaining such control shall impose no prohibition, restriction or delay on the transfer of payment for any article the growth, produce or manufacture of the other country which is not imposed on the transfer of payment for the like article the growth, produce or manufacture of any third country. With respect to rates of exchange and with respect to taxes or charges on exchange transactions, articles the growth, produce or manufacture of the other country shall be accorded unconditionally treatment no less favorable than that accorded to the like articles the growth, produce or manufacture of any third country. The foregoing provisions shall also extend to the application of such control to payments necessary for or incidental to the importation of articles the growth, produce or manufacture of the other country. In general, the control shall be administered so as not to influence to the disadvantage of the other country the competitive relationships between articles the growth, produce or manufacture of the territories of that country and like articles the growth, produce or manufacture of third countries.

ARTICLE V

1. In the event that the Government of either country establishes or maintains a monopoly for the importation, production or sale of any article or grants exclusive privileges, formally or in effect, to any agency to import, produce or sell any article, it is agreed that the commerce of the other country shall be accorded fair and equitable treatment in respect of the foreign purchases of such monopoly or agency. To this

end such monopoly or agency will, in making its foreign purchases of any article, be influenced solely by those considerations, such as price, quality, marketability and terms of sale, which would ordinarily be taken into account by a private commercial enterprise interested solely in purchasing such article on the most favorable terms.

2. The Government of each country, in the awarding of contracts for public works and generally in the purchase of supplies, shall accord fair and equitable treatment to the commerce of the other country as compared with the treatment accorded to the commerce of any third country.

ARTICLE VI

1. Articles the growth, produce or manufacture of the United States of America enumerated and described in Schedule I annexed to this Agreement shall, on their importation into Iran, be exempt from ordinary customs duties in excess of those set forth and provided for in the said Schedule, subject to the conditions therein set out. The said articles shall also be exempt from all other duties, taxes, fees, charges or exactions, imposed on or in connection with importation, in excess of those imposed on the day of the signature of this Agreement or required to be imposed thereafter under laws of Iran in force on the day of the signature of this Agreement.

2. Schedule I and the notes included therein shall have full force and effect as integral parts of this Agreement.

ARTICLE VII

1. Articles the growth, produce or manufacture of Iran enumerated and described in Schedule II annexed to this Agreement shall, on their importation into the United States of America, be exempt from ordinary customs duties in excess of those set forth and provided for in the said Schedule, subject to the conditions therein set out. The said articles shall also be exempt from all other duties, taxes, fees, charges or exactions, imposed on or in connection with importation, in excess of those imposed on the day of the signature of this Agreement or required to be imposed thereafter under laws of the United States of America in force on the day of the signature of this Agreement.

2. Schedule II and the notes included therein shall have full force and effect as integral parts of this Agreement.

ARTICLE VIII

The provisions of Articles VI and VII of this Agreement shall not prevent the Government of either country from imposing at any time on the importation of any article a charge equivalent to an internal tax imposed in respect of a like domestic article or in respect of a commodity from which the imported article has been manufactured or produced in whole or in part.

ARTICLE IX

1. If the Government of either country should consider that any circumstance, or any measure adopted by the other Government, even though it does not conflict with the terms of this Agreement, has the effect of nullifying or impairing any object of the Agreement or of prejudicing an industry or the commerce of that country, such other Government shall give sympathetic consideration to such written representations or proposals as may be made with a view to effecting a mutually satisfactory adjustment of the matter. If agreement is not reached with respect to the matter within thirty days after such representations or proposals are received, the Government which made them shall be free, within fifteen days after the expiration of the aforesaid period of thirty days, to terminate this Agreement in whole or in part on thirty days' written notice.

2. The Governments of the two countries agree to consult together to the fullest possible extent in regard to all matters affecting the operation of the present Agreement.

ARTICLE X

1. The provisions of this Agreement relating to the treatment to be accorded by the United States of America and Iran, respectively, to the commerce of the other country shall apply to the respective customs territories of the two countries.

2. Furthermore, the provisions of this Agreement relating to most-favored-nation treatment shall apply to all territory under the sovereignty or authority of the two countries, except that they shall not apply to the Panama Canal Zone.

ARTICLE XI

1. The advantages now accorded or which may hereafter be accorded by the United States of America or Iran to adjacent countries in order to facilitate frontier traffic, and advantages accorded by virtue of a customs union to which either country may become a party, shall be excepted from the operation of this Agreement.

2. The advantages now accorded or which may hereafter be accorded by the United States of America, its territories or possessions or the Panama Canal Zone to one another or to the Republic of Cuba shall be excepted from the operation of this Agreement. The provisions of this paragraph shall continue to apply in respect of any advantages now or hereafter accorded by the United States of America, its territories or possessions or the Panama Canal Zone to one another, irrespective of any change in the political status of any of the territories or possessions of the United States of America.

ARTICLE XII

Nothing in this Agreement shall be construed to prevent the adoption or enforcement of measures

(a) imposed on moral or humanitarian grounds;

(b) designed to protect human, animal or plant life or health;

(c) relating to prison-made goods;

(d) relating to the enforcement of police or revenue laws;

(e) relating to the importation or exportation of gold or silver;

(f) relating to the control of the export or sale for export of arms, ammunition, or implements of war, and, in exceptional circumstances, all other military supplies;

(g) relating to neutrality;

(h) relating to public security, or imposed for the protection of the country's essential interests in time of war or other national emergency.

ARTICLE XIII

The Government of the United States of America and the Imperial Government of Iran declare that the purpose of this Agreement is to grant mutual and reciprocal concessions and advantages for the promotion of commercial relations between the two countries; and that each and every one of the provisions contained herein shall be complied with and interpreted in accordance with this spirit and intention.

ARTICLE XIV

This Agreement shall be proclaimed by the President of the United States of America and shall be ratified by the National Assembly (Majlis) of Iran. It shall enter into force on the thirtieth day following the exchange of the proclamation and the instrument of ratification, which shall take place in Washington as soon as possible.

ARTICLE XV

Subject to the provisions of Article IX, this Agreement shall remain in force for a term of three years from the date of entry into force pursuant to Article XIV, and, unless at least six months before the expiration of the aforesaid term of three years, the Government of either country shall have given notice to the other Government of intention to terminate the Agreement upon the expiration of that term, the Agreement shall remain in force thereafter, subject to the provisions of Article IX, until six months from the date on which the Government of either country shall have given notice to the other Government of intention to terminate the Agreement.

In witness whereof the respective Plenipotentiaries have signed this Agreement and have affixed their seals hereto.

Done in duplicate, in the English and Persian languages, both authentic, in Washington, this eighth day of April 1943.

> For the President of the United States of America:
> CORDELL HULL   [SEAL]
> *Secretary of State of the*
> *United States of America*

> For His Imperial Majesty the Shah-in-Shah of Iran:
> M. SHAYESTEH   [SEAL]
> *Envoy Extraordinary and Minister*
> *Plenipotentiary of Iran at Washington*

The Iranian Minister to the Secretary of State (Hull)

No. 108   *April 8, 1943*

SIR: During the course of the negotiations of the Trade Agreement signed this day, and with direct reference to the tariff concession on opium imported into the United States as provided in Schedule II thereof, it has been explained that the general policy of the Government of the United States is to issue permits for the importation of opium only in cases where the producing country has established a system of import permits and export authorizations at least equivalent to that described in the International Opium Convention signed at Geneva on February 19, 1925.

It has been further explained that in accordance with this policy, which is of general application, the issuance of permits for the importation of Iranian opium into the United States in the future would depend largely upon the measures which may have been taken by the Government of Iran for controlling effectively traffic in opium.

I am directed by my Government to state that it fully appreciates the reasons which have led to the general policy of the Government of the United States with respect to the importation of opium and to the adoption of the above means to carry out this policy. I am further directed to state that my Government has always been in full accord and sympathy with the international efforts made in the past to suppress the contraband traffic in opium, and that it is my Government's intention to establish at any early date any additional regulations which may be necessary to confine the trade in opium produced in Iran to legitimate international channels, including a system of import permits and export authorizations at least equivalent to that described in the Geneva drug convention of 1925.

Accept, Sir, the renewed assurances of my highest consideration.

M. SHAYESTEH

The Secretary of State to the Iranian Minister (Shayesteh)

Department of State
Washington, April 8, 1943

SIR: I have the honor to acknowledge the receipt of your note of today's date and to confirm the statement therein set forth concerning the general policy of the Government of the United States with respect to the importation of opium.

My Government is deeply interested in measures designed to suppress the illicit international traffic in opium. It is, therefore, gratifying to learn that it is the intention of your Government to establish at an early date any additional regulations which may be necessary to confine the trade in opium produced in Iran to legitimate international channels, including a system of import permits and export authorizations at least equivalent to that described in the Geneva drug convention of 1925.

Accept, Sir, the renewed assurances of my highest consideration.

CORDELL HULL

Agreement Regulating United States Air Transport Services to Iran

November 8, 1945	*Exchanges of notes at Tehran.*
December 17, 1945	*Exchanges of notes at Tehran.*
December 17, 1945	*Entered into force.*
April 17, 1958	*Replaced by agreement of January 16, 1957.*

The Under Secretary of State for Foreign Affairs to the American Ambassador

[TRANSLATION]

Ministry of Foreign Affairs
No. 5164   *November 8, 1945*

MR. AMBASSADOR: As you know, the Imperial Government took favorable (active) part in the International Civil Aviation Conference in Chicago. However, according to the basic regulations of the Empire, the accords which were signed at the said Conference become definitive only when they have been ratified by the National Consultive Assembly (Majlis).

With regard to the proposed bilateral air transport agreement, the text of which was sent to the Imperial Ministry of Foreign Affairs as an enclosure to the United States Embassy's note No. 223 dated April 5, 1945, the following matters are brought to your attention.

1. With a view to strengthening the happy relations existing between our two Governments and establishing serial communications between our two countries, the Imperial Government has received the said proposed agreement with favor, and will be most pleased when it becomes possible to take the necessary decisions in this respect and to put these decisions into effect.

2. However, as a matter of general policy, the Imperial Government is refraining, prior to the departure of the last foreign soldier from Iran, from concluding an agreement of this kind with any foreign Government.

3. Under the circumstances existing at present, the Imperial Government, with a view to showing evidence of its goodwill towards the American Government and people, grants unexclusively and temporarily, and as an exception, to any American airline, which may be recommended and presented by the American Government, the permission for civil flight in Iran, and also permission for the planes of the said airline to land at Mehrabad airport for the purpose of technical and commercial needs and for the transport of passengers.

4. The American airline must furnish the Imperial Government in advance with complete information as to the flights scheduled, including the dates and hours of arrival in, and departure from, Iranian territory; and full information as to the markings and specifications of the planes to be used on this route. The Imperial Government must also be informed in advance of any changes in the schedules furnished.

5. Flights within Iran for the purpose of carrying goods, passengers, mail, et cetera, are the monopoly of the air services of the Iranian Government and are outside the scope of the permission mentioned in paragraph numbered 3 of this note.

6. It goes without saying that the present air service between Tehran and Baghdad will be maintained as in the past, the Imperial Iranian Government being determined to extend and develop its air service between Iran and Baghdad, and to establish airlines to other countries in the Middle and Near East.

7. This permission which the Iranian Government has granted temporarily and unexclusively, and as an exception, for the establishment of an airline between Iran and America should in no way impair or harm the development of any Iranian national or international airlines which may be established in the future.

8. The following points will be considered and observed:

a. The authorized airplanes must, in each of the two countries, upon the occasion of arrival and departure, and during flights and stops, carry out and observe the laws and regulations of that country.

b. In order to make use of the landing fields and facilities needed by authorized planes, the airline to which the planes belong must pay the just and reasonable charges prescribed by the appropriate authorities of the country in which the planes are operating. Also, customs duties must be paid on shipments in accordance with the regulations of the country concerned.

9. Whenever the Imperial Government, or an Iranian aviation service presented by the Iranian Government, should wish to establish an aviation service between Iran and the United States, the provisions of articles 3, 4, 5, 8 and 10 of this note must also be applied to Iran.

10. This permission may be cancelled by either party on three months notice.

I avail myself of this opportunity to renew to Your Excellency the assurances of my highest consideration.

MOHAMMED ALI HOMAYOUNDJAH

ALLIED MINUET ON IRAN, 1943-45

The Tehran Conference (The Tripartite Declaration)
November 28-December 1, 1943

Declaration of the Three Powers Regarding Iran

December 1, 1943

The President of the United States, the Premier of the U.S.S.R. and the Prime Minister of the United Kingdom, having consulted with each other and with the Prime Minister of Iran, desire to declare the mutual agreement of their three Governments regarding their relations with Iran.

The Governments of the United States, the U.S.S.R., and the United Kingdom recognize the assistance which Iran has given in the prosecution of the war against the common enemy, particularly by facilitating the transportation of supplies from overseas to the Soviet Union.

The Three Governments realize that the war has caused special economic difficulties for Iran, and they are agreed that they will continue to make available to the Government of Iran such economic assistance as may be possible, having regard to the heavy demands made upon them by their world-wide military operations, and to the world-wide shortage of transport, raw materials, and supplies for civilian consumption.

With respect to the post-war period, the Governments of the United

States, the U.S.S.R., and the United Kingdom are in accord with the Government of Iran that any economic problems confronting Iran at the close of hostilities should receive full consideration, along with those of other members of the United Nations, by conferences or international agencies held or created to deal with international economic matters.

The Governments of the United States, the U.S.S.R., and the United Kingdom are at one with the Government of Iran in their desire for the maintenance of the independence, sovereignty and territorial integrity of Iran. They count upon the participation of Iran, together with all other peace-loving nations, in the establishment of international peace, security and prosperity after the war, in accordance with the principles of the Atlantic Charter, to which all four Governments have subscribed.

WINSTON S. CHURCHILL

J. STALIN

FRANKLIN D. ROOSEVELT

Conclusions of the Potsdam Conference between the U.S.S.R., U.S., and U.K. July 17-August 2, 1945 Regarding Iran

XIV. IRAN

It was agreed that Allied troops should be withdrawn immediately from Tehran, and that further stages of the withdrawl of troops from Iran should be considered at the meeting of the Council of Foreign Ministers to be held in London in September, 1945.

Report by Secretary Byrnes on Moscow Meeting

December 30, 1945

The purpose of my talk tonight is to render a report on the recent meeting of the Foreign Secretaries of Great Britain, the United States, and the Soviet Union at Moscow.

With President Truman's approval and encouragement I had urged the calling of this meeting in fulfillment of the understanding reached at Yalta that the three Foreign Secretaries should meet every three or four months.

I was well aware of the risk involved in suggesting this meeting without any definite assurance that the three governments would be able to reach agreement on the points under discussion. I knew the risk of another impasse such as occurred in London. I felt this risk had to be taken.

It is just when there are genuine difficulties in reaching agreement that Foreign Secretaries should meet in an effort to understand each other's problems and troubles. . . .

The Foreign Ministers reached understanding on all important items placed on our agenda with the exception of Iran. At one time it looked as if we might agree on a tripartite commission to consider Iranian problems which have been accentuated by the presence of Allied troops in Iran. Unfortunately, we could not agree. I do not wish to minimize the seriousness of the problem. But I am not discouraged. I hope that the exchange of views may lead to further consideration of the grave issues involved and out of such consideration a solution may be found. . . .

3

Cold War Imbroglio

The years immediately following World War II were marked by a substantial strengthening and extension of U.S.-Iranian ties. This development was both a symptom and a result of U.S.-Soviet rivalry. As far as Iran was concerned, the development first manifested itself when the Soviet Union not only refused to withdraw its troops from Iran by the prearranged deadline, but also supported the establishment of a separatist government in the province of Azerbaijan.

Although the war was only a few months over when these events occurred, the United States already had reason to mistrust Soviet intentions. Iran's appeals thus found a ready ear in Washington. From the U.S. standpoint it was important to minimize Soviet influence in the Middle East and to safeguard the West's supplies of oil. Iran's national integrity and, quite possibly, her independence, were threatened by Soviet machinations.

Iran had two objectives: the withdrawal of Soviet troops and the cessation of Soviet support for the separatist government of Azerbaijan. To accomplish these objectives, it sought the help of the United States, which responded with notes of protest to the Soviet Union, and with diplomatic support at the United Nations. The main burden of bilateral negotiations fell, of course, on Iran. Those negotiations were long and tortuous. The documentation printed herein bears this out, and it constitutes only a segment of what is available.

With the encouragement of the United States, Iran complained to the Security Council of the United Nations about the presence of Soviet troops on her soil. Unhappy at being indicted before the world body, the Soviet Union expressed its willingness to withdraw its troops and urged that Iran's complaint thus should be removed from the agenda. The Soviet Union put tremendous pressure on Iran and on its chief negotiator, Prime Minister Qavam, who was disposed toward conciliatory tactics vis-à-vis the Soviet Union in any event. The Russians proposed that they obtain an oil concession as a price for withdrawal. Qavam appeared to give in, the issue was withdrawn from the agenda, and the Soviet troops were withdrawn from Iran. But the Majlis never ratified the concession agreement. Moreover, Iran stiffened its stance and complained a second time to the United Nations, citing Soviet interference in Azerbaijan. Again it did so with the support and assistance of the United States.

When Iran summoned up the courage to send troops to Azerbaijan, they met no resistance. Lacking overt Soviet support in the form of troops, the separatist government collapsed. The assessment of the U.S. ambassador at the time, George V. Allen, was that the Soviets backed down because they had no wish to risk a military confrontation with the United States. This was a perception that was widely shared. The United States took advantage of its standing with the Iranian government to recommend a liberal policy toward the Azerbaijanis. Both the ambassador's evaluation and the note from Secretary Byrnes urging moderation are printed in this chapter.

By 1947, the West was becoming thoroughly alarmed at what was perceived as the relentless thrust of Soviet expansionism. George Kennan elaborated the doctrine of containment, which was given practical form in the Truman Doctrine and the Marshall Plan. The former stated that it must be the policy of the United States "to support free peoples who are resisting attempted subjugation by armed minorities or by outside pressures." The latter provided for economic assistance to the countries of Western Europe, where communism had made substantial inroads because of an economy still shackled by the destruction of the war. The new structure of U.S. security was capped by the North Atlantic Treaty Organization (NATO), the first peacetime military alliance in U.S. history.

Iran's national interests dovetailed with the new U.S. policy. Fearful of Soviet designs and anxious to build up his nation, the young Shah, Reza Mohammed Pahlavi, sought U.S. military and economic assistance. From the Shah's standpoint, if the United States was assisting Turkey economically and militarily, it was only logical to do the same for Iran.

The United States obliged, but not without hesitation and not in the full measure sought by the Shah, as the documentary record shows. Even in those early days, the Shah displayed an inordinate interest in military hardware (at that time tanks), which his untrained and largely

*illiterate peasant army could not realistically be expected to handle. The
United States did not accept the comparison of Iran with Turkey. The
latter, after all, had a long history as a European power, and its troops
had fought in many European wars, including World War I. Nor was
the United States prepared, at this juncture, to assign Iran the stature
given to the countries of Western Europe.*

*But the United States did recognize that the location of Iran,
together with its oil resources, gave it a strategic value. Thus it entered
into a Mutual Defense Agreement with the Shah's government in 1950.
In the same year, the United States announced that Iran would receive
technical assistance under the new Point Four program. A new basis
was thereby formed for future U.S.-Iranian relations. Iran would be assigned a higher priority and a more important role in the security of the
entire Middle East.*

UNITED STATES POSTWAR POLICY TOWARD IRAN

*Memorandum by the Director of the Office of Near Eastern and
African Affairs (Henderson) to the Secretary of State*

[*Washington,*] *August 23, 1945*

I. THE BACKGROUND

Historically, relations between the United States and Iran were of
minor importance, both from the American and the Iranian viewpoints,
until 1941. During the entire course of Iran's modern history, its foreign
relations have been influenced principally by Russia and Great Britain,
which have been engaged in a continuous struggle for political and
economic ascendancy in Iran. The steady increase in Germany's interest
in Iran, beginning in the 1920's, introduced a complicating factor into
Iranian foreign affairs. The extension of German influence, and the
failure of Reza Shah Pahlevi to reply satisfactorily to repeated Anglo-
Soviet demands for the expulsion of German fifth-columnists, finally
resulted in a coordinated invasion of Iran by Russian and British forces
in August 1941.

A. *Effects of Allied Occupation of Iran.*   Iran's occupation by
British and Russian troops, subsequently augmented by United States
Army service forces, had far-reaching economic and political conse-

quences. The authoritarian government of Reza Shah Pahlevi was replaced, under his young son, by a weak, constitutional regime for which Iran was ill prepared by tradition or experience. Iran's internal security forces collapsed, semi-autonomous conditions prevailed in the provinces, tribal security deteriorated, the administrative machinery of the government was disrupted, the morale of the population was badly shaken, foreign and domestic commerce were drastically curtailed, and an inflationary trend began.

Faced with this critical internal situation, the Iranians turned for advice and assistance to the United States, which had maintained a traditional policy of disinterested friendship toward Iran. This period, beginning in the autumn of 1941, marks the turning point in Irano-American relations, and the beginning of a trend toward ever deeper American interest in Iran.

B. *American advisory assistance.*   The American response to Iran's need was sympathetic. Since 1942, the principal expression of the closer relations prevailing between the two countries has been the provision of American advisers in various fields of governmental activity, upon specific Iranian request. The largest of these advisory groups is the economic and financial mission, charged with supervision of finance, internal revenue, customs, price control and stabilization, rationing, collection and distribution of food and commodities, public domains, et cetera. A military mission is charged with the reorganization of the Iranian Army's services of supply. A second military mission has for its task the reorganization and administration of the Iranian *gendarmerie* (rural police). Other Americans serve or have recently served as advisers in public health, pharmacy, municipal police administration, and irrigation.

C. *American economic and military assistance.*   In addition to the adviser program, assistance has been extended to Iran in the form of goods essential to the maintenance of the economy and internal security of the country. Civilian goods, such as pharmaceuticals, vaccines, motor transport, and tires, have been furnished through the machinery of the Middle East Supply Centre. Military goods in some volume have been supplied under Lend-Lease, as a result of recommendations from the American military missions.

This policy of assistance to Iran, from the American point of view, had for its immediate objective the desire to respond sympathetically to the appeals of a friendly nation. Its long-range objectives, however, were to contribute to the reconstruction of Iran as a sound member of the international body politic, and thereby to remove a future threat to Allied solidarity and international security.

D. *Declaration on Iran.*   American interest in Iran was publicly acknowledged by our participation in the Declaration on Iran, signed at Tehran on December 1, 1943, by President Roosevelt in conjunction with Prime Minister Churchill and Marshal Stalin. This declaration acknowledged Iran's contribution to the common war effort, recognized the special economic problems created for Iran by the war, pledged Iran such economic assistance as might be possible within the limits imposed by the war, promised consideration of Iran's economic problems in the postwar period, and expressed the desire for the maintenance of Iran's independence, sovereignty, and territorial integrity.

II. CURRENT STATUS OF AMERICAN POLICY

The basic objectives of the American policy of assistance to Iran still obtain.

A. *Current status of advisory program.*   Therefore the Department is continuing to extend its political and moral support to the two military missions and is endeavoring to find means of making available to the Iranian Government the supplies and equipment necessary to the implementation of the mission's tasks. At the same time we are pressing the Iranian Government to give to the missions more effective administrative and legislative support, in the interests of internal security.

With respect to the Financial Mission, the Department is aware that its economic benefit is steadily diminishing, and that the present weak Iranian Government is unable and perhaps unwilling to afford it the support and authority necessary to the accomplishment of its objectives. The Department, therefore, is currently giving consideration to the withdrawal of the mission, provided this can be accomplished without contributing to the political and economic instability of Iran. It should be emphasized, however, that the Financial Mission is not an official United States Government mission, each of the American advisers having been employed individually by the Iranian Government. The Department's role in regard to this mission has been to advise both the members and the Iranian Government when appropriate.

B. *Economic assistance to Iran.*   In the meantime, other forms of economic assistance are being provided. With the termination of the mission of the Persian Gulf Command for supply to Russia, large quantities of American installations and equipment are being or will soon be declared surplus. In conjunction with the surplus disposal authorities, the Department is undertaking to make available for purchase by the Iranian Government such equipment and installations as may be necessary to facilitate restoration of Iran's economy and to augment the capacity of the Trans-Iranian Railway in a manner consistent with Iran's expanded postwar needs. In this connection, the Department is requesting other American Government agencies, which have priority rights to such surpluses, to re-examine their needs with a view to waiving their claims to specified surpluses in favor of the Government of Iran. Moreover, the Department is undertaking interdepartmental discussions directed towards insuring the operational stability of the Iranian railroad system, by endeavoring to obtain for the Iranian Government remuneration for the services which it extended to the Allies in transporting supplies to Russia.

C. *Attitude toward evacuation of Iran.*   Political assistance is being rendered with respect to the Iranian Government's request for evacuation of foreign troops. The Department's attitude towards this request has been sympathetic, since the withdrawal of foreign forces is regarded as an essential preliminary to the restoration of Iran's administrative stability and economy. Accordingly the Department has indicated to the British and Soviet Governments its attitude of sympathy towards the Iranian request, and, through consultation with the War Department, has endeavored to expedite the departure of American forces. These efforts have been furthered in the Potsdam commitment calling for evacuation of Tehran, and the Department has recommended American participation on the Mixed Evacuation Commission in Tehran, which is designed to implement that commitment. It is hoped that the Council of Foreign Ministers will be able to expedite the complete evacuation of foreign troops from Iran.

D. *Attitude toward Allied censorship in Iran.*   The Department has endeavored on a number of occasions to effect the relaxation or abolition of Anglo-Soviet political censorship controls in Iran, which also constitute a limitation on Iran's sovereignty. These controls, chiefly exercised by the Russian authorities, prevent the dissemination of unbiased news to and from Iran. In accordance with its general interest in free access to news and its desire to assist Iran in recovering its independence, the Department will continue to urge the Soviet and British Governments to effect the immediate abolition of all censorship controls in Iran.

E. *Results of American aid policy.*   This policy of political and economic assistance to Iran has had beneficial results. During the war, the provision of economic advice and essential commodities contributed to the tranquilization of the country and thereby helped to insure the uninterrupted flow of supplies to Russia. The efforts of the military missions in some measure restored the organizational stability and the morale of Iran's internal security forces. The presence of American missions to the Iranian Government, as an expression of the United States' interest in preserving the latter as an entity, had a stabilizing effect upon the population and perhaps served as a moderating influence upon the British and Russians.

F. *American commercial, aviation, and petroleum interests.* American national interests in Iran are not being disregarded.

It is desired that American trade with Iran be restored and expanded as rapidly as possible. In this connection, the Department is endeavoring to indicate to the Iranian Government the desirability of relaxing its monopolistic controls, which extend to foreign trade, raw materials, the major part of Iranian industry, and foreign exchange. American business interests are already reopening trade channels with Iran, and have expressed interest in participating in development projects. At present American interests are bidding on a large municipal power project in Tehran, and it is probable that American companies will endeavor to construct certain irrigation projects for the Iranian Government.

The Department, in accordance with its policy of assisting in the development of commercial aviation, is pressing the Iranian Government to sign the Chicago aviation agreements and the proposed bilateral agreement. Because of the present weakness of the Iranian Government, it is doubtful whether it will undertake to sign the agreements in the near future. However, the Iranian Government has given informal assurances that it will extend to American commercial aviation temporary landing and traffic rights in Iran, regardless of whether the Iranian Government signs the air transport agreement in the immediate future. From the Iranian point of view, the recently formed Iranian Airways Company has indicated its desire to obtain American equipment and operating personnel, and the Department is endeavoring to assist the company in this respect.

With regard to the possiblity of assisting in the development of American petroleum reserves outside the Western Hemisphere, the attitude of the Iranian Government towards the granting of further oil concessions to any foreign interest is somewhat uncertain, since the Soviet Government has made it clear that it desires to acquire petroleum concessions if they are granted to any other foreign power. However, the Iranian Government has given the Department assurances that, in the event that it decides in the future to reopen negotiations for concessions in Iran, American applications will be given consideration.

III. FUTURE POLICY

A. *Deterioration of Iran's internal and international position.* In the course of the past year, certain modifications in Iran's internal and international position have occurred, which directly or indirectly affect the application of American policy to Iran. Of these modifications, the most important is the intensification of the traditional Anglo-Soviet conflict for supremacy in Iran, which had been subordinated temporarily to a policy of outward cooperation in the interests of military expediency. Apart from the obvious effects of this conflict upon Anglo-Soviet relations and upon Allied solidarity, it is reflected in Iranian internal affairs in the form of a steadily widening politico-social schism between leftist and conservative forces, which makes impossible the maintenance of governmental stability and administrative continuity in Iran. With the progressive weakening of the Iranian Government, a political vacuum is being created in which continued foreign interference is inevitable. Because of the weakening of the Iranian Government, moreover, the American advisers' tasks of strengthening and stabilizing the Government have been rendered difficult through lack of adequate support and authority.

With the termination of supply to Russia through the Iranian corridor, the Government is also faced with critical economic problems with which it is unable to cope, such as resettlement of labor, reconversion of industry, transition from an inflated to a rapidly deflating economy, and the general problems arising out of the relaxation of war-time economic controls.

The disturbing developments which are taking place in Iran make it increasingly clear that Iran threatens to become one of the major security problems of the future, and one of the great threats to Allied solidarity, unless there can be achieved both the reconciliation of British and Soviet interests and the stabilization of Iran's internal affairs. The formulation of American policy towards Iran, therefore, will be governed in the future, as at present, primarily by the requirements of international security.

It would appear, however, that the present means of implementing American policy require re-examination.

B. *American policy toward Iran as an international problem.* Although the Department has for some time been considering the possibility of reorganizing the American advisory program on an intergovernmental basis through an amendment of Public Law No. 63, the advisability of attempting to continue a unilateral American aid program on a long-range basis is now open to question. The ideal solution would be the formation of a tripartite advisory commission, on which the two great powers which have enduring interests in Iran would also share the responsibility for and participate in the stabilization of Iran and its reconstitution as a strong nation. While the Department is fully aware of the obstacles which stand in the way of the achievement of this goal, it will continue to take the initiative in seeking to attain this objective, and in seeking to impress upon the British and Soviet Governments the multilateral character of the obligation towards Iran.

C. *American policy toward Iran's internal problems.* As a corollary, this Government will also attempt to encourage the Iranian Government to assume the responsibilities and functions of a sovereign state, and to establish a legitimate and strong government which will be representative of the population and effectively responsive to its needs. It will also urge the Iranian Government to reconcile the political and separatist differences which now threaten to produce a fragmentation of Iran.

D. *Implementation of American policy.* In pursuit of these objectives, consideration should be given to the initiation of conversations in the Council of Foreign Ministers regarding Iran's economic problems in the postwar period. Should such conversations give promise of effecting any real cooperation for the betterment of Iran, the Department would consider the advisability of offering to replace its unilateral advisory program by an Anglo-Soviet-American program or a broader United Nations program dedicated to the reconstruction of Iran. This would constitute an effective implementation of the economic guarantees of the Declaration of Tehran.

In implementation of the Tehran Declaration's guarantees of Iranian sovereignty and independence, the Department will continue to press for the rapid abolition of Allied censorship controls, evacuation of all foreign forces from Iran, and restoration to Iran of those communications facilities which still remain under Allied control. Once these are restored, it will endeavor to assist Iran in the maintenance of their operational stability, so as to prevent any power from having a pretext for assuming their operation or control. From a broader point of view, moreover, it will make every effort to prevent the development of any situation which might constitute a limitation on Iranian sovereignty, such as the situation implicit in the Russian desire for access to the Persian Gulf, or any attempt by a third power to exploit the internal difficulties of Iran for its own expansionist purposes or in pursuit of a policy of regionalism. . . .

The Secretary of State to the Secretary of War (Patterson) on Interest of United States in Maintaining Postwar Military Mission in Iran

Washington, October 17, 1945

MY DEAR MR. SECRETARY: . . .Continuance of the Military Missions to Iran, at the request of the Iranian Government, is considered to be in the national interest of the United States. Strengthening of Iran's internal security forces by the American Missions contributes to the stabilization of Iran and, thereby, to its reconstruction as a sound member of the international community. By increasing the ability of the Iranian Government to maintain order and security, it is hoped to remove any pretext for British or Soviet intervention in Iran's internal affairs and, accordingly, to remove such future threat to Allied solidarity and international security. The stabilization of Iran, moreover, will serve to lay a sound foundation for the development of American commercial, petroleum, and aviation interests in the Middle East.

The American Military Missions to Iran have, as the War Department indicated, experienced considerable difficulty in achieving their objectives. This has been due, principally, to the unwillingness or inability of the Iranian Government to provide the Missions with the authority and support necessary to the accomplishment of their tasks.

The Russian occupation of northern Iran has also added materially to the difficulties of the Missions.

Recent assurances given by the Iranian Government, together with the imminent evacuation of all foreign troops from Iran, should permit the more complete accomplishment of the objectives of the Missions. On September 29, 1945, Colonel Schwarzkopf in Tehran informed Colonel Starbird* in Washington that the American Ambassador "has obtained completely satisfactory documents from the Iranian Government, thus opening the way for renewal of the contract. Under these circumstances, additional instructions are unnecessary and the Mission will proceed as heretofore." On October 1, 1945, the Embassy advised the Department that Colonel Schwarzkopf had had "a most satisfactory interview with the Shah" and that notes had been exchanged with the Iranian Foreign Office agreeing to one year's extension of the contract covering the *Gendarmerie* Mission. This favorable situation will, however, be subject to constant reassessment by this Government, with the view to withdrawal of the Missions in the event that their presence in Iran no longer serves American national interests.

While the contracts controlling the two Missions can be terminated by this Government if it is considered desirable "in the public interest" of the United States, the Missions are presently committed to the following duration: The Schwarzkopf Mission, for one year beginning October 1, 1945, but not exceeding the declared national emergency; the Ridley Mission, for the period of the declared national emergency. As indicated above, proposed legislation would permit the continuation of the Missions in peacetime.

The problem of supplying both the Ridley and the Schwarzkopf Missions, now that their lend-lease source has been stopped, has reached the point of solution. Discussions between representatives of the War Department, the U.S. Commercial Company, and the State Department, have resulted in a tentative arrangement whereby the Iranian Government would purchase necessary supplies through the U.S. Commercial Company for dollars, cash in advance. Details of the arrangement are embodied in a message, copy attached, to the American Embassy in Tehran requesting the approval of Major General Ridley, Colonel Schwarzkopf, and appropriate Iranian authorities. . . .

BYRNES

---

* Col. Alfred D. Starbird, Chief, European Section, Theater Group, Operations Division, War Department.

Agreement between the United States and Iran on the Establishment of a Postwar American Military Mission in Iran

October 6, 1947: Agreement signed at Tehran.
October 6, 1947: Entered into force.
December 29, 1948; January 5, 1949; November 28, 1949; January 10, 1950; April 10, 1961; June 14, 1961; November 12, 1961; February 7, 1962; March 19, 1962: Amended by agreements.
December 29, 1943; January 5, 1949; November 28, 1949; January 10, 1950; September 17, 1950; November 18, 1950; April 18, 1954; September 22, 1954; November 22, 1954; February 13, 1956; April 10, 1961; June 14, 1961; November 12, 1961; February 7, 1962; March 19, 1962; December 3, 1967; December 28, 1967; November 25, 1968; December 14, 1968; November 7, 1970; January 18, 1971: Extended by agreements.

In conformity with the request of the Government of Iran to the Government of the United States of America, the President of the United States of America has authorized the appointment of officers and enlisted men of the United States Army to constitute a military mission to Iran under the conditions specified below:

TITLE I

Purpose and Duration

ARTICLE 1.   The purpose of this Mission is to cooperate with the Ministry of War of Iran and with the personnel of the Iranian Army with a view to enhancing the efficiency of the Iranian Army.

ARTICLE 2.   This agreement shall be effective from the date of signing of the agreement by the accredited representatives of the Government of the United States of America and the Government of Iran and shall continue in force until March 20, 1949, unless sooner terminated or extended as hereinafter provided.

ARTICLE 3.   If the Government of Iran should desire that the services of the Mission be extended beyond the stipulated period, it shall make a written proposal to that effect prior to September 21, 1948. The Government of the United States of America agrees to act upon such proposal prior to December 21, 1948.

ARTICLE 4.   This agreement may be terminated prior to March 20, 1949, in the following manner:

(a) By either government subject to three months notice in writing to the other government;

(b) By either government at any time, upon written notice, if that government considers it necessary due to domestic disturbances or foreign hostilities;

(c) By the Government of the United States of America at any time upon written notice that the present statutory authority under which this arrangement is concluded has terminated and that Congress has provided no other authority for the continuation of the Mission;

(d) By the recall of the entire personnel of the Mission by the Government of the United States of America in the public interest of the United States of America, without necessity of compliance with provision (a) of the article;

(e) The termination of this agreement, however, shall not effect or modify the several obligations of the Government of Iran to the members of the Mission or to their families as set out in Title IV hereof.

TITLE II

Composition and Personnel

ARTICLE 5.   Initially the Mission shall consist of such numbers of personnel of the United States Army as may be agreed upon by the Minister of War of Iran through his authorized representative in Washington and by the War Department of the United States of America. The Individuals to be assigned shall be those agreed upon by the Minister of War of Iran or his authorized representative and by the War Department of the United States of America or its authorized representative.

TITLE III

Duties, Rank, and Precedence

ARTICLE 6.   Members of the Mission shall be assigned to the Department of the Ministry of War designated the Advisory Department. The Advisory Department shall be organized under a table of organization prepared with the agreement of the Chief of Mission and approved by the Minister of War of Iran. Members of the Mission shall be assigned to position vacancies shown on this table, and their assignment shall be published in Iranian Army General Orders.

ARTICLE 7. The senior officer of the Mission shall be appointed Chief of the Mission. Other members of the Mission shall be assigned duties by the Chief of Mission as indicated by the table of organization and approved by the Minister of War of Iran, or such other duties as may be agreed upon between the Minister of War of Iran and the Chief of the Mission.

ARTICLE 8. The duties of the Mission shall be to advise and assist the Ministry of War of Iran and its several departments as well as subordinate sections of the General Staff with respect to plans, problems concerning organization, administrative principles and training methods. These duties involve the principles of work of the General Staff and all departments of the Ministry of War in Tehran and their field agencies except tactical and strategical plans or operations against a foreign enemy, which are not related to the duties of the Mission.

ARTICLE 9. Members of the Mission will assume neither command nor staff responsibility in the Iranian Army. They may, however, make such official inspections and investigations as may be necessary and are approved by the Minister of War of Iran and directed by the Chief of the Mission.

ARTICLE 10. Each member of the Mission shall serve in the Mission with the rank he holds in the United States Army but shall have precedence over all Iranian Army officers of the same rank. Each member of the Mission shall be entitled to all benefits and privileges which the regulations of the Iranian Army provide for officers of corresponding rank of the Iranian Army. Members of the Mission shall wear the United States Army uniform with a shoulder sleeve insignia indicating service with the Iranian Army.

ARTICLE 11. Members of the Mission in case of violation of the laws and regulations of the Iranian Government, may be separated from the service of the Iranian Army and in such case will have only the right to draw travel expenses back to America.

ARTICLE 12. In the normal execution of their duties as defined in Article 8 and 9, the Chief of the Mission, and other members when so directed by him, are authorized to visit and inspect any part of the Iranian military establishment, and officers in authority shall facilitate such inspections and make available plans, records, reports, and correspondence as required. Members of the Mission will not concern themselves with secret matters except when it is essential to their duties and then only with the approval of the Ministry of War. Each member of the Mission has the obligation not to divulge or in any way to disclose to any foreign government or any person whatsoever any secret or confidential matter of which he may have become cognizant in his capacity as a member of the Mission. This obligation shall continue in force after the termination of the services of the member of the mission and after the expiration or cancellation of this agreement.

TITLE IV

Compensation and Perquisites

ARTICLE 13. Members of the Mission shall receive from the Government of Iran such fixed annual compensation and emoluments, payable in American currency or dollar draft or check, allowances as may be agreed upon between the Government of the United States of America and the Government of Iran for each member. Such compensation and emoluments shall be paid in twelve (12) equal monthly installments, each due and payable on the last day of the month. The compensation and emoluments shall not be subject to any tax, now or hereafter in effect, of the Government of Iran or of any of its political or administrative subdivisions. Should there, however, at present or while this agreement is in effect, be any taxes that might affect such compensation and emoluments, such taxes shall be borne by the Ministry of War of Iran, in order to comply with the provisions of this Article that the compensation agreed upon shall be met.

ARTICLE 14. The compensation and emoluments indicated in the preceding article shall commence for each member of the Mission upon arrival in Iran and, except as otherwise expressly provided in this agreement, shall continue, following the termination of duty with the Mission, or following the termination of the Mission under Article 4 of this agreement, likewise for the return trip to the United States of America and thereafter for the period of any accumulated leave which may be due the member.

ARTICLE 15. The additional compensation and emoluments due for the period of the return trip and accumulated leave shall be paid to each member of the Mission before his departure from Iran and such compensation and emoluments shall be computed for travel by the shortest route usually travelled to the port of entry in the United States of America, regardless of the route and method of travel used by the member of the Mission.

ARTICLE 16. During the period of the present national emergency in the United States of America, expense of transportation of each member of the Mission and his household effects, baggage and automobile from and to the United States of America shall be paid by the Government of the United States of America. If the period of this agreement extends beyond the date on which the national emergency in the United States of America is terminated, notification of the termination of the national emergency having been communicated to the Government of Iran in writing by the Government of the United States of America, expenses (except in case a member is replaced with less than two years service in the Mission for the convenience of the Government of the United States of America) for transportation of each member of the Mission and his household effects, baggage and automobile shall be paid by the Government of Iran. First-class accommodations for travel will be furnished the members of the Mission via the shortest usually traveled route between the port of embarkation in the United States of America and their official residence in Iran, both for the outward and return journey.

ARTICLE 17. At any time during the period of this agreement, as may be elected by each member, the family of each member of the Mission shall be furnished by the Government of Iran with first-class accommodations for travel, via the shortest usually traveled route between the port of embarkation in the United States of America and the official residence of the member in Iran, both for the outward and for the return journey. Throughout this agreement the term "Family" is limited to mean wife and dependent children.

ARTICLE 18. Compensation for transportation and travel expenses on official business of the Government of Iran shall be provided by the Government of Iran in accordance with the travel regulations of the Iranian Army.

ARTICLE 19. In addition to the United States Government transportation available to the Mission, the Government of Iran shall place other means of transportation (vehicle and aircraft) at the disposal of the Mission, when deemed necessary for the performance of official duties and will provide one third of the gasoline and oils required for the United States Government vehicles at the disposal of the Mission, as determined by the Chief of the Mission. The number and type of United States Government vehicles shall be determined by the War Department of the United States of America and authority is granted for the entry and exit from Iran, in accordance with the existing law, of one United States Army aircraft with crew as considered necessary by the Chief of the Mission, in the performance of official duties, provided that the Chief of the Mission previously informs the Iranian authorities concerned of the matter according to existing rules and regulations of Iran. All the United States Government vehicles placed at the disposal of the Mission for operation within Iran will be subject to the laws of Iran.

ARTICLE 20. The Government of Iran shall provide for members of the Mission suitable office space and facilities such as office equipment, stenographic and clerical help, civilian interpreters and orderlies, as indicated on the table of organization of the Advisory Department, and shall give necessary assistance for the smooth operation and improvement of the work of the Mission.

ARTICLE 21. If any member of the Mission, or any of his family, should die in Iran, the Government of Iran shall have the body transported to such place in the United States of America as the surviving members of the family may decide, but the cost to the Government of Iran shall not exceed the cost of transporting the remains from the place of decease to New York City. Should the deceased be a member of the Mission, his services with the Mission shall be considered to have terminated fifteen (15) days after his death. Return transportation to New York City for the family of the deceased member and for their baggage, household effects, and automobile shall be provided as prescribed in Article 17. All allowances due the deceased member, including salary for fifteen (15) days subsequent to his death, and reimbursement for expenses and transportation due the deceased member for travel performed on official business of the Government of Iran, shall be paid to the widow of the deceased member or to any other person who may have been designated in writing by the deceased while serving under the terms of this agreement; but such widow or other person shall not be compensated for accrued leave due and not taken by the deceased. All compensations due the widow, or other person designated by the deceased, under the provisions of this article, shall be paid within fifteen (15) days of the decease of said member.

ARTICLE 22. If a member of the Mission becomes ill or suffers injury, he shall, at the discretion of the Chief of the Mission, be placed in such hospital as the Chief of the Mission deems suitable, after consultation with the Ministry of War of Iran, and all expenses incurred as the result of such illness or injury while the patient is a member of the Mission and remains in Iran shall be paid by the Government of Iran. If the hospitalized member is a commissioned officer, he shall pay his cost of subsistence. Families will enjoy the same privileges agreed upon in this article for members of the Mission, except that a member of the Mission shall in all cases pay the cost of subsistence incident to hospitalization of a member of his family. Any member of the Mission unable to perform his duties with the Mission by reason of long continued physical disability shall be replaced.

TITLE V

Stipulations and Conditions

ARTICLE 23. Each member of the Mission shall be entitled to one month's annual leave with pay, or to a proportional part thereof with pay for any fractional part of the year. Unused portions of said leave shall be cumulative from year to year during service as a member of the Mission. This leave may be spent in Iran, in the United States of America, or in other countries, but the expense of travel and transportation not otherwise provided for in this agreement shall be borne by the member of the Mission taking such leave. All travel time on leave shall count as leave. The Government of Iran agrees to grant the leave herein specified according to the written application approved by the Chief of Mission with due consideration for the convenience of the Government of Iran.

ARTICLE 24. So long as this agreement, or any extension thereof, is in effect, the Government of Iran shall not engage the services of any personnel of any other foreign government for duties of any nature connected with the Iranian Army, except by mutual agreement between the Government of the United States of America and the Government of Iran.

ARTICLE 25. The Government of Iran shall grant exemption from custom duties or other imports on articles imported into Iran by members of the Mission for their personal use or the use of their families, provided that their request for free entry has received the approval of the Ambassador of the United States of America or the Chargé d'Affaires, ad interim, and from all export duties on articles purchased in Iran for their personal use or the use of their families. The Government of Iran shall grant free and unrestricted passage of mail to and from members of the Mission from and to the United States when transportation of such mail is furnished by the Government of the United States of America. The Chief of the Mission is responsible that no contraband is sent or received by members of the Mission or their families.

In witness whereof, the undersigned Mahmoud Djam, Minister of War of Iran, and George V. Allen, Ambassador Extraordinary and Plenipotentiary of the United States of America, have signed this agreement in duplicate in the English and Persian languages, at Tehran, this sixth day of October one thousand nine hundred and forty seven.

GEO. V. ALLEN
Ambassador of the United States of America

M. DJAM

THE AZERBAIJAN CRISIS: EFFORTS TO OUST SOVIET TROOPS FROM POSTWAR IRAN AND TO NEUTRALIZE SOVIET-SUPPORTED SEPARATIST MOVEMENTS

Soviet Failure to Withdraw Troops

The Iranian Ambassador (Ala) to the Secretary of State

No. 2936   *Washington, March 5, 1946*

SIR: In the course of my conversation with Your Excellency yesterday morning, I had the honour to request that the United States Government, which is a signatory of the Declaration of Teheran and of the United Nations Charter, be good enough to protest in Moscow against the breach of faith of the Soviet Government in failing to withdraw their forces from the whole of the North of Iran by the second of March 1946,—the ultimate date fixed by the Tripartite Treaty of Alliance of January 29, 1942.

Your Excellency observed that before taking action, the State Department would need to be informed of the attitude of the Prime Minister of Iran, who is at present negotiating in Moscow, in the matter of the Soviet default.

As I had surmised, it is now officially confirmed by a cable received from our Prime Minister by my colleague in London and communicated to me this morning, that Mr. Ahmad Qavam, Premier of Iran, protested in writing against the failure of the Soviet Government to live up to its solemn pledge, and would welcome and appreciate American intervention at this critical juncture.

It would, therefore, appear that there is no longer any obstacle to prevent Your Excellency from issuing the necessary instructions to your Chargé d'Affaires in Moscow.

I would also like to draw your attention to the fact that in accordance with information received from well-informed quarters the Soviet Government are making the evacuation of Iran depend upon the acceptance by the Persian Government of certain very important demands whereas the withdrawal of foreign allied forces at the end of the war has always been considered unconditional.

May I venture to ask Your Excellency to use the great influence of the American Government to obtain the unconditional evacuation of Iran by the Soviet forces?

Please accept [etc.]   HUSSEIN ALA

The Secretary of State to the Chargé in the Soviet Union (Kennan)

Washington, March 5, 1946, 7 p.m.

385. Please deliver immediately the following note to Mr. Molotov:

"I have the honor to inform your Excellency that I have been instructed by my Government to deliver to the Government of the Soviet Union the following message:

The Government of the United States has been informed that the Government of the Soviet Union has decided to retain Soviet troops in Iran after March 2, 1946, that this decision was taken without the consent of the Iranian Government, and that Soviet troops continue to remain on Iranian territory in spite of the protests of the Iranian Government.

It will be recalled that in reply to a note addressed on November 24, 1945 by the Government of the United States to the Government of the Soviet Union suggesting the immediate withdrawal of all foreign troops from Iran, the Soviet Government on November 29 stated that the period of the stationing of Soviet troops in Iran was governed by the Anglo-Soviet-Iranian Treaty of January 29, 1942. The Government of the United States understood from this statement that it was the intention of the Government of the Soviet Union that all Soviet troops would be withdrawn from Iran not later than March 2, 1946, six months after the date of the signing of the instrument of surrender with Japan on September 2, 1945. This understanding was based upon Article Five of the Tripartite Treaty referred to above which states:

'The forces of the Allied Powers shall be withdrawn from Iranian territory not later than six months after all hostilities between the Allied Powers and Germany and her associates have been suspended by the conclusion of an armistice or armistices, or on the conclusion of peace between them, whichever date is the earlier.'

So far as the Government of the United States is aware, this commitment was not questioned at the recent meeting of the Security Council in London which agreed that the Soviet Union and Iran should seek a solution of their differences by direct negotiation.

The decision of the Soviet Government to retain Soviet troops in Iran beyond the period stipulated by the Tripartite Treaty has created a situation with regard to which the Government of the United States, as a member of the United Nations and as a party to the Declaration Regarding Iran dated December 1, 1943, can not remain indifferent. That Declaration announced to the world that the Governments of the United States, the Union of Soviet Socialist Republics and the United Kingdom were 'at one with the Government of Iran in their desire for the maintenance of the independence, sovereignty and territorial integrity of Iran.' In the opinion of the Government of the United States, the maintenance of troops in Iranian territory by any one of the three signatories to that Declaration, without the consent and against the wishes of the Government of Iran, is contrary to the assurances contained in that Declaration. Furthermore it was generally accepted during the various discussions which took place at the meeting of the Security Council in London that the retention by a member of the United Nations of its troops in the territory of a country which is also a member of the United Nations, without the consent of the Government of that country, is not in accordance with the principles of the United Nations and that the withdrawal of such troops should not be made contingent upon other issues.

The Government of the United States, in the spirit of the friendly association which developed between the United States and the Soviet Union in the successful effort against the common enemy and as a fellow member of the United Nations, expresses the earnest hope that the Government of the Soviet Union will do its part, by withdrawing immediately all Soviet forces from the territory of Iran, to promote the international confidence which is necessary for peaceful progress among the peoples of all nations.

The Government of the United States trusts that the Government of the Soviet Union, no less than itself, appreciates the heavy responsibility resting upon the great powers under the Charter to observe their obligations and to respect the sovereign rights of other states.

The Government of the United States requests that it be promptly advised of the decision of the Government of the Soviet Union which it hopes will be in accord with the views herein expressed."

Sent to Moscow, repeated to London and Tehran.

BYRNES

The Ambassador in Iran (Murray) to the Secretary of State

Tehran, March 11, 1946, 4 p.m.

. . . 2. Qavam said he had raised three points in Moscow: (a) He had tried obtain Soviet promise to withdraw troops before March 2; (b) He had asked for Soviet moral support in settling Azerbaijan difficulties; (c) He had requested appointment of new Russian Ambassador to Iran (which has been done).

With regard point (a), Stalin at first advanced 1921 Irano-Soviet treaty as justification for retaining troops, which Qavam had countered by citing text and accompanying notes to show clearly treaty was inapplicable and by recalling that he himself had been in office at time treaty signed and knew from personal knowledge what was intended.

Soviets had then raised "hostile attitude" of Iranian delegation at Paris
Conference, to which Qavam replied that head of delegation had been
Moshavar-ol-Mamalek (Ali Gholi Kahn Ansari)* who had later negotiated and signed 1921 treaty to which Soviets so often pointed with
pride. Russians ultimately fell back on bald and unexplained statement
that their "interests" required retention of troops in Iran.

On point (b) Stalin had said Azerbaijan was internal question for
Iran. Why should Iranian Government be so disturbed, since Azerbaijanis were asking only autonomy, not independence? In any case, USSR
could do nothing because "Soviet honor was involved." This statement
was not explained.

Qavam answered that constitution did not allow autonomy. If
Azerbaijan were autonomous other provinces would follow and central
government would lose all control. Iran [apparent omission] Molotov
suggested that Iranian Government recognize existing Azerbaijan
regime minus Minister of War and Minister Foreign Affairs. Qavam
indicated he was willing to compromise on Azerbaijan but could go
only so far as provincial councils law allowed and could not possibly
accept present arrangement.

3. Both Stalin and Molotov separately had raised question of oil
concession to Russia. Molotov had insisted upon discrimination shown
in making grant to Britain and refusing anything to USSR. Qavam had
refused to discuss question because of Majlis law prohibiting oil negotiations with foreign countries. He had pointed out that present Majlis
would never repeal law and only hope of reopening question lay in
election of new Majlis which was impossible so long as Russian troops
remained in Iran. Molotov then asserted that Bayat, when Prime Minister, had offered to form Russo-Iranian company, 51% Russian and 49%
Iranian, to develop north Iran oil. USSR had rejected this but was now
willing to accept it. Molotov embodied this proposal in a written note
to Qavam which also contained suggestion that Iranian Government
should recognize existing Azerbaijan regime. When Qavam reiterated
his inability to do anything contrary to constitution or law, Molotov
withdrew offer to accept asserted Bayat proposal and said Soviet
Government would insist on full oil concession.

I gathered this request for oil grant was only affirmative demand
made by [Soviets?] during course of conversations.

4. In strictest confidence and without explaining context out of
which remark arose, Qavam told me that at one point Stalin and
Molotov had burst out with statement that, "We don't care what US and
Britain think and we are not afraid of them." (He asked me not to report
this to my Government and said he had not told Shah.)

. I suspect this may have been elicited by some effort on Qavam's part

* Persian Foreign Minister. The Peace Conference, meeting in 1919, refused to seat the
Persian delegation.

to advance American and British attitude as reason for his inability to comply with Soviet wishes.

5. In one talk Stalin had stressed necessity for social reforms in Iran saying that if England had made reforms in America she would not have lost us and if she did not make reforms in India she would lose India. Even in England itself reforms were essential. Qavam had replied he wished to make reforms but this would be possible only if Iran were left alone.

6. At end of talks Soviets had proposed text of joint communiqué including statement that "negotiations had been conducted in spirit of friendship and good understanding" and that they "would be continued in Tehran thru new Soviet Ambassador." Fearing this phraseology was intended to indicate that negotiations had ended in agreement and so prevent further recourse to UNO Qavam crossed out words "good understanding." Likewise to prevent possible assertion that negotiations were still in progress he had changed final sentence to read that two Governments would make every effort through new Ambassador to consolidate friendly relations.

. . . 9. Prime Minister said that throughout he had made every effort to avoid provoking Russians. Nevertheless it appeared some of conversations had taken on very strained note.

. . . Because Qavam's attitude did not seem entirely clear as regards UNO action I arranged audience with Shah this morning. I told His Majesty that I had no grounds for suspecting Prime Minister of weakening but would like him (Shah) to make sure Qavam understood situation and vital importance of Iranian action. I am sure Shah is completely clear on this.

His Majesty expressed grave concern over rumors of possible Soviet *Putsch* in Tehran to seize capital and gain control of Government. He pointed out that if this should happen Soviets could dictate instructions to Ala, prevent Iranian appeal to UNO and so make parallel Irano-American action impossible. He suggested that in such a case US and Britain could nevertheless act on own initiative on basis their obligations and voice true Iranian sentiments.

MURRAY

The Ambassador in Iran (Murray) to the Secretary of State

Tehran, March 15, 1946, 1 p.m.

343. Confidential emissary from Qavam came to see British Ambassador and myself this morning with following message:

Soviet Chargé called on Prime Minister yesterday and said Soviet Government had heard he planned to make complaint to Security Council. Chargé said this would be regarded as unfriendly and hostile act and would have unfortunate results for Iran. He therefore advised Qavam not to take any such step.

Prime Minister replied that presence foreign troops Iran after expiration Tripartite Treaty was unconstitutional and that if he failed to act he would be called to account by his people and eventually by Majlis. Further cited fact that case remains before Security Council which can ask for report on basis London decision.

Apparently because of the stout resistance shown by Qavam during their long conversation Soviet Chargé finally shifted his position slightly and pressed Prime Minister at least to refrain from taking initiative himself and to await request from Security Council for report.

(Qavam asks that no reference ever be made to this conversation with Chargé, whether in Security Council or elsewhere.)

Through his emissary Qavam asked Sir Reader and me for our advice as to his course in light of Soviet threat. Further asked what support he could expect from US and British if he took risk of bringing complaint to Security Council. Our visitor explained that Prime Minister feels his responsibility keenly and would be glad of any loophole to escape Soviet wrath while at same time protecting interests of Iran. He is therefore tempted to follow Chargé's advice and leave it to Security Council itself to raise question.

Sir Reader and I replied that we could not give official advice on matter of such gravity without consulting our Govts. Personally, however, we felt Iran's case would be gravely prejudiced if she did not herself speak out soon since Soviets would undoubtedly exert even greater pressure on Iran Govt at time of Security Council meeting to force her to keep silent and would then argue that Iran's silence indicated all was well.

In this connection our visitor (who is highly intelligent and holds high position though not member of Cabinet) suggested that Soviets would probably send new Ambassador here in very few days to hold out hopes to Qavam and persuade him to renew Moscow conversations here. Having accomplished this he would advise Qavam that any recourse to Security Council in midst of negotiations would be highly improper and unfriendly and would destroy all hope of Irano-Soviet reconciliation thus at one and same time tempting Prime Minister with hopes of salvation and bludgeoning him with threats of utter distaste [disaster?]. Visitor also suggested as a possible alternative line of Soviet action that, after persuading Qavam to delay appeal, they would overthrow his Cabinet between now and March 25 and see to it that new Cabinet would be completely under their control thus eliminating all possibility of Iranian appeal to Security Council. I concur entirely in this reasoning and believe Sir Reader does too.

Although I remain convinced, as I have told Shah and Prime Minister repeatedly, that Iran's sole frail hope of salvation lies in quick appeal to Security Council, direct and ominous threat by Soviet Chargé makes immediate situation so grave that I hesitate to say anything further to Qavam without definite word from Dept as to its present position. I therefore request urgent instructions as to official reply I should give to his request for advice and his query regarding support he could expect from US if he defies Soviet warning.

Sent Dept 343, repeated Moscow 104, London 61.

MURRAY

United States Ambassador in Iran (Murray) to Secretary of State

Tehran, March 22, 1946, 2 p.m.

. . . Essence of Qavam's thinking as it developed in course of conversation was:

1. He fears that if SC censures USSR and asks withdrawal of troops Russians will vent their wrath on himself and on Iran, which could be harrassed in many ways by Soviet Govt, and that UNO could not provide adequate protection.

2. He considers that from viewpoint of practical politics understanding with USSR on northern Iranian oil is long overdue. He asserted that Soviet complaints that Iran had discriminated in favor of Britain by granting AIOC concession were hard to meet in light of fact controlling interest in AIOC is held by British Govt. He believes any future Majlis will approve concession to Soviets and that such concession is inevitable.

3. He believes he can get around law prohibiting oil negotiations by arranging for a joint Irano-Soviet Company with the two Govts sharing control. He admits even such company would ultimately need Majlis' approval for its operations but is confident this can be obtained. Meanwhile during period before new Majlis assembles, he asserts approval can be granted by Cabinet decree subject to later Majlis confirmation. (I would hesitate to pass on correctness of his legal position in this reasoning, which seems to me open to grave doubt. However he might be able to carry it off in circumstances.)

4. He is considering preparation of an agreement in very general terms which would provide in principle for joint Irano-Soviet oil exploitation as inducement for Soviets to withdraw troops. He would draft this very carefully to make troop withdrawal a condition precedent. He added this agreement might be expanded to include subjects other than oil. . . .

MURRAY

Statement by the Secretary of State Made before the United Nations Security Council

March 26, 1946

I cannot agree with the representative of the Union of Soviet Socialist Republics nor support the amendment he offers to the agenda.

The facts before the Council are that the Iranian Government, through its representative, brought to the attention of the Council a dispute between Iran and the USSR which it declared was likely to endanger international peace and security. The Iranian Government further stated that contrary to the provisions of the Treaty of 29 January

1942, the USSR was maintaining troops on Iranian territory after 2 March. In its letter to the Council, it further declared that the USSR was continuing to interfere in the internal affairs of Iran through the medium of USSR agents, officials and armed forces.

The Iranian Government, through its representative, referred to these facts as constituting new developments arising since the action of the Council on 30 January.

Today the representative of the USSR states that there has been an agreement. If that information is correct, then the USSR Government should have presented to the Council for its consideration a joint statement from the Iranian Government and the USSR Government stating that an agreement had been arrived at and asking that there be no further consideration of the question. But that is not the case. The Iranian Government has not withdrawn its letter.

Though we have tried to ascertain the facts, we have not ascertained from the Iranian Government that there has been an agreement.

Therefore, when a Member of the United Nations advises the Council that a situation exists which is likely to threaten the peace and security of the world, we cannot deny to that nation the opportunity to be heard, to say whether or not there has been an agreement, to say whether or not it wishes to withdraw its complaint.

If that is not correct, then all that a Government represented on the Council would have to do when a complaint was made against it would be to advise the Council that there had been an agreement, and on the strength of that statement, to ask that the complaining Government should be denied the opportunity to have a hearing.

All that is contemplated now is the adoption of an agenda which would give to the Iranian Government an opportunity to present facts which in the opinion of that Government constitute a threat to international peace. Surely the Council cannot deny to any Member of the United Nations the opportunity to present a request of that kind, filed in complete accord with the provisions of the Charter.

If there has been an agreement, certainly the Council would want to hear that fact stated by the representative of the Iranian Government. If there has been an agreement, we must assume that the representative of the Iranian Government will make a statement as to the agreement. We must put this matter on the agenda; we must give to the Iranian Government an opportunity to say whether or not there has been an agreement.

If there is not a complete understanding between the Iranian Government and the USSR Government, that fact will be disclosed when opportunity is given to both parties to the dispute to make a statement. When that is done, the Council can take the matter under consideration and determine whether it can take any action to bring about complete agreement. But certainly it cannot deny to a Member of the United

Nations that states that a condition exists which is likely to threaten international peace and security, even the opportunity to present its case.

The United States Representative at the United Nations (Stettinius) to the Secretary of State

New York, April 4, 1946, 6:45 p.m.

35. The Security Council, at a 95-minute meeting on Thursday, April 4, agreed on a solution to the Iranian question. The vote was 9-0 with Australia abstaining.

With the Soviet delegate still absent, the session was called to order at 11:10 a.m. by the Chairman, Dr. Quo Tai-Chi. The agenda was adopted without comment. Hussein Ala, Iranian Ambassador, was invited to take a seat at the Council table.

U.S. Secretary of State James F. Byrnes submitted a resolution, which deferred action on the Iranian issue until May 6, 1946, under the following conditions:

1. That the Council note the statements of the Iranian representative that the appeal to the Council arises from the presence of Soviet troops in Iran and their continued presence there beyond the date stipulated for their withdrawal in the Tripartite Treaty of January 29, 1942.

2. That the Council note the responses on April 3, 1946, of the Soviet and Iranian Governments pursuant to the Secretary General's request for information as to the status of negotiations between the two Governments, and as to whether the withdrawal of Soviet troops was conditioned upon agreement on other subjects.

3. That the Council, in particular, note and rely upon the assurances of the Soviet Government that the withdrawal of Soviet troops from Iran has already commenced and that Russia expects that the complete evacuation of its troops from the whole of Iran will be accomplished within 5 or 6 weeks.

4. That the Council note that the proposals under negotiation between the Iranian and Soviet Governments are not connected with the withdrawal of Soviet troops.

5. That the Council is solicitous to avoid any possibility of the presence of Soviet troops in Iran being used to influence the course of negotiations between the two Governments.

6. That the Council recognizes that the withdrawal of Soviet troops from the whole of Iran cannot be completed in a substantially shorter period of time than that within which the Soviet Government has declared it to be its intention to complete such withdrawal.

The resolution also provides that the Soviet and Iranian Governments shall report to the Council on May 6 whether or not the withdrawal of all Soviet troops from the whole of Iran has been completed, and that the Council will then decide what, if any, further proceedings on the Iranian appeal are required.

The resolution left the way open for the Council to consider at any time, as the first item on its agenda, reports from any member of the Security Council on developments which may retard or threaten to retard the prompt withdrawal of Soviet troops from Iran.

In support of his proposal Byrnes said that it spoke for itself, but pointed out that it rested upon his earlier suggestion that the Soviet and Iranian Governments should be communicated with through their representatives. He added that he had stated then that if the Council were able to ascertain adequate and exact information as to the status of the negotiations, the Council might be able to satisfy itself that the assurances of the Soviet Government as to the prompt withdrawal of troops from Iran were in fact, for all practical purposes, unconditional.

. . . Chairman Quo then called on the Iranian representative. Ala said that the fundamental problem was to have all foreign troops removed from Iran. He added that the people of Iran were willing to accept the Soviet pledge, as the Security Council had, that its troops would be withdrawn unconditionally by May 6. Once this is accomplished, Ala said that he believed the Iranian Government will be able to negotiate with the Soviet Union on other questions.

Ala praised the Council for its firmness and courage. He said that the Council action already had instilled a feeling of confidence among the smaller nations, and concluded that the results achieved have significance of permanent value and that Iran has received something from the Council which it could not have obtained alone.

Secretary Byrnes expressed appreciation for the adoption of his resolution and said that he was happy to hear the Iranian representative agree to the solution. He added that the withdrawal of troops from Iran without condition was the only sane method to follow. The U.S. Secretary concluded by expressing the opinion that the United Nations today was truly a center for harmonizing international differences. . . .

[STETTINIUS]

The Secretary of State to the Ambassador in Iran (Murray)

Washington, April 12, 1946, 7 p.m.

308. Please inform PriMin that I have given careful consideration to his views as reported in your 510 Apr 11 and fully appreciate his difficulties. You should point out to him, however, that any indication of willingness on his part to have the Iranian case dropped from the agenda of the Security Council would be likely to create an impression on world opinion and among members of the Council that Iran wished to have the Council act merely to help it in its negotiations and not

because it believed as it stated, that the presence of troops of another Govt threatened international peace. Furthermore, a feeling might be engendered that the members of the Security Council should not be expected to engage in protracted and at times acrimonious discussions for the purpose of endeavoring to uphold the integrity and independence of a country which is unwilling to maintain a firm stand on its own behalf.

The one request urged by Iran above all others was that this case remain on the agenda until foreign troops had withdrawn. The Council granted Iran's request. If Iran now says it wishes to have case removed from agenda before troops are withdrawn how can it hereafter expect any Govt give serious attention to its appeals.

The most friendly and sincere advice that I can give to the PriMin, in the interests of Iran and of developing a United Nations strong enough to maintain peace, is that he take the attitude that the question whether the Iranian case should be dropped or remain on the agenda is one entirely for the Security Council to decide. The Council and not Iran placed it on the agenda and did it by a unanimous vote. Iran should stand firm in respecting the decision already taken by the Council and be prepared to report to the Council on May 6 as requested.

BYRNES

The Ambassador in Iran (Murray) to the Secretary of State

Tehran, April 13, 1946, 10 a.m.

515. Jernegan saw Qavam at 7 tonight and conveyed in full message transmitted urtel 308, April 12.

Qavam was obviously still uncertain as to his best course and extremely reluctant to risk offending Soviets. He again pointed out that if he failed comply their wishes they might turn against him on Azerbaijan question, in which he must have their moral support to achieve settlement. They could withdraw Soviet troops from Iran as agreed but supply arms to Azerbaijanis and encourage them resist. Tehran Govt would be forced send troops and precipitate fighting, whereupon Russians could assert right to intervene to protect security their frontiers.

He admitted however that Soviets might also break their agreements even if he acquiesced in their demand to withdraw case from Security Council. Jernegan pointed out in such case Iran would be left completely defenseless and urged that in long run Iran would face fewer dangers if she relied on UNO and made it possible for that organization to become real force for security.

Ultimately with evident misgivings, after long discussion, Prime Minister agreed that he would not instruct Ala to request withdrawal of question from Security Council. However he did not want Ala to continue his aggressive tactics in opposing Soviet move. At Jernegan's suggestion, based on final paragraph urtel under reference, he decided he would direct Ambassador that, if called upon by Security Council to make statement, he should say only that Iran left matter entirely in hands of Council for whatever decision it might choose to take.

MURRAY

The United States Representative at the United Nations (Stettinius) to the Secretary of State

New York, April 15, 1946, 6:10 p.m.

73. Letter from the Iranian Ambassador to the President of the Security Council, dated 15 April 1946:

Iranian Embassy New York, 15th April, 1946

SIR: On April 9, 1946, I had the honour to state, in accordance with the instructions of my Government, its position regarding the request of the Soviet representative on the Security Council that the Council remove from its agenda the matters relating to the continued presence of Soviet troops in Iran and the interferences in the internal affairs of Iran. In my letter, I informed the Council of the desire of my Government that these matters remain on its agenda as provided by the resolution adopted on 4 April, 1946.

Yesterday, April 14, my Government instructed me to make to the Security Council the following statement:

"As the result of the signature of the agreement between the Iranian Government and the Government of the Soviet Union, it has been agreed that the Red Army evacuate all Persian territory by the 6th May, 1946. The Iranian Government has no doubt that this agreement will be carried out, but at the same time has not the right to fix the course the Security Council should take."

This morning I received a further telegram from my Government reading as follows:

"In view of the fact that the Soviet Ambassador has again today, 14 April, categorically reiterated that the unconditional evacuation of Iranian territory by the Red Army will be completed by the 6 May, 1946, it is necessary that you immediately inform the Security Council that the Iranian Government has complete confidence in the word and pledge of the Soviet Government and for this reason withdraws its complaint from the Security Council."

STETTINIUS

The Ambassador in Iran (Murray) to the Secretary of State

Tehran, April 16, 1946, 9 a.m.

532. Embtels 515, April 13 and 518, April 15. Qavam last night gave Jernegan following account of developments resulting in instructions to Ala to request withdrawal Iranian appeal to Security Council: Soviet Ambassador learned of new instructions sent Ala to leave matter for

decision of Security Council and protested to Prime Minister this was illogical because Iran simultaneously professed confidence in Soviet evacuation yet did not follow Soviet action in asking Council to drop complaint. Qavam replied his action not illogical in view initial Soviet qualification that troops would be withdrawn if "nothing unforeseen occurred."

Sadchikov then stated that this qualification had been made before agreement had been reached between Iran and USSR and at time when it seemed possible elements hostile to Russia might be able to force out Qavam. Since that time agreements had been signed and Qavam's friendly Govt remained in power, therefore reservation no longer obtained. Under circumstances he insisted Prime Minister must direct Ala join in request to drop question from agenda.

Qavam drew up formula which was approved by Cabinet to effect that since Soviet Ambassador on April 14 had given assurances that evacuation would be completed unconditionally by May 6, Iran Govt wished to withdraw its appeal to Security Council. After consulting Moscow, Sadchikov informed Qavam at 9:30 yesterday morning that this was acceptable and instructions were despatched accordingly.

Qavam apologized to Jernegan for having failed to inform us of his action, saying it was due solely to rapidity of events and not to any intent to slight American Govt in any way. (From talks with British Chargé we learn British had been even more in ignorance of developments than we.)

Jernegan said he feared Prime Minister's decision would be regretted by American Govt but he hoped and was sure American Govt hoped that it would achieve results Prime Minister desired.

Qavam said that in addition to renewed assurances re evacuation, Sadchikov had again given assurances that Soviets would use their influence with Azerbaijanis to have latter keep their demands within limits Prime Minister felt he could grant, as stated Embtel 424, March 29. (Mozaffar Firuz told Jernegan last night that preliminary, indirect negotiations with Azerbaijan are under way and it is hoped get Azerbaijan delegation to Karaj soon.)

MURRAY

Soviet Interference in the Azerbaijan Province after Troop Withdrawals

The Chargé in Iran (Ward) to the Secretary of State

Tehran, May 4, 1946, 8 p.m.

639. Qavam told me this evening his negotiations with Azerbaijanis are deadlocked. Principal point of disagreement is disposition of

Azerbaijan Army. Prime Minister is insisting it must be completely disbanded and that any armed forces stationed that province in future shall be composed of regular conscripts with officers appointed by Tehran. Pishevari* has refused accept this. Other disputed points are:

(1) Prime Minister demands that National Majlis Azerbaijan be dissolved and completely new elections be held for Provincial Council. Pishevari wants present Majlis preserved intact and simply converted bodily into Provincial Council.

(2) Qavam wants Azerbaijan finances controlled by commissioner appointed by Tehran, with locally appointed "comptroller" under him to represent provincial interests. Pishevari insists Chief Finance Officer must be locally named with Tehran appointee as subordinate comptroller. . . .

WARD

The Chargé in Iran (Ward) to the Secretary of State

Tehran, May 5, 1946, 4 p.m.

640. Deptel 386, May 2. After consulting both British and Iranian authorities and other sources, Embassy feels it may safely be said that to date all of Northern Iran except possibly for Azerbaijan has been completely evacuated. British Military Attaché has just returned from trip along Caspian Littoral all the way from Astara to Bandar Shah and reports complete evacuation except for scattered units engaged in miscellaneous duties connected with physical details of evacuation. Reliable gendarme officer has returned from trip through all of Mazanderan and reports evacuation completed.

Information on number of Soviet troops left behind in civilian clothes is contradictory but in any case there do not appear to be many. This does not apply to Azerbaijan, accurate information on developments there not being available in Tehran. Gagarine who left for Tabriz by car May 3 should by now have arrived and he and Dooher should be able to provide reports on progress evacuation in Azerbaijan.

Our estimate is that evacuation of uniformed troops will be complete by specified date but that number of troops in civilian clothes will be left in Azerbaijan.

Sent Dept 640; repeated Moscow on 85.

WARD

The United States Representative at the United Nations (Stettinius) to the Secretary of State

New York, May 8, 1946, 9:30 p.m.

158. Security Council. The Security Council at its 40th meeting

---

* Jafar Pishevari was the leader of the Democratic Party of Azerbaijan.

Wednesday, May 8, unanimously adopted a U.S.-sponsored resolution deferring further proceedings on the Iranian question in order that the Government of Iran may have time in which to ascertain whether all Soviet troops have been withdrawn from the whole of Iran. The Soviet Union was not represented at this session.

Mr. Stettinius was accompanied by Herschel Johnson, his recently appointed deputy, who arrived in New York yesterday.

Following adoption of the provisional agenda, Chairman Hafez Afifi Pasha called on Mr. Stettinius. The latter pointed out that the Security Council in its resolution of April 4 requested the USSR and Iran to report to the Council on May 6 whether the withdrawal of all Soviet troops from the whole of Iran had been completed. He said that the Soviet Government had not complied with the request and Iran has replied only in a preliminary manner, but apparently as fully as conditions have permitted.

Mr. Stettinius called attention to the Iranian statement that it would report to the Council on the true state of affairs in Azerbaijan as soon as it was able to ascertain the facts through its own official representatives before introducing the following resolution:

"Resolved: That in view of the statement made by the Iranian Government in its preliminary report of May 6, submitted in compliance with the resolution of April 4, 1946, that it was not able as of May 6 to state whether the withdrawal of all Soviet troops from the whole of Iran had been completed, the Council defer further proceedings on the Iranian matter in order that the government of Iran may have time in which to ascertain through its official representatives whether all Soviet troops have been withdrawn from the whole of Iran; that the Iranian government be requested to submit a complete report on the subject to the Security Council immediately upon the receipt of the information which will enable it so to do; and that in case it is unable to obtain such information by May 20, it report on that day such information as is available to it at that time; and that immediately following the receipt from the Iranian Government of the report requested, the Council shall consider what if any further proceedings are required."

[STETTINIUS]

The Acting Secretary of State to the Chargé in Iran (Ward)

Washington, May 9, 1946, 6 p.m.

408. Conversation with Ala before Security Council meeting May 8 revealed Amb's feeling that Council resolution should recognize existence of two Iranian complaints; should treat at this time only one complaint dealing with presence of Soviet troops in Iran; and should anticipate future Council action upon other complaint charging interference by Soviet agents, officials and armed forces. Henderson pointed out that whole context of Council proceedings on Iranian matter seemed to treat Iranian appeal as single complaint and reminded Ala that Iranian letter of April 15 referred to the withdrawal of "its com-

plaint" from Security Council. Ala admitted use of word in singular in Iranian withdrawal note was most unfortunate. Henderson said he doubted that US, particularly in absence of clear statement by Iran to Security Council on subject, would be able to maintain position that Iran had withdrawn only that portion of its complaint regarding presence of Soviet forces and had not withdrawn portion regarding Soviet interference in internal affairs. . . .

ACHESON

The Acting Secretary of State to the United States Representative at the United Nations (Stettinius)

Washington, May 13, 1946, 3 p.m.

58. For Stettinius. Urtel 156, May 8. We have given careful consideration to question raised by Mr. Ala whether a finding by Security Council that all Soviet troops have been withdrawn from whole of Iran would justify Council action in dropping that portion of Iranian complaint relating to interference by Soviet agents, officials, and armed forces in the internal affairs of Iran, as well as that portion relating to continued presence of Soviet forces in Iran.

Mr. Ala has taken position that Iranian Govt, in its letter of Apr 15, did not intend to inform Security Council that its complaint with re[gard] to such interference was being withdrawn. According to Mr. Ala, it intended to limit its request for withdrawal to that portion of its letter of Mar 18 relating to continued presence of Soviet troops in Iran.

We have thus far been under impression that Iran, in its note to Security Council of Apr 15, had in using the words "withdraws its complaint" meant to withdraw both aspects of its complaint. We would not be in position to support contention that Iran had not intended to withdraw every aspect of its complaint against Soviet Union in its letter of April 15 unless Iran itself should on its own behalf make a clear statement to Security Council to that effect.

If Iranian Govt does make such a statement, we should accept it at face value on the ground that Iran alone is able to give a true interpretation of its note. If Iran should insist that Soviet agents and officials are continuing to interfere in internal affairs of Iran and that its complaint in this regard has not been withdrawn, we should take position that this allegation represents continuation of complaint of Mar. 18.

We would have no objection, of course, if Iran should desire to raise the interference issue as an entirely new case, which action would not in our opinion be precluded by any action of Security Council in disposing of matter of presence of Soviet armed forces in Iran.

In either event, if the matter of interference comes up on Council's agenda, we should advocate that procedure in Council follow past practice under which Iranian Govt would first be asked to appear before

Council and make statement in support of complaint of interference, and that Soviet Govt be given an opportunity to reply.

This position should be taken in Council itself and may, in your discretion, be imparted to other representatives on Security Council who may approach you on subject.

Sent to New York, repeated to Tehran, Moscow and Paris, and London.

ACHESON

The Secretary of State to the United States Representative at the United Nations (Stettinius)

Washington, May 21, 1946, 8 p.m.

67. For Stettinius. We suggest that at tomorrow's meeting of the Security Council you make a statement along the following lines with respect to the Iranian matter:

In view of the record of Soviet-Iranian difficulties and differences and in view of the conflicting reports relating to the current situation in northern Iran, particularly in Azerbaijan, my Government would consider it most unfortunate for the Security Council at this time to drop the Iranian matter from its agenda. It will be recalled that in the Council's resolution of April 4 the Council called upon the Soviet Government and the Iranian Government to report by May 6 whether the withdrawal of all Soviet troops from the whole of Iran had been completed. The Soviet Government has made no report and no statement on this subject. Until today the Iranian Government was unable to report factually as to Azerbaijan. It has today made a report which on its face is incomplete and deals with only a portion of the province of Azerbaijan. Moreover we must bear in mind that the presence of Soviet troops on Iranian territory has been only one of the subjects which has been a matter of dispute between the Soviet and the Iranian Governments. For these reasons my Government earnestly recommends that the Security Council should not at this time drop the Iranian matter from its agenda.

I wish to add that my Government, which, as is well known, has followed developments in the Iranian matter with the greatest concern, has recently been giving careful consideration to requesting upon its own initiative an investigation by the Council of the situation in northern Iran in order to assist the Council to determine whether the continuation of the situation in northern Iran was likely to endanger the maintenance of international peace and security. I do not at this time propose that the Council take further action with respect to the Iranian matter but I do wish to emphasize the feeling of my Government that it is most desirable that the Council continue to remain seized of the Iranian matter and indicate thereby its continuing concern in the developments with respect to northern Iran.

BYRNES

The Vice Consul at Tabriz (Rossow) to the Secretary of State

[EXTRACTS]

Tabriz, June 5, 1946, noon

183. Following is summary of political situation this district:

There has been no lessening of Soviet penetration of Azerbaijan govt and Democratic Party. At present this penetration consists chiefly of tutelage and instruction on high level policy, and control of political security thru strategic placement of personnel who are plainly of Soviet origin. Latter personnel are continually observed on streets in Azerbaijan uniforms or in civilian clothes and can be identified not only by their constant use of Russian language but frequently by features, for numbers of them are obvious north Russian types, although Soviet Caucasians are in the majority. All observers also agree that Soviet railroad personnel, who wear uniforms of military type, have been at least tripled for no known reason. Popular belief is that they are Soviet political agents.

. . . All reports, supported by analysis of recent public pronouncements, indicate that Soviet Union has instructed Azerbaijan Govt to come to terms with Tehran. Both Azerbaijan Govt and Soviet Union appear to have adopted a definitely defensive policy now with respect to Azerbaijan problem. Timing of this shift of policy together with reports of explanations from within party and Azerbaijan Govt, and press attacks against US, show plainly that it resulted from strong American stand at Security Council coupled with strong attitude of world press. Everyone here gives US full credit for this weakening of Azerbaijan Soviet policy, and bitterness of party and government hierarchy against US has accordingly increased. This has produced a series of violent editorial attacks against US, coupled with protestations of Azerbaijan govt's innocence and altruism, and continually reiterate insistence that Azerbaijan problem is internal affair. Propaganda crudely follows straight line.

. . . Sent Dept 183; Tehran 179; Moscow 120; London 56.

ROSSOW

The Ambassador in Iran (Allen) to the Secretary of State

Tehran, September 30, 1946, 1 p.m.

1293. In long conference with Prime Minister yesterday, held at his request, Qavam told me he realized that policy of conciliation towards Azerbaijan had not yielded favorable results and had merely encouraged other sections of country to make impossible demands. Qavam said he was contemplating sharp change of policy, based on strong insistence upon Iranian sovereignty throughout country. He fully realized he would be immediately castigated as turncoat and Fascist reactionary and would face serious internal difficulties. City of Tehran would even be in danger from almost certain Tudeh Party disturbances.

Qavam said new policy would in no way lessen his determination to institute far-reaching economic reforms which Iran needed so urgently. But to reestablish Iran as a nation and create conditions which would have some permanence, Iran needed immediate assistance along two major lines, military supplies and substantial financial credits. Iran could only look to United States for these. Before he undertakes new policy he would welcome assurance that United States would render assistance. He asked me to report conversation promptly and expressed hope for an early favorable reply.

I said I would naturally report his request immediately.

During conversation I expressed confidence that United States had in no way altered policy stated in Declaration Regarding Iran which contained assurances of American respect for Iranian sovereignty and our desire to assist Iran economically. I read to him Department's 810, September 27, 7 p.m. (sent to Paris as Secdel 1005) which fortunately had just reached me. I pointed out, however, that subsequent to signature of Declaration in 1943, both United States and Iran had become parties to a broader and more important instrument, the United Nations Charter. United States bases its foreign policy squarely on that Charter and encouraged other member states to do likewise. Nations like Iran which felt threatened with foreign interference for [and?] aggression should place reliance in UN for assistance. We should face the fact realistically that America could probably be moved to aid Iran seriously only to the extent its aid was regarded by American public as being given to support UN. Iran was making direct request of United States for combat military equipment and for credits which I understand Iranians felt should total 250 million dollars. I expressed opinion that sooner we came down to earth and viewed situation realistically the more progress we would make. My Government had told me 10 million dollars was most Iran could expect in credit from Export-Import Bank. As for combat equipment we had refused to sell any even to Latin America or China. I said I hoped in [my?] views were unduly negative since I would like nothing better than to be able to give him fullest encouragement. I knew Soviets had already offered him combat equipment to fight southern tribes. I hoped he would not yield to obvious temptation to accept this help which would have political strings attached. I could not encourage him to expect more direct American help than I honestly felt he was likely to get, but if my Government would give a more favorable response, no one would be more pleased than I. . . .

ALLEN

Memorandum of Conversation, by the Chief of the Division of Middle Eastern and Indian Affairs (Minor)

[*Washington,*] *October 8, 1946*

Participants: Mr. Hussein Ala, Iranian Ambassador; Mr. Acheson; Mr. Minor, MEI.

The Iranian Ambassador called today at his request. He said that he wished to emphasize to the Department the seriousness of the situation in Iran. He said that the Province of Azerbaijan is now entirely under the control of the Democrats, who are under Russian influence, so that the central Government has virtually lost control of this important state. In addition to this grave difficulty, the southern part of Iran is now torn by civil strife. Whatever the degree of British complicity in the southern rebellion, the Ambassador gave his opinion that the movement is a normal and natural reaction of the tribes against Russian infiltration into Southern Iran and domination over the central government. It all, in his opinion, goes back to the original "sin" of Russian aggression in northern Iran. Ambassador Ala declared that Iran now stands at a cross road, and the next moves may well determine Iran's destiny. He stated frankly that, while he has up to this point been sure that Qavam is following a patriotic course designed to protect Iran's independence, he is not now so sure of this. His general impression is still that Qavam has followed his present course because of necessity, since the Russians are on top of Iran and since little hope of assistance from any other power is evident. Iran, the Ambassador said, continues to pin its hope on the United States. He sincerely believes that Qavam has followed this course by default and that he will alter his course if encouragement is given by the United States.

The situation in Iran is made critical by the fact that Qavam has now agreed to hold elections. The Ambassador said he was at a loss to understand how Qavam could agree to hold elections for the Majlis at a time when Azerbaijan and part of the South are [not?] under the control of the central Government. The elections will certainly have the effect of returning to the Majlis a solid bloc of Soviet dominated deputies from Azerbaijan and possibly from other northern areas. The result of this Soviet bloc will be to give the Russians virtual control of the central Government and all that that entails. If this course of action is carried through, Iran will have lost a major degree of sovereignty.

With this background in mind, Ambassador Ala suggested that the United States should now help Iran in the following three ways:

1. The Iranian case should be reopened before the Security Council by the United States. The Ambassador said that conditions in Iran are much worse than in May when the case was postponed temporarily. With Russian aggression still effective in the North and rebellion in the

South, a full inquiry should now be made and a commission sent to Iran to investigate.

2. The United States should express to Iranian officials, through its Ambassador at Tehran, the serious view this government takes of the trend of events and recommend that the impending elections in Iran should be postponed.

3. In addition to bringing American views to the attention of Soviet officials through our Ambassador, it would be very helpful if this Government could send an official of the State Department to Iran with a more personal message from this Government, to express the American Government's viewpoint more fully and carefully than could be done by telegraph.

Mr. Acheson assured the Ambassador of the very close interest this Government has in the course of events in Iran. As to the possibility of reopening the Iranian case before the Security Council, Mr. Acheson did not wish to express an off-hand opinion without full consultation on the subject. However, he told the Ambassador frankly that it would be very difficult for this Government to reopen the Iranian case when there is no indication that the Iranian Government has altered the stand it took before the Security Council in the spring when it requested that the Iranian case be dropped from the agenda. We are not at all sure of what the Iranian reaction to such a move might be, and we do not know that Qavam would approve of reopening the case or sending a commission of inquiry. This is a question which should be carefully considered before any action is taken. Concerning the second of the Ambassador's points, Mr. Acheson said that this Government has on many occasions expressed a great interest in the Iranian affairs and only recently instructed Ambassador Allen to express to Qavam the dangers which appear to be inherent in the proposed aviation agreement with Russia. We will continue to take a close interest in Iran and make every effort to implement our declared policy of economic assistance to that country. As to the specific point of recommending to Qavam that elections not be held, Mr. Acheson said he had some misgivings about such definite interferences in Iranian internal affairs. He thought that the appropriate course of action would be to give Qavam assurances of American interest and support so that he might feel strengthened to take whatever action he might feel suitable in the circumstances to protect Iran's sovereignty. Replying to the third of the Ambassador's points, Mr. Acheson said that the possibility of sending an official of the State Department to Iran on a special mission will be discussed with officials of the Department. In closing Mr. Acheson said he wished the Ambassador to take away the impression that the United States Government is sincerely interested in Iran and desires to be of assistance at this critical time.

The Acting Secretary of State to the Ambassador in Iran (Allen)

Washington, November 22, 1946, 7 p.m.

976. We have given careful consideration urtels urging US implement more fully its declared policy assistance Iran. In view great importance we attach Iranian problem, not only in terms Iran-US relations but also in terms UN principles supporting independence small countries and US strategic interests Middle Eastern area as a whole, we feel measures listed below should be taken in implementing our announced policies re Iran.

1. You may express to appropriate Iranian officials on appropriate occasions genuine interest US in independence Iran and assure them this Govt is prepared, so long as Govt Iran sincerely desires independence and demonstrates willingness stand up for its sovereignty against external pressure, support independence Iran not only by words but also by appropriate acts.

2. We are prepared to consider sympathetically pending Iranian request sale reasonable quantities nonaggression military material to assist Iran in maintaining internal order. Conversations at present taking place between Iranian military mission and appropriate US officials. For your info, possibilities of credit for arms purchase are now being explored.

3. We hope to be able maintain US military missions Iran if desired by Iranian Govt and will continue to support before Congress legislation permitting their detail beyond period national emergency. Recommendations these missions would be appreciated re present requests Iranian Military Purchasing Mission.

4. We are hoping to be able intensify our informational and cultural program Iran. In this connection, revision surplus property obligations would make funds available purposes increased cultural exchange.

In connection with this program Dept is earnestly endeavoring obtain Exim Bank approval in principal to loan for Iran. Since we have not yet been able obtain Bank's approval you should make no commitment or statement to Iranian Govt other than to indicate Dept is giving question sympathetic consideration.

In bringing these measures attention Iran authorities, you should make clear US assistance Iran is based on assumption Govt Iran is working in true interests people Iran and to this end will endeavor steadfastly preserve Iranian sovereignty and independence.

ACHESON

The Ambassador in Iran (Allen) to the Secretary of State

Tehran, November 24, 1946, 2 p.m.

1517. PriMin Qavam informed me today that he had definitely

determined to send security forces into Azerbaijan and that if the authorities there resist (and he expects they will), he will appeal to Security Council for assistance. In response to my inquiry he said perhaps 2 or 3 weeks would be required to despatch the forces and bring matters to head. He contemplates making immediate appeal to SC whenever fighting starts.

I pointed out that SC concerns itself with matters threatening international peace. He said he was aware of this and that if fighting broke out in Northern Iran he would inform Council that situation existed which might endanger world peace. I asked specifically whether he had in mind any appeal or statement to General Assembly, possibly informing that body of action he was taking to reassert Iranian sovereignty over Azerbaijan. He replied in negative, stating that his appeal would be to Security Council where, he said, Iranian case was fortunately still on agenda.

I reminded him that last April he had informed SC that all differences between Iran and Soviet Union had been settled and that there was no longer any case for SC to consider. I said Soviet representative on Council would be certain to cite this statement of Iranian Govt and that consequently Iranians would need new evidence of interference or threat to peace as answer to Soviet argument. He said his appeal, if made, would present new evidence.

In order to obtain this he was thinking of sending 1,000 soldiers to Azerbaijan, 500 to be concerned with elections and 500 to patrol Soviet border to seize Soviet agents or supplies coming south.

As regards type of assistance SC would render, Qavam realized troops could probably not be sent to aid Iran but he felt Iran must bring to Council's attention situation which threatened peace and leave it to Council to determine what assistance it would render. He hoped members of Council would at least show their approval of Iranian Govt's efforts to maintain its sovereignty.

At the end of conversation I said I wanted to inform my Govt specifically regarding situation. He said "I will send troops to Azerbaijan, there will inevitably be fighting, consequently the probabilities are very strong that Iran will appeal to Security Council for aid soon."

Since we have been urging Iran and other UN members to base their policy on UN, I hope Department will again feel in position to support Iran's case strongly if presented. While every effort must be made to assure that case presented is strong one and that Iranian Govt goes through with it wholeheartedly, Qavam appreciates difficulties he placed US in last time and I do not think he will repeat his previous performance. He said he would like to coordinate his plans with US in closest detail when he prepares appeal.

ALLEN

The Ambassador in Iran (Allen) to the Secretary of State

Tehran, November 29, 1946, 4 p.m.

1536. Prime Minister asked me to come to see him urgently this morning. He said the Soviet Ambassador had demanded to see him last night and had informed him on instructions from Moscow, that the sending of Iran troops into Azerbaijan was considered by the Soviet Govt as undesirable because it would create difficulties "within Azerbaijan and on the Soviet-Iran frontier."

Qavam considers these Soviet representations to be in the nature of a threat and consequently interference in Iranian affairs. He says he is determined to carry out his announced intention of sending forces into Azerbaijan, mentioning the figure 10,000 as being necessary to do the job, but he is afraid, in view of the Soviet Govt's attitude, that USSR will send Soviet troops to support the Azerbaijan Govt.

Prime Minister asked me to obtain American Govt's reaction most immediately to his idea of notifying Security Council of Soviet Ambassador's representations to him. Qavam's idea is that Iran would make such notification under Iran's obligation to inform Security Council of any situation which might threaten international peace. He would not make any specific request of Council, leaving any action which Council might desire to make, up to the Council. . . .

I hope Dept will authorize me to inform Prime Minister that American Govt considers Iran fully justified, if it so desires, in notifying Security Council in above sense. . . .

ALLEN

The Acting Secretary of State to the Ambassador in Iran (Allen)

Washington, December 2, 1946, 10 p.m.

. . . 2. It seems to us that Iranian Central Govt is justified in taking appropriate measures, including the dispatch of troops, in order to restore its authority in Azerbaijan. We do not see how valid elections can be held in Azerbaijan so long as that province is not under control of Central Govt.

3. If Qavam should refrain from taking appropriate measures to restore authority of Central Govt in Azerbaijan merely because of pressure brought to bear upon him by Soviet Amb, he will be adding to difficulties which we have been encountering in carrying out our policy of supporting integrity and independence of Iran. If on other hand following dispatch by Qavam of troops into Azerbaijan he should have reason to believe that Soviet Govt is interfering in Iranian affairs by giving support to Azerbaijan movement and he should bring this matter to attention of Security Council, American Govt will be prepared to pursue matter energetically. You can assure Qavam that this Govt will

give its unqualified support to Iran or to any other power the integrity and independence of which may be threatened by external forces, provided that power shows courage and determination to maintain its own independence and freedom of action and provided it is willing to make its position clear to world.

4. You may further inform Qavam that we feel that he would be justified at this point in informing SC of situation with regard to Azerbaijan. If he decides to do so he might care to incorporate in his communication some of the following points: (a) Iranian Central Govt, despite protracted negotiations, has not as yet been able by peaceful means to reassert its authority over the province of Azerbaijan; (b) he has therefore decided to send Iranian forces into Azerbaijan to supervise elections and to reestablish order and restore authority of Iranian Govt; (c) he has taken this decision notwithstanding a message delivered to him by Soviet Amb on behalf of Soviet Govt to effect that if Central Govt forces are sent to Azerbaijan there will be disturbances in that province and along the Soviet border; (d) his present communication to SC is in nature of further report on developments in Iranian question pending before SC and he hopes that in view of situation in Azerbaijan SC will continue to be seized of Iranian question.

5. Such communication would not of course be considered as invitation for SC to act at this juncture. It would however place SC upon notice re possibility that Iranian case might again become active in immediate future.

ACHESON

The Acting Secretary of State to the Ambassador in Iran (Allen)

Washington, December 6, 1946, 7 p.m.

1012. For your confidential info Iranian Amb states following communication sent to SYG, UN, N.Y. Dec. 5:

"SIR: In connection with the dispute arising out of the interferences in the internal affairs of Iran previously complained of, I have the honour to submit for the attention of the Security Council a report respecting the present state of affairs in the Province of Azerbaijan. No request for action is made at the present time, though it will be apparent that the decision of the Security Council to continue seized of this question should remain unchanged. The purpose of the report is to keep the Security Council informed of the further consequences of the interferences previously complained of. I am, Sir, your obedient servant, Hussein Ala, Iranian Ambassador and Representative of Iran before the Security Council."

[ATTACHMENT]

"His Excellency, The Honorable Herschel V. Johnson, President of the Security Council, Lake Success, New York. Sir: My Government has instructed me to submit this report in connection with the complaints previously made to the Security Council against interferences in the internal affairs of Iran. It will be recalled that a result of these interferences is that the Central Government has been denied the exercise of effective control in the Province of Azerbaijan. Unfortunately, in spite of every effort to remove by conciliatory means the consequences of these interferences, the Central Government has not yet been able to re-establish its authority in that Province.

Elections to provide for the selection of the Majless, our National Legislature, have been called to take place throughout Iran beginning December 7th. In order to assure that the election procedures are duly followed, it has been arranged that military forces shall be stationed in all the provinces of Iran. Those in control of affairs in Azerbaijan have objected to the entry of such Government forces into that Province. The Soviet Ambassador at Teheran, acting under instructions from his Government, has given friendly admonition that the movement of Government forces into this part of Iran may result in disturbances within that Province and on the Persian borders adjacent to Russia, and advised that the Government's plans be abandoned.

It is, of course, the duty of my Government to exercise its sovereign responsibilities, and to assure that the elections are carried out impartially in Azerbaijan as well as in the rest of Iran; and my Government for that purpose must station its troops in Azerbaijan no less than in other parts of the Country. It is hoped that this will not be used as a pretext for hostile demonstrations, but my Government will not fail to take the action necessary to maintain law and order throughout Iran, even though disturbances may be threatened.

The decision of the Security Council to remain seized of the questions raised by the complaints of Iran has demonstrated its concern regarding the consequences of the interferences that have occurred in the past. My Government has, therefore, felt it to be its duty to furnish the information contained in this report in order that the Council may be in a position better to interpret the course of events in the Northwestern portion of my Country. I am, Sir, your obedient servant, Hussein Ala, Iranian Ambassador and Representative of Iran before the Security Council."

Sent Tehran rptd London, 8064, Moscow 2093.

ACHESON

Memorandum of Telephone Conversation, by the Director of the Office of Near Eastern and African Affairs (Henderson)

[*Washington,*] *December 7, 1946*

The Iranian Ambassador telephoned from New York today at noon to tell me the contents of two important telegrams he had received from Prime Minister Qavam in Tehran.

The first telegram reported a second interview with the Soviet Ambassador in Tehran. The Soviet Ambassador referred to the "friendly advice" which he had given, on instructions from his Government, to Mr. Qavam a few days ago, namely that "difficulties" would ensue from the despatch of Iranian Central Government forces into the province of Azerbaijan abutting on the Soviet frontier. He recalled that Mr. Qavam promised to take the matter up with the Iranian Council of Ministers and stated that he had awaited the decision of the Council. The Soviet Ambassador reiterated that the action contemplated by the Iranian

Central Government would lead to "disturbances" to which "the Soviet Government cannot be indifferent." . . .

The Soviet Ambassador concluded by saying that he had fulfilled his mission undertaken on instruction from his Government. He stated that if Mr. Qavam does not accept Soviet advice and persists in his course toward Azerbaijan, the Soviet Government "will have to revise its attitude toward you personally."

Mr. Qavam concluded his statements by saying that if he were subject to threat, should abandon his efforts on behalf of Iran and step aside, anyone chosen to succeed him as Prime Minister would take the same action that Qavam is taking now. Mr. Qavam stated that his decision was not a personal one but reflected the public opinion of Iran. . . .

The second telegram was received at 10 p.m. Friday, December 6. Mr. Qavam referred to the statement which Mr. Acheson had made to him recently concerning Iranian relations with the United States and the United Nations. Mr. Qavam stated that he had sent instructions to Mr. Ala before receipt of Mr. Ala's telegram embodying that statement. Mr. Qavam said he was "steadfast" before the Soviet Ambassador and that Iranian forces would soon move into Azerbaijan to maintain security there during elections. He reported that Azerbaijan was considering hostile measures and had mined the roads at the provincial border. Mr. Qavam stated that the Tabriz radio had been violent in its attacks upon him and the Central Government, that the Tudeh press had apparently taken the lead of the Soviet Government, and that the Soviet Ambassador had threatened him personally. In spite of all this, Mr. Qavam emphasized that he will not change his position. He recalled that the subject of Iran is still on the agenda of the Security Council and that Council action is the only hope Iran has of preventing Soviet interference.

L[OY] W. H.[ENDERSON]

The Ambassador in Iran (Allen) to the Secretary of State

Tehran, December 12, 1946

1582. Azerbaijan situation is not entirely clear but it seems very probable the war is over. There has been very little fighting, in fact Gaflaneu Pass was left undefended for some inexplicable reason, only one bridge in the pass being blown. Tehran troops occupied Mianeh at 3 p.m. yesterday without meeting resistance. Djavid telegraphed Qavam requesting termination of hostilities and saying he would go to Mianeh to arrange for peaceful occupation of Azerbaijan by govt troops. Qavam, in consultation with Shah, replied that his officers would discuss matter with Djavid in Tabriz. Meanwhile Chief of Staff ordered army to proceed to Tabriz in all haste. . . .

Soviets are said to have let Azerbaijans know that USSR could furnish them little more than moral support, which was not enough in face of determined move by Central Govt forces. Qavam's notification to Security Council seems to have been well-timed.

Tehran Govt and populace are rather in a daze, incredulous that war could be over so easily and hesitant to celebrate too early lest there be a hitch somewhere.

Repeated London 186 and Moscow 311.

ALLEN

The Ambassador in Iran (Allen) to the Secretary of State

Tehran, December 17, 1946, 2 p.m.

1597. Principal reason for sudden collapse of Azerbaijan movement, in Shah's opinion, was (1) surprising weakness of Tabriz military organization, (2) high morale and determination of Tehran forces, and (3) most important, conviction by all concerned (Soviets, Iranians and Azerbaijanis) that United States was solidly supporting Iranian sovereignty.

In view of Soviet Ambassador's strenuous efforts to prevent sending of Tehran forces to Azerbaijan and his frequent declarations to Shah and Qavam that USSR would not remain indifferent if those forces proceeded, people are asking why Soviets failed to give Azerbaijan any significant material assistance. Practically every Iranian, including notably the Shah, thinks answer lies primarily in fact that Soviets were finally convinced that US was not bluffing and would support any United Nations member threatened by aggression.

Embassy has received numerous visits from Iranian Cabinet officers and officials, including Minister of War, Minister of Finance, Governor of National Bank, President of last Majlis, et cetera, to express appreciation to America for "giving back Azerbaijan to Iran.["]

At an informal social gathering last night Shah made a fulsome and even embarrassing tribute to our help. Azerbaijan was referred to by others present as the "Stalingrad of the western democracies" and the "turn of the tides against Soviet aggression throughout the world." I emphasized that Iranians themselves had regained Azerbaijan and that any credit for enabling Iran to accomplish this free from outside interference, was due to existence of a world organization which could mobilize opinion against such interference.

Repeated Moscow 314.

ALLEN

The Secretary of State to the Ambassador in Iran (Allen)

Washington, December 20, 1946, 7 p.m.

1054. Now that Iran Govt has been able reassert authority over

Azerbaijan we hope Qavam will adopt conciliatory attitude toward people that province and refrain from repressive or retaliatory measures against Russians, Azerbaijanis and Kurds. We believe that granting of general amnesty and limiting of punishment to judicial process against few guilty leaders would have good effect on world opinion and tend to counter Soviet statements that Iran is reactionary.

We feel that Qavam has splendid opportunity at this point to show statesmanlike qualities, mold Iran into homogeneous nation and put into effect reforms which he has stated are basis of his program and in general lead Iran toward a fuller life for the people and an improved place among the United Nations. It would be regrettable if through inaction or lack of publicity Soviet view that political trend in Iran is retrograde should gain currency in world. To prevent this we feel Qavam should lose no time in announcing and giving full publicity to a clear-cut program of social, constitutional and tribal reform which will leave no doubt that Iran is looking forward and not backward. In this connection we believe Qavam should refrain to extent possible from suppressing opposition parties and press but rather should encourage democratic processes and establishment of reponsible press through positive leadership and by issuing official clarifying statements where misstatements have been made or truth distorted.

You may in your discretion make these views known to Qavam.

BYRNES

COLD WAR COOPERATION

**State Department and United States Embassy in Iran
Exchanges on Strategic Importance of Iran
and Proposed United States Aid**

The Acting Secretary of State to the Embassy in Iran

Washington, January 3, 1948, 1 p.m.

5. Arms purchase discussions Washington (Deptel 776, Dec 13) and communications Tehran (urtel 1213, Dec 9) point up question of possible direct US aid to Iran (ur letter to Henderson Nov 18 and Deptel 740, Nov 22), in context over-all Iran-US relations vis-à-vis Soviet Union (Deptel 434, July 29). Since provision arms is only one aspect total problem, we consider it advisable analyze whole picture with view to determining how best we can serve essential US interests in Iran. Fol-

lowing represents Dept thinking at this time:

1. Security of Iran is substantially as important to US as is security Greece and Turkey. Question to be solved is how best to assure Iran's independence, stability, and friendship, recognizing remoteness of Iran and inherent weaknesses Iranian Govt.

2. Basic considerations re Soviet threat to Iranian security stated Deptel 434 July 29 are, in our opinion, still generally valid. We recognize that Soviet "hostile action" note to Iranian Govt Nov 20 may represent effort lay basis anticipated action against central Govt. It is still felt, however, that Soviet military and political disposition vis-à-vis Iran, in light of over-all U.S.-USSR relations (urtel 1092, Nov 11) makes overt aggression improbable in near future.

3. US military assistance should continue be aimed at internal security, not national defense, of Iran. (MA-R539, Dec 10) Power relations Iran and USSR cannot be altered appreciably by provision US military supplies. Iranian arms program intended (1) replace lost or obsolete equipment Iranian Army to permit effective display central Govt power, patrol border areas and insure quick repression of foreign-inspired uprisings, and (2) increase effectiveness Gendarmerie in maintaining law and order throughout country. We inclined think provision of arms for first-line defense would be fruitless and provocative to USSR.

4. In view non-availability substantial quantities supplies from surplus (Deptel 776, Dec 13) it is virtually certain special assistance by US Govt to Iran on any large scale could be provided only by act of Congress. Indicated attitude of Congressmen who have devoted attention to Iranian situation gives some hope that Congress might be favorably disposed. However, only convincing ground we can see for requesting legislation would be to support Iranian independence in face of Soviet threat. Iran would have to make strong appeal and Dept would have to speak out frankly and publicly. Result would be to place Iran definitely in same category as Greece and Turkey in minds of Russians and world public.

We believe this would be displeasing to many Iranians who are anxious avoid open break with USSR. Apart from this consideration, such open alignment of Iran in opposition to Soviet Union might deprive Iran Govt of opportunities for diplomatic maneuver, delaying tactics, conciliatory gestures, and the like which it has employed with considerable success in past. US might assume very serious responsibility if it encouraged Iran to burn its bridges in this fashion in view of fact we could not guarantee to protect it in event of Soviet attack.

5. We believe US should be especially careful avoid any appearance of forcing loan or gift on Iran both because of adverse effect such appearance would have on Iranians, who are pehaps justifiably hesitant obligate themselves financially to foreign Govts, and because of plausi-

bility it would lend to Soviet-inspired charges of American dollar imperialism. Consequently, it seems to us that any initiative in discussion of special assistance to Iran from US should always be left to Iran Govt and we should make no move this regard without specific and formal request. It should also always be kept in mind that even if request were made and favorably considered by Dept, political situation in US might make action impracticable. Limitations imposed by financial and economic demands of US interim aid and ERP should be recognized.

6. Dept hopeful transportation charges for surplus purchases will be reduced by possible provision ships to Iran following strong Dept appeal favorable reconsideration Iranian application by Maritime Commission. Financial strain arms purchase upon Iranian dollar resources might be alleviated to some extent by Iran purchase available items or substitutes from British.

7. Important US contribution to Iranian security forces can be made, we think by Iranian acceptance advice Grow and Schwarzkopf re organization, administration, and personnel. On our part, we will press strongly for Congressional passage Military Missions Bill permitting continuance missions beyond national emergency.

8. We continue feel that US objectives in Iran can be best achieved by economic development to strengthen social structure and popular loyalty to central Govt. World Bank currently giving favorable preliminary study Iranian intention apply for loan. We reiterate we are prepared support reasonable request for loan. Should such loan materialize, we will give every possible assistance in obtaining material and personnel for Iran, even in present short-supply situation. Iran should be prepared permit considerable Bank supervision loan expenditure for broadest, most economical benefits to country.

9. There is considerable opinion here supporting earlier Emb view that by modification of currency reserve requirements plus modest World Bank loan, Iran could obtain all foreign exchange it could effectively utilize for economic purposes during next two or three years. Would like your present views on this.

10. Implementation Fulbright Bill, passage Mundt Act, and availability Imbrie funds should contribute to furtherance US objectives Iran. Voice of America expected to reach Iran soon in Persian and Turkish languages.

Foregoing represents only tentative thinking subject modification in light any additional info you may be able to furnish or additional considerations you may suggest. Our attitude will of course also be affected by course of developments in Iran and in relations between Iran and USSR.

This message cleared with Army who will advise Grow concerning current thinking Iran's strategical importance upon his return.

Sent Tehran 5 repeated London 16 Moscow 9.

LOVETT

The Ambassador in Iran (Allen) to the Secretary of State

Tehran, January 5, 1948, 2 p.m.

10. In my first official call on Prime Minister Hakimi today I reviewed background of military credit, emphasizing that while we did not press our military supplies on anyone, I felt I should press Iran Government for early decision on question. Hakimi declared himself in favor of ratification of credit and said he would press matter to Majlis following receipt of vote of confidence.

I also referred to recent opposition expressed by certain Iranians (Embtel 2, January 2) to American Military Mission in Iran, emphasizing that we were anxious to assist Iran whenever possible and that we maintained our missions here, despite urgent need for American military personnel elsewhere, only as result of Iran Government's request and in desire to help develop Iran's security forces. I said that at any moment Iran Government desired termination of these missions, they would leave promptly. I said I felt I should say, to be entirely frank, that Iranian request for withdrawal of American missions would be interpreted by American public as lack of interest by Iran in American assistance, adding that I did not mention this factor in order to urge retention of advisors but merely to state a fact. Hakimi interrupted my statement several times to assure me that he strongly desired retention of American advisors and said Iran could turn nowhere else for disinterested expert assistance. . . .

ALLEN

The Ambassador in Iran (Allen) to the Secretary of State

Tehran, January 9, 1948, 5 p.m.

. . . As regards question of placing Iran in Greek-Turkish category . . . this subject has many aspects. I concur that in absence of ability to assure Iran prompt support, we would assume considerable responsibility by forcing Iran off fence onto our side. At same time, I am not certain that policy of diplomatic maneuver, delaying tactics and conciliatory gestures is desirable basis for foreign policy of Iran or any other country when issue is totalitarian aggression against democracy. Difference between American policy of support for Iranian independence and Soviet policy here during past two years has been difference between white and black, and everyone should recognize it. Soviets are forever telling Iranians to beware of American imperialism, and many Iranians who follow policy of balance or neutrality swallow this line at least half way. They profess to see no distinction between "Soviet imperialism" and "American imperialism" and cry plague on both houses. Continued policy of neutrality would result, if hostilities should come, in disinterested attitude by Iranians who would regard conflict as being between two imperialisms. Even now we face great difficulties in strengthening Iran economically, since Iranians who follow policy of balance hesitate to request economic aid from either side.

Moreover, for better or worse, Iran's geographical location and petroleum resources of Persian Gulf will make it impossible for Iran to remain neutral in any future war and I am not certain we are benefiting Iranians by encouraging them to hope they might. It is entirely true that many, perhaps most, Iranians wish fervently that all great powers, including US, would go away and leave Iran alone. But no great power will or can abandon it to another. Stakes here are too important. Since Iran must choose sides eventually, it should be on side of freedom and independence. Sooner whole free world is lined up clearly on that side, less likelihood there will be of totalitarian aggression. I agree that we should avoid pushing Iran off fence against her will. However we should emphasize to Iranians in every possible way difference between American and Soviet policy in Iran and should encourage Iran to show her recognition of this difference and to realize that US and Iranian interests are parallel. . . .

ALLEN

The Secretary of State to the Ambassador in Iran (Wiley)

Washington, May 16, 1949

DEAR JOHN: Thank you for your letter of March 29. I have, indeed, realized from your telegrams that you are concerned about Iran's position vis-à-vis its great northern neighbor. I need hardly tell you that we in the Department share your concern and had it very much in mind when we inserted the paragraph on Greece, Turkey and Iran in my talk of March 18 as well as in the special statement I made to the press a few days later. It was our hope, which seems so far to have been fulfilled, that these statements and the President's reference to the Near East in his speech of April 4 would sound enough of a warning note to deter the Russians from embarking on any new major adventures in the direction of Iran.

The evidence which we can assemble here points to the conclusion that the Soviet Union does not want to risk war in the near future and that its activities in the Near East, including Iran, will therefore not go beyond the sort of pressures and subversive attempts to which it has resorted during the past two years. The evidence also seems to lend itself to the interpretation that the Kremlin fears open aggression against Iran would involve it in grave risk of conflict with the United States. If this were not the case, it would be difficult to explain why Soviet forces have so far refrained from entering Iran despite the obvious Russian designs on that country and the equally obvious physical weakness of Iran.

The essential thing, therefore, is to keep the Iranians firm in their resistance to Soviet pressures short of war. This is undeniably difficult, but we have been successful so far and I think we are justified in having good hope of success in the future. . . . We must endeavor to steer Iran on a middle course between undue complacency and undue fear.

The question of what concrete support, diplomatic and material, we can give to Iran remains a knotty one. In the diplomatic field, the Department continues to believe it desirable that the Iranians should make some non-provocative report to the Security Council regarding the various threats and pressures Russia has employed in the past year and a quarter. We would expect to follow up such a report with a statement of our own regarding American activities in Iran and our view as to the duty of the USSR to complain to the Security Council if she genuinely feels threatened. However, we have become somewhat concerned lest our repeated indications of this view to the Iranian Government should be construed as pressure exerted on our part and lest the Iranians, if they do take action, should do so unwillingly, merely out of a desire to avoid offending the United States. Apart from the fact that the Iranian Government could not be relied upon to back up a *démarche* made under such circumstances (you will recall Qavam's vacillations in 1946), I am afraid such a situation would impose upon us a tremendous moral responsibility to stand behind Iran whatever the consequences of her action. I do not want to be in the position of egging on a small country to do something it is reluctant to do in its own interest. . . .

In the field of material aid, we have succeeded so far in keeping an amount of approximately 12 million dollars allocated to Iran in the draft Military Aid Program. Whether this will stay in the bill is, of course, for Congress to decide. It is not politically feasible to increase this amount, although we hope the bill will also include a "contingency fund" of perhaps 50 million dollars from which some small additional sum might conceivably be drawn to assist Iran if it seemed necessary. I realize that this would seem very small to the Iranians as compared with 75 or 100 million dollars for Turkey. We shall strive to minimize this difficulty by avoiding any revelation of the amounts allocated. Perhaps we can also diminish Iranian disappointment or resentment by continuing to emphasize, as you have done, the inability of the Iranian forces to absorb large quantities of additional equipment in the coming year and the need for extensive training before highly technical modern weapons and equipment could profitably be provided. A further argument which occurs to me, and on which I would like your opinion, is the economic one. Even though we might supply all of the foreign exchange costs of an enlarged and modernized Iranian Army, I should think the internal costs would be an extremely severe drain on the Iranian budget and would handicap the implementation of the economic development program. As you know, in the European arms program we are emphasizing that economic recovery is the first objective and all military programs must be subordinated to that. In our view, this applies equally to Iran. . . .

DEAN ACHESON

Intelligence Report on Soviet Designs on Iran

Memorandum for the President by the Central Intelligence Agency

July 27, 1950

Unless the Soviet Union definitely modifies what appears to have been its previous policy of abstaining from open military action by Soviet forces, it seems probable that the USSR will not attack Iran but will intensify its efforts to build up subversive forces within Iran and to weaken the country by means of propaganda, border activities, and diplomatic pressure. (Note: The basic question of general Soviet intentions with respect to the open military action is not discussed here.)

Recent reports of increased activity along the Iranian border have obscured the fact that, for almost four years, Soviet forces have been in a position to overrun Iran without warning. In view of the advantages that would have accrued to the USSR from the acquisition of Iran and of the means at its disposal for cloaking aggressive action in a semblance of legality, it seems reasonable to assume that the USSR has been reluctant to employ its own troops in direct aggression. Although in attacking Iran, the USSR could make initially effective use of Iranians-in-exile, Soviet Azerbaijanis, and disaffected elements within Iran, Soviet troops would also have to be used—a condition that does not apply in other sensitive areas such as Formosa, Southeast Asia, and the Balkans.

Soviet domination of Iran would give the USSR important advantages:

(a) The extension of the Soviet frontiers to Iraq and Pakistan would facilitate penetration of the Near East and the Indian subcontinent.

(b) The USSR would also be in a more favorable position for extending its control over these areas in the event of global war.

(c) The USSR would have access to Iran's great oil resources.

(d) The US would be denied an important potential base of operations against the USSR. Conversely, the USSR would obtain buffer territory between its vital Baku oil fields and the bases from which Baku might be attacked.

If the USSR were to decide upon an invasion of Iran, it would have open to it several courses which would, either singly or in combination, have the effect of cloaking its action with a semblance of legality. It could:

(a) Set out to "liberate" Iranian Azerbaijan with a "volunteer" army of Iranians-in-exile and Soviet Azerbaijanis. Clashes between the invaders and the Iranian armed forces would provoke the USSR to send in troops allegedly to restore order. The Soviet forces could overrun northern Iran in a few days and the entire country shortly thereafter.

(b) Create provocative border incidents and instigate disturbances in northern Iran through the use of such elements as Soviet agents, dissident Kurdish factions, or Tudeh Party members. Claiming that such disorders jeopardized Soviet security, the USSR would send in troops to restore order as in para. (a) above.

(c) Invade Iran with Soviet troops under the pretext that, in violation of the 1921 Irano-Soviet Treaty of Friendship, US activities in Iran were making that country a base for attack on the USSR by a third power. Recent Soviet notes have made this allegation and have requested Iran to rectify the situation. The treaty provides that if Iran is unable to comply with such a request, the USSR may intervene.

Past Soviet attempts to subjugate Iran through subversion and intimidation have achieved little success, and the present government is firmly committed to a policy of withstanding Soviet threats and pressures and of maintaining a pro-US alignment. If, however, Iran loses confidence in the ability of the US to fulfill its commitments or comes to believe that the US has little interest in the preservation of Iranian independence, the Iranian Government may feel compelled to seek an accord with the USSR or at least to attempt a course of neutrality. In either case, the USSR would be in a greatly improved position for taking over the country without the use of force.

United States Caution Regarding the Shah's Military Aid Requests

The Ambassador in Iran (Wiley) to the Secretary of State

Tehran, September 1, 1948, 1 p.m.

1025. Saw Shah for more than two hours yesterday. Almost entire period was devoted to arms credit program with Shah manifesting greatly aggravated discontent. As is inevitably the case in all such conversations with him he persistently raised the question of Turkey with, I think, erroneous and jealously exaggerated ideas of the military and economic aid which the US is furnishing that country. He alleged that it was obvious that in case of war with the Soviet Union we were planning to use airfields in Turkey against the Soviet Union and would let Iran go down the drain. He manifested deepest concern that the US had apparently ignored completely the great strategic importance of his country and felt moreover that we were wasting invaluable time. . . . He emphasized and reemphasized what he considered to be the vital importance to the US in the event of war for Iran to be able to impede Soviet access to Absdan and the Persian Gulf.

During our conversation I used all possible counter arguments with no apparent success. He is obviously obdurately stubborn. I insisted that he should discuss military matters with General Grow since it was field in which I was not qualified. He will see General Grow tomorrow but he urgently requested that in meantime I inform you of our interview.

The state of mind of the Shah is clearly something that should be taken seriously.

WILEY

The Acting Secretary of State to the Embassy in Iran

Washington, October 1, 1948, 8 p.m.

948. You should in ur discretion make following points to Shah and appropriate Iranian officials as general comment on Shah's and PriMin's recent complaints as set forth Embtels 1025, Sept 1; 1041, Sept 3; 1083, Sept 14; 1111, Sept 19 re alleged inadequacy of US military and economic aid to Iran.

1. Shah must realize every free country in world is under Soviet pressure or attack in form of military, political, economic or social pressure or combinations of these methods in varying degrees and forms to suit local circumstances as understood by Kremlin and in pursuance overall Soviet objectives.

2. Since no country is perfect in all respects no country is completely impervious to these tactics. All feel more or less vulnerable in their respective weak spots.

3. US, all things considered, being strongest country in world, all other countries look to US to bolster up their weaknesses.

4. This too large order for US to fill even assuming, which is not case, that other countries are using their own resources and capabilities to greatest advantage.

5. US must, accordingly, be its own judge of where, how and to what extent it can extend assistance. Decision, in all cases where important policy determinations are dependent on substantial appropriations rests with Congress which, of course, must act within limits set at any given moment by American public opinion.

6. We hope Shah will agree that, on any broad view, US has not been either inconsiderate of or irresponsive to problems of other countries resulting from Soviet policies and practices. Moreover, we hope he will agree that US choice of locales and methods for application of assistance, judged by results achieved and emerging, have in main been correct.

7. As was bound happen, critics have arisen in various countries to complain with respect to one or another aspect of US cooperation and assistance, with resulting pressure on govts concerned and upon US. Obviously we cannot take "keeping up with Joneses" type of appeal into serious account. On other hand we are always glad to give most

affirmative consideration we can to realistic and urgent needs.

8. US cooperation and assistance on even smallest scale must be premised on concrete efforts of country concerned to stand on own feet. In our considered opinion, most effective means whereby Iranian Govt can resist Soviet expansionist aims are within competence of Iranian Govt itself, namely: (a) persistent refusal of Soviet demands which would impair Iran's independence, (b) constant vigilance in preventing and suppressing Soviet-sponsored attempts to infiltrate country or undermine Govt, and (c) conscientious efforts to improve provincial administration immediately (Tabriz A-35, Aug 14) and raise standards of living gradually, thereby increasing people's allegiance to Iranian Govt and decreasing proportionately their susceptibility to Soviet subversion.

9. There is one point in particular which you should drive home: That if worse comes to worst in international sphere, we are not worried over eventual outcome. Shah may wish to keep this conviction in mind in considering general Iranian policy.

LOVETT

The Ambassador in Iran (Wiley) to the Secretary of State

No. 281   *Tehran, November 18, 1949*

. . . I strongly urge that the Director take such extraordinary measures as may be necessary to include in this first year's program the six (6) 75 mm recoilless rifles requested. I realize that this weapon is in short supply and that we do not have sufficient numbers for our own forces. Its use by the Iranian Army, under the instruction of our Military Mission, will be of tremendous psychological value and will balance to some extent the bitter disappointment of the Shah and the Iranian Government in what both they and I regard as a totally inadequate program.

I have advised the Department of the Shah's early ambitious plans and of my successful efforts to reduce them to something within reason. The Shah remains adamant, however, on the subject of tanks. His position amounts to an obsession. I believe he will be satisfied with 50 M4-83 medium tanks equipped with a 76 mm gun. It has been impossible to furnish these tanks within the present program. Therefore we should seek some means outside of the program to satisfy the Shah's minimum desires for tanks. This should be justified on political grounds. I fear that we must take this question most seriously. A "token aid" approach is worse than no approach at all. . . .

Respectfully yours,   JOHN C. WILEY

Message from ARMISH Chief (Evans) in Iran to the Department of the Army

Teheran, September 20, 1949

Matter discussed with Ambassador Wiley and he sent reply yesterday. If I were charge Iran Army I wouldn't ask for med tanks. Military justification this time non existent. Have repeatedly said so to all incl Shah and given reasons. Believe many Iran mil agree but can't say no to Shah.

2. Ref JCS decision. We should not deny med tanks merely because aggressive label. If they help Iran help us they should be considered. To consider Iran aggressive ridiculous. Versus USSR Iran bound to be defensive. Any weapon useful Iran in such war should be considered. Let's not get tangled up by acad classification of weapons. Think we are splitting hairs and gaining nothing. Shah will so believe.

3. Lt tank units are more mobile than medium. The tank itself more mobile, Maint and supplies more mobile. Unless medium has 90 MM gun armament about same. With 90 MM gun med units less mobile. Cannot visualize Iran using massed tanks against USSR. Couldn't mass them and shouldn't. From very nature operations visualized here must use hit and run tactics of small mobile tank units, tank offensive roles. Iran will have difficulty absorbing present tanks, destroyers, and armd cars. Should cut their teeth on these before biting off mediums and armd divisions. Iran support of combat units in field weak, cannot yet effectively support all equip now have. Don't increase difficulties by adding med tanks.

4. Reur Item D concur. Other items worth far more than med tanks. Reur B don't stress, few roads or bridges here. Except for mountains and during floods tanks wouldn't need use many roads or bridges.

5. Med tanks and jet planes obsession with Shah. Has heard all arguments still wants them. Political appeasement thru giving him 50 tempting but not at new production price. Latter would knock out too many useful items. Four Items C and D together appear best defense against request for med tanks.

[EVANS]

United States Concern with Internal Communist Movement in Iran

Central Intelligence Agency Report
The Tudeh Party: Vehicle of Communism in Iran

[EXCERPT]

July 18, 1949

SUMMARY

Although the now banned Tudeh (Masses) Party of Iran purports to be only a homegrown reformist movement of Marxist leanings, it is, for all practical purposes, the Communist Party of Iran. Party propaganda has consistently parroted the Communist line, while the party organization in the field has repeatedly acted to advance the Soviet interest. The party machinery, organized along Communist lines of "democratic centralism," has been dominated from the outset by a combination of veteran Soviet-trained agitators and Marxist intellectuals, most of whom have been comrades in arms ever since they were thrown together in the prisons of Iran during the Reza Shah regime. There is every indication that the Tudeh Party, like the openly Communist parties of other countries, enjoys direct command liaison with the USSR.

The Tudeh Party is significant not only because of its Soviet connections, which make it the logical nucleus for a quisling government should the USSR accelerate its efforts to interfere in Iran, but also because of the head start it has obtained in rousing certain important elements of the Iranian people from their political apathy. The other parties which have sprung up in Iran since the fall of the Reza Shah dictatorship are at present chiefly loose associations of notables, leaving the Tudeh Party as the only political group which has achieved any degree of genuine popular support. Although the Tudeh organization has scarcely begun to organize Iran's vast peasantry, it has made notable strides in the towns, which constitute the principal centers of power and control in Iran. Utilizing the Tudeh-created Central United Council of Trade Unions, the party at one time had more than 70,000 members—about one-third of Iran's industrial population—and has been particularly active in such key installations as the Iranian State Railway, the Anglo-Iranian Oil Company, and government-owned factories.

Thus far the party has not been completely successful in capitalizing on its opportunities. Its various attempts to obtain power in 1946, culminating in the establishment of the Azerbaijan People's Republic by a Tudeh offshoot, proved premature; the party received a severe setback just as its strength was increasing most rapidly. In February 1949, when membership was believed to number some 25,000 and the party's comeback was far from complete, the Tudeh organization was outlawed by the Iranian Government, and a number of its leaders were arrested (and later convicted) on charges of treasonable activity.

Despite these reverses, the Tudeh Party will continue to be an important factor in Iran's future so long as the lagging of social and economic reform creates a reservoir of popular unrest upon which to draw. While the party has been temporarily driven underground, it will undoubtedly proceed with its announced intentions of carrying on the struggle, although the leadership may eventually feel it wise to set up a new organization ostensibly free of Communist associations. It is hardly likely that the Tudeh leadership has any real hope of gaining power through peaceful means, especially in view of the tight control over electoral processes exercised by Iran's present ruling class. As a more or less conspiratorial group, however, the Tudeh organization is well fitted to further Soviet policy by undertaking sabotage, work stoppages, and disturbances at critical points within Iran or by setting up a new group of regional autonomist movements. Although such acts would not constitute a decisive threat to the Iranian Government if unaccompanied by active Soviet assistance, they could be arranged so as to furnish a pretext for Soviet intervention in Iran.

Aid Discussions during the Shah's Visit to the United States

Memorandum by the Assistant Secretary of State for Near Eastern, South Asian, and African Affairs (McGhee) to the Secretary of State

[*Washington,*] *November 17, 1949*

The following briefly summarizes the subjects the Shah of Iran is likely to raise with you when you call on him at the Prospect House on November 18. The subjects are outlined in detail in the "Background Memorandum" on the visit:

1. *Military Assistance.*   The Shah will probably describe his strategic plans in the event of a Soviet invasion and his consequent need for an army larger and more elaborately equipped than is possible under both Iran's present budgetary position and our plans for military assistance. We feel the Shah should be listened to sympathetically but without commitment. If he asks concerning the present status of the list of military equipment, he might be told the program is not sufficiently far advanced for the presentation of any detailed lists at this time. It can be pointed out that our military assistance to Iran is limited by

(a) The fact that effective use of military equipment depends on an army tailored to fit the military budget and any increase in Iran's budget would have serious repercussions on its Seven Year Plan for economic development;

(b) Our own security considerations and the fact that our resources are not unlimited;

(c) The fact that Iran is the only country with a favorable foreign exchange program to receive military assistance on a grant basis;

(d) The availability of trained personnel capable of handling and maintaining the more complex varieties of modern military equipment.

2. *Economic Assistance.*   The Shah is likely to raise the question of economic assistance to his government. In this connection, Iran has embarked upon a Seven Year Program involving about $650 million. Financing of this program, which involves agricultural, irrigation, highway, railway, industrial, public health, and education projects, depends primarily on oil royalties. The IBRD may also be asked for loans up to $250 million to provide additional funds. Immediate aims of the program include raising standards of education and public health, improving agricultural methods and transportation facilities, and reforming tax administration.

Last September, in answer to a specific Iranian request for an economic grant of $147 million, the Department replied that no authority existed for a grant, and that it would be impossible to obtain such authority from Congress since Iran has a favorable foreign exchange position (mainly because of an arrangement under which the British Government freely converts its sterling royalties to dollars) and has not yet exhausted other sources of financial assistance, i.e., the IBRD. We added that the U.S. would be willing to support an adequately documented Iranian application for a loan from the International Bank.

You may want to convey a general idea to the Shah of the part that the Point Four Program might play in assisting Iran in its Seven Year Plan, reiterating the program's emphasis on technical rather than financial assistance and stressing the role that private capital must assume. You might also say that the first step that Iran could take in preparing the way for its Point Four participation should be the negotiation of a Treaty of Friendship, Commerce and Navigation with the United States, which would include suitable clause on investment guarantees.

3. *Extension of the Truman Doctrine to Include Iran.*   Since preparation of the Background Memorandum, Iranian Ambassador Ala has suggested that upon the departure of the Shah, a joint statement be issued reaffirming the principles of the Tehran Declaration on Iran, promising Iran further military and economic assistance and "extending the Truman Doctrine" to include Iran. If the Shah raises this point, it might be pointed out that our position regarding the maintenance of the independence and territorial integrity of Iran is well known, that we will consider a public reiteration of it in connection with his visit here, but that we cannot make any commitments towards further financial, military, or other aid at this time.

4. *Regional Defense Pacts.*   If the Shah suggests a regional Middle East defense pact, with or without a guarantee by the United States, he might be informed that this Government is not in a position to give consideration to any other pacts until the ramifications of the North

Atlantic Pact become clear and can neither encourage nor discourage consideration of such pacts by the countries concerned. It is important, however, that any remarks on this subject be phrased in such a way as to avoid the impression that if Iran were attacked she would be left to her own resources.

5. *General Line.*   Whether or not the Shah raises the question of military or economic aid or further American commitments to Iran, I believe it is desirable that you should make our position on these points and our general attitude toward Iran as clear as possible. He has probably heard all of these things before, but they have come to him through intermediaries in whom he does not appear to have complete confidence or who have not been able themselves to make the situation completely clear. One of the main objectives we should seek during the Shah's visit to the United States is to demonstrate to him that our own Ambassador in Iran and his Ambassador here have in fact been correctly representing the policies and problems of the United States Government with regard to Iran.

The Shah must be convinced that we have a genuine interest in his country and that we are prepared to assist it within reasonable and practicable limits, and he must also be convinced that when we reject his requests we do so for sound logical reasons rather than out of any prejudice against Iran or in favor of other countries.

The two main lines which, I think, can be used to get this point across are:

(a) That we must insist with Iran, as we do with all other countries, that she do everything she can to help herself before requesting American assistance; (this is especially applicable to the question of economic aid) and

(b) That we must make haste slowly and not attempt over night to make up for the deficiencies developed over many years (i.e., even if our resources were unlimited, we could not renovate the Iranian Army in a year or two simply by pouring in great quantities of equipment).

[WILEY]

Memorandum by the Secretary of State: Interview between the President and the Shah of Iran

[Washington,] November 18, 1949

. . . [The Shah] described the situation in the Near East vis-à-vis the Soviet Union as being that Greece constituted the left flank, Turkey the center, and Iran the right flank. He spoke of the interest which we had shown in developing the capacities of the countries which wished to resist foreign domination and of the sums which we had spent in strengthening the left flank and the center in the Middle East. He then pointed out that from a military point of view this effort would be largely wasted if the right flank remained so weak as to invite attack there.

He stated that he might be told that Iran was not ready at the present time to absorb military equipment. That might be true, but it was necessary to start now in order that Iran might be ready within a year or two years. He said he was looking forward to explaining in detail this afternoon at the Pentagon to General Bradley* and the Chiefs of Staff the military situation as he saw it and the military needs of Iran.

The President said that this was the proper course to follow; that His Majesty's ideas would receive the most respectful attention, and would be discussed by the President with his military advisers and with the Secretary of State. The President pointed out that he was necessarily operating under limitations. The Congress, which held the purse strings, had, after considerable debate and in the face of some opposition, passed a Military Assistance Bill. The funds provided were not as large as the President would have wished; however, in face of the difficulties with which the Administration was confronted, he was satisfied with the result. Under this bill, 27 million dollars was available for Iran, the Philippines, and Korea, and there remained the possibility of some transfers in case of necessity from one category to another. The Shah expressed complete familiarity with the terms of the Military Assistance Bill. The President then repeated that he would assure the Shah of the most careful consideration of his views and that both he and the Secretary of State were strong advocates of Iran. He hoped that all our friends appreciated that, with our responsibilities in this hemisphere, in Europe, the Far East, and the Middle East, it was often necessary to leave undone many things which we would wish to see accomplished when the purpose had to be to use the funds available in the wisest way.

The Shah then turned to the economic situation. He spoke of Iran's desire to develop the very great natural resources of the country, of the 7-year plan, and of the bad harvest last year. He said that the income from the oil royalties was to be used for the 7-year plan and for certain other current necessities. This left the military requirements of which he had already spoken and certain other economic ones unprovided for. Among these other needs, he mentioned specifically the need for such items as wheat and of his hope that some way could be found, either through the barter of strategic materials which the United States needed or through some form of Lend-Lease, to provide current consumable items such as wheat.

He then mentioned the need of the railways for new equipment. He said that if the needs of the oil companies were subtracted, the capacity of the railroads for all other needs was only at the present time about 700 tons per day. This he wished to increase to 60,000 tons per day. He had

---

* General Omar Bradley, Chairman of the U.S. Joint Chiefs of Staff.

placed orders in England and in Germany for locomotives and freight cars. He was informed that it would take 17 months to get the equipment ordered in Great Britain because of large prior orders placed by South Africa. The German orders, he understood, could be delivered in approximately 10 months. However, he was anxious to obtain some locomotives and, if possible, cars from the United States at once. He asked whether this matter could be investigated.

The Secretary of State said that he was not quite clear as to just what the matter was which the Shah wished to have investigated. Was it the possibility of immediate availability of equipment in the United States, or was it the question of financing such purchases? The Shah indicated that it was both, and spoke of the possibility of providing this equipment under some sort of Lend-Lease. The Secretary of State observed that there was no present legislation under which this sort of financing could take place. The President remarked that he had only recently filed the last report under the Lend-Lease Act, but that authority under that Act had expired some time ago. The Shah then asked whether the Marshall Plan could be extended to Iran, and was told that under its terms it applied only to countries in Europe.

This led the Shah to observe that he did not think Turkey was a country in Europe. The President pointed out that Turkey had been considered to be in this capacity, partly for geographical reasons, but primarily because of the prior legislation providing aid for Greece and Turkey which arose out of special circumstances and which was incorporated into the Marshall Plan legislation.

The President concluded that if the Iranian representatives would present us specifically with the requests for these suggestions which they had in mind, we would give these careful and sympathetic consideration within the limits of the authority provided by law.

The Iranian Embassy to the Department of State

[AIDE-MÉMOIRE]

Washington, November 29, 1949

. . . In order to combat the aggression and the subversive activities it faces, the Iranian Government must possess a military force, not only for internal security, but powerful enough in defense to be a factor to be reckoned with by the aggressor. To enable it to become such a factor, it is necessary to give the Iranian army adequate equipment, suitable modern weapons of defense, and sufficient mobility.

Having assigned its entire oil royalties to the execution of the Seven Year Plan, Iran neither has the economic ability nor the foreign exchange to enable her to purchase the necessary arms and equipment herself. The Military Aid Program is therefore most timely and for that reason is doubly appreciated. To be effective, however, it must be substantial enough to fulfill its object and continue for some years. Needless to say, too little help will not achieve its objective and will therefore be useless and wasteful.

The limited amount allocated this year under the Military Aid Program to the three countries, of which Iran is one, would appear to be inadequate for the purpose. Iran therefore hopes that its share will be supplemented substantially from the $50 million credit left at the discretion of the President; also that the equipment to be delivered being in the main surplus, will be included in categories supplied at a nominal charge.

While the assistance given to rearm and reequip the Iranian army is most helpful, the Government of Iran wishes to point out that it is desirable for the Government of the United States to supplement that aid politically by extending the Truman Doctrine to Iran and by adopting a policy in the Middle East, as in Western Europe, of encouraging the creation of a union of peace-loving nations, strong enough collectively, to resist Communist domination and capable of serving as effective allies against aggression in the event of a general conflict.

The necessity for assistance to rehabilitate the railway, ports and industrial plants and to raise the standard of living of the Iranian people is so well known that it is superfluous to dilate on the economic needs of Iran. As far back as 1943 these were fully recognized in the Declaration of Tehran, which bears the signature of the late President Roosevelt. Unfortunately its promise of Economic Aid has so far remained unfulfilled. For obvious reasons referred to in this Embassy's Memorandum of August Fourth 1948, the Iranian Government can only look to the Government of the United States for the implementation of the Aid promised and implied by that Declaration, and it would appear that the present visit of His Imperial Majesty The Shah would be a most suitable occasion for such a gesture.

It is suggested that Economic Aid might be extended by the United States Government in the following ways:

1. By the inclusion of Iran in the Act for Aid to Greece and Turkey and in future enactments for economic assistance to other countries.

2. By the extension of a line of credit of $100,000,000—from the Export-Import Bank over a period of seven years at the rate of about $15 million a year, partly to guarantee American investments in Iran in terms of Point Four and partly to finance self-liquidating projects to be carried out by private Iranian enterprise.

3. By giving urgent and special consideration to a barter or lend-lease agreement to supply wheat to Iran to tide over the present scarcity and famine conditions in many parts of the country.

4. By the act implementing Point Four of the President's inaugural speech. Special consideration should be given to Iran under this act

because her development program is under way, whereas other beneficiaries have still to undertake their preliminary studies.

5. By the inclusion of Khouzistan in any development of the nature adumbrated by the President in a recent speech. It is to be noted that its geographical and strategic situation, its proximity to highlands, its fertility and its oil and mineral resources give Khouzistan potentialities far superior to any other area in the Middle East.

Promise of financial and economic aid within the scope of the above-mentioned suggestions will not only give moral strength to the Iranian Government but will also serve as the best answer to insidious communistic propaganda among the masses.

Joint Statement Following Discussions with the Shah of Iran

December 30, 1949

His Imperial Majesty, Mohammed Reza Pahlevi, Shahinshah of Iran, today completed his tour of the United States and departed for Iran. The Shah came to this country at the invitation of the President and his visit has enabled him to become acquainted at first hand with the United States and its institutions. The President said today that the existing friendly relations with Iran have been strengthened still further by the Shah's visit. The President is most happy that His Majesty has paid the United States the honor of this visit, which enabled not only the President but many officials of the Government, as well as the American people, more clearly to know and understand Iran, its great traditions, and its present achievements and objectives.

Following a stay of several days in Washington, the Shah visited many parts of the country and inspected various institutions and industrial and agricultural enterprises whose technical operation might be usefully applied in Iran. He also saw military, naval, and air installations. His Majesty had the opportunity of meeting civic, industrial and educational leaders, as well as other representatives of broad segments of the American population.

While in Washington His Majesty had conversations with the President, the Secretary of State and other senior officials of the United States Government. These conversations took place in an atmosphere of frankness and cordiality, and the interchange of views was most valuable in arriving at a mutual understanding of problems in which both the United States and Iran have interest. Pursuant to these conversations His Majesty and the President have decided to issue the following joint statement on the relations between the two countries:

"His Imperial Majesty, the Shah of Iran, and the President of the United States have examined the relations between their two countries and the problems which they face in common. In the course of their conversations it has been brought out that:

"1. They believe the United Nations offers the best means of assuring a peaceful world. Both countries will continue to give the United Nations their unfaltering support and to work in close cooperation with it and its agencies.

"2. A serious threat to international peace and security anywhere in the world is of direct concern to the United States. As long ago as December 1, 1943, when President Roosevelt, Prime Minister Churchill, and Marshal Stalin signed the Three Power Declaration at Tehran, the United States made clear its desire for the maintenance of the independence and integrity of Iran. The great interest of the United States in this regard has been repeatedly affirmed in its foreign policy declarations and the United States Government intends to continue that policy.

"3. His Imperial Majesty believes, and the President concurs, that the ability of any country to maintain its independence is based on a sound and prosperous economy. For this reason, as far back as 1946, upon His Majesty's advice, the Iranian Government took steps to prepare a Seven-Year Plan for economic and social progress which now, embodied into law, is being carried out with all the means at the Government's disposal. The President appreciates the importance of this program to the economic development of Iran, and applications by the Iranian Government to the International Bank for Reconstruction and Development for economically justifiable loans to be used in the furtherance of the program will therefore receive the support of the United States. Subject to favorable Congressional action on the Point IV program, the United States also stands ready to facilitate Iranian economic development through the provision under Point IV and otherwise of technical advisory assistance if requested by Iran. His Majesty welcomes the assistance envisaged under the Point IV program and is particularly aware of the desirability of increased investments of private capital in the Iranian economy. The Iranian Government will consider measures to be taken to encourage such investments.

"4. It is the policy of the United States to help free peoples everywhere in the maintenance of their freedom wherever the aid which it is able to provide can be effective. As the result of recent Congressional authorization, and in response to the request of the government of Iran, the Government of the United States is currently prepared to offer certain military assistance essential to enable Iran, as a nation dedicated to the purposes and principles of the United Nations Charter, to develop effective measures for its self-defense in support of those purposes and principles. The United States will continue to bear in mind Iran's defense needs in connection with further foreign assistance which may be considered by the United States Government."

**Mutual Defense Assistance Agreement between
the United States and Iran**

May 23, 1950   *Agreement effected by exchange of notes signed at
Washington.*
May 23, 1950   *Entered into force.*

The Acting Secretary of State (Webb) to the
Iranian Chargé d'Affaires ad interim (Aram)

Department of State
Washington, May 23, 1950

SIR: I refer to the conversations which have recently taken place between the representatives of our two Governments concerning the transfer of military assistance by the Government of the United States of America to the Government of Iran pursuant to Public Law 329, Eighty-first Congress of the United States of America, and to confirm the understandings reached as a result of those conversations as follows:

1. The Government of the United States of America, recognizing this principle that economic recovery is essential to international peace and security and must be given clear priority, undertakes to make or continue to make available to the Government of Iran on a grant basis such equipment, materials and services as the Government of the United States of America may authorize. The furnishing of any such assistance as may be authorized pursuant hereto shall be consistent with the Charter of the United Nations and shall be subject to all of the applicable terms and conditions and termination provisions of the Mutual Defense Assistance Act of 1949 and such other applicable laws of the United States of America relating to the transfer of military assistance. The two governments will, from time to time, negotiate detailed arrangements necessary to carry out the provisions of this paragraph.

2. The Government of Iran undertakes to make effective use of assistance received pursuant to paragraph 1 for the purposes for which such assistance was furnished and will not devote such assistance to purposes other than those for which it was furnished in accordance with these understandings.

3. In the common security interest of both governments, the Government of Iran undertakes not to transfer to any person not an officer or agent of such government or to any other nation title to or possession of any equipment, materials or services received on a grant basis pursuant to paragraph 1, without the prior consent of the Government of the United States of America.

4. The Government of Iran, after giving due consideration to reasonable requirements for domestic use and commercial export of Iran, which are to be determined by the Iranian Government itself, agrees to

facilitate the production, transport, export and transfer to the Government of the United States of America, for such period of time, in such quantities and upon such terms and conditions as to the value, method of payment, et cetera, as may be agreed upon, of raw and semi-processed materials required by the United States of America as a result of deficiencies or potential deficiencies in its own resources, and which may be available in Iran.

5. (a) The Government of Iran will take appropriate measures which are not inconsistent with security and the interests of the country to keep the public informed of operations pursuant to these understandings.

(b) Each government will take such security measures as may be agreed in each case between the two governments in order to prevent the disclosure or compromise of materials, services or information furnished by the other government pursuant to these understandings.

6. The Government of Iran, except as may otherwise be agreed between the two governments, shall grant duty-free treatment and exemption from internal taxation on importation or exportation to products, property, materials or equipment imported into its territory in connection with this understanding.

7. The Government of Iran agrees to receive technical personnel of the Government of the United States of America who will discharge in its territory the responsibilities of the Government of the United States of America for implementing the provisions of these understandings and to accord them necessary facilities to observe the progress of assistance furnished pursuant thereto.

8. The two governments will, upon request to either of them, negotiate appropriate arrangements between them respecting responsibility for patent or similar claims based on the use of devices, processes, technological information or other forms of property protected by law in connection with equipment, material or services furnished pursuant to paragraph 1. In such negotiations, this point shall be considered: that each government will assume the responsibility for all such claims of its nationals and such claims arising in its jurisdiction of nationals of any third country.

9. The two governments will, upon the request of either of them, consult regarding any matter relating to the application of these understandings or to operations or arrangements carried out pursuant to these understandings.

10. Nothing herein shall be construed to alter, amend or otherwise modify the agreements between the United States of America and Iran, signed at Tehran November 27, 1943, and October 6, 1947, as amended or extended.

I propose that, if these understandings meet with the approval of the Government of Iran, this note and your note concurring therein will be considered as confirming these understandings, effective on the date of your note and thereafter until one year after the date of receipt by either Government of a notification in writing of the intention of the other Government to terminate these understandings.

Accept, Sir, the renewed assurances of my high consideration.

JAMES E. WEBB

The Iranian Chargé d'Affairs ad interim (Aram) to the Acting Secretary of State (Webb)

Iranian Embassy
Washington, D.C., May 23, 1950

EXCELLENCY: . . . I have the honor to concur in the proposals made in your note and to inform you that the understandings set forth therein meet with the approval of the Government of Iran. That note and the present note, accordingly, are considered as confirming these understandings, effective on this date and thereafter until one year after the date of receipt by either Government of a notification in writing of the intention of the other Government to terminate these understandings.

I avail myself of this opportunity to renew to Your Excellency the assurances of my highest consideration.

G. ARAM

State Department Announcement of Point Four Project in Iran

Press Release   *October 19, 1950*

The first comprehensive technical cooperation project under the new Point 4 Program—an integrated health, agriculture, and education project for improving living conditions in rural villages in Iran—was announced today by the Governments of Iran and the United States.

The project, to be undertaken at the request of the Government of Iran, will be carried out under authority of the Act for International Development (Public Law 535) recently enacted by the Eighty-first Congress.

Supervision of the cooperative program will be exercised by an Iranian-U.S. Joint Commission for Rural Improvement, composed of four representatives of the Government of Iran and three representatives of the Government of the United States, with an Iranian member as chairman. The Commission will designate a technical director for the project and will determine what personnel and facilities are required for each country.

The United States has allocated $500,000 for technical cooperation in Iran from the Point 4 appropriation for the current fiscal year. It is expected that the rural improvement program will require $300,000 between now and June 30, 1951, with the remaining $200,000 being available for expansion of this program or for undertaking other technical cooperation projects in Iran.

The Iranian Government will contribute personnel, land, buildings, and locally produced equipment to the cooperation program, in addition to funds for operating expenses. The United States will provide the services of agricultural, health, and educational experts and equipment not produced in Iran.

An integrated program with major emphasis on health, agriculture, and education will be carried out by American and Iranian personnel working together in rural villages near the principal centers of population. These centers will serve as demonstration and training areas, in which action programs will be carried out both to improve the living conditions and productivity of the inhabitants and to train Iranian teachers and demonstration agents who can apply the same methods in other villages.

Each demonstration area will be a nucleus from which the techniques for increasing food production, reducing disease, raising the education level, and otherwise improving the living conditions of the people will be gradually extended to other villages throughout Iran. These activities are essential to the general economic development of the country.

The first demonstration center will be established immediately and three more are expected to be in operation by next June 30. It is expected that 10 such centers will be in operation by June 30, 1952. . . .

4

The Nationalist Groundswell

It was not long after Iran and the United States had concluded the Mutual Defense Agreement that a controversy erupted which was to have a profound and long-lasting effect on the ties between the two countries. That controversy concerned the nationalization of the Anglo-Iranian Oil Company.

This quarrel was one which the United States probably wished had never broken out, for it involved a NATO partner on the one hand and a country of growing importance for U.S. policy on the other. It also brought to the forefront of Iranian politics Dr. Mohammed Mossadeq, an ardent nationalist, who had been chairman of the Oil Committee of the Majlis, and who had actually proposed the nationalization policy. The oil nationalization bill was passed by the Majlis and the Senate in March of 1951 and was given the royal assent of the Shah, who did not have the right of veto. The next month Mossadeq became Prime Minister, and thus bore chief responsibility for implementing the legislation which he was so instrumental in having adopted.

For Iran, the most important objective in this crisis was to establish title to her own resources, and in this aim she was eventually successful. Britain took Iran to the International Court of Justice on the seizure, but

Iran refused to recognize the court's jurisdiction. The court decided that it did not, in fact, have jurisdiction, and in effect upheld Iran's position.

When Iran won this victory, Prime Minister Mossadeq was riding the crest of his popularity. All shades of opinion in Iran that had any claim to the nationalist label wanted to extirpate foreign influence as embodied in the Anglo-Iranian Oil Company. Yet such was Iranian ambivalence that many who favored the seizure of the Anglo-Iranian Oil Company were apparently prepared to accept foreign influence as represented by the United States, particularly if this country would come to Iran's aid, operate the oil industry, and purchase Iranian production.

The traditional Iranian tactic of playing off foreign powers against each other may have been another factor in this mix. Some believed that the United States would come to Iran's aid in order to complete the expulsion of the British, while others assumed that the United States would have to assist Iran to prevent the Iranians from requesting help from the Soviet Union in operating the oil installations. This latter belief was buttressed by the emphasis given in both the United States and Britain to the importance of Iranian oil to the Western world.

As it was, the United States had to steer a tricky course between Iran and Britain. The U.S. was not unsympathetic with Iran's nationalist aspirations, but Britain was our most important ally. Besides, there was always the possibility that Iran's action would touch off a chain of nationalizations in other oil producing countries. For these reasons the United States urged compromise on both parties.

Negotiations did go forward and at one point a solution seemed possible, but in the end they failed. In the three years that followed until a settlement was finally reached, the Iranian oil industry was idle for all practical purposes. There were few foreign buyers, and the shortfall in Iranian production was quickly made good by increased production elsewhere. The result was increased suffering for Iran and increased political opposition for Mossadeq.

As his support slipped away, Mossadeq's relations with the United States became increasingly strained. Disappointed that the United States had not sided with Iran, he appealed to the incoming President, Eisenhower, for support. This correspondence is printed in the ensuing chapter. He asked for American assistance in the sale of Iranian oil and, failing that, for economic assistance to exploit Iran's other resources. He hinted broadly that if such assistance were not forthcoming Iran might go communist.

In playing the communist card, Mossadeq not only overreached himself, he was actually going against his nationalist principles. Moreover, this tactic simply served to ensure U.S. opposition by persuading those in authority that the situation was getting out of control and that if Mossadeq remained in power Iran might in fact fall under Soviet domination.

As his power declined, Mossadeq became more dictatorial, thus further shrinking his support. In August 1953 he ordered a plebiscite to dissolve the Majlis. The Shah then appointed a new prime minister, but Mossadeq refused to recognize him and took control of the army, the main prop of the Shah's regime. The Shah fled the country, but his exile was short-lived. Street rioters called for his return and for the ouster of Mossadeq, and both were accomplished within a few days. The United States has often been accused of complicity in this turn of events. Whatever the facts, there is no doubt that from this time until his downfall, a quarter of a century later, U.S. policy in Iran was inextricably linked with the government and policies of the Shah.

While all of these events were occurring, so was the ordinary intercourse of U.S.-Iranian relations. The American military mission was continued, and additional Point Four programs were inaugurated, as the documents show. It thus seems fair to say that during this period of national upsurge the United States believed it was acting as a friend of Iran, even if it could not fully accept all the policies of the Iranian government.

THE ANGLO-IRANIAN OIL DISPUTE

Statement by the Department of State on the United States Position Regarding Oil Negotiations

May 18, 1951

The United States is deeply concerned by the dispute between the Iranian and British Governments over Iranian oil. We are firm friends of both Iran and Great Britain and are sincerely interested in the welfare of each country. The United States wants an amicable settlement to this dispute, which is serious not only to the parties directly concerned but also to the whole free world. We have followed the matter closely and have told both countries where we stand. The views which we have expressed have related to the broad aspects of the problem, as it has not been appropriate for us to advise with respect to specific terms of arrangements which might be worked out.

Since the United States attitude has been the subject of some speculation, it is deemed advisable to describe the position which we have taken in our talks with representatives of Iran and Great Britain.

We have stressed to the Governments of both countries the need to solve the dispute in a friendly way through negotiation and have urged them to avoid intimidation and threats of unilateral action.

In our talks with the British Government, we have expressed the opinion that arrangements should be worked out with the Iranians which give recognition to Iran's expressed desire for greater control over and benefits from the development of its petroleum resources. While the United States has not approved or disapproved the terms of any particular British proposal, it is pleased to note a sincere desire on the part of the British to negotiate with the Iranians on all outstanding issues.

We fully recognize the sovereign rights of Iran and sympathize with Iran's desire that increased benefits accrue to that country from the development of its petroleum. In talks with the Iranian Government, we have pointed out the serious effect of any unilateral cancellation of clear contractual relationships which the United States strongly opposes. We have stressed the importance of the Iranians achieving their legitimate objectives through friendly negotiation with the other party, consistent with their international responsibilities. This would have the advantage of maintaining confidence in future commercial investments in Iran and, indeed, in the validity of contractual arrangements all over the world.

Iran has been urged, before it takes final action, to analyze carefully the practical aspects of this problem. In this connection, we have raised the question of whether or not the elimination of the established British oil company from Iran would in fact secure for Iran the greatest possible benefits. We have pointed out that the efficient production and refining of Iranian oil requires not only technical knowledge and capital but transport and marketing facilities such as those provided by the company. We have also pointed out that any uncertainty as to future availability of Iranian supplies would cause concern on the part of customers which might lead to shifts in their source of supply with a consequent decreased revenue to Iran.

Those United States oil companies which would be best able to conduct operations such as the large-scale and complex industry in Iran have indicated to this Government that they would not in the face of unilateral action by Iran against the British company be willing to undertake operations in that country. Moreover, petroleum technicians of the number and competence required to replace those presently in Iran are not, due to extreme shortages of manpower in this specialized field, available in this country or in other countries.

The United States believes that Iran and Great Britain have such a strong mutuality of interests that they must and will find some way, through friendly negotiation, of reestablishing a relationship which will permit each party to play its full role in the achievement of their common objectives. Through such negotiation it is felt that Iran's basic desires and interests can best be realized, the legitimate British interests preserved, and the essential flow of Iranian oil into the markets of the free world maintained.

The United States has repeatedly expressed its great interest in the continued independence and territorial integrity of Iran and has given and will continue to give concrete evidence of this interest.

The American Ambassador at Tehran to the Iranian Minister for Foreign Affairs Stressing United States Nonintervention

[AIDE-MÉMOIRE]

May 26, 1951

The aide-mémoire of His Excellency, the Minister for Foreign Affairs of Iran, which was handed to the American Ambassador in Tehran on May 21, has been carefully considered by the Government of the United States.

It is unfortunate that the public statement made by this Government on May 18, has been misconstrued by the Iranian Government as intervention in the internal affairs of Iran. The United States wishes to make it clear that it did not then intend, nor does it now intend, to interfere in the internal affairs of Iran, nor to oppose Iran's sovereign rights or the expressed desires of the Iranian Government in regard to control of Iranian resources.

There is, however, legitimate basis for deep and proper interest on the part of this Government in a solution of the oil problem in Iran. A serious controversy exists between Iran and Great Britain, a controversy which could undermine the unity of the free world and seriously weaken it. The United States is bound to both countries by strong ties of friendship and has attested its sincere concern for the well-being of both. It has, therefore, in view of the importance of the matter, discussed the issues with both parties and has stated publicly the principles it considers important in reaching a solution of this controversy.

The United States continues in its firm belief that an issue of this kind can be settled satisfactorily only by negotiation by the parties concerned. While the United States has urged upon both parties the need for moderation, it has taken no position on details of any arrangement which might be worked out. It has, however, reaffirmed its stand against unilateral cancellation of contractual relationships and actions of a confiscatory nature. The United States is convinced that through negotiation a settlement can be found which will satisfy the desires of the Iranian people to control their own resources, which will protect legitimate British interests and which will assure uninterrupted flow of Iranian oil to its world markets. Such a settlement is, in the opinion of this Government, of the utmost importance not only to the welfare of the two powers concerned but to that of the entire free world. The United States wishes to state again its deep interest in the welfare of the

Iranian people and in the maintenance of the independence and territorial integrity of Iran, which is a cardinal principle of United States
policy.

Exchange between Prime Minister Mossadegh and
President Truman on the Breakdown of Oil Negotiations

July 8, 1951

MY DEAR MR. PRIME MINISTER: I am most grateful to Your Excellency for giving me in your recent letter a full and frank account of the
developments in the unhappy dispute which has arisen between your
government and the British oil interests in Iran. This matter is so full of
dangers to the welfare of your own country, of Great Britain and of all
the free world, that I have been giving the most earnest thought to the
problems involved. I had hoped that the common interests of the two
countries directly involved and the common ground which has been
developed in your discussions would open the way to a solution of the
troublesome and complicated problems which have arisen. You know
of our sympathetic interest in this country in Iran's desire to control its
natural resources. From this point of view we were happy to see that the
British Government has on its part accepted the principle of nationalization.

Since British skill and operating knowledge can contribute so
much to the Iranian oil industry I had hoped—and still hope—that
ways could be found to recognize the principle of nationalization and
British interests to the benefit of both. For these reasons I have watched
with concern the breakdown of your discussions and the drift toward a
collapse of oil operations with all the attendant losses to Iran and the
world. Surely this is a disaster which statesmanship can find a way to
avoid.

Recently I have come to believe that the complexity of the problems
involved in a broad settlement and the shortness of the time available
before the refinery must shut down—if the present situation continues—require a simple and practicable *modus vivendi* under which
operations can continue and under which the interests of neither side
will be prejudiced. Various suggestions to this end have failed. The time
available is running out.

In this situation a new and important development has occurred.
The International Court of Justice, which your Government, the British Government and our own all joined with other nations to establish
as the guardian of impartial justice and equity has made a suggestion
for a modus vivendi.

Technical considerations aside, I lay great stress on the action of the
Court. I know how sincerely your Government and the British Government believe in the positions which you both have taken in your

discussions. However, I am sure you believe even more profoundly in the idea of a world controlled by law and justice which has been the hope of the world since the San Francisco Conference. Apart from questions of jurisdiction no one will doubt the impartiality of the World Court, its eminence and the respect due to it by all nations who signed the United Nations treaty.

Therefore, I earnestly commend to you a most careful consideration of its suggestion. I suggest that its utterance be thought of not as a decision which is or is not binding depending on technical legal considerations, but as a suggestion of an impartial body, dedicated to justice and equity and to a peaceful world based upon these great conceptions. A study of its suggestion by your Government and by the British Government will, I am sure, develop methods of implementing it which will carry out its wise and impartial purpose—maintaining the operation of the oil industry and preserving the positions of both Governments. Surely no government loses any element of its sovereignty or the support of its people by treating with all possible consideration and respect the utterance of this great court. Our own government and people believe this profoundly. Should you take such a position I am sure that the stature of Iran would be greatly enhanced in the eyes of the world.

I have a very sincere desire, Mr. Prime Minister, to be as helpful to you as possible in this circumstance. I have discussed this matter at length with Mr. W. Averell Harriman who as you know is one of my closest advisers and one of our most eminent citizens. Should you be willing to receive him I should be happy to have him go to Tehran as my personal representative to talk over with you this immediate and pressing situation.

May I take this opportunity to assure Your Excellency of my highest consideration and to convey to you my confidence in the future well-being and prosperity of Iran.

HARRY S TRUMAN

July 11, 1951

DEAR MR. PRESIDENT: I have the honor to acknowledge receipt of your friendly message of 8th July handed to me by His Excellency the Ambassador of the United States in Teheran just after the government of Iran had taken its decision with regard to the findings of the International Court of Justice at The Hague. I deem it my duty to thank you once again, Mr. President, for the care you have always taken in the welfare of this country.

As I mentioned in my previous letter, the government and people of Iran recognize the government and the people of the United States as the staunch supporters of right and justice and appreciate therefore, with complete sincerity, the interest you are taking in the solution of the economic difficulties of Iran in general and in the oil question in particular.

I am extremely glad to note your reference, Mr. President, to the sympathy and interest of the American Nation in the realization of Iran's national aspirations and the acceptance of the principle of nationalization of the oil industry; for Iran has had and is having no aim other than the acceptance of this principle by virtue of the laws ratified by the two Houses of Parliament, and has always been ready, within the terms of these laws to take any measures for the removal of the present disputes. It is, therefore, a matter of great regret that, insofar as Iran can judge, no proposal or suggestion has been made, up to the present, by the former oil company denoting their acceptance of the principle of nationalization of the oil industry in accordance with the laws ratified by the Parliament—laws which the government is duty bound to put into force. On the contrary, in their note of 29th June, the representatives of the former oil company made proposals which were against the provisions of these laws and which resulted in the termination of the discussions.

Provided, of course, that our indisputable national rights are respected in accordance with the laws concerning the nationalization of the oil industry, the government and the people of Iran are ready to enter into immediate discussions with the aim to remove all the disputes so that there may be no stoppage in the production and exploitation of oil—a situation which the government of Iran has always been anxious to avoid and which, as you have mentioned, Mr. President, is causing losses to all concerned.

With reference to your desire, Mr. President, to help our country I must state without hesitation that the Iranian nation and government fully appreciate this high intent in all sincerity and candor, more so when they find that you have shown your readiness, Mr. President, to send to Teheran as your Special Representative, Mr. Averell Harriman, one of the most distinguished American citizens, for consultations.

In the light of our knowledge of Mr. Harriman's personality and his vast experiences, and considering the fact that he will act as your representative, the Iranian government welcomes this gesture and hopes to take full advantage of consultations with a man of such high standing. In the meanwhile it would also give him the opportunity to become directly acquainted with our views and to obtain first hand knowledge of our living conditions and requirements.

May I avail myself of this opportunity to offer you, Mr. President, the expressions of my best and most sincere regards.

MOHAMMED MOSADEQ

Observations on the Iranian Position in the Oil Controversy:
Note from the President's Special Representative
(W. Averell Harriman) to the Prime Minister of Iran

September 15, 1951

Your Excellency's message of September 12 has been communicated to me by the Iranian Ambassador. I share your regret that the discussions between the Iranian Government and the British delegation under Lord Privy Seal Stokes did not culminate in an agreement upon a settlement of the oil controversy. I know that the continued interruption to the production and shipment of Iranian oil imposes a very considerable hardship upon the economy of Iran as it does upon the economy of Great Britain. The United States and the entire free world looked anxiously upon these discussions in the hope that some solution could be found which would satisfy the legitimate interests of both parties.

I assure Your Excellency that I continue to stand ready to assist in any way that I can in finding a just solution. In my efforts thus far I have endeavored to be frank and objective in the advice that I have given to the Iranian Government, as well as to the British Government. It is in this objective and friendly spirit, and in an effort to be helpful to you in arriving at a settlement, that I should like to comment upon the substance of your communication.

With reference to the proposals in general, I should say at the outset that they appear to be the same as proposals made by the Iranian Government during the course of the negotiations in Tehran, which the British Mission did not accept since they did not conform to practical and commercial aspects of the international oil industry. In some respects the proposals in fact represent a retrogression from the positions taken during the discussions.

Your Excellency has suggested that the various departments of the Anglo-Iranian Oil Company be retained; insofar as this does not conflict with the terms of the Nationalization Law, and that the managers and other responsible personnel of the technical sections be employed in the National Oil Company of Iran with the same authority which they enjoyed previously. You have also stated that the Iranian Government is prepared to create a mixed executive board composed of Iranian and neutral foreign technicians who would jointly manage the administrative and technical affairs of the National Oil Company of Iran.

In discussing this possiblity during the negotiations in Tehran, I endeavored to point out to the Iranian representatives the impracticability of attempting to operate a large and complex industry on the basis of a number of section heads reporting to a board of directors, with no single individual being given executive authority. I believe that no organization can operate effectively in this manner and I understood Mr. Stokes' position in Tehran to be that the British would not consider it workable. Moreover, I have pointed out that effective operations, particularly of a refinery of the size and complexity of that in Abadan, require the employment of an integrated organization rather than the employment of individual foreign specialists. Competent technicians would not themselves consent to employment except under conditions satisfactory to them. Such conditions would include assurance that the industry was under capable management and operated in a manner which would assure safety and efficiency.

Your Excellency has expressed concern that the arrangements for the operation of the oil industry must take into account the requirements of the Nationalization Law. I am convinced that arrangements are possible which would meet this objective and at the same time would assure that the oil industry is conducted on an efficient basis. During our visit in Tehran Mr. Levy and I discussed with Iranian officials arrangements under which a competent organization could be employed to operate under the control of the National Oil Company of Iran. Such arrangements are a common business practice throughout the world.

Your Excellency has reiterated that the Iranian Government has not intended and does not intend to confiscate the property of the Anglo-Iranian Oil Company and has suggested methods for the determination of the amount of compensation.

While I have no comments upon your suggestions for determining the value of the assets, it is obvious that payment of compensation must depend upon and will be affected by arrangements for the efficient operation of the oil industry to assure that the products continue to be made available for sale to world markets. As I have pointed out to Your Excellency, in the view of the United States Government the seizure by any government of foreign-owned assets without either prompt, adequate and effective compensation or alternative arrangements satisfactory to the former owners is, regardless of the intent, confiscation rather than nationalization. There must be more than a willingness to pay; there must be the ability to do so in an effective form. I believe, however, that if arrangements for the sale of oil are made with the British interests the compensation problem could be worked out satisfactorily and that the net oil income accruing to Iran could be as large as that of any other oil-producing country under comparable circumstances.

Your Excellency has stated that the Iranian Government is prepared to sell to the British ten million tons of oil per year, this quantity representing an estimate of Iranian oil previously used in Great Britain. It is specified that sales would be at prevailing international prices on the basis of the f.o.b. value at Iranian ports. It is also stated that this oil would be delivered to any company or transport agency designated by the British.

As I pointed out to Your Excellency in Tehran, in order to be assured of continuous sales of substantial quantities of its oil in world markets Iran must make arrangements with customers that can make available large transportation and distribution facilities for marketing it on a world-wide basis. Potential customers would not make such arrangements unless they could obtain Iranian oil on a basis as favorable as that on which they could buy or develop oil in other producing countries. This, of course, is a practical business consideration. It is also true that only those who have developed markets for Iranian oil are in a position to commit themselves for its purchase in the large quantities produced.

[HARRIMAN]

Joint Chiefs of Staff Memorandum for the Secretary of Defense
Subject: The Anglo-Iranian Problem

October 10, 1951

1. This memorandum is in response to your memorandum, dated 8 October 1951, on the above subject.

2. If Iran passes to the domination of the USSR, the following consequences are to be expected:

a. Immediate loss of Iranian oil and probable eventual loss of all Middle East Oil with the consequent greatly increased and possible intolerable deficiency in oil resources;

b. Demonstration of the strength of the Soviet system and of the weak position of the Western World in opposition thereto;

c. Expansion of the Soviet empire to the Persian Gulf and the Indian Ocean;

d. Major threat to the position of Afghanistan, Pakistan, and India;

e. The almost inevitable collapse of Afghanistan to Communism;

f. Such enhancement of the Soviet position in the Middle East as to increase greatly the danger of Communist domination during peacetime of Pakistan, Iraq, Saudi Arabia, and India; and in the event of war to permit prepositioning of USSR military forces with oil immediately available which would greatly increase the chances of their military success against the Middle East and/or Pakistan-India; and

g. Turkey would be so flanked and uncovered as greatly to threaten its military position.

3. If Iran comes under Soviet domination in peacetime:

a. The Truman Doctrine would be breached;

b. The USSR would be provided with a springboard for domination of the entire Middle East, including the Eastern Mediterranean and the Suez Canal areas; prior development by the USSR of bases, facilities, and military stockpiles (including oil) would permit the Soviets to advance greatly any time table for military operations against the Middle East and/or Pakistan-India; and

c. The USSR would be permitted to develop facilities for delivery of Iranian oil to the territory of the USSR.

4. If the Iranian oil problem results in the complete denial to the British of any stake in Iranian oil, the position and prestige of the United Kingdom in the Middle East and possibly throughout the world would, in all probability, be further weakened. Events in Iran cannot be separated from the world situation and specifically from developments in Egypt.

5. The following is responsive to the three specific questions in the third paragraph of your memorandum:

a. If Iranian oil should fall to the USSR a greater and, in all probability, a longer effort by the Western Powers would be required to bring about the defeat of the USSR and its satellites;

b. Whether or not any alteration of our strategic targets would be required in the eventuality of control of Iranian oil by the USSR would depend largely upon the length of time available to and the scale of effort by the Soviets for development of facilities for delivery of that oil to the USSR; and

c. If the USSR achieves control of Iran in peacetime, the Soviet power position (including its logistical position) would be so improved that, in all probability, an increase in the level of the military establishments of the Western World would be required.

6. The Joint Chiefs of Staff consider that the United States should take most energetic measures, as a matter of urgency, to support or arrive at the achievement of a solution of the Iranian problem which will:

a. Provide for the continued orientation of Iran toward the Western World (this should receive overriding priority);

b. Make possible an effective command organization for the defense of Iran in coordination with the other areas of the Middle East; and

c. Assure the continued supply of Iranian oil to the Western World, at least during peace.

Accordingly, they would support action which would achieve those objectives, such as an offer by the United States of its "good offices," as outlined in the first paragraph of your memorandum.

7. Strictly from the United States military point of view, Iran's orientation towards the United States in peacetime and maintenance of the British position in the Middle East now transcend in importance the desirability of supporting British oil interests in Iran. The Joint Chiefs of Staff would be forced immediately to re-examine their global strategy in the event that the USSR breached the Truman Doctrine in regard to Iran by measures short of war.

For the Joint Chiefs of Staff:
/s/   HOYT S. VANDENBERG
Chief of Staff, United States Air Force

Central Intelligence Agency Special Estimate:
The Current Crisis in Iran

March 16, 1951

CONCLUSIONS

1. The political situation in Iran has long been unstable. This instability has been increased by the assassination of Razmara, which has led to a new outburst of extreme nationalism, expressed in a vigorous demand for nationalization of oil resources of the Anglo-Iranian Oil Company.

2. We do not believe, however, that the situation is such that there is imminent danger of the government's losing control, barring armed intervention by the USSR. This estimate is based on the following considerations:

(a) Available information indicates that the Iranian armed forces, including the gendarmerie and police, are adequate to maintain order. There is no evidence to suggest that they are not under effective control of the government.

(b) The extreme nationalists have only a very small representation in the Majlis. Their popular following, though large and widespread, is nevertheless unorganized.

(c) The illegal pro-Soviet Tudeh Party is not believed to be capable of taking advantage of the current tension to gain control of the government or even seriously to disrupt the government's control.

(d) Although the main issue in the present crisis is nationalization of Iran's oil resources and although this issue has evoked overwhelming popular support, responsible government officials, led by the Shah, are aware of the difficulties involved in nationalization. Given the cooperation of the British, they may be expected to make a real effort to find a face-saving settlement with the Anglo-Iranian Oil Company.

3. Nevertheless, the possibility cannot be excluded that the situation may be aggravated and the crisis prolonged by an unyielding attitude on the part of the British, or by some unpredictable development such as assassination of the Shah. In such circumstances the opportunity might be created for an attempt by the Tudeh Party to seize power, or even for armed intervention by the USSR.

DISCUSSION

The Background of the Crisis

4. The assassination of Premier Razmara by a religious fanatic on 7 March and the ensuing period of uncertainty are direct results of the agitation for nationalization of the Anglo-Iranian Oil Company, which has been building up ever since the rejection by the Majlis in December

1950 of a revised concession agreement offered by the company. This agitation has been led by a very small group of ultra-nationalists in the Majlis known as the National Front. One of its leaders, the violently anti-British religious figure, Mulla Kashani, was reportedly implicated in the assassination, also by religious fanatics, of another high official in 1949.

5. Tension over the oil issue increased sharply in the period just preceding the assassination. The National Front stepped up its demands for nationalization, using that issue as a club to attack Razmara, whose attempts to provide strong government had run counter to its own attempts to gain a controlling influence. The National Front reportedly approached the British with an order to drop the nationalization issue entirely if the British would help get rid of Razmara in favor of a more acceptable Premier. The British, irritated with Razmara's failure to line up support for their position, delivered strong official warnings against any attempts at nationalization, meanwhile, however, indicating to Razmara that they were willing to grant a more generous concession agreement along the lines of that recently concluded by Saudi Arabia and the Arabian-American Oil Company. Razmara was persuaded to go before the Majlis Oil Commission with a statement prepared for him by the British emphasizing the practical difficulties of nationalization. In his presentation on 3 March, Razmara (to the irritation of the British) was careful to label the statement as one prepared by technical experts rather than his own. The statement, however, still brought down the wrath of the ultra-nationalists upon him and may well have furnished the immediate incentive (or pretext) for his murder.

The Development of the Crisis

6. The assassination produced no immediate repercussions. Tehran was quiet, with the public evidently unconcerned. The pro-Soviet Tudeh Party was evidently taken by surprise. The Shah, after briefly considering the invocation of martial law, decided against such a move and contented himself with the designation of an innocuous elder statesman as acting Premier.

7. This situation, however, soon changed. On the evening of 8 March the Majlis Oil Commission, under pressure from the exultant ultra-nationalists, unanimously passes a resolution endorsing nation-alization but asking a two-month extension for study of the practical problems involved. On the following morning the pro-Soviet element went into action with an anti-US and anti-UK demonstration outside the US Embassy, while in the afternoon Mulla Kashani held a mass meeting which, though orderly, was marked by inflammatory speeches denouncing the British and Razmara. The organization responsible for the murder, the Friends of Islam, threatened violence against other op-ponents of nationalization and indicated that reprisals would be forth-

coming if the assassin were not released. Although the provinces apparently continued to be quiet, and the government's control of the security forces was apparently unshaken, uneasiness in Tehran, particularly in political circles, mounted sharply. No one appeared capable of forming a strong government satisfactory to the Shah, and most of those who would normally have participated in such a government were deterred by fear of personal reprisal and by the sheer difficulty of coping with the question of nationalization. Proclamation of martial law would require approval of a demoralized Majlis, while dissolution of the Majlis involved a risk of increasing the tension. Under the circumstances, the Shah apparently decided to avoid a head-on clash with the ultra-nationalists, making do with a weak interim government until tension abated.

8. The situation has clarified somewhat during the last few days. Upon rejection by the Majlis on 11 March of the Shah's first choice for interim Premier, the Shah persuaded his widely respected Minister of Court, former Ambassador to the US Ala, to assume the premiership. Ala, who has been approved by both the Senate and the Majlis, is described as apparently "cheerful and optimistic" about what he regards as the task of effecting a reconciliation among the various factions, including Kashani's. Meanwhile, the impending adjournment of Parliament for the Noruz holidays offers a breathing spell, and it has been reported that the police have been quietly rounding up members of the reportedly small Friends of Islam group and of the Tudeh Party. At the same time, however, the unanimous Majlis vote in favor of the resolution on oil nationalization indicates that the National Front is determined to exploit its present psychological advantage. The Oil Commission has been granted a two-month extension to study the practical aspects of the problem. In addition, the warning note on nationalization which the UK has sent Iran may actually provoke rather than discourage further ultra-nationalist outbursts.

9. A major indication of the trend will be provided by Ala's presentation of his proposed Cabinet to the Majlis on 18 March.

Proposals for Settlement of the Controversy: Joint Message and Proposals from the President of the United States and the Prime Minister of the United Kingdom to the Prime Minister of Iran

August 30, 1952

To His Excellency Dr. Mohammad Mossadegh: We have reviewed the messages from our two Embassies in Iran regarding recent talks with you, as well as your communication of August 7, 1952, to the British Government. It seems clear to us, that to bring about a satisfactory solution to the oil problem will require prompt action by all three of our Governments. We are attaching proposals for action which our two Governments are prepared to take and which we sincerely hope will meet with your approval and result in a satisfactory solution. We are motivated by sincere and traditional feelings of friendship for the Iranian nation and people and it is our earnest desire to make possible an early and equitable solution of the present dispute.

HARRY S TRUMAN
WINSTON S. CHURCHILL

Proposals

1. There shall be submitted to the International Court of Justice the question of compensation to be paid in respect of the nationalization of the enterprise of the AIOC in Iran, having regard to the legal position of the parties existing immediately prior to nationalization and to all claims and counterclaims of both parties.

2. Suitable representatives shall be appointed to represent the Iranian Government and the AIOC in negotiations for making arrangements for the flow of oil from Iran to world markets.

3. If the Iranian Government agrees to the proposals in the foregoing two paragraphs, it is understood that (a) representatives of the AIOC will seek arrangements for the movement of oil already stored in Iran, and as agreements are reached upon price, and as physical conditions of loading permit, appropriate payments will be made for such quantities of oil as can be moved; (b) Her Majesty's Government will relax restrictions on exports to Iran and on Iran's use of sterling; and (c) the United States Government will make an immediate grant of $10 million to the Iranian Government to assist in their budgetary problem.*

---

* On Sept. 3, 1952, the Secretary of State pointed out at a press conference that "the purpose of this grant would be to provide Iran with funds for a short term to assist that nation financially until flow of Iranian oil to world markets could be resumed" (Department of State *Bulletin* Sept. 15, 1952, p. 406). On Sept. 24, 1952, Prime Minister Mossadegh rejected the proposals of Aug. 30, 1952, and made counter-proposals (*ibid.*, Oct. 6, 1952, pp. 532-535). On October 5, 1952, the American Ambassador at Tehran delivered to Prime Minister Mossadegh a message from the Secretary of State pointing out that the rejection had apparently been based on certain misunderstandings of the Anglo-American proposals, and correcting the misunderstandings concerning the management of the oil industry and the purchase of the oil produced (*ibid.*, Oct. 13, 1952, p. 569). On Oct. 7, 1952, Prime Minister Mossadegh replied saying that he had gratefully examined the explanations which were furnished with a view to removing the ambiguity of the joint message of Aug. 30, 1952, and that he had now proposed to the British Foreign Secretary that plenipotentiary representatives of the former Anglo-Iranian Oil Company be sent to Tehran to discuss the terms of his counter-proposals of Sept. 24, 1952, if the British Government would pay prior to the departure of the plenipotentiary representatives a sum of 20 million pounds (*ibid.*, Oct. 20, 1952, p. 624). There was no reply to this suggestion (*ibid*, Dec. 8, 1952, p. 894). The Department of State observed on Dec. 6, 1952, that as regards the purchase of oil from Iran by American nationals or American firms, it was the position of the U.S. Government that the decision on this point must be left to such individuals or firms as might be considering purchases. The legal risks involved were matters to be resolved by them (*ibid.*, Dec. 15, 1952, p. 946).

United States Attitude toward Purchase of Oil from Iran

Press Release 906

State Department
December 6, 1952

Questions have been raised regarding the present attitude of the U.S. Government toward the purchase of oil from Iran by American nationals or American firms. It would seem advisable at this time to clarify the Department's position on this matter.

Prior to the passing of the oil nationalization law in Iran, some 32 million tons or approximately 240 million barrels of oil and refined products were produced in that country and marketed per year. The gross income on royalties, taxes, and wages received by Iran exceeded 100 million dollars. As will be recognized at once, this constituted a vast commercial operation engaging the world's largest fleet of tankers and required the services of an enormous distributing and marketing organization.

Ever since the oil ceased to flow and the refinery at Abadan was shut down, the United States has made every effort to assist in resolving the differences between the parties to this dispute. The United States wished to see as rapidly as possible the resumption of Iran's revenue. Also in the interests of the entire free world, the United States wished to minimize the dislocation of a great industry and avoid the attendant waste in manpower and monetary resources.

Since the passing of the oil nationalization law in Iran the Anglo-Iranian Oil Company (AIOC) has turned to other sources for its supplies, and in the absence of an over-all settlement, facilities of the AIOC have not been available to move and market oil from Iran. The question of moving relatively small quantities of oil or oil products has seemed to us as of minor importance in comparison with the necessity to find some solution which could drive to the heart of the matter and result in resumption of large-scale movement of Iranian oil. Thus we believe that the relatively small amount of oil which could be moved without the assistance of large tanker fleets and distribution and marketing organization will not solve the problem nor enable Iran to benefit from significant revenues from its great resources. Indeed on occasions it has seemed to us more likely than not that such shipments with the attendant legal complexities involved could be harmful to a general settlement of the major problem.

Under present circumstances, this Government believes that the decision whether or not such purchases of oil from Iran should be made must be left to such individuals or firms as may be considering them, and to be determined upon their own judgment. The legal risks involved are matters to be resolved by the individuals or firms concerned.

The Department of State will continue to address itself to the main problem which is the resolution of the dispute so that the essential international principle of adequate and effective compensation may be given effect and Iran may again benefit from the large scale resumption of its oil production.

Exchange between Prime Minister Mossadegh and President-Elect Eisenhower on American Neutrality

January 9, 1953

MR. PRESIDENT ELECT: I take this opportunity to convey to you the cordial congratulations of the Iranian people on your election to the high office of President of the United States and to wish you every success in the carrying out of the important tasks which that office imposes.

I dislike taking up with you the problems of my country even before you assume office. I do so partly because of their urgency and partly because I have reason to believe that they have already been presented to you by those who may not share my concern for the future of Iran and its people.

It is my hope that the new administration which you will head will obtain at the outset a true understanding of the significance of the vital struggle in which the Iranian people have been engaging and assist in removing the obstacles which are preventing them from realizing their aspirations for the attainment of [omission] life as a politically and economically independent nation. For almost two years the Iranian people have suffered acute distress and much misery merely because a company inspired by covetousness and a desire for profit supported by the British Government has been endeavoring to prevent them from obtaining their natural and elementary rights.

I am happy to say that during this struggle so injurious to the people of Iran the American people on many occasions have demonstrated their sympathy for the Iranian nation and an understanding of its problems. I personally witnessed many manifestations of this sympathy and understanding when I was in the United States. Unfortunately the government of the United States while on occasions displaying friendship for Iran has pursued what appears to the Iranian people to be a policy of supporting the British Government and the former company. In this struggle it has taken the side of the British Government against that of Iran in international assemblies. It has given financial aid to the British Government while withholding it from Iran and it seems to us it has given at least some degree of support to the endeavors of the British to strangle Iran with a financial and economic blockade.

It is not my desire that the relations between the United States and the United Kingdom should be strained because of differences with regard to Iran. I doubt however whether in this day and age a great nation which has such an exalted moral standing in the world can afford to support the internationally immoral policy of a friend and ally merely in order not to disturb good relations with that friend and ally. The Iranian people merely desire to lead their own lives in their own way. They wish to maintain friendly relations with all other peoples. The former company which for years was engaged in exploiting their oil resources unfortunately persisted in interfering in the internal life of the country.

The Iranian people finally became convinced that so long as this company continued to operate within Iran its systematic interference in Iranian internal life would continue. The Iranian people therefore had no choice other than to exercise their sovereign rights by nationalizing their oil and terminating the activities of the former company in Iran. The Iranian Government made it clear at the time of nationalization that it was willing to pay fair compensation to the former company due consideration being given to such claims and counter claims as Iran might have against the former company. The former company instead of entering into negotiations with Iran for the purpose of determining the amount of compensation due took steps with the support of the British Government to create an economic and financial blockade of Iran with the purpose of forcing the Iranian people again to submit to the will of the former company and to abandon their right to exploit and utilize their own natural resources.

It is my sincere hope that when the new Administration of which you are to be the head will come into power in the United States it will give most careful consideration to the Iranian case so that Iran would be able to attain its just aspirations in a manner which will strengthen the cause of world peace and will renew confidence in the determination of the United States to support with all its power and prestige the principles of the charter of the United Nations.

Please accept the assurances of my high esteem.

DR. MOHAMMAD MOSSADEGH

January 10, 1953

HIS EXCELLENCY DR. MOHAMMAD MOSSADEGH: Please accept my thanks for your kind greetings and felicitations. Likewise I am happy to have a summary of your views on your country's situation and I shall study those views with care and with sympathetic concern. I hope you will accept my assurances that I have in no way compromised our position of impartiality in this matter and that no individual has attempted to prejudice me in the matter. This leads me to observe that I hope our own future relationships will be completely free of any suspicion, but on the contrary will be characterized by confidence and trust inspired by frankness and friendliness. I shall be delighted to receive either personally and directly or through established diplomatic channels at any time a communication regarding your views on any subject in which we may have a common interest.

With renewed thanks for the kindly courtesy of your message and with expression of my continued esteem.

Sincerely,   DWIGHT D. EISENHOWER

Exchange between Prime Minister Mossadegh and President Eisenhower on the Oil Dispute and the Problem of United States Aid to Iran

May 28, 1953

DEAR MR. PRESIDENT: In the kind reply which you sent to my message of last January you suggested that I might inform you direct or through diplomatic channels of any views that may be of mutual interest.

In that message I had briefly referred to the hardships and privations which the Iranian people had undergone during the last two years in their efforts to attain their aspirations and also to the difficulties which the British Government has created for Iran in its support of the illogical claims of an imperialistic company.

During the few months that have elapsed since the date of that message the Iranian people have been suffering financial hardships and struggling with political intrigues carried on by the former Oil Company and the British Government. For instance, the purchasers of Iranian oil have been dragged from one court to another, and all means of propaganda and diplomacy have been employed in order to place illegal obstacles in the way of the sale of Iranian oil. Although the Italian and Japanese courts have declared Iranian oil to be free and unencumbered, the British have not as yet abandoned their unjust and unprincipled activities.

Although it was hoped that during Your Excellency's administration attention of a more sympathetic character would be devoted to the Iranian situation, unfortunately no change seems thus far to have taken place in the position of the American Government.

In the message which the Secretary of State sent me from Karachi, he expressed regret that the efforts of the United States to contribute to the solution of the problem of compensation had thus far been unsuccessful. It should be recalled that the Iranian Government was prepared to pay the value of the former Company's properties in Iran in such amount as might be determined by the International Court of Justice. It was also prepared to accept the jurisdiction of the said court with regard to the amount of compensation provided the British Government would state the amount of its claim in advance and that claim would be within the bounds of reason. Obviously the Iranian Government also had certain claims against the former Oil Company and the British Government which would have been presented at the time of the hearing of the case.

The British Government, hoping to regain its old position, has in effect ignored all of these proposals.

As a result of actions taken by the former Company and the British Government, the Iranian nation is now facing great economic and political difficulties. There can be serious consequences, from an international viewpoint as well, if this situation is permitted to continue. If prompt and effective aid is not given this country now, any steps that might be taken tomorrow to compensate for the negligence of today might well be too late.

We are of course grateful for the aid heretofore granted Iran by the Government of the United States. This aid has not, however, been sufficient to solve the problems of Iran and to ensure world peace which is the aim and ideal of the noble people and of the Government of the United States.

The standard of living of the Iranian people has been very low as a result of century-old imperialistic policies, and it will be impossible to raise it without extensive programs of development and rehabilitation. Unfortunately the aid heretofore granted has been in principle primarily of a technical nature, and even in this respect the assistance needed has not at times been accorded. For example, the Export-Import Bank which was to have advanced Iran twenty-five million dollars for use in the sphere of agriculture did not do so because of unwarranted outside interference.

The Iranian nation hopes that with the help and assistance of the American Government the obstacles placed in the way of sale of Iranian oil can be removed, and that if the American Government is not able to effect a removal of such obstacles, it can render effective economic assistance to enable Iran to utilize her other resources. This country has natural resources other than oil. The exploitation of these resources would solve the present difficulties of the country. This, however, is impossible without economic aid.

In conclusion, I invite Your Excellency's sympathetic and responsive attention to the present dangerous situation of Iran, and I trust that you will ascribe to all the points contained in this message the importance due them.

Please accept, Mr. President, the assurance of my highest consideration.

DR. M. MOSSADEGH

June 29, 1953

DEAR MR. PRIME MINISTER: I have received your letter of May 28 in which you described the present difficult situation in Iran and expressed the hope that the United States might be able to assist Iran in overcoming some of its difficulties. In writing my reply which has been delayed until I could have an opportunity to consult with Mr. Dulles and Ambassador Henderson, I am motivated by the same spirit of friendly frankness as that which I find reflected in your letter.

The Government and people of the United States historically have cherished and still have deep feelings of friendliness for Iran and the Iranian people. They sincerely hope that Iran will be able to maintain its independence and that the Iranian people will be successful in realizing their national aspirations and in developing a contented and free nation which will contribute to world prosperity and peace.

It was primarily because of that hope that the United States Government during the last two years has made earnest efforts to assist in eliminating certain differences between Iran and the United Kingdom which have arisen as a result of the nationalization of the Iranian oil industry. It has been the belief of the United States that the reaching of an agreement in the matter of compensation would strengthen confidence throughout the world in the determination of Iran fully to adhere to the principles which render possible a harmonious community of free nations; that it would contribute to the strengthening of the international credit standing of Iran; and that it would lead to the solution of some of the financial and economic problems at present facing Iran.

The failure of Iran and of the United Kingdom to reach an agreement with regard to compensation has handicapped the Government of the United States in its efforts to help Iran. There is a strong feeling in the United States, even among American citizens most sympathetic to Iran and friendly to the Iranian people, that it would not be fair to the American taxpayers for the United States Government to extend any considerable amount of economic aid to Iran so long as Iran could have access to funds derived from the sale of its oil and oil products if a reasonable agreement were reached with regard to compensation whereby the large-scale marketing of Iranian oil would be resumed. Similarly, many American citizens would be deeply opposed to the purchase by the United States Government of Iranian oil in the absence of an oil settlement.

There is also considerable sentiment in the United States to the effect that a settlement based on the payment of compensation merely for losses of the physical assets of a firm which has been nationalized would not be what might be called a reasonable settlement and that an agreement to such a settlement might tend to weaken mutual trust between free nations engaged in friendly economic intercourse. Furthermore, many of my countrymen who have kept themselves informed regarding developments in this unfortunate dispute believe that, in view of the emotions which have been aroused both in Iran and the United Kingdom, efforts to determine by direct negotiation the amount of compensation due are more likely to increase friction than to promote understanding. They continue to adhere to the opinion that the most practicable and the fairest means of settling the question of compensation would be for that question to be referred to some neutral international body which could consider on the basis of merit all claims and counter-claims.

I fully understand that the Government of Iran must determine for itself which foreign and domestic policies are likely to be most advantageous to Iran and to the Iranian people. In what I have written, I am not trying to advise the Iranian Government on its best interests. I am merely trying to explain why, in the circumstances, the Government of the United States is not presently in a position to extend more aid to Iran or to purchase Iranian oil.

In case Iran should so desire, the United States Government hopes to be able to continue to extend technical assistance and military aid on a basis comparable to that given during the past year.

I note the concern reflected in your letter at the present dangerous situation in Iran and sincerely hope that before it is too late, the Government of Iran will take such steps as are in its power to prevent a further deterioration of that situation.

Please accept, Mr. Prime Minister, the renewed assurances of my highest consideration.

DWIGHT D. EISENHOWER

Exchange between President Eisenhower and the Shah of Iran Concerning the Settlement of the Oil Dispute

August 4, 1954

YOUR IMPERIAL MAJESTY: The important news that your Government, in negotiation with the British, French, Dutch and United States oil companies, has reached, in principle, a fair and equitable settlement to the difficult oil problem is indeed gratifying.

Your Majesty must take great satisfaction at the success of this significant phase in the negotiations to which you personally have made a valuable contribution. I am confident that implementation of this agreement, under Your Majesty's leadership, will mark the beginning of a new era of economic progress and stability for your country.

Like myself, all Americans have a deep concern for the well-being of Iran. With them I have watched closely your courageous efforts, your steadfastness over the past difficult years, and with them I too have hoped that you might achieve the goals you so earnestly desire. The attainment of an oil settlement along the lines which have been announced should be a significant step in the direction of the realization of your aspirations for your people.

There is concrete evidence of the friendship that exists between our two countries and of our desire that Iran prosper independently in the family of free nations. We have endeavored to be helpful in the form of economic and technical assistance and we are happy to have helped in finding a solution to the oil problem.

I can assure Your Majesty of the continued friendly interest of the United States in the welfare and progress of Iran, and of the admiration of the American people for your enlightened leadership.

With sincere best wishes for the health and happiness of Your Majesty and the people of Iran,

Sincerely,   DWIGHT D. EISENHOWER

August 9, 1954

MR. PRESIDENT: I am deeply grateful for your letter of August 5th [4th] and appreciate the friendly feelings which have inspired it.

It is, indeed, a source of satisfaction to me that my government has been able to arrive, in principle, at a settlement of the oil dispute, which, in the light of present world conditions, appears to be as equitable a solution of a difficult problem as could have been reached.

Ever since nationalization of the oil industry, which corresponded with the aspirations of my people, it has been my constant endeavor to facilitate and hasten a fair agreement within the framework of the relevant laws.

You can rest assured that the valuable contribution which you personally, Mr. President, The American Government and your distinguished Ambassador, Loy Henderson, have made to this end is highly prized.

It is now my hope that the implementation of the agreement will not be long delayed.

With the attainment of this goal and with increased American assistance, I share your feeling that we may look forward to an era of economic and social development which will improve the lot of my people, as well as further consolidate the security of the Middle East.

I cannot sufficiently lay stress on the fact that American assistance to Iran has been most timely and helpful. My people reciprocate to the full the friendship of your noble nation.

Whilst renewing the expression of my gratitude for your cooperation, I tender warm wishes for the welfare of the American people under your wise leadership.

Yours sincerely,   MOHAMMAD REZA PAHLAVI

MILITARY RELATIONS IN THE EARLY 1950s

Joint Chiefs of Staff Memorandum for the Secretary of Defense:
Continuation of the United States Military Mission with the
Iranian Army (ARMISH)

February 12, 1952

1. A memorandum dated 2 January 1952 states that the Joint Chiefs of Staff consider it in the security interests of the United States to continue military assistance to Iran, particularly through the U.S. Military Assistance Advisory Group (MAAG), and that negotiations for the renewal of the contracts for the U.S. Military Mission with the Iranian Army (ARMISH) and the U.S. Training Mission to the Iranian Gendarmerie (GENMISH) should not be allowed adversely to affect obtaining the assurances required by the Mutual Security Act of 1951 for the continuation of MAAG. These assurances have not been forthcoming, but the Joint Chiefs of Staff consider that the United States should persist in seeking legal ways and means to continue MAAG as a matter of priority.

2. It is recognized that it may be impossible to obtain the required assurances and MAAG may have to be eliminated. Under these circumstances, ARMISH would provide the only remaining vehicle of direct U.S. government influence on the military leaders of the Iranian Army.

3. The contract which governs the existence of ARMISH expires on 20 March 1952. One of the conditions guaranteed by the present contract is that the Government of Iran shall not engage the services of any personnel of any other foreign government for duty of any nature connected with the Iranian Army except as mutually agreed between the two governments. If the ARMISH contract is allowed to terminate, this influential position in Iran may be taken over by the USSR.

4. Due to Iran's desperate need for financial assistance, Prime Minister Mossadegh may be willing to accept an offer from the United States to provide financial support, in whole or in part, for the mission. The Joint Chiefs of Staff do not believe that ARMISH should be discontinued because of Iran's inability to support the mission financially. FY 52 budget funds for ARMISH are $122,760 in addition to normal pay and allowances. The Iranian Government, in accordance with the present contract, has been providing approximately $30,000 per month in extra pay and allowances for support to ARMISH in addition to rent-free office space. Assuming that United States provides complete financial support and agrees to the compensation now paid U.S. personnel by the Iranian Government necessary funds must be made available as they are not now included in either the FY 52 or FY 53 budget for ARMISH.

5. The Joint Chiefs of Staff prefer that ARMISH be continued at its present strength; however, it is possible that Iran will insist upon a reduction in strength. In this event, the United States should agree to a mission of sufficient size to represent effectively the interests of the United States. A reduced strength mission may well be used as a nucleus for increased operation when and if it becomes politically feasible. In this connection, it is felt that the importance of prestige in Iran requires a chief of mission of general officer rank and a minimum supporting staff.

6. A day-to-day agreement for the continuation of a military mission is not acceptable. This type of agreement would permit the present Iranian Government to use continually the retention of the mission as a lever to obtain financial and/or economic assistance. A day-to-day agreement would allow Iran to order withdrawal of our mission with little or no notice, creating a situation which could seriously damage the prestige of the United States.

Joint Chiefs of Staff Memorandum for the Secretary of Defense: Continuation of Military Assistance Advisory Group, (MAAG) Iran

March 19, 1952

1. The United States has three military missions in Iran. One mission is with the Imperial Iranian Gendarmerie whose contract expires 2 October 1952; the second mission is with the Iranian Army whose contract expires on 20 March 1952. Contract negotiations for the latter are now in progress, but there has been no indication on the part of the Iranian Government that it has any intention of renewing this contract. The third mission is the Military Assistance Advisory Group, Iran (MAAG-Iran).

2. The Iranian Government has failed to provide the assurances required by Section 511 (a) of the Mutual Security Act of 1951 (Public Law 165, 82nd Congress) in order to be eligible for military assistance and, as a result, the activities of MAAG-Iran have been suspended except for residual functions. Delivery of military grant aid en route to Iran by 8 January 1952 has been authorized; similarly, Iranian students who had departed Iran prior to 8 January 1952 have been authorized to complete their schooling in the United States and return to Iran. Personnel of MAAG-Iran are continuing to perform their assigned mission; however, no replacement of personnel has been authorized.

3. To preclude emergency action in the event that the present suspension of advisory activities should result in cancellation by the United States, the Office of Military Assistance (OMA)-Office of Secretary of Defense (OSD) requested the Department of the Army to prepare an orderly phase out plan. This plan contemplates that 25% of the

personnel will leave Iran prior to 1 May 1952; 50% prior to 1 July 1952; and the remainder by 20 August 1952 when the return of Iranian students will have been completed.

4. General Wayne C. Zimmerman, Chief, MAAG-Iran, states that there has been no indication by the Iranian Government that they expect the group to be withdrawn, and accordingly, requests information as to whether it can be legally maintained indefinitely.

5. The opinion presented to the Department of the Army by legal counsel, OMA-OSD, is that it is consistent with the provisions of the Mutual Security Act of 1951 for MAAG-Iran, to be maintained while there is reasonable possibility of obtaining the assurances required by Section 511(a) of the Mutual Security Act of 1951. This is based on the theory that the mere presence of MAAG-Iran is not "military assistance," but is being maintained pending negotiations for resumption of advisory activities and can be considered similar to a diplomatic mission. The Joint Chiefs of Staff do not believe that Congress intended, on the one hand, to terminate military grant aid and training of Iranian students and, on the other hand, to permit expenditure of Mutual Security Act and Defense funds to maintain MAAG-Iran indefinitely. However, in the opinion of OMA legal counsel, it was also pointed out that the basic question appears to be one of policy rather than of legality and the continued presence of Military Assistance Advisory Group personnel in Iran must be justified on military and political considerations.

6. The Joint Chiefs of Staff believe that it is in the security interests of the United States to find legal ways and means to continue MAAG-Iran. As the group is now constituted under the Mutual Defense Assistance Act of 1949 (Chap. 626, 63 Stat. 714) as amended (22 U.S.C. 1571-1604), its continued maintenance in Iran, pursuant to the Act, is unauthorized because of Iran's refusal to give the assurances required thereby. Further, there is no indication that the Iranian Government will furnish, in the foreseeable future, such assurances. Regardless of the legal aspects, to continue an advisory group in Iran without the assurances required may be the forerunner of pressures to provide military assistance to other countries who find the Mutual Security Act of 1951 not in accordance with their present interests.

7. It must be emphasized that, if legal ways and means are found prior to 20 August 1952, military assistance can be resumed. Lacking these means, the Joint Chiefs of Staff recommend that: (a) The plan for the phase-out of MAAG-Iran, commencing not later than 1 May 1952 and terminating by 20 August 1952, be approved, and the Joint Chiefs of Staff be authorized to implement it; and (b) the above information be forwarded to the Secretary of State and the Director of Mutual Security.

Joint Chiefs of Staff Memorandum for the Secretary of Defense:
Suspension of Military Assistance to Iran

April 9, 1952

1. Reference is made to your memorandum, subject as above, dated 14 February 1952, requesting that the Joint Chiefs of Staff recommend an alternate use of the FY 1952 funds for Iran to indicate necessary distribution of funds by country and military department.

2. The Joint Chiefs of Staff, feeling that the question of the disposition of previous programs for Iran is in some ways more important than redistribution of the FY 1952 program, have taken the liberty of broadening the scope of this reply to embrace the undelivered materiel of the earlier programs. The undelivered materiel of the earlier programs, almost in entirety, represents firm obligations to producers for equipment not yet completed for delivery. In lesser measure, this is also true of that portion of the FY 1952 funds made available for procurement under interim procedures. In light of the above, the Joint Chiefs of Staff invite attention to the fact that any redistribution of funds involves also the redistribution of a substantial portion of the associated materiel.

3. The Joint Chiefs of Staff have concluded that:

(a) Alternate plans for the use of Mutual Defense Assistance (MDA) FY 1952 funds presently allocated to Iran should be based on the transfer of the entire amount to fill, insofar as possible, the unsatisfied priority deficiencies in military equipment which exists in other Title II countries.

(b) In connection with the above-mentioned transfer to other Title II countries, there should be no redistribution of funds among the military departments.

(c) Any further delay in the resolution of the question of grant aid to Iran would be prejudicial to the economical use and orderly administration of MDA funds.

(d) Pending possible future acceptance by the Iranian Government of the assurances required by Section 511(a) of the Mutual Security Act of 1951, all undelivered materiel and all unobligated funds of the Fiscal Year 1952 and previous programs for Iran should now be reprogrammed for Greece and Turkey, but deliveries of this materiel to Greece and Turkey should not be made prior to 30 June 1952. Furthermore, the Governments of Greece and Turkey should not be informed of this possible transfer of the Iranian programs prior to the above-mentioned date.

4. The Joint Chiefs of Staff recommend that grant military aid to Iran be reprogrammed to Greece and Turkey as indicated in paragraph 3(d) above and in conformity with the following approximate percentages:

Iran MDAP	Greece	Turkey
Army, FY 50-51	40%	60%
Air Force, FY 50-51	0%	100%
Army, FY 52	30%	70%
Air Force, FY 52	0%	100%

5. The Joint Chiefs of Staff further recommend that the Army and Air Force be directed to submit revised programs, to reflect the recommended redistribution of the Iran programs set forth in the preceding paragraph.

A Report of the Joint Strategic Plans Committee to the Joint Chiefs of Staff on United States Military Courses of Action with Respect to Iran

December 31, 1952

Facts Bearing on the Problems and Discussion

I. *Conduct a show of force by periodic flights of carrier aircraft, or aircraft from land bases outside of Iran over key cities. . . .*

1. The Strategic Air Command has the capability of carrying out this mission with medium bombardment aircraft now deployed in North Africa. This effort could be augmented with jet fighter bombers now assigned to Commander in Chief, U.S. Air Forces, Europe, utilizing the aerial refuelling technique and obviating the necessity for redeployment or the use of intermediate staging bases. This mission could be accomplished by deploying aircraft carriers for operations in the Persian Gulf or by deploying VP Rons for operations from Cyprus, Dhahran or Turkey. Planning for this course of action should be initiated by the Chief of Staff, U.S. Air Force and by CINCNELM. These plans should be coordinated with USCINCEUR prior to final approval by the Joint Chiefs of Staff.

II. *Assist the loyal Iranian Army with logistic support by augmenting the present policy of arms aid. . . .*

2. Advance planning for this course of action should be done by the Chief of Staff, U.S. Army, who should consider the recommendations of the Chief, U.S. Military Mission with the Iranian Army. Since there is no way of foretelling what assistance might be needed or requested by the Iranians, however, it appears that meaningful plans cannot be prepared at this time.

III. *Furnish additional arms aid to appropriate Middle East countries so as to eventually enable them to possess the strength to secure their frontiers against effective communist infiltration. . . .*

3. This is a matter of political and military interest. The Department of State, with the concurrence of the Department of Defense, has recommended to the Bureau of the Budget that the United States provide

grant military assistance in the amount of $100 million to the States of the Middle East in FY 1954. . . . The Secretary of Defense on 3 December 1952 requested the views of the Joint Chiefs of Staff concerning grant military aid to Egypt. . . . Planning for this course of action is a continuing project.

IV. *In the event of a Tudeh Coup in Iran, deploy appropriate Air Force units on the order of 1½ wings plus support units, to Southern Turkey with a mission of Assisting Middle East governments in preventing the spread of communist power to their countries. . . .*

4. The Chief of Staff, U.S. Air Force should recommend the composition of the forces to be deployed and initiate broad preliminary planning. It would be improper to approach the Turkish Government with regard to the matter at this time.

V. *In the event of a Tudeh Coup in Iran, deploy U.S. forces on the order of 1 Division reinforced and necessary supporting air and naval forces to the vicinity of Basra with a mission of assisting Middle East governments in preventing the spread of communist power to their countries. . . .*

5. Assuming that this mission is to be assigned to a commander under the Joint Chiefs of Staff, responsibility for the development of operational plans for it would properly be delegated to such commander, who in turn would properly delegate a major part of the planning responsibility to the commander of the forces to be deployed to Basra. Under the Unified Command Plan, . . . CINCNELM is the appropriate specified commander under the Joint Chiefs of Staff to conduct such planning. However, there is no commander in the Middle East under the Joint Chiefs of Staff with the required forces for the mission. In view of this, it appears advisable to withhold the delegation of operational planning responsibility for this course of action at this time.

6. Planning by the Joint Strategic Plans Committee at this time should proceed with the objective of obtaining from the Joint Chiefs of Staff tentative approval as to the forces by Service to be earmarked for the task, the general type and makeup of the command organization for those forces, and the way that the forces will be integrated into the U.S. command structure. With these matters decided, the Services will have a good idea of the support which will be required of them and can plan accordingly. Also the Joint Chiefs of Staff will be in a position to delegate responsibility for the operational planning when this appears advisable.

7. As a first step toward the objective mentioned in paragraph 6 above it appears advisable to obtain the comments and recommendations of CINCNELM.

8. Our present state of preparedness is such that the 82nd Airborne Division or the 2nd Marine Division could be moved on short notice

provided the necessary shipping were made available. It is estimated that the 82nd Airborne Division, the 2nd Marine Division or an infantry division in Europe could be moved to Basra and unloaded within a period of 60 days. However, the logistic support required to maintain the deployment of these forces, including the necessary combat reserve and the establishment of the supply pipeline, could be accomplished at this time only at the expense of critical supplies now destined for operations in Korea.

AMERICAN TECHNICAL AND ECONOMIC AID

Expansion of Point Four Activities in Iran

Press Release

State Department
January 21, 1952

The Point Four Program in Iran will be greatly expanded as a result of an understanding reached on January 19. An exchange of notes embodying the general scope and terms of the expanded program was concluded between Prime Minister Mosadeq on behalf of the Government of Iran and William E. Warne, director of technical cooperation in Iran, on behalf of the Government of the United States.

The United States may contribute as much as $23,450,000 toward the program of technical cooperation and economic development in Iran in the current fiscal year, compared with approximately $1,460,000 in fiscal year 1951.

Specific projects to be undertaken under the terms of the new understanding will be worked out between representatives of the United States Government and the individual ministries concerned, or such other representatives as the Prime Minister may designate.

After the expanded Point Four Program had been approved by the Council of Ministers, Mr. Mosadeq immediately appointed a four-man committee to work with United States officials in carrying out the plan. Members of the new committee are Mr. Maleki, Minister of Health, chairman; Mr. Hessabi, Minister of Education; Engineer Taleghani, Minister of Agriculture; and Mr. Zangeneh, Managing Director of the Plan Organization.

It is expected that the major part of the United States contribution will be used for enlarging and extending the rural improvement program which is already under way. Ten regional centers, of which seven are already in operation, help to develop specialized services in agriculture, health, sanitation, and education. Teams of specialists work among the people of the villages, helping them dig wells for clean water, obtain better seeds, improve their farming methods, make better use of irrigation water, adopt more efficient tools, establish new schools, and generally improve their standards of living and farming. Iranian technicians work with the Americans assigned to these centers, gaining knowledge and skills which they in turn hand on to other villages and other people.

The rural improvement program is the basis of Iran's long-range plan for raising the level of food production and the health and living standards of the people. Point Four has been assisting in this program under a memorandum of understanding between the two Governments signed October 19, 1950. The agreement set up a Joint Commission, consisting of five Iranians and four Americans, with an Iranian chairman, which continues to plan and carry out this work.

Also under consideration is the use of approximately 4 million dollars for urgently needed industrial rehabilitation and modernization. The main purpose is to develop small industries for processing local raw products, including food and housing materials, as well as goods and equipment needed for economic development.

It is expected that about 250 thousand dollars will be spent on training (in the United States or at regional training centers) of Iranian nationals selected by their Government.

At present, 62 American technicians and administrative personnel are working in Iran on the Point Four Program under the direction of the Technical Cooperation Administration, Department of State. It is expected that by the end of the current fiscal year there will be more than 150 such personnel in Iran. The great majority of these will be technicians in the fields of agriculture, public health and sanitation, and education, working directly with the people in the villages and on the farms.

Point Four Agreements Concluded with Iran

	State Department
Press Release	*April 15, 1952*

The Department of State announced on April 15 that project agreements for technical cooperation in the fields of agriculture, public health, and education have been concluded with the Government of Iran. The project agreements were signed on April 1, 1952, in Tehran by William E. Warne, U.S. Director of Technical Cooperation, for the United States, and Khalil K. Taleghani, Minister of Agriculture, Mohammad Ali Maleki, Minister of Health, and Mahmoud Hessabi, Minister of Education, representing Iran.

The three project agreements, calling for an expenditure of approximately $11,000,000 by the United States, describe the detailed operations of the expanded Point Four Program provided for in the exchange of notes at Tehran on January 19, 1952. At that time the United States agreed to contribute up to $23,450,000 for the 1952 fiscal year toward the program of technical cooperation.

The agricultural program includes such projects as the development of an agricultural extension service, improved livestock practices, irrigation development, soil and water conservation, and plant development.

The public-health program provides for the establishment of sanitary engineering, nursing, and public-health education divisions in the Ministry of Health to combat communicable diseases, improve sanitary conditions, and provide maternal and child-health care, and other services necessary for the development of a rural public-health service.

The objectives of the education program are to provide for improved rural facilities by establishing demonstration schools, better training for a greater number of rural teachers, and the extending of the program to remote areas.

As an emergency measure to meet the local currency costs of the Point Four Program, which the Iranian Government is unable to pay at the present time, agreements have also been entered into which will make rials available for the technical-cooperation projects in the amount of $6,000,000.

The first of these is the student emergency assistance program to provide dollars in the United States for subsistence and tuition of stranded Iranians whose sources of funds have been cut off by the Iranian Government currency restrictions. Under this program, rials must be deposited by the students' sponsors in Iran before the students may receive dollars in the United States. The rials go into a special account to be used by the Point Four director in Iran to meet local currency requirements. The United States has agreed to use up to $1,000,000 in this program.

The other is a program whereby the United States will supply approximately 34,000 metric tons of sugar valued at $5,000,000. The agreement to cover the terms of the sugar purchase was concluded on March 31, 1952, in Tehran.

Under the terms of the consumer goods (sugar) agreement the Government of Iran will sell the sugar through regular commercial channels and will deposit the equivalent of the $5,000,000 in rials in a special account for the Point Four director to use in meeting local expenses of the program.

The sugar will be shipped to Persian Gulf ports of Iran in three separate shipments in May, June, and July.

Emergency Assistance for Iranian Students

Press Release

State Department
April 7, 1952

A program to provide emergency assistance for approximately 1,000 Iranian students stranded in the United States by reason of their sources of funds having been cut off by the new currency restrictions adopted by the Government of Iran because of the shortage of dollars, was announced by the Department of State on April 7.

The purpose of the emergency program is to provide dollars in the United States only for maintenance and tuition in amounts equivalent to Iranian currency made available by the students' sponsors or parents in Iran. The rials (Iranian currency) deposited by the sponsors will go into a special account to be used by the Point Four director in Iran to meet local currency requirements of the technical-cooperation and economic-development program.

The Near East Foundation, 54 East 64th Street, New York City, will administer this Iranian Student Emergency Assistance Program under an agreement with the Technical Cooperation Administration of the Department of State.

The Point Four Program in Iran is one of rural development—improvement in agriculture, health, and education at the village level. There is an inadequate number of Iranian specialists in most fields and much of the success of the Point Four Program will depend on increasing the number of urgently needed technicians.

The emergency student assistance program covers Iranians enrolled as regular or special students in recognized colleges and universities and also visiting professors and research workers attached to educational and scientific institutions. The majority of the Iranian students in the United States is studying technical subjects such as agriculture, engineering, and medicine. . . .

Point Four Aid to Iran in Land Distribution

Press Release

State Department
September 18, 1952

The long-range plan of the Shah of Iran for dividing his vast holdings into small farms and selling them to nearly 50,000 peasants living on them will be carried out with American technical advice and financial assistance through the Point Four Program.

The Shah in a brief ceremony in Tehran on September 17 inaugurated the Bank for Rural Credit, an integral part of the joint program in which the Technical Cooperation Administration (TCA) is cooperating with the Crown Lands Commission. The bank will finance cooperatives and other rural services and provide trained Iranian farm supervisors to help the peasants through the first 5 years of their new undertaking in self-management and independent ownership.

William E. Warne, Point Four director in Iran, informed the Shah that TCA would contribute $500,000—half the initial capital—to get the bank started. Point Four will also provide an American financial adviser to assist the bank in developing its policies and carrying out its operations.

The Shah said, in thanking Mr. Warne,

"The help of the United States through Point Four in this program is greatly appreciated by myself and Iran. This program cannot be permitted to fail. Your interest in it is most encouraging."

The Near East Foundation will help train the village supervisors. Ultimately, the bank will receive nearly 25 million dollars from the proceeds of the land sales. No part of these proceeds is to revert to the Crown, nor are they to be used for general economic or industrial development. All of the money from the sale of lands is to be devoted to rural services and other benevolent purposes for the direct benefit of the peasants, according to the terms of the Shah's decree.

Arrangements with the Crown Lands Commission covering Point Four participation in this program are expected to be completed later this week.

This marks the first major step by the United States to implement in the Middle East its policy of cooperating with other governments in carrying out programs of land reform which they initiate themselves.

The Shah of Iran, on January 27, 1951, ordered the crown lands distributed to the peasants living on them. Since then the Crown Lands Commission has made surveys, divided up some of the lands, and transferred title to about 900 small farms in the Varamin area, about 30 miles east of Tehran.

Several months ago the Crown Lands Commission sought American advice on development of basic policies and machinery for assuring the success of this immense and highly significant undertaking. The agreement which was signed today is the result of intensive study and recommendations made in Iran earlier this year by Paul V. Maris, one of the foremost experts in the United States in matters of land tenure, supervised agricultural credit, and rural improvement. Following the request of the Crown Lands Commission for American advice, Mr. Maris, a veteran of 37 years with the Department of Agriculture, was sent to Iran in April by the Technical Cooperation Administration.

During the ensuing 9 weeks, Mr. Maris made a series of detailed recommendations covering every aspect of the crown-lands program, from the training of Iranian farm supervisors all the way through to completion of the distribution some 20 years from now. TCA Director Warne described Mr. Maris' work as "the best job of its kind I have ever seen done at home or abroad."

These recommendations were accepted in principle by the Crown Lands Commission and the TCA mission in Iran.

Basic U.S. Contribution

The most important American contribution to the program in the long run may prove to be the application of principles which are considered to be essential in all efforts to improve tenancy conditions among peasant-type farmers. These principles include division of lands into family-size units; intensive advice and supervision in farm management during the first few years of independent operation; extension of credit in direct combination with such supervision; organization of cooperatives for buying, marketing, and supplying of needed services; and help in organizing rural services for education, health, transportation, water supply, and the like.

The Shah's program for distributing the crown holdings, a plan which is entirely benevolent in character, was intended as a model and an inspiration to other landlords to follow suit. As such, it is considered imperative by the Shah and the Crown Lands Commission that the scheme be successful. The Commission has moved with great care and deliberation, first making a general survey of the extensive holdings, with their 300,000 acres now in cultivation, 131,000 acres of arable land not presently in cultivation, and 494,000 acres suitable for cultivation if properly irrigated. It was decided first to survey and divide into fairly uniform plots the 17,000 acres in the Varamin Plains area. Distribution of these lands to the peasants living on them has now been completed.

But land reform is much more than simply dividing up lands and transferring title. It was in recognition of this fact that American advice was sought by the Crown Lands Commission.

The prospective farm owners have a tradition of many years of peasanthood behind them, in which they have had few management decisions to make and few business responsibilities. As a rule, they have little education, their tools are simple and inefficient, their livestock is of inferior quality, they know little of modern farming techniques. Suddenly finding themselves in the position of ownership and responsibility, with annual payments to make, they would have little chance for success unaided, in spite of a great capacity for hard work.

To guard against the discouragement and failure which would be the lot of many of the new owners, the heart of the program is a plan to make available to each group of about 75 peasant families the services of a technically trained Iranian farm supervisor.

A service charge of 1 percent of the price of the peasant's land allotment will be levied annually for 15 years to meet the cost of supervisory service. This means that the peasant's annual payments will be about 75 dollars a year while he is receiving the benefits of technical guidance, whereas they would be about 15 dollars less than that if the help of supervisors were not provided. The returns to the farmer from such a guidance are expected to exceed the cost many times.

Villagers to Be Trained as Supervisors

The supervisors, all of whom will be Iranian villagers, trained in a special school conducted by the Near East Foundation under the auspices of the Iranian Ministry of Education, will help the farmers with advice, planning, and supervision in developing cropping systems, applying proper fertilizers, controlling insects and diseases, organizing and using cooperative services, installing and maintaining farm irrigation works, and in various other ways.

The cost of training the supervisors will be borne by Point Four. Inasmuch as the proceeds of the 1-percent service charge will not be sufficient at the outset to cover costs of supervision, the salaries of supervisors in the Varamin Plains demonstration area will be paid out of the Point Four contribution to the Rural Credit Bank funds.

The bank will make loans to farmers and will finance cooperatives and other enterprises of direct benefit to farmers, for purposes such as acquiring improved livestock and seeds, needed machinery and supplies; providing basic community facilities in the villages; developing irrigation works, and so on. Its activities will include 1-year crop loans, 1-to-5 year farm improvement and equipment loans, and longer-term community facility loans.

The funds of the bank will be progressively augmented by the annual purchase-price payments by farmers on the crown lands. These will average about 60 dollars each (not including the service charge for farm supervision), amounting in 20 years to almost 25 million dollars. The purchase price of the farms will be about 80 percent of the assessed valuation, without any interest charge. None of the proceeds revert to the Crown.

The surveying, allotment, distribution, sale, and settlement of the crown holdings will take a good many years to complete. Under present plans, the peasants will be given 25 years to pay off their interest-free notes, and it will be almost 20 years before all the 49,117 farm families on the Shah's estates will be started on the road to ownership. Approximately 3,000 farms will be laid out and transfered to the peasants each year after the program gains momentum.

Point Four work in village improvement, health, education, water development, irrigation, and other fields is being planned and carried out in Iran with a view to supporting the basic objectives of the crown-land program. The farm supervisors will develop and encourage participation in these and other community activities and services. The Point Four Program will assist in meeting village needs in these respects.

THE DOWNFALL AND RETURN OF THE SHAH

Communist Activities in Iran: Press Conference Remarks
by Secretary of State Dulles

July 28, 1953

The growing activities of the illegal Communist party in Iran [the Tudeh Party] and the toleration of those activities by the Iranian Government have caused our Government great concern. These developments certainly make it more difficult for the United States to grant assistance to Iran.

Ambassador Loy Henderson Conveyed to the Shah of Iran the
Following Message from President Eisenhower

August 27, 1953

In the spirit of friendliness which has always been the basis for the relations of our two countries, I offer you my sincere felicitations on the occasion of your happy return to your country, and my continuing good wishes for every success in your efforts to promote the prosperity of your people and to preserve the independence of Iran.

[DWIGHT D. EISENHOWER]

FOA Program of Assistance

The Foreign Operations Administration (FOA) announced on September 3 that 23.4 million dollars would be made available to Iran during the 1954 fiscal year to continue the present U.S. program of technical assistance in Iran.

This agreement, concluded in an exchange of letters between U.S. Ambassador Loy Henderson and Iranian Prime Minister Gen. Fazlollah Zahedi, does not include the special economic assistance for Iran which is currently being discussed by representatives of the two Governments.

The technical cooperation program with Iran involves 12 programs and 71 projects which have been developed during the last 2 years.

Following are the texts of the letters.

Exchange between Ambassador Henderson
and Prime Minister Zahedi

August 27, 1953

EXCELLENCY: I have the honer to refer you to prior notes between the

Governments of Iran and the United States establishing a joint program of technical cooperation for economic development of Iran, as follows:

(a) Memorandum of understanding for Technical Cooperation on rural improvement between the United States of America and Iran, executed October 19, 1950, between Henry F. Grady, Ambassador Extraordinary and Plenipotentiary, U.S. of America, and Ali Razmara, Prime Minister of Iran;

(b) Note of William E. Warne, Director of Technical Cooperation Mission of the U.S. of America, January 19, 1952, to Dr. Mohammad Mossadegh, Prime Minister, Imperial Government of Iran, and his reply thereto under date of January 20, 1952;

(c) Note of W.E. Warne, U.S. Director of Technical Cooperation for Iran, to Dr. Mohammad Mossadegh, Prime Minister of Iran, December 27, 1952, and his reply thereto under date of December 30, 1952. Pursuant to and on the terms and conditions contained in these notes and hereinafter set forth, the U.S. of America is prepared to make available for technical and economic aid during the current fiscal year ending June 30, 1954, up to $23,400,000 including costs of U.S. technicians and training costs outside Iran, which costs will not be included in program or project agreements.

The Governments of Iran and the U.S. have heretofore executed, pursuant to above referenced notes and memorandum, twelve program agreements and 71 project agreements providing detailed plans and creating operational responsibilities and duties. It is, therefore, proposed that the Government of the U.S. of America, by this note, and the Government of Iran, by its reply thereto, signify their acceptance and approval of the Technical Cooperation program in Iran by affirming all memoranda, correspondence, agreements and other documents relating to the Technical Cooperation program in Iran, and by rededicating their joint efforts to the social and economic development of Iran.

If these proposals are acceptable to Your Excellency's Government, it is requested that you notify me of Your Excellency's concurrence on behalf of the Government of Iran. I shall be pleased to meet at an early date with the Joint Commission to take up continuing problems and plans.

Accept, Excellency, the assurances of my highest consideration.

LOY W. HENDERSON

September 1

EXCELLENCY: Your note of September 1, 1953, offering up to $23,400,000 for technical and economic aid during the current fiscal year ending June 30, 1954, and proposing the confirmation of the Technical Cooperation program now in operation in Iran, has received the approval of my government.

In response to your proposals, this government will expedite the

fulfillment of programs designed to advance the welfare of the people of
Iran. The Joint Commission will be continued as before with the
following members representing the Government of Iran: Minister of
Interior, Minister of Agriculture, Minister of Health, Minister of Education, Minister of National Economy, Managing Director of the Plan
Organization.

The formation of the Commission is entrusted to the Managing
Director of the Plan Organization.

In the absence of any of the above Ministers their respective under-
secretaries will take part in the meetings of the Joint Commission.

GENERAL FAZLOLLAH ZAHEDI

Exchange between President Eisenhower and Prime Minister Zahedi Concerning the Need for Increased Aid to Iran

August 26, 1953

DEAR MR. PRESIDENT: I wish to express to you and through you to
the American people the appreciation of the Iranian Government and
people for the aid which the United States has extended to Iran during
recent years. This aid has contributed much to the security of the
country and to the raising of its technical efficiency. The assistance
which the United States is already rendering Iran, helpful as it is, is
unfortunately not sufficient in amount and character to tide Iran over
the financial and economic crisis which I find it to be facing. The
treasury is empty; foreign exchange resources are exhausted; the
national economy is deteriorated. Iran needs immediate financial aid to
enable it to emerge from a state of economic and financial chaos.

Iran also requires aid of an economic character to enable it to carry
out programs which the government is preparing for developing its
agriculture and industry, for exploiting its rich mineral resources, for
improving its transport and communications, for strengthening its
internal and foreign trade, and for raising the health, education and
technical levels of the Iranian people.

The people of Iran are anxious to have a prosperous, orderly
country in which they can enjoy higher standards of living and make
greater use of their talents and resources. They are willing, if given an
opportunity, to work hard in order to obtain these objectives, but the
realization of their aspirations may be delayed for some time unless they
receive technical, financial, and economic aid from abroad. I hope that
the United States will find it possible at this critical moment in Iranian
history to come to my country's assistance as it has done on occasions in
the past.

In conclusion, I would like to emphasize that it is the intention of
the new Government of Iran not only to strengthen the country internally but also to improve its international position. The government

desires to maintain friendly relations with the other members of the family of nations on a basis of mutual respect. It will pursue a policy of eliminating such differences as may exist or which may develop between other countries and itself in a spirit of friendliness and in accordance with accepted principles of international intercourse. I am sure that I voice the feelings of the great majority of the people of Iran when I state that Iran desires to contribute its share to the maintenance of peace and to the promotion of international goodwill.

Please accept, Mr. President, the assurance of my highest consideration.

GENERAL F. ZAHEDI

September 1, 1953

DEAR MR. PRIME MINISTER: I have received your letter of August 26 regarding the problems which you face in Iran. The American people continue to be deeply interested in the independence of Iran and the well-being of the Iranian people. We have followed policies in Iran, as in other countries of the free world, designed to assist peoples of those countries to bring about economic development which will lead to higher standards of living and wider horizons in knowledge and opportunity. I am gratified that the aid which we have extended has contributed to the security of Iran and to the raising of the technical efficiency of the Iranian people. I am also pleased to have your assurance that your Government desires to maintain friendly relations with other members of the family of nations and that it will pursue a policy of eliminating such differences as may exist or which may develop with other countries in a spirit of friendliness and in accordance with accepted principles of international intercourse.

In an effort to assist you in dealing with your immediate problems, I have authorized my Ambassador to Iran to consult with you regarding the development of our aid programs there. I recognize that your needs are pressing. Your request will receive our sympathetic consideration and I can assure you that we stand ready to assist you in achieving the aspirations for your country which you have outlined.

Please accept, Mr. Prime Minister, the assurances of my highest consideration.

DWIGHT D. EISENHOWER

President Makes Available $45 Million in Emergency Aid

White House Office
Press Release   *September 5, 1953*

In response to a request for urgent assistance from the new Government of Iran, the President has made available on an emergency basis

$45 million which will be used for the immediate economic assistance of Iran in accordance with the procedures of the Foreign Operations Administration under the Mutual Security Act. This amount is in addition to existing U.S. technical assistance and military programs in Iran.

There is great need for immediate assistance to restore a measure of stability and establish a foundation for greater economic development and improvement in the living standards for all of the people of Iran. It is hoped that, with our assistance, there will be an increase in the internal stability of Iran which will allow the development of a healthy economy to which an early effective use of Iran's rich resources will contribute.

Agreement on Extending United States Relief Supplies and Packages to Iran: Duty-Free Entry and Free Inland Transportation

September 22, 1953	*Effected by exchange of notes.*
October 5, 1953	*Effected by exchange of notes.*
October 13, 1953	*Effected by exchange of notes.*
October 13, 1953	*Entered into force.*

The American Ambassador to the Iranian Minister for Foreign Affairs

American Embassy
No. 301   *Tehran, September 22, 1953*

EXCELLENCY: I have the honor to refer to the Embassy's Note No. 1519 of June 10, 1953, and to conversations between representatives of our two Governments concerning measures to facilitate private manifestations of friendship between the people of our two countries through voluntary gifts of food and other basic supplies by individuals and organizations in the United States to individuals and organizations in Iran. I also have the honor to confirm the understandings reached as a result of these conversations, as follows:

1. The Imperial Government of Iran shall accord duty-free entry into Iran, as well as exemption from internal taxation, of supplies of goods approved by the Government of the United States, donated to or purchased by United States voluntary, non-profit relief and rehabilitation agencies qualified under United States Government Regulations, and consigned to such organizations, including branches of these agencies in Iran which have been or hereafter shall be approved by the Imperial Government of Iran.

2. Such supplies may include goods of types qualified for ocean freight subsidy under applicable United States Government Regulations, such as basic necessities of food, clothing and medicines, and other relief supplies and equipment in support of projects of health,

sanitation, education and recreation, agriculture and promotion of small self-help industries, but shall not include tobacco, cigars, cigarettes, alcoholic beverages, or items for the personal use of agencies' field representatives.

3. Duty-free treatment on importation and exportation, as well as exemption from internal taxation, shall also be accorded to supplies and equipment imported by organizations approved by both governments for the purpose of carrying out operations under this Agreement. Such supplies and equipment shall not include items for the personal use of agencies' field representatives.

4. The cost of transporting such supplies and equipment (including port, handling, storage, and similar charges, as well as transportation) within Iran to the ultimate beneficiary will be borne by the Imperial Government of Iran.

5. The supplies furnished by the voluntary agencies shall be considered supplementary to rations to which individuals would otherwise have been entitled.

6. Individual organizations carrying out operations under this Agreement may enter into additional arrangements with the Imperial Government of Iran, and this Agreement shall not be construed to derogate from any benefits secured by any such organizations in existing agreements with the Imperial Government of Iran.

I have the honor to propose that, if these understandings meet with the approval of the Imperial Government of Iran, this note and Your Excellency's note in reply constitute an agreement between our two Governments, effective on the date of Your Excellency's reply, to remain in force until three months after the receipt by either Government of written notice of the intention of the other Government to terminate it.

Accept, Excellency, the renewed assurances of my most distinguished consideration.

LOY W. HENDERSON

The American Embassy to the Iranian Ministry of Foreign Affairs

American Embassy
No. 349   *Tehran, Iran, October 5, 1953*

The Embassy of the United States of America presents its compliments to the Imperial Iranian Ministry of Foreign Affairs and has the honor to refer to conversations between officers of this Embassy and Mr. Afshar Qasemlu, Chief of the Ministry's Fourth Political Division, regarding the intent and purpose of paragraph number 6 of the American Ambassador's Note No. 301 dated September 22, 1953, to His Excellency the Minister of Foreign Affairs concerning the agreement relative to the distribution in Iran of certain goods donated to or purchased by certain United States voluntary, non-profit relief and rehabilitation agencies.

Paragraph number 6 of the Note under reference reads as follows:

"6. Individual organizations carrying out operations under this agreement may enter into additional arrangements with the Government of Iran, and this Agreement shall not be construed to derogate from any benefits secured by any such organizations in existing agreements with the Imperial Government of Iran."

This paragraph provides, in effect, that the existence of the agreement in question between the Imperial Government of Iran and the Government of the United States shall not prevent any organization distributing goods in Iran in accordance with such agreement from making additional arrangements directly with the Imperial Government of Iran, and that it shall not reduce or limit any facilities or concessions already granted to any such organization by the Imperial Government of Iran.

The Embassy avails itself of this opportunity to renew to the Imperial Iranian Ministry of Foreign Affairs the assurances of its highest consideration.

The Iranian Ministry of Foreign Affairs to the American Ambassador (Henderson)

[TRANSLATION]

October 13, 1953

MR. AMBASSADOR: I respectfully acknowledge receipt of your Note No. 301, dated September 22, 1953, whereby proposals are made by the Government of the United States of America to send to Iran free of charge some foodstuffs, and have the honor to state the following:

The Imperial Government of Iran, with due consideration of the elaboration made in the Embassy's Note No. 349, dated October 5, 1953, hereby conveys its agreement to the proposals as set forth in Your Excellency's Note and expresses its sincere gratitude for the help which will be rendered in this manner. As suggested in your Note No. 301, dated September 22, 1953, my reply in this connection shall be considered as an agreement between the Governments of Iran and the United States of America.

I avail myself of this opportunity to renew the assurance of my highest consideration.

ABDOLLAH ENTEZAM

Statement by Secretary of State Dulles upon Receiving the New Iranian Ambassador*

October 22, 1953

It is a pleasure to greet Dr. Nazrollah Entezam as Ambassador-Designate of Iran to the United States and as a respected friend of long standing.

Dr. Entezam is no stranger here, having served his country in a similar capacity in the past. He also has served his country with distinction as Iran's representative to the United Nations, being president of the General Assembly 2 years ago, and has furthered the cause of free people everywhere through his devotion to and energetic support of the principles and purposes of the United Nations Charter.

Under the leadership of the Shah and Premier Zahedi, Iran today is recovering from the effects of the recent Communist-abetted disorders and is striving to overcome serious economic dislocations which have come about during the past 2 years. The United States, as a means of helping Iran carry out urgent measures to stabilize her economy, has extended $45 million in emergency aid, in addition to that previously granted under the technical-cooperation program.

These constitute concrete evidence of the friendship and concern of the United States toward Iran and our desire that Iran prosper as an independent country and a respected member of the family of free nations.

It is with genuine pleasure that I look forward to working with Dr. Entezam in furthering the mutual feeling of friendship and respect that already exists between our two countries, sharing as they do the desire for freedom and the hope that peace shall prevail in the world.

Excerpt from a Draft of President Eisenhower's Speech to the National Governor's Conference

July 12, 1954

. . . The Iranian problem confronted me even before I was inaugurated; Prime Minister Mossadegh cabled me in early January while I was still living on the Columbia University campus. After a brief congratulatory sentence on the election results, he expounded at great length on the problems of Iran which he feared had already been presented to me by those who did not see eye to eye with him on the future of Iran and its people.

Through two years, according to his message, the Iranian people had suffered acute distress and much misery merely because an oil

---

* Made on receiving the new Iranian Ambassador on October 22 (press release 586). Dr. Entezam previously served as Ambassador in Washington from September 1950 to September 1952.

company inspired by covetousness and a desire for profit supported by the British Government had been endeavoring to prevent them from obtaining their natural and elementary rights.

I immediately assured Dr. Mossadegh in my answering cable that I had in no way compromised a position of impartiality and that no individual had attempted to prejudice me in the matter. I expressed the hope that our own future relationships would be completely free of any suspicion and that I would be delighted to receive either personally and directly or through established diplomatic channels at any time a communication of his views on any subject in which we might have a common interest.

During the next three months, Mossadegh balked successive efforts of our Ambassador to find a new basis for settlement of the oil dispute. In May, he declared that no acceptable settlement was possible. And, on the 28th of that month, in a long personal letter to me, he declared flatly that his hopes of a more sympathetic attention by my administration had not been realized.

In the meantime, the political and economic situation in Iran greatly deteriorated. Turmoil, created by Mossadegh and his followers, nullified any possible effectiveness of United States aid and, at the end of June, I refused any further aid until an oil settlement was reached. Matters came to a head in August when Mossadegh, for three days, backed up by the communistic Tudeh party, seemed the irresistible dictator of Iran after the Shah's flight from the country.

I was advised that we would now have to take a whole new look at the Iranian situation and, in the words of a senior adviser, "probably have to snuggle up to Mossadegh if we're going to save anything there." Fortunately, loyalty to the Shah and fear of communism started a popular groundswell. Street mobs and the army completely turned the tables on August 19. Mossadegh and his principal supporters were imprisoned. The Shah returned in triumph from exile in Bagdad. I quickly cabled him my congratulations. I also sent a congratulatory message to General Fazollah Zahedi, whose appointment as Prime Minister by the Shah had precipitated Mossadegh's seizure of dictatorial powers.

The news, naturally, was heartening to me. I had met the Shah four years earlier at Columbia when I conferred on him an honorary degree. At lunch and in a long private conversation, I there recognized in him a profound respect for constitutional processes, a sense of responsibility and obligation and an enlightened purpose to further the Iranian people's welfare. His conduct as a constitutional monarch, during the turbulence of the Mossadegh period, strengthened my regard for him. . . .

The Present Situation in Iran: A Statement made before the
Middle East Conference, Washington, D.C.

December 12, 1953

Henry A. Byroade, Assistant Secretary for Near Eastern,
South Asian and African Affairs

Iran is a land of ancient culture and tradition, in which the eloquent wisdom of poets and sages is held in the highest respect. We in the West are sometimes inclined to overstress the practical. We delight in shrewd Yankee injunctions. The Iranians, however, choose to express themselves in a more poetic fashion.

A Persian poet, Nezami, wrote the following beautiful sentences: "At times of difficulty, do not despair, for the black cloud pours forth white rain. Continue your efforts to find a way out, for many a bitter drug results in sweet remedies."

I suggest that this might almost be taken as a text for the discussions of this conference. Not all of the wisdom in sound international relationships is to be sought in immediate practical measures designed to deal with specific situations. The sensitive statesman recognizes that an atmosphere, indefinable as it might appear to be, is often more potent in achieving results than some formula of accommodation.

It will not be thought too fanciful, I hope, if I paraphrase the poet Nezami to put it that out of the black cloud of the severance of diplomatic relations between Iran and the United Kingdom white rain has descended. It was a week ago today, as you all know, that diplomatic relations between the two countries were renewed. A few months ago such a decision on the part of Iran would have been impossible. Iran was in turmoil. Constructive, ameliorating action seemed to be a matter for the remote future.

Now, from the bitter drug of the past, His Majesty the Shah and Prime Minister Zahedi are producing sweet remedies. The wisdom of the poet has become a graphic expression of official action. The new Iranian Government, although firm in its adherence to the national honor and integrity of Iran, seems to be free from the inflexible emotional commitments of the immediate past. It does not stand in fear of the exaggerated pressures of organized groups, but rather is subject to legitimate public opinion. Under such circumstances, it is in its power to make careful and far-reaching decisions. I believe it safe to say that the future of Iran and of Iranian relations with the rest of the world, for the visible and even for the far future, will be largely shaped by the decisions which this government has made and will make within the next few months.

Decision means action and action inevitably creates opposition. The problems faced by Iran are massive. To any action proposed there are bound to be opponents both inside and outside the country. It may be that advocates of conflicting courses will be ready to abandon the government if it is not prepared to follow their whim. To please everyone is impossible. An attempt to do so usually results in nothing being accomplished. It may temporarily enable a government to retain power, but only at the cost of letting current problems grow more acute.

No one seems to realize this better than the present leaders of Iran. Otherwise they would certainly not have taken the step of resuming relations with the British. This action was very unpopular in some quarters. It has been vociferously denounced. But the government realized that the original cause for severing relations, the oil problem, could best be solved were the two parties involved in direct contact with each other, rather than obliged to deal through intermediaries. It therefore decided to go ahead no matter how much opposition might temporarily come from certain segments of the Iranian political scene.

Rumors have been spread to the effect that the United States brought pressure to bear on Iran, through the threat of withholding economic aid, in order to bring about resumption of relations. Let me, as one in close touch with Iranian relations, categorically deny this. It has repeatedly been stated that the United States Government will not use its influence to threaten or intimidate others. The United States did not depart from that principle in this case. It is true that we welcomed the establishment of direct official contacts between Iran and the United Kingdom. At his November 3 press conference Secretary Dulles stated that he hoped the renewed friendliness between the Iranians and the British would lead to resumption of diplomatic relations between the two governments. Likewise the Iranian Government, as Prime Minister Zahedi said in his address of December 5, saw that resumption would facilitate the settlement of existing differences and, therefore, in conjunction with Great Britain, proceeded to take the necessary steps.

Other decisions of comparable importance have yet to be made and these, too, will probably receive their share of criticism. Yet Prime Minister Zahedi and His Majesty the Shah seem ready to proceed as the need arises. Zahedi's advent to power was a repudiation of the sterile negative policies of the past. The Prime Minister has repeatedly said he would prefer to resign rather than stay in power if unable to advance the real interests of Iran. Accordingly it is reasonable to believe that the new government will act solely according to its conception of what is in the interest of the Iranian people.

New Government's Constructive Measures

Much has already been done. The Prime Minister has reported to the Iranian people that the new government is rapidly establishing law and order, that there has been some measure of success achieved in stabilizing what was less than two months ago a chaotic financial situation. Another significant step, taken by the Shah himself, was the resumption of his land distribution program whereby tenant farmers will eventually become land owners. This is highly important for Iran's stable future progress. Still further reports tell of improved working conditions for factory workers and implementation of social insurance laws.

We Americans applaud these constructive measures. More than that, we have backed our applause with additional aid, a special $45 million grant made by President Eisenhower on September 5. This fund is given in the hope that it will facilitate the new government's task of starting Iran on the road to progress. It has been made available in a reasonable expectation of a better future for the Iranian people, whose independence is so important in the maintenance of world peace. It is also hoped that the charting of an orderly path toward increased prosperity will lessen the attraction of the Tudeh party's cynical promises.

I am sure the Iranians look upon our aid only as a means of implementing their own efforts. They realize that eventually the bettering of conditions in Iran must be their own handiwork. An example of recent accomplishment is the Iranian Government's program to combat malaria which for many years had afflicted large areas of Iran. Today, this century-old scourge is virtually extinguished. In this project, as in many others, our technical assistance mission was able to help by making available to the Iranians latest developments in Western research and technology.

The Iranians will have to bring to the task before them the full use of their manpower and their natural resources. Of the latter the most important is, of course, their huge reserve of oil. To settle the oil problem and once more enjoy the revenue which would result from the large-scale flow of petroleum to world markets is the most pressing need of the Iranian Government. It would greatly simplify the carrying out of its program for the welfare of the country.

This settlement, while so much desired, will be far from easy to reach. In both Iran and Great Britain the problem has its emotional and historic aspects. In addition there have been changes in the world oil situation which will affect the negotiations.

Mr. Hoover's Mission

The United States is anxious to see a settlement reached both for the benefit it would bring Iran and for the added friendliness which would result between two important countries of the free world. We stand ready at any time to offer our good offices in helping to find a solution. Herbert Hoover, Jr., Special Assistant to the Secretary of State for petroleum matters, has lately been devoting his entire attention to investigating the facts of the Iranian oil problem. As you all know, he has visited both Iran and the United Kingdom. He has been in touch with representatives of all the major and many of the small British and

American oil companies. He has not been empowered to negotiate, nor has he proposed to either side any full and final solution. He represents the United States interest in bringing about an early settlement to the dispute, but he is guided by the principle that we will avoid any unwanted interference.

A solution to this problem will not mean the beginning of paradise on earth for Iran. The deserts will not bloom in Kerman nor the melons grow bigger in Isfahan the day oil begins to flow in Ahadan. But it can be the beginning of a new era of constructive achievement. The revenues which the nation will receive from its oil sales, together with the hard work of its leaders and citizens, can play an important role in increasing the well-being of Iran and the rest of the Middle East. A wise decision now by their elders will give the youth of Iran wider horizons looking toward renewed glory and progress for their ancient land.

It is not too much to say that Iran is once again a focus of world interest. Our own particular concern is reflected by the recent visit of Vice President Nixon which has just ended. The Vice President has expressed his appreciation for the warm welcome he received and for the opportunity which was given him for a first hand look at Iran. We hope that his trip will lead to a greater mutual understanding, on our part, of the hopes of the Iranian people and of the magnitude of the task to which they are now devoting their efforts, and, on their part, a fuller realization of the desire of America to assist the Iranian people in all feasible and practical ways.

The temptation to offer specific suggestions is strong. But while we are, of course, interested in the decisions Prime Minister Zahedi will make, we are in no sense prepared to bear down upon him with some inflexible program that would meet the exclusive desires of the United States. It will be for Mr. Zahedi, under the guidance of the Shah, to decide what actions are for the good of the Iranian nation. I would far rather see him proceed according to the sincere convictions of his heart and mind than take with reluctance one or another step for the purpose of pleasing the United States or some other government, much less of some clique or faction within Iran.

As Secretary Dulles said last week:

"Indeed, we do not want weak or subservient allies. Our friends and allies are dependable just because they are unwilling to be anyone's satellites. They will freely sacrifice much in a common effort. But they will no more be subservient to the United States than they will be subservient to Soviet Russia.

Let us be thankful that they are that way and that there still survives so much rugged determination to be free. If that were not so, we would be isolated in the world and in mortal peril."

During the coming years we hope to witness the continuance of Iran's traditional determination to remain free. We are impressed with the new government's stated intention not to bow to expediency as a means of remaining in power. Only decisions made with the enduring national interest at heart, and after a realistic appraisal of the obstacles and of the chances of failure or success, can set a true course toward the goal of national independence and survival.

The Middle East Institute is to be congratulated for its efforts in organizing this important meeting and Georgetown University for the loan of its facilities. I share the hope of all here that these discussions will lead to a more informed understanding of the present situation in Iran at a time when it is of such vital national and international interest.

You will permit me, perhaps, to close as I began, with a quotation from a Persian poet whose thoughts are living legacies in the lives of all Iranians, the master poet, Ferdowsi. He wrote: "Only he who walks will reach his destination; only he who endeavors will attain happiness."

We are all walking together in this perilous world toward the goal of a prosperous, peaceful future. I like to think that Iran and the United States, each pursuing its separate national course, are walking side by side. God grant that these two great peoples reach their common destination.

5

Consolidating
the Alliance

*The period of consolidation which followed the downfall of Mos-
sadeq was marked by a number of major developments: the Shah
increased his power in Iran; the relationship between Iran and the U.S.
solidified; Iran assumed an even greater strategic significance in U.S.
eyes; and Iran committed itself more and more firmly to its connection
with the U.S. As a result, economic ties and other nonmilitary relations
between Iran and the U.S. were strengthened.*

*This activity in the economic sphere attracted the attention of
Congress, which has the constitutional power to inquire into the operations of the executive departments. This chapter presents the conclusions of a Congressional report which, though not unanimous, was
nevertheless quite critical of the results achieved in Iran from programs
of American assistance.*

*In 1955, Iran joined the Baghdad Pact, previously consisting of
Turkey, Iraq (then under a pro-Western government), Britain, and
Pakistan. After the Iraqi regime was overthrown in the revolution of
1958, Iraq withdrew, and the group became known as the Central
Treaty Organization (CENTO). Although the United States was not a*

member of CENTO, the organization was part of the network of pacts that Secretary of State Dulles sought to erect as a barrier against Soviet aggression.

Rather than CENTO, however, the most important component of U.S. policy in the Middle East during the last half of the 1950s was the Eisenhower Doctrine. This consisted of Presidential proposals which were embodied in a joint resolution of Congress. It authorized the President to employ American armed forces, as he deemed necessary, to protect the independence and integrity of any nation or group of nations in the Middle East requesting such aid against overt armed aggression from any nation controlled by international communism. James P. Richards, (former) Democratic chairman of the House Foreign Affairs Committee, was sent to the Middle East as a special ambassador to explain what the United States was willing to do under the doctrine. Iran supported the policy, but continued to prefer U.S. membership in CENTO and increased U.S. military aid. When the doctrine was invoked to land U.S. troops in Lebanon in 1958, Iran supported the action. This is the general background of the last segment of this chapter.

GROWING UNITED STATES STRATEGIC INTERESTS IN IRAN

United States Policy toward Iran: A Report to the National Security Council by the N.S.C. Planning Board

[DRAFT]

December 21, 1953

GENERAL CONSIDERATIONS

1. It is of critical importance to the United States that Iran remain an independent nation, not dominated by the USSR. Because of its key strategic position, oil resources, vulnerability to intervention or armed attack by the USSR, and vulnerability to political subversion, Iran must be regarded as a continuing objective of Soviet expansion. The loss of Iran, particularly by subversion, would:

 a. Be a major threat to the security of the entire Middle East, as well as Pakistan and India.

 b. Increase the Soviet Union's oil resources for war and its capability to threaten important free world lines of communication.

c. Damage United States prestige in nearby countries and with the exception of Turkey and possibly Pakistan, seriously weaken, if not destroy, their will to resist communist pressures.

d. Permit the communists to deny Iranian oil to the free world, or alternatively to use Iranian oil as a weapon of economic warfare to disrupt the free world pattern of petroleum production and marketing.

e. Have serious psychological impact elsewhere in the free world.

2. Due to the events of mid-August, 1953, there is now a better opportunity to achieve U.S. objectives with respect to Iran. The Shah's position is stronger and he and his new Prime Minister look to the United States for counsel and aid. Some Iranian leaders now seem to realize that Iranian oil is not vital to the world and that it must be sold in substantial quantities if Iran is to achieve stability. There is accordingly a possibility for the United States to help bring Iran into active cooperation with the free world and thus strengthen a weak position in the line from Europe to South Asia. An essential step in this direction is the receipt by Iran of substantial revenues from its oil resources. In the absence of such revenues, Iran will be dependent on external assistance which, if doled out only in minimum quantities to meet emergencies, will do little to create real stability, permit development or avoid future emergencies.

3. If the Shah cooperates, the Zahedi Government should be able to stay in power for some time. However, the Government is confronted with many serious problems, springing primarily from the basic changes taking place in Iranian society. Zahedi must cope with the Majlis, composed of heterogeneous groups, motivated by self-interest, upon whose support the enactment of essential economic and social legislation will depend. The Communist and other opposition groups will continue to pose a threat. The problem of Mossadegh must be solved. Zahedi's position is also threatened by the Shah's inherent suspicions of any strong Prime Minister. Any non-Communist successor government would encounter similar difficulties.

4. The United States now has an opportunity to further its national objectives with respect to Iran by: (a) facilitating an early oil settlement leading to substantial oil income for Iran at the earliest possible date; (b) technical assistance and economic aid; (c) U.S. military aid.

Importance of an Oil Settlement

5. The Iranian economy is basically dependent upon agriculture. Despite revenues from the oil industry, the great majority of the Iranian people have lived in poverty. However, if it receives substantial revenue from the renewed operation of its oil industry on a sound basis, Iran should be in a position to establish a self-supporting, stable govern-

ment, and carry out much-needed economic and social welfare programs. Without such revenues from the renewed operation of its oil industry, the Iranian Government will proceed from crisis to crisis, thereby greatly increasing both Tudeh Party opportunities to cause disorder or to infiltrate the government, and pressures on the United States for substantial aid. Even if Iran again receives oil revenues, there will be the continuing problem of insuring their application to programs of permanent value, and minimizing corruption.

6. In recent months some progress has been made in clarifying the positions of Iran and the U.K. toward a settlement. The resumption of UK-Iran diplomatic relations removes one obstacle to a settlement. However, the Iranian Government will continue to fear public reaction to any apparent concessions, and the British may be reluctant to accept necessary terms.

Economic Aid

7. In September 1953, the United States granted emergency assistance of $45 million to permit the Zahedi Government to meet the operating deficit inherited from the Mossadegh regime and to initiate essential monetary reforms. This aid is believed sufficient to carry the regime until May or June of 1954.

8. Until the oil revenues become substantial, emergency aid in some form will have to be continued and may have to be increased. In considering the timing and extent of such aid, the following factors must be kept in mind:

a. Too long a delay in the institution of economic and social reforms in Iran may make it impossible to seize the opportunity presented by present circumstances to increase Iran's political stability and economic health.

b. Granting of other than emergency aid prior to an oil settlement may make Iran less interested in coming to an early settlement and at the same time harm our relations with the U.K.

c. The timing and extent of U.S. aid to Iran should not be such as to encourage other nations to emulate the method employed by Iran in nationalizing her oil resources.

d. While the present government of Iran has shown itself to be favorably disposed to seek an early settlement of the oil dispute, too great or too obvious pressure from the outside may, because of internal political reasons in Iran, have the opposite effect.

9. In addition to emergency aid, the United States has [*illegible in original*] technical and economic assistance program for Iran of approximately $23 million for FY 1954. Even when substantial oil revenues are realized, it will be desirable to continue limited technical assistance to Iran for a number of years. Insofar as such assistance may effectively be provided through international or private agencies, local fears of U.S. imperialism will be minimized.

Military Aid

10. Iran has thus far received approximately $46 million in military aid from the U.S., and an additional $58 million is currently programmed. Inadequate training, maintenance and supply capabilities, and low caliber personnel restrict Iran's ability to absorb U.S. military equipment, even at the present rate of delivery. At present, the Iranian armed forces are capable of maintaining internal security against any uprising short of a nation-wide tribal revolt. It is possible that Iran will, in perhaps one or two years, be willing to move in the direction of regional security arrangements, assuming: (a) an early oil settlement; (b) continuation in power of a government friendly toward the West, which has the Shah's and widespread public support; and (c) a steady increase in the capability of the Iranian army. Iranian forces may be able to improve their capability for guerrilla and limited mountain operations, although it is unlikely that they could in themselves become capable within the foreseeable future of effectively delaying a strong Soviet thrust toward Iraq or the Persian Gulf. A long-range program of improving the Iranian armed forces should be related to the progress made toward effective regional defense plans which will provide Iran, in case of attack, with military assistance from adjacent states.

11. However, military aid to Iran has great political importance apart from its military impact. Over the long term, the most effective instrument for maintaining Iran's orientation toward the West is the monarch, which in turn has the Army as its only real source of power. U.S. military aid serves to improve Army morale, cement Army loyalty to the Shah, and thus consolidate the present regime and provide some assurance that Iran's current orientation toward the West will be perpetuated.

12. Neither the solution of the oil problem nor U.S. moral and financial support for Iran should be viewed as panaceas, but rather as measures which may permit Iran to achieve a condition of stability in which some modest progress may be made by Iran toward the working out of its own underlying problems. However, it should be recognized that physical execution of an economic development program, itself a time-consuming process, will be hampered by (1) lack of qualified Iranian administrative personnel, (2) the opposition of various vested interests, and (3) historically engendered suspicion of the West. Iran's long frontier with the USSR and the Soviet-Iranian Treaty of 1921 may affect the degree of Iranian cooperation, particularly military cooperation, with the United States.

OBJECTIVES

13. An independent Iran free from communist control.

14. A strong, stable government in Iran, capable of maintaining internal security, using Iranian resources effectively, and actively coop-

erating with the anti-communist nations of the free world.

COURSES OF ACTION

15. a. Assist Iran again to obtain substantial revenues from its oil resources.

b. Assist in every practicable way to effect an early and equitable settlement of the oil controversy between the United Kingdom and Iran.

c. If no such settlement has been arranged by July 1954, be prepared (insofar as practicable)* to take independent action with Iran, in order to bring about a sufficient resumption of revenues from its oil resources to terminate the need for U.S. emergency economic assistance.

16. Pending the time when Iran shall receive substantial revenues from her natural petroleum resources, provide emergency economic aid as necessary to the government of Iran, provided that it remains friendly to the U.S.

17. Continue limited technical and economic aid to Iran. Where appropriate utilize such private institutions and international organizations as may provide technical assistance more effectively.

18. In carrying out the courses of action in paras. 15, 16 and 17 above, the United States should:

a. Maintain full consultation with the United Kingdom.

b. Avoid unduly impairing United States-United Kingdom relations.

c. Not permit the United Kingdom to veto any United States actions which the United States considers essential to the achievement of the objectives set forth above.

d. Continue efforts to have the United Kingdom and Iran agree to a practical and equitable solution of the oil problem at the earliest possible moment and, at the same time, have the United Kingdom give full support to the Zahedi Government.

e. Be prepared to avail itself of the authority of the President to approve voluntary agreements and programs under Section 708(a) and (b) of the Defense Production Act of 1950, as amended.

19. Provide United States grant military aid for Iran designed to:

a. Improve the ability of the Iranian armed forces to maintain internal security and provide resistance to external aggression.

b. Enhance the prestige of the monarchy and the morale of the Iranian Government and military services.

20. The amount and rate of such military aid to Iran should take into account:

---

* The Defense and JCS Members propose deletion of the phrase in parenthesis, subparagraph c. The State Member proposes the following as a substitute for subparagraph c: If such a settlement has not been reached in a reasonable period of time, review U.S. policy toward the problem in the light of circumstances then existing.

a. The attitude of Iran with regard to this aid and with regard to political, economic and military cooperation with the free world, including Turkey, Pakistan, and possibly Iraq.

b. Iran's ability satisfactorily to absorb military equipment and training, and its willingness at an appropriate time to formalize necessary contracts for military aid and training.

21. Encourage Iran to enter into military cooperation with its neighbors as feasible, and to participate in any regional defense arrangement which may be developed for the Middle East.

22. Recognize the strength of Iranian nationalist feeling; try to direct it into constructive channels and be ready to exploit any opportunity to do so, bearing in mind the desirability of strengthening in Iran the ability and desire of the Iranian people to resist communist pressure.

23. Encourage the adoption by the Iranian Government of necessary financial, judicial and administrative and other reforms, including provision for an orderly succession to the crown.

24. [1 line deleted from the original copy] in achieving the above purposes.

[3 pages deleted from the original copy]

Memorandum by the Joint Chiefs of Staff for the Secretary of Defense on the MDA Program for Iran

[DRAFT]

JCS Memo 1714/68   October 12, 1954

ENCLOSURE A

1. The Joint Chiefs of Staff have reviewed the enclosed plan for reorganizing and enlarging the Iranian army at an estimated cost of $360 million over a three-year period. This cost can be divided into $122 million required from the Foreign Operations Administration for defense support and economic aid, and $238 million required from the Department of Defense for military assistance. In their estimate of the funds required to support the Iranian army over the same period, as reported in their memorandum, subject "MDA Programs FY 1955-1958 Which Will Support U.S. Military Strategy," dated 17 June 1954, the Joint Chiefs of Staff considered that approximately $62 million would be necessary. The proposed program therefore represents an increase of $176 million for military assistance above this estimate.

2. A build-up of Iranian military potential would be consistent with the military objectives of the United States in the Middle East. It may be assumed, however, that major increases in the Iranian program are likely to cause immediate pressure from other Middle Eastern countries for enlarged military and economic assistance programs. Approval

of any major increase in a military assistance program for Iran or any other Middle Eastern country should therefore be withheld until the military requirements for the Middle East have been reviewed by the Joint Chiefs of Staff, either as a result of combined United States-United Kingdom-Turkey planning studies or development of a regional defense organization. Furthermore, the value of material to be programmed for Iran should not be increased over that already planned until the Iranian army has demonstrated the capability to utilize additional materiel effectively.

3. Appropriate defense support and economic aid are desirable in conjunction with the present Mutual Defense Assistance Program for Iran. When and if an expanded military program for Iran is considered justified, additional assistance in these fields must be provided. It is therefore recommended that the Department of State and the Foreign Operations Administration be requested to determine whether the defense support and economic assistance recommended by the Chief, MAAG Iran can be partially, or totally, implemented in support of the present MDA program both with and without regard to his proposals for military expansion. . . .

ENCLOSURE C

Discussion

1. A build-up of Iranian military potential would contribute to the achievement of the military objectives in the Middle East, particularly the establishment of an adequate defense, based on the Zagros Mountain line, of the NATO right flank and essential air base sites in the area.

2. While new demands for military and economic assistance are constantly being received, the funds appropriated each year by Congress for support of these programs are decreasing. It may be assumed that major increases in the Iranian program are likely to cause immediate pressure from other Middle Eastern countries for enlarged military and economic assistance programs. Increased funds can be provided for Iran only at the expense of military and economic assistance programs in other countries.

3. In view of the above, approval of any major increase in a military assistance program for Iran or any other Middle Eastern country should be withheld until the military requirements for the defense of the Middle East have been reviewed, either by combined U.S.-U.K.-Turkey planning studies or by a regional defense organization.

4. At the same time, the friendly and cooperative attitude of the present Iranian Government should be encouraged. Some recognition should be given to the new receptiveness of the Iranian armed forces to guidance from U.S. Mission and MAAG personnel and to the marked improvement over the past year in Iran's ability to receive and utilize MDAP equipment. Accordingly, as an interim solution designed to

provide the framework for an expanded program if and when determined to be necessary, the proposed force basis should be approved in order to bring it into consonance with the existing force structure. However, it should be emphasized that the value of materiel to be programmed will not be increased over that already planned until such time as defense plans for the Middle East have been reviewed, the Iranian Army has demonstrated the capability to utilize effectively additional materiel, and the necessary defense support and economic assistance have been made available.

5. In this connection it is noted that the Department of the Army is supporting the provision of training teams intended to function at division and brigade level. The provision of these teams will provide further evidence of the interest of the United States in Iran and will at a later date permit a clear evaluation of the future capabilities of the Iranian Army.

6. As part of his recommended program, the Chief, MAAG, Iran has proposed that the Army force basis for Iran be changed as follows:

Present Force Basis	Recommended Force Basis
12 Inf Brig	8 Light Inf Div
3 Armd Brig	4 Light Armd Div
	5 Independent Inf Brig

The recommended change in force basis corresponds to the actual organization of the Iranian Army, is in fact primarily a change in nomenclature (i.e. Brigade to Light Division) and involves only an increase equivalent to one regimental combat team and one armored combat command—a total of 7,000 additional personnel.

7. The recommended program includes items such as pay and allowances for the Iranian Armed Forces, construction of barracks and quarters, relocation of stores and others which are military requirements for defense support and economic aid from Foreign Operations Administration (FOA). These aspects of the program should be reviewed by the Department of State and the FOA in order to determine their desirability and feasibility from an economic and political point of view.

Joint Chiefs of Staff Joint Intelligence Committee Memorandum for the Joint Strategic Plans Committee and the Joint Logistics Plans Committee

[ENCLOSURE-DRAFT]

April 13, 1955

INTERIM MILITARY OBJECTIVES FOR IRAN

The Joint Intelligence Committee has considered J.S.P.C. 961/48, as amended by PM-80-55, from an intelligence viewpoint, noted the divergent Service views contained therein, and concurs subject to the following changes to J.S.P.C. 961/48: . . . .

c. ENCLOSURE "A"
(1) Page 8, subparagraph 1(a)—Delete and substitute the following:

"a. From the viewpoint of attaining U.S. military objectives in the Middle East, the natural defensive barrier provided by the Zagros Mountains must be retained under Allied control indefinitely. Because Western Iran includes the Zagros Mountain barrier, geographically, Iran is the most important country in the Middle East, excluding Turkey. Iranian participation in a regional defense organization would permit the member countries to take full advantage collectively of the natural defensive barrier in Western Iran and would permit utilization of logistical facilities of the area. The relative importance of Iran in relation to other countries of the Middle East would be significantly increased if she became a partner in a regional defense organization which included Turkey, Iraq and Pakistan. Although there would be no immediate increase in military strength as a result of such a defense organization, the commitment of Iran's allies to come to her aid in the event of a Soviet attack would probably have a deterrant effect on the USSR."

(2) Page 9, subparagraph 1b—Delete and substitute the following:

"b. Within the level of the current U.S. aid program for Iran, the Iranian armed forces are capable of maintaining internal security but alone could hold none of the areas in the Middle East of critical importance to the United States for more than one month in the event of attack on Iran by a major power. The effectiveness of Iranian forces alone in defending the Zagros Mountain passes is questionable regardless of the amount of U.S. financial aid provided."

d. APPENDIX "A" TO ENCLOSURE "A"
(1) Page 18, subparagraph 6c—Delete and substitute the following:

"c. From the foregoing, it is apparent that U.S. military, as well as other interests and objectives, would be critically jeopardized should Iran come under Communist domination either through aggression or subversion; this is considered to be equally true whether Iran assumes the role of an active participant in the regional defense arrangement or serves only as an ally in spirit to the extent that her geography and topography are available to the Allies. In light of the above, and from a U.S. military viewpoint, because Western Iran includes the Zagros Mountain barrier, geographically, Iran is the most important country in the Middle East, excluding Turkey."

(2) Page 20, subparagraph 7g—Delete and substitute the following:

"g. The immediate effects of a loose regional defense grouping based on the Turkey-Pakistan-Iraq defense arrangements and backed by U.S. military aid programs would be primarily political and psychological rather than military. Creation of such a grouping would:
"(1) Tend to create a favorable climate for development of greater awareness of the Soviet threat and closer regional defense cooperation.
"(2) Possibly encourage participating states to cooperate more closely on other matters, both with the Western allies and among themselves.

"(3) Strengthen the position of Western-oriented elements in participating countries.

However, such developments would not materially affect the internal weaknesses which have thus far undermined Middle East strength and stability, and
would by no means eliminate the tensions and fears which have thus far
alienated much of the area from the West. Such a loose grouping would not per
se result in any significant reduction of the area's military vulnerability. However, together with U.S. military aid programs, it would create greater opportunities than in the past for reducing existing Middle East defense deficiencies.
The requirement for outside ground forces might eventually be significantly
reduced. However, achievement of even this limited goal would be a long and
costly operation, involving considerable training and equipment over a period
of years, and effective Middle East defense will continue to depend for the
foreseeable future on substantial Western force contributions." . . .

Message from the Chief of ARMISH and MAAG (McClure) to the Department of the Army on a Conference with the Shah Concerning United States Military Aid

April 20, 1955

. . . H.I.M. outlined his conversation in Washington substantially as reported to us. Reiterated willingness to join Middle East Pact
when Iranian military posture improved and stated military talks necessary now to determine requirements. Reassured no rpt no US policy
changes as result of pending change in Army Chief of Staff. Shah
conferred with Iraqi Government officials and Iraq Army Chief of Staff
on return from US. Iraq Army Chief of Staff concurred with concept for
defense of Khanigan Pass consisting of 1 infantry division in Hamadan
area, armored division with air support in Kerman Shah area, an Iraqi
division backstopping them in Zagros Mountains inside of Iran, with
Iraqi armor remaining mobile to protect any exits from passes into Iraq.
Also, Shah pointed out probable requirement to establish Iranian
supply depots inside of Iraq.

H.I.M. stated that Turkish President had been invited to visit Iran
and that he expected him to come. No date established. Further discussing defense of Iran, Shah recognizes there are areas which would be
extremely difficult to defend or even delay in with his limited forces.
Prepared to radioactivate these areas and desires if practicable, US
consider sending engineer to make survey of possibilities of this use. In
connection with defenses of Khanigan Pass he stated they must have
tactical air support in small quantities. He believes 3 to 5 wings consisting of 30 to 35 planes per wing would meet Iran's requirements and that
it would be necessary for outside air support to make defense of the
Zagros truly effective. Any power coming to support of Iran with aircraft would require landing facilities and base facilities in this country
and should take immediate opportunity to get them developed. He

desires engineers to make a survey for proper sites because let down procedures for jets precludes large areas of this mountainous country for utilization for jet airfields. He commented further that the conversion of the 12 Infantry Division at Kerman Shah to an armored division should be expedited. He was told that this required a JCS decision.

He asked specifically about development of the aid program, realizing that Washington's attitude for increased aid will be based on success of training teams. Shah was informed of our budget procedures and that any funds in FY 55 would have to be taken from other commitments or be surplus to other requirements. Further that Iran's position had to be viewed with respect to the world situation. Deliveries made during FY 55 were related to him and made quite an impression. He was told that requests for defense support and direct support in consonance with the program submitted to Washington in August 1954 had been made and that further information on this program depended on Congress and appropriations for FY 56.

H.I.M. stated that he would give full support to training teams and asked what the reaction of training team personnel was to the task involving them and what progress they were making. He was informed that they were making considerable progress and they were quite optimistic. He was also informed that General Bullock offered assistance in developing information program which would enhance prestige of armed forces and explain to civilian population obligations of citizens toward their country and necessity of serving in the Army as well as benefits gained by individuals. Detailed report follows in diplomatic pouch.

Department of State Office of Intelligence Research: The Formulation of Iranian Foreign Policy

[ABSTRACT]

September 1, 1955

Iran's present foreign policy is based on two assumptions—that the United States will exert all feasible efforts to prevent the loss of Iranian independence to the USSR or, probably to a lesser degree, the UK; and that there are very real though unpublicized differences between the US and the UK which can be exploited to maintain Iranian bargaining power. So long as Iranian policymakers remain confident of these assumptions, the government will feel free to engage in actions and attitudes which are regarded primarily as enhancing Iranian prestige. Thus, they can be expected frequently to disregard US advice, develop closer relations with the Soviet bloc and India, resist settlement of disputes with Pakistan, Afghanistan, and Iraq, and even press irridentist claims to Bahrein Island. With these calculated deviations, Iran is likely to continue to adhere to its present policy of relying primarily on the United States, but to counterbalance rising US military influence by encouraging UK preponderance in the economic sphere.

With the marked improvement in Iran's financial prospects as a result of the oil settlement, the Shah has set his sights once more on his dream of an effective modern army as the key to enhancing his personal prestige and that of the dynasty, raising the national morale, and increasing Iran's international prestige. With this aim in mind, he is likely to continue to press for US military aid, to complain that whatever is forthcoming is insufficient, and to compare such aid unfavorably with US aid to Turkey. He will probably hold off on making any public formal commitment, such as adherence to the Turkish-Iraqi Pact, for two reasons: (1) he sees advantages in maintaining a flexible, bargaining position, and (2) he is not entirely a free agent on foreign policy commitments. Adherence to a regional pact would require Majlis ratification. The strong component of vested interests in the Majlis is lukewarm to any build-up of the armed forces which would cut seriously into oil revenues and any steps which could lead to the kind of authoritarian military regime imposed by the present Shah's father. Should he press too fast in implementing his reform program and strengthening Western ties, he runs the risk of bolstering his opposition—i.e., Mosadeq's nationalistic followers and the conservative politicians. Although this opposition would probably not be united, it could be effective on specific issues. The possibility of the Shah's assassination would be increased. If there were a serious reduction of oil revenues within the next five years, a recurrence of the anti-foreign emotionalisms of the Mosadeq period would be a distinct probability with potentially disastrous consequences for Iran.

ECONOMIC AND DIPLOMATIC RELATIONS SOLIDIFY AS UNITED STATES ECONOMIC AND TECHNICAL ASSISTANCE CONTINUES

FOA Announces Program of Aid to Iran, 1954

State Department Press Release   *November 1954*

The Foreign Operations Administration on November 2 announced that the United States is prepared to offer aid to Iran in the form of loans and grants totaling $127.3 million.

Both Iranian and U.S. Government circles have concerned themselves recently with the indication that, even with an oil settlement accomplished, it would be 3 years until Iran's oil revenues would permit it to finance large-scale development from its own resources. To help Iran during the interim period, the United States has decided to make available up to $127.3 million which would be provided from both Foreign Operations Administration and Export-Import sources. This total includes $21.5 million for a technical-cooperation program; $52.8 million for consumer-goods imports, which will be sold by the Iranian Government for local currency (rials), which in turn will be used to support basic governmental expenditures as has been done in the past year; and an additional $53 million largely for short-term developmental assistance, which would be provided for specifically approved projects.

Iran has not yet fully developed its own plans for economic development although it has submitted proposed projects to the Export-Import Bank for preliminary considerations. Some time, however, will be required for Iran fully to prepare project plans and establish priorities among them, and for the bank to make its required investigations. Of the above $127.3 million, $85 million is being offered in the form of loans, the balance in grants; $15 million of the latter has already been allotted on an emergency basis.

With this assistance the Iranian Government will be able to finance essential Government operations as well as develop and initiate a sound economic development program.

FOA Loan to Iran, 1955

State Department Press Release   *April 25, 1955*

An agreement for a $32 million loan to Iran was announced on April 4 by the Foreign Operations Administration. The agreement was signed by Nasrollah Entezam, the Iranian Ambassador to the United States, and Glen E. Edgerton, chairman of the board and president of the Export-Import Bank of Washington.

FOA loans, made under provisions of section 505 of the Mutual Security Act, are negotiated by the Department of State and FOA. FOA is responsible for disbursement of the loans, and other administration is handled by the Export-Import Bank.

Section 505 provides that, of funds made available to FOA this year for assistance to foreign countries, the equivalent of $200 million or more, including foreign currencies received from the sale of surplus agricultural commodities, is to be in the form of loans.

The Iranian loan, which is repayable in U.S. dollars over a 25-year period at an average rate of interest of 2.41 percent, is part of FOA's $74.3 million allotment to that country for technical cooperation and development assistance during the current fiscal year. The loan funds will help Iran carry out its extensive plan for economic development.

The overall U.S. program of economic assistance to Iran during the current year totals $127 million. This total includes the new FOA loan, an FOA grant of $42.3 million, and a $53 million Export-Import Bank loan, largely for development projects.

Detailed plans for projects will be formulated by the Government of Iran; negotiations between Iran officials and a mission from the Export-Import Bank will begin in the near future.

Treaty of Amity, Economic Relations, and Consular Rights between the United States and Iran

August 15, 1955	*Treaty signed at Tehran.*
July 11, 1956	*Ratification advised by the Senate of the United States of America.*
September 14, 1956	*Ratified by the President of the United States of America.*
April 30, 1957	*Ratified by Iran.*
May 16, 1957	*Ratifications exchanged at Tehran.*
June 27, 1957	*Proclaimed by the President of the United States of America.*
June 16, 1957	*Entered into force.*

By the President of the United States of America
A PROCLAMATION

Whereas a treaty of amity, economic relations, and consular rights between the United States of America and Iran was signed at Tehran on August 15, 1955, the original of which treaty, being in the English and Persian languages, is word for word as follows:

The United States of America and Iran, desirous of emphasizing the friendly relations which have long prevailed between their peoples, of reaffirming the high principles in the regulation of human affairs to which they are committed, of encouraging mutually beneficial trade and investments and closer economic intercourse generally between their peoples, and of regulating consular relations, have resolved to conclude, on the basis of reciprocal equality of treatment, a Treaty of Amity, Economic Relations, and Consular Rights, and have appointed as their Plenipotentiaries:

The President of the United States of America:

Mr. Selden Chapin, Ambassador Extraordinary and Plenipotentiary of the United States of America at Tehran; and

His Imperial Majesty, the Shah of Iran;

His Excellency Mr. Mostafa Samiy, Under Secretary of the Ministry of Foreign Affairs;

Who, having communicated to each other their full powers found to be in due form, have agreed upon the following articles:

ARTICLE I

There shall be firm and enduring peace and sincere friendship between the United States of America and Iran.

ARTICLE II

1. Nationals of either High Contracting Party shall be permitted, upon terms no less favorable than those accorded to nationals of any third country, to enter and remain in the territories of the other High Contracting Party for the purpose of carrying on trade between their own country and the territories of such other High Contracting Party and engaging in related commercial activities, and for the purpose of developing and directing the operations of an enterprise in which they have invested, or in which they are actively in the process of investing, a substantial amount of capital.

2. Nationals of either High Contracting Party within the territories of the other High Contracting Party shall, either individually or through associations, and so long as their activities are not contrary to public order, safety or morals: (a) be permitted to travel therein freely and reside at places of their choice; (b) enjoy freedom of conscience and the right to hold religious services; (c) be permitted to engage in philanthropic, educational and scientific activities; and (d) have the right to gather and transmit information for dissemination to the public abroad, and otherwise to communicate with other persons inside and outside such territories. They shall also be permitted to engage in the practice of professions for which they have qualified under the applicable legal provisions governing admission to professions.

3. The provisions of paragraphs 1 and 2 of the present Article shall be subject to the right of either High Contracting Party to apply measures which are necessary to maintain public order, and to protect public health, morals and safety, including the right to expel, to exclude or to limit the movement of aliens on the said grounds.

4. Nationals of either High Contracting Party shall receive the most constant protection and security within the territories of the other High Contracting Party. When any such national is in custody, he shall in every respect receive reasonable and humane treatment; and, on his demand, the diplomatic or consular representative of his country shall without unnecessary delay be notified and accorded full opportunity to safeguard his interests. He shall be promptly informed of the accusations against him, allowed all facilities reasonably necessary to his defense and given a prompt and impartial disposition of his case.

ARTICLE III

1. Companies constituted under the applicable laws and regulations of either High Contracting Party shall have their juridical status recognized within the territories of the other High Contracting Party. It is understood, however, that recognition of juridical status does not of itself confer rights upon companies to engage in the activities for which

they are organized. As used in the present Treaty, "companies" means corporations, partnerships, companies and other associations, whether or not with limited liability and whether or not for pecuniary profit.

2. Nationals and companies of either High Contracting Party shall have freedom of access to the courts of justice and administrative agencies within the territories of the other High Contracting Party, in all degress of jurisdiction, both in defense and pursuit of their rights, to the end that prompt and impartial justice be done. Such access shall be allowed, in any event, upon terms no less favorable than those applicable to nationals and companies of such other High Contracting Party or of any third country. It is understood that companies not engaged in activities within the country shall enjoy the right of such access without any requirement of registration or domestication.

3. The private settlement of disputes of a civil nature, involving nationals and companies of either High Contracting Party, shall not be discouraged within the territories of the other High Contracting Party; and, in cases of such settlement by arbitration, neither the alienage of the arbitrators nor the foreign situs of the arbitration proceedings shall of themselves be a bar to the enforceability of awards duly resulting therefrom.

ARTICLE IV

1. Each High Contracting Party shall at all times accord fair and equitable treatment to nationals and companies of the other High Contracting Party, and to their property and enterprises; shall refrain from applying unreasonable or discriminatory measures that would impair their legally acquired rights and interests; and shall assure that their lawful contractual rights are afforded effective means of enforcement, in conformity with the applicable laws.

2. Property of nationals and companies of either High Contracting Party, including interests in property, shall receive the most constant protection and security within the territories of the other High Contracting Party, in no case less than that required by international law. Such property shall not be taken except for a public purpose, nor shall it be taken without the prompt payment of just compensation. Such compensation shall be in an effectively realizable form and shall represent the full equivalent of the property taken; and adequate provision shall have been made at or prior to the time of taking for the determination and payment thereof.

3. The dwellings, offices, warehouses, factories and other premises of nationals and companies of either High Contracting Party located within the territories of the other High Contracting Party shall not be subject to entry or molestation without just cause. Official searches and examinations of such premises and their contents, shall be made only according to law and with careful regard for the convenience of the occupants and the conduct of business.

4. Enterprises which nationals and companies of either High Contracting Party are permitted to establish or acquire, within the territories of the other High Contracting Party, shall be permitted freely to conduct their activities therein, upon terms no less favorable than other enterprises of whatever nationality engaged in similar activities. Such nationals and companies shall enjoy the right to continued control and management of such enterprises; to engage attorneys, agents, accountants and other technical experts, executive personnel, interpreters and other specialized employees of their choice; and to do all other things necessary or incidental to the effective conduct of their affairs.

ARTICLE V

1. Nationals and companies of either High Contracting Party shall be permitted, within the territories of the other High Contracting Party: (a) to lease, for suitable periods of time, real property needed for their residence or for the conduct of activities pursuant to the present Treaty; (b) to purchase or otherwise acquire personal property of all kinds; and (c) to dispose of property of all kinds by sale, testament or otherwise. The treatment accorded in these respects shall in no event be less favorable than that accorded nationals and companies of any third country.

2. Upon compliance with the applicable laws and regulations respecting registration and other formalities, nationals and companies of either High Contracting Party shall be accorded within the territories of the other High Contracting Party effective protection in the exclusive use of inventions, trade marks and trade names.

ARTICLE VI

1. Nationals and companies of either High Contracting Party shall not be subject to the payment of taxes, fees or charges within the territories of the other High Contracting Party, or to requirements with respect to the levy and collection thereof, more burdensome than those borne by nationals, residents and companies of any third country. In the case of nationals of either High Contracting Party residing within the territories of the other High Contracting Party, and of nationals and companies of either High Contracting Party engaged in trade or other gainful pursuit or in non-profit activities therein, such payments and requirements shall not be more burdensome than those borne by nationals and companies of such other High Contracting Party.

2. Each High Contracting Party, however, reserves the right to: (a) extend specific tax advantages only on the basis of reciprocity, or pursuant to agreements for the avoidance of double taxation or the mutual protection of revenue; and (b) apply special requirements as to the exemptions of a personal nature allowed to non-residents in connection with income and inheritance taxes.

3. Companies of either High Contracting Party shall not be subject, within the territories of the other High Contracting Party, to taxes

upon any income, transactions or capital not attributable to the operations and investment thereof within such territories.

ARTICLE VII

1. Neither High Contracting Party shall apply restrictions on the making of payments, remittances, and other transfers of funds to or from the territories of the other High Contracting Party, except (a) to the extent necessary to assure the availability of foreign exchange for payments for goods and services essential to the health and welfare of its people, or (b) in the case of a member of the International Monetary Fund, restrictions specifically approved by the Fund.

2. If either High Contracting Party applies exchange restrictions, it shall promptly make reasonable provision for the withdrawal, in foreign exchange in the currency of the other High Contracting Party, of: (a) the compensation referred to in Article IV, paragraph 2, of the present Treaty, (b) earnings, whether in the form of salaries, interest, dividends, commissions, royalties, payments for technical services, or otherwise, and (c) amounts for amortization of loans, depreciation of direct investments and capital transfers, giving consideration to special needs for other transactions. If more than one rate of exchange is in force, the rate applicable to such withdrawals shall be a rate which is specifically approved by the International Monetary Fund for such transactions or, in the absence of a rate so approved, an effective rate which, inclusive of any taxes or surcharges on exchange transfers, is just and reasonable.

3. Either High Contracting Party applying exchange restrictions shall in general administer them in a manner not to influence disadvantageously the competitive position of the commerce, transport or investment of capital of the other High Contracting Party in comparison with the commerce, transport or investment of capital of any third country; and shall afford such other High Contracting Party adequate opportunity for consultation at any time regarding the application of the present Article.

ARTICLE VIII

1. Each High Contracting Party shall accord to products of the other High Contracting Party, from whatever place and by whatever type of carrier arriving, and to products destined for exportation to the territories of such other High Contracting Party, by whatever route and by whatever type of carrier, treatment no less favorable than that accorded like products of or destined for exportation to any third country, in all matters relating to: (a) duties, other charges, regulations and formalities, on or in connection with importation and exportation; and (b) internal taxation, sale, distribution, storage and use. The same rule shall apply with respect to the international transfer of payments for imports and exports.

2. Neither High Contracting Party shall impose restrictions or

prohibitions on the importation of any product of the other High Contracting Party or on the exportation of any product to the territories of the other High Contracting Party, unless the importation of the like product of, or the exportation of the like product to, all third countries is similarly restricted or prohibited.

3. If either High Contracting Party imposes quantitative restrictions on the importation or exportation of any product in which the other High Contracting Party has an important interest:

(a) It shall as a general rule give prior public notice of the total amount of the product, by quantity or value, that may be imported or exported during a specified period, and of any change in such amount or period; and

(b) If it makes allotments to any third country, it shall afford such other High Contracting Party a share proportionate to the amount of the product, by quantity or value, supplied by or to it during a previous representative period, due consideration being given to any special factors affecting the trade in such product.

4. Either High Contracting Party may impose prohibitions or restrictions on sanitary or other customary grounds of a non-commercial nature, or in the interest of preventing deceptive or unfair practices. provided such prohibitions or restrictions do not arbitrarily discriminate against the commerce of the other High Contracting Party.

5. Either High Contracting Party may adopt measures necessary to assure the utilization of accumulated inconvertible currencies or to deal with a stringency of foreign exchange. However, such measures shall deviate no more than necessary from a policy designed to promote the maximum development of nondiscriminatory multilateral trade and to expedite the attainment of a balance-of-payments position which will obviate the necessity of such measures.

6. Each High Contracting Party reserves the right to accord special advantages: (a) to products of its national fisheries, (b) to adjacent countries in order to facilitate frontier traffic, or (c) by virtue of a customs union or free trade area of which either High Contracting Party, after consultation with the other High Contracting Party, may become a member. Each High Contracting Party, moreover, reserves rights and obligations it may have under the General Agreement on Tariffs and Trade, and special advantages it may accord pursuant thereto.

ARTICLE IX

1. In the administration of its customs regulations and procedures, each High Contracting Party shall: (a) promptly publish all requirements of general application affecting importation and exportation; (b) apply such requirements in a uniform, impartial and reasonable manner; (c) refrain, as a general practice, from enforcing new or more burdensome requirements until after public notice thereof; (d) provide

an appeals procedure by which prompt and impartial review of administrative action in customs matters can be obtained; and (e) not impose greater than nominal penalties for infractions resulting from clerical errors or from mistakes made in good faith.

2. Nationals and companies of either High Contracting Party shall be accorded treatment no less favorable than that accorded nationals and companies of the other High Contracting Party, or of any third country, with respect to all matters relating to importation and exportation.

3. Neither High Contracting Party shall impose any measure of a discriminatory nature that hinders or prevents the importer or exporter of products of either country from obtaining marine insurance on such products in companies of either High Contracting Party.

ARTICLE X

1. Between the territories of the two High Contracting Parties there shall be freedom of commerce and navigation.

2. Vessels under the flag of either High Contracting Party, and carrying the papers required by its law in proof of nationality, shall be deemed to be vessels of that High Contracting Party both on the high seas and within the ports, places and waters of the other High Contracting Party.

3. Vessels of either High Contracting Party shall have liberty, on equal terms with vessels of the other High Contracting Party and on equal terms with vessels of any third country, to come with their cargoes to all ports, places and waters of such other High Contracting Party open to foreign commerce and navigation. Such vessels and cargoes shall in all respects be accorded national treatment and most-favored-nation treatment within the ports, places and waters of such other High Contracting Party; but each High Contracting Party may reserve exclusive rights and privileges to its own vessels with respect to the coasting trade, inland navigation and national fisheries.

4. Vessels of either High Contracting Party shall be accorded national treatment and most-favored-nation treatment by the other High Contracting Party with respect to the right to carry all products that may be carried by vessel to or from the territories of such other High Contracting Party; and such products shall be accorded treatment no less favorable than that accorded like products carried in vessels of such other High Contracting Party, with respect to: (a) duties and charges of all kinds, (b) the administration of the customs, and (c) bounties, drawbacks and other privileges of this nature.

5. Vessels of either High Contracting Party that are in distress shall be permitted to take refuge in the nearest port or haven of the other High Contracting Party, and shall receive friendly treatment and assistance.

6. The term "vessels," as used herein, means all types of vessels, whether privately owned or operated, or publicly owned or operated; but this term does not, except with reference to paragraphs 2 and 5 of the

present Article, include fishing vessels or vessels of war.

ARTICLE XI

1. Each High Contracting Party undertakes (a) that enterprises owned or controlled by its Government, and that monopolies or agencies granted exclusive or special privileges within its territories, shall make their purchases and sales involving either imports or exports affecting the commerce of the other High Contracting Party solely in accordance with commercial considerations, including price, quality, availability, marketability, transportation and other conditions of purchase or sale; and (b) that the nationals, companies and commerce of such other High Contracting Party shall be afforded adequate opportunity, in accordance with customary business practice, to compete for participation in such purchases and sales.

2. Each High Contracting Party shall accord to the nationals, companies and commerce of the other High Contracting Party fair and equitable treatment, as compared with that accorded to the nationals, companies and commerce of any third country, with respect to: (a) the governmental purchase of supplies, (b) the awarding of government contracts, and (c) the sale of any service sold by the Government or by any monopoly or agency granted exclusive or special privileges.

3. The High Contracting Parties recognize that conditions of competitive equality should be maintained in situations in which publicly owned or controlled trading or manufacturing enterprises of either High Contracting Party engage in competition, within the territories thereof, with privately owned and controlled enterprises of nationals and companies of the other High Contracting Party. Accordingly, such private enterprises shall, in such situations, be entitled to the benefit of any special advantages of an economic nature accorded such public enterprises, whether in the nature of subsidies, tax exemptions or otherwise. The foregoing rule shall not apply, however, to special advantages given in connection with: (a) manufacturing goods for government use, or supplying goods and services to the Government for government use; or (b) supplying at prices substantially below competitive prices, the needs of particular population groups for essential goods and services not otherwise practically obtainable by such groups.

4. No enterprise of either High Contracting Party, including corporations, associations, and government agencies and instrumentalities, which is publicly owned or controlled shall, if it engages in commercial, industrial, shipping or other business activities within the territories of the other High Contracting Party, claim or enjoy, either for itself or for its property, immunity therein from taxation, suit, execution of judgment or other liability to which privately owned and controlled enterprises are subject therein.

ARTICLE XII

Each High Contracting Party shall have the right to send to the other High Contracting Party consular representatives, who, having presented their credentials and having been recognized in a consular capacity, shall be provided, free of charge, with exequaturs or other authorization.

ARTICLE XIII

1. Consular representatives of each High Contracting Party shall be permitted to reside in the territory of the other High Contracting Party at the places where consular officers of any third country are permitted to reside and at other places by consent of the other High Contracting Party. Consular officers and employees shall enjoy the privileges and immunities accorded to officers and employees of their rank or status by general international usage and shall be permitted to exercise all functions which are in accordance with such usage; in any event they shall be treated, subject to reciprocity, in a manner no less favorable than similar officers and employees of any third country.

2. The consular offices shall not be entered by the police or other local authorities without the consent of the consular officer, except that in the case of fire or other disaster, or if the local authorities have probable cause to believe that a crime of violence has been or is about to be committed in the consular office, consent to entry shall be presumed. In no case shall they examine or seize the papers there deposited.

ARTICLE XIV

1. All furniture, equipment and supplies consigned to or withdrawn from customs custody for a consular or diplomatic office of either High Contracting Party for official use shall be exempt within the territories of the other High Contracting Party from all customs duties and internal revenue or other taxes imposed upon or by reason of importation.

2. The baggage, effects and other articles imported exclusively for the personal use of consular officers and diplomatic and consular employees and members of their families residing with them, who are nationals of the sending state and are not engaged in any private occupation for gain in the territories of the receiving state, shall be exempt from all customs duties and internal revenue or other taxes imposed upon or by reason of importation. Such exemptions shall be granted with respect to the property accompanying the person entitled thereto on first arrival and on subsequent arrivals, and to that consigned to such officers and employees during the period in which they continue in status.

3. It is understood, however, that: (a) paragraph 2 of the present Article shall apply as to consular officers and diplomatic and consular employees only when their names have been communicated to the appropriate authorities of the receiving state and they have been duly recognized in their official capacity; (b) in the case of consignments, either High Contracting Party may, as a condition to the granting of

exemption, require that a notification of any such consignment be given, in a prescribed manner; and (c) nothing herein authorizes importations specifically prohibited by law.

ARTICLE XV

1. The Government of either High Contracting Party may, in the territory of the other, acquire, own, lease for any period of time, or otherwise hold and occupy, such lands, buildings, and appurtenances as may be necessary and appropriate for governmental, other than military, purposes. If under the local law the permission of the local authorities must be obtained as a prerequisite to any such acquiring or holding, such permission shall be given on request.

2. Lands and buildings situated in the territories of either High Contracting Party, of which the other High Contracting Party is the legal or equitable owner and which are used exclusively for governmental purposes by that owner, shall be exempt from taxation of every kind, national, state, provincial and municipal, other than assessments levied for services or local public improvements by which the premises are benefited.

ARTICLE XVI

1. No tax or other similar charge of any kind, whether of a national, state, provincial, or municipal nature, shall be levied or collected within the territories of the receiving state in respect of the official emoluments, salaries, wages or allowances received (a) by a consular officer of the sending state as compensation for his consular services, or (b) by a consular employee thereof as compensation for his services as a consulate. Likewise, consular officers and employees, who are permanent employees of the sending state and are not engaged in private occupation for gain within the territories of the receiving state, shall be exempt from all taxes or other similar charges, the legal incidence of which would otherwise fall upon such officers or employees.

2. The preceding paragraph shall not apply in respect of taxes and other similar charges upon: (a) the ownership or occupation of immovable property situated within the territories of the receiving state; (b) income derived from sources within such territories (except the compensation mentioned in the preceding paragraph); or (c) the passing of property at death.

3. The provisions of the present Article shall have like application to diplomatic officers and employees, who shall in addition be accorded all exemptions allowed them under general international usage.

ARTICLE XVII

The exemptions provided for in Articles XIV and XVI shall not apply to nationals of the sending state who are also nationals of the receiving state, or to any other person who is a national of the receiving state, nor to persons having immigrant status who have been lawfully admitted for permanent residence in the receiving state.

ARTICLE XVIII

Consular officers and employees are not subject to local jurisdiction for acts done in their official character and within the scope of their authority. No consular officer or employee shall be required to present his official files before the courts or to make declaration with respect to their contents.

ARTICLE XIX

A consular officer shall have the right within his district to: (a) interview, communicate with, assist and advise any national of the sending state; (b) inquire into any incidents which have occurred affecting the interests of any such national; and (c) assist any such national in proceedings before or in relations with the authorities of the receiving state and, where necessary, arrange for legal assistance to which he is entitled. A national of the sending state shall have the right at all times to communicate with a consular officer of his country and, unless subject to lawful detention, to visit him at the consular office.

ARTICLE XX

1. The present Treaty shall not preclude the application of measures:

    (a) regulating the importation or exportation of gold or silver;

    (b) relating to fissionable materials, the radio-active by-products thereof, or the sources thereof;

    (c) regulating the production of or traffic in arms, ammunition and implements of war, or traffic in other materials carried on directly or indirectly for the purpose of supplying a military establishment; and

    (d) necessary to fulfill the obligations of a High Contracting Party for the maintenance or restoration of international peace and security, or necessary to protect its essential security interests.

2. The present Treaty does not accord any rights to engage in political activities.

3. The stipulations of the present Treaty shall not extend to advantages accorded by the United States of America or its Territories and possessions, irrespective of any future change in their political status, to one another, to the Republic of Cuba, to the Republic of the Philippines, to the Trust Territory of the Pacific Islands or to the Panama Canal Zone.

4. The provisions of Article II, Paragraph 1, shall be construed as extending to nationals of either High Contracting Party seeking to enter the territories of the other High Contracting Party solely for the purpose of developing and directing the operations of an enterprise in the territories of such other High Contracting Party in which their employer has invested or is actively in the process of investing a substantial amount of capital: provided that such employer is a national or company of the same nationality as the applicant and that the applicant

is employed by such national or company in a responsible capacity.

ARTICLE XXI

1. Each High Contracting Party shall accord sympathetic consideration to, and shall afford adequate opportunity for consultation regarding, such representations as the other High Contracting Party may make with respect to any matter affecting the operation of the present Treaty.

2. Any dispute between the High Contracting Parties as to the interpretation or application of the present Treaty, not satisfactorily adjusted by diplomacy, shall be submitted to the International Court of Justice, unless the High Contracting Parties agree to settlement by some other pacific means.

ARTICLE XXII

1. The present Treaty shall replace the following agreements between the United States of America and Iran:

(a) the provisional agreement relating to commercial and other relations, concluded at Tehran May 14, 1928, and

(b) the provisional agreement relating to personal status and family law, concluded at Tehran July 11, 1928.

2. Nothing in the present Treaty shall be construed to supersede any provision of the trade agreement and the supplementary exchange of notes between the United States of America and Iran, concluded at Washington April 8, 1943.

ARTICLE XXIII

1. The present Treaty shall be ratified, and the ratifications thereof shall be exchanged at Tehran as soon as possible.

2. The present Treaty shall enter into force one month after the day of exchange of ratifications. It shall remain in force for ten years and shall continue in force thereafter until terminated as provided herein.

3. Either High Contracting Party may, by giving one year's written notice to the other High Contracting Party, terminate the present Treaty at the end of the initial ten-year period or at any time thereafter.

In witness whereof the respective Plenipotentiaries have signed the present Treaty and have affixed hereunto their seals.

Done in duplicate, in the English and Persian languages, both equally authentic, at Tehran this fifteenth day of August one thousand nine hundred fifty-five, corresponding with the twenty-third day of Mordad one thousand three hundred and thirty-four.

SELDEN CHAPIN	MOSTAFA SAMIY
[SEAL]	[SEAL]

Whereas the Senate of the United States of America by their resolution of July 11, 1956, two-thirds of the Senators present concurring therein, did advise and consent to the ratification of the said treaty;

Whereas the said treaty was ratified by the President of the United States of America on September 14, 1956, in pursuance of the aforesaid advice and consent of the Senate, and has been duly ratified on the part of Iran;

Whereas the respective instruments of ratification of the said treaty were duly exchanged at Tehran on May 16, 1957;

And whereas it is provided in Article XXIII of the said treaty that the treaty shall enter into force one month after the day of exchange of ratifications;

Now, therefore, be it known that I, Dwight D. Eisenhower, President of the United States of America, do hereby proclaim and make public the said treaty to the end that the same and every article and clause thereof may be observed and fulfilled in good faith on and after June 16, 1957, one month after the day of exchange of ratification, by the United States of America and by the citizens of the United States of America and all other persons subject to the jurisdiction thereof.

In testimony whereof, I have hereunto set my hand and caused the Seal of the United States of America to be affixed.

Done at the city of Washington this twenty-seventh day of June in the year of our Lord one thousand nine hundred fifty-seven and of the Independence of the United States of America the one hundred eighty-first.

[SEAL]   DWIGHT D. EISENHOWER
By the President:
  JOHN FOSTER DULLES
    Secretary of State

Agreement on Cooperation for Civil Uses of Atomic Energy between the United States and Iran

March 5, 1957   Agreement signed at Washington.
April 27, 1959   Entered into force.

Whereas the peaceful uses of atomic energy hold great promise for all mankind; and

Whereas the Government of the United States of America and the Government of Iran desire to cooperate with each other in the development of such peaceful uses of atomic energy; and

Whereas the design and development of several types of research reactors are well advanced; and

Whereas research reactors are useful in the production of research quantities of radioisotopes, in medical therapy and in numerous other research activities and at the same time are a means of affording valuable training and experience in nuclear science and engineering useful in the development of other peaceful uses of atomic energy including civilian nuclear power; and

Whereas the Government of Iran desires to pursue a research and development program looking toward the realization of the peaceful and humanitarian uses of atomic energy and desires to obtain assistance from the Government of the United States of America and United States industry with respect to this program; and

Whereas the Government of the United States of America, acting through the United States Atomic Energy Commission, desires to assist the Government of Iran in such a program;

The Parties agree as follows:

ARTICLE I

For the purposes of this Agreement:

(a) "Commission" means the United States Atomic Energy Commission or its duly authorized representatives.

(b) "Equipment and devices" means any instrument or apparatus and includes research reactors, as defined herein, and their component parts.

(c) "Research reactor" means a reactor which is designed for the production of neutrons and other radiations for general research and development purposes, medical therapy, or training in nuclear science and engineering. The term does not cover power reactors, power demonstration reactors, or reactors designed primarily for the production of special nuclear materials.

(d) The terms "Restricted Data," "atomic weapon," and "special nuclear material" are used in this Agreement as defined in the United States Atomic Energy Act of 1954.

ARTICLE II

Restricted Data shall not be communicated under this Agreement, and no materials or equipment and devices shall be transferred and no services shall be furnished under this Agreement to the Government of Iran or authorized persons under its jurisdiction if the transfer of any such materials or equipment and devices or the furnishing of any such services involves the communication of Restricted Data.

ARTICLE III

1. Subject to the provisions of Article II, the Parties hereto will exchange information in the following fields:

(a) Design, construction, and operation of research reactors and their use as research, development, and engineering tolls and in medical therapy.

(b) Health and safety problems related to the operation and use of research reactors.

(c) The use of radioactive isotopes in physical and biological research, medical therapy, agriculture, and industry.

2. The application or use of any information or data of any kind whatsoever, including design drawings and specifications, exchanged

under this Agreement shall be the responsibility of the Party which receives and uses such information or data, and it is understood that the other cooperating Party does not warrant the accuracy, completeness, or suitability of such information or data for any particular use or application.

ARTICLE IV

1. The Commission will lease to the Government of Iran uranium enriched in the isotope U-235, subject to the terms and conditions provided herein, as may be required as initial and replacement fuel in the operation of research reactors which the Government of Iran, in consultation with the Commission, decides to construct and as required in the agreed experiments related thereto. Also, the Commission will lease to the Government of Iran uranium enriched in the isotope U-235, subject to the terms and conditions provided herein, as may be required as initial and replacement fuel in the operation of such research reactors as the Government of Iran may, in consultation with the Commission, decide to authorize private individuals or private organizations under its jurisdiction to construct and operate, provided the Government of Iran shall at all times maintain sufficient control of the material and the operation of the reactor to enable the Government of Iran to comply with the provisions of this Agreement and the applicable provisions of the lease arrangement.

2. The quantity of uranium enriched in the isotope U-235 transferred by the Commission under this Article and in the custody of the Government of Iran shall not at any time be in excess of six (6) kilograms of contained U-235 in uranium enriched up to a maximum of twenty percent (20%) U-235, plus such additional quantity as, in the opinion of the Commission, is necessary to permit the efficient and continuous operation of the reactor or reactors while replaced fuel elements are radioactively cooling in Iran or while fuel elements are in transit, it being the intent of the Commission to make possible the maximum usefulness of the six (6) kilograms of said material.

3. When any fuel elements containing U-235 leased by the Commission require replacement, they shall be returned to the Commission and, except as may be agreed, the form and content of the irradiated fuel elements shall not be altered after their removal from the reactor and prior to delivery to the Commission.

4. The lease of uranium enriched in the isotope U-235 under this Article shall be at such charges and on such terms and conditions with respect to shipment and delivery as may be mutually agreed and under the conditions stated in Articles VIII and IX.

ARTICLE V

Materials of interest in connection with defined research projects related to the peaceful uses of atomic energy undertaken by the Government of Iran, including source materials, special nuclear materials, byproduct material, other radioisotopes, and stable isotopes, will be sold or otherwise transferred to the Government of Iran by the Commission for research purposes in such quantities and under such terms and conditions as may be agreed when such materials are not available commercially. In no case, however, shall the quantity of special nuclear materials under the jurisdiction of the Government of Iran, by reason of transfer under this Article, be, at any one time, in excess of 100 grams of contained U-235, 10 grams of plutonium, and 10 grams of U-233.

ARTICLE VI

Subject to the availability of supply and as may be mutually agreed, the Commission will sell or lease, through such means as it deems appropriate, to the Government of Iran or authorized persons under its jurisdiction such reactor materials, other than special nuclear materials, as are not obtainable on the commercial market and which are required in the construction and operation of research reactors in Iran. The sale or lease of these materials shall be on such terms as may be agreed.

ARTICLE VII

It is contemplated that, as provided in this Article, private individuals and private organizations in either the United States or Iran may deal directly with private individuals and private organizations in the other country. Accordingly, with respect to the subjects of agreed exchange of information as provided in Article III, the Government of the United States will permit persons under its jurisdiction to transfer and export materials, including equipment and devices, to and perform services for the Government of Iran and such persons under its jurisdiction as are authorized by the Government of Iran to receive and possess such materials and utilize such services, subject to:

(a) The provisions of Article II.

(b) Applicable laws, regulations and license requirements of the Government of the United States and the Government of Iran.

ARTICLE VIII

1. The Government of Iran agrees to maintain such safeguards as are necessary to assure that the special nuclear materials received from the Commission shall be used solely for the purposes agreed in accordance with this Agreement and to assure the safekeeping of this material.

2. The Government of Iran agrees to maintain such safeguards as are necessary to assure that all other reactor materials, including equipment and devices, purchased in the United States under this Agreement by the Government of Iran or authorized persons under its jurisdiction shall be used solely for the design, construction, and operation of research reactors which the Government of Iran decides to construct and operate and for research in connection therewith, except as may otherwise be agreed.

3. In regard to research reactors constructed pursuant to this Agree-

ment, the Government of Iran agrees to maintain records relating to power levels of operation and burn-up of reactor fuels and to make annual reports to the Commission on these subjects. If the Commission requests, the Government of Iran will permit Commission representatives to observe from time to time the condition and use of any leased material and to observe the performance of the reactor in which the material is used.

4. Some atomic energy materials which the Government of Iran may request the Commission to provide in accordance with this arrangement are harmful to persons and property unless handled and used carefully. After delivery of such materials to the Government of Iran, the Government of Iran shall bear all responsibility, in so far as the Government of the United States is concerned, for the safe handling and use of such materials. With respect to any special nuclear materials or fuel elements which the Commission may, pursuant to this Agreement, lease to the Government of Iran or to any private individual or private organization under its jurisdiction, the Government of Iran shall indemnify and save harmless the Government of the United States against any and all liability (including third party liability) from any cause whatsoever arising out of the production or fabrication, the ownership, the lease, and the possession and use of such special nuclear materials or fuel elements after delivery by the Commission to the Government of Iran or to any authorized private individual or private organization under its jurisdiction.

ARTICLE IX

The Government of Iran guarantees that:

(a) Safeguards provided in Article VIII shall be maintained.

(b) No material, including equipment and devices, transferred to the Government of Iran or authorized persons under its jurisdiction, pursuant to this Agreement, by lease, sale, or otherwise will be used for atomic weapons or for research on or development of atomic weapons or for any other military purposes, and that no such material, including equipment and devices, will be transferred to unauthorized persons or beyond the jurisdiction of the Government of Iran except as the Commission may agree to such transfer to another nation and then only if in the opinion of the Commission such transfer falls within the scope of an agreement for cooperation between the United States and the other nation.

ARTICLE X

It is the hope and expectation of the Parties that this initial Agreement for Cooperation will lead to consideration of further cooperation extending to the design, construction, and operation of power producing reactors. Accordingly, the Parties will consult with each other from time to time concerning the feasibility of an additional agreement for cooperation with respect to the production of power from atomic energy in Iran.

ARTICLE XI

1. This Agreement shall enter into force [April 27, 1959] on the day on which each Government shall receive from the other Government written notification that it has complied with all statutory and constitutional requirements for the entry into force of such Agreement and shall remain in force for a period of five years.

2. At the expiration of this Agreement or of any extension thereof the Government of Iran shall deliver to the United States all fuel elements containing reactor fuels leased by the Commission and any other fuel materials leased by the Commission. Such fuel elements and such fuel materials shall be delivered to the Commission at a site in the United States designated by the Commission at the expense of the Government of Iran and such delivery shall be made under appropriate safeguards against radiation hazards while in transit.

In witness thereof, the Parties hereto have caused this Agreement to be executed pursuant to duly constituted authority.

Done at Washington, in duplicate, this fifth day of March, 1957.

For the Government of the United States of America:

WILLIAM M. ROUNTREE
*Assistant Secretary of State for
Near Eastern, South Asian
and African Affairs*

LEWIS L. STRAUSS
*Chairman, United States
Atomic Energy Commission*

For the Government of Iran:
DR. AMINI
Ambassador of Iran

Conclusions of the Investigation on United States Aid Operations in Iran by the Foreign Operations Subcommittee of the Committee on Government Operations, U.S. House of Representatives

January 28, 1957

1. United States aid and technical-assistance programs in Iran which, between 1951 and 1956, totaled a quarter billion dollars, were administered in a loose, slipshod, and unbusinesslike manner.

2. The so-called expanded technical-assistance program which began in January 1952 and resulted in United States obligations of over $100 million in a 5-year period, was neither technical assistance nor economic development, but an ad hoc method of keeping the Iranian economy afloat during the years of the oil dispute.

3. The expenditure of technical-assistance funds during these years was undertaken without regard to such basic requirements of prudent management as adequate controls and procedures, with the inevitable

consequences that it is now impossible—with any accuracy—to tell what became of these funds. The resulting opportunities for waste and loss of funds were considerable, but the extent to which loss and waste actually occurred cannot be determined since management practices and control procedures were so poor that records of the operation, especially in the early years, are not reliable.

4. Amounts requested for United States aid to Iran seem to have been picked out of the air. There is no evidence that they were based on advance study of what the Iranian economy needed, the amount it could absorb, or programs which could be intelligently administered by the United States personnel available at the time to expend the funds.

5. The conduct of the United States operations mission's affairs appears to have been based on the assumption that as long as United States aid funds were spent promptly it was not a matter of great consequence as to what they were spent for. Members of the mission who openly objected to the uncontrolled nature of the operation were either disciplined or labeled as incompetent. To those familiar with the involved and time-consuming processes for financing public works in the United States, in whole or in part with Federal funds, the cavalier, free-wheeling casual fashion in which huge sums of United States funds were committed in Iran must necessarily be shocking.

6. The participation of Iran in sharing the expense of the program appears to have been little more than nominal, and it is clear that, from the Iranian standpoint, the program's virtue was that it supplied a source of foreign exchange. It was not United States know-how but United States dollars which was Iran's chief gain.

7. Under the expanded operations begun in 1952, about $10 million in direct aid was furnished for a series of industrial, or capital improvement projects. Under statutory criteria the eligibility of the projects is questionable. United States officials sought to justify these expenditures on the grounds that the various plants involved were not only badly needed for the economy of the country but would supply excellent demonstrations of the feasibility of such undertakings. However, the more important of these enterprises still are not fully operating after 4 years, due to poor planning and faulty engineering. Thus their value in terms of economic development has been almost nil, and as demonstrations they appear chiefly to be monuments to a fumbling aid program.

8. A major effort on the part of the United States mission in 1953 to promote the construction of a multi-million-dollar dam on the Karadj River has resulted in virtually nothing but the relocation, at a cost to the United States Government of nearly $3 million, of a road around the proposed site; while not only has there been no construction started on the dam, the Iranian Government has not even concluded a firm contract for its financing.

9. Among the programs undertaken was one of supplying nearly

$5 million over a 4-year period to support Iranian students who were completing their college training abroad. Involved in the program was a $2 million subsidy, through a special exchange rate for dollars, to the well-to-do sponsors and parents of these students. The nature and scope of the program were not revealed to the Congress and the Comptroller General has ruled that the expenditure of technical assistance funds for this purpose was unauthorized.

10. On top of annual grants of about $20 million for technical assistance, the United States began, in 1953, to supply supposedly temporary budgetary assistance to the Iranian Government at a rate of $5 million a month. In spite of the alleged temporary nature of this increased aid, the United States has continued to make budget aid grants and loans at about this same rate for 3 years.

11. United States control over what Iran did with this budget aid was practically nonexistent and the subcommittee notes that Iranian budget deficits increased rather than decreased during this period.

12. United States aid, alleged to be granted on the basis of austerity levels of Iranian Government expenditures, was utilized to pay for many extraordinary items, like the payroll of the National Iranian Oil Co. The fact that these items had not previously been considered appropriate charges against the Government budget casts doubt upon the propriety of treating them as budget items to be supported with United States aid dollars.

13. Whatever Iranian efforts may have been made to solve their own difficulties through appropriate reforms in Government spending and tax collection, their successes in this regard do not appear to have been noteworthy during the period when United States aid was financing Iranian budget deficits.

14. Iran's oil revenues are, and have been for some time, adequate to finance both the Government's operating budget and their ambitious development plans. Thus, their chronic budget deficits appear to be an outgrowth of financial management methods rather than lack of resources.

15. A factor in continued United States aid appears to be an aversion on the part of Iran to receive help in the form of United States loans, even though such loans are feasible and Iran is in a good position to repay them.

16. Each year's allotment to Iran has been justified as a temporary measure for a given set of reasons which have changed each year while the level of aid has remained about the same throughout. Presentations to the authorizing and appropriating committees of the Congress have been vague and misleading. This may be due, in part, to the paucity of factual information available to those testifying before the committees of Congress. It may also be due to awareness that a clearer picture would have led Congress to reduce the program by eliminating items of expenditures which could not be reasonably justified.

17. Program presentations to the Congress have consistently failed to point out that Iran was and is an essentially solvent country.

18. The use of the so-called illustrative method of presenting budget requests to the Congress is a major factor in the almost complete loss of control by the Congress over-spending in this type of program. Under this system the Congress is given a description of a hypothetical program which might be carried out if requested funds are furnished. However, when funds are granted by the Congress, there is no commitment by the executive branch to expend them for any of the activities used as hypothetical illustrations.

19. Congressional control over expenditures in this type of program is further defeated by the fact that information supplied Congress on how funds granted on the illustrative basis were actually spent consistently omits the elementary facts needed for an intelligent post-audit.

Minority Dissent (in Letter Form) from the Conclusions of the House Subcommittee's Investigation on United States Aid Operations in Iran

[EXCERPTS]

Johnson City, Tennessee
December 29, 1956

Hon. PORTER HARDY, *Chairman, Subcommittee on International Operations, House Committee on Government Operations, Washington, D.C.*

DEAR PORTER: After reading the draft of the subcommittee's report, I find that I do not concur in several of its conclusions and recommendations. I believe it to be inaccurate and misleading in its presentation and in its analysis of the factual material. I also find that its general tone is biased and unfair.

Furthermore, in my opinion, the report taken as a whole, tends to cast reflections upon the intentions, character, and good faith of those who were responsible for the aid program during this most trying and difficult period of Iranian history. I do not believe that it is worthy of our committee to resort to indirection in order to convey impressions which cannot be factually supported by such evidence as has been adduced. . . .

It should be noted that the report concentrates its criticism of administrative shortcomings almost wholly on the years 1951-53, when our program in Iran jumped from a small point 4 program of $1.6 million to $23 million during the most critical years of that country's history, so far as the Soviet threat is concerned. Obviously, no program could operate smoothly and efficiently under the circumstances. To be critical of its detailed operations without giving due credit to the success of the program in accomplishing its major objectives is more than nearsighted. As to waste, to which reference is made in several places in the report, this would surely have to be judged in the light of the objectives of the program and its real accomplishments.

There is almost a complete omission from the report of any reference to, or explanation of, the political emergency in which the expanded Iran program was undertaken. Nowhere does it sufficiently take into account the circumstances that attended our operations in Iran at any given period; consequently, it neglects to mention the evident success which marked the attainment of our major objectives. I do not believe that we are contributing to an intelligent understanding of the efficiency and economy of the means employed to achieve foreign policy goals (to borrow the introductory language of the report) by eliminating meaningful references to these goals and the extent to which they were achieved. We cannot evade our obligation to evaluate the results of the program in the light of the security interests of the United States and the free world.

In the particular case of Iran, a bankrupt economy had opened the gates to communism. At the time of the emergency aid program, the conduct of which the proposed report so severely criticizes, there was rioting and bloodshed in the streets. The threat of the Soviets was very real. Disciplined Communist fifth columns terrorized the population. Communists had already penetrated many segments of Iranian life. The lives of our own Mission personnel were endangered. Point IV offices were attacked and pillaged. Yet the report makes no reference to the continuity of operations during this period of stress; operations, in fact, which contributed to the saving of Iran. Surely the work of American officials in Iran and in Washington at that time deserve recognition in the light of the results achieved. Even more important, there is no recognition of the successful efforts of the Iranian people themselves.

Again, I find nowhere an adequate discussion of Iran's internal problems, which constituted major obstacles to be overcome in the administration of United States aid programs. The political and administrative chaos in years substantially accounts for some of the practices which the Mission found itself forced to tolerate in order to implement the program rapidly. As for the later period, to take another instance, Iranian budget deficits are treated in the proposed report without due reference to the expanded defense burden shouldered by Iran, an effort which was directly in the interest of the security of the Middle East. . . .

The report dwells on the administrative shortcomings of the early years in Iran, but places little emphasis on the development of better practices when it became possible to do so. I believe it was testified that, at one critical period, recruitment of American personnel for Iran had to be stopped, because of danger to American lives. The report seems to lead to the conclusion that the program in Iran should have been held up, or drastically curtailed, for lack of adequate personnel to guarantee in every respect good management and administrative practices. . . .

These examples are drawn at random to illustrate why I dissent from the proposed report. The list could be extended.

Therefore, I urge that publication of this report be postponed until it can be adequately reviewed and commented upon both by members of the committee and by the affected agencies.

Efforts to force through its premature publication are neither fair nor in the best interests of our Government.

However, in the event that this report is published despite my request, I ask that this letter be appended to it as an indication of my dissent.

Sincerely,   B. CARROLL REECE

An Examination of the Economic and Technical Assistance Program for Iran Administered by the International Cooperation Administration, Department of State, Fiscal Years 1956-1960: A Report to the United States Congress by the Comptroller General of the United States

[EXCERPTS]

June 1961

SUMMARY OF FINDINGS AND RECOMMENDATIONS

General Comments

Our previous audit report of 1956 and the subsequent hearings of the Subcommittee of the House Committee on Government Operations disclosed a number of serious deficiencies and problems in the administration of the program which hampered an efficient and economical use of United States aid funds. Our report directed attention to the overly complex joint United States-Iranian administrative machinery under which the program was operating and the need for simplification, the need for Iran to assume a fair share of the financial burden and the operating responsibility which need had been recognized by ICA but was awaiting implementation, the large amounts of unused farm equipment financed by ICA and other defects in property management, the lack of end-use investigations and related audit checks to determine proper utilization of ICA-financed commodities, the planning and operating deficiencies which contributed to delays in the successful completion of several major development projects, the need for effective joint procedures governing the use of local currency generated by ICA-aid activities, the need for strengthening internal controls to help prevent irregularities in the accounts of the privincial offices, and several other unsatisfactory conditions.

The Subcommittee found that the program between 1951 and 1956 was administered in a loose and unbusinesslike manner and expenditures of aid funds were undertaken without regard to basic requirements of prudent management and that the lack of adequate controls and procedures, especially in the earlier years, resulted in unreliable records and offered considerable opportunities for waste and loss of funds. The Subcommittee reported numerous deficiencies in planning and carrying out projects and other program activities.

Our follow-up examination in 1960 showed that various corrective measures had been taken by ICA and responsible Iranian agencies. Thus, the ICA Mission had strengthened internal control procedures for property management, procurement, and cash transactions and had improved the administration of the commodity import program. Obstacles to the completion of several major projects were removed and the projects appeared to be operating satisfactorily. The agency established an effective program of overseas audit activities. The Iranian Government had taken over an increasing share of administrative responsibilities. On the other hand, we found that some of the basic weaknesses persisted throughout a major part of the period covered by our examination and were the subject of recommendations made by the ICA Internal Audit Branch which performed an overseas audit during March and April 1960 immediately preceding our field visit to Iran.

In particular, we found that ICA and Iran had continued cumbersome and costly administrative arrangements, the anticipated absorption of United States-supported aid projects into Iran's regular governmental programs had not been fully accomplished, and several ICA-financed projects showed unsatisfactory progress because of planning and operating deficiencies. Principally because of the recent internal audit findings together with the results of the Mission's own periodic end-use investigations and audit activities, responsible Mission employees were generally aware of the deficiencies requiring correction. The principal task which the agency faces is to develop a realistic plan of action, enlist the necessary cooperation of the Iranian Government, and carry out this plan with energy and dispatch.

The status of our prior audit findings and recommendations is summarized in a separate section of this report, . . . Following are our principal findings regarding the administration of the ICA program during the period 1956-60, with a more detailed discussion in succeeding pages as indicated.

Need for Improvement of Over-All Program Direction

We believe that the United States assistance program for Iran requires more effective over-all direction and coordination by responsible United States and Iranian agencies.

The Joint Commission for Social and Economic Development, which was established by the United States and Iran in 1952 as a top-level coordinating body, did not fulfill its intended function during fiscal year 1960 as it has held no meetings since May 9, 1959, except for the work of certain subcommittess. The Iranian Government has a multiplicity of agencies carrying on social and economic development activities but has designated no single agency to direct these efforts and coordinate them with United States and other foreign aid. Also, ICA has been joined in recent years by other United States agencies, namely, DLF and the Export-Import Bank, in financing Iranian development activities; we noted that several of these activities required better coordination and cooperation among the several agencies.

ICA advised us that negotiations with Iran for a more effective arrangement than was possible under the Joint Commission will be undertaken at the time the new bilateral agreement is negotiated (see next finding) and, also, that the Iranian Government has made some progress in assigning increased responsibility to the Plan Organization for long-range planning. Further, ICA believes that the pending reorganization of the United States aid program, announced by the executive branch, will take into account any problem of coordination among the several United States agencies.

Need for Over-All Bilateral Agreement

The United States Government has no over-all agreement with Iran covering the nature, conditions, and terms of the economic aid program. In 1958, and again in 1960, the ICA Internal Audit Branch stressed the need for such a basic agreement to take the place of some 70 individual agreements and exchanges of notes which have governed the various activities and projects financed by ICA and its predecessor agencies.

The agency advised us that a new basic agreement is to be negotiated with the Iranian Government. . . .

Deficiencies in Financial Controls Over Joint Project Funds

An examination by a United States public accounting firm of the financial controls and transactions of the jointly financed Special Activities Accounts (SAA) through March 1957 disclosed that both prescribed procedures and those actually in effect were deficient in many respects. The auditors reported significant weaknesses in budgetary controls, financial reporting, disbursement of funds, and internal controls and concluded that the accounts were "unauditable."

We found no evidence that the Mission had evaluated the audit findings and recommendations and taken corrective action, and the ordering of such a comprehensive review under the circumstances may not have been warranted. Accordingly, we believe that the benefits obtained from this audit were not commensurate with its substantial cost ($233,600 equivalent). We were advised by the Mission that the principal problem was to obtain compliance by the Iranian authorities with the prescribed control procedures which were considered generally adequate for this type of operation representing principally an Iranian responsibility. The Mission believes that the Iranian agencies have been gradually influenced in the direction of sound management.

On the basis of our observations, we suggested a number of actions which we believed were needed for a more orderly financial administration of SAA projects. The Mission subsequently informed us that its advisors were working closely with Iranian officials to improve financial procedures in the several areas outlined by us and that progress was being made. . . .

CENTO AND THE "EISENHOWER DOCTRINE"

*The Richards Mission to Iran on Behalf of the "Eisenhower Doctrine":
Joint Communiqué Issued at Tehran by the Government of Iran
and the Special Assistant to the President*

March 27, 1957

His Excellency Prime Minister Hussein Ala and members of his Cabinet, and Ambassador James P. Richards, Special Representative of President Dwight D. Eisenhower, have met in common cause and interest to discuss the purposes and aims of the American Doctrine, proposed by President Eisenhower and decisively adopted by the American Congress.

During these discussions Prime Minister Ala reaffirmed his Government's endorsement of the purposes of the new American policy to strengthen the national independence and defense the territorial integrity of the countries in the general area of the Middle East against international communism and its imperialistic aims.

Ambassador Richards outlined the philosophy of President Eisenhower's policy, emphasizing that the foremost hope and purpose of the United States was, in company with its likeminded friends, to build peace with justice. He pointed out that the peoples of the Middle Eastern area and the people of America have a common interest in their joint efforts to preserve liberty and freedom through the maintenance of security against encroachments by international communism in the Middle East. International communism is incompatible with the aspirations of the people of the Middle East for political independence, national integrity, religious, cultural and social freedom. It is likewise incompatible with the freedom heritage of the American people. Should international communism succeed in its imperialistic aims, the security, freedom, integrity and independence of all peoples throughout the free world would face extinction.

The two Governments intend to continue their close cooperation to attain their mutual objectives.

Ambassador Richards explained that the President of the United States and the American Government and people have declared it their policy to use, if necessary and appropriate and if requested, the armed forces of the United States in support of any country in the area of the Middle East which is attacked by a country under the control of international communism.

He emphasized that the United States, in accordance with its historical traditions, has no territorial designs in the area, nor is it desirous of creating a so-called sphere of influence. Its desires are solely to assist the nations in the Middle Eastern area to achieve security and economic well-being. It is not seeking to fill a power vacuum. If one exists, the United States believes it should be filled by the increasing strength of the Middle Eastern nations themselves.

The Governments of Iran and the United States, in accordance with their long established policies, continue to oppose any form of intervention or interference in the internal affairs of one state by another. They are determined, in conformity with the United Nations Charter, to cooperate together in protective measures against the threat of aggression from any source.

Substantial American aid in the form of economic, technical and military assistance is continuing. Because of past experience and Iran's own increasing capabilities, it is anticipated that American aid will accelerate progress in Iran's economic development program and toward the Government's goal of a better standard of living, with full national security, for its people.

The representatives of the Government of Iran and the special Mission of Ambassador Richards have agreed on procedures in which the development of economic and military aid to Iran can serve best to achieve the aims and purposes of the Middle East proposals.

Ambassador Richards stated that the United States was prepared to offer assistance toward several joint regional projects which have been or may be approved by the Economic Committee of the Baghdad Pact. These would be in addition to the large economic aid programs already in progress in Iran. As further evidence of America's deep interest and belief in the defensive objectives of the countries of the Baghdad Pact, the United States has expressed a willingness to join the Military Committee of the Pact, if invited to do so.

Ambassador Richards agreed that the United States would provide increased financing for an already planned large military construction program to meet the needs of the Imperial Iranian armed forces and would also provide certain additional items of military equipment to those forces.

Multilaterial Declaration Respecting the Baghdad Pact, Including Express United States Cooperation with Pact Nations

July 28, 1958   Signed at London.
July 28, 1958   Entered into force.

DECLARATION

1. The members of the Baghdad Pact attending the Ministerial meeting in London have re-examined their position in the light of recent events and conclude that the need which called the Pact into being is greater than ever. These members declare their determination to maintain their collective security and to resist aggression, direct or indirect.

2. Under the Pact collective security arrangements have been instituted. Joint military planning has been advanced and area economic projects have been promoted. Relationships are being established with other free world nations associated for collective security.

3. The question of whether substantive alterations should be made in the Pact and its organization or whether the Pact will be continued in its present form is under consideration by the Governments concerned. However, the nations represented at the meeting in London reaffirmed their determination to strengthen further their united defence posture in the area.

4. Article 1 of the Pact of Mutual Co-operation signed at Baghdad on February 24, 1955 provides that the parties will cooperate for their security and defence and that such measures as they agree to take to give effect to this co-operation may form the subject of special agreements. Similarly, the United States in the interest of world peace, and pursuant to existing Congressional authorization, agrees to co-operate with the nations making this Declaration for their security and defence, and will promptly enter into agreements designed to give effect to this co-operation.

Made and signed at Lancaster House, London, on the twenty-eighth day of July, 1958, in five copies.

For the United States of America: For Iran:
    JOHN FOSTER DULLES   M. EGHBAL

    For Pakistan: For Turkey:
    FIROZ KHAN NOON   A. MENDERES

For the United Kingdom of Great Britain and Northern Ireland:
    HAROLD MACMILLAN

Agreement of Defense Cooperation between the Government of the United States of America and the Imperial Government of Iran

March 5, 1959   Agreement signed at Ankara.
March 5, 1959   Entered into force.

The Government of the United States of America and the Imperial Government of Iran,

Desiring to implement the Declaration in which they associated themselves at London on July 28, 1958;

Considering that under Article I of the Pact of Mutual Cooperation signed at Baghdad on February 24, 1955, the parties signatory thereto agreed to cooperate for their security and defense, and that, similarly, as stated in the above-mentioned Declaration, the Government of the United States of America, in the interest of world peace, agreed to cooperate with the Governments making that Declaration for their security and defense;

Recalling that, in the above-mentioned Declaration, the members of the Pact of Mutual Cooperation making that Declaration affirmed their determination to maintain their collective security and to resist aggression, direct or indirect;

Considering further that the Government of the United States of America is associated with the work of the major committees of the Pact of Mutual Cooperation signed at Baghdad on February 24, 1955;

Desiring to strengthen peace in accordance with the principles of the Charter of the United Nations;

Affirming their right to cooperate for their security and defense in accordance with Article 51 of the Charter of the United Nations;

Considering that the Government of the United States of America regards as vital to its national interest and to world peace the preservation of the independence and integrity of Iran;

Recognizing the authorization to furnish appropriate assistance granted to the President of the United States of America by the Congress of the United States of America in the Mutual Security Act of 1954, as amended, and in the Joint Resolution to Promote Peace and Stability in the Middle East;

Considering that similar agreements are being entered into by the Government of the United States of America and the Governments of Turkey and Pakistan, respectively,

Have agreed as follows:

ARTICLE I

The Imperial Government of Iran is determined to resist aggression. In case of aggression against Iran, the Government of the United States of America, in accordance with the Constitution of the United States of America, will take such appropriate action, including the use of armed forces, as may be mutually agreed upon and as is envisaged in the Joint Resolution to Promote Peace and Stability in the Middle East, in order to assist the Government of Iran at its request.

ARTICLE II

The Government of the United States of America, in accordance with the Mutual Security Act of 1954, as amended, and related laws of the United States of America, and with applicable agreements heretofore or hereafter entered into between the Government of the United States of America and the Government of Iran, reaffirms that it will continue to furnish the Government of Iran such military and economic assistance as may be mutually agreed upon between the Government of the United States of America and the Government of Iran, in order to assist the Government of Iran in the preservation of its national independence and integrity and in the effective promotion of its economic development.

ARTICLE III

The Imperial Government of Iran undertakes to utilize such military and economic assistance as may be provided by the Government of the United States of America in a manner consonant with the aims and purposes set forth by the Governments associated in the Declaration signed at London on July 28, 1958, and for the purpose of effectively promoting the economic development of Iran and of preserving its national independence and integrity.

ARTICLE IV

The Government of the United States of America and the Government of Iran will cooperate with the other Governments associated in the Declaration signed at London on July 28, 1958, in order to prepare and participate in such defensive arrangements as may be mutually agreed to be desirable, subject to the other applicable provisions of this agreement.

ARTICLE V

The provisions of the present agreement do not affect the cooperation between the two Governments as envisaged in other international agreements or arrangements.

ARTICLE VI

This agreement shall enter into force upon the date of its signature and shall continue in force until one year after the receipt by either Government of written notice of the intention of the other Government to terminate the agreement.

Done in duplicate at Ankara, this fifth day of March, 1959.

For the Government of the United States of America:	For the Imperial Government of Iran:
FLETCHER WARREN	GENERAL HASSAN ARFA
[SEAL]	[SEAL]

Statement Issued by the White House Following a Meeting between the President of the United States (Eisenhower) and the Prime Minister of Iran (Eqbal) Affirming the Grave Concern of the United States Regarding Soviet Threats to Iran

October 9, 1959

The President today had the pleasure of meeting with Prime Minister [Manuchehr] Eqbal of Iran, who represented his country at the Central Treaty Organization meeting which has just terminated. There was a very useful and interesting discussion concerning matters of mutual interest.

The President told the Prime Minister that Iran's courageous and unyielding stand in the face of the intensive and unwarranted propaganda attacks of recent months has evoked the admiration of all free nations. The President reaffirmed United States support for the collective efforts of Iran and other free nations to maintain their independence. In stressing the gravity with which the United States would view a threat to the territorial integrity and political independence of Iran, the President recalled the provisions of the bilateral agreement of cooperation with Iran and the joint resolution to promote peace and stability in the Middle East.

The Eisenhower Visit to Iran

Remarks upon Arrival at Mehrabad Airport, Tehran

December 14, 1959

YOUR MAJESTY, LADIES AND GENTLEMEN: Your Majesty, before I proceed further, may I express my gratitude for the warmth and generosity of the sentiments you have expressed toward my country and toward me personally. I am truly grateful.

This morning, as I set foot on the soil of Iran, I realize a long-held ambition, to see something of this historic land and a courageous people. I have wanted also to return the visit of Your Majesty to my own country, so that here on this spot we may renew our association and friendship.

In my boyhood, ancient Persia, its kings and their adventures, the nation's marvels of building, its religion, made up a fascinating realm of wonder and romance for a high school student who lived on the Plains of Kansas many thousands of miles away, and half a century ago.

Years later, as a soldier, as a University President, and then President of the United States, Iran became for me one of the most important nations of the world. Three times in the past decade I have had long and searching talks with His Majesty the Shahinshah. He concentrates, in his plans and dreams for Iran, the hopes and aspirations of his people. From him I learned more vividly than from books and papers the present greatness of his country's spirit.

I learned, too, its problems, its strengths, its advances, its vital role in the defense of the free world, and the golden future that is assured Iran and its people in a world of peace with justice.

Now I am here—bringing you from the American people their salute to your courage, their congratulations on their achievements, their best wishes for growth in the years ahead, their pledge of friendship for you and your people.

Address to the Members of the Parliament of Iran

December 14, 1959

MR. PRIME MINISTER, MR. PRESIDENT, MR. SPEAKER, MEMBERS OF THE SENATE, MEMBERS OF THE MAJLIS: The honor you do me with this reception in your handsome new Senate buiding is a clear indication of the high mutual regard which the Iranian and American peoples have for each other.

Personally, I am deeply touched by your welcome.

We know that people, by meeting together, even if for a limited time, can strengthen their mutual understanding. To increase this mutual understanding has been one of the purposes of my trip to Iran; as it has been to the other countries in which I have stopped along the way.

My conversation this morning with His Imperial Majesty, this convocation, my knowledge of the state of relations between our two countries—and indeed, the cordial warmth of the reception that I received upon the streets of your beautiful city—have all been heartening assurances that our two countries stand side by side. This visit reinforces my conviction that we stand together. We see eye to eye when it comes to the fundamentals which govern the relations between men and between nations.

The message I bring from America is this: "We want to work with you for peace and friendship, in freedom." I emphasize freedom—because without it there can be neither true peace nor lasting friendship among peoples.

Consequently, Americans are dedicated to the improvement of the international climate in which we live. Though militarily we in America devote hugh sums to make certain of the security of ourselves and to assist our allies, we do not forget that—in the long term—military strength alone will not bring about peace with justice. The spiritual and economic health of the free world must be likewise strengthened.

All of us realize that while we must, at whatever cost, make freedom secure from any aggression, we could still lose freedom should we fail to cooperate in progress toward achieving the basic aspirations of humanity. The world struggle in which we are engaged is many sided. In one aspect it is ideological, political, and military; in others it is both spiritual and economic.

As I well know, you, and the people of Iran, are not standing on the sidelines in this struggle.

Without flinching, you have borne the force of a powerful propaganda assault, at the same time that you have been working at improving the living standards in your nation.

The people of Iran continue to demonstrate that quality of fortitude which has characterized the long annals of your history as a nation. I know I speak for the American people when I say we are proud to count so valiant a nation as our partner.

Your ideals, expressed in the wise and mature literature of your people, are a source of enrichment to the culture of the world.

By true cooperation with your friends—and among these, America considers herself one—we can proceed together toward success in the struggle for peace and prosperity.

Through trust in one another, we can trust in the fruitful outcome of our efforts together to build a brighter future.

This future—the world we will hand on to our children and to our grandchildren—must occupy our thinking and our planning and our working. The broad outline of our goal is, I think, clear to everyone—to achieve a just peace in freedom.

But peace will be without real meaning—it may even be unattainable—until the peoples of the world have finally overcome the natural enemies of humanity—hunger, privation, and disease. The American people have engaged considerable resources in this work. I am proud of the many dedicated American men and women who have gone out into the world with the single hope that they can ease the pain and want of others.

Some of them are at work in Iran, and I have heard that the people of Iran have found these efforts beneficial.

Of course, their work is effective only because the government of Iran has sturdily shouldered its responsibilites for the development of their country. There are reports of significant accomplishments throughout the length and breadth of your land.

America rejoices with you that this is so.

On the long and difficult climb on the road to true peace, the whole world must some day agree that suspicion and hate should be laid aside in the common interest.

Here, I think, is our central problem. I know that you, too, and all men of good will, are devoting thought and energy to the practical and realistic steps to this great objective.

One such step is, of course, an enforceable agreement on disarmament, or, to be more exact, arms reduction of the arms burden can be made. To such a realistic beginning, there is no feasible alternative for the world.

In the meantime, we cannot abandon our mutual effort to build barriers, such as the peaceful barrier of our Central Treaty Organization, against the persistent dangers of aggression and subversion. This organization, CENTO, has no ulterior or concealed purpose; it exists only to provide security.

Such an effort erects a shield of freedom for our honor and for our lives. With such a shield, we preserve the cherished values of our societies.

To be sure, the people of Iran need no reminder of these simple facts. Only yesterday you celebrated the anniversary of the day on which justice triumphed over force in Azerbaijan. The full weight of world public opinion, as represented in the United Nations, supported you in those difficult times. It will always support the rights of any people threatened by external aggression.

Justice—the rule of law—among nations has not yet been effectively established. But in almost every nation in the world there is a great awakening to the need for such a development. Certainly this is true among the free nations. Because there is such an awakening, the act of any government contrary to the rights of mankind is quickly resented and keenly sensed by people everywhere.

This is the wellspring of our hope. This is why we are right to believe as we do—despite centuries of human turmoil and conflict—that true peace can and will one day be realized.

The impulse toward justice, toward the recognition of the worth and dignity of each and every human being, will not be denied. This is the mainspring of the movement toward freedom and peace.

Now, may I offer my heartfelt thanks for the opportunity you have given me to speak to you, and through you, the representatives of the people of Iran, to your entire nation.

You have conferred upon me an honor which I shall always remember.

Thank you very much.

Joint Statement Following Discussions with the Shah of Iran

December 14, 1959

President Eisenhower visited Iran on December 14, 1959. The President and his party were welcomed warmly by the Iranian people. The feelings of the Iranian people shown during this significant visit demonstrated again the strength of the ties between the governments and people of Iran and the United States. The visit attested to the confidence of both countries that their cooperation is of benefit both to themselves and to the world.

During the visit talks were held at the Palace of His Imperial Majesty between the two leaders assisted by Prime Minister Eqbal, Foreign Minister Aram, Ambassador Murphy, and Ambassador Wailes. The President addressed a joint session of the Iranian Parliament.

His Imperial Majesty and the President discussed the CENTO alliance and both emphasized the importance of CENTO in preserving stability and security in the area. They reiterated the determination of their Governments to support CENTO and further recognized the usefulness of their bilateral agreement while, of course, continuing to participate in the action of the United Nations for the furtherance of world peace. Both leaders emphasized their adherence to the goals of peace and freedom.

In the course of their talks the world situation was reviewed. Both leaders expressed their belief in the principles of negotiation as a means of finding just and peaceful solutions to problems which arise between nations. It was agreed that disarmament with adequate controls should be sought in the interest of lasting peace. His Imperial Majesty and the President also exchanged views on various problems, especially those relating to the Middle East. The President recognized the significant contribution Iran is making to the stability of this important world area.

His Imperial Majesty outlined the economic and social progress achieved in Iran and expressed appreciation for the help given by the American people. The President congratulated His Imperial Majesty on the service which Iran is rendering the free world and for his vigorous effort to sustain stability and to further economic development. The President noted that such programs undertaken by Iran have the objective of creating a more bountiful life for the Iranian people. President Eisenhower also expressed interest in the steps His Imperial Majesty is taking to promote social progress. The President said that the United States intends to continue to assist Iran in the mutual interest of both nations.

The President took the opportunity to express the admiration of the people of the United States for the brave stand of the Iranian people and Government in the face of outside pressure.

6

Reconsideration and Reaffirmation

Until the advent of the 1960s, relations between Iran and the United States proceeded on the assumptions that had governed them since the immediate postwar era. Those relations had generally been good, although not without certain strains. Iran, for instance, had frequently expressed dissatisfaction with the size of the U.S. aid package. For its part, the United States had shown flashes of impatience at this attitude, particularly after the oil nationalization controversy had been settled and oil revenues began to flow into Iran once again. Also, Iran would have liked U.S. guarantees against any aggression, a commitment the United States was not prepared to make. The United States was committed, however, to support Iran against possible Soviet aggression. Furthermore, there were indications that U.S. policy operated on the assumption that support for Iran required support for the regime of the Shah.

Nevertheless, for a time it appeared that this latter assumption was being reconsidered. A story in the Christian Science Monitor *reported that the United States was going to cultivate the Iranian opposition, just in case the Shah's regime was overthrown. The State Department officially denied the story in a press release which is printed in this chapter. However, other documents do indicate that the State Department gave some internal consideration to the question of possible alternatives to the Shah. It is not clear from these sources whether this was done by the direction of high officials or merely represented an initiative of lower-ranking State Department personnel. Whatever the origins of these papers, the United States did not switch its support to any anti-Shah elements.*

There was little doubt, though, that the U.S. government's dissatisfaction with Iran's economic progress was deepening. According to New York Times reports in March and April of 1962, President Kennedy informed the Shah that future U.S. aid would stress long-term economic development over military strength. In the U.S. view it was important that Iran undertake fundamental economic reform, and the sooner the better. Land reform, which Iran had just instituted, was seen as particulary critical. The Shah's personal convictions did coincide with U.S. demands for land reform, but his continuing desire to upgrade his military establishment did not diminish. Additionally, it may not be unfair to suggest that the Shah also envisioned land reform as strengthening his position internally.

The land reform law was actually passed in January of 1962. It was the showpiece of the Shah's "White Revolution," and the Shah was widely praised at the time for sponsoring such a fundamental change. It is interesting to note that although the United States had strongly advocated such reform, a number of American officials were uneasy when it actually got underway, as some of the documentation in this chapter indicates. They feared it might prove too destabilizing. In the light of results, however, such fears seemed exaggerated.

The economic effects of the White Revolution proved to be quite positive, which pleased the United States. The White Revolution validated the U.S. analysis of Iran's economic problems, and it reduced Iran's need for outside assistance. Thus the United States began to cut down on grant aid in both the military and economic spheres, and in 1967 aid under the annual U.S. appropriation was eliminated altogether. Again, the documents in this chapter have been selected in order to outline these developments.

Just as the United States had considered the possibilities of an alternative Iran policy, Iran began to think in terms of pursuing a policy more independent of the United States. The Iranians were encouraged to think in this way by a new and softer Soviet policy, which dropped the characteristic threats and bluster toward Iran in favor of easy-term economic credits and professed mutual respect.

In 1962, perhaps nettled by U.S. criticisms of his military spending, the Shah informed the Soviet Union that Iran would never permit foreign missile bases on Iranian soil. However, there were no U.S. missile bases on Iranian soil, and as the United States did not contemplate putting any there, the Shah's overture to the Soviet Union was received with equanimity. In any event, the Iranians made no promises to the Soviet Union concerning other types of U.S. installations. Later,

Iran was to buy certain Soviet equipment, such as communications systems and trucks, but the Soviet Union never displaced the United States as Iran's principal weapons supplier. Nor, indeed, did Iran ever take any serious steps under the Shah's government to align itself with the Soviet Union.

But Iran did take advantage of Soviet offers of economic credits, particularly where they took the form of advances against the future sale of Iranian natural gas to the Soviet Union. These credits were proposed for the future and were not granted at the time, but they offered a market for an Iranian resource that had hitherto simply been wasted. Even these economic arrangements, however, did not really pry Iran away from its alignment with the United States. In short, each partner had given some thought to severing the bonds, but each had decided against a real separation.

RETHINKING SUPPORT OF THE SHAH

United States Denies Rumored Shift in Policy

Press Release 30   *January 22, 1960*

The Department of State has categorically denied that there is any substance whatsoever to the report contained in an article appearing in the *Christian Science Monitor* on January 15. Specifically it is denied, as alleged in the article, that the United States is considering a change in policy toward Iran, which would supposedly entail encouraging opposition elements as a result of allegedly growing internal dissatisfaction with the present Government and its policies.

The United States has the closest and most cordial relations with the present Government of Iran, which, under the able leadership of the Shah, is striving effectively to maintain Iran's independence and to improve conditions within the country.

The Current Internal Political Situation in Iran: A Report by the Deputy Director of the Office of Greek, Turkish, and Iranian Affairs (John W. Bowling), United States Department of State to the President

February 11, 1961

Present Position of the Shah

The elections now being concluded have been a test of the Shah's

ability to control a difficult political situation through his prestige and
the utilization of his security forces. The elections were largely rigged,
and diverse opposition political forces have not been able to force their
cancellation, despite several minor riots in Tehran and a few disturbances in other parts of the nation. There were no deaths in Tehran. The
possibility, however, of a combination of circumstances in the future
leading a combination of opposition political elements and disaffected
members of the security forces toward an attempt to overthrow the
regime cannot be discounted, and will probably increase over the long
run if present political trends continue.

The Shah has been ruling through the security forces, which have
been loyal to him personally, and through an alliance with a part of the
traditionalist elements of Iranian society. He would like to enlist the
support and enthusiasm of the restive urban middle-class and intellectual classes, but he cannot forget that under Mosadeq they attempted to
unseat him, and he realizes the danger that they would raise popular and
demagogic emotions against him if they were to be given footholds
within the government.

At the present time, communist influence in the main opposition
groupings appears to be limited—such influence as exists will probably
increase slowly. The communists by themselves pose no direct threat to
the regime, and are unlikely to do so in the foreseeable future. Their
primary potential lies in the infiltration of opposition groups. This
potential is accentuated by the absence of first-class political leadership
or a unifying political issue among groups opposed to the present
regime. . . .

Pro-Westernism and Neutralism

The Shah and his supporters, both military and civilian, are
strongly pro-Western at present. The majority of the Mosadeqists hate
the United Kingdom but are still not overtly hostile toward the United
States and Germany. This group resents Iran's openly pro-Western
foreign policy and military alignment, however, and there is a growing
tendency, particularly among the younger and more radical elements, to
identify the United States with the Shah and with the security forces and
to hold the United States responsible for the Shah's misdeeds and mistakes, real and alleged. The general tendency of opinion among these
groups is neutralist along "Indian" lines, with a strong admixture of
the traditional Iranian distrust and fear of Russia. Leaders of the traditional elite are divided between a minority favoring formal Iranian
alignment with the West and a majority favoring the traditional Iranian
policy of playing off big powers against each other and avoiding commitments to any large power, while extracting the maximum in aid
from all sides.

Iran's formal alignment with the West is popularly regarded as the
Shah's personal venture, and he is judged by its consequences. . . .

The Security Forces

The security forces of Iran, including the Army, are relatively noninstitutionalized. Peasant conscripts do as they are told, and in the officer class can be seen a spectrum of the elements and forces of contemporary urban society, with an admixture of (a) personal loyalty to the Shah in the sense that an American ward heeler is loyal to a political boss, and (b) a small but growing professionalism concentrating on the techniques of the military.

The Army exists in part, as it did under the Shah's father, as a tool of personal power for the ruler. The Shah devotes an inordinate amount of his time and energy to military matters, and is almost obsessed with increasing its size and obtaining the most modern military equipment. The fulfillment of these ambitions was probably the primary purpose which he had in mind when he formally aligned Iran with the West. With the physical power of the Army solidly behind him, the Shah could probably remain in power indefinitely, playing his traditionalist and Mosadeqist enemies off against one another. The Shah very cleverly plays off individuals and groups in the military against one another in order to prevent the rise of key personalities who could possibly take the machine away from him.

The loyalty of the security forces remains doubtful, however. The Chief of Army Intelligence in 1958 was caught at plotting with moderate conservative opposition leaders and has just emerged from jail. Several key conservative generals have in the past approached the United States and the United Kingdom for help in plots to overthrow the Shah with some civilian help. It is probable that "nationalist" sentiment of the Mosadeq type is widespread and is increasing among that majority of junior officers who have urban middle class backgrounds. There is, however, no single key military figure and no philosophy of government peculiar to the military which could be posed as an alternative to the present Shah-Army key ruling element. A purely military and conservative successor regime would have little hope for a long life, since the military as it exists is disliked and distrusted by opposition elements even more than is the Shah.

Underlying Factors

Under the Shah, Iran has made considerable progress in economic development, in social welfare, and in internal security and administrative efficiency. The progress has, however, taken place without participation in the government by the main opposition groups. To some extent, the Shah's isolation from these groups has been due to his unwillingness to ride demagogic issues appealing to the lower popular passions—he could even now, for instance, rally popular support behind himself by launching a self-defeating demagogic campaign against the Oil Consortium, against minority racial and religious groups, or against Iraq or the United Kingdom on territorial issues. To an equal extent, however, it has been due to his unwillingness to listen to critical advice, to his unwillingness to share power, and to his near-obsession with military affairs.

With the confidence and support of the Mosadeqists, the Shah could easily control his rightist opposition. The converse, however, is not true. The force and power of the urban semi-Westernized elements continue to grow at the expense of other elements of society. Unless and until the Shah can come to terms with them and bring them, or part of them, into the process of policy making, he faces a remorseless and slowly increasing pressure, which will become sharper and more dangerous to the West as moderate leadership elements are displaced by the radicals. It seems unlikely, however, that the Shah can capture the loyalty of this element without abandoning the military as his internal political base, without giving up much of his power, without abandoning his openly pro-Western foreign alignment, and without taking steps inimical to internal security and to practical economic development. He is unlikely to be willing to pay such a price.

Another very important element is the Shah's alternative with regard to foreign policy. The Shah, though highly intelligent, is emotionally insecure, and shares with other Iranians a deep suspicion that the West may abandon him in the course of a detente with the USSR or by supporting his internal opposition. The recent change of administration in Washington has heightened his anxieties. He is bitterly disappointed with the quantity of United States military aid in terms of money and hardware;* he is only slightly less unhappy about the quantity and procedures of United States economic aid to Iran in the context of a current difficult and unpopular economic stabilization program, undertaken last year at IMF insistence, and he suspects that the United States is cooling toward CENTO and hence toward its military assistance plans for the CENTO regional allies. He is under strong Soviet propaganda attack, and the Soviets have made it clear to him that if he will move toward neutralism, he can escape this pressure and can expect economic and even some military assistance from the USSR as well as assistance from the United States, citing Afghanistan and India.

The Shah is capable of making such a switch—one of our Ambassador's main tasks has been to dissuade him, to soothe him, and to reassure him of United States support. Even so, the Shah has authorized his Prime Minister to go to Moscow on a "good-will" visit in March or April, though he continues to resist Soviet demands for political concessions.

---

* In FY 1961 total MAP aid to Iran amounted to about $75 million, plus about $19 million in Defense Support. From the overthrow of Mosadeq in 1953 to the present, United States military aid of about $450 million and the United States economic aid (including Defense Support) of about $567 million has been extended to Iran.

Two other factors of the internal political situation often mentioned as important are corruption and the suppression of civil liberties. The former has always been a feature of Iranian administrations, and, though the Shah himself is honest, many of his family and entourage are not. Such dishonesty is not a major factor in the economic situation, and is probably decreasing slowly. It is normal for any political attack in Iran to be accompanied by charges of corruption.

There is a limited press censorship in Iran, and arrests and temporary deportations are rather common measures to avert political disorders. Freedom of assembly is often limited, but there is great freedom of speech. Iran is far from being a "police state" in the ordinary sense of the word.

What Can the United States Do?

It is often suggested that the United States, using its aid programs as leverage, could issue orders to the Shah which would, by their implementation, result in political tranquillity. It has been suggested that some of these "reform" measures would be the ending of corruption, the establishment of genuine democratic institutions, the downgrading of the military, further land reform, and the sharing of power with Mosadeqist leaders.

These suggestions presuppose that the Shah is a creature of the United States and the United Kingdom, a common misconception in Iran. Any United States ultimatums or even heavy-handed hints would be regarded by the Shah as an intolerable interference in his affairs and would probably result in corresponding moves on his part toward the USSR and neutralism.

Granted that this difficulty could be overcome, it is evident that the suggested "reform" measures are not simple matters. Corruption in our sense is a part of the Iranian culture, often associated with family ties, and the Shah relies on traditional elements of society in his government. Civil servants will probably continue to accept bribes unless they are able to afford a European standard of living on their salaries alone. This would entail an unacceptable gap in living standards between them and the mass of the population. Free elections to the Parliament today would result in a Majlis controlled by reactionary landlords and the clergy, with a vociferous and demagogic Mosadeqist minority from the big cities. Iranian politics would be polarized to the point of civil war. The restriction of suffrage to literates would result in a Mosadeqist majority, but there is no indication that a Mosadeqist government, representing perhaps fifteen percent of the population, would represent the submerged rural masses even as well as the present government does. In any case, this kind of freedom would be tantamount to asking the Shah to abdicate, and would entail a foreign policy shift away from the United States.

To ask the Shah to de-emphasize the military element in the Iranian Government would be to attack his most sensitive personal quirk, and would completely dishearten him. He would have to deprive himself of a highly practical element of his personal power, as well as to abandon the military dreams so dear to him.

Hasty and sweeping land reforms without careful preparation and heavy expenses would disrupt rural society, turn most landlords into bitter personal enemies of the Shah, result in immediate hardship to the peasants, retard mechanization and soil conservation, and decrease agricultural production. Urban opposition groups would be pleased, not because of any solicitude for the peasantry, but because of the discomfiture of the landlords.

The admission of Mosadeqist leaders to the government, while the most promising of the suggested reforms, would mean a reduction of the Shah's powers, an eventual reduction of the role of the military, and a danger of cutting the moderate Mosadeqists off from their following. The Shah would regard such a suggestion as proof positive that the United States had turned against him.

Another broad and basic suggestion for United States policy would be to increase its support of the Shah. To satisfy His Majesty, this would have to involve very heavy expenses in military, as well as financial assistance, would identify the United States even more with the Shah's authoritarian regime, and would accentuate rather than solve the basic political dilemma.

Still another suggestion involves United States and United Kingdom support to a conservative military group, perhaps with ties to the moderate Amini conservatives, to take over power by a coup. The resulting successor regime, without charismatic and practical leadership not in sight today, would have all the Shah's problems without the tremendous stabilizing force represented by the monarchical institution, and would solve nothing.

The most forthright and extreme suggestion involves Western support to a hypothetical Mosadeqist-oriented coup, with support from junior officers. While the resulting regime would not be strongly anti-United States and would have popular urban support, it would entail the following probable awesome disadvantages, which would accrue at an early date should such a regime remain in power:

(a) The breakup of CENTO,

(b) The withdrawal of the United States military mission from Iran,

(c) The abandonment of the current economic stabilization program,

(d) Undetermined moves to extract more money from the Oil Consortium,

(e) A great blow to the global prestige of the United States,

(f) Opportunity for communist infiltration into the regime,

(g) The loss of Iran's friendly United Nations vote,

(h) Neutralism as a positive policy, probably midway between the Nehru and Kassem models,

(i) The acceptance of Soviet economic, and possibly of military, aid.

These probable short-range costs would have to be balanced against the long-range advantages of a more popularly based regime in Iran. The cost does not appear to be worth the advantages, but a proper appreciation of the choice could only be made in the light of global national security consideration.

It would appear preferable that the United States would be best advised to continue its present policy of reassurance to the Shah of United States sympathy and support, along with persistent but delicate inferences by our Ambassador to the effect that the Shah should devote his attention to his internal political problems rather than to foreign and military affairs. We would also continue our policy of monitoring the Shah's dealing with the USSR, pointing out Soviet traps, depreciating the effect of Soviet propaganda, and warning him of Soviet intentions. We should continue to provide him with reasonable economic and military assistance, and, in the context of more general changes in our mutual security mechanisms, reduce the delays and contradictions in our assistance programs which tend to irritate and demoralize him.

The implementation of this program will require, as it has in the past, the greatest possible delicacy on the part of our Ambassador in handling his personal relationship with the Shah.

We should, of course, continue to be on the alert for the rise of competent and creative alternate leadership, in or out of the military, which might allow a reconsideration of our alternatives. This latter, along with the requirement that we do what we can to support moderate as against extreme opposition leadership, is very difficult in Iran, since Embassy contacts with the important Mosadeqist opposition elements have met and will continue to meet with violent objections from the Shah. CAS has done, and will continue to do, whatever it can along this line, but all such contacts run a risk of alienating the Shah.

At the present moment, we could hearten the Shah and reduce the possibility of his dealing with the Soviets by

(a) Making an immediate decision as to Defense Support for Iran in FY 1962, preferably in the scheduled amount of $20 million,

(b) Informing the Shah now of this figure so that he can count on it in his upcoming annual budget, which begins March 21, 1961, and

(c) Modifying procedures and regulations in order that the sum can be made available by this fall, halfway through the Iranian budget year.

It might be noted that the JCS has recently indicated that it desires to "assist" the Shah by United States adherence to CENTO, stationing atomic weapons in Iran, and similar measures. Unless such strengthening of CENTO were accompanied by greatly increased military assistance to Iran, it would be of only temporary effect, or even counterproductive, as regards preserving the Shah's pro-Western orientation, and it would not affect the internal political situation to the advantage of United States interests and objectives.

Political Characteristics of the Iranian Urban Middle-Class and Implications Thereof for United States Policy: A Report by the Deputy Director of Greek, Turkish, and Iranian Affairs (Bowling), United States Department of State, to the President

March 20, 1961

Definition

A meaningful definition of the Iranian urban middle class must be sociological and historical, not primarily economic. The urban middle class constitutes that element of Iranian society in which there are present two cultures, two value systems, the traditional and the Western. Those elements of society in which the traditional value systems are overwhelmingly predominant are excluded, i.e., the peasantry, both in the countryside and recently arrived in the large cities, most landlords, older religious leaders, and the great majority of small merchants and artisans outside the capital. Similarly excluded are the very small minority of thoroughly Westernized individuals, in high levels of society, who are really strangers in their own society. . . .

Psychological Characteristics

It is well known that individuals the world over tend to rationalize political behavior which stems from deep emotional needs. This is particularly true with regard to extremist views aimed at radical changes in an existing society. To take at face value the rationalizations of an Iranian middle class leader is as unrewarding as to accept the rationalizations of anti-Semites, Negro-haters, or communists in the United States. Some understanding of the psychological background of such individuals is necessary in order to be able to understand them and to predict their behavior.

The political reactions of the key elements of the Iranian middle class find their psychological roots in the fact that these people are partly Westernized and partly attached to their traditional culture. The result is an inability to adjust to society, and an inability to find security. Thus, if a student tries to "date" a girl, and to choose his own wife, one side of his "super-ego" tells him that he is behaving atrociously; if he asks his parents to find him a wife and does not expect to become acquainted with her until after the marriage, the other side says he is behaving atrociously. He is continually frustrated, unhappy, and unable to achieve adjustment to, and security within, his society.

At the same time, he is oppressed by feelings of inferiority. He has lost the deft understanding which enables one to fit into the traditional society in its small middle niches; he is unable to sense the nuances which allow for security through sycophancy, flattery, and the manipulation of chains of influence. He is likewise, with only a few exceptions, quite incompetent by Western standards. There is enough of the traditional culture in him that is not able to work for the sake of the results, and to view a task as separate from considerations of personal prestige and status.

He is not willing to accept now the old idea of status, self-fulfillment, and success resting upon traditional values, nor can he adjust to the ideally Western concept of rewarding an individual strictly according to how he performs. Too often, he tends to accept the basic idea of rewards based on membership in an autocratic group, but wishes to substitute for the badges of the traditional autocracy what he conceives as the badge of Western autocracy—"educational qualifications." He feels, understandably enough, that he should, by virtue of formal educational qualifications, be allowed to attain the security and status of an informal autocracy. The traditionalist element of society refuses to recognize this claim, holding rather that "qualifications" are based on traditional values; the Westerner laughs at him and tells him that performance, continual performance against competition, is the only standard by which status can be achieved.

Our typical member of the urban middle class now becomes desperate. He becomes anxious and then angry. He cannot, as a normal human being, admit of his inadequacy to meet either system, much less the confused mixture of both which confronts him. He suspects that he is being persecuted and plotted against, and develops aggressive desires for revenge against "the system."

These desires are channelled, naturally, against both of the structures which form the underpinnings of his society. He applies Western standards against the traditional element of his society, and finds it wanting. He applies traditional standards in a critique of the Western element in his society, and naturally finds it wanting, too. It is a short step from these judgments to an uncritical aggressive desire for revenge, and for a final justification of himself by punishing and humiliating the two figures who seemingly mock at his plight, the self-assured member of the traditional upper class and the self-assured Westerner.

Good and Evil

There are certain key concepts of the world which are born and bred into Iranians which unfortunately tend to sharpen the terrible psychological dilemma outlined above. They are rooted in Iranian history, and can be traced back to Zoroastrianism and picked up again in the Iranian interpretation of Shi'a Islam.

Persians tend to believe in the all-pervasive presence of a powerful force of evil in the world. All actions, all motives, are divisible into good and evil. It is probable at any time in history that the forces of evil control the world, while the good man, like the hidden Imam, is forced to hide and remain inconspicuous, to lie and pretend if need be, until the moment arrives for battle. Thus, most Persians cannot ascribe political actions with which they disagree to error, or to grant good intentions to the author of such actions. The term "political compromise" cannot be translated into colloquial Persian without a connotation of "sell-out."

Two results follow from this—first, since the forces of evil are strong and organized, actions by others which one disapproves are not isolated, they are linked together in a mesh of intertwining conspiracies with an overall evil motive behind them. Second, public and private morality are inextricably confused—no politician with a reprehensible private life can be other than evil in his public actions, and no saintly man can be really wrong in his public life.

As a corollary of the above, Persians tend to follow blindly a man who has convinced them that he is on the side of right, without examining political issues critically. Since members of the urban middle class have deep aggressive drives against the traditional ruling class and the Westerner, it is natural to associate a saintly leader with opposition to these two forces. All the ingredients are present for what we would call demagogic politics directed against them as scapegoats and as evil forces.

Foreigners

Persians, and especially the urban middle class, have, from historical experience and from their own peculiarities, evolved an amazing political mythology whereby almost all political developments are viewed in terms of foreign influence, usually selfish and malignant. Most such influence has been ascribed to the Russians and the British; practically every national leader was in the past characterized as "pro-British" or "pro-Russian." Since German and U.S. power were far away and supposedly disinterested, members of the urban middle class for a long time tended to describe themselves as "pro-German" or "pro-American." Nowadays, with the U.S. obviously in the Shah's graces, the term "pro-American" is taking on the evil overtone which "pro-British" has had; the Germans are out of the picture.

There is a deep residue of hatred and distrust of Russia in Iran, but communism has its attractions. This attraction for the urban middle class is based primarily on (a) the communist opposition to the existing scheme of things, and (b) a hope that communism really means that the "educationally qualified" urban middle class displaces the traditional autocracy and thereafter enjoys status, security, and justification. However, even the most angry and frustrated Persian tends to draw back in alarm when he suspects that a Russian lurks behind the fair mask of communism.

Economics

Let us set aside immediately the common conception that the urban middle class is primarily concerned with national economic development. Nothing interests it less. It would like an aristocratic standard of living, but it channels this desire primarily through the idea of stepping into the seats of the traditional ruling class and the high-living Westerners resident in Iran. It has repeatedly shown its almost total lack of concern for the peasantry and even for the urban proletariat, except insofar as it can turn these groups against the traditional ruling class and the West. It is noteworthy that the consumption levels of the urban middle class have been rising sharply over the past eight years, while its political discontent has been rising even more sharply.

Members of this class, with Western tastes whetted by an addiction to movie-going, often bemoan the absence of "a decent standard of living" for themselves. This "decent standard" is measured in Western terms. Its provision, in a society still desperately poor, would obviously result in a profound increase in the gap between the educated and the uneducated, and therefore of "social injustice."

This class has, over the past ten years, shown itself to be ready at any time to put almost all other factors ahead of economic development for the nation. They have opposed infrastructure development and have instead demanded relatively non-productive amenities such as hospitals, colleges, asphalt streets, and urban water and sewage systems. They have been particularly opposed to any development involving foreign contractors or suppliers, which they feel is by definition somewhat nefarious.

It is important to note, however, that an expanding economy and a high rate of investment, particularly in the private sector, provide (a) attractive outlets for the energies of the more intelligent and better-educated members of the class, and (b) obviate the dangers of mass urban unemployment. They do not effectively modify political and psychological attitudes, but they dilute the readiness of the urban population to take drastic action along the lines indicated by these attitudes.

Political Aspirations

Most members of the class look back on the Mosadeq era with undisguised nostalgia. We are thus not operating in a vacuum when we attempt to determine the results of a political change or changes in which power would come into the hands of this group.

In 1957, one urban middle class group indicated in a public manifesto that it was willing to live with CENTO and with the Consortium

Agreement. We must note, however, that the leader of this particular group is probably the most moderate of all potential leaders of the class, and that he and his followers admitted openly that the promise represented the stiff price which they were willing to pay for American "support" in a bid for power. In practice, it seems highly unlikely that any leader would be able to hold to such a position for long. His rivals would make life intolerable for him by accusing him of being a stooge of the West. It is almost a certainty that any government responsive to the urban middle class would as a minimum be forced to withdraw from CENTO and initiate some kind of squeeze on the Consortium, at least to the extent that it could prove to its followers that it was hostile to Western interests. Similarly, in the international arena, such a government would be forced to display its opposition to Western interests in the Arab world, the Congo, the Far East, and other trouble spots, and to extend sympathy to urban middle class leaders in those areas who are now opposing the West.

It is highly probable that, as another minimum, the U.S. military mission to Iran would be invited to leave. The Army is highly unpopular with the urban middle class, and to retain any position whatever in society, the Army itself would have to acquiesce in good grace.

The urban middle class has historically had no interest in or knowledge of financial realities. The degree of financial stability which has been maintained recently would almost certainly go overboard. One cannot imagine school teachers agreeing to postpone wage demands, for example, in view of esoteric and complicated financial factors, nor a government responsive to the urban middle class refusing to embark on a highly desirable hospital-building program because there was not enough money in the kitty. After all, as in the Mosadeq era, the printing press is always available.

Democracy in the Western sense means nothing to the urban middle class. It is probable that the oft-proposed measure to disenfranchise the illiterate classes would be brought up again and adopted, if there were any desire to utilize a freely-elected assembly.

The urban middle class complains bitterly about corruption in the government, but shows little interest in reducing corruption at low levels. Rather, it sympathizes with low-level officials in trouble for this reason, and insists that nothing can be done to remedy the basic problem until high-level corruption, involving the traditional upper class and foreigners, is eliminated. Almost all members of the upper class and most foreigners are believed to be guilty of corruption, unless they are openly sympathetic to the Mosadeqist groups. It seems quite likely that this middle class concern over corruption is actually a rationalization of its deeper emotional antipathies, and its justification in terms of the actual situation is coincidental.

The traditional upper classes, and the upper strata of the upper middle class as well, would probably be victimized in one way or another, ranging from confiscatory taxation to hanging. These policies would naturally quickly dry up the sources of capital formation for the private sector of the economy. Economic enterprise would turn toward the statist road, primarily because it is in the bureaucracy that the urban middle class is closest to having a vehicle through which it can institutionalize status and security for itself.

Political Realities

The aspirations described above do not constitute a prediction of the future. They represent the existing political raw material provided by the urban middle class. When one considers that they are inchoate, contradictory, and emotional in essence, it is obvious that they will be shaped by leadership. They cannot be disregarded. They are growing and spreading every day at an accelerating rate, upward into the younger sons of the aristocracy and downward into the proletariat, pushed by increasing urbanization. Their spread can only be stopped by stopping the process of culture clash, and that is impossible in the world of today.

There is no discernible competent leadership in the urban middle class at present. Should its incompetent leadership of today be catapulted into power, it is likely that a process of confused demagoguery would ensue, which would result in uncoordinated moves in the direction of the various negative aspirations listed above and increased potential for the communists, who obviously, by virtue of their program and organization, would have a good chance of eventually filling the vacuum if they have learned to stop bowing publicly in the direction of the hated Russians.

The Iranian military does not offer potential leadership which could deal with these aspirations and satisfy them. Most junior officers share the prejudices of the middle class families from which they sprang; senior officers are roundly hated as members of the traditional aristocracy.

Traditional leaders—clergy, landlords, and the really big merchants—offer little hope of providing competent leadership, and are blind to the threat which the urban middle class represents. It might conceivably still be possible to "bypass" the urban middle class by providing a dynamic to the inert traditional-minded peasantry and proletariat, perhaps based on a regeneration of Shi'a Islam with new values adjustable to semi-Western values and to modern techniques of production and organization. But there is no sign of the gigantic creativity which would be necessary for such a reversal of the current historical trend.

There is one potential leader who has the necessary ability, personality, and talent, and whose political capital is not yet quite exhausted. That is the Shah himself. The Shah would still be capable, if he could only see the truth, of taking steps like the following which might allow him to seize and mold middle class aspirations.

(a) Channelling current resentments against Ministers rather than against himself.

(b) Dumping his family, or most of it, in Europe.

(c) Abstaining from state visits abroad and discouraging state visits to Iran.

(d) Reducing his military forces gradually to a small, tough force of infantry and artillery capable of internal security and guerrilla activities.

(e) Removing gradually most U.S. advisers from the Iranian Government except those few engaged in health, education, and welfare work in the field.

(f) Publicly excoriating the traditional ruling class for a lack of social responsibility.

(g) Withdrawing from his openly pro-Western international posture with as little damage as possible to Free World morale and to his own prestige.

(h) Ostentatiously reducing his personal standard of living, and the pomp and panoply of his life.

(i) Proceeding loudly with at least a token land distribution program against the big landlords.

(j) Making menacing gestures against the Oil Consortium and "extracting" concessions from it, in such a way as to make it appear that the Consortium was reluctantly bowing to his power and determination.

(k) Making public scapegoats of scores of "corrupt" high officials, whether or not the "corruption" could be proved.

(l) Appointing respected moderate Mosadeqists to positions such as those of Minister of Finance and Head of the Plan Organization, where they could assume responsibilities without being able to reverse policy.

(m) Making public all details of the operations of the Pahlavi Foundation, and appointing as its supervisors a few moderate Mosadeqists.

(n) Employing his personality to make constant personal contact with the members of the middle class.

The foregoing items are not intended to be a comprehensive program of action for the Shah. They are rather examples of actions which would have a positive effect on relations between the Shah and the class under discussion, and as indications of the types of action and gesture by the Shah to which the class would respond. Many of them would be demagogic in nature and would be hard for the West to swallow. But it is still possible that the Shah could turn the trick. He has the brains, the personality, and the cunning to do it.

United States Policy

Elements of U.S. policy which are presently open and which would serve to protect U.S. interests against the dangers represented by the rise of the urban middle class in Iran are as follows:

(a) Inducing the Shah to turn his political talents and his attention, as a matter of priority over military and foreign affairs, to the broad task of winning the confidence of the urban middle class by providing them with a sense of participation in, and identification with, his regime.

(b) Providing economic assistance to Iran sufficient to prevent economic and financial collapse, maintain a high rate of economic growth in both the public and private sectors, and provide for the continuing provision of a reasonable amount of relatively non-productive urban amenities.

(c) Watching political developments carefully with a view to the identification and analysis of effective and responsible alternative political leaders who might, as a last resort, be available to replace the Shah should he fall completely as a political leader.

State Department Report on a Discussion with the Iranian Ambassador (Zahedi)

March [23?] 1961

The following items of interest were mentioned by the Iranian Ambassador during our luncheon engagement on 22 March 1961. . . .

2. *Iran's Policy on Western Alignment.*   Mr. Zahedi appeared to be particularly depressed by the feeling of uncertainty regarding future U.S.-Iranian relations caused by the current U.S. Government reappraisal of foreign aid policies. He explained that despite frequent advice to the contrary, the Shah wants to remain closely allied to the United States but that this is an extremely difficult task in view of U.S. vacillation, our dependence on a budget that can be projected only one year ahead and our periodic economy drives that occasionally result in the cancellation of existing and truly worthwhile programs (i.e. Persian Voice of America program).

Mr. Zahedi feels that his country should not remain tied to "the American apron strings" unless the United States Government can formulate a clearcut policy, valid for at least four to five years and not subject to yearly budget appropriations.

To illustrate his point he stated that Iran's current difficulties with the USSR are caused in a large measure by Iran's joining of the Baghdad Pact (CENTO), that Iran joined CENTO as a result of American recommendations, that Iranian Armed Forces were expanded to their current size also on U.S. recommendations and on the assumption that the U.S.

will continue its Military Assistance Program. He explained that the Iranian Government could not, by itself, support the current military expenses and since there are no firm indications as to whether the United States is willing to continue its military assistance, Iran is left "holding the bag." This situation is further aggravated by the fact that a reduction in military forces would result in considerable dissatisfaction among the military, which is the last thing the Shah wants. In this connection he discussed Mr. Harriman's recent visit to Iran and with particular bitterness described how Mr. Harriman had avoided making any commitments to support Iran, while only a few days later in New Delhi he publicly stated that the United States would continue to support Pakistan's army. Mr. Zahedi's bitterness stemmed from the fact that Mr. Harriman's remarks were made in India even though Mr. Harriman was aware of the rivalry between India and Pakistan and knew that such statements would not be welcome. In a further discussion of this matter, Mr. Zahedi said that General Ayub Kahn of Pakistan advised the Shah that the only way to deal with the United States is to insult and threaten; if this is not done the United States takes its allies for granted and concerns itself only with countries threatening to join unfriendly blocs.

3. *U.S. Government Public Relations.* Mr. Zahedi was bitter about what he considers a lack of proper U.S. Government public relations effort toward his country and the awkwardness of his own position resulting from his efforts to explain and defend the United States' position to the Shah. To illustrate this point, he described the ease and promptness with which visiting American officials can visit anyone in Iran including the Shah himself and compared this with the excessively long time it required him, when he first arrived, to present his credentials. He said that the recent visit by General Bakhtiar as special emissary from the Shah was intended as an effort to reach the President and Secretary of State, and was caused by the troubles he had experienced in accomplishing this. Mr. Zahedi said that upon his return to Teheran General Bakhtiar complained about the shoddy treatment he received in Washington, and of the fact that it took him some three weeks to get to the President, Mr. Zahedi said that he had to insist that the Shah re-interview General Bakhtiar in his presence in order to refute some of Bakhtiar's anti-American charges.

In further discussion of this general matter, Mr. Zahedi said that the Shah would like to be invited to the United States; that he (Zahedi) had dropped a number of hints to this effect but without any success; that he was finally asked about it but in such manner that to save face he had to say that the Shah did *not* wish to come. . . .

Returning to the U.S. foreign policy, Mr. Zahedi pointed out that his self-assigned task of developing friendly relations with the U.S. was becoming increasingly difficult to accomplish since his constant pro-American arguments caused him to be considered in Iran as an American "pigeon." Returning to the subject of U.S. government economy drives, he again cited the unfortunate case of the Persian Voice of America Program and said that Iran was completely saturated by a Soviet propaganda barrage partially devoted to attacks against American "imperialism" in Iran. He explained that Iranian efforts to answer these Soviet charges only resulted in the Iranian Government being called American lackeys and he emphasized that the United States could and should defend its own policies in Iran in a much more effective manner, but that, instead of doing this, we cancelled the half-hour Persian Voice of America program beamed to Iran. . . .

Comments

I met and became friends with Ardeshir Zahedi in 1950 when he returned to Teheran upon graduating from an American college. Since then, I have seen him on a number of occasions in Europe, Pakistan and of course here in Washington. I consider him to be genuinely interested in maintaining the closest possible ties between Iran and the United States. Unfortunately, it appears that occasionally there develops a lack of understanding between him and the appropriate U.S. Government officials. This misunderstanding seems to be caused either by a lack of organization in the Iranian Embassy or more likely by Mr. Zahedi's somewhat complex sense of mission and national pride. Further, he does not desire to "make a nuisance of himself" by appearing to insist on appointments with key U.S. Government officials who he feels may not wish to see him. Since any changes in the orientation of the current Iranian Government, or any changes of that government, will probably result in a deterioration of U.S.-Iranian relations, it appears desirable that special effort be made to facilitate Mr. Zahedi's mission to the United States.

Central Intelligence Agency Report on Iran's Foreign Relations with the United States, the U.S.S.R., Afghanistan, and Iraq

[EXCERPT]

1961

32. There has been no significant change in Iran's international position during the past year. The Shah's regime has remained under heavy political and propaganda pressure from the U.S.S.R. and has continued cautious negotiations aimed at relieving this West openly on most important international issues, has continued to pledge his allegiance to the Central Treaty Organization (CENTO), and has maintained close relations with the U.S.

Relations with the U.S.

33. Assuming that the Shah remains in power and continues to

enjoy U.S. support, we foresee little change in Iran's international position in the next year or so. The Shah and many influential Iranians are generally well disposed toward the West and are deeply suspicious of the U.S.S.R.'s intentions. The Shah knows that he would be unable to resist Soviet pressure without U.S. support. He probably realizes that under present circumstances U.S. support is important, if not essential, to his maintenance of power at home, inasmuch as it deters coup moves against him and provides the military aid which helps him keep his army in hand.

34. Nevertheless, there will remain important problems in U.S.-Iranian relations. The Shah is uneasy over the new U.S. administration's attitude toward his regime and he is likely to remain suspicious that U.S. policy is shifting toward support of neutralist states, particularly in the under-developed area, at the expense of allies such as Iran. He will persist in his dissatisfaction with the level of U.S. aid and his misgivings over the degree of U.S. support for CENTO. This will probably be expressed particularly strongly in the weeks immediately ahead, prior to approval of the Iranian budget and the CENTO Ministerial Council Meeting in April.

35. In these circumstances, a continuing problem for the US will be how to give the Shah sufficient support to preserve his present pro-Western policy without encouraging excessive demands for aid. It is difficult to say what the minimum requirement for this purpose is, but in view of the Shah's preoccupation with his armed forces, it undoubtedly includes some military aid. While he would find it acceptable to have this in the context of increasing the importance of CENTO, with himself in a prominent position, he would almost certainly be willing, if CENTO were to recede into the background, to rely primarily on bilateral arrangements with the U.S., provided he felt such arrangements ensured him a considerable amount of military, as well as economic and political, support.

Relations with the U.S.S.R.

36. A stalemate in Soviet-Iranian relations has persisted during the two years since the Shah broke off negotiations for a nonaggression pact with the U.S.S.R. This stalemate grows out of the essentially contradictory objectives and attitudes of the two parties. The Shah's concept of improved relations is limited to the cessation of hostile Soviet propaganda, modest expansion of trade, and the settlement of a few minor commercial and border matters. The Soviet objective, on the other hand, is to force Iran out of its alliance with the West. We believe the odds are against a break in this stalemate for some time to come. There may be ups and downs in the degree of active tension between the Soviets and Iran, but basic incompatibilities will probably prevent any real rapprochement in the short run.

37. It is possible that over the longer run, the Shah and the U.S.S.R.

may achieve some kind of *modus vivendi*. The Shah is deeply worried about the pressure which is being brought against him by the Soviet Union, and no amount of rational argument or moral support from the West is likely to be completely successful in reassuring him. A general reduction in tension with the U.S.S.R. would probably be popular with most of the nationalist elements in Iran and would receive support from many conservatives who remain devoted to the traditional Iranian policy of neutrality. Thus, we believe that the Shah will continue to seek to relieve Soviet pressure by such measures as his often-repeated offers to ban foreign missile bases from Iran and the sending of a good will mission to Moscow now scheduled for this spring.

38. Should the Shah become convinced that the U.S. was withdrawing or significantly reducing its support for him, the chances of his working out an accommodation with the U.S.S.R. would be much greater. Such an accommodation could lead to a broadening of Iranian relations with the Soviet Union to include substantial economic aid, and conceivably even military aid.

Regional Relations

39. During 1959 and early 1960 the Shah was very worried about the danger of aggression from Iraq and Afghanistan, but he has become less concerned about such dangers in recent months. The Shah will continue to fear the antimonarchial character of the Iraqi revolution. Iran's recurrent quarrel with Iraq over navigation on the Shatt al Arab probably will remain potentially explosive and no settlement is likely. A new flare up could affect the operations of the oil complex at Abadan and the flow of foreign trade through the port of Khorramshar.

40. There has been some improvement in Iranian-Afghan relations during the past year. Iran has undertaken to supply Afghanistan with substantial quantities of oil and eventually to develop special facilities at a Persian Gulf port for Afghan imports and exports. These measures, if implemented, will tend to reduce Afghan dependence both on Pakistan and the U.S.S.R. Nevertheless, the Shah will remain apprehensive about Afghanistan as long as the flow of Soviet aid—particularly military equipment—continues. If Iranian-Afghan relations deteriorate, he will seek U.S. support. Although both Iran and Afghanistan appear to have adopted somewhat more flexible positions on the Helmand River waters dispute, they remain far apart and no settlement is likely in the near future.

41. Iran will probably continue to seek to extend its influence in the Arab areas of the Persian Gulf. The Iranians will continue to regard Nasser's pan-Arab nationalism as a serious threat to Iran and relations between the UAR and Iran are likely to continue strained. On the other hand, the present cordial relations with Jordan will probably be maintained. Iran's membership in the recently formed Organization of Petroleum Exporting Countries (OPEC) was probably designed more to

protect its interests against the Western oil companies. Cooperation with Israel will probably continue, although in a cautious manner designed to minimize Arab reaction of the kind which caused the UAR to break relations in July 1960 when the Shah publicly repeated his "de facto" recognition of the Jewish state.

Joint Statement by President Kennedy and the Shah of Iran upon the Shah's Visit to Washington

April 13, 1962

The President and His Imperial Majesty have had a cordial and useful exchange of views during the past three days. The visit afforded an opportunity for the President and the Shah to become acquainted personally and to discuss matters of mutual interest to their countries.

Their talks included a review of political and military situations in the world; a discussion of the progress which Iran is making in economic and social advancement; a review of defense arrangements in which the two countries are associated; and aspects of United States economic and military aid programs in Iran.

Secretary of State Dean Rusk, Secretary of Defense Robert S. McNamara and Iranian Foreign Minister Abbas Aram also participated in the talks.

His Imperial Majesty described the form and goals of the Third Iranian Economic Development Plan, which is scheduled to start later this year. The President and His Imperial Majesty agreed on the necessity for further acceleration of economic development in Iran, and on the need for continued external assistance to Iran to enable that country to pursue the goals of its economic development plans.

They discussed and were in complete agreement on the subject of the nature of the threat to the Middle East and to all free peoples. They reaffirmed the provisions of the bilateral agreement of 1959 concerning the maintenance of the independence and territorial integrity of Iran, and agreed on the necessity of collective security arrangements to achieve this end. They also agreed on the necessity of achieving a high level of internal economic development and social welfare in order to continue the internal stability necessary to resist external threats.

The friendly and extensive exchange of views between the President and His Imperial Majesty has been consonant with the close relationship between the two countries and has strengthened the bonds of friendship between them in their quest for common objectives of peace and well-being.

In taking leave of the President, His Imperial Majesty expressed his thanks for the friendly reception accorded him in the United States. Both the President and His Imperial Majesty were gratified by their fruitful discussions and by the spirit of cooperative understanding which marked those discussions.

THE UNITED STATES STRESSES ECONOMIC
DEVELOPMENT OVER MILITARY BUILDUP

*Agricultural Commodities Agreement between the United States
and Iran under Title I of the Agricultural Trade
Development and Assistance Act, As Amended*

[Note: Similar agreements under Title I of the Agricultural Trade Development and Assistance Act were concluded and entered into force on February 20, 1962 (13 UST 174), February 3, 1963 (14 UST 215), June 11, 1964 (15 UST 755), and September 29, 1964 (15 UST 1959). In each case, the U.S. subsidy for Iranian wheat sales was substantially larger than in this first agreement, totalling $7.5 million, $7.7 million, $6.2 million and $11.5 million, respectively. The U.S. also concluded agricultural commodities agreements under Title IV of this Act for $2.1 million in November of 1964 (15 UST 2140) and on December 20, 1966 (17 UST 2372).]

July 26, 1960	*Agreement signed at Tehran.*
July 26, 1960	*Entered into force.*
July 26 and 28, 1960	*With exchanges of notes, signed at Tehran.*

The Government of the United States of America and the Government of Iran:

Recognizing the desirability of expanding trade in agricultural commodities between their two countries and with other friendly nations in a manner which would not displace usual marketings of the United States in these commodities, or unduly disrupt world prices of agricultural commodities or normal patterns of commercial trade with friendly countries;

Considering that the purchase for Iranian rials of surplus agricultural commodities produced in the United States of America will assist in achieving such an expansion of trade;

Considering that the Iranian rials accruing from such purchase will be utilized in a manner beneficial to both countries;

Desiring to set forth the understandings which will govern the sales, as specified below, of surplus agricultural commodities to Iran pursuant to Title I of the Agricultural Trade Development and Assistance Act, as amended, (hereinafter referred to as the Act) and the measures which the two Governments will take individually and collectively in furthering the expansion of trade in such commodities;

Have agreed as follows:

ARTICLE I

Sales for Iranian Rials

Subject to the availability of commodities for programming under the Act and to issuance by the Government of the United States of

America and acceptance by the Government of Iran of purchase authorizations, the Government of the United States of America undertakes to finance the sale for Iranian rials to purchasers authorized by the Government of Iran of the following agricultural commodities determined to be surplus pursuant to the Act, in the amounts indicated:

Commodity	Export Market Value (millions)
Wheat	$3.075
Ocean Transportation	.615
Total	$3.690

Applications for purchase authorizations will be made within 90 calendar days after the effective date of this Agreement. Purchase authorizations will include provisions relating to the sale and delivery of commodities, the time and circumstances of deposit of the Iranian rials accruing from such sale, and other relevant matters.

It is understood that the sale of wheat under this Agreement is not intended to increase the availability of this or like commodities for export and is made on the condition that no exports of such commodities will be made from Iran during the period that the wheat is being imported and utilized.

ARTICLE II

Uses of Iranian Rials

The two Governments agree that the Iranian rials accruing to the Government of the United States of America as a consequence of sales made pursuant to this Agreement, will be used by the Government of the United States of America, in such manner and order of priority as the Government of the United States of America shall determine, for the following purposes, in the amounts shown:

a. For United States expenditures under subsections (a), (b), (c), (d), (f), (h), (i), (j), (k), (l), (m), (n), (o), (p), (q), and (r) of Section 104 of the Act or under any of such subsections, the Iranian rial equivalent of $1.29-million.

b. For loans to be made by the Export-Import Bank of Washington under Section 104(e) of the Act and for administrative expenses of the Export-Import Bank of Washington in Iran incident thereto, the Iranian rial equivalent of $.74-million but not more than 25% of the currencies received under the Agreement. It is understood that:

(1) Such loans under Section 104(e) of the Act will be made to United States business firms and branches, subsidiaries, or affiliates of such firms in Iran for business development and trade expansion in Iran, and to United States firms and Iranian firms for the establishment of facilities for aiding in the utilization, distribution, or otherwise increasing the consumption of and markets for United States agricultural products.

(2) Loans will be mutually agreeable to the Export-Import Bank of Washington and the Government of Iran, acting through the Bank Melli. The Governor of the Bank Melli, or his designate, will act for the Government of Iran, and the President of the Export-Import Bank of Washington, or his designate, will act for the Export-Import Bank of Washington.

(3) Upon receipt of an application which the Export-Import Bank is prepared to consider, the Export-Import Bank will inform the Bank Melli of the indentity of the applicant, the nature of the proposed business, the amount of the proposed loan, and the general purposes for which the loan proceeds would be expended.

(4) When the Export-Import Bank is prepared to act favorably upon an application, it will so notify the Bank Melli and will indicate the interest rate and the repayment period which would be used under the proposed loan. The interest rate will be similar to that prevailing in Iran on comparable loans, and the maturities will be consistent with the purposes of the financing.

(5) Within sixty days after the receipt of the notice that the Export-Import Bank is prepared to act favorably upon an application, the Bank Melli will indicate to the Export-Import Bank whether or not the Bank Melli has any objection to the proposed loan. Unless within the sixty-day period the Export-Import Bank has received such a communication from the Bank Melli it shall be understood that the Bank Melli has no objection to the proposed loan. When the Export-Import Bank approves or declines the proposed loan, it will notify the Bank Melli.

(6) In the event the Iranian rials set aside for loans under Section 104(e) of the Act are not advanced within 3 years from the dates of this Agreement because the Export-Import Bank of Washington has not approved loans or because proposed loans have not been mutually agreeable to the Export-Import Bank of Washington and the Bank Melli, the Government of the United States of America may use the Iranian rials for any purpose authorized by Section 104 of the Act.

c. For a loan to the Government of Iran under subsection (g) of Section 104 of the Act, the Iranian rial equivalent of not more than $1.66-million for financing such projects to promote economic development, including projects not heretofore included in plans of the Government of Iran, as may be mutually agreed. The terms and conditions of the loan will be set forth in separate agreements between the two Governments. In the event that agreement is not reached on the use of the Iranian rials for loan purposes within three years from the date of this Agreement, the Government of the United States of America may use the Iranian rials for any purposes authorized by Section 104 of the Act.

d. In the event the total of Iranian rials accruing to the Government of the United States of America as a consequence of sales made is less than the Iranian rials equivalent of $3.69-million, the amount available for a loan pursuant to this Agreement to the Government of Iran under Section 104(g) will be reduced by the amount of such difference; in the event the total Iranian rial deposit exceeds the equivalent of $3.69-million 45% of the excess will be available for a loan under Section 104(g), 20% for loans under Section 104(e), and 35% for any use or uses authorized by Section 104 as the Government of the United States of America may determine.

ARTICLE III

Deposit of Iranian Rials

The deposit of Iranian rials to the account of the Government of the United States of America in payment for the commodities and for ocean transportation costs financed by the Government of the United States of America (except excess costs resulting from the requirement that United States flag vessels be used) shall be made at the rate of exchange for United States dollars generally applicable to import transactions (excluding imports granted a preferential rate) in effect on the dates of dollar disbursement by United States banks, or by the Government of the United States of America, as provided in the purchase authorizations.

ARTICLE IV

General Undertakings

1. The Government of Iran agrees that it will take all possible measures to prevent the resale or transshipment to other countries, or the use for other than domestic purposes (except where such resale, transshipment or use is specifically approved by the Government of the United States of America), of the surplus agricultural commodities purchased pursuant to the provisions of this Agreement, and to assure that the purchase of such commodities does not result in increased availability of these or like commodities to nations unfriendly to the United States of America.

2. The two Governments agree that they will take reasonable precautions to assure that all sales or purchases of surplus agricultural commodities, pursuant to the Agreement, will not unduly disrupt world prices of agricultural commodities, displace usual marketings of the United States of America in these commodities, or disrupt normal patterns of commercial trade with friendly countries.

3. In carrying out this Agreement, the two Governments will seek to assure conditions of commerce permitting private traders to function effectively and will use their best endeavors to develop and expand continuous market demand for agricultural commodities.

4. The Government of Iran agrees to furnish, upon request of the Government of the United States of America, information on the pro-

gress of the program, particularly with respect to arrival and condition of commodities, and the provisions for the maintenance of usual marketings, and information relating to exports of the same or like commodities.

ARTICLE V

Consultation

The two Governments will, upon the request of either of them, consult regarding any matter relating to the application of this Agreement or to the operation of arrangements carried out pursuant to this Agreement.

ARTICLE VI

Entry into Force

The Agreement shall enter into force upon signature.

In witness whereof, the respective representatives, duly authorized for the purpose, have signed the present Agreement.

Done at Tehran in duplicate this twenty-sixth day of July, 1960.

For the Government of the   For the Government
United States of America: of Iran:
EDWARD T. WAILES   MUSA KHATATAN

Agreement for Economic and Technical Cooperation between the United States and Iran

December 21, 1961   Agreement signed at Tehran.
December 21, 1961   Entered into force.

PREAMBLE

Whereas the Imperial Government of Iran desires to raise the standard of living of the people of Iran by promoting economic and social development of the country, and,

Whereas the Government of the United States of America is willing to extend economic, technical and related assistance to Iran, and the Government of the United States of America and the Imperial Government of Iran, desiring to strengthen the traditional ties of friendship between the two countries, have agreed as follows:

ARTICLE I

The Government of the United States of America will furnish such economic, technical and related assistance hereunder as may be requested by representatives of the agency designated by the Imperial Government of Iran to cooperate in the planning and implementation of such assistance and approved by representatives of the agency designated by the Government of the United States of America to administer its responsibilities hereunder, or as may be requested and approved by other representatives designated by the Government of the United States of America and the Imperial Government of Iran. The furnishing of such assistance shall be subject to the applicable laws and regulations of the Government of the United States of America; the utilization of such assistance shall similarly be subject to the constitution, laws and regulations of Iran. It shall be made available in accordance with written arrangements agreed upon between the above-mentioned representatives.

ARTICLE II

The Imperial Government of Iran agrees to make the full contribution permitted by its manpower, resources, facilities and general economic condition in furtherance of the purposes for which assistance is made available hereunder; to bear a fair share of the costs of such assistance and to give the people of Iran full publicity concerning programs and operations hereunder. The Imperial Government of Iran will take appropriate steps to insure the effective use of assistance furnished pursuant to this Agreement and will afford every opportunity and facility to representatives of the Government of the United States of America to observe and review programs and operations conducted under this Agreement and will furnish whatever information they may need to determine the nature and scope of operations planned or carried out and to evaluate results.

ARTICLE III

1. In any case where commodities or services are furnished on a grant basis under arrangements which will result in the accrual of proceeds to the Imperial Government of Iran from the import or sale of such commodities or services, the Imperial Government of Iran, except as may otherwise be agreed upon by the representatives referred to in Article I hereof, will establish in its own name a Special Account in the Bank Markazi Iran, and will deposit promptly in such Special Account the amount of its currency equivalent to such proceeds.

2. Except as may otherwise be agreed upon by the representatives referred to in Article I hereof, the currency in the Special Account will be utilized as follows: Upon notification from time to time by the Government of the United States of America of its requirement for the currency of Iran, the Imperial Government of Iran will make available to that government in the manner requested by it out of any balances in the Special Account such sums as are stated in such notifications to be necessary for such requirements. The Imperial Government of Iran may draw upon any remaining balances in the Special Account for such purposes beneficial to Iran as may be agreed upon from time to time by the representatives referred to in Article I hereof. Whenever funds from such Special Account are used by the Imperial Government of Iran to make loans, all funds received in repayment of such loans prior to the termination of assistance hereunder shall be reused only as may be

agreed upon by the representatives referred to in Article I hereof. Any unencumbered balances of funds which remain in the Special Account upon termination of assistance hereunder to the Imperial Government of Iran shall be disposed of for such purposes as, subject to approval by Act or joint resolution of the Congress of the United States of America, may be agreed upon by the representatives referred to in Article I hereof.

ARTICLE IV

The Imperial Government of Iran will receive a special mission and its personnel to discharge the responsibilities of the Government of the United States of America hereunder; will consider this special mission and its personnel as part of the diplomatic mission of the United States of America in Iran for the purposes of enjoying the privileges and immunities accorded to that diplomatic mission and its personnel of comparable rank; and will give full cooperation to the special mission and its personnel, including the furnishing of facilities and personnel necessary for the purpose of carrying out the provisions hereof. It is understood that the detailed application of this Article would, when necessary, be the subject of intergovernmental discussion.

ARTICLE V

In order to assure the maximum benefits to the people of Iran from the assistance to be furnished hereunder:

(a) Any supplies, materials, equipment, commodities, or funds introduced into or acquired in Iran by the Government of the United States of America or any contractor financed by that Government, for purposes of this Agreement shall, while such supplies, materials, equipment, commodities, or funds are used in connection with this Agreement, be exempt from any taxes on ownership or use of property and any other taxes, investment or deposit requirements and currency controls in Iran, and the import, export, purchase, use or disposition of any such supplies, materials, equipment, commodities or funds in connection with this Agreement shall be exempt from any tariffs, customs duties, import and export taxes, taxes on purchase or disposition of property, and any other taxes or similar charges in Iran.

(b) All personnel, except citizens and permanent residents of Iran, including employees of the Government of the United States of America or its agencies or individuals under contract, or employees of public or private organization under contract, with the Government of the United States of America, the Imperial Government of Iran, or any agencies of either the Government of the United States of America or the Imperial Government of Iran, who are present in Iran to perform work in connection herewith, shall be exempt from income and social security taxes levied under the laws of Iran and from taxes on the purchase, ownership, use, or disposition of personal movable property (including one automobile) intended for their own use. Such personnel and members of their families shall receive the same treatment with respect to the payment of customs, import, and all other duties and fees on personal effects (including one automobile), equipment, and supplies imported into Iran for their own use as is accorded by the Imperial Government of Iran to diplomatic personnel of the Embassy of the United States of America.

(c) Funds introduced into Iran for purposes of furnishing assistance hereunder shall be convertible into currency of Iran at the rate providing the largest number of units of such currency per United States dollar, which, at the time the conversion is made, is not unlawful in Iran.

(d) The Imperial Government of Iran will deposit, segregate, or assure title to all United States funds allocated to, or derived from, any program of assistance undertaken hereunder by the Government of the United States of America so that such funds shall not be subject to garnishment, attachment, seizure, or other legal process by any person, firm, agency, corporation, organization or other government when the Imperial Government of Iran is advised by the Government of the United States of America that any such legal process would interfere with the attainment of the objectives of the program of assistance hereunder.

ARTICLE VI

1. This Agreement shall enter into force on the date on which it is signed by the two governments and it shall terminate six months after the close of the first regular session of the Iranian Parliament, i.e., the Majlis and the Senate whichever closes later, held after the signing of this Agreement, unless, before the expiration of said six months, the Imperial Government of Iran shall have notified the Government of the United States of America that this Agreement has been ratified, in which case it shall remain in force until ninety days after receipt by either government of written notification of the intention of the other to terminate it. It is understood, however, that the provision of this Agreement shall remain in full force and effect after termination of the Agreement with respect to assistance furnished pursuant to this Agreement before such termination.

2. All or any part of the program of assistance provided hereunder may, except as may otherwise be provided in arrangements agreed upon pursuant to Article I hereof, be terminated by either government if that government determines that because of changed conditions the continuation of such assistance is unnecessary or undesirable. The termination of such assistance under this provision may include the termination of deliveries of any commodities hereunder not yet delivered. delivered.

3. The two governments or their designated representatives shall, upon request of either of them, consult regarding any matter on the application, operation or amendment of this Agreement.

4. This Agreement supersedes the Agreement relating to the program of Technical Cooperation and Economic Development effected by an exchange of notes signed at Tehran on January 19 and 20, 1952. Arrangements or agreements implementing the above-mentioned Agreement and concluded prior to the entry into force of this Agreement shall hereafter be subject to this Agreement.

Done in Tehran on December 21, 1961, in the Persian and English languages.

<table>
<tr><td>For the Government of the
United States of America:
J.C. HOLMES
[SEAL]</td><td>For the Imperial
Government of Iran:
H. GHODS NAKHAI
[SEAL]</td></tr>
</table>

Agreement between the United States and Iran on Furnishing American Peace Corps to Iran

September 5, 16, 1962   *Agreement effected by exchange of notes.*
September 16, 1962   *Signed at Tehran.*
September 16, 1962   *Entered into force.*

The American Ambassador to the Iranian Minister of Foreign Affairs (Aram)

No. 107   *Tehran, September 5, 1962*

EXCELLENCY: I have the honor to refer to recent conversations between representatives of our two Governments and to propose the following understandings with respect to the men and women of the United States of America who volunteer to serve in the Peace Corps and who, at the request of your Government, would live and work for periods of time in Iran.

1. The Government of the United States will furnish such Peace Corps Volunteers as may be requested by the Government of Iran and approved by the Government of the United States to perform mutually agreed tasks in Iran. The Volunteers will work under the immediate supervision of governmental or private organizations in Iran designated by our two Governments. The Government of the United States will provide training to enable the Volunteers to perform more effectively these agreed tasks.

2. The Government of Iran will accord equitable treatment to the Volunteers and their property; afford them full aid and protection, including treatment no less favorable than that accorded generally to nationals of the United States residing in Iran; and fully inform, consult and cooperate with representatives of the Government of the United

States with respect to all matters concerning them. The Government of Iran will exempt the Volunteers from all taxes on payments which they receive to defray their living costs and on income from sources outside Iran, from all customs duties or other charges on their personal property introduced into Iran for their own use at or about the time of their arrival, and from all other taxes or other charges (including immigration fees) except license fees and taxes and other charges included in the prices of equipment, supplies and services.

3. The Government of the United States will provide the Volunteers with such limited amounts of equipment and supplies as our two Governments may agree are needed to enable the Volunteers to perform their tasks effectively. The Government of Iran will exempt from all taxes, customs duties and other charges, all equipment and supplies introduced into or acquired in Iran by the Government of the United States, or any contractor financed by it, for use hereunder.

4. To enable the Government of the United States to discharge its responsibilities under this agreement, the Government of Iran will receive a representative of the Peace Corps and such staff of the representative and such personnel of United States private organizations performing functions hereunder under contract with the Government of the United States as are acceptable to the Government of Iran. The Government of Iran will exempt such persons from all taxes on income derived from their Peace Corps work or sources outside Iran, and from all other taxes or other charges (including immigration fees) except license fees and taxes or other charges included in the prices of equipment, supplies and services. The Government of Iran will accord the Peace Corps Representative and his staff the same treatment with respect to the payment of customs duties or other charges on personal property introduced into Iran for their own use as is accorded personnel of comparable rank or grade of the Embassy of the United States. The Government of Iran will accord personnel of United States private organizations under contract with the Government of the United States the same treatment with respect to the payment of customs duties or other charges on personal property introduced into Iran for their own use as is accorded Volunteers hereunder.

5. The Government of Iran will exempt from investment and deposit requirements and currency controls all funds introduced into Iran for use hereunder by the Government of the United States or contractors financed by it. Such funds shall be convertible into currency of Iran at the highest rate which is not unlawful in Iran.

6. The Peace Corps may assign a physician to its staff for the purpose of medical supervision of the Volunteers. In order to carry out this work the physician will travel to the areas of Volunteer assignment. The doctor will be available to work in the Government medical facilities to the extent permitted by his duties with the Peace Corps.

7. Appropriate representatives of our two Governments may make

from time to time such arrangements with respect to Peace Corps Volunteers and Peace Corps programs in Iran as appear necessary or desirable for the purpose of implementing this agreement. The undertaking of each Government herein are subject to the availability of funds and to the applicable laws of that Government.

I have the further honor to propose that, if these understandings are acceptable to your Government, this note and your Government's reply note concurring therein shall constitute an agreement between our two Governments which shall enter into force on the date of your Government's note and shall remain in force until ninety days after the date of the written notification from either Government to the other of intention to terminate it.

Accept, Excellency, the renewed assurance of my highest consideration.

J.C. HOLMES

September 16, 1962

EXCELLENCY: I have the honor to refer to your note No. 107, dated September 5, 1962 and to the conversations between representatives of our two Governments with respect to the service of the Peace Corps Volunteers in Iran, and to inform you that the Imperial Government of Iran agrees to the understandings proposed therein, which are set forth below [agreement as proposed in Holmes' letter above].

This agreement shall enter into force as of the date of this note, and shall remain in force until ninety days after the date of the written notification from either Government to the other of intention to terminate it.

Accept, Excellency, the renewed assurance of my highest consideration.

ABBAS ARAM

Message from United States Ambassador in Tehran (Holmes) to the President and Secretary of State on Chester Bowles's Visit to Iran (February 10-14, 1962)

February 19, 1962

I consider that Chester Bowles's visit to Iran was successful, beneficial and timely. It was successful in that it gave Iranians assurance of continued interest and support. This is something they need to receive at frequent intervals. It was beneficial in that my staff and I got an enhanced knowledge and comprehension of the attitudes and trends of thought in Washington, and I venture to suggest that Mr. Bowles has an increased understanding of the situation here. It was timely as it went a long way to mitigate the disappointment created by the cancellation of the Attorney General's visit. . . .

Having expressed concern about Iran's military budget, the Prime Minister responded enthusiastically to a suggestion by Mr. Bowles that surplus conscripts be organized into special battalions as an expansion of the Army Corps of Engineers with enhanced training and equipment to engage in development construction projects. Mr. Bowles cited the role of the U.S. Army Corps of engineers in civil-type work and pointed out the advantages of such a Corps with high competency and morale. He also suggested that these units be generally retained in the home districts of the men and that they be trained and armed for guerrilla warfare. Mr. Bowles indicated a willingness to furnish the necessary engineering equipment and small arms.

During an hour's conversation with the Minister of Agriculture, the latter gave his standard impression of enthusiasm, determination and courage coupled with a hit or miss, unorganized approach to the complicated and difficult problem of land reform. I believe that Mr. Bowles shares my view that the Minister is the right man to break the eggs but will have to have help in making the omelet. This help can come from the Prime Minister and the Plan Organization.

In response to Minister Arsanjani's expression of need for modernization of agriculture, Mr. Bowles pointed out that a tractor is largely a labor and timesaver; that in his view available capital would be better employed in putting down tube wells. He expressed the opinion that such wells should constitute an acceptable project for a loan on easy terms. These wells should be located in distributed land as an indication of the benefits of the land reform program.

The heads of the several sections of the Plan Organization participated in the hour and a half briefing given Mr. Bowles. This was well done without too much detail and, I believe, very useful to Mr. Bowles. At its conclusion the latter spoke for a few minutes, congratulating the planners on the prominence they are giving agriculture and rural development in the Third Plan and gave them a brief statement of his views on this subject resulting from years of study and experience. This was a very good thing to do and was genuinely appreciated by these young men who are dedicated to their work and are making a very great contribution to the future of Iran.

The visit to the villages of the Varamin Plain gave Mr. Bowles the opportunity to inspect several in various stages of development and to get an idea of the magnitude of the task which lies ahead to change this feudal and backward society into a more enlightened one.

Except for the overnight trip to Bandar Abbas, the visit culminated in the meeting with the Shah. This was unusual in at least two respects; it was a dinner with only the Foreign Minister present in addition to the Shah, Mr. Bowles and myself, and it lasted four hours and a quarter. Mr. Bowles presented the President's invitation to which the Shah responded with obvious pleasure. His acceptance will no doubt be transmitted without delay.

Mr. Bowles will, of course, report his own impressions of this long conversation. My own view is that it was very useful but largely inconclusive. The talk was frank and cordial but did not result in a meeting of the minds, especially with regard to military aid. The Shah stated his case for budgetary support and modernization of his Armed Forces in his usual terms but much less persuasively than he has done so on previous occasions. He bore down heavily on the disparity between military aid to Iran and to Turkey, citing a recent press statement that $120,000,000 had been granted to Turkey more than half of which was for budgetary support. . . . The Shah also compared the quantity and quality of military equipment furnished Turkey and Iran, laying special stress on early warning systems and aircraft. The Shah made a plea for an examination of the role of the Iranian Armed Forces and military needs by an American-Iranian group. We were able to avoid a direct answer.

Although I had told the Shah several weeks ago that he should not count on any budgetary support for the future, including the next Iranian fiscal year, he made a strong plea for such help, stressing the need for decision within a month's time because the next fiscal year begins on March 22nd. He said that if the U.S. is committed to end budgetary support, Iran could use its own resources for military needs, provided economic aid in sufficient amount and on sufficiently favorable terms could be expected. In this connection, the Shah expressed regret that the invitation from the President to visit the U.S. was too late to discuss this matter.

There was an exchange of opinion with regard to the military threat to Iran on which there was no agreement. There was agreement on Iran's strategic importance to the Free World.

Throughout the conversation Mr. Bowles strongly maintained that the assurance of an independent Iran, increasing in economic, social and political strength, lay in economic and social progress. He said that he expected a decision with regard to this year's military program would be made before the end of the month. He would not return to Washington before the decision was made but would be able to communicate about it.

Mr. Bowles explained the new Administration's philosophy with regard to aid to developing countries, particularly concerning its long-term aspects. He defined the attitude with regard to countries in various stages of development and suggested that Iran would fall in the second category of nations not yet sufficiently advanced to warrant commitment to a five-year program, but one to which a year's commitment could be made with a contingency for subsequent years depending on continuing progress.

Mr. Bowles expressed praise and support for the reform program of the Government, especially the land reform law. The Shah indicated complete agreement and reaffirmed his support of Dr. Amini, and specifically the land reform program.

Mr. Bowles expressed the opinion that by the time the Shah visits America in late September the pattern of relations with the USSR would be clearer than at present; that he believed the intervening months might result in the Russians either becoming tougher and more difficult or they might reveal a greater willingness to reach reasonable accommodation. However, there was still the most likely prospect that no permanent change in relationship would occur. In any event, he thought that September would be a good time for the President and Shah to assess the future together. . . .

HOLMES

Testimony of the Secretary of Defense (McNamara) before a Defense Department Subcommittee of the United States Senate Appropriations Committee

February 3, 1964

. . . With respect to Iran, our objective has been to help build up their military forces to the point where they could ensure internal security and provide at least an initial defense against a Soviet attack across borders. Although the Iranian military forces, with our aid, have improved significantly during the last decade, they are still not and never can be a match for even those Soviet forces presently deployed along the Iranian borders, even though the terrain favors the defense. Thus Iran could not be expected to stand alone for very long against a major attack from its northern neighbor and would require immediate assistance from the United States; and in this event, the defense of Iran could not be separated from the larger problem of the collective defense of the free world.

Despite the strategic vulnerability of Iran, it seems quite unlikely that the Soviet Union would, in view of our mutual cooperation agreement with Iran, deliberately undertake a major aggression against that country in the near future. In fact, if Chairman Khrushchev's pronouncement of a few years ago regarding Iran can be taken at face value, the Soviet Union does not believe that military aggression is necessary to bring Iran into the Soviet orbit. Given the economic and social conditions prevailing in Iran a few years ago, Chairman Khrushchev said that Iran would in time "fall like a ripe fruit" into the Soviet lap. Recent vigorous Soviet efforts to improve relations with Iran and Communist efforts to take credit for the Shah's reforms indicate that Chairman Khrushchev may not be so sure today.

Regardless of the validity of that statement, it is certainly clear that the more likely contingency is a covert or ambiguous aggression, using dissident elements in Iran or neighboring nations to pave the way for ultimate Communist takeover. In Iran, as elsewhere in the world, the best defense against the spread of communism is a steady improvement in economic and social conditions, which is the primary aim of our economic aid efforts. These efforts are meeting with considerable success in Iran. The modernization of Iranian society under the leadership of the Shah is in full swing and the economic and social reforms generated by the Shah are making Iran an example for other underdeveloped nations. . . .

THE "WHITE REVOLUTION": UNITED STATES RESPONSE AND CONCERNS

Message from the United States Ambassador in Tehran (Holmes) to the Secretary of State (Rusk)

May 15, 1963

I very much appreciate your 811 and welcome the opportunity to review with you the Iranian economy as a whole. I completely agree that the success of the reform program is fundamental to our interests and that we need to exploit every occasion which presents itself for our assistance both in following up land distribution and in stimulating recovery in the economy. We have made one proposal concerning PL-480 to Washington to which I refer again below. I have a couple of additional suggestions to make in this message on which we need Dept's help. Moreover, while we have been exploring among ourselves and with the Iranians additional ways in which we can help, we have been indicating with increasing frequency some of the steps the GOI* could take to help itself. For example I have a number of times emphasized to the Shah and the PriMin the importance of getting idle money to work and of developing constructive projects. As I mention below, the PriMin told me last night that the GOI now appears to be taking some steps along these lines for which we can probably take some credit.

The problems which beset Iran's reform efforts, of which land reform is by far the most important, and which are preventing economic recovery are basically twofold. Firstly, land reform is not merely "reform." It is a revolution aimed at the destruction of the political and, to a great extent the economic, power of the traditionally most influential class of the country and the replacement of this class with the previously disenfranchised peasantry. Although the revolution has been sparked and, in initial destructive stages, directed from the top, it

---

* Government of Iran.

will by its very nature not lend itself easily to direction in its later stages.

Secondly, there is an incredible dearth of managerial competence and economic knowledge in the government, from the Shah on down. As the difficulties here are fundamentally political and managerial, there are very real limits to what we can do to help overcome them. Were we to intervene directly it would lead us into the midst of Persian politics and personal interests. If we give advice in these areas and our advice is accepted, we run a high risk of being held responsible for such failures as may result from our inability to control subsequent events. Revolutions can't be controlled by foreigners. And in trying to do so, we could endanger all we have gained in this country in the past ten years. With respect to the land reform program, the revolution and managerial shortcomings have created a number of specific problems. Like most revolutions, it was launched without careful preparation and with a tempo which outstripped available administrative, technical and financial resources. Although the tempo has slowed since Arsanjani's departure, these fundamental problems remain. Managerial shortcomings, in particular, manifest themselves in such things as divided responsibility between the Mins of Agriculture and Interior, the Agriculture Bank and the PlanOrg, the slowness in evaluating the government factories to permit their issuing shares against the paper being received by the landlords in payment for their lands, and the delays in establishing new cooperatives and getting assistance to the farmers.

With respect to the economy as a whole, the revolution has directly affected the moneyed classes as many businessmen are either landlords themselves or are connected by family ties with the great landlords. In addition, another facet of the revolution, worker profit sharing, has scared potential investors. But these problems could probably be overcome if it were not for the administrative inefficiency and economic illiteracy of the Govt. For even in the original and revised third plans, in which—given current circumstances—private investment appears greatly over-estimated, the importance of the private sector in terms of economic growth was considerably less than that of the public sector. And private investment could be stimulated if the Govt were to administer consistently and equitably such things as land reform, tax policy, worker profit-sharing, etc., and if the Govt were to launch an effective and large-scale public investment program. The Govt is doing neither. Its policies towards the private sector are constantly changing. Its own investment program is bogged down, the transition to the third plan, involving the transfer of project control to the ministries from the PlanOrg, continues to cause problems. The PlanOrg lacks effective leadership and is unable to organize its work or prepare projects quickly or properly. The Minister of Finance seems to want to launch public works projects but can't get them organized. He is preoccupied with controlling expenditures, balancing his budget and paying his debts and has little understanding of how to achieve economic growth nor attachment to development planning. Parenthetically it should be pointed out that some advantages, in terms of budgetary controls and stabilizing the economy, have been gained from the GOI's conservative fiscal policy of recent months and that balanced budgets are good politics in Iran. Nevertheless the policy of public debt retirement and credit restriction has further dampened the possibility of recovery from the recession and hindered effective implementation of the reform program and we have therefore, as I noted above, been suggesting to the GOI that it would be well to find ways to loosen the purse strings for constructive purposes. Now we have some evidence that our approach may be getting some results, although we were careful to stay out of the discussions concerning the appointment, and excellent man and friend of the embassy has just been named as the new head of the Central Bank, and the PriMin told me last night that the Govt and the new Governor agreed before the appointment was made that certain measures would be taken to make more money available to the Govt for use in the agricultural sector. The PM said it had been agreed that the Central Bank would make advances to the AG Bank for credits to farmers and to the Min of Finance for purchases of wheat and tobacco.

In addition, it was agreed, with some important details still to be worked out, that AG Bank will discount paper given to landlords for their lands provided landlords guarantee money will be spent on constructive industrial or agricultural projects. Such an expansion of credit in the public sector should have its effects on the private sector where factors such as price stability, foreign exchange reserves and bank liquidity now all favor recovery. Monetary authorities have within past year greatly loosened credit and relatively cheap money is available if potential investors can be stimulated to use it.

But, and to come to the principal recommendation of this message, there remain real limits to how far we can go in influencing GOI decisions and I therefore believe that it would be extremely useful if the IBRD could be brought actively back into the picture in Iran. From my discussions in Washington last fall and my letter of November 26, 1962 to Secretary Dillon you know that this is not a new idea of mine. But I think it is becoming increasingly urgent that the IBRD get to work in this country and I urge that representations to this effect be made to the top command of the bank. A major problem, of course, remains the reluctance of the bank's lawyer to approve assistance to Iran in the absence of a Majlis. But we have every reason to believe that elections will be held this summer and in view of this fact and the fact that much preparatory work on the part of the bank will be required before anything firm develops. I urge that a high-level team from the bank come here now.

What I think the bank's objective should be in its discussions with the GOI is not only financing Third Plan projects but establishing on a long-term basis a group in the Plan Organization and perhaps in other developmental and financial agencies of the GOI to assist in improving governmental organization and administration for development and in the preparation and implementation of projects. The IBRD is in a far better position than we are to make its assistance and such things as the formation of a lenders' club conditional on proper planning and project implementation and therefore both to render technical assistance in these areas and to speak frankly to the GOI about its shortcomings. That is the first and principal recommendation I have to offer at this time. Secondly, there are a number of things we can do ourselves in addition to the help we now give which includes technical assistance, financial assistance, PL-480 and moral suasion. What I have in mind, and I mention where we need help from Washington are the following:

1. *PL-480:* We have submitted a PL-480 program (TOAID-A-1736) designed to support the land reform program and to overcome anticipated shortages in agricultural production. As a matter of fact we were surprised to receive AIDTO 787 which suggests considerably stiffer and less flexible PL-480 approach then we recommend and therefore appears inconsistent with your message. We have reiterated our recommendations in TOAID 646 and urge prompt approval of them.

2. *Financial assistance:* Several applications for assistance—or third plan projects are now before the Export-Import bank. I believe it possible that other useful projects will be presented to us. In particular, there are possibilities for loans for the purchase of U.S. agricultural machinery and equipment such as pumps, casing, drilling equipment, tractors, harvesting machinery, etc. I believe that both the Agriculture Bank and the Industrial Mining and Development Bank might be interested in this type of assistance.

One of the problems we face in this area is, however, the insistence of the ExIm Bank that the GOI set aside oil revenues for the repayment of outstanding loans before the ExIm will extend additional credits. The GOI, most recently the PriMin in his conversation with you, has indicated that it opposes this requirement. I do not think we will be able soon, if ever, to overcome this opposition because it is based on emotional factors, the GOI believing, rightly or wrongly, that such an arrangement reflects on Iranian dignity and credit. I fully understood and as you know supported Harold Lindler's stand on this problem last fall. But I wonder if conditions have not now changed. Not only is the GOI current in its payments to the ExIm, but the dispute about the set-aside is eliminating the possibility of ExIm assistance here just at a time when such assistance would be especially useful. I urge that the Dept consult the ExIm on this problem with a view to determining if a way can be found out of the current impasse. One possibility might be to send an ExIm representative here to go over the ground with the GOI and attempt to reach some conclusion which would permit the ExIm to resume a lending program in Iran.

3. *Technical assistance.* The atmosphere for U.S. technical assistance is considerably more favorable than in time of Arsanjani. We are again working closely with officials in agriculture ministry on programs for more effective follow-up of land reform, including rural credit, proved irrigation, mobilization of Iranian field staff, and establishment of production goals in selected areas. We also are cooperating closely with the new Interior Minister in preparation of a new village council law and administration of food-for-work projects on decentralized basis. U.S.AID has taken the initiative in speeding up emergency food distribution for the tribes in the southern areas, and is seeking to develop a long-term rehabilitation program for politically sensitive tribal areas.

I will of course make additional recommendations as the situation develops and opportunities present themselves. I hope we can have early action on the problems I have mentioned above.

HOLMES

National Security Council Report on United States Strategy for Iran

Undated [circa 1963]

I. *Current U.S. Policy Objective*

The basic U.S. objective is the preservation of Iran as an independent country, free from all foreign domination, with a stable government oriented toward the West and an economy capable of self-sustaining economic growth.

This principal objective, and the lines of action now being followed to implement it, are described more fully in Tab A.

The U.S. has a large, shared interest with the Shah both in foreign and domestic political fields. Where there are areas of divergence, e.g., about the initial speed of the land reform program and the role of the Third Plan in economic development, they are differences more of emphasis than of essence. The Shah's estimate of internal requirements for the political stability of his regime does not always coincide exactly with ours. However, the monarchy, which provides the stability not yet available through popular institutions or long popular experience in political affairs, is in fact the sole element in the country that can at present give continuity to public policy. The Shah, therefore, remains a linchpin for the safeguarding of our basic security interests in Iran.

II. *Policy Recommendations*

We believe that the thrust of our policy, as detailed in Tab A, is still basically valid and that the strategy there implied remains feasible in the present situation. To adapt to the rapid changes occurring in Iran we have already made a number of tactical adjustments in our programs (see below, Section III and Tab B). In addition, in view of these changes and to meet circumstances that can now be foreseen, we recommend that you approve the following specific U.S. policies toward Iran:

1. That the U.S. prepare itself, as opportunities are offered by Iranian needs and requests, to give timely and expeditious support to the major elements of the Shah's program of social reform—particularly the land reform—and to influence this program in the direction of efficiency and rationality; that in implementation of this recommendation continuing review should be made to determine whether the criteria for U.S. assistance and loans in regard to local currency are suitable for accomplishing our objectives in the context of current requirements in Iran; that the U.S. abide by its decision not to reinstitute the practice of dollar grants or long-term loans for budgetary support, either direct or indirect.

2. That the U.S., while continuing to stress sound financial management and avoidance of inflation, encourage the GOI, in the short-term, to loosen up its excessively conservative fiscal policies and give the economy an expansionist boost by promoting increased levels of both public and private investment.

3. That the U.S. support the Iranian Third Development Plan and the high priority in the allocation of the country's resources to developmental activities which it envisages, and encourage the evolution of practices and administrative procedures within the Iranian Government which will contribute to the Plan's effective implementation.

4. That the U.S. in the fulfillment of its obligations under the multi-year MAP agreement with Iran, continue to require satisfactory implementation by Iran of its obligations thereunder, including the implied obligation to maintain its military effort within a broader security concept which also includes internal political strengthening, orderly and efficient economic development, and an appropriate balance between military and non-military expenditures.

The above recommendations include the changes in lines of action occasioned by reassessments that have derived from examination of AID strategy for FY 1964 and the review undertaken in response to NSAM 228.

III. *Recent Changes in Iran and Their Implications for U.S. Policy*

A. *General*

Recent changes in Iran are linked, to some indeterminable extent, with U.S. programs and policies. They probably would have occurred in any case, though perhaps at a different time and in a different way. . . .

1. *Major Changes.* The major changes, with the most important effects on U.S. policies and programs, have been the following:

(a) The action of the Shah in suddenly and drastically setting forth on a program of broad social reform such as he had been only talking about for the past decade;

(b) The weakening of the Iranian Government's concept of a broad national political-economic approach based on the institutions and practices of centralized, rational, economic planning and financial controls; and

(c) The swing of the general financial situation from one of a relatively high level of economic activity to one of recession and slowdown of private investment.

2. *Principal U.S. Policy Initiatives in Past Year.* In the period marked by these changes, the principal U.S. policy initiatives have been the termination of direct budgetary support to the Iranian Government and the negotiation of a long-range military agreement.

(a) *Termination of Supporting Assistance.* The termination of budgetary support, in addition to being an expression of basic U.S. aid policy, was also designed to stimulate sound Iranian self-help with regard to economic management problems. This termination has been accomplished without any significant diminution of Iran's pro-Western attitude. While this may have reduced the leverage of the U.S. in influencing the actions of the Iranian Government, there has been a compensatory increase in Iranian self-respect and sense of responsibility, which is necessary for the long-term solution of Iran's problems. Recent changes in the situation in Iran have not been such as to lead the U.S. to reverse its decision to discontinue overt or disguised budgetary assistance.

(b) *Military Program.* The basic strategy underlying the earlier approval of the military commitment was to effect, through a long-range MAP program along with active support of a long-range economic program, a redirection of Iranian attention, resources and efforts away from a reoccupation with military force expansion toward that which appeared to be the greatest threat to Iranian security—the insufficiency of economic development and internal reforms. (Report to the NSC of March 8, 1962 "A Proposed Approach to the Shah of Iran" is attached as Tab C.)

The Five-Year MAP Program discussed with the Shah in Washington in April 1962, refined during the months following and agreed to in September, appears to have been reasonably successful in achieving objectives foreseen by providing the Shah with a sense of security which allowed him to turn his attention increasingly to internal reforms, by planned reduction of GOI military force levels and by initiating steps to increase the efficiency and effectiveness of the GOI military force. However, developments on the economic front did not proceed as anticipated by the underlying strategy which was devised during a period when Prime Minister Amini ppeared to be laying a base for GOI acceptance of comprehensive planning as well as an overriding priority for planned economic development. We are now faced with a government committed to and making far greater strides in land reform (as well as other reforms) than anticipated a year ago but less prepared to accept and mount a comprehensive development plan.

3. *Current Changes in U.S. Policy.*   In response to the changes in Iran, our strategy and programs have had to be re-evaluated and adjusted to new opportunities and dangers. The first occasion for re-evaluation came in the consideration of the FY 64 AID strategy for Iran (See Tab D for the AID strategy formulated in January 1963). There are certain inhibiting factors on the formulation of more specific lines of action than are contained in the AID paper, but the basic thrust of our policy is clear. It is spelled out in detail in the following analysis, in which the factors that will affect our formulation of more specific policies are also identified.

B. *The Shah's Reform Program*

1. *Promise and Risks.*   The Shah's reform program should in the long run bring added stability and prosperity to Iran. It coincides in large measure with what we have long been urging on the Shah and he considers that his course was approved in the President's February message of congratulations.

But for the short run it has involved the Shah in additional risks. He has aroused the animosity of the dispossessed elite and the fanatical clergy, and having not yet consolidated the support of the emancipated peasantry, he is dependent in the immediate future to a greater degree than ever on the support of the military and security forces. Although these forces might not be able to put down a coordinated country-wide rising of tribal and urban elements, such a development is unlikely. It is believed that the support of the military and security forces can probably be counted upon and they can probably deal with any internal security problems likely to arise.

Although the Shah has recently slowed the pace of land reform, the political motivations of the program have already caused it to be carried further than Iran's administrative machinery rationally admits. In the short run, at least, this will create serious difficulties, including, undoubtedly, disruption of agricultural production and marketing, some disorders in the countryside, and dislocations in other sectors of the economy.

2. *Lines of U.S. Support.*   The preservation of Iran's internal stability and its pro-Western orientation would, in any case, justify our continued support for the Shah. Now he has unexpectedly launched a

reform program which expresses in essence significant aspects of our ideals of self-help but which poses great dangers for him. U.S. support for the program is dictated by the fact that only by supporting it can we influence a broad and sweeping change which we could not effectively halt even if we wanted to. There remains the complicated problem of how and by what means we can contribute to the success of the reform program and influence its direction into rational and constructive channels.

(a) *The Pitfalls of Direct Involvement.* The U.S. is strongly identified with the regime and the reform program. Any major failure by the Shah would inevitably adversely affect U.S. interests. However, after consideration we have rejected the possibility of attempting to involve ourselves directly in the decision making required for implementing land reform and other thorny aspects of the Shah's program, such as the workers' profit-sharing scheme. We believe that our leverage can be better used in other ways, since most basic decisions in the early stage of the program are so loaded with purely domestic political, social and religious factors that the decision of any reasonably intelligent Persian would probably be more valid than those of a foreign adviser. We are unsure in any case that we could substantially influence the basic decisions being made at this stage. Yet we do have some latitude in determining the degree of our involvement on specific issues and problems.

The history to date of the Shah's management of land reform supports the validity of our decision. Until two months ago, land distribution, under the direction of the Shah and Minister of Agriculture Arsanjani, was moving so rapidly that, while it ensured the breaking of the political power of the large landholders and far outstripped the government's capacity to manage the program, it also so frightened business interests that the recession deepened and new investment slowed down.

[13 lines censored]

Instead of attempting such active and undoubtedly unproductive intervention, we have taken the attitude that this is an Iranian revolution which will evolve at a Persian tempo and produce Persian results; that bloodless destruction by the Iranians themselves of an ancient and unprogressive system of land tenure and political monopoly is a good thing which we can only view sympathetically; that, like any revolution, these events bring with them great problems which perhaps we can help the Iranians solve or meet but which we cannot solve by ourselves. In any event, the success of the program over the long run may well rest on the extent to which it is identified as an indigenous effort; to the extent that it becomes known as an American-dominated movement, it will lose popular appeal and its directors will lose self-confidence and a sense of responsibility. It must not be forgotten that the Shah's greatest single liability may well be his vulnerability to charges by both reactionary and radical opposition elements that he is a foreign puppet.

(b) *Aid Strategy for the Reform Program.* As stated in the latest AID Strategy Paper (Tab D), we intend to use U.S. assistance to influence the GOI land reform programs in directions conducive to maximum rationality, long-range economic development, and social justice. It is in our interest to help Iran keep the program in the best balance possible between the political requirement of maintaining peasant enthusiasm and Iranian capabilities to develop viable new institutions to fulfill the essential functions once performed by the landlords. As the Government of Iran has only partially anticipated the administrative and technical problems, the needs are great. However, the opportunities for the U.S. to influence through its aid program the future course of land reform are both limited and not yet clearly defined. The situation is one requiring considerable flexibility both in aid strategy and in the types of aid through which that strategy is to be carried out.

(1) *PL-480.* The principal element in our aid strategy is the use of PL-480 as a flexible tool both to offset the anticipated short-run deficit in Iranian agricultural production as a result of land reform and to provide local currency to meet some of the agricultural credit requirements, expecially for the cooperatives, arising from the program. The Embassy and USAID are currently working with the GOI in developing such a PL-480 program.

(2) *Technical Assistance.* We still endorse the emphasis on rural development activities and manpower training in the Aid Strategy Paper (Tab D), and are also studying possible opportunities for the Peace Corps in connection with the land reform program. When Arsanjani was in the Cabinet, the Government of Iran showed no inclination to request U.S. technical assistance for the land reform program. It appears likely that the new Minister of Agriculture will seek such assistance. We believe that the United States should be prepared to respond promptly and as favorably as we can to requests for this type of aid, and to encourage third countries to assist in this area as in others.

(3) *Development Lending.* We are now examining possibilities considered in the AID Strategy Paper of providing Ex-Im Bank and/or AID loans to finance the importation into Iran of U.S. farm machinery, pumps, well-drilling, and other similar equipment, as well as fertilizer and insecticides. The limit to our activity in this regard will be the Iranian ability to develop concrete projects along these lines which will meet our aid criteria. . . .

D. *Military Program*

U.S.-Iranian agreement on a multi-year MAP program, tied to quantitative reductions and qualitative improvements in the Iranian military establishments, is being implemented according to plan. (See Tab F for a review of our military assistance program in Iran and the status of the reorganization of the Iranian armed forces as envisaged in the U.S.-Iranian agreement).

One of the principal reasons for the multi-year MAP agreement was our desire to protect the economic development program against inroads from constantly burgeoning military expenses. Although the development effort we wish to protect is now smaller, it now encompasses the various special and regular categories of government expenditure which affect directly the success or failure of the "White Revolution," in particular the land reform program. U.S. and Iranian implementation of the provisions of the multi-year MAP agreement are thus more, not less, desirable and necessary in view of the recent changes which have taken place in Iran. At present we do not feel that the devotion of roughly 25% of total budgetary expenditures (developmental plus ordinary) to the military establishment (including the Gendarmerie: See Tab E) is incompatible with overall U.S. national security interests. We consider this conclusion is justified by Iran's geographical position, and the nature of potential external and internal threats. The military forces are now playing a key role in maintaining in power a progressive and pro-Western monarch over the next few years. During this time he will face the near-unanimous opposition of old elite elements and will not be able to mobilize effectively for political purposes the mass support upon which the success of the "White Revolution" will eventually depend. If this effort is successful, there is a chance that, for the first time since the twenties, the military may come to be viewed by the Iranian public as a force on the side of progress. Participation in the literacy campaign, growing attack on corruption in the forces, and programs for civic action could do much to bridge the gulf of mistrust and misunderstanding that has existed for so long between the civilian society and the military.

TABS*

A. Our Current Policy toward Iran
B. SNIE 23-63: The Iranian Situation
C. Report to the NSC of March 8, 1962, "A Proposed Approach to the Shah"
D. AID Strategy for Iran
E. Iran's Basic Resource Allocation
F. U.S. Military Assistance to Iran

* Only Tab A attached.

TAB A

Our Current Policy toward Iran

The principal objective of U.S. policy toward Iran is to keep this country out of the hands of the Soviet Union. This policy is based upon tangible U.S. interests involved here: the protection of the flanks of the NATO alliance and our Pakistani ally, the safeguarding of the oil supplies to the United Kingdom and Western Europe, the maintenance of a barrier to Soviet political penetration of the Arab world and Africa, and the inhibition to the expansion of Soviet influence and power which would accompany Soviet access to the Persian Gulf. The reality of the threat to these interests is apparent from the long, documented history of Russian and Soviet designs on this country and the vulnerability of an underdeveloped country with much the longest common border (more than 1100 miles) with the USSR.

A corollary objective is to assist Iran to strengthen its institutions and its economy so that Iran itself can assume more of the responsibility for its own independence.

The lines of action now in force to achieve our objectives consists primarily of the following:

A. Deterring communist aggression against Iran, by

(1) Persuading Iran and the USSR that Iran cannot be attacked without grave risks of direct U.S. military counteraction;

(2) Equipping, training, and encouraging Iranian armed forces with an improving and maximal capacity to fulfill a tripwire function, to delay a communist advance, and to combat indirect communist aggression with a minimum of direct involvement by Free World military sources.

B. Keeping Iran's foreign policy on a pro-Western line of vigilance against the real threats and dangers to national security and independence, by

(1) Maintaining the Shah in a position of ultimate control over Iran's foreign policies;

(2) Persuading the Iranian government and people that the U.S. is willing to assist Iran without threatening its sovereignty;

(3) Persuading the Iranian Government to show maximum understanding of the problems faced by Iraq and Afghanistan;

(4) Encouraging the Iranians to maintain an attitude of dignified, non-provocative, but firm resistance to communist diplomatic threats and blandishments.

C. Maintaining internal political stability and preventing the coming to power of neutralist elements, by

(1) Encouraging the Shah in his "White Revolution" on a course fast enough to maintain lower class support of the regime but slow enough to avoid social and/or economic collapse;

(2) Maintaining the armed forces' morale and loyalty to the regime;

(3) Improving the counter-insurgency capacity of the military and of rural and urban police forces;

(4) Discouraging governmental impulses toward unduly harsh and repressive measures against non-communist opposition elements;

(5) Encouraging the detaching of moderate conservative and liberal opposition elements and the enlistment of their loyalties and energies in the Shah's program of social reform and emancipation.

D. Maximizing Iran's prospects for economic prosperity and for long-term economic development, by

(1) Encouraging Iran to take measures to recover from its current economic recession and to stimulate private and public investment activities;

(2) Stimulating continued vigilance against "boom and bust" policies such as those which led Iran to inflationary and foreign exchange difficulties in 1960;

(3) Persuading Iran to resist *ad hoc* distortions of the Third Economic Development Plan for short-term political purposes;

(4) Pressing Iran to increase governmental revenues at an appropriate time through tax adjustments and improved tax collection;

(5) Encouraging the development of centralized budgetary controls and of improved civil service and other basic administrative arrangements;

(6) Controlling and discouraging the Iranian tendency to give military expenditure increases a priority over other demands on government revenues;

(7) The provision of technical, financial, and administrative assistance to essential and creditable elements of the Shah's reform program, as the need is realized, as opportunities for such assistance arise, and as the U.S. is capable of providing the needed assistance;

(8) Encouraging international support of the Third Plan and providing development loans for Iranian projects within the Plan.

MUTUAL CONGRATULATIONS ON
IRANIAN ECONOMIC PROGRESS

*President Johnson and the Shah Exchange Greetings upon
the Shah's Arrival in Washington*

August 22, 1967

President Johnson

It is an honor and a very real pleasure to welcome you again to our country.

When Your Majesty was here in Washington three years ago, you spoke of Iran's determination to build "a society in which men may prosper and feel happy and secure, a society in which the benefits of a sound education and healthy economy are shared not by a few but by all." We have admired Iran's steady progress toward that goal which you announced.

The changes in Iran represent very genuine progress. So far as economic growth rates tell the story of a nation's achievements, Iran's recent record—an annual growth of about 10 percent—is surpassed by very few countries on this earth. In the five years since we visited Iran, 6,500 village schools have been established by your new Literacy Corps. In 1962 only 8 percent of the rural population went to elementary schools. Now, a short five years later under your leadership, the figure is more than 20 percent and still rising.

Iran has risen to the challenge of new times and new generations, through its land reform, through a drive against illiteracy, through a sharp increase in private investment, and through so many other vital reforms, all of which you discussed with me in your planning when I was privileged to visit there.

Iran is a different country now from the one that we saw in 1962. The difference has sprung from Your Majesty's dedicated inspirational and progressive leadership.

I see another difference, another lesson that your leadership provides for all who prize real progress. Because you are winning progress without violence and without any bloodshed, a lesson that others still have to learn.

To destroy the existing order, to dismiss the past without a plan for the present and future—that is never enough.

We Americans challenge every propagandist and demagog— whether he speaks on the radio waves of the world or in the streets of our own cities—to demonstrate his commitment to progress with the facts and figures. The people of the world cry out for progress, not propaganda. They hunger for results, knowing they cannot eat rhetoric.

Progress in Iran has not meant discarding the past; it has meant keeping the best of the past and forging it to a brighter future.

Your Majesty, we understand this kind of progress. We are proud to have seen you make it, and we are pleased that we could help along the way. But the accomplishments are yours.

You and your people, we think, have sown good seed. I hope to hear a great deal more about that harvest after we go to the office. I hope also to draw on Your Majesty's very wise counsel—so valuable to me in the past—as we discuss our common interest in building peace and security, particularly in the Middle East.

Mrs. Johnson and I are very pleased that you are with us here again. We hope to return now, with special warmth, the welcome that you have so generously extended to many Americans over many years, and particularly to us on our cherished visit to Tehran five years ago.

His Imperial Majesty

Mr. President, I am overwhelmed by the warmth of your words and your welcome.

Since the day I first met with you and Mrs. Johnson, I developed a very special sense of admiration for your personality, your ideas, and what you stood for.

I can say now that it is always a source of inspiration to see someone defending his principles and his ideals with such reserve, with such steadfastness, which creates confidence in the present and in the future.

I would like to thank you for the very kind words you have had toward my country; what we have realized. We believe that what we do is for the sake of the majority of our people.

That is why the economic steps are taken. They present results of this magnitude, because this is done not for a few but for the majority of the people.

Our fight is against illiteracy, our fight is against disease, and now in the future we hope to be able to contribute to the fight that the whole world—the community of nations—must undertake against these same evils and shortcomings: illiteracy, shortage of food, and diseases.

In many ways we have always found inspiration in your great country, the ideals that you have always represented, the humanitarian aspects of the characteristics of your people, of your policies, the wonderful principles of freedom, equity, that you have always upheld with valor and dignity.

We also try to inspire ourselves in the betterment of the life of the individual. We put a great deal of importance to the betterment of the life of the society—but a society in which the individual counts.

We shall try always to inspire ourselves by the wonderful technology of your people—your breakthroughs in agriculture, science, and technique.

We shall always remember that your country and your office, yourself, Mr. President, have stood for truth, for the principles of justice and international equity—but also for the special friendship that you have always had for us.

The only way we can repay you this debt of gratitude is to remain true to the same principles for which you are standing and defending.

I would like to thank you once more for affording me the opportunity of seeing you again and visiting your wonderful country. I am sure that during our exchange of views we can discuss so many things of interest to both of our countries and maybe to the world at large.

Thank you again, Mr. President.

An Exchange of Toasts between the President and the Shah at a White House Dinner

August 22, 1967

President Johnson

The poet Emerson has said that "The ornament of a house is the friends who frequent it."

Our one regret this evening is that our warm friend and honored guest has not been able to ornament the occasion more—by bringing along his very beautiful and charming Empress. We miss her very much, because this administration champions beauty in all its forms.

His Majesty's coronation will take place in October, after a reign of nearly 26 years. This gathering of friends offers you heartfelt good wishes and prayers for still brighter success.

To them I must add special congratulations on Your Majesty's superb sense of timing. You have had the foresight to schedule your coronation when your polls are up.

You also have the satisfaction of looking back on a most impressive record of very progressive leadership. You have taught Iran's people that they have in their own strength and imagination the power to solve their own problems and to realize their own dreams.

When I visited Iran with Mrs. Johnson, just five years ago next week, the land reform program, that we discussed until late in the evening, was just beginning. Tonight, 50 percent of Iran's rural families farm their own land. Some 7,000 or more rural cooperatives have already been established, and more than 800 extension corpsmen are out helping the farmers of that country to acquire new agricultural skills.

This promise of new progress and dignity beckons all the Middle East. The people of that region have just suffered a very great shock. But that shock should and must not obscure the vision of what they can do to solve their problems constructively, peacefully—by working together, by working with their neighbors.

We stand ready tonight, as before, to help those who ask our help—to strengthen the independence of all who seek it in purposeful partnership. Now, as always, America seeks no domination—by force of arms, by influence of wealth, by stealth or subversion.

We seek to build in brotherhood. We want to continue giving and learning, as we will again when Iranian and American scientists soon begin to study ways to exploit Iran's water resources and to employ the exciting new technology of desalting. Our cooperation will continue to grow in this and many other ways.

We take great pride in having with us this evening Mr. David Lilienthal, who has done so much to plan and develop our own land and who is now giving his talented energies to your country.

But turning the dreams we all share into a shared reality asks a long journey of both our countries. We take heart from the knowledge that the people of Iran, under Your Majesty's leadership, have the fortitude and vision to continue their advance and to so inspire all who would follow in hope.

Ladies and gentlemen, I can conclude this statement in no better way than to recall for you the words of a great Persian poet:

> Dig deep and sow good seed;
> Repay the debt you owe your country's soil;
> You need not then be beholden to any man.

Our distinguished guest this evening has truly sown good seed. I ask those of you who have come from throughout our land to join me in a toast to the architect of Iran's future, the distinguished sovereign and leader of the Iranian people, and our most valued and trusted friend, His Imperial Majesty the Shah of Iran.

His Imperial Majesty

This is the second time today, Mr. President, that you have showered upon myself, my country, and my countrymen such words of encouragement and friendship.

I want to thank you from the bottom of my heart that you think this way and appreciate what we are trying to do in our part of the world.

As I said before, we have been inspired in so many ways by the Americans—in your humanitarian approach to the problems of life, in the wonderful achievements of your people in every domain, also in many of your great leaders.

If I may say so, the pleasure of meeting you, Mr. President, and Mrs. Johnson five years ago coincides, incidentally, with the reforms that we have undertaken in our recent history.

What you represent, the morality that you represent—and trying to really uphold it in our world—the confidence that you have created that your word can be taken as the word of a man and a judgment, and so many other aspects of your great qualities are a real contribution to all of us.

So I will always take this as a nice augury that your coming to our country coincided with our great effort to bring our country, even after 2,500 years of history, into the modern age.

We are proud of our history, but we cannot live only with the memory of our past glories. We have to live with the present and live with not only decency but with pride and, if possible, with plenty, with happiness, and with joy.

Again, in that respect, your people and your countrymen have done a great deal and can still do a great deal.

I remember the first time I met and talked with this distinguished gentlemen of yours, Mr. David Lilienthal. He spoke with me and talked about things in my own country that I personally didn't know about.

Because of his knowledge, because of his experience, he told me
what could be done in one of the regions of my country, the fantastic
prospects of development, the happiness that could be brought in that
part of my country—in that part of the world.

The plan has been initiated. We have made some progress. But this
progress cannot be as rapid as we wish it to be. We cannot wait a long
time—neither for ourselves nor really the world—we cannot wait a long
time before seeing all its resources tapped, developed, and put at the
disposal of the human race.

Again, I think in that field, in the promotion of agriculture, in the
promotion of food production, speaking of so many other aspects and
possibilities that exist in my country, you can do a lot by showing us
how to best develop a land.

You have done it in your own country. Not many people can come
and see it for themselves. But if you can do the same things in our part of
the world, many more people could succeed and try maybe to do the
same.

The interest that you show in the desalinization of sea water is
something of the utmost importance. There must be an early solution to
the economic way of doing it. I am sure that before long your scientists
will come up with the answers.

Then, again, our region of the world may be one of the most
interesting cases for experiencing this wonderful technological break-
through. Water is the essence of life. Today it is needed more than ever.

I could continue on for a very, very long time praising the unselfish,
humanitarian contribution of the American people in our country.
That is the cause of this deep friendship existing between us—the trust
that we have in you and, I hope, the trust that you have in us.

I think we are both trying to serve the same cause—the cause of
human dignity, freedom, decency—in what we do. That is why it is also,
again, a great pleasure for me to be once more in your beautiful land,
among such good friends, and especially of having this opportunity of
seeing you again, Mr. President, and having the friendly talks that we
have had, as usual.

I would like to thank you, also, for the words that you have had for
my wife, who had to stay back home. She has a lot to do, because, for the
first time, I think, a woman will be crowned in our country.

Lately women have attained many rights—first, franchise, then
equality with men, and now even equality in wearing a crown. We are
considering now a change also in our Constitution to automatically
appoint the mother of the Crown Prince as the Regent of the Realm if
anything happens to the King before the Crown Prince comes of age or
is 20 years old.

This is to show that we are recognizing the value and the qualities
of the women in our country. I think that really we all, everywhere, owe
so much to the women of our country. I am not going very far. I just

want to mention what Mrs. Johnson is doing in this country and the great contribution that she is making for the betterment of so many things.

As for the future, I can only say that I hope that with God's help and will we shall make the contribution that we can for the betterment of our own people and also in the humble way that we can for all the people in our world, and especially cherish the unselfish, solid, reliable friendship binding our two people together.

It is with the hope of good health to you, Mr. President, and to Mrs. Johnson, success in your work, the welfare of your Government and your people that I would like to propose a toast to the President of the United States of America.

Joint Statement by President Johnson and the Shah upon Concluding Discussions

August 23, 1967

The Shahanshah and the President had very cordial and useful discussions covering a broad range of topics of common interest. Their talks reflected the long-standing friendly relations that exist between Iran and the United States. The President congratulated the Shahanshah on the progress of Iran's program of economic development and social reform and reviewed with the Shahanshah the scope for continued United States Government collaboration with Iran's development efforts. The two leaders also had a useful exchange of views on world food, water and illiteracy problems and the efforts of both countries to enrich the lives of their peoples.

In this connection, the Shahanshah and the President reviewed preliminary plans for cooperation in studying the development of water resources in certain areas of Iran. A U.S. team of water experts will join an Iranian team to begin the study this fall. President Johnson assured His Majesty that the United States Government stands ready to share the technology it has developed so that adequate water may be available to meet Iran's needs.

The Shahanshah and the President reviewed the world situation and particularly the situation in the Middle East, and they agreed that a solution to the current tensions in the area should be sought in strict compliance with the principles of the United Nations Charter. The two leaders agreed to remain in close touch about the Middle East situation. The Shahanshah also reaffirmed Iran's determination to sustain adequate modern defense forces to ensure Iran's national security.

The Shahanshah and the President also discussed problems of building peace in other parts of the world and the President informed the Shahanshah about efforts of the United States to achieve peace in Vietnam. The Shahanshah and the President agreed on the importance of avoiding a widening of hostilities and the need to continue the search for a settlement on the basis of the 1954 Geneva Agreements which would also respect the rights of the Vietnamese people to determine their own destiny in freedom.

The Shahanshah expressed his thanks for the warm and friendly reception accorded him. Both the Shahanshah and the President agreed that the considerations which have motivated Iranian and American cooperation are today more pertinent than ever.

United States Commemorates the Closing of Its Successful AID Mission to Iran

November 29, 1967

Remarks by Secretary Rusk

We are gathered to celebrate the completion of a major foreign aid program. Tomorrow, November 30, direct economic aid to Iran under our Foreign Assistance Act will end. We celebrate because Iran has arrived at the point where it can support its own continuing economic development.

This is a varied group—businessmen, churchmen, and engineers and others in private life, as well as officials of our Government and representatives of Iran. Our interests in Iran are in its safety and its prosperity, in its people and its capacity to enrich the cultural heritage of us all, in its progressive but stable government and its constructive role in the family of nations.

This is an especially moving occasion for me. In the spring of 1946, as a junior officer in the Department of State, I accompanied Secretary of State Byrnes to the Security Council of the United Nations in New York. Our mission was to get the Soviet troops out of northern Iran.

Last December I arrived in Tehran on the great national holiday celebrating the 20th anniversay of the reoccupation of Azerbaijan by Iranian troops.

Plutarch once used the metaphor of "a rich Persian carpet, the beautiful figures and patterns of which can be shown only by spreading and extending it out." What is true of Persia's carpets is also true of her history. Its patterns can be appreciated only when seen in broad dimension.

For thousands of years Iran has been at the center of cycles of growth and development, violence and change. Millennia before Christ, cultures appeared there which used the wheel, copper tools, and woven cloth. In the sixth century B.C., the Persian tribes were welded into a single nation by Cyrus the Great and became the foremost people of the world.

In historic perspective, Iran's recent period of growth is only an instant in time. Iran began to become a modern national political entity only about half a century ago. The first railroad linked the Caspian Sea with the Persian Gulf in 1933.

The United States and Iran have had close and friendly relationships for many years. In 1911 we responded to an invitation to send a financial adviser to Iran. In 1922, at the request of Iran, another American financial mission went out. Iran employed American engineers to build roads in the 1920's and to prepare feasibility studies for the trans-Iranian railroad.

The United States has long supported the independence and territorial integrity of Iran. That was one of our vivid concerns in discussions with our allies in the Second World War about the peace settlement.

The economic assistance program which ends tomorrow night began in 1952 as a technical assistance program under Point 4. The next year, when oil production came to a halt, it was expanded to include direct budgetary support. It has totaled $605 million in direct loans and grants for economic development. But only $37 million of that has been provided in the last five years.

In the same period—15 years—Iran invested more than $3 billion in public programs—half of that in the last 5 years.

Last year oil production yielded more than $600 million in revenues to the Government of Iran, and this year the figure will be still higher. Oil revenues are paying for 80 percent of Iran's development budget.

In 10 years Iran's industrial production has increased 88 percent and its exports by more than one-third. Its GNP increased 11.8 percent in 1965 and 9.5 percent in 1966.

In 1950, more than three-quarters of the available water in Iran was not being used productively; a handful of irrigation facilities covered a few thousand acres. Today, dams, irrigation systems, and well-drilling projects are multiplying.

The use of fertilizer has more than quadrupled since 1960, and the capacity of Iran to produce its own fertilizer is being expanded, partly in cooperation with American firms.

Rice, sugar, tea, and cotton crops have all doubled in the last 10 years. The production of wheat has risen substantially. Poultry and dairy farming have grown from almost scratch to significant levels.

American aid has helped Iran to establish an agricultural extension service with more than 1,000 trained technicians. We have assisted Iran's new hydrographic program and government service to conserve and utilize ground waters. Only 11 percent of Iran's land is now cultivated. With adequate irrigation, an estimated 30 percent can be farmed.

The list of concrete results from Iran's development programs is too long to repeat here. But perhaps we can be forgiven for citing just a few more programs in which American assistance played a significant role.

The American people deserve to know this record:

—Building of the new port at Bandar Abbas on the Persian Gulf, which will open Iran's entire southern region.

—Loans totaling $77½ million to help complete a nationwide network of improved highways.

—Loans of about $9 million to help with a master electrification program.

—Aid in building or improving schools in which 100,000 Iranians are enrolled this year.

—A drastic reduction in the incidence of malaria.

—Immunization of 95 percent of the population against smallpox.

—The insuring, as of last year, of $55 million of industrial development in Iran by American business—in ventures in petrochemicals, mining, rubber products, dairy products, and pharmaceuticals.

But, I would emphasize, the American role has been to help. The main job has been done by Iran.

And certainly, strong and wise leadership deserves a large share of the credit for the remarkable progress of Iran.

The Shah's land reform has given 14 million Iranians a direct stake in agricultural progress. His far-reaching social and educational reforms, including equal rights for women, are producing results. His "white revolution" has made dramatic progress. I have never met a chief of state or head of government who could speak with more precision, detail, and real expertness about the economy of his country than does the Shah of Iran. And I know also from experience that His Majesty is extensively informed about world affairs. We in the United States Government value his judgments. We are proud to have Iran as a friend and partner.

There is every reason to believe that Iran's forward march will continue. Loans from the Export-Import Bank will not be affected by tomorrow's termination. American private enterprise carries on. Many American companies and firms—some of them represented here today—are demonstrating their confidence in Iran's future. Assisted by AID's investment guarantee and investment survey programs, they will provide a continuing partnership that will help to maintain Iran's momentum toward an ever-higher level of prosperity.

There is a Near Eastern proverb which pleads: "May God make our end better than our beginning."

That has been Iran's goal and Iran's accomplishment.

Only a few weeks ago the Shah was crowned—he had postponed the event until his aspirations and policies and programs for his people had produced substantial results. The verdict throughout the free world was that he had thoroughly earned his crown.

Indeed, the story of modern Iran is one of the great success stories of our time. And the realization that in some small measure we have been able to help Iran to accomplish this success should give all of us in the United States satisfaction and joy.

November 29, 1967

Messsage from President Johnson

Today American and Iranian hands join in mutual congratulations. We mark a great success.

It may seem strange that we celebrate when an enterprise goes out of business. It may seem odd that we are pleased that the American AID Mission that has long channeled much of America's economic assistance to Iran will close its doors tomorrow.

But we are celebrating an achievement—not an ending. This is a milestone in Iran's continuing progress and in our increasingly close relations.

What we mark today is Iran's success. What we celebrate is Iran's economic and social progress. What we honor are the effective work of the men and women of Iran and the enlightened and progressive leadership of His Majesty the Shah.

In 1962, I visited Iran and saw its farms, cities, and schools when Iran was on the doorstep of its reform program.

Just three months ago, I had the pleasure of hearing from the Shah himself of Iran's progress in land reform and its drive against illiteracy, its far-reaching development program and emphasis on private investment, and its many other vital reforms.

That story is impressive.

What is even more impressive is Iran's impatience with ways no longer useful—and yet its respect for traditions of the past and its willingness to face hard decisions and to do those difficult things necessary for a better future.

We are glad that we have been able, in an important way, to assist in Iran's rapid strides forward. Our commitment to Iran's progress has been enthusiastically given and of long standing.

Since the dark years following World War II, we have moved from emergency economic support to exciting development efforts which have now paid visible dividends. Careful joint planning has had much to do with the success we mark today.

We cannot depart one era without looking toward another that lies ahead. The similarity of needs and mutuality of purpose that Iran and the United States have long shared do not stop simply because Iran's well-being enables it to shoulder greater burdens.

Now is the time when even stronger ties become possible.

We will turn our hands now to new fields of cooperation. Exchanges in science and technology, expanded business relationships, continued cooperation in development, and a common determination to work for peace and security—these are but a few of the ways in which Americans and Iranians will phrase their new plans for cooperation.

With one milestone behind us, we begin planting for a new harvest of friendship, trust, and shared hopes.

President Nixon and Shah Exchange Remarks upon the Shah's Departure from His Visit to Washington, October 1967

October 23, 1969

President Nixon

As you leave this Capital after your visit here, I can echo what the Secretary of State just said in reflecting on your visit. He said: "The weather today is like our relations."

And certainly on this beautiful day as we complete our talks, I believe that the relations between Iran and the United States have never been better. That is due to your leadership. It is due also to the fact that we feel a special relationship not only to your country but to you, a relationship which, in my case, goes back many years.

We have had bilateral talks which have been most constructive.

But I, too, want to thank you for giving the Secretary, myself, and our colleagues the benefit of your analysis of the problems in the Mid-east, which are tremendously explosive at the present time, and also the problems in the world; because Iran, in a sense, is a bridge between the East and West, between Asia and Europe, and, for that matter, Africa.

And at that vantage point you are able to see those problems perhaps better than almost any leader in the world.

We thank you for coming to us.

And I can say, in conclusion, that I look forward to visiting Iran again. I have not yet set a date. But you have very cordially invited me to come. I accept the invitation and we will set a date at a later time.

Thank you.

His Imperial Majesty

Thank you very much, Mr. President.

I must say once more how honored I was by your hospitality and friendship that you have shown to me once more and how deeply appreciative I am of the frankness and the friendliness in which we have had our talks with you, Mr. President, and your associates.

As you very well mentioned, our relations have never been as good as they are now, because they are based on an absolute trust and mutual interests.

We are defending the same principles, upholding the same moral values that we understand and for which we are living and, if necessary, dying; the interest of your country that the world should be a good place to live in, a free place to live in; that everybody should be given the opportunity of progressing, of living better without fear and in health and happiness.

For these ideals that we respect, we wish you an ever-growing strength.

We wish you success in all your enterprises and, in addition to this, we hope that you will always feel—maybe sometimes it is a burden—but feel the responsibility that you have toward the human race, because you can provide it. When you can provide it, if I could be bold enough to say, you must provide it.

We shall continue on our part to play whatever constructive role that we can in our part of the world, upholding the same principles, trying to be of any assistance and cooperation for the maintenance of peace, stability, and assistance to all those who would ask for it without any second thought and as liberally as possible.

The state of relationships between our two countries, I hope, will continue in this manner for the better of our two countries, of our region, and I hope maybe even for the world.

As you mentioned, Mr. President, my country is a crossroad between various civilizations and various interests. It will be our duty to be able to honor this task faithfully, with dignity, and, I hope, also in a constructive way.

We will be more able to do it always when we have the moral support, assistance, of our friends, the greatest of them being this great country of yours, and your personal friendship, Mr. President, which I personally, and I am sure my people, value to the greatest possible extent.

Thank you very much.

United States Foreign Policy 1969-1970: A Report of the Secretary of State

[EXCERPT]

By the end of 1970, Iran, at one time the beneficiary of substantial U.S. military and economic assistance, was essentially self-reliant. The closeness of U.S.-Iranian relations has been demonstrated by a similarity of views and action on important bilateral and international issues, as well as by visits of the Shah to the United States and by the Secretary of State to Iran.

Stable and progressive, Iran is a constructive force in the region. Internally, Iran has maintained the momentum of progress and reform that has marketed the country's history since the early 1960's. Iran has emphasized economic progress, reform, and reconstruction in pragmatic and largely effective ways, establishing a real GNP growth rate of more than eight percent.

Although Iran no longer requires economic assistance, we have sought to be responsive to Iran's continuing drive toward economic development and diversification. Export-Import Bank loans of $24 million in 1969 and $47 million in 1970 were authorized for improvements in communications, transportation, and agriculture. Iran purchases much more from us than we buy from them—in 1969 we exported $353 million worth of goods to Iran and imported $88 million worth.

U.S. investment in Iran in 1969 approached $465 million of which a major portion was in the oil industry. Negotiations over production and price levels between Iran and the companies owning oil concessions were major elements in Iran's external relations during 1969 and 1970. While the U.S. Government was not directly involved, we maintained close contact with the Iranian Government and the companies concerned. While U.S. companies are involved in much of the oil production in Iran, the oil is exported primarily to Europe and Japan and little enters the United States. Toward the end of 1970, as Iran and other oil-producing countries joined in common negotiations with the interested corporations, we consulted with U.S. companies and with the governments involved with a view to producing an acceptable agreement. Agreement was reached in early 1971.

We have also cooperated closely with Iran in supplying some of its military requirements, largely through programs of military advisers, military credit sales, and more recently with an Export-Import Bank loan of $120 million in fiscal year 1971.

7

High Tide

In the early years of the 1970s, relations between the United States and Iran reached the zenith of the entire era that had begun at the end of World War II. Not only was there close cooperation in the economic sphere, but Iran was given U.S. blessings in its drive to become the regional power in the Persian Gulf area.

This all-out support for Iran's political and military aspirations was the result of changing world conditions, rather than any sudden enthusiasm for the sometimes grandiose ideas of the Shah. The first of these changes was the impact of the Vietnam war on the United States. It aroused so much domestic opposition that many people, both in America and abroad, wondered whether the United States would be able to keep the commitments it had made to come to the assistance of nations all over the globe whose security might be threatened by communist aggression.

The incoming Nixon administration recognized this dilemma, and the new President, on two separate occasions, pronounced his formula for dealing with it. In Guam, in June 1969, he emphasized that regional powers would have to take on greater responsibility for collective security. They would get U.S. arms, but not necessarily U.S. forces. In a 1970 report to Congress, President Nixon stated that the United States would participate in the defense and development of allies and friends, but that it could not conceive all of the plans, design all of the programs, execute all of the decisions, or undertake all of the defense of the free nations. The U.S. would help where such help would make a difference and where it would be in U.S. interests. The Nixon Doctrine thus proclaimed a more cautious, less exposed world role for the United States.

Another change in the world scene was the decision of the British, announced in January 1968, to withdraw their forces from the Persian Gulf by the end of 1971. From the U.S. standpoint some friendly power had to fill that vacuum, since the United States was not prepared to do so itself. The result was the adoption of what was called the "twin pillars" policy for the region. The United States decided to rely on Iran and Saudi Arabia to maintain security in the Persian Gulf. It was a case of confluence of interests.

Once that decision had been made, the logic of increased arms sales became persuasive. By the time the British withdrew from the Gulf in 1971, Iran had become a significant military power in the area. After that, the policy of military acquisitions went on at a sustained pace. Arguing that Iran was prepared to make a significant effort in its own defense and that its commitment to its security was a major factor for stability in the Middle East, U.S. policy became, for the most part, one of uncritical acquiescence in Iran's requests for new weapons. Some of the latest weapons systems in the U.S. inventory were purchased by Iran. These included a wide range of aircraft, naval vessels including submarines and landing craft, tanks, various types of missiles, "smart bombs," self-propelled artillery, and many others. Documents in this chapter illustrate various aspects of U.S. policy regarding the Iranian arms build-up.

Iran obtained the wherewithal to pursue its arms acquisition program as a result of the quantum increase in oil prices adopted by the Organization of Petroleum Exporting Countries (OPEC) in 1973. As early as 1969 the Shah had suggested that the United States purchase $100 million worth of Iranian oil every year in return for a guarantee that this money would be spent by Iran for U.S. arms and other military equipment. The United States had turned down that suggestion, but after the rise in OPEC oil prices Iran had no problem in finding the funds to pay for its arms purchases. Indeed, numerous media reports have contended that Iran was among the OPEC leaders in lobbying for drastic price increases—certainly not a friendly attitude from the standpoint of the U.S., although the Shah insisted that such increases were necessary to compensate for the higher prices Iran and others had to pay for imports from the West because of inflation.

It has been asserted that the allocation of so much oil money to military procurement damaged Iran's economic development program, destabilized her economy, and hence contributed substantially to the revolution that eventually overthrew the Shah. Whether this thesis is wholly accurate or not, there is no doubt that by the mid-1970s Iran's economic program was experiencing many difficulties. The depth of these difficulties is not fully reflected in the communiqué of the U.S.-Iranian Joint Commission which is published in this chapter. That Joint Commission, which could be described as a board of directors for the combined interests of Iran and the United States, was a short-lived bilateral experiment that testified to the special position given the U.S.-Iranian relationship by both countries.

Even this special relationship, however, could not provide Iran with immunity from a certain degree of condemnation concerning its alleged violations of human rights, the last subject of this chapter. Before the Carter administration assumed office in January 1977, Iran had already been criticized on the issue of human rights. As the Carter administration quickly placed even greater emphasis on the importance of human rights, U.S. assistance to the Shah's regime was seriously questioned in many quarters. Time would tell just how vulnerable the Shah would become on this issue.

NARCOTICS RESTRICTION

Joint Communiqué of President Nixon and the Shah of Iran upon the President's Visit to Iran

Tehran, May 31, 1972

. . . The President and His Imperial Majesty agreed that the security and stability of the Persian Gulf is of vital importance to the littoral States. Both were of the view that the littoral States bore the primary responsibility for the security of the Persian Gulf.

His Imperial Majesty reaffirmed Iran's determination to bear its share of this responsibility.

The President and His Imperial Majesty also agreed that the economic development and welfare of the bordering States of the Persian Gulf are of importance to the stability of the region. Iran declared itself ready and willing to cooperate with its neighbors in fostering an atmosphere in which stability and progress can flourish.

The President and His Imperial Majesty voiced the hope that Pakistan and India would find ways to reach a just and honorable settlement of the existing issues. They noted with satisfaction the initiative taken by both countries for meetings which hold the promise through further talks of progress toward a peaceful settlement in South Asia built on lasting relationships of friendship and mutual respect.

The President expressed his admiration for Iran's impressive record in the development of a strong economy and the successful implementation of His Imperial Majesty's "White Revolution." His Imperial Majesty outlined the main features of Iran's new five-year plan with particular emphasis on agro-industry and socio-economic projects. The President reiterated the readiness of the United States to cooperate with Iran as appropriate in this extensive program and important enterprise.

The President and His Imperial Majesty also discussed the worldwide narcotics problem. They noted that Iran and the United States were taking vigorous action against the illicit international narcotics traffic. Both took satisfaction in Iran's effective measures to control domestic opium production. The President expressed understanding of Iran's declared policy to cease internal cultivation of the opium poppy when Iran's neighbors also cease internal cultivation of the opium poppy. They agreed that the two governments should continue their close cooperation in international forums dealing with narcotic matters. The President noted with appreciation the active support provided by Iran at the recent United Nations conference which adopted a protocol amending the 1961 single convention on narcotic drugs. The President reaffirmed United States' support for regional cooperation in solving international narcotics problems.

Both sides expressed deep satisfaction over the excellence of relations between their two countries and the expectation that they would continue in the future. His Imperial Majesty stressed once again Iran's determination to strengthen its defensive capability to ensure the nation's security. The President confirmed that the United States would, as in the past, continue to cooperate with Iran in strengthening its defenses. They reaffirmed their respect for the sovereign right of every nation to choose its own destiny in its own way without any outside interference.

In expressing appreciation for the warm hospitality shown him and Mrs. Nixon, the President invited Their Imperial Majesties to visit the United States at a mutually convenient time. The invitation was accepted with deep appreciation.

Attempts to Control Opium Production in Iran: A Report of the Department of State, Office of Intelligence Research*

[ABSTRACT]

December 28, 1950

Although the United States, the United Kingdom, and such inter-

---

* Although the Nixon Administration became increasingly vigorous in the effort to restrict world narcotics traffic, the issue itself did not fall into neglect after U.S. participation in the Geneva Conference of the 1920s. This document helps fill in the post-1920s record of U.S. concern with Iranian opium cultivation.

national organizations as the League of Nations and the UN have repeatedly attempted to induce Iran to institute controls on opium cultivation, consumption, and trade, these efforts have met with little success. While the Iranian Government has often gone on record with promises to reduce or eliminate opium production, no real attempt has ever been made to enforce these pledges.

There are several reasons for this failure to implement controls: (1) the continuing instability and lack of continuity in Iranian governments; (2) public apathy to any moral issue involved in opium addiction, since most Iranians attach little more stigma to opium smoking than Americans do to cigarettes; (3) the inability of agricultural experts to suggest any one substitute crop that would bring as high a return for as little effort as opium, which now contributes an estimated five percent of Iran's gross farm income; (4) the combined pressure of landowners, merchants, and consumers to invalidate any opium legislation passed; (5) the fact that many Iranian promises for action on the opium problem were obviously made as temporary salves to strong Western pressure; Iranian delegates to international conferences have been particularly prone to make sweeping promises which, owing to domestic pressures, were impossible of fulfillment. In the past, an additional excuse for the lack of official support for controls has been the revenue which the government receives from opium sales. However, this reason is no longer valid, since the government now actually pays more for the opium it buys (including storage and transport costs) than the world market price.

Even without a perfect crop substitute for opium, it might be possible to institute production cuts without undue hardship to farmers as soon as the Seven-Year Economic Development Plan, now underway, begins to bring about a general improvement in the Iranian economy. However, the Iranians are not likely, of their own accord, to establish effective controls as long as such action can be postponed. In the absence of any public or moral pressure within Iran to stimulate action, intensive foreign prodding would be required to induce Iran to regard the opium problem seriously. It is extremely doubtful if an effective control program will be adopted until Iranian officials are convinced that their country will be completely barred from the world legitimate opium market unless illicit production and trade are eliminated.

Iran ranks second only to Turkey as the world's largest producer of opium. The bulk of Iran's current output of about 1,000 metric tons a year is consumed domestically by more than a million addicts, but Iran also supplies about one-third of world opium exports.

Since 1911 the Iranian National Assembly (Majlis) has twice passed legislation prohibiting the production and consumption of opium; on another occasion, the Council of Ministers decreed a similar prohibition. In none of these instances was any serious effort made to enforce the legislation. In 1926, at the request of Iran, the League of Nations sent a mission to study the question of crop substitution, but the Iranian Government failed to take any action on the mission's recommendation. Numerous Iranian commissions have made similar studies since that time, but no effort has been made to put these reports to practical use.

The United States expressed concern on several occasions during the 1930s regarding Iran's growing illicit opium trade in the Far East. When Iran continued to procrastinate about establishing controls over this traffic, the United States (in 1937) placed an embargo on the importation of Iranian opium. This ban was lifted after the outbreak of World War II because (1) Iran's controversial Far Eastern market had been eliminated and (2) opium had become a critical war material in the United States.

In 1943, on the occasion of the signature of a trade agreement with the United States, Iran agreed to institute an opium expert control system, primarily designed to prevent opium exports to the Far East. Since Iran made no effort to carry out this promise, the United States re-imposed its ban on the importation of Iranian opium in 1947. Although Iranian authorities objected strenuously to the "injustice" of this new embargo, they gave no indication that they were prepared to institute an export control system; several U.S. notes to the Iranian Government offering suggestions for opium control were never answered, and an offer of assistance in facilitating crop substitution has not been acknowledged.

In response to strong U.S. urging, the Iranian Council of Ministers finally issued a decree in February 1949 prohibiting opium exports to the Far East. The U.S. embargo was subsequently lifted, and American purchasers have since been buying most of Iran's opium stocks for their current needs and for the government's strategic stockpile program. Recently Iran, together with the other opium producing countries, agreed in principle to the establishment of an export quota and to control production. It would be premature, however, to regard this as a significant step in opium control, since it will require the passage of adequate legislation by the Majlis and the cooperation of the government in enforcing it.

ECONOMIC, TECHNICAL, AND MILITARY
TIES INTENSIFIED

Memorandum of Understanding between the United States and Iran on Sharing Remote-Sensing Satellite Data

July 25, 1974   *Memorandum of understanding signed at Washington and Tehran.*
October 29, 1974   *ton and Tehran.*
October 29, 1974   *Entered into force.*

1. The purposes of this agreement are to set forth the responsibilities of the parties and the procedures for providing for (a) direct access, by a ground station to be built and operated in Iran by The Plan and Budget Organization, to NASA ERTS-1* and ERTS-B satellite data and to the data from any future ERTS experimental satellites which NASA may launch, and (b) availability to NASA of data acquired by the Iranian station pursuant to (a) above, subject to the provisions which follow.

2. For its part, the Plan and Budget Organization will use its best efforts to:

(a) Develop and operate a facility in the Greater Tehran Area for acquisition and processing of ERTS data as well as other data of interest to the Plan and Budget Organization entirely at its own cost, including the cost of the necessary communication links with the NASA ERTS OCC/NDPF (Operations Control Center/NASA Data Processing Facility) at the Goddard Space Flight Center.

(b) Provide during Phase B, as described below, processed data to ERTS Principal Investigators duly selected by NASA whose test sites are in range of the Iranian data acquisition station for the period of coverage promised to them and under the same conditions as NASA provides data to Principal Investigators. Should another country in the region establish ERTS facilities, the Plan and Budget Organization's obligation to provide data to Principal Investigators in that country will terminate as soon as the new facilities are capable of providing this service. The Plan and Budget Organization will continue to serve Principal Investigators in countries within range of the Tehran station which do not have ERTS facilities unless and until alternative arrangements are concluded.

(c) Provide, to the best of its ability, any support requested by NASA in a spacecraft emergency condition, such as the provision of data indicated in paragraph 2(e) below should the on-board tape recorders fail.

(d) Provide quarterly reports in English to NASA on the progress and results of the Plan and Budget Organization's experimental program with respect especially to the ability to apply data and analyses obtained to real-time decision making, and the principal applications made.

(e) Make available to NASA, on a cost-free basis and in the NASA-preferred format (negative imagery format with identifying annotation) such copies of the ERTS data it acquires and processes as NASA may request in reasonable quantities (except in emergency conditions as noted in paragraph 2(c) above). These data provided to NASA by the Plan and Budget Organization will be made availa-

---

* Earth Resource Technology Satellite (recently it has been changed to LANDSAT).

ble to the public from U.S. sources on precisely the same terms as data acquired directly by NASA. These provisions apply as well to selected duplicate compatible tapes. Public requests (for data) from the area covered by the Tehran station will be referred as appropriate to the Plan and Budget Organization or to other regional facilities which may be established in the area. Coordination among such facilities would be highly desirable.

(f) Include as output data from the Tehran station Computer Compatible Tapes (CCT's) and 70mm roll film.

3. For its part, NASA will use its best efforts to:

(a) Program ERTS-1 and any subsequently experimental ERTS-type satellites to acquire data in areas accessible for direct read-out by the Iranian station. The frequency of such programming will be subject to mutual agreement by the Project Managers (see below). It will be limited to test purposes in Phase A and expanded as agreed in Phase B.

(b) Provide to the Plan and Budget Organization as necessary antenna pointing elements for acquisition of the ERTS spacecraft transmitted signal and updated definitive orbital information for use in processing the data.

(c) Process, on time-available basis and as may be agreed by the Project Managers, a limited number of data tapes acquired by the Iranian station in Phase A for initial evaluation and calibration of the station's performance.

(d) Provide, during Phase A, ERTS data to any NASA-selected Iranian Principal Investigators to the extent of the time-coverage promised for them.

(e) Make available, for comparison purposes, a limited number of selected NASA data tapes covering portions of the area accessible to the Tehran station.

(f) Keep the Plan and Budget Organization informed of other prospective ERTS facilities in the area so that regional coordination can be effected.

4. The course of the project will be divided into two phases. Phase A is for the test and checkout of the Tehran station. Phase B is for the following period of routine data acquisition and processing at the Tehran station. Phase A will begin when the Project Managers agree on the readiness of the technical and operational interfaces required to carry out the project and on a schedule for accomplishing Phase A and B. Phase A will be concluded and Phase B begun by mutual agreement of the Project Managers.

5. To implement the agreement, the Plan and Budget Organization and NASA will each designate Project Managers to be responsible for coordinating the agreed functions and responsibilities of each side with the other. The Project Managers will be co-chairmen of a Joint

Working Group (JWG) which will be the principal instrument for assuring the execution of the project and for keeping both sides continuously informed of the project status. The Joint Working Group may establish such committees as required to carry out the project.

6. The following additional understandings are confirmed:

(a) The Plan and Budget Organization will resolve any radio frequency difficulties in the region to the satisfaction of the parties concerned so this cooperation can proceed without difficulty.

(b) The responsibility for spacecraft control, health and status will remain with NASA throughout the program.

(c) There will be no exchange of funds between the Plan and Budget Organization and NASA for ERTS-1 operation. This agreement assures the Plan and Budget Organization access to the ERTS-B satellite throughout its design life of one year without charge by NASA. It is understood, however, that NASA may thereafter establish some cost-sharing arrangement, such as users' fees, for participating ground stations.

(d) It is understood at this stage that NASA cannot make a firm commitment for future ERTS-type satellites.

(e) Decisions taken by the International Telecommunications Union require that radio frequencies for future operational ERTS satellites will differ from those currently used for experimental satellites.

(f) It is understood that the Plan and Budget Organization and the other Iranian agencies participating in the program will pursue an ERTS open-data policy comparable to that of NASA and other U.S. agencies participating in the program, particularly with respect to the public availability of data. The Plan and Budget Organization will thus ensure unrestricted public availability of the earth resources satellite data at a fair and reasonable charge based on actual cost.

(g) Training and exchange of technical personnel will take place as mutually agreed.

(h) The Plan and Budget Organization and NASA will freely share and exchange data and technical information as mutually agreed and consistent with the laws and regulations of the two countries.

(i) It is understood that this project is experimental in character and subject to change in accordance with changes in technical requirements and opportunities.

(j) The Plan and Budget Organization and NASA may each release general information to the public regarding the conduct of their own portion of the project as desired and, insofar as participation of the other agency is concerned, after suitable coordination.

(k) The Plan and Budget Organization and NASA will assure

that the project is appropriately recorded in still and motion picture photography and that the photography is made available to the other agency upon request for public information purposes.

(l) It is understood that the ability of the Plan and Budget Organization and NASA to carry out the responsibilities of this agreement is subject to the availability of appropriated funds.

7. This Memorandum of Understanding shall enter into force upon signature by the Plan and Budget Organization and NASA and shall continue in force for four years, subject to extension as may be agreed by the Plan and Budget Organization and NASA.

<table>
<tr><td>For the Plan and
Budget Organization:
A.M. MAJIDI
Minister of State and Director of
the Plan and Budget Organization
October 29, 1974</td><td>For the National Aeronautics
and Space Administration:
JAMES C. FLETCHER
Administrator

July 25, 1974
RICHARD HELMS
Ambassador</td></tr>
</table>

Joint Communiqué Issued at the Conclusion of Secretary of State Kissinger's Visit to Iran, Announcing the Establishment of a United States-Iran Joint Commission

November 2, 1974

At the invitation of the Government of Iran the Secretary of State of the United States, Dr. Henry A. Kissinger, visited Iran November 1-3, 1974. The visit was another expression of long-standing close and friendly relations between the two countries and their interest in further strengthening the ties between them.

During the visit Dr. Kissinger was received by His Imperial Majesty, Mohammad Reza Shah Pahlavi, Shahanshah of Iran. Secretary Kissinger conveyed to His Majesty the warm personal greetings of President Ford, together with the President's expressions of appreciation for His Majesty's leadership and statesmanlike role in world affairs. His Majesty and the Secretary of State reviewed the international situation and discussed matters of bilateral interest in the spirit of mutual respect and understanding that has long characterized U.S.-Iranian relations. Dr. Kissinger also met with Minister of Foreign Affairs Dr. Abbas Ali Khalatbary and Minister of Economic Affairs and Finance Hushang Ansary.

In their review of the international situation the two sides expressed satisfaction with the progress toward global détente and agreed on the need for further efforts to reduce tensions. The two sides also noted their close similarity of views on regional security issues. The U.S. side expressed its continuing support for Iran's programs to strengthen itself and to work cooperatively with its neighbors in the Persian Gulf and wider Indian Ocean regions. It also stated appreciation for Iranian efforts to promote peaceful solutions to disputes among its neighbors. The Iranian side explained its concept of increasing economic cooperation among the countries on the Indian Ocean littoral. Both sides reaffirmed their continued support of CENTO and the contribution which it makes to regional security and economic development.

Secretary Kissinger described the efforts the United States is making in search of a lasting peaceful resolution of the Arab-Israeli conflict. The Secretary reaffirmed the determination of the United States to press its efforts to help maintain the momentum of the negotiations begun earlier this year. The Iranian side reaffirmed its support for the peace-making efforts of the United States.

The two sides engaged in a full, constructive and friendly discussion of the global petroleum price and supply question in the context of a review of the overall world economic situation. The two sides also reviewed other aspects of the world economic situation and agreed on the need for cooperative efforts to check inflation and avert the common misfortune of a major economic crisis. The Iranian side explained its programs of bilateral financial assistance to other countries and its proposal for a new multilateral organization to aid developing countries. The American side welcomed Iran's far-sighted policies in this respect. The two sides agreed to cooperate in global and regional programs to eliminate the world food deficit. The two sides agreed to form a U.S.-Iran Joint Commission designed to increase and intensify the ties of cooperation that already exist between the two countries. It was decided that the U.S. Secretary of State and the Iranian Minister of Economic Affairs and Finance would serve as the co-chairmen of the Commission. The first meeting of the Joint Commission, which was held November 2, laid out a broad program of cooperation in the political, economic, cultural, defense, scientific, and technological fields. Joint working groups will be formed to carry out the work of the Commission and to enlist the energies and skills of governmental and private institutions in fulfilling the aims of the Commission. The next meeting of the Commission will be held in Washington next year.

A major element in the work of the Joint Commission will be a program in the field of nuclear energy, especially power generation, for which an agreement for cooperation is now under discussion. Meanwhile, contracts have been signed under which the United States is to provide enriched fuel for two power reactors. Contracts for fuel for six additional reactors will be signed in the near future. Iran will be discussing construction of the reactors with American firms. The Iranian side has also expressed interest in participating in a proposed commercial uranium enrichment facility to be built in the United States. The two sides were in full agreement on the need for better national and international controls over nuclear materials to prevent them from falling into irresponsible hands. They further agreed that every effort should be made to discourage further national development of nuclear weapons capabilities building on the principles of the Non-Proliferation Treaty to which both are parties.

Among other fields in which cooperation is already underway and will be further expanded are joint ventures with Iran in the fields of agriculture, the development of petrochemical and electronics industries, as well as animal husbandry, telecommunications, highway construction, geology, space technology, education and social services. Other fields of cooperation will be developed as the work of the Joint Commission progresses.

Joint Communiqué Issued by the United States-Iran Joint Commission

March 4, 1975

The U.S.-Iran Joint Commission completed its second session in Washington on March 3-4, 1975. The Iranian Delegation was headed by His Excellency Hushang Ansary, Minister of Economic Affairs and Finance, and the U.S. Delegation by the Secretary of State, Dr. Henry A. Kissinger, who are the co-chairmen of the Commission. Other high officials of both governments participated in the meeting.

The Joint Commission was established in November 1974 in order to broaden and intensify economic cooperation and consultation on economic policy matters. . . .

In the light of the strong desire on the part of the two sides to extend areas of mutual cooperation, the Commission set a target of $15 billion in total non-oil trade between the two countries during the next five years.

Major Iranian development projects selected for cooperation between the two countries include a series of large nuclear power plants, totaling 8,000 electrical megawatts, with associated water desalination plants; 20 prefabricated housing factories; 100,000 apartments and other housing units; five hospitals with a total of 3,000 beds; establishment of an integrated electronics industry; a major port for handling agricultural commodities and other port facilities; joint ventures to produce fertilizer, pesticides, farm machinery, and processed foods; super highways; and vocational training centers. The total cost of these projects is estimated to reach $12 billion.

The Commission also recognized the special importance of cooperation between the two countries in the field of petrochemicals, and took note of major projects under study for joint ventures between

Iran and major companies in the United States to produce petrochemical intermediates and finished products for general use in Iran and for export. . . .

Substantial progress was made toward conclusion of an Agreement on Cooperation in the Civil Uses of Atomic Energy. This Agreement will provide for a broad exchange of information on the application of atomic energy to peaceful purposes, and for related transfer of equipment and materials, including enriched uranium fuel for Iran's power reactors.

In order to facilitate exchange of technical specialists, the two co-chairmen signed a reciprocal agreement for technical cooperation. Technical cooperation projects were agreed upon in agriculture, manpower, science and higher education, and health services.

The Commission agreed to emphasize scientific programs in the fields of oceanography, seismic studies, geological and mineral surveys, remote sensing applications, and radio astronomy. In the field of higher education and advanced study, the Commission also agreed that the two governments should increase exchanges and develop a network of inter-institutional relationships.

The Commission noted that, concurrent with the meeting of the Commission, agreement in principle was reached between Iranian and U.S. private interests on projects for production of graphite electrodes, sanitary wares and trailers, and for establishment of a hotel chain in Iran.

It was agreed to hold the next meeting of the Joint Commission in Tehran before the end of 1975.

Leader of the Iranian
Delegation:
HUSHANG ANSARY
*Minister of Economic
Affairs and Finance*

Leader of the United
States Delegation:
HENRY A. KISSINGER
The Secretary of State

Remarks by Secretary Kissinger and Finance Minister Ansary upon the Conclusion of the United States-Iran Joint Committee Meeting

March 4, 1975

Secretary Kissinger: Mr. Minister, on behalf of the President and the U.S. Government I would like to express our very great gratification at the agreed minutes and the technical cooperation agreement that we have just signed.

The economic cooperation agreement between Iran and the United States that is foreseen is the largest agreement of this kind that has been signed between any two countries. It represents an attempt to underline the interdependence to which both of our countries have been committed, in which the resources of the producers are combined with the technological experience of some of the consuming countries to enhance the development and the progress of both sides.

It reflects also the very deep political bonds that exist between Iran and the United States.

The economic cooperation agreement foresees projects on the order of $12 billion which will be completed or the negotiation for which is in the process of being completed or will be completed in the very near future.

Out of this economic cooperation we expect that there will develop a trade between the two countries, excluding oil, over the next five years in the amount of $15 billion. These projects will represent a major step forward in the very vast scheme of development that Iran has undertaken, and the United States is happy that it can ply its part in this enterprise. It also reflects the conviction of both sides that an expanding world economy is in the interests of progress and peace. . . .

Minister Ansary: Thank you, Mr. Secretary. May I join you in expressing the gratification and appreciation of the Iranian team in the talks that we have had in the course of the past two days in the second session of our joint ministerial commission for economic cooperation. We are extremely pleased on our side that the outcome of these negotiations is entirely satisfactory to both sides. We have managed to reach agreement on the use of the comparative advantages of the two countries for the benefit not only of our respective nations but also of the world at large.

To your remarks, Mr. Secretary, I may add that Iran is the first major oil-producing country to go nuclear in a major way, and one important aspect of the agreement that we have reached on the areas of cooperation between the two countries is of course the readiness that has been expressed in principle on the part of the Atomic Energy Organization of Iran to place orders for a large number of nuclear power plants in the United States.

Of the other agreements that we reached, I think the most important in terms not only of the development for our relations but also of the problems facing the world today is where this cooperation entails the production of additional amounts of food and agricultural products not only for the use of domestic needs of Iran but also for the region at large.

This includes also the development of a center for agricultural technology that would be used regionally by all the countries concerned.

In addition to this, of course, it is highly satisfactory to us that, the end result of economic cooperation being increasing trade, the amount envisaged in the agreement for the exchange of commodities between the two countries in the next five years is a rather impressive figure of

$15 billion that the Secretary has just mentioned.

May I take the opportunity also, Mr. Secretary, to express my appreciation and sincere thanks for the opportunity that I had to call on the President this morning and for his support and encouragement in the efforts that are being made by the two sides for the development for our relations. . . .

Agreement on Technical Cooperation between the United States and Iran

March 4, 1975   Agreement signed at Washington.
April 5, 1976   Entered into force.

The Government of the United States of America, and the Imperial Government of Iran,

Desiring to expand and strengthen their friendly relations,

Confirming their mutual interest in the expansion of economic cooperation between the two countries,

Recognizing the importance of technical cooperation for the expansion of economic relations, and

Wishing to create the most appropriate conditions for the development of technical cooperation.

Have agreed as follows:

ARTICLE 1

The Contracting Parties undertake to develop technical cooperation, on the basis of mutual respect for sovereignty and noninterference in each other's domestic affairs.

ARTICLE 2

Technical cooperation as mentioned in Article 1 shall cover a wide variety of economic activities including industry, agriculture, social affairs, and the development of infrastructure, and may take the form of furnishing technical and training services, advisory personnel and the supply of related commodities and facilities, for the implementation of joint projects, as may be mutually agreed between the Contracting Parties.

ARTICLE 3

The Contracting Parties shall adopt mutually agreeable administrative, organizational and staff arrangements to facilitate implementation of this Agreement.

ARTICLE 4

The Contracting Parties or their agencies or ministries may enter into specific agreements to implement technical cooperation described in Article 2.

ARTICLE 5

The implementation agreements described in Article 4 will contain, *inter alia*, standard provisions on:

A. Advance payment, as mutually agreed upon for costs incurred in the technical cooperation described in Article 2 including costs of project development, program implementation, administrative and staff support and project termination;

B. Privileges and immunities, when applicable, of personnel assigned to engage in such technical cooperation in the territory of the other Contracting Party; and

C. Claims arising from such technical cooperation.

ARTICLE 6

When requested by either Contracting Party, representatives of both Contracting Parties shall meet to review progress toward achieving the purposes of this Agreement, and to negotiate solutions to any outstanding problems.

ARTICLE 7

This Agreement shall be inapplicable to agreements and transactions relating to the sale of defense articles and services by the Government of the United States to the Imperial Government of Iran.

ARTICLE 8

This Agreement shall enter into force on the date of an exchange of notes confirming this fact between the Contracting Parties.

ARTICLE 9

This Agreement shall remain in effect for five years from the date it enters into force, subject to revision or extension, as mutually agreed, and may be terminated at any time by either Contracting Party by one hundred and eighty days' advance notice in writing.

Done in Washington in duplicate on March 4, 1975, both originals being equally authentic.

For the Government of the United States of America: HENRY A. KISSINGER	For the Imperial Government of Iran: HUSHANG ANSARY

Memorandum of Understanding on United States Assistance Regarding Civil Emergency Preparedness to Iran

November 22, 1975   Memorandum of understanding signed at Tehran.
November 22, 1975   Entered into force.

PREAMBLE

Throughout late 1974 and 1975, representatives of the Supreme Commander's Staff, Imperial Iranian Army, Government of Iran, and the Federal Preparedness Agency, General Services Administration, Government of the United States of America, have conducted a series of exchanges concerning a program of cooperation between the Imperial Iranian Armed Forces and the Federal Preparedness Agency that would provide advisory technical assistance to the Imperial Iranian Armed Forces in organizing all aspects of its civil emergency preparedness capability.

I. *Purpose of the Memorandum of Understanding*

Under this Memorandum of Understanding between the Government of Iran, Imperial Iranian Army, hereinafter referred to as the IIA, and the Government of the United States of America, General Services Administration, Federal Preparedness Agency, hereinafter referred to as the FPA, the FPA will provide advisory technical assistance in the form of consultants to the IIA in several emergency preparedness areas, to include the fields of mobilization, national readiness, and non-military defense, comprising, overall, the civil emergency preparedness capability of the Government of Iran.

II. *Services to Be Provided*

The FPA is prepared to share its experience and place it at the disposal of the IIA and to assign the requisite temporary duty consultative personnel to a study/working group chaired by an Iranian official and consisting of personnel of both nationalities, organized by and under the direct guidance and supervision of the Supreme Commander's staff. The purpose of the study/working group will be to:

(1) Develop a clear conceptual statement of the overall mission to be accomplished in all aspects of civil emergency preparedness (CEP);

(2) Develop an organizational structure to carry out the mission;

(3) Review the basic CEP tasks to be assigned to specific offices, ministries and agencies and recommend modifications to existing agencies, as appropriate;

(4) Develop clear guidelines governing the relationships between elements of the government concerned with CEP to include the kind and degree of authority needed to coordinate and implement the total CEP effort;

(5) Assess the adequacy of existing authorities to deal with all potential contingencies, review the delegations of authority for compatibility with organizational arrangements and recommend modification, as appropriate;

(6) Recommend an approach to personnel requirements and training to carry out CEP functions;

(7) Outline a definitive time-phased program for the development of an effective CEP capability to include implementation of the measures proposed.

The FPA will provide the necessary technically competent personnel (estimated to be 30 man months) to be integrated into the Iranian-directed study/working group. Consultants are expected to be thoroughly familiar with the CEP operations of the FPA, the Defense Civil Preparedness Agency, and the Federal Disaster Assistance Administration.

The IIA will organize a study/working group consisting of personnel of both nationalities and will provide overall policy guidance and operating instructions directly to the study/working group.

III. *Personnel*

To provide the foregoing services, the FPA expects to assign personnel for a total of thirty man months, whose combined qualifications will include expertise in the following areas: national security affairs; continuity of government; economic evaluation; resource management; disaster relief; and civil defense. The numbers of personnel assigned to Iran at any one time is expected to approximate the thirty man months figure.

IV. *Estimated Costs*

Estimated costs associated with the advisory technical assistance, as discussed with the IIA, total $171,384.80 and are broken down as follows: salaries (six months basis), $83,000; transportation (to and from Iran and in-country), $20,000; per diem, $49,500; incidental costs (rental of in-country transportation, with driver, etc.), $15,000; pre-trip preparations, $3,884.80.

These are the best estimates that the FPA can develop at this time. They may be more or less than the actual expenses which the consultants may entail as part of the group composed of both U.S. and Iranian nationals participating in the Iranian-directed planning effort.

All expenses incurred in the performance of services in connection with the advisory technical assistance program which are to be performed by the FPA will be paid or reimbursed by the IIA. Such expenses shall include cost of salaries, transportation and traveling expenses, and all other properly reimbursable expenses incurred in the performance of such services. All such expenses incurred and reimbursement claimed will be in accordance with applicable United States status and regulations.

The compensation of consultative personnel will include salary or fee applicable at the time of payment of the same, per diem as prescribed by applicable United States statutes and regulations in force at the time of payment of the same, and travel expenses from point of residence to Iran and return.

If expenses exceed the estimated figures, the IIA will be expected to defray them, since the FPA is merely providing consultants and a mechanism through which payments to the consultants are made.

V. *Method of Reimbursement for Costs*

The compensation for all services provided to the IIA in connection with this Memorandum of Understanding will be paid by the FPA from funds advanced by the IIA. The IIA will provide the amount of the estimated costs, or one hundred seventy-one thousand, three hundred eighty-four and eighty one-hundredths dollars (Dols. 171,384.80), by means of a bank draft in U.S. dollars, payable to the Federal Preparedness Agency, General Services Administration. The FPA will create a dollar working fund in this amount and will control disbursements from this fund in accordance with this Memorandum of Understanding. The FPA will also provide the IIA with periodic reports on the status of the account.

The IIA will replenish the working fund, upon the request of the FPA and the agreement of the IIA, should costs incurred to the date of the request plus estimated costs required to complete the advisory technical assistance program exceed the amount already advanced by the IIA.

Any such requests will be accompanied by itemized statements setting forth all expenditures made from the fund which have not been reported in any previous itemized statement and by such supporting documents as the IIA may reasonably request. The amount of any such replenishment shall equal the amount by which the total of costs to date plus estimated costs to completion exceeds the amount previously advanced. If the IIA does not agree to a requested replenishment, the FPA is not obligated to provide the services estimated to be necessary to complete the advisory technical assistance program and will be reimbursed for any uncovered costs incurred prior to or because of termination.

Promptly following the last expenditure from the dollar working fund and completion of the advisory technical assistance program, the FPA will submit a final itemized statement setting out all expenditures made from the fund which have not been reported in any previous itemized statement and will return to the IIA any balance remaining in the fund after such last expenditure.

VI. *Exemptions from Liabilities*

The IIA agrees to hold the FPA and the Government of the United States of America harmless against any and all claims that may arise as a result of the technical services furnished under this Memorandum of Understanding.

The IIA will, on the basis of existing laws, cause the appropriate authorities of the Government of Iran to grant to American personnel assigned to Iran in connection with this advisory technical assistance program exemption from all Iranian taxes. In the absence of such exemption, the IIA will pay all such Iranian taxes as may be assessed.

VII. *Local Services in Iran*

The IIA will provide the following local services, to the extent necessary for the performance of the services envisioned in this Memorandum of Understanding, to personnel assigned in Iran in connection with the advisory technical services program: necessary office space and facilities; secretarial-clerical, translating, and other local office help; transportation for official business; assistance in obtaining any necessary local permits, licenses, et cetera; and other logistical support.

VIII. *Effective Date*

This Memorandum of Understanding shall enter into effect on the date upon which it has been signed by the Iranian Deputy Minister of War for the Imperial Iranian Army and the Director of the Federal Preparedness Agency, General Services Administration, and will remain in force until December 30, 1976. It may be renewed, amended, or extended by the mutual consent of the parties thereto. The Memorandum of Understanding may be terminated by either party thereto on sixty-days written notice; such termination will not, however, impair any obligations or commitments properly incurred under it by either party up to and including the effective date of termination.

United States of America   Government of Iran
General Services Administration   Imperial Iranian Army
Federal Preparedness Agency   LT. GEN. M. MASSUMI
LESLIE W. BRAY, JR.
Director

Statement of the Iranian Finance Minister (Ansary) at the Conclusion of the United States-Iran Joint Commission

August 7, 1976

Minister Ansary: Ladies and gentlemen, we just concluded the deliberations of our third session of the Joint Iran-U.S. Commission on Economic Cooperation; and together with the Secretary of State and the members of the American delegation, I'm glad to say that we have reached some very important decisions. This session has started, as you know, with meetings of experts at committee levels, and the Secretary's visit started with an audience yesterday with His Imperial Majesty the Shahanshah, following which the work of the Commission began this morning.

The Commission, as you know, was set up to concretize decisions and policy matters and provide directions for the development of trade and economic cooperation between Iran and the United States; and in that context I am very pleased to say that this session—this particular session—has been highly successful. The highlights of these agreements which you have just signed with the Secretary of State are as follows.

In the field of trade you may recall that at the last session of the Commission in Washington last year, an estimate was provided for an amount of trade between the two countries in the order of about 15 billion U.S. dollars. At this particular session we reached an agreement for the figure of trade to be more comprehensive and to present a very clear picture of what we envisage would lie ahead in the exchange of goods and services between the two countries.

We must revise our previous estimate to include the additional potentials that we feel lie ahead in the course of the next few years until 1980. We have therefore revised the figure upward, in the order of about $40 billion, to include exports of oil from Iran to the United States, exports of industrial and traditional goods from Iran to the United States, and the import of goods and services from the United States, but not inclusive of military input.

I would like to say here and now that we are appreciative of the readiness that has been expressed on the part of the U.S. Government to facilitate and cooperate with us for the expansion of Iranian exports to the United States so that we will over the years attain a reasonable proportion in the amount of exports and imports between the two countries.

In the field of energy I would like to say that as far as nuclear energy is concerned, we are pleased that we have made very good progress forward in our discussions for cooperation in this field between the two countries. Iran, as you know, is a signatory to the Nonproliferation Treaty, and we very strongly believe in the measures that are needed to assure safeguards in this particular area. We are ready to support measures on an international level aimed at preventing proliferation in the world at large. We therefore, quite naturally indicated our readiness to agree to safeguards that are necessary, as long as we are assured of the supply of enriched uranium—not plutonium—needed for our fast-breeders. We are hoping that in the light of this progress and our talk with the Secretary of State and the American delegation, we will, hopefully, reach the final phase of our agreement in the near future.

We also reached an agreement to cooperate between the two countries in the field of solar energy and in other fields of energy, including gas, in connection with which we have two important multibillion-dollar agreements now under consideration. Because of this we have created a new Research and Development Committee in this field so that the experts and the officials of the two sides may continue their active cooperation because primarily—not only for the concern of the two sides that need to meet the energy requirements of the two countries but also of the requirements of the world at large in the next decade.

In the field of agriculture, we agreed to some important decisions in pinpointing the areas of cooperation including the possibilities of cooperation between the two countries for the purpose of manufacturing agricultural machinery and implements as well as insecticides and petrochemicals and chemicals for use not only in Iran but also for meeting the needs of the general region as a whole.

Because of our mutual concern for active steps that are necessary for the purpose of meeting food requirements of the world at large and this general region as a whole, we feel therefore that the discussions that were held in the past two days for the purpose of selecting a special region in Iran for development with U.S. cooperation in the field of agriculture are also important in this particular field.

In the field of housing we have reached agreement to encourage the private sector on both sides as well as the public sector in Iran to engage in ventures that would be aimed at manufacturing and producing construction material and housing components and participating in the development of construction technology for mass production of housing in Iran. This, of course, would also include participation, on the part of Iran and on the part of the United States, in commercial exhibitions in this particular field, as well as engagement in training programs.

In the field of science, technology, and education, the cooperation will continue in oceanography, fishery studies, geological and mineral surveys and environmental protection, health care education, and the like.

In the field of health we have reached an agreement in principle to cooperate for the purpose of establishing a Food and Drug Administration in Iran and the development of procedures for specific techniques in the laboratories for drug and food control. On the Iranian side, we attach a great deal of importance to this particular field of cooperation between our two countries.

In the field of industry, we have reached an agreement to encourage further activities on the part of the private sector on both sides to an active participation on the part of the Joint Business Council that was established as a result of the decisions of the Commission previously, and we feel that in various big industries it would result in agreement for joint ventures in promising areas to both countries, especially in the field of petrochemicals and mining as well as in other fields of interest.

As far as investment is concerned, we have expressed our readiness in principle on both sides to encourage movement in the private sector in accordance with the laws and regulations of the two countries, and we believe that the measures that will be introduced as a result of these decisions in principle will encourage movement in that direction.

I want to express my sincere appreciation to the Secretary of State for his invaluable contributions to the deliberations of the Commission and for the very friendly atmosphere in which the talks were conducted. I believe we have taken some very important steps forward, the results of which should be witnessed in the coming 12 months and in the years that we have ahead of us, as a result of which we are certain the friendship between our two peoples will advance and the trade and economic relations between the two countries will further consolidate our friendship. . . .

Communiqué of United States-Iran Joint Commission Issued at Tehran*

August 7, 1976

The Iran-U.S. Joint Commission met in Tehran for its third session August 6 and 7, 1976. His Excellency Hushang Ansary, Minister of Economic Affairs and Finance, and the Secretary of State, the Honorable Henry A. Kissinger, Co-Chairmen of the Commission, headed the Iranian and the U.S. delegations.

During his visit to Iran, the Secretary of State was received in audience by His Imperial Majesty, the Shahanshah, at Nowshahr and conveyed to him the personal greetings of President Ford. In their talks, His Imperial Majesty and Secretary Kissinger discussed the current world situation and reviewed bilateral matters in the spirit of mutual respect and understanding characteristic of relations between Iran and the United States.

Trade and Investment

The Commission noted with satisfaction that the trade between the two countries had expanded well beyond earlier expectations. In March 1975 a target of $15 billion in trade (exclusive of oil and military items) over the following five years was established. The Commission agreed that a target of $26 billion for the period 1975-80 is now attainable, and agreed that the two governments would cooperate to reach that goal. If Iran's oil exports to the United States are taken into account, total non-military trade is expected to exceed $40 billion over the period 1975-80.

In their desire to achieve continued expansion of trade and economic cooperation between the two countries, the two parties recognized the need for considerable expansion of Iranian industrial exports to the United States. In this connection the U.S. delegation expressed its readiness to cooperate in the Iranian efforts to increase such exports. The Iranian side emphasized that exclusion of Iranian exports from the U.S. generalized system of preferences [GSP] runs counter to the

---

* For the official agreed minutes of the 1976 U.S.-Iran Joint Commission elaborating the points made in the communiqué, see 27 UST-4329-49.

aim and determination of the two sides in facilitation and expanding trade between the two countries. The U.S. side stated that while any change in GSP eligibility would require an act of Congress, the U.S. Executive Branch supports legislation recently introduced to provide GSP benefits covering Iran and will continue to use its best efforts to achieve passage in the current session of Congress. . . .

Energy

Both delegations agreed that one of the major problems facing mankind in the decades ahead will be the availability of adequate energy to meet the demands of growing populations and industrial expansion throughout the world. Iran, as a major supplier of petroleum with vast natural gas reserves, and the United States as a center of advanced technology, have the shared responsibility to work together to contribute to solutions of this problem. In order to facilitate broad cooperation throughout the spectrum of energy research and development, the Commission established an Energy Research and Development Committee and instructed it to initiate rapidly an innovative and practical program.

The Commission noted that substantial progress has been made in defining the principles of a new cooperative agreement in nuclear power, which takes into account Iran's interest in developing the peaceful uses of nuclear energy and the concern of both countries to prevent the proliferation of nuclear weapons. Good progress has been made in reconciling these two objectives and as a result of this discussion, a realistic basis for proceeding with final negotiations now exists. The Commission agreed that these negotiations should be pursued promptly in order to reach an early agreement.

The Commission particularly noted cooperation between the two countries in the evaluation of sites for the establishment of nuclear power plants in Iran, exploration in Iran for uranium resources, training of Iranian engineers and scientists, and fabrication of slightly enriched fuel uranium for nuclear power reactors.

The Commission noted that solar energy must have an increasingly prominent role in meeting man's energy needs, and agreed to develop a program of cooperation in this field. As the first step, a team of experts from Iran will visit the United States in the near future to consult with officials of the Energy Research and Development Administration. It is anticipated that the cooperative research program will be coordinated with multilateral arrangements in this field.

Further discussions will be held looking to collaboration in research and development in alternative energy fields.

The Iranian party reviewed recent natural gas developments in Iran, noting that proven reserves may now exceed those of any other country and that the Imperial Government of Iran has well-advanced plans for the utilization of these resources. Two multibillion-dollar joint ventures involving the National Iranian Gas Company and U.S. private companies are under consideration. The American delegation reported President Ford's recent decisions establishing the United States policies on natural gas imports. These policies enable the U.S. Executive Branch to encourage and support projects for the production and delivery of natural gas to the United States on economically attractive terms.

Technical Cooperation

The two delegations reviewed existing and planned programs of technical cooperation. In particular, the Commission noted the following activities:

—The agreement between the U.S. Department of Transportation's Federal Highway Administration and the Iranian Ministry of Roads and Transport.

—The initiation of a new program by the Manpower and Technical Cooperation Committee, concerning the measurement and improvement of Iranian labor productivity.

—The continuation of vocational training program development and employment service units. In this connection, the Commission noted Iran plans to acquire 40 more mobile training and employment service units for use in non-urban areas. These units and the 23 centers which have been already obtained and will start operation during the current year will increase the annual capacity of training skilled workers by 1,700, and will facilitate the mobility of the workers according to the requirements of the country.

—The Commission agreed to expand cooperation in the field of agriculture with an emphasis on encouraging the respective sectors of the two countries to form joint ventures for intensive production, and distribution of agricultural products as well as machinery, pesticides, fertilizers, etc.

—Tentative plans have been developed for cooperation between the two countries in animal health, plant pest control, forest and range management, agricultural extension and education.

—A team of American experts will visit Iran in October 1976 in order to cooperate with the Iranian party in preparing a program for the establishment of an integrated agricultural region.

Housing

The Commission observed that considerable exchange of information has taken place in the field of large-scale housing, with the U.S. private sector gaining a better understanding of Iranian housing and building plans and regulations and Iranian officials gaining greater knowledge of U.S. housing methods and technology. The Commission approved plans to broaden the scope of cooperation in the coming year. These will include the encouragement of private sector joint ventures and provision of know-how and services related to the manufacture of housing and housing components. It also includes the transfer of technology in housing and urban management, housing finance, and technical information. Participation in commercial exhibits and training activities also will be expanded.

Science and Technology

The Commission noted the expansion of scientific and technological cooperation, particularly with regard to programs underway or planned in the field of oceanography, seismic studies and geological and minerals surveys. Both delegations agreed that environmental protection, health care education, biomedical sciences and arid land sciences were promising areas for cooperation.

The United States noted with appreciation the generosity of Her Imperial Majesty's Committee for the American Bicentennial, in establishing an American Studies endowment fund, capitalized at $1 million to support American studies programs in Iran. The U.S. delegation also expressed appreciation for the Imperial Government of Iran's creation of a $100,000 Bicentennial scholarship fund to assist American students to study in Iran.

The Commission expressed satisfaction at the completion of the study, undertaken by the U.S. Government in accordance with a decision of the last meeting of the Commission, of ways to facilitate and expedite education linkages between U.S. and Iranian institutions of higher learning.

The Commission agreed that the two countries will cooperate in food and drug administration, and, in particular, development of specific techniques in laboratory procedures for drug and food control and exchange of know-how and experts. Cooperation in the field of health will also cover control of drug addiction and rehabilitation of addicts.

It was agreed to hold the next meeting in Washington at a mutually convenient time, in 1977.

CARTE BLANCHE ON ARMS SALES

Statement of State Department Under Secretary for Political Affairs (Joseph J. Sisco) before the Special Subcommittee on Investigations of the House Committee on International Relations

[EXCERPT]

June 10, 1975

Iran's Security and Development Programs

Iran shares a lengthy border with the Soviet Union. While seeking cooperation with the powerful northern neighbor, any prudent Iranian leader has to remain concerned about long-term Soviet intentions. Looking east and west, he can see substantial Soviet involvement in Afghanistan and Iraq; to the south he sees growing Soviet naval activity in the Indian Ocean. Possessing half of the shoreline of the Persian Gulf, a waterway of vital importance to its burgeoning economy and oil exports, Iran has a natural strategic interest in maintaining free passage through the gulf and the Strait of Hormuz, through which pass all of Iran's and two-thirds of the world's oil exports, and the Indian Ocean, through which the gulf is reached.

Iran's size, harsh terrain, relatively limited transportation network, and great distance from foreign suppliers of military equipment have required it to develop comprehensive defense plans which correspond to these conditions. The result has been a concept that keeps the standing armed forces relatively small in number (about 350,000) while providing advanced equipment for air, naval, and armored forces and the means to move ground forces by air rapidly from one location to another.

While using a portion of its oil wealth to equip itself for its defense, Iran has sought to develop a cooperative approach to regional security among states. It has recently been able to settle a longstanding territorial dispute with Iraq. At the same time, it has offered support to its gulf neighbors in dealing with radical threats. Iranian units are presently in Oman to help the Sultan end the insurgency in Dhofar, which has its sanctuary and base in the Soviet-backed People's Democratic Republic of Yemen.

The size of Iran's population, coupled with its rapid social and economic development, gives it a capability to exercise leadership in the gulf. The United States has welcomed Iran's taking on greater security responsibilities. We have agreed to sell it a substantial quantity of defense material, especially aircraft and naval craft. The progress which Iran has made in improving its military capability has given Iran a credible deterrent, enabled it to play a more active role in protecting the vital trade routes of the gulf, and was undoubtedly a factor in the recent decision of the Iraqi and Iranian leadership to resolve a major bilateral dispute by negotiation. I would note it is only recently that Iran's armed forces have drawn level with Iraq's military capabilities and strength.

Much has been said regarding the resources which the Iranian Government is putting into building its defense military capacity. But too little has been said about the impressive strides which the government has made in economic development and in improving the welfare of its people. Iran's domestic investment program is more than twice what it spends on defense. The Iranian five-year plan (1973-78) calls for the expenditure of roughly $70 billion in the civilian sector. A substantial portion is for industrial growth, but $19 billion is earmarked for housing, free education, urban and rural development, and a massive increase in medical facilities.

Statement of Secretary Kissinger upon the Conclusion of the United States-Iran Joint Commission

August 6, 1976

. . . There are about 24,000 Americans in Iran. Of those, about 1,000 are military personnel; 2,000 are engaged in training activities that will end when the training is completed; another thousand are engaged in combined training and maintenance activities, which will also end when the capabilities are developed. Five thousand are here in the oil business, and 2,000 are here in other businesses. And the rest are dependents.

So it is true there are 24,000 Americans here. There are 11,000 who are working here, 7,000 in civilian pursuits, and their families. So when people talk lightly about "hostages," the hostages are created by the nature of the connection of our societies and not by any particular decision having to do with military affairs alone or even primarily.

Iran is the country where in 1946 President Truman considered it important to the interest of the United States to confront the Soviet Union over Azerbaijan, when there were only a few hundred Americans in this country, because we thought then that the territorial integrity of Iran was important for the United States.

Iran is the country about which in 1949, again, President Truman developed Point 4, to express the close connection we felt not only with the territorial integrity but with the development of Iran.

Iran is the country with which President Eisenhower in 1959 made an executive agreement in which he pledged that the United States would come again to the assistance of Iran against Communist attack or Communist-inspired attack, according to our constitutional processes. And while one can debate today, in the sophisticated period in which we have the great fortune of living, what the legal significance of an executive agreement was, there can be no question that it reflected the conviction of an American President that the security of Iran was an important interest of the United States.

And now, in 1976, when the efforts of 1946 and the efforts of 1949 have led to the result that Iran's security is no longer as precarious as it was right after the war and Iran's progress economically has reached a point where it is part of the plan of Iran that within 10 years this country will have the economic level of activity of Western Europe today—under those conditions it goes without saying that Iran has not become less important to the United States.

At the time when Iran and the United States first encountered each other in the postwar period, we were predominant in the world; and we, in our innocence of international affairs, assumed all the burdens for defense and for economic advance. And it was indeed necessary that we do so, because there was no one else to man the ramparts.

Now, in 1976, the world has become much more complicated. Other centers of power have developed. The threats have become more complex. The United States cannot assume all the responsibilities. Under those conditions we especially value those friends who are prepared to make their own efforts for their economic advance and who are prepared to make a significant contribution to their own defense.

As the recent period has made amply clear, the Middle East, always a pivot of world affairs, has become one of the potentially most tense areas of the globe. In the circumstances, the stability of Iran, the commitment of Iran to its security, is a major factor for global peace and a major factor in the stability of the Middle East.

There are at least some Americans who do not take it for granted, because they remember that even in Iran things were not always that way and that they do not always have to be that way and that we owe something to the farsighted leadership of His Imperial Majesty, which has brought matters to this point.

It is true that Iran has made great economic progress. It is also true that Iran has made strenuous efforts in its own defense. And finally, it is true that it has been the policy of the United States to support both of these efforts.

The first, the economic effort, no longer requires American support. In fact, it may be a little bit the reverse, if Hushang keeps raising the oil prices.

But in assessing the relationship between the two countries, we note a number of factors. First, on all major international issues, the policies of the United States and the policies of Iran have been parallel and therefore mutually reinforcing. Those countries which have represented the greatest threat to the security of Iran are also those countries whose domination of Iran would have a profound effect on the global balance of power or on the regional balance of power and would therefore have profound consequences for the United States.

In all the years of our cooperation, Iran has never gone to war, or threatened to go to war, for any purpose which would not have been parallel to our own.

And this cooperation has been all the more significant because it grew out of a leadership that is clearly independent, that pursues its conception of its own national interest based on a history of 2,500 years of Iranian policy; and this is what has made the cooperation all the more effective.

I do not want to paint too idyllic a picture. There have been conferences where we have not seen eye to eye—not involving questions of peace and war. Unfortunately, the technical competence of your personnel is such that when we do not agree you can make life extremely unpleasant for us. But those occasions have been rare; and they have not gone to the central issues of global stability and global peace, not to the strategy toward the Middle East nor to the strategy toward the Soviet Union, both key elements in the global balance.

I have taken the liberty of speaking in this manner because I wanted our Iranian friends to understand that, not out of sentimentality, though we are always happy here, but out of a calculation of our own national and global interests—just as Iranian policy is based on its calculation of its national interests—there has developed a parallelism of views on many key problems that has made our cooperation a matter that is in the profound national interest of both countries. This is the conviction of our Administration. It is this conviction that has brought me here, and it will be pursued in the period ahead. . . .

Testimony of Philip C. Habib, Under Secretary for Political Affairs to a Subcommittee of United States House Committee on International Relations

[EXCERPT]

September 21, 1976

Now I would like to comment on the specific proposals for sales included among the notifications before you.

Let me first speak of Iran. There are eight letters of offer for Iran, which total $4.4 billion. Over $3.8 billion, or over half of the total amount of all 43 notifications, is attributable to Iran's request to purchase 160 F-16's, with follow-on support.

Iran wishes to have the F-16 aircraft as its aircraft of the 1980's and 1990's. Deliveries will not begin until the early 1980's and will take several years to complete. The delivery schedule has been planned in order not to overburden Iranian facilities or available trained manpower and not to interfere with our own or NATO acquisition of the plane. Although, if this transaction is approved, some payments will be made by Iran next year, the schedule of payments and deliveries will stretch well into the 1980's.

This purchase is characteristic of the Iranian Government's desire to project its development requirements into the future and to act now rather than to delay a decision which might be adversely affected by inflation or other external factors.

To put in perspective the sums involved in the F-16 sales package, we should not ignore the fact that our nonmilitary trade with Iran will, it is estimated, total $22-$23 billion during the period 1975-80, with a $6-$7 billion surplus in our favor in civilian goods alone.

More basically, our military sales to Iran add to the strength of a valued ally and to that nation's ability to continue to carry out a policy on which we and the Iranians agree. They also provide the essential assurances that the United States has not changed its mind about Iran, that we remain committed to a close relationship in all fields, and that close coordination with the United States on the part of the Iranians is still justified. For we are not only talking about past and present policies, including relevant military sales, but also about our future relations.

Chronology of Events Relating to Sale of United States F-14 Aircraft to Iran, Submitted to Senate Foreign Relations Committee by United States Department of Defense September 10, 1976

Memorandum for Mr. T.R. Hullin, Principal Deputy Assistant Secretary, Public Affairs: Press Inquiry Concerning Sale of F-14 to Iran

Department of Defense
Office of General Counsel
Washington, D.C., August 26, 1976

Pursuant to your request, I have prepared the attached Chronology setting forth the pertinent facts concerning the decision not to award Grumman any additional profit points on DOD's procurement contract with Grumman in implementation of the FMS case with Iran for the sale of F-14 aircraft.

The Chronology is based on my examination of the record of DSAA and of the notes kept by Admiral Carr of meetings attended by him. Because of the limited time available for preparation of the Chronology, I made no effort to search for the existence of files in the Office of the Secretary of the Navy or of the Chief of Naval Operations.

BENJAMIN FORMAN
Assistant General Counsel, International Affairs

[ATTACHMENT]

CHRONOLOGY

May 1972: Deputy Secretary of Defense Rush transmits to the White House, for President Nixon's trip to Iran. DOD briefing papers and recommendations with respect to anticipated Iranian purchase requests.

May 1972: President Nixon, during trip to Iran, informs the Government of Iran that the United States is willing in principle to sell to Iran the F-14 and F-15 aircraft as soon as the United States Government is satisfied as to their operational effectiveness.

August 1973: Government of Iran requests information on price and availability of F-14 and F-15 aircraft.

September 1973: U.S. Government informs Government of Iran that reasonably accurate price and availability information would be available for the F-14 in early 1974 and for the F-15 in 1975; however, definite information would not be available until procurement for U.S. Armed Forces had been authorized by Congress.

September 1973: Government of Iran replies that it must have a firm commitment on the availability of these aircraft. The Government of Iran requested that this commitment be made in the form of a signed statement, and that, if prices could not then be quoted, the statement could include language to the effect that the price charged to Iran would not exceed the price to be charged to the United States Government.

October 1973: Department of State instructs the American Ambassador in Iran to inform the Government of Iran in writing that the United States Government confirms its willingness to sell both the F-14 and F-15 aircraft to the Government of Iran, and that, apart from the recoupment charge for the United States R&D investment and the administrative costs surcharge, the cost to the Government of Iran will be the same as it would be for coincident procurement for the U.S. forces. . . .

June 6, 1974: Secretary Schlesinger sends letter to the Government of Iran concerning the payments schedule contemplated for the Iranian purchase of F-14 aircraft. In pertinent part, the letter states: "It is our understanding with you that we will purchase the F-14 aircraft for you on the basis that we do so for ourselves. . . ."

A Staff Report to the Subcommittee on Foreign Assistance of the Committee on Foreign Relations, United States Senate: United States Military Sales to Iran

July 1976

SUMMARY

Iran is the largest single purchaser of U.S. military equipment. Government-to-government military sales to Iran increased over seven-fold from $524 million in Fiscal Year (FY) 1972 to $3.91 billion in FY 1974, slackening off a little to $2.6 billion in FY 1975. The preliminary sales estimate for FY 1976 is $1.3 billion. Sales in the 1972-76 period totalled $10.4 billion. The number of official and private American citizens in Iran, a large percentage of whom are involved in military programs, has also increased from approximately 15,000-16,000 in 1972 to 24,000 in 1976; it could easily reach 50,000-60,000 or higher by 1980.

Iran is and will remain an extremely important country to the U.S. and its allies because of its geographical location and oil. Iran, on the other hand, places great importance on its relationship with the U.S., in large part because of the Iranian belief that the U.S. may come to Iran's defense if it is threatened. Iran has undertaken a major military expansion and modernization program in recent years to protect its interests from numerous perceived threats. Iranian officials also view the military buildup as the spearhead of a broader program to transform Iran into a modern economic as well as military power within twenty years.

U.S. officials share many of Iran's defense concerns, and U.S. and

Iranian foreign policy interests coincide in most instances, with the notable exception of oil pricing. Thus, Iran wants to buy its most sophisticated arms and defense equipment from the U.S. for political as well as economic reasons; it prefers to contract through the Department of Defense on a government-to-government basis rather than deal directly with U.S. private companies. Arms sales are, therefore, an important component of U.S.-Iranian foreign relations.

Because the U.S. has a major interest in the military security of Iran, most Iranian arms requests have been favorably received.

In May, 1972, President Nixon and then National Security Advisor Kissinger, agreed for the first time to sell Iran virtually any conventional weapons it wanted and so instructed the bureaucracy in a memorandum in late July, 1972. In 1973, oil prices were quadrupled and from that time on Iranian purchases from the U.S. boomed. The direct participation of U.S. Government and industry in Iranian defense programs, which increased after this bonanza, has raised important procedural and policy questions about the magnitude and nature of the programs, the manner in which they have been implemented, and the implications they pose for the future.

In this study we focused our attention on the U.S. decision-making process, the U.S. involvement (managerial and operational) in implementing the arms sales programs to Iran, and on identifying and analyzing future policy and programmatic implications inherent in the U.S.-Iranian military relationship as it has emerged. Based upon our research, extensive interviews with U.S. and Iranian officials and private citizens both in the U.S. and Iran, and a close examination of the current data on U.S. arms programs, the following findings emerge concerning U.S.-Iranian military relations and U.S. arms sales policy.

Findings

1. Iran has purchased large quantities of some of the most sophisticated equipment in the U.S. inventory including the F-14 Tom Cat Fighter and the DD993 modified Spruance Class destroyer. The F-14 system is so complicated that the United States Navy is having major difficulty keeping it operational; Iran's Spruance Class destroyer will be even more sophisticated than those being procured by the U.S. Navy. Iran is already the dominant military power in the Persian Gulf area. Upon delivery between now and 1981 of equipment ordered to date, Iran, on paper, can be regarded as a regional superpower. Although future purchases of new U.S. equipment and related services are likely to decline in absolute terms from the fiscal year 1974 and 1975 levels, any additional sales will add to an already sizeable inventory.

   —Iran is considering the purchase of additional sophisticated equipment such as the F-16, or F-18, and AWACS aircraft;

   —To pay for new systems and complete its planned purchases of such systems as the Spruance Class destroyer, Iran has proposed barter arrangements (weapons for oil) to compensate for a reduction in normal oil revenues.

2. The Government of Iran is attempting to create an extremely modern military establishment in a country that lacks the technical, educational and industrial base to provide the necessary trained personnel and management capabilities to operate such an establishment effectively. Iran also lacks experience in logistics and support operations and does not have the maintenance capabilities, the infrastructure (port facilities, roads, rail nets, etc.), and the construction capacity to implement its new programs independent of outside support.

—Most informed observers feel that Iran will not be able to absorb and operate within the next five to ten years a large proportion of the sophisticated military systems purchased from the U.S. unless increasing numbers of American personnel go to Iran in a support capacity. This support, alone, may not be sufficient to guarantee success for the Iranian program;

—The schedule for virtually every major program except equipment deliveries to the point of entry into Iran has slipped considerably due to the limitations noted above;

—In the face of immense obstacles, our investigation indicated that the Iranian Armed Forces are making a maximum effort to ensure the success of the modernization program; their efforts, however, are hampered because of rapid expansion in the civilian sector as well. The military, for example, has difficulty in matching civilian salary offers to the growing, but still insufficient numbers of trained personnel.

3. The 1972 decision by President Nixon to sell Iran the F-14 and/or the F-15 aircraft and, in general, to let Iran buy anything it wanted, effectively exempted Iran from arms sales review processes in the State and Defense Departments. This lack of policy review on individual sales requests inhibited any inclinations in the Embassy, the U.S. military mission in Iran (ARMISH-MAAG), or desk officers in State and DOD to assert control over day-to-day events; it created a bonanza for U.S. weapons manufacturers, the procurement branches of the three U.S. services and the Defense Security Assistance Agency.

—Between 1973-75, the activities of U.S. arms salesmen, official and private, were not closely supervised by Executive Branch officials charged with doing so, or by the Congress;

—Each of the U.S. services, particularly the Air Force and Navy, was trying to sell equipment for its own reasons, usually to lower per-unit costs of its own procurements or to recoup part of its prior research and development investment. On occasion, the services fiercely competed with each other for sales to Iran, e.g. the Air Force and Navy to sell the F-15 and F-14 respectively;

—The services often did not inform the Iranians of the full

extent of the training, logistics, and maintenance implications of the systems they were trying to sell. Thus, Iran may have been unaware of the complexities involved in translating its purchases into an effective fighting force. Problems in all of these areas are very serious;

—Discussions both in Washington and Iran have confirmed that until recently U.S. appreciation of the management problems of the arms programs in Iran was extremely limited;

—Secretary Schlesinger's decision to appoint a senior civilian Defense Representative in Iran in September, 1975, to oversee and coordinate U.S. military programs in Iran is considered by virtually everyone to be a positive and necessary development, given the chaos and problems that had emerged in program management and implementation. Nevertheless, until there is clear policy direction and effective program management in Washington, the problems in the field (Iran) will continue. Deputy Secretary Ellsworth issued a directive in February, 1976, that he hopes will ensure coordination and policy direction within the DOD;

—Evidence gathered indicates that the Iranian arms sales program is not yet fully under control. Only with more effective control from Washington can the inherent propensity of civilian contractors and U.S. armed services to sell in an unrestrained manner be curbed.

4. The presence of large and growing numbers of Americans in Iran has already given rise to socio-economic problems. Although many of these have proven to be manageable, they could become worse should there be a major change in U.S.-Iranian relations.

—On the whole, U.S.-Iranian personal relationships are excellent, if somewhat formal;

—We were told that some of the early problems were due to the presence of large numbers of young, single American male civilians without adequate recreational outlets. Decisions by some of the private companies to limit the number of unattached male employees have improved social relations, especially in more traditional cities such as Isfahan;

—There are many other foreigners in Iran as well as Americans, including British, German, South Korean, French, Filipino, Indian and Pakistani;

—Anti-Americanism could become a serious problem in Iran, as it has elsewhere, if there were to be a change in government in Iran. The possibility of a future crisis situation cannot be totally ignored and for this reason contingency plans to deal with such an emergency are necessary.

5. The U.S., having sold sophisticated arms in large quantities to Iran, has assumed a growing and significant "commitment" in terms of supporting that equipment—an unstated but nevertheless real obligation to train Iranians and to provide logistical support for the lifetime of the equipment. To the extent that the decisions to sell the arms were

politically motivated, a failure to provide follow-on support to the satisfaction of Iran would vitiate the political benefits of having made the sales. The deep involvement of U.S. personnel assisting Iran in program implementation has significant foreign policy implications for the United States in the Persian Gulf.

—The U.S. cannot abandon, substantially diminish, or even redirect its arms programs without precipitating a major crisis in U.S.-Iranian relations;

—If Iran is not able effectively to use the equipment it has purchased, it may blame the U.S. for the failures;

—There is general agreement among U.S. personnel involved with the Iranian programs that it is unlikely that Iran could go to war in the next five to ten years with its current and prospective inventory, i.e., purchases to date, of sophisticated weapons (as distinct from some of the less sophisticated ground equipment) without U.S. support on a day-to-day basis.

6. The symbiotic relationship, and Iranian dependence on the U.S., has political advantages and disadvantages for both countries. In theory, the U.S. has the capability to immobilize major components of the Iranian armed forces, especially the Air Force, by cutting off spares, munitions and maintenance support should Iran try to use U.S. equipment for purposes contrary to important U.S. interests. Iran knows this could happen and is therefore unlikely to precipitate a showdown, e.g. by aiding the Arabs against Israel. However, if, *in extremis,* there were a crisis, the United States personnel in Iran could become, in a sense, hostages. The most difficult potential problems are likely to arise in those hypothetical "gray areas" when it is not self-evident that Iran's use of U.S. equipment is contrary to U.S. interests but when its use may embroil U.S. personnel in an on-going conflict situation, e.g. a new war between India and Pakistan in which the Iranians might participate with U.S. equipment. In this type of situation:

—Any attempt to limit the end-use of U.S. equipment could result in a sharp deterioration in U.S.-Iranian relations;

—Failure to limit the Iranians given our capabilities would amount to implicit endorsement of their action and tacit approval of the use of U.S. equipment which, in turn, would almost certainly mean the use of U.S. personnel in a support capacity. Whether this would mean *front-line,* i.e. base level, participation by uniformed U.S. personnel or *rear-line* involvement by U.S. official or contractor personnel would depend upon the actual weapons used and the duration and intensity of the conflict. Clearly the most serious case would be the former;

—Since Iran has memories of the abrupt cut-off of U.S. arms to Pakistan in 1965, and to Turkey in 1974, and because of the political symbolism that stems from a close supplier-client arms relationship, it is not clear who really has influence over whom in time of an ambiguous crisis situation. Senior U.S. officials have expressed concern about the U.S. being labeled as an unreliable supplier; this concern undoubtedly inhibits the U.S. will to exercise its capability to terminate support;

—Thus far the U.S. has not had to face any serious problems concerning the use of U.S. arms by Iran. Iran's participation in counterinsurgency operations in Oman has not involved any U.S. personnel and the U.S. has not opposed the use of U.S. equipment in that conflict.

7. Iranian officials see actual or potential military threats from all directions; they are particularly concerned about protecting Iran's oil "lifeline," the source of virtually all of the country's wealth and revenue. Iran views the Soviet Union as the major threat at the present time, having resolved its immediate differences with Iraq over the Kurds and the Shatt-al-Arab waterway. Iranian officials expressed concern about indirect, as well as direct, Soviet threats in the future through the latter's ties with neighboring India, Afghanistan, and Iraq. These officials are also worried about Soviet support for radical groups on the Arab side of the Gulf and Soviet encouragement of separatist tendencies among certain tribes in Iran. U.S. officials are also concerned about many of these threats to Iran; in particular, U.S. officials stress the importance of stability in the region and the uninterrupted flow of oil. The U.S., however, has officially neither endorsed nor rejected the Iranian perception of the threat. . . .

10. Although Iran is arming against a number of potential threats ranging from the Soviet Union to blockage of the mouth of the Gulf (the Straits of Hormuz) and external support for separatism in Baluchistan, it is clear from our discussions that factors other than operational effectiveness, such as deterrence and prestige, seem to motivate Iran's hardware purchases.

—Iran apparently believes that possession of the most advanced systems may serve as a deterrent;

—Many U.S. military personnel believe that weapons such as the F-14 aircraft and the DD993 Spruance class destroyers are not very useful to Iran in the probable contingencies that it might face in the next ten years;

—We were told that because of the priority given to "prestige" systems such as the F-14, already trained personnel assigned to other systems that are more relevant to near-term threats (F-5E and F-4), have been transferred to the newer systems with a resultant unmeasurable degradation in overall force effectiveness;

—Iran's military programs are having a profound effect upon the socio-economic development of the country. Thousands of young Iranians are learning skills that have application to the economy as a whole. The creation of new bases, e.g. Chah Bahar, and the expansion of existing ones, e.g. Bandar Abbas, are resulting in the development of basic infrastructure and the creation of new communities in sparsely populated regions of the country. Thus the bases may be a catalyst for population redistribution and industrial growth.

11. The recent history of U.S. arms sales to Iran highlights some of the inherent strengths and weaknesses of the Executive Branch in coordinating arms transfer policy and reconciling short with mid-to-long-term foreign policy interests.

—The State Department and the Embassy in Tehran have tended to take a strong, united position on the Iran issue. Senior State Department officials appear not to have been prepared to tolerate open debate on possible adverse implications of unrestricted arms sales to Iran;

—Within the Department of Defense, on the other hand, there were more diverse opinions due in part to the different missions, interests and power bases of its numerous components. The sales and procurement representatives of the Defense Security Assistance Agency (DSAA) and the military services tended to support high levels of sales to Iran; those responsible for policy formulation, training, and logistics and supply tended to be more critical;

—There have been no interagency studies in recent years dealing with arms sales to Iran or the Persian Gulf. A portion of a study of U.S. policy on arms transfers, pursuant to a directive issued in May, 1975, deals with this subject. As of June, 1976, this study had still not been completed, reflecting both the complexity of the subject and the considerable disagreement within the Executive Branch;

—A current study of U.S. policy toward the Persian Gulf, begun in April, 1976, is not yet completed.

12. Irrespective of the benefits and costs of U.S. sales programs to Iran, its history provides valuable insights concerning (1) the policy-making process which determined the nature and level of our current and future involvement; and (2) the policy and programmatic implications of a deep U.S. military involvement with a major arms recipient.

—The Iran case demonstrates that there needs to be more explicit recognition that when the United States sells major weapons in large numbers to a non-industrial state, it is, in effect, entering into a long-term commitment to provide support to those weapons. This life cycle support has military, political, economic and sociological implications which are not easy to anticipate and may eventually create new problems for the U.S.

—Although the nature of U.S.-recipient relationships will vary depending upon circumstances, there is no such thing as a "non-binding" arms sales agreement. Even if the U.S. Government were to play *no* administrative role in foreign military sales, i.e. rely on the private sector for implementing arms sales, U.S. personnel and inevitably the U.S. Government, would still be involved.

General Conclusions

Our first general conclusion is that for at least three years U.S. arms sales to Iran were out of control and the programs were poorly managed. Badly managed arms sales programs are not in U.S. interests. We, therefore, believe that the Iran program demonstrates the importance of and need for effective Congressional oversight to focus attention on these issues and thereby ensure that the Executive Branch takes further action immediately to correct the management deficiencies in Iranian arms sales programs.

Our second general conclusion is that, over time, the so-called "back-end" implementation aspects of arms sales can have a strong influence upon the flexibility of political leaders to change or modify their "front-end" choices. Events leading up to a sale itself, the so-called "front-end" issues, attract attention because they often deal explicitly with grand strategies and require high level policy decisions. The "back-end" process, i.e., what happens after a sales contract has been signed, involves the entire spectrum of military operations—procurement, finance, logistics, maintenance, and training—and may continue for ten or more years after the sale itself. The participation of large numbers of uniformed and civilian Americans, both in the recipient country and in the United States, may be necessary. This creates mutual commitments: the U.S. assumes the obligation of long-term support for the equipment it has sold; the purchaser becomes dependent on the U.S. in much the same manner as a local automobile dealer is dependent on Detroit.

The long-run policy implications of these commitments or obligations are important. On the one hand, the United States has considerable leverage over the recipient, who could not sever its military ties with the U.S. without a devastating effect upon its military capabilities for years to come. On the other hand, the United States reputation as a dependable supplier is at stake and it may be reluctant to use the leverage it has. . . .

VII. CONCLUDING COMMENTS

A. *U.S. Interests and Iranian Security Policy*

The prevailing view within the Executive Branch is that the United States has a major interest in a strong, pro-Western Iran for political, economic and strategic reasons:

—It is a large, populous, resource-rich country located on the periphery of the Soviet Union and between the Near East and South Asia;

—The flow of oil from the Persian Gulf is vital to the economies of Western Europe and Japan and to a lesser extent the United States itself;

—A hostile presence or political instability in Iran or the lower Gulf region could threaten access to this oil;

—U.S. trade with and investment in Iran is large and growing.

The foregoing perception of U.S. interests combined with a policy decision by the U.S. in the late 1960's not to replace the British with a direct U.S. presence in the Persian Gulf, and Iran's desire to develop a deterrent capability to protect its own interests and oil life line, are the factors that explain the positive U.S. responses to Iranian arms requests.

However, the sweeping nature of the 1972 Presidential decision to permit the Shah to purchase without prior review led to problems, many of them unanticipated. The evidence indicates that the 1972 decision was not reassessed following the oil bonanza in 1973; apparently senior officials did not believe that the increase in Iranian oil revenues fundamentally changed the reasons for the 1972 decision. Hence, the U.S. sought to avoid short-term negative political repercussions that might have resulted from occasional negative sales decisions at the cost of contributing to future problems associated with high levels of sales. The Executive Branch began to lose control of the situation.

Since the late 1960's the U.S. Government has been both arms salesman and adviser to Iran. These roles have not been easy to reconcile. ARMISH-MAAG was supposed to offer professional, neutral advice on arms acquisitions; at the same time the military services to whom ARMISH-MAAG reports and the civilian contractors, who are in frequent contact with ARMISH-MAAG personnel, had strong interests in selling weapons systems for their own purposes. Given the 1972 decision, the salesman's role often predominated.

One significant reason advanced by Executive Branch officials to explain U.S. policy is that since Iran had other sources of military supply and was a leader of OPEC, the U.S. should not confront the Shah concerning the difficulties that would be incurred in absorbing his proposed acquisitions. This attitude probably underestimated U.S. leverage with Iran, or rather, the importance that Iran placed on its relationship with the United States. There is no question that Iran would have purchased equipment from other suppliers if it determined that a given capability was vital and the U.S. refused to sell it. In the case of the F-14 and F-15, however, there were no comparable alternatives available.

Iranian officials regard the relationship with U.S. as vital to Iranian interests. If Iran is attacked by the Soviet Union, they believe that the survival of Iran would be dependent on U.S. intervention; no other country has the capability or the will to assist Iran in this ultimate contingency. Thus Iran appears consciously to view the defense link with the U.S. as a form of insurance. Iran may, and has, purchased equipment from third countries, but it is very doubtful to most observers that Iran would have risked its U.S. relationship had the U.S., as a good friend, openly and forthrightly given its unvarnished opinion on several of the proposed large-scale purchases.

B. *Policy Implications of U.S. Military Involvement in Iran*

Barring a dramatic change in Iran's leadership, the future course of the U.S.-Iranian military relationship is already being determined by the level of U.S. activity in the country. Iran has invested so heavily in American weapons and technology that through the early 1980's it will have to rely upon American maintenance and logistics support to the extent that most Iranian decisions regarding a major and sustained use of military power must inevitably take into account attitudes of the United States.

The two most potentially difficult issues that, in the future, may confront U.S. policymakers as a result of this relationship are: (1) what to do if the current programs run into further trouble and Iran requests an even deeper U.S. involvement and (2) what to do if, on the contrary, the Iranians are in a position to use sophisticated equipment effectively in combat and, in fact, do so. In both cases there is the potential for friction or serious tension in U.S.-Iranian relations.

The first issue may arise if Iran is unable, over time, to develop the trained personnel and the support infrastructure to utilize effectively the large amounts of sophisticated military (and civilian) equipment that it has purchased. If the weapons systems do not "work," Iran may blame the United States for the fact that its equipment is not fully operational. . . .

At this point it is important to elaborate on what is actually meant by U.S. "involvement." This includes activities performed for the Iranian armed forces by *uniformed* or *contractor* personnel who participate in two types of roles: (1) advisory and managerial; (2) logistics and support. Each of these roles can involve either: (1) *front line service* with the Iranian military in the field or at Iranian bases; or (2) a *supporting role* in Iran at rear bases and headquarters, or U.S.-based logistical support.

From a political perspective, U.S. uniformed personnel actually helping the Iranians maintain F-4's and F-14's in day-to-day combat is quite different from providing long-term logistics support from the United States; phrased differently, the greater the possibility of Americans, especially uniformed Americans, being drawn into fighting, the greater the immediate political problems.

Thus, while it is true that a "visible" U.S. involvement entails greater political risks, the less controversial but nonetheless real involvement resulting from a common logistics base also has important political and military implications for the United States. Although it is correctly assumed that the United States has less influence over the choice of systems purchased by a country on a cash basis than those provided under the grant military assistance program, it is less appreciated that recipient countries, such as Iran, are taking advantage of certain economies of scale that come from buying into the U.S. armed services logistics systems. In practice, this means that an Iranian logistics officer obtains spare parts for the F-4 aircraft in the same manner, within the same system, as does a U.S. F-4 logistics officer. The net result is that the Iranian forces are, in many instances, integrated into the U.S. logistics and support system. In theory, therefore, the U.S. Air Force has the ability, literally, to halt the operations of the IIAF over time by cutting off spare parts. While Iran has greater freedom to choose the weapons it buys, its freedom to operate that equipment is, in the last resort, dependent upon the good graces of the U.S. Government.

This dependency can only grow as recipient countries such as Iran buy increasingly sophisticated U.S. weapons systems. Iran cannot become "self-sufficient" in F-4E or F-14/Phoenix operations anymore than a local automobile dealer can become independent of Detroit. Understanding the umbilical relationship between the supplier and recipient of advanced weapons becomes particularly important in view of the frequently heard arguments that a recipient such as Iran or Egypt can easily "switch" suppliers if it is not satisfied with its treatment by a supplier. Theoretically, this is true, and there are undoubted political advantages in stressing this option; in reality, however, once a recipient has committed itself to a particular supplier for the maintenance of its active combat forces, it can only "switch" at the risk of losing its operational capabilities for a very long time. More specifically, if there were a revolution in Iran and the Shah were replaced by an anti-U.S. regime, that regime would find it virtually impossible to maintain the current inventory of U.S. weapons without sustained cooperation with the United States. This might moderate a new regime's policies. However, if the regime were intent upon eliminating the U.S. role and presence in Iran, the United States could retaliate by bringing Iran's military machine to a virtual standstill.

While the U.S. could "ground" Iranian forces (particularly the Air Force), its ability to do so is circumscribed by the political implications of such an act. The U.S. has been and is the largest seller of arms in the world. The forces of many nations are almost entirely equipped with U.S. weapons and are, consequently, dependent on the U.S. for follow-on support. Indeed, the U.S. Government often provides assurances that new weapons systems can be supported throughout the "lifetime" of the equipment purchased.

A decision by the U.S. to terminate such support to Iran in a combat situation could cause other past or potential purchasers to call into question the wisdom of relying on the U.S. as a military supplier. The ramifications of such a decision would not be limited to Iran. Senior Iranian officials, for example, have indicated that Iran's decision not to stretch out delivery schedules of equipment it has purchased from the U.S., notwithstanding its unreadiness to receive the equipment, is in large part based on lessons learned from the 1974 U.S. embargo on arms sales to Turkey.

Countries such as Iran, who are deeply involved militarily with the U.S., seem to have, therefore, a curious kind of "reverse influence" on the U.S. (the original U.S. decision to sell arms to Iran was based, in part, on the presumed influence that an arms relationship would provide the U.S. in and over Iran). The effect of this "reverse influence," is to seriously limit, in political terms, the ability of the U.S. to exercise the policy option of cutting off military support to Iran. This option is thus limited to extreme situations such as an Iranian military involvement that is diametrically opposed to or threatens important U.S. interests.

C. The Executive Branch Decision-Making Process on Iran Arms Transfers

Some important general lessons can be drawn from the Iran experience concerning the U.S. arms transfer decision-making process.

Washington

At the most conceptual level it can be argued that once a potential recipient of U.S. arms assumes, for whatever reason, great importance to the U.S., the "normal" arms transfer review processes that determine whether or not to sell what types of goods and services in what numbers become less relevant. Decisions on arms sales to such countries are often taken at the highest level (President and Secretary of State) and must be viewed differently from more routine arms sales.

In the case of Iran, absent any other explanation or evidence, it must be inferred that the 1972 decision was based upon broad geostrategic and political considerations rather than exacting calculations about the balance of military power in the Persian Gulf. When arms decisions are made at the highest level, the probability that potential future policy and programmatic problems will take a back seat to perceived tangible political benefits is increased.

Once the basic policy decision was made, the Iranian armed forces, the U.S. Defense Department and private U.S. defense contractors became the primary actors. The ensuing problems might never have occurred but for the hike in oil prices in 1973 which gave Iran the means to buy *far more* arms than had been anticipated at the time of the decision. The increased oil revenues made billions of dollars available for new military orders. The immediate effect was to increase the stakes in arms to sell to Iran.

The overall effect was to overwhelm the U.S. Government systems that normally execute routine arms sales. The only institution in the

United States (or Iran) capable of managing and monitoring this boom in sales was the Department of Defense. During the period 1973-75, various factions within the DOD, especially the Navy and the Air Force, pursued their own, often competing, objectives with respect to major sales to Iran. "Alliances" between private industry and the procurement branches of the Air Force and Navy resulted in major sales efforts in Iran. In practical terms, it would have been extremely difficult for the U.S. Embassy in Tehran, ARMISH-MAAG, the policy desks in State and DOD and DSAA to exercise control over events had they chosen or been able to do so.

Thus for a period of time a situation approaching anarchy existed within the Executive Branch. A telling indicator of this is that when Schlesinger and Ellsworth came to the conclusion, somewhat independently, that all was not well with DOD activities in Iran, their respective efforts to deal with the problems were not fully coordinated. If the DOD leadership was in doubt over what was actually happening in Iran, it would be unreasonable to expect other Executive Branch agencies to be better informed.

Once the various elements in the DOD, including those responsible for program implementation, began to recognize the extent of the problems of the FMS program in Iran, Schlesinger and Ellsworth began to exert policy level control over the entire operation. The appointment of a Defense Representative to Iran in September 1975 by Schlesinger, and the issuance of a directive by Ellsworth in February 1976 on DOD activities and interests in Iran were intended to ensure coordination within the DOD, and were seen as first but essential steps to bring the situation under firm policy control within the DOD.

Since the expertise on weapons systems management, logistics, training and manpower requirements is in Washington, not Iran, all DOD departments and agencies, including the services who are involved in programs in Iran, are now required to cooperate and provide analytical backup in support of the Defense Representative's tasks in Iran.

The foreign policy problems resulting from the U.S. military involvement in Iran have been less explicitly noted in the State Department and the White House. However, the current review of U.S. policy in the Persian Gulf, at least acknowledges the need for a re-examination of policy.

Iran

In Iran the major difficulties with *current* U.S. defense programs relate to some but not all of the so-called "back end" (implementing) operations—logistics, maintenance, training, etc. This is now clearly recognized within U.S. defense circles, and has been communicated to senior Iranian officials by the U.S. Defense Representative in Iran. If the Defense Representative's mandate is to be performed effectively and routinely, ARMISH-MAAG will need to have a larger percentage of its personnel trained in weapons system management, planning, and resource management. General Miles, the current Chief of ARMISH-MAAG, has a weapons systems management background himself and acknowledges the importance of such expertise. Whether the three services respond remains to be seen.

The DOD's task is particularly difficult (1) because the U.S., directly or indirectly, is responsible for not having fully briefed the Iranians on the implications of its proposed purchases, and (2) because the issues are politically sensitive in that the responsibility for many of the current problems and delays lies ultimately with the Iranians. On the whole, the U.S. Government and U.S. contractors have met their schedules but the Iranians have not. Indeed, one of the most serious problems is that the delivery schedules for U.S. equipment have been on time while Iranian training and construction schedules have slipped, and the entire support infrastructure in Iran, is inadequate. The Iranian armed forces are working diligently to overcome these obstacles; the tasks confronting them, however, are enormous.

That Iran is considering additional purchases of large quantities of sophisticated weapons, perhaps on a barter basis, indicates that Iran has not altered its "front-end," i.e. new purchases, policies because of the "back-end" difficulties of which it is now fully aware.

IRAN IN OPEC

News Conference by Secretary Kissinger and Minister Ansary

[EXCERPTS]

Tehran, November 2, 1974

Q: Put maybe overly simply, the United States favors lower oil prices, and Iran has favored higher oil prices. Based on your visit here, do you think there will be any narrowing of the views on prices?

Secretary Kissinger: I think of course the statement of the issue, as you yourself said, is overly simple. I think that you of course all have to keep in mind that Iran cannot make these decisions unilaterally and will have to consult its partners in OPEC about any conclusions that it may reach with respect to oil prices. I think the views with respect to the linked problems of oil prices and inflation have been brought closer.

Q: The suggestion of that, sir, is that you would hope that Iran at some point in the near future would use its influence in the direction of lowering prices. Is that correct?

Secretary Kissinger: Well, as I've tried to explain on a number of occasions, the oil price problem has many aspects. When prices have been rising, there are many other things that can be done other than immediately lowering them. But, first of all, some of you will have an opportunity to meet with His Imperial Majesty. Secondly, I do not think it would be appropriate for me to go into details except to say that we had a constructive and positive talk on the subject and that our views have been brought closer.

Q: Mr. Secretary, are you hopeful that in the medium run that oil prices might be reduced?

Secretary Kissinger: I'm hopeful that the impact of oil prices on the world economy can be brought under control, and I believe that this requires, on the other side, some recognition of the impact of the inflation of the world on the oil-producing countries. But I think in that framework progress is possible.

Q: But in the immediate future, do you anticipate any further rise in oil prices, perhaps not a very great one, but a further rise as a result of the OPEC meeting in Vienna?

Secretary Kissinger: Well, I think we should wait until we see what His Imperial Majesty will propose at the OPEC meeting. Of course the hope of the United States is that further rises can be avoided.

Q: Mr. Secretary, did you discuss with the Shah the prospects for a possible meeting between producers and the consumers anytime soon?

Secretary Kissinger: Yes, we discussed the initiatives that have been made with respect to meetings of producers and consumers. I explained to His Imperial Majesty the general American approach to the problem of the dialogues. We, in any event, will remain in close contact with His Majesty, as we traditionally do, to make sure that we understand each other's views. The United States is not opposed to a dialogue between consumers and producers, and the problem is to conduct it in such a manner that it will achieve the desired results for both parties.

Q: Mr. Secretary, on the Middle East, did you have a considerable discussion with the Shah on this issue, and would you tell us whether there is any fundamental difference in U.S. and Iranian views?

Secretary Kissinger: I had an extensive discussion with His Imperial Majesty on the Middle East and benefited from his evaluation of the situation. I believe that, as has been the case in the past, our analysis is substantially congruent.

Q: Mr. Secretary, what is the American view on His Imperial Majesty's proposal for a fixed price of just under $10?

Secretary Kissinger: We are not, in principle, opposed to the idea of a fixed price, but we are studying it further.

Q: Mr. Secretary, has the question of food supply been linked with the question of energy supply?

Secretary Kissinger: No, the issue of food supply has not been linked with the issue of energy supply. But on the other hand, there is an inherent connection between the willingness of the world to take a global view to one problem and the ability of the world to take a global view to the other problem. This is not a question of a condition; this is a question of the approach.

We will proceed with our food policy without reference to any decisions that have been made or will be made. But any thoughtful person must recognize that reality establishes a connection between the ability of the world to deal globally with its problems in various fields.

But I would also like to add that, at least as far as Iran and the United States are concerned, this is not a problem. . . .

Q: Mr. Secretary, does what you have said on oil previously mean that you now expect Iran to support efforts to hold the line on oil prices?

Secretary Kissinger: I don't think I should be any more specific than I have been, and I think that you will just have to wait to see what position Iran will take.

Q: Mr. Secretary, nevertheless, in speaking of the United States and leaving Iran out of it, you said that the hope of the United States is that further rises can be avoided. What happens to our hope for lower prices?

Secretary Kissinger: Before you can have lower prices, you have to have stable prices.

Q: Mr. Secretary, Iran has proposed this unitary price of $9.85 in the gulf. Do you regard this as a true weighted average reflecting current rates in the gulf, or as an increase?.

Secretary Kissinger: I was warned before I got here under no circumstances to get myself involved in a detailed discussion of oil prices, because my Iranian counterpart would be infinitely more competent than I and would overwhelm me with statistics. So I'm not prepared to go into a discussion of what price would be considered the current price by the United States or a price from which indexing might be considered appropriate. But it is one of the problems that has to be discussed.

Q: Can we ask, perhaps, the question from Mr. Ansary? How would Iran regard an arbitration of the present oil price?

Minister Ansary: Well, as you know, His Imperial Majesty has proposed that he would be prepared to link the price of oil with the rate of inflation in the industrial countries. Once you link the two together, they can move in either direction together.

Q: Mr. Minister, when you say once you link them together they can move in either direction, do you believe that, in a period when there is massive world inflation, it is realistic to expect a downward trend in oil prices linked to a downward trend in other commodity prices?

Minister Ansary: I stand on my statement that the idea is to link the two together. Once you do that, they both have the same destiny. Now, whether it's realistic or not depends on the approach that we all make to the problem, toward inflation.

Q: Mr. Ansary, I wasn't challenging your statement by any means, sir. I was seeking further amplification of it.

Minister Ansary: As you know, we're all concerned with the rampant inflation with which the world has been faced. This proposal was made initially by His Imperial Majesty in the context of his desire for the entire community of nations to cooperate in lowering the rate of inflation, which is only beneficial to the entire world community.

Q: Mr. Minister, does Iran want to mate the two at the present levels, when the price of oil is artificially high, or would it be willing to go back to some previous index level from previous years?

Minister Ansary: All I can say is that linking can only take place at the time you talk about it. There was no question of making the link retroactive.

Q: Mr. Secretary, did you and His Majesty specifically discuss his plan for indexing and for linking 20 or 30 commodities to the price of oil? And if so, I assume you're familiar with the criticism of that, that it amounts to institutionalizing inflation. Did that come up?

Secretary Kissinger: Yes, that came up, and I will have to stand on what I said; I cannot go into more detail about it. I repeat what I said, that what we discussed was within the context of considering the impact on the world economy, especially on the industrialized nations as well as on the least developed nations, of the energy crisis, as well as the impact, on the producers, of inflation.

Now, obviously it is in neither side's interest to build an institutionalized system that accentuates the tendencies on both sides. And some means will have to be found to take account of these objectives, and I left the meeting with some encouragement that an evolution in a constructive direction was possible. Now, what form this will take, one will have to await Iran's proposals at the OPEC meetings and other discussions that may take place.

News Conference by Secretary Kissinger and the Shah

[EXCERPTS]

Zurich, February 18, 1975

Q: Is Iran prepared to play a role in the Secretary's step-by-step diplomacy? Specifically, I have in mind supplying oil to Israel, should Israel be compelled to give up the Sinai oilfields.

The Shah of Iran: Well, I think that I have answered this question before by saying that our policy is to sell oil to [remainder of sentence inaudible]. Once the tankers are loaded it doesn't matter where or to whom the oil goes, because it is a strictly commercial transaction for my country.

Q: So certainly you would be part of no boycott of Israel, which seems to be growing big?

The Shah of Iran: We have never really boycotted anybody. It is not part of our policy. We think that politics and commerce are separate. We have not taken part in the first oil embargo, and we will not take part in any other embargo. No embargo can work anymore, because we have tremendous oil reserves in both Europe and other countries of the world. I believe they have 90 days' reserve, and today's wars cannot last more than three weeks. So I don't really believe in that. But if it comes, we are not going to put an embargo on oil.

Q: Your Majesty, you and the Secretary discussed prices surely. What do you see as a future price [inaudible] and Mr. Kissinger's plan for a floor price on oil?

The Shah of Iran: We are going to go to the OPEC meeting in Algiers very soon. Anything I say before that meeting you will hear about. What I want to say is that in my opinion, for good or bad, the price of oil has increased. If we consider inflation and that the Western countries—or the industrialized countries—are selling their goods to us at about 35 percent more, and then, with the devaluation of the dollar, in the matter of fact of purchasing power a barrel of oil corresponds today to about $7 or $8, if you want my opinion. So the price of oil has gone up.

Q: Excuse me, but that brings up indexing. We are familiar with your position. Are you and the Secretary getting together on a view of the value of indexing?

The Shah of Iran: In principle he agrees with me on the indexing of prices. The question is a floor price for oil and also a floor price for other commodities. But the other commodities are 20 or 30, and oil is one. It won't be easy to index it, but it can be done.

Q: Mr. Secretary, what was the main concern between yourself and His Majesty?

Secretary Kissinger: Well, as you know, the relations between Iran and the United States are extremely close; and I think that His Imperial Majesty and I have agreed that they have probably never been better. Therefore it was natural that as a result of my tour to the Middle East I would inform His Imperial Majesty of what the United States is intending to do and to get the benefit of his advice on those matters. It naturally gave us an opportunity to review other issues such as the general issue of energy and the bilateral Iranian-American relations. We will have a meeting in Washington of the Iranian-U.S. Commission.

Q: [Inaudible.]

The Shah of Iran: I am not one of those to believe that the price of oil will go lower—

Q: Will go up, did you say?

The Shah of Iran: No, go lower. If you force us to raise the prices by your inflation, it might go up. But what will be the purchasing power? I am not interested in raising the price of oil. But if I have to go and buy more expensive goods, what really concerns me is to keep a constant purchasing power.

Q: Mr. Secretary, in context with His Majesty's remarks about the decline of the dollar, I understand the United States is planning to do something about the dollar now.

Secretary Kissinger: As I understand it, the value of the dollar has stabilized; and we are very interested in maintaining it. We will do our best to do so.

Q: We have not seen it in Switzerland yet.

Secretary Kissinger: It will come here. Everything comes here sooner or later.

Q: What, according to your ideas, are the means of getting down inflation? For instance, you buy products from industrialized countries, but at the same time you are paying much more. But what is the way out?

The Shah of Iran: The way out is for you people to check your inflation.

Q: Mr. Secretary, how can one check this inflation?

Secretary Kissinger: That is an extremely complicated matter; but as you know, the Administration is attempting to deal simultaneously with both inflation and recession, and we agree with the concern of His Imperial Majesty about bringing inflation under control and, above all, to have a fruitful dialogue.

Q: Your Majesty, I am sorry, but we did not hear your answer about the possibility of selling oil to Israel. Would you please repeat it?

The Shah of Iran: I said that when we sell our oil and fill up the tankers in our terminal ports we do not mind and do not care where it goes.

Q: Would you be willing to play an active role in promoting step-by-step diplomacy?

The Shah of Iran: I am not one of those who loses his head very easily in believing that he is a big deal, but for the little influence that we could eventually have, is to see every possible way of defusing the present, maybe explosive, situation that will permit more meaningful and constructive talks later.

Q: Your Majesty, do you believe that after your meeting in Algiers the price of oil will be higher?

The Shah of Iran: I can't say what will be the result of that meeting. This meeting will probably study what to do if the inflation in Europe and elsewhere continues. And if our purchasing power becomes less and less, we will have to defend ourselves somehow.

Q: You see a direct link between inflation and the price of oil that will be set? If inflation goes higher, the price of oil could go higher?

The Shah of Iran: If inflation goes on the price of everything will get out of control.

Q: Your Majesty, have you discussed with the Secretary recent reports that Diego Garcia is to be built up as a naval position, in view of your disagreement with big powers moving in the Indian Ocean?

The Shah of Iran: I have spoken about it before, but our principal first-choice policy will be first to see the Persian Gulf and then the Indian Ocean eventually free of outside powers. That means nonriparian states. But as long as some powers are there, we would not only not object to the presence of the United States but on the contrary we would welcome it.

TREMORS ON THE HUMAN RIGHTS ISSUE

Testimony of Alfred Atherton, Assistant Secretary for Near Eastern and South Asian Affairs, before House Subcommittee on International Organizations

September 8, 1976

. . . In Iran the large landholders and the leaders of large tribal groups have seen the bases of their strength severely eroded by land reform and the other reforms which I previously mentioned. The religiously conservative elements in the society, powerful in varying degrees in all Moslem countries, have at times vigorously opposed the whole process of modernization, which they consider to be sectarian and anti-Islamic.

The voting rights proposal referred to earlier, for example, brought about large-scale rioting in the streets of Tehran in 1963. These riots, which were put down with force by the government, had been organized by a leading cleric who exploited the strong antifeminist sentiment in the society.

Extremist Opposition Movements

There is another important source of opposition to the Iranian changes of recent years. To this day, Mr. Chairman, the Government of Iran is confronted by the opposition—using at times brutal and harsh methods—of extremists from the Left and the Right. . . .

Thus the Government of Iran has faced during the past 30 years strong opposition from an extreme leftist movement, tied in various ways to the outside, and opposition from the indigenous, extremely traditional forces who resent change and modernity.

As I noted above, the opposition to the Government of Iran has frequently taken a violent and brutal turn. By this I mean terrorist actions, which we saw senselessly reflected only a week ago in the murders of three American civilians.

Terrorism as a form of political action is not a new phenomenon in Iranian history. It has long historical and cultural roots. Since the 1960's a number of separate terrorist groups whose principal platform has been the violent overthrow of the regime have come and gone, but this phenomenon continues. The victims of the terrorists have included an Iranian Prime Minister, numerous police and government officials, and six Americans. Plots to kidnap the Empress of Iran and the Crown Prince were uncovered, and several efforts to murder the Shah were made. You will also recall that in 1949 the Shah was wounded by a terrorist attack. Relatively little is known about the numbers of terrorists involved—they are not particularly large, we are told—but through stealth and individual murder, they are able to make their presence felt.

Neither do we know a great deal about the various political programs of these groups, for their principal motivation appears to be the destruction of the current society and its leaders; these groups have not promoted constructive alternatives. It appears that, in effect, the terrorists come from two ideological currents—one extreme leftist if not neo-anarchist, and the other strongly influenced by extreme religious conservatism.

At times there have appeared to be two separate movements, both of which can be hazily linked to earlier terrorist organizations. But it also appears that the two groups have often worked together in individual political murders and may in fact be wings of the same movement brought together in a loose federation—having in common their hatred of the regime. We do know that elements representing at least one of these groups were involved in the murder of the two American colonels last year in Tehran.

It is also very clear that in addition to the indigenous support that the terrorists receive, they have established links with a variety of terrorists movements abroad and have received substantial financial assistance and very large quantities of arms. In recent successful attacks on terrorist safehouses in Tehran, large caches of foreign arms—machine guns, hand grenades, pistols, et cetera—have been found, as well as sums of money.

All of us have been horrified by the Lod massacre, the murders at the Olympic games, the numerous hijackings of civilian airliners, and the numerous individual assassinations, including the murder of American Ambassadors and other officials, which have taken place throughout the world. The media, except on rare occasions, have not paid as much attention, quite understandably, to the fact that the Iranian leadership is faced today, and has been faced for many years, with a terrorist movement which need not take second place to any group in its brutality. This problem—this cancer—must be kept in mind when we view events in Iran.

Investigation and Trial Procedures

In view of these disruptions and their threat to the security of the state and to its leaders, the Government of Iran through its legislative processes has determined that persons charged with actions against the security of the state or of actions against official persons and property will be tried by the military court system.

The International Commission of Jurists and others have criticized this procedure and have made a number of charges concerning the treatment given to people who fall within the military court system. The procedures of that court system do not, in fact, meet the criteria set forth in relevant international conventions or those we have established for our court systems, although the courts do operate according to Iranian law.

Investigating authorities in Iran have the power to detain suspects during investigations of alleged crimes without formal charges being immediately placed. Detention for persons involved in crimes having to do with state security can either last only a few hours for the initial questioning—which is probably the case for the vast majority of cases—or up to one to four months for the rare fuller investigations of detainees on whom prima facie evidence of a crime has been gathered or who have a previous record.

When formal charges are made, the accused has a right to select counsel from a list and, to the best of my knowledge, this right is generally observed in practice. If the accused prisoner does not make a choice of counsel from the list, the court appoints counsel.

We understand that visits from family and friends are not permitted during the investigatory stage but that during the trial and later, if the individual is sentenced, such visits are generally permitted.

We have also seen reports from individuals who claim that torture has been used in the investigatory period. While we have no direct verifiable evidence of this, it is difficult to discount the many persistent reports, particularly in the context of terrorist violence, that there have been cases of harsh methods being used by the Iranian police and security services. I do not condone such treatment in the Iranian system or any other system. I simply must reiterate again the context of the charges. Most of the charges of torture are at least two to three years old. The only recent charges, largely made by Iranians abroad, all concerned terrorists who were allegedly killed or maimed under torture. . . .

I should at the same time point out that while the Iranian penal code imposes severe penalties on those who order or practice torture, we have no information on cases where these penalties have been imposed.

Political Crimes and Sentences

Mr. Chairman, a fair amount has been written about the number of "political prisoners," and in your invitation to me you requested that I comment on this matter. There is no precise definition of the term "political prisoner" in the Iranian context, but there may well be a number—perhaps 100 to 150—who would fall within the definition in your letter; that is, "persons who have been detained, arrested or punished for their beliefs or opinions but who have neither used nor advocated violence."

As I said earlier, membership in a Communist movement or the advocacy of communism is illegal under Iranian law. I simply do not know how many persons are jailed for what we would consider normal political dissent. I am reasonably certain that the large majority of prisoners who have gone through the military court system were convicted for involvement in planning or carrying out violent acts against the security of the state or overtly engaged in acts of terrorism or were associated in some way with the terrorists. The number of such people in prison today is probably in the range of 2,800 to 3,500. . . .

You also wished me to comment upon the number of persons convicted of "political crimes" and the sentences which they have received. We have no information on the numbers convicted, but sentences have ranged from a few years to life imprisonment and to the death sentence. In his report Mr. Butler wrote that if the 424 prisoners whose names were listed, ". . . 75 have been executed, 55 have been given life sentences, 33 have been sentenced to between 10 and 15 years imprisonment and others have been given lesser sentences." Mr. Butler's statistics are probably within a reasonable order of magnitude, but let me add that recently an American journalist from a major U.S. newspaper visited an Iranian prison and was introduced to and interviewed a number of prisoners who opponents of the Government of Iran have long claimed had died in prison from torture. . . .

Mr. Chairman, I would like briefly to address two other questions which you put to me and to submit as an enclosure to this statement, in order to save time, answers to a few other matters in which you have shown interest. I would be glad to answer questions on those matters as well.

We believe that the Iranian Government has no doubt as to U.S. views on the observance of human rights. The Iranian Government is also aware of the legislation in which you have played a prominent role, Mr. Chairman.

However, we have not made official representations to Iran on the condition of human rights in that country for two reasons. First, we believe that the administration of Iranian judicial and penal systems is above all a matter of internal Iranian responsibility and that one sovereign country should not interfere lightly in another's domestic affairs. This is admittedly a matter of fine judgment on which there can be honest differences. In reaching our judgment, we have also taken into account the remarkable progress which has been made in Iran in many areas of human rights as well as the unique and extraordinarily difficult problems of terrorism and other manifestations of social disruption. If Iran's internal practices in matters relating to human rights were a growing affront to international standards, we would of course reconsider our judgment. The trend appears to us, however, to be in the opposite direction.

In applying section 502B of the Foreign Assistance Act to Iran, we are about to begin the formulation of fiscal year 1978 security assistance programs. Available evidence regarding Iran's observance of internationally recognized human rights will be taken into account in this process, and a report to Congress on human rights in Iran will accompany our fiscal year 1978 legislative request. . . .

State Department Report on Human Rights in Iran (Pursuant to the Arms Export Control Act of 1976) to the House Committee on International Relations

December 31, 1976

A. *Human Rights Information*

1. *Political Situation*

For the past century Iranian leadership has been attempting to create a modern national state against a backdrop of entrenched traditional conservatism, poverty, and illiteracy. During this period Iran has confronted severe challenges to its governmental structure, as well as economic turmoil and outside pressures. It has been twice invaded and partially occupied by the Soviet Union. In the post-World War II period, an indigenous Communist party with substantial external support grew in influence to the point where it was able to precipitate a governmental crisis in 1953 which resulted in the Shah fleeing the country temporarily. He returned shortly thereafter and began to lay the basis for major economic and social reforms now known as the Shah people revolution. Implementation of these reforms brought the Government and modernizing elements into conflict with landlords and reactionary religious personalities and, in 1962, resulted in a week of confrontation and physical violence in the streets of Tehran. The Government carried the day and since that time its reform programs, which have benefited the majority of the population, have had wide public support.

These reforms, along with Iran's economic development programs, form the core of the government's domestic activities. In the past 15 years, they have resulted in major progress in fields related to landownership, education, the local court system, rural development, health, and the rights of women. In sum, they amount to a significant improvement in the quality of life and rights of most Iranians.

Beginning in the late 1960's, Iran has also been confronted with a small number of terrorist organizations operating within the country. These terrorist groups have not delineated fully their economic and social programs, but they appear to be motivated by either the extreme conservative desire to oppose the social-economic changes in the society brought about by the Shah or to advocate even more sweeping, radical leftist changes. There is evidence that they have received substantial foreign support and training. While those groups pose no serious political threat to the Government, terrorists have been responsible for the murders of Iranian Government officials and Americans, including three colonels and three civilian defense contractor personnel over the past 34 months.

The present governmental system is a constitutional monarchy headed by the Shah and a two-chamber parliament. Until March 1975, Iran had a multiparty system. This was replaced by a new broad-based single party, the Resurgency Party of the People of Iran. Elections for both the Majles (lower house) and the Senate were held in June 1975 and were recognized as among the most honest in Iran's history. However, these democratic institutions have limited powers; the Shah makes all important decisions.

2. Legal Situation

Iranian constitutional law provides a comprehensive system of guarantee of basic human rights, combining traditional Moslem legal principles with codification largely patterned after the French system.

Civil and criminal cases are handled with full guarantees of civil rights. The civilian court system which handles the large majority of civil and criminal cases has been recognized by outsiders as giving fair and balanced treatment to those brought before it. Most recently a team from the International Commission of Jurists praised certain aspects of this regular Iranian judicial system.

On the other hand, the same team recommended reforms in the handling of civilians charged with crimes involving state security. These recommendations stemmed from the fact that the security police (SAVAK) are empowered, without supervision of the regular courts, to function as military magistrates with regard to persons they may detain while protecting state security and carrying out other functions described in the Establishment of Security Organization Act of 1957. The great majority of those so detained are released within a few hours. Others are held for varying periods pending military trial or release.

Crimes against state security or which involve destruction of government property or bodily harm to government officials must under Iranian law be before a military tribunal.

As a result of this process, there are currently in prison about 2,800-3,500 persons. They are sometimes referred to as "political prisoners." These figures are based on a definition of "political prisoners" which includes those convicted of crimes related to terrorism and other forms of violence. If instead the definition used is "persons who have been detained, arrested or punished for their beliefs or opinions but who have neither used nor advocated violence" the total of political prisoners in Iran is much smaller, probably about 100-150. Most persons in the latter group have been convicted for what the Iranian Government considers to be communist activities which are in violation of Iranian law.

In 1975, Iran agreed to a request by the International Commission of Jurists to send two observers into the country. Iranian authorities cooperated fully with the visitors. Also in 1975, the U.N. Human Rights Commission reviewed accusations of violations of human rights by Iran, based on material presented by Iranian students studying abroad and decided, on the basis of information before it, that no action was called for in the case of Iran.

3. Observance of Internationally Recognized Human Rights

(a) Integrity of the Person

Article 3: Iranian law provides for the protection of life, property, home and honor. These legal provisions are generally observed. Charges that these legal provisions are not properly observed are generally met by the Government's reference to its efforts to suppress the terrorist movement and other threats to national security.

Article 5: The Iranian penal code specifically prohibits torture and provides severe penalties for anyone who tortures a prisoner or orders the use of torture. While we have no verifiable evidence of the use of torture, one cannot discount the reports, particularly with regard to persons alleged to be involved in terrorist violence, that such methods have been used by the Iranian police and security services. We also have no information that any official has ever been prosecuted for the use of torture. Fewer allegations of torture have been brought to our attention in recent years than in the past.

Important recent reports on the subject include the following: Amnesty International wrote in May 1976 that "torture of political prisoners during interrogation appears to be a routine practice, but persons may be subjected to torture again at any time during their imprisonment." An observer from the International Commission of Jurists reported in 1976: "The following reports on cases involving human rights violations occurred between 1963 and 1975. In most of them those brought to trial alleged they were tortured or held in custody for excessively long periods before trial." The report that followed related to from 200 to 400 persons brought to trial. The same observer, an American human rights legal expert, stated: "In the opinion of the writer there can be no doubt that torture has been systematically practiced over a number of years against recalcitrant suspects under interrogation by the SAVAK. The number of detailed allegations which have been made, the absence of any impartial investigation, and the fact that the SAVAK is, and knows itself to be, a law unto itself, point inevitably to this conclusion."

The Shah has stated on several occasions that torture was probably used in the past, but has added that it is no longer used: he has said that "intelligent ways of questioning" prisoners are used.

Article 8: In most cases, Iranians can obtain an effective remedy for violations of their rights with the judicial system. However, the persons who allege that their rights were violated during the prosecution of their cases by SAVAK and the military courts have more limited possibilities of obtaining redress. Decisions by military courts can be and are appealed to a military appellate court, but are not subject to review by the Supreme Court. The Shah has final review of these decisions and has on occasion lessened sentences.

In cases involving state security, terrorism or similar crimes of violence, detention without initial charges does occur and pretrial confinement has been lengthy. Internal exile is permitted by law but has been used in recent years only with respect to price fixing and corruption cases after full and fair, usually public trials.

Article 10: Iranian law provides for equal treatment before the law. Persons suspected of violating civil and most criminal laws are normally charged shortly after arrest and many are able to gain release by posting bond.

Article 11: Except in state security cases trials in Iran are generally public and fair and afford guarantees necessary for defense. Security cases are tried in military courts, often in camera, and without the possibility of appeal to the civil judiciary. A military officer is assigned to act as defense counsel.

(b) *Other freedoms*

While there are some manifestations of discrimination in Iranian society, largely related to traditional religious practice, equal rights before the law are guaranteed. Freedom of movement, both within the country and abroad, the right to property, and freedom of thought and religion are observed in Iran, which has a long tradition of religious freedom.

The constitution provides for freedom of the press except for a prohibition against publications harmful to Islam, but all publishers and writers are also required to conform with the press law. The observers from the International Commission of Jurists noted that "in practice" freedom of the press did not exist.

Special rules govern the behavior of the Iranian military. There are restrictions on the peaceful assembly of groups which the Government considers political or subversive.

B. *U.S. Government Action in Human Rights Area*

1. *Promotion of Observance of Human Rights*

Over the past two years, U.S. Government officials have discussed privately with Iranian officials our views about human rights in general and the human rights situation in Iran specifically. These contacts have been guided by our belief that handling this subject privately would be most effective in the Iranian context. To do otherwise would certainly become widely known and would put the matter of human rights in confrontational and self-defeating terms. We have made clear in private conversations our views and laws.

Iranian officials are aware of our views about human rights both from those contacts and from other U.S. Government activities. These latter include our prominent role in human rights matters in the U.N. and elsewhere. Most recently the hearings on human rights in Iran before the Subcommittee on International Organizations of the House International Relations Committee were followed carefully by the Government of Iran. In addition, our Embassy in Tehran keeps itself informed on developments related to human rights and that fact is certainly obvious to the Iranians.

2. *Disassociation of U.S. Security Assistance from Violations of Human Rights*

. . . There is in Iran no U.S. public safety or other assistance program having to do with the Iranian police or penal authorities. There have been some sales of U.S. equipment to the Iranian gendarmerie, but we are not aware of any case in which that equipment has been used in connection with a possible violation of human rights.

Iranian officials are well aware of the provisions in the current law linking possible violations of human rights to the entire U.S. security assistance program.

C. *U.S. Interests Justifying a Security Assistance Program*

The U.S. security assistance program for Iran is composed only of cash sales of military equipment to Iran. In fiscal year 1976, including the transitional quarter, Iran received deliveries from the United States valued at $1.6 billion. That same figure for fiscal year 1977 will probably be about $1.2 billion.

These Iranian purchases are the heart of a program designed to develop a strong Iran. Iran's strength is important to us because of the parallel in Iranian and U.S. national interests found in (1) Iran's defense of its long border with the Soviet Union; (2) the transportation and communications bridge between Europe and Asian countries to the east; (3) Iran's interest in assuming major Persian Gulf security responsibilities previously carried out by the British; (4) Iran's willingness to serve as a reliable source of critical amounts of oil for the United States, Israel, our European allies and Japan; and (5) Iran's activities as a politically stabilizing force throughout that important region from Turkey into the Indian subcontinent.

For these reasons, the Department of State is of the opinion that continuation of our security assistance program with Iran is in the U.S. national interest.

8

Prelude to Revolution

In 1977 and 1978, while the forces of revolution were gathering strength in Iran, relations between the United States and that country remained unchanged with regard to closeness and cordiality. Iran, together with Saudi Arabia, was the anchor of U.S. policy in the Persian Gulf, and its economic progress remained an object of U.S. concern. Cooperation moved forward in a number of fields, highlighted by the agreement on atomic energy in 1977 which is printed in this chapter.

Two aims which President Carter had outlined during his 1976 campaign, however, foreshadowed changes in the relationship between the U.S. and Iran. One aim called for a limitation on U.S. arms sales overseas; the other proposed to make human rights a central focus of U.S. foreign policy. If both were vigorously pursued, differences with Iran could hardly be avoided.

As matters developed, the United States did proceed with a reduced but still large arms sales program to Iran because, in the words of the Under Secretary of State for Security Assistance, "the Shah is sitting on an area of the world we consider necessary for our own national security." This decision was made despite the Shah's increasing internal troubles—troubles whose meaning was not accurately assessed by U.S. intelligence agencies.

Insofar as human rights were concerned, the Shah appears to have been desirous of placating the United States. He instituted a number of reforms in this area early in 1977, or roughly simultaneously with the advent of the new administration. These reforms included a prohibition of the use of torture by security forces (there had been many allegations of such practices in Iran), a selective release of political prisoners, a loosening of censorship, and other measures.

There was certainly ambivalence in pursuing the human rights program with respect to Iran. This first shows up in the testimony (included in this chapter) of the State Department's Director of the Office of Iranian Affairs. Indeed, the Shah's limited liberalization may have fueled demands for still further liberalization and may have actually contributed to his downfall. There have been reports that he believed this to be the case.

In November 1977 the Shah paid the new U.S. President a visit, a practice which had become almost a ritual. While the Shah was being welcomed, anti-Shah Iranian students were demonstrating within sight of the White House. The target of the demonstrators was not only their ruler, but also the U.S. policy which supported him. President Carter visited Tehran at the turn of the year, 1977-78. He spoke warmly of the Shah and favorably of Iran as an "island of stability in one of the more troubled areas of the world." During 1978 he reaffirmed the strategic importance of Iran and expressed support for the Shah's attempts to modernize his country. As the internal crisis in Iran deepened, however, President Carter stated several times that the people of Iran would have to decide their own future, free of outside interference.

CLOSE COOPERATION CONTINUES

Agreement between the United States Nuclear Regulatory Commission and the Atomic Energy Organization of Iran for the Exchange of Technical Information and Cooperation in Nuclear Safety Matters

April 11, 1977   *Agreement signed at Shiraz.*
April 11, 1977   *Entered into force.*
           With letter of understanding.

The United States Nuclear Regulatory Commission (hereinafter called the U.S.N.R.C.) and the Atomic Energy Organization of Iran (hereinafter called the A.E.O.I.), considering the desirability of a continuing exchange of information pertaining to regulatory matters, and collaboration in standards of the type required or recommended by these organizations for the regulation of safety and environmental impact of nuclear facilities, conclude the following arrangement of cooperation.

I. SCOPE OF THE AGREEMENT

I.1 *Technical Information Exchange*

The U.S.N.R.C. and A.E.O.I. agree to exchange the following types of technical information related to the regulation of safety and environmental impact of designated nuclear energy facilities:

a. Topical reports concerned with technical safety and environmental effects written by or for one of these parties as a basis for, or in support of, regulatory decisions and policies.

b. Significant licensing actions and safety and environmental decisions affecting these facilities.

c. Detailed descriptive documents on the U.S.N.R.C. regulatory process of certain U.S. facilities designated by the A.E.O.I. as being similar to certain facilities being built in Iran and reciprocal documents on these Iranian facilities.

d. Information in the field of reactor safety research which the parties have the right to disclose, either in the possession of one of the parties or available to it, including light water reactor safety information from the technical areas described in Addenda "A" and "B," attached hereto and made a part hereof. Each party will transmit to the other urgent information concerning research results that require early attention in the interests of public safety, along with an indication of significant implications.

e. Reports on operating experience, such as reports on incidents, accidents and shutdowns, and compilations of historical reliability data on components and systems.

f. Regulatory procedures for safety and environmental impact evaluation of these nuclear facilities.

g. Each party will make special efforts to give early advice to the other of important events, such as serious operating incidents and government-directed reactor shutdowns, that are of immediate interest to the other.

I.2 *Collaboration in Development of Regulatory Standards*

The U.S.N.R.C. and the A.E.O.I. further agree to cooperate in the development of regulatory standards for these nuclear facilities.

a. Each party will inform the other of specific subjects on which regulatory standards development work is underway.

b. Copies of regulatory standards required to be used, or proposed for use, by the regulatory organizations of the respective countries will be made available by each party on a timely basis.

I.3 *Cooperation in Safety Research and Development*

The execution of joint programs and projects of safety research and development, or those programs and projects under which activities are divided between the two parties, including the use of test facilities and/or computer programs owned by either party, will be agreed upon on a case-by-case basis. Temporary assignments of personnel by one party in the other party's agency will also be considered on a case-by-case basis.

I.4 *Training and Assignments*

The U.S.N.R.C. will assist the A.E.O.I. in providing certain training and experience for A.E.O.I. safety personnel. Costs of salary, allowances and travel of A.E.O.I. participants will be paid by A.E.O.I. Participation will be permitted within the limitation of available resources. The following are typical of the categories of such training and experience that will be provided:

a. A.E.O.I. inspector accompaniment of U.S.N.R.C. inspectors on reactor and reactor construction inspection visits in the U.S., including extended briefings at U.S.N.R.C. regional inspection offices (anticipated 1-2 persons per year, each visit 1-3 weeks in length).

b. Participation by A.E.O.I. employees in U.S.N.R.C. staff training courses.

c. Assignment of A.E.O.I. employees for 1-2 year periods within the U.S.N.R.C. staff, to work on U.S.N.R.C. staff duties and gain experience (1-2 assignees at a time).

I.5 *Additional Safety Advice*

To the extent that the documents and other information provided by U.S.N.R.C. as described in SCOPE OF THE AGREEMENT, above, are not adequate to meet A.E.O.I. needs for technical advice, the parties will consult on the best means for fulfilling such needs. U.S.N.R.C. will attempt, within the limitations of appropriated resources and legislative authority, to assist A.E.O.I. in meeting these needs. For example, within these limitations, U.S.N.R.C. will attempt to meet requests that come through the IAEA for technical assistance missions to Iran by U.S.N.R.C. safety experts.

II. ADMINISTRATION

II.1   The exchange of information under this Arrangement will be accomplished through letters, reports, and other documents, and by visits and meetings arranged in advance on a case-by-case basis. A meeting will be held annually, or at such other times as mutually agreed, to review the exchange activity, to recommend revisions, and to discuss topics within the scope of the exchange. The time, place, and agenda for such meetings shall be agreed upon in advance. Visits which take place under the arrangement, including their schedules, shall have the prior approval of the administrators.

II.2   An administrator will be designated by each party to coordinate its participation in the overall exchange. The administrators shall be the recipients of all documents transmitted under the exchange, including copies of all letters unless otherwise agreed. Within the terms of the exchange, the administrators shall be responsible for developing the scope of the exchange, including agreement on the designation of the nuclear energy facilities subject to the exchange, and on specific documents and standards to be exchanged. These detailed arrangements are intended to assure, among other things, that the maximum possible exchange providing access to available information from both sides is achieved and maintained.

II.3   The administrators shall determine the number of copies to be provided of the documents exchanged. Each document will be accompanied by an abstract, less than 250 words, describing its scope and content.

II.4   This Arrangement shall have a term of five years; it may be extended further by mutual written agreement, and terminated by either party upon ninety-day notice.

II.5   The application or use of any information exchanged or transferred between the parties under this Arrangement shall be the responsibility of the receiving party, and the transmitting party does not warrant the suitability of such information for any particular use or application.

II.6   Recognizing that some information of the type covered in this Arrangement is not available within the agencies which are parties to this Arrangement, but is available from other agencies of the governments of the parties, each party will assist the other to the maximum extent possible by organizing visits and directing inquiries concerning such information to appropriate agencies of the government concerned. The foregoing shall not constitute a commitment of other agencies to furnish such information or to receive such visitors.

II.7   Nothing contained in this Arrangement shall require either party to take any action which would be inconsistent with its existing laws and regulations. Should any conflict arise between the terms of this Arrangement and those laws and regulations, the parties agree to consult before any action is taken.

II.8   Information exchanged under this Arrangement shall be subject to the patent provisions in Addendum C of this document.

III. EXCHANGE AND USE OF INFORMATION

III.1 *General*

The parties support the widest possible dissemination of information provided or exchanged under this Arrangement, subject both to the need to protect proprietary or other confidential or privileged information as may be exchanged hereunder, and to the provisions of Addendum C.

III.2 *Definitions* (As used in this article)

a. The term "information" means nuclear energy-related regulatory, safety, safeguards, scientific, or technical data, results and any other knowledge intended to be provided or exchanged under this Arrangement;

b. The term "proprietary information" means information which contains trade secrets or commercial or financial information which is privileged or confidential.

c. The term "other confidential or privileged information" means information, other than "proprietary information," which is protected from public disclosure under the laws and regulations of the country providing the information and which has been transmitted and received in confidence.

III.3 *Marking Procedures for Documentary Proprietary Information*

A party receiving documentary proprietary information pursuant to this Arrangement shall respect the privileged nature thereof, provided such proprietary information is clearly marked with the following (or substantially similar) restrictive legend:

"This document contains proprietary information furnished in confidence under an Arrangement dated _____ between the United States Nuclear Regulatory Commission and the Atomic Energy Organization of Iran and shall not be disseminated outside these organizations, their consultants, contractors, and licensees, and concerned departments and agencies of the Government of the United States and the Government of Iran without the prior approval of *(name of submitting party)*. This notice shall be marked on any reproduction hereof, in whole or in part. These limitations shall automatically terminate when this information is disclosed by the owner without restriction."

III.4 *Dissemination of Documentary Proprietary Information*

a. Proprietary information received under this Arrangement may be freely disseminated by the receiving party without prior consent to persons within or employed by the receiving party, and to concerned Government department and Government agencies in the country of the receiving party.

b. In addition, proprietary information may be disseminated without prior consent

(1) to prime or subcontractors or consultants of the receiving party located within the geographical limits of that party's nation, for use only within the scope of their contracts with the receiving party in work relating to the subject matter of the proprietary information; and

(2) to organizations permitted or licensed by the receiving party to construct or operate nuclear production or utilization facilities, or to use nuclear materials and radiation sources, provided that such proprietary information is used only within the terms of the permit or license; and

(3) to the contractors of such licensed organizations for use only in work within the scope of the permit or license.

Provided that any dissemination of proprietary information under (1), (2), and (3), above, shall be pursuant to an agreement of confidentiality.

c. With the prior written consent of the party providing proprietary information under this Arrangement, the receiving party may disseminate such proprietary information more widely than otherwise permitted in the foregoing subsections (a) and (b). The parties shall cooperate in developing procedures for requesting and obtaining approval for such wider dissemination, and each party will grant such approval to the extent permitted by its existing national policies, regulations, and laws.

III.5 Marking Procedures for Other Confidential or Privileged Information of a Documentary Nature

A party receiving under this Arrangement other confidential or privileged information shall respect its confidential nature, provided such information is clearly marked so as to indicate its confidential or privileged nature and is accompanied with a statement indicating

a. the reason or reasons for the requirement of confidentiality;

b. that the information is protected from public disclosure by the Government of the transmitting party; and

c. that the information is submitted under the condition that it be maintained in confidence.

III.6 Dissemination of Other Confidential or Privileged Information of a Documentary Nature

Other confidential or privileged information may be disseminated within the same manner as that set forth in paragraph (III.4). . . .

III.7 Non-documentary Proprietary or Other Confidential or Privileged Information

Non-documentary proprietary or other confidential or privileged information obtained under this Arrangement shall be treated by the parties according to the principles specified in this Article for documentary information; provided, however, that the party communicating such proprietary or other confidential or privileged information provides the same information as in paragraph (III.5) above.

III.8 Consultation

If, for any reason, one of the parties becomes aware that it will be, or may reasonably be expected to become, unable to meet the nondissemination provisions of this Article, it shall immediately inform the other party. The parties shall thereafter consult to define an appropriate course of action.

III.9 Other

Nothing contained in this Arrangement shall preclude a party from using or disseminating information received without restriction by a party from sources outside of this Arrangement.

Signed in Shiraz on the 11th day of April 1977.

M.H. FARZIN
*On behalf of
the Atomic Energy
Organization of Iran*

JAMES R. SHEA
*On behalf of
the United States Nuclear
Regulatory Commission*

ADDENDUM "A"

U.S.N.R.C.-A.E.O.I. Reactor Safety Research Exchange Areas in which the NRC is Performing LWR Safety Research

1. Primary Coolant System Rupture Studies
2. Heavy Section Steel Technology Program
3. LOFT Program
4. Power Burst Facility—Subassembly Testing Program
5. Separate Effects Testing—Loss of Coolant Accident Studies
6. Loss of Coolant Accident Analyses—Analytical Model Development
7. Design Criteria for Piping, Pumps, and Valves
8. Alternate ECCS Studies
9. Core Meltdown Studies
10. Fission Product Release and Transport Studies
11. Probabilistic Studies
12. Zirconium Damage
13. All computer codes applicable to the above at whatever stage of development they may be.*
14. Data from all experiments applicable to the above.*

ADDENDUM "B"

A.E.O.I.-U.S.N.R.C. Safety Research Exchange Areas in which the A.E.O.I. is Performing Research

1. Vibrations induced by Earthquake: Application to Nuclear Reactor Structural Safety Analysis Design

ADDENDUM "C"

Patent Addendum for N.R.C.-A.E.O.I. Arrangement

1. *Definitions*

When used in this Addendum, unless the context otherwise indicates

(i) The term "personnel" means: (a) the employees of a party to

---

* Data and computer codes will be "as is" at the time of the request. N.R.C. or contractor manpower will generally not be available for interpretation of uncompleted work.

this Arrangement and (b) the employees of a contractor of a party to this Arrangement.

(ii) The term "inventing party" means the party of this Arrangement whose personnel have made or conceived an invention or discover during the course of or under the activities covered by the terms of this Arrangement.

2. *Reporting and Allocation of Rights*

(i) Except as otherwise provided in paragraph (ii) hereinafter, if an invention or discovery is made or conceived by the personnel of the inventing party during the course of or under the activities covered by the terms of this Arrangement, or if such invention was made or conceived as a direct result of information acquired by such personnel from the other party, then the inventing party:

(a) agrees to promptly disclose such invention or discovery to the other party;

(b) agrees to transfer and assign to the other party, all right, title, and interest in and to such invention or discovery in the country of the other party subject to the reservation of a nonexclusive, irrevocable, royalty-free license to make, use and sell such invention or discovery in such other country; and

(c) may retain the entire right, title, and interest in and to such invention or discovery in the country of the inventing party and in third countries but shall grant to the other party, upon request of the other party, a nonexclusive, irrevocable, royalty-free license to make, use, and sell such invention or discovery in such country of the inventing party and in such third countries.

(ii) In the event an invention or discovery is made or conceived by the personnel of the inventing party during the course of or under the activities covered by the terms of this Arrangement and such invention was made or conceived while such personnel were assigned to the other party, the inventing party:

(a) agrees to promptly disclose such invention or discovery to the other party;

(b) may retain the entire right, title, and interest in and to such invention or discovery in the country of the inventing party;

(c) shall grant to the other party, upon request of the other party, a nonexclusive, irrevocable, royalty-free license to make, use, and sell such invention or discovery in the country of the inventing party; and

(d) agrees to transfer and assign to the other part all right, title, and interest in and to such invention or discovery in the country of the other party and in third countries subject to the reservation of a nonexclusive, irrevocable, royalty-free license to make, use, and sell such invention or discovery in such other country and in such third countries.

(iii) As employed in this Arrangement, a license to a party to make, use, and sell an invention or discovery shall include the right to have others make, use, and sell such invention or discovery on behalf of such licensed party.

3. *Claims for Compensation*

Each party agrees to waive, and does hereby waive, any and all claims against the other party for compensation, royalty or award as regards any invention, discovery, patent application or patent made or conceived in the course of or under this Arrangement, and agrees to release, and does hereby release, the other party with respect to any and all such claims, including any claims under the provisions of the United States Atomic Energy Act of 1954, as amended.

Sale of Airborne Warning and Control System (AWACS) Aircraft to Iran: Statements before the House Subcommittees on International Security and Europe and the Middle East

Prepared Statement of Alfred L. Atherton, Jr., Assistant Secretary, Bureau of Near Eastern and South Asian Affairs, Department of State

July 29, 1977

Proposed Sale of AWACS to Iran

I am pleased to have the opportunity, together with my colleague from the Department's Bureau of Politico-Military Affairs, the Department of Defense and ACDA, to discuss with you the Administration's proposal to sell to Iran seven E-3A aircraft, the Airborne Warning and Control System or AWACS aircraft. This is a significant sale, and we appreciate your desire to understand fully the reasons behind it. As we have provided substantial information on this proposal, both in written responses to your requests and in informal consultations with Members and your staffs, it is appropriate to limit my remarks to a brief statement of the key issues so that we may devote the greater part of this meeting to a discussion of questions that may be of particular interest to you.

There are three central considerations that bear on this sale:

First, the proposal to sell AWACS to Iran has a lengthy background in that country's search for an effective air defense system. AWACS provides a sound answer to that requirement.

Second, the sale is of significant importance in terms of our overall relationship with Iran.

Third, we want to discuss the sale in the context of the President's arms transfer policy as announced on May 19.

Let me elaborate briefly on each of these considerations.

First, our efforts to assist Iran in the development of an effective air defense system have been an integral element in our defense ties with Iran, dating from World War II. Over the years we have provided Iran, for example, with radar systems, air interceptor fighters and the improved HAWK anti-aircraft missile system. But these programs have been limited in scope; they have not provided the kind of integrated, broad protection that a modern air defense system requires. In the period 1972-73, the Iranian military leadership began to discuss with us the requirements for such a comprehensive system. A number of studies were commissioned. The question has not been whether Iran needs a comprehensive air defense system, but which system is best suited to its requirements. The first Iranian Government request to purchase AWACS aircraft dates from January 1974, three and one-half years ago. During that period there were additional studies and projections of possible air defense arrangements, culminating in the U.S. Air Force study last fall which concluded that seven to nine AWACS and a mix of ground stations would form an effective air defense system. In all of these discussions, the AWACS was considered for the fundamental role it could play as a defensive system—which could for the first time give Iran an effective capability to deter, delay and help repel air attack by an unfriendly power or powers. Like any military system, AWACS can also play additional roles, but it is the air defense capacity which has been the fundamental factor in the U.S. and Iranian studies.

For outsiders who have not traveled there, Iran is a surprisingly large country equal in area to the U.S. east of the Mississippi. The border facing the powerful and sophisticated forces of the U.S.S.R. is 1,200 miles in length. Iran is also a country of harsh geography, a land broken by vast deserts and rugged mountains with little in the way of a developed road or rail network. The job of constructing an air defense system based on those stations with skilled personnel would also place a heavy burden on the nation's trained manpower base and military training facilities.

The answer that we and the Iranian Government believe is the most sensible is the deployment of AWACS aircraft. The use of that aircraft would reduce the need for ground stations from about 40 specially-designed radars to as few as 12 standard models, eliminating many of the most remote radar locations. It would cut the requirement for Iranian personnel from 6,500 trained personnel and 20,000 non-technical workers to about 3,000 trained staff and 6,900 other personnel. The cost of the air defense program by using AWACS would be reduced from an estimated $10-15 billion to about $3 billion. The AWACS component of the latter figure would total about $1.2 billion, compared to over $3 for radars alone in the ground-based system. Some 400 U.S. technicians would be required initially to support the AWACS program.

When this Administration took office, the AWACS sale and this background were presented to the President for his decision, a decision that was clearly deeply rooted in the past and intertwined in the good relations we have valued with Iran over three decades.

This brings me to the second consideration: The importance of the AWACS sale to our relations with Iran. I do not think that it can be disputed that a strong and secure Iran, sharing our objectives of global peace, stability and economic well-being, is essential to the peace and continued progress of the states of the Persian Gulf region and to our own interests there. It is only necessary to reflect for a moment on the potential consequences if there were in this strategic area a weak, unstable regime or one hostile to our interests.

Negotiating from a position of strength and confidence, the Iranian Government in 1975 was able to resolve its differences with Iraq and Iran now enjoys stable and for the most part satisfactory relations with all of its neighbors. But the history of the region underscores the need to maintain a vigilant defense. Iran, invaded and occupied by Soviet forces within the memory of many of its citizens, highly vulnerable to foreign attack against the oil-producing and refining installations at the head of the Persian Gulf and responsible for the security of its oil exports, which must transit the narrow Hormuz Straits choke point, plainly requires—and is determined to create—a modern and effective defense force.

In addition to the substantial dollar and manpower savings that AWACS can make possible, the improvement in Iran's air defense and Iranian confidence in the security of its borders also serve important U.S. interests. The resources and energies of the nation can be directed toward the priority task of internal development.

A peaceful region, concentrating on its own modernization, assures the continuing flow of Persian Gulf oil to our friends in Europe, Japan, Israel and to our own ports. If we refuse to provide this important component, Iranian air defense would have serious deficiencies and the fundamental problem would remain to be solved.

This leads to the last point, the relationship of this sale to the President's policy on conventional arms transfers. I would like to ask Mr. Gelb, Director of the Bureau of Politico-Military Affairs, to speak to that point.

My colleagues and I will be pleased to respond to your questions on any aspect of this proposal.

Statement of Hon. Leslie Gelb, Director, Bureau of Politico-Military Affairs, Department of State

President's Arms Transfer Policy

The President, as you know, has recently enunciated a new arms transfer policy that states that henceforth arms transfer will be treated as an exceptional instrument of foreign policy to be used only when it is clearly demonstrated that our national security interests are involved.

This statement of policy is an attempt to balance his desire for restraint, consistent with longstanding congressional intent to bring about reductions, with a continuing need to use arms transfers to bolster our own security and the security interests of our friends and allies.

It is not an easy task to balance these interests, especially when one is faced with particular cases; one must make judgments. The President's guidelines are intended to create a different presumption about arms sales, to put the burden of proof henceforth on those who want to authorize sales, rather than those who are opposing them.

Six Guidelines of the Arms Transfer Policy

There are six guidelines that the President has publicly put forward. One deals with his intention to make reductions in arms transfers generally, beginning in the next fiscal year.

The second guideline relates to the transfer of advanced technology. The third to weapon systems significantly modified or produced solely for purposes of export. The fourth, to place limits on coproduction activities. The fifth, to tighten up procedures on retransfers of armaments, and the sixth, to limit promotional activities by the U.S. Government.

The second of these guidelines pertains specifically to the issue at hand today, our proposed sale of the AWACS to Iran. Let me read that guideline and explain the Presidential determination on that guideline in this instance.

The guideline states that:

The United States will not be the first supplier to introduce into a region newly developed advanced weapon systems which could create a new or significantly higher combat capability.

Also, any commitment for sale or coproduction of such weapons is prohibited until they are operationally deployed with U.S. forces, thus removing the incentive to promote foreign sales in an effort to lower unit costs for defense procurement.

There are two sentences here that apply to the AWACS. The first is that we will not be the first supplier to introduce a new level of technology, a new higher combat capability into a region. The President has determined that this case, the proposed sale of the AWACS to Iran, is an exception to this provision of that guideline.

We are not contending that the AWACS does not represent a new higher level of combat capability. It does. I don't think there is much question about that. We could have come forward and argued that since it is basically a defensive system, the combat capability, overall, is not affected; but the fact of the matter is, AWACS does increase Iran's combat capability.

The President has determined, for the reason Mr. Atherton has stated, that he will make an exception in this instance.

AWACS Operationally Deployed in U.S. Forces

The second provision—which says that we will not commit a weapon for sale until it has been operationally deployed with U.S. forces—is met in our judgment, in this particular case. We have two AWACS at Tinker Air Force Base. We are defining operationally deployed with U.S. forces, for purposes of implementing this guideline, as the use of production models rather than prototypes, or R.&D. models, by U.S. forces. They are, for our purposes, operationally deployed at that time.

White House Statement upon the Meeting of President Carter and the Shah of Iran

November 15, 1977

. . . The President reaffirmed to His Majesty that he fully supports the special relationship which the two countries have developed over the last 30 years and gave his personal commitment to strengthen further our ties. The President emphasized the broad mutuality of our interests in the region and globally and expressed appreciation for the support which Iran has extended in achieving our shared objectives. The President reiterated the importance that he attaches to a strong, stable, and progressive Iran under the leadership of His Imperial Majesty. To that end, he emphasized that it remains the policy of the United States to cooperate with Iran in its economic and social development programs and in continuing to help meet Iran's security needs.

The President and His Majesty discussed in some detail the current situation in the Middle East. The President reviewed the diplomatic efforts the United States is making to bring about a reconvening of the Middle East Peace Conference in Geneva. The President noted that Iran has a unique position in the area in that it has good ties with all the countries involved and that Iran's economic assistance to several of these countries and its trade with them were valuable contributions to the stability of the area. The President welcomed the support Iran has extended for our diplomatic efforts to achieve peace in the area.They also discussed developments in the Middle East region as a whole and such matters of mutual interest as developments in Africa and South Asia and our discussions with the Soviet Union on SALT II and the Indian Ocean.

The President expressed his disappointment that it has been necessary to postpone his visit to Iran but reiterated his desire to make the trip as soon as possible. The President emphasized his determination to obtain the comprehensive national energy program, which is currently before Congress. His Majesty expressed his support for the President's effort. They gave special attention to the needs to develop alternative energy sources, including solar, and agreed that both countries would work closely together in this area. They agreed that effective energy conservation programs are essential to help meet future world energy needs as oil supplies dwindle. In this discussion, they exchanged views on how to maintain a healthy world economy. The President emphasized the very great importance to the international community of maintaining world oil price stability and expressed his strong hope that there would be no oil price increase over the coming year. He expressed his pleasure at His Imperial Majesty's understanding of this issue.

The President also expressed his appreciation for the strong support we have received from Iran on nuclear nonproliferation matters.

His Majesty stated that he looks forward to receiving the President in the near future in Tehran.

Communiqué of the United States-Iran Joint Commission

February 28, 1978

The U.S.-Iran Joint Commission for Economic Cooperation held its fourth session in Washington on February 28, 1978. The Delegation of the United States was headed by the Honorable Cyrus Vance, Secretary of State, and the Iranian Delegation was led by H.E. Mohammed Yeganeh, Minister of Economic Affairs and Finance. High officials of both governments also took part in the discussion.

During his visit to Washington, Minister Yeganeh also met with Secretary of the Treasury Michael Blumenthal and other U.S. officials for discussions on a broad range of economic and other issues of mutual interest.

Minister Yeganeh and Secretary Vance reviewed the current international economic situation and discussed bilateral matters in the spirit of mutual respect and understanding that has long characterized U.S.-Iranian relations. The U.S. side noted with satisfaction Iran's recent efforts to apply a freeze on oil prices during 1978, and assured Iran of the U.S. determination to meet its long-term energy needs by promoting conservation and the development of alternate sources of energy, and also to take effective measures in curbing inflation and improving the international monetary situation.

The two sides emphasized the importance of carrying out the recommendations of the Conference on International Economic Cooperation (CIEC) and agreed to pursue the positive dialogue in the United Nations overview mechanism established by United Nations General Assembly Resolution 32/174 of December 1977.

The U.S. side expressed its appreciation for Iran's efforts in the Economic and Social Council of the United Nations to conclude an international agreement on illicit payments. The two sides explored possibilities for further cooperation towards this end.

The Joint Commission meeting followed several days of preparatory meetings by its five standing joint committees, each of which had prepared detailed proposals for the full Commission's consideration. The two sides reviewed the status of progress in the programs approved at the last Joint Commission meeting in Tehran in August 1976, and considered the recommendations for cooperation in new areas offered by the committees. The Commission concluded that there is a vast scope for cooperation between Iran and the United States for their mutual benefit.

Economy and Finance. Both sides reaffirmed their belief that the potential for expansion of commercial relations between the two countries is very great. They registered their determination to work towards that end and discussed ways of doing so. In this connection the Iranian Delegation expressed Iran's interest in being made eligible for the U.S. Generalized System of Preferences, which it considers important for the development of future trade relations between the two countries.

The Commission agreed that cooperation in development of various fields of industries, such as chemical, pharmaceutical, engineering, basic metals, petrochemicals, transportation equipment, electronics, and other industries in Iran will be greatly facilitated if it involved capital participation as well as financing, transfer of technology and export financing.

Both sides noted with pleasure the broad range of cooperative activities envisaged in the field of health, including the establishment of the Imperial Medical Center of Iran. The Commission expressed particular satisfaction that the two countries had successfully cooperated in the establishment of the Food and Drug Administration (FDA) in Iran.

Housing. The Commission noted the priority attached by Iran to the development of middle and low income housing, and agreed that there are significant opportunities for cooperation in this area.

Transportation. The Commission discussed cooperation of the two countries in the field of transportation, including construction of toll roads in Iran and expressed satisfaction at the conclusion in June 1977 of a technical service agreement between the U.S. Federal Aviation Administration and the Iranian Civil Aviation Organization to upgrade the air traffic control system of Iran.

Energy. The two sides expressed satisfaction over the recent progress towards conclusion of a bilateral Agreement for the Peaceful Uses of Nuclear Energy, which should be signed in the near future. It is anticipated that the final accord will open an era for wide collaboration under a Most Favored Nation basis, and in accordance with International Atomic [Energy] Agency (IAEA) safeguards and the objectives of the Non-Proliferation Treaty (NPT) for the participation of the United States in the Iranian nuclear power program.

The Commission reviewed the recent cooperation between the two countries in the training of Iranian nuclear power engineers and discussed possible future programs for the establishment of an export refinery in Iran and exchange of information in respect to enhanced oil and gas recovery technology, as well as uranium exploration and solar energy training and application.

Agriculture. The Commission agreed to encourage further cooperation between the private sectors of the two countries in agriculture.

Both delegations expressed satisfaction with the current and proposed training and consultancy programs in extension, soya and cotton production, forestry, veterinary services, plant quarantine and data collection.

Manpower and Technical Cooperation. The Commission reviewed cooperation between the two countries in the field of manpower and technical cooperation and noted with satisfaction the completion of joint activities in vocational training, manpower statistics, audio-visual techniques, on-the-job training and expatriate employ-. ment practices.

Experts of the two sides will meet in Iran in the near future to initiate several cooperative programs in technical education, productivity improvement, data processing and vocational training.

Science, Technology and Education. The Commission noted progress achieved since the August 1976 meeting in Tehran, particularly in the fields of education, oceanography, meteorology, remote sensing application and environment. Proposals for future cooperation in educational technology, geological research, earthquake effects mitigation, and lands sciences and establishment of links between research laboratories and industry were welcomed by both delegations.

HUMAN RIGHTS TO THE FORE

Statement by Charles W. Naas, Director of the Office of Iranian Affairs, Made before the Subcommittee on International Organizations of the House International Relations Committee

October 26, 1977

I welcome the opportunity to appear before the subcommittee this morning. In his testimony last year Assistant Secretary Atherton sketched out the historical, economic, cultural, and political context within which we view the subject of human rights in Iran. I will not repeat the important points Mr. Atherton made. They are now part of the official record. However, my comments today should be seen in that context.

Mr. Butler has testified about the important changes made in the military court system which would improve substantially due process protection of the individuals who come into that system because of their involvement, or suspected involvement, in crimes against state security.

Briefly, changes in the law provide that: (1) persons arrested must be arraigned or released within 24 hours; (2) the defendant may select a civilian lawyer of his own choice; (3) the defense counsel will be given adequate time to prepare his brief; and (4) except in unusual circumstances, trials will be open to the public.

The Iranian Parliament approved the amendments in August 1977. Implementing regulations have now been prepared, and the law will become effective November 7. The revisions are partly retroactive in the sense that they will apply to individuals who were arrested but not tried before enactment of the legislation. During the summer a law was passed which provides penal measures—6 months to a year and heavy fines—for discrimination on grounds of race, creed, or sex.

Finally a bill is presently before the Iranian Parliament which is designed to streamline the civilian court system and improve the administration of justice.

A number of developments concerning prisoners should be placed on the record in this status report. Late last year BBC was permitted access to one of the prisons to film interviews with some security prisoners. At about the same time, a Belgian journalist of Le Soir asked to interview, by name, a number of prisoners whom opponents of the regime in Europe had claimed were crippled by torture or in fact executed. He was given access to these prisoners for interview and permitted to photograph them to insure their identity. All of the prisoners were in good health.

In April of this year, a public trial was held for a number of prisoners who had been arrested in December 1976 for Communist activity. This was the first public trial of security prisoners in 5 years, and the Iranian press gave extensive coverage to the event. A number of foreign observers, including an American, were present.

The total number of prisoners who had been found guilty of state security crimes has been substantially reduced since the turn of the year by the government's amnesty program. An additional 131 are to be released today—the birthday of His Imperial Majesty—thus bringing the total held to around 2,200, down from the 3,700 held at one point in 1976.

Earlier this year the Iranian Government requested the International Committee of the Red Cross (ICRC) to carry out a thorough survey of Iran's penal institutions and to report to the Government of Iran on what improvements should be instituted. This action is quite unusual and represented, in part, the government's desire to put to rest the allegations about prison conditions which have been made in Europe and the United States. Such reports are, according to ICRC practice, confidential and for the use only of the government which has requested the study. The ICRC just recently completed a second visit to follow up the earlier report. . . .

A few months ago, the Shah of Iran publicly commented that he had previously ordered the ending of the use of torture. We have had no reports of the use of inhumane treatment against prisoners this year.

I will address briefly your question about freedom of opinion and expression, including freedom of the press. Foreign newspapers and magazines containing criticism of the Government of Iran have long circulated freely in Iran. Increasing relaxation with respect to internal criticism is clearly visible. The evidence of this more relaxed attitude is best exemplified by two open letters—one to the Shah and the other to the Prime Minister— articulating liberal aspirations. The letter to the Shah was signed by senior members of the former National Front. The second letter, which called for increased intellectual freedom and the reestablishment of the Writers Guild, was addressed to the Prime Minister by 40 intellectuals. . . .

Iran is a one party state. Within the Rastakhiz Party there is considerable opportunity for political debate and criticism of governmental performance. A major stated goal of this relatively new organization is to expand further such opportunities.

Let us turn briefly to organized labor. The Iranian Workers Organization represents 17 federations, which in turn are composed of 750 unions having about 600,000 members. Strikes are illegal, but a substantial number of wildcat walkouts do occur.

Progress in the field of women's rights continues, although not without the opposition of conservative forces. Of the 268 seats in the lower body (the Majlis) of Parliament, 21 are held by women, and two women are in the Senate which has 60 members. The employment of women is growing, but slowly; by next year it is estimated that 14 percent of all women will be in the labor force. Also, by next year literacy among women will be in the 45-50 percent range. . . .

As I said earlier, these actions and developments, taken cumulatively, reinforce the gratifying trend which we noted last year. We shall watch developments with interest.

A Report by the United States State Department on Human Rights Practices in Iran (in Accordance with Sections of the Foreign Assistance Act of 1961, as Amended) to the Senate Committee on Foreign Relations and the House Committee on International Relations

February 3, 1978

For the last three decades Iran has been engaged in a forced pace modernization of its economy and social system. During this period the Iranian Government has faced major internal and external challenges. Twice in this century, Iran has been partially occupied by the Soviet Union, whose objectives continue to be of major concern to the Iranian Government. Internally, Iran has faced strong opposition to its modernization and reform programs—from both the entrenched landowners and conservative religious leaders and from the far left. Following a near takeover of the government by the communist Tudeh Party in 1953, the advocacy of communism was made illegal. In more recent years, small groups of extreme rightist and leftist terrorists, who have received substantial foreign support and training, have murdered a number of Iranian officials and six Americans.

Since World War II, Iran has given high priority to economic development, providing such human needs as health care, social services, housing and education, and to the national integration of an ethnically and linguistically diverse population. Political power increasingly was concentrated in the monarchy. The government has dealt firmly—and at times harshly—with persons from both left and right charged with committing acts against state security, or believed to constitute a serious political threat. Iran has relied on a military court system separate from the normal civilian court system when dealing with persons suspected of crimes against state security. Although procedures of this court have not adequately protected due process, some potentially significant improvements in this system were instituted during the past year.

1. *Respect for the Integrity of the Person, Including Freedom from:*

a. *Torture*

The Iranian Penal Code prohibits torture and provides severe penalties for violators. While the Government of Iran has not said so publicly, there are reliable reports that several relatively low-ranking officials have been tried and convicted for violations of the code. The Shah has publicly stated that torture is not now practiced.

The 1976 report of Amnesty International offered documentation on specific cases of alleged torture going as far back as the 1960s. Amnesty's 1977 report does not refer to any cases of torture. The International League for Human Rights 1976-77 annual review mentions torture. In Congressional testimony of October 26, 1977, the Chairman of the Executive Committee of the International Commission of Jurists (ICJ) stated that the ICJ was not aware of any case of torture in Iran for at least the previous ten to eleven months. The Department of State itself has received in recent months significantly fewer allegations of torture in Iran than was the case in previous years and does not believe torture has been used recently.

b. *Cruel, Inhuman or Degrading Treatment or Punishment*

Individual complaints as well as the reports of various international human rights organizations allege that prison conditions and the treatment of prisoners continue to be inadequate. The Government of Iran is attempting to improve prison conditions and treatment of prisoners. In 1977, at the initiative of the Iranian Government, the International Committee of the Red Cross twice inspected Iranian prisons. The U.S. Government has not seen the ICRC's reports of these inspections inasmuch as they are confidential and only for the use of the government concerned. Several foreign journalists also visited prisons within the last year. We believe the Iranian Government is committed to prison reform and that prison conditions have indeed improved.

c. *Arbitrary Arrest or Imprisonment*

Cases of arbitrary arrest and imprisonment have occurred. In 1976, it was our estimate that the number of state security prisoners ranged between 3,300-3,700. During 1977, however, a series of amnesties and the normal completion of prison terms reduced the total to about 2,200, of which the large majority were in jail for crimes involving violence or conspiracy to commit violence.

Iranian law combines in one organization—SAVAK (The State Organization for Security and Intelligence)—the duties of both the police and the examining magistrate. In some cases, SAVAK has appeared to use its authority to arrest without a warrant anyone suspected of involvement in a crime against state security. Pursuant to the French system, from which the procedure was copied, SAVAK then has carried out an initial investigation and determined initial charges. Some individuals have been held up to several months while investigations were being conducted. During initial detention, counsel has not been provided for the detainee, and contact with family and friends has been prohibited or severely restricted.

Amnesty International and the ICJ have criticized the combining in SAVAK of police and magistrate duties and the holding of prisoners for lengthy periods, sometimes incommunicado, without formal charging. An ICJ official representative presented to the Shah specific proposals for separating the police and magistrate functions and Amnesty

International has also discussed the possibility of change with the government.

We also believe that the separation of these two functions would improve due process procedures.

The Code of Military Procedures section dealing with bail and initial charges against detainees has been changed by an amendment, which went into effect in December 1977. The key portion of the wording requires that a detainee "be questioned within 24 hours after he is brought before the examining magistrate who shall thereupon issue an appropriate warrant, be it a warrant for the release of the accused on bail or for his imprisonment." The ICJ representative questioned whether this wording will offer sufficient protection to an individual in view of possible delay before the arrested person is brought before the magistrate.

d. Denial of Fair Public Trial

Civil and criminal cases, except for the relatively few having to do with state security, are tried in the civilian court system in which full guarantees of civil rights exist. In its 1976 report, the ICJ examined this regular judicial system and found it generally satisfactory. Administrative reforms enacted in the summer of 1977 have significantly speeded up trials in these civilian courts. Students and others brought to trial in civilian criminal courts have come before a judge within four days to three weeks time, depending on the complexity of the case. This is a significant improvement over conditions which pertained through most of the 1970s.

Those accused of a crime related to state security, as defined in Iranian law, are tried before Iranian military courts and under the relevant legal code for these courts. Between 1973 and 1977 most of the state security were *in camera*, and the system appears to have contained important due process deficiencies.

Potentially significant amendments to the military court code came into effect in December 1977. Now "civilian defendants may make their choice among civilian defense attorneys" (Article 182). The same article grants "complete" freedom to the defense counsel. Under Article 184, counsel is now granted "up to 15 days" (previously, five days) to study the case prior to trial. Article 192 has been changed so that "military tribunals shall always hold public sessions unless, in exceptional cases where a public session may be deemed to be against the public order, national interest or accepted moral standards." In the latter cases, the court will make a decision on the basis of the prosecutor's request for trial *in camera*. Article 203 previously declared that "in the pronouncement of the verdict, the judges are free subject to the provisions of law." The new wording says judges "subject to provisions of law and with due regard to the character of the defendant will pronounce their verdict in complete liberty and independence."

The ICJ representative has stated that his organization views these amendments with "cautious optimism," while other non-governmental organizations have questioned the adequacy of the changes. The coming months should demonstrate the real significance of the changes and the extent to which important due process deficiencies have been removed.

e. *Invasion of the Home*

Iran's constitutional law of 1907 states "Everyone's house and dwelling is protected and safeguarded. No one may enter forcibly into any dwelling except by order of and in conformity with the law." In normal practice, police officials apply to local magistrates for a warrant when they wish to search a home. Security police have acted in some instances without such a warrant.

2. *Governmental Policies Relating to the Fulfillment of Such Vital Needs as Food, Shelter, Health Care and Education*

Meeting the economic and social needs of Iranians, particularly the poor, has been emphasized by the government for nearly two decades, especially since the Shah gained secure control of the government in the early 1960s and instituted major economic and social development plans and the reform program known as the Shah-People Revolution.

Iran has had five-year development plans since the late 1940s, but it has been only since the 1973 increase in oil prices that the government has had significant financial resources to implement its plans. Roughly two-thirds of the Iranian Government's total spending in the period 1973-78 can be classified as outlay for economic development and social welfare programs. Per capita income is now about $2,000. The Shah-People Revolution emphasizes the fulfillment of human needs. A major land distribution and reform program, initiated in the early 1960s, ended Iran's traditional feudalism and beneficially affected at least a third of the population directly and perhaps another 30 percent indirectly. An early reform involved a profit-sharing scheme for industrial workers. A more recent addition to the program provides a stock divestiture system to pass 49 percent of the ownership of certain industries to workers and farmers. A literacy corps has helped over two million Iranians to read and write. A similar program related to health has helped move the services of doctors and nurses out into rural areas. During the past 15 years, life expectancy has increased from 41 to 53 years. An extension and development corps gives basic technical advice to the rural poor. Houses of Equity have been formed in many villages to provide prompt court service in minor cases covering a wide range of subjects.

3. *Respect for Civil and Political Liberties, Including:*

a. *Freedom of Thought, Speech, Press, Religion, and Assembly*

Iranian law prohibits the advocacy of communism, attacks on the monarchy or the basic tenets of the political system, and advocacy of violence. The interpretations given at any particular time by the authorities as to what constitute violations of these prohibitions have on some instances limited freedom of speech, press and assembly.

Foreign publications of many viewpoints, including some sharply critical of Iran and the Shah, are widely sold. Domestic newspapers and journals (radio and TV are government-owned) are bound by the restrictions noted above and receive governmental guidance on how to treat what the government regards as sensitive issues—particularly foreign policy and security matters. Government domestic policy and program implementation are discussed and criticized in the local media.

In a March 1976 report on Iran, an ICJ representative concluded that there are limitations on freedom of the press and freedom of speech resulting from the penalties which have been imposed for expression of dissent. In a brief comment in its November 1976 report, Amnesty International referred to "the suppression of political opposition" and an "atmosphere of fear."

The PEN American Center has protested the government of Iran's alleged mistreatment of some writers and urged the re-activation of the Writers Association of Iran. So far, the government has not permitted the re-establishment of the Writers Association.

According to law, labor in Iran is free to organize. The Iranian Workers Organization, a governmentally controlled union, represents 17 federations which in turn are composed of 750 unions having about 600,000 members. Strikes are illegal, but a substantial number of wildcat walkouts do occur.

The Shiah sect of Islam predominates in Iran, but the country is proud and supportive of its long history of religious tolerance which permits religious minorities to practice their faith openly and participate fully in civil life.

Restrictions on the right of assembly are applied to persons seen by the Iranian authorities as advocating subversion, violence or communist doctrines. Restrictions have been particularly tight on university campuses and have led periodically to clashes between security forces and students and other dissidents. In November 1977, several gatherings involving students and others expressing opposition to the political system or complaining about alleged human rights violations were forcibly disbanded by the police. Some injuries resulted from this police action. About 200 individuals were arrested, but most were later released; fewer than 100 have been charged. It is expected that they will be tried for misdemeanors before the civil court system.

In January 1978, a clash took place in Qom between local police and demonstrators. The demonstrators were objecting to a newspaper attack on a conservative religious leader, living in exile in Iraq, on the anniversary of the land reform and liberalization of women's rights carried out by the Shah's government 15 years before. After unsuccessful police efforts to halt the protest march, shots were fired and up to 14 people were killed.

b. *Freedom of Movement within the Country, Foreign Travel and Emigration*

Iranians enjoy extensive freedom of movement within Iran and abroad. The government has denied passports to some individuals who the government believes will engage in activities abroad detrimental to the country. The provision, rooted in Islamic law, that a wife must have her husband's permission to travel abroad and a child under 18 must have his father's permission can in effect also restrict freedom of travel. These latter restrictions have been eased over the past year.

Iranian law does not provide for emigration. However, Iranians who acquire citizenship in another country without previously informing the Government of Iran may apply to the government for recognition of their new citizenship status. Approval of such applications is normally extended. Also, Iranian citizens over 25 years old who have completed their military obligations may submit a renunciation of citizenship, which requires the approval of the Council of Ministers.

c. *Freedom to Participate in the Political Process*

Iran is a constitutional monarchy with a lower legislative body and a senate. The lower house and half the senate are elected under full adult suffrage. The other half of the senate are chosen by the Shah. Power and decision-making are concentrated around the Shah.

Two years ago one political party (Resurgence), which by decree encompasses all citizens, was established. This is the only political party permitted to operate in Iran. The Government's stated objective is to develop a broad political movement to support its development and modernization programs. Within the new party, there is critical debate, particularly on local bread-and-butter issues. Royal commissions and inspectorates, which have been increasingly active in recent months, directly criticize government performance—often on TV—and the press is attentive to problems of waste and corruption. Over the past 18 months, decentralization has begun to pass modest decision-making and resource—allocating power to provincial and local government units. Elected provincial councils comment frequently on local administrative shortcomings.

Some Iranians overseas, including students, regularly criticize the Iranian political system, including the limitations on political expression. Private letters objecting to specific aspects of the Iranian governmental system have been freely circulated in Iran recently. Amnesty International has objected to the creation of a one-party system.

4. *Government Attitude and Record Regarding International and Non-Governmental Investigation of Alleged Violations of Human Rights*

Until 1975 Amnesty International was the principal outside organization monitoring Iran's human rights practices. The Government of Iran, which was very irritated by Amnesty's criticisms of human rights conditions in Iran, particularly its allegation that there were 100,000 political prisoners, would not cooperate with that organization. During 1977, however, the Shah met privately with the Secretary General of Amnesty International and contacts with Amnesty have been maintained at other levels.

On the other hand, the Government of Iran has been more forthcoming in dealing with the International Commission of Jurists. In 1975 government officials cooperated extensively with ICJ officials who were preparing a report on human rights in Iran which was published in 1976. The Chairman of the Executive Committee of the International Commission of Jurists had a long audience with the Shah in 1977, during which a number of amendments to the military penal code were discussed, many of which were enacted into legislation later in the year.

The Iranian Government invited the International Committee of the Red Cross to carry out two inspections of Iranian prisons. We do not know of any Iranian reply so far to the International League of Human Rights 1976-77 report. Finally, prison visits and interviews with prisoners by foreign journalists were arranged during 1977.

UNITED STATES REACTS TO IRANIAN UNREST

Official United States Press Statements

Presidential News Conference
[EXCERPT]

October 10, 1978

Q: I'd like to ask you about Iran. How do we view the situation involving the Shah there now? Is he secure? How important is it to U.S. interests that the Shah remain in power? And what, if anything, can the U.S. Government do to keep him in power?

President Carter: The strategic importance to our country—I think to the entire Western world—of a good relationship with a strong and independent Iran is crucial. We have historic friendships with Iran. I think they are a great stabilizing force in their part of the world. They are a very important trade partner. They've acted very responsibly.

My own belief is that the Shah has moved aggressively to establish democratic principles in Iran and to have a progressive attitude toward social questions, social problems. This has been the source of much of the opposition to him in Iran.

We have no inclination to try to decide the internal affairs of Iran. My own hopes have been that there could be peace there, an end to bloodshed, and an orderly transformation into more progressive social arrangements and also increased democratization of the government itself which I believe the Shah also espouses. He may not be moving fast enough for some; he may be moving too fast for others. I don't want to get involved in the specifics.

News Conference Held by Secretary of State Vance

[EXCERPTS]

November 3, 1978

Q: Last night on public television your Iran desk officer, Henry Precht, appeared, and he reported that there were quiet talks going on between the Shah and some of the moderate opposition leaders to achieve a compromise, and that these talks involve political and economic issues. I wonder what you could tell us about those talks and what the prospects are that they might achieve some sort of stability there?

Secretary Vance: Let me say a few words about Iran and the situation in Iran, and then I will speak briefly to your question.

Iran over the past decade has made a very important contribution to the stability of the Middle East. The United States has worked very closely with the Shah, and Iran is a close and valued ally.

Iran has recently reached a stage in its development where the Shah has believed it is essential to broaden participation in the political life of Iran, and we have supported this plan of liberalization.

The continuing violence and the strikes in Iran are a serious problem for the government, and we fully support the efforts of the Shah to restore order while continuing his program of liberalization. And we hope that everyone in Iran will recognize that continuing turmoil and destruction serve no one's interest.

As to the specific question that you raise, this is an internal question as to what the exact nature of the discussions are and a question which I think should be addressed by the Iranians rather than by the United States.

Q: Could you explain how the United States believes that it will be possible for you, at one and the same time, to restore order and continue liberalization?

Secretary Vance: I think that they are not at all inconsistent. I think that law and order can be restored. I think at the same time one can continue along the course which the Shah has charted for himself and for his nation. As you know, he has set forth a plan which would lead to elections in the year 1979; and there is no inconsistency in reestablishing stability within the nation and moving on subsequently to the holding of elections according to his liberalization plan.

Presidential Interview with Bill Moyers of the Public Broadcasting Company

[EXCERPTS]

November 13, 1978

Q: Let me apply the multiple choice difficult options equation to a couple of other contemporary and very live issues. One is Iran. What are the options facing you there?

President Carter: We look on the Shah, as you know, as a friend, a loyal ally, and the good relationship that Iran has had and has now with ourselves and with the other democracies in the world, the Western powers, as being very constructive and valuable. Also, having a strong and independent Iran in that area is a very stabilizing factor, and we would hate to see it disrupted by violence and the government fall with an unpredictable result. The Shah has been primarily criticized within Iran because he has tried to democratize the country and because he's instituted social reforms in a very rapid fashion.

Some of his domestic adversaries either disagree with the way he's done it, or think he hasn't moved fast enough, or too fast, and deplore his breaking of ancient religious and social customs, as Iran has become modern.

Q: But he was also criticized for running a police state—political prisoners—

President Carter: That's exactly right. I think the Shah has had that criticism, sometimes perhaps justified—I don't know the details of it. But I think there's no doubt that Iran has made great social progress and has moved toward a freer expression of people. Even in recent months, for instance, the Shah has authorized or directed, I guess, the Parliament to have all of its deliberations open and televised, something that we don't even do in our country here.

Q: You think this is all too late?

President Carter: I hope not. I don't know what will come eventually. I would hope that a coalition government could be formed rapidly.

At the present time, there's a quasimilitary government. The Shah has reconfirmed his commitment to have open and democratic elections, maybe within 6 months, or 8 months. I hope that would be possible.

Our inclination is for the Iranian people to have a clear expression of their own views and to have a government intact in Iran that accurately expresses a majority view in Iran.

Q: But can we do anything to encourage that, or are our hands tied?

President Carter: No, we don't try to interfere in the internal affairs of Iran.

Q: We did put the Shah in, but you're saying we can't keep him in.

President Carter: I think that's a decision to be made by the people of that country.

Question-and-Answer Session at a Breakfast with Members of the White House Correspondents Association

[EXCERPTS]

December 7, 1978

Q: Mr. President, I was going to ask you about the Shah. Do you think he could survive now, and how?

President Carter: I don't know. I hope so. This is something that is in the hands of the people of Iran. We have never had any intention and don't have any intention of trying to intercede in the internal political affairs of Iran.

We primarily want an absence of violence and bloodshed, and stability. We personally prefer that the Shah maintain a major role in the government, but that's a decision for the Iranian people to make.

Q: Do you think there's still any chance that he'll form a civilian coalition government?

President Carter: I think he has offered that publicly. And as you know, yesterday, I believe, he released two of his top political opponents. And I think, I would guess, surmise, that one of the reasons for those political leaders being released was to encourage them and their followers to join in some form of coalition government. That's the Shah's desire that's expressed to me personally by him and through his own Ambassador here, and I take him at his word.

The President's News Conference

[EXCERPTS]

December 12, 1978

Q: Mr. President, what will be the domestic and international effect if the Shah fails to maintain power in Iran?

President Carter: I fully expect the Shah to maintain power in Iran and for the present problems in Iran to be resolved. Although there have been certainly deplorable instances of bloodshed which we would certainly want to avoid, or see avoided, I think the predictions of doom and disaster that came from some sources have certainly not been realized at all. The Shah has our support and he also has our confidence.

We have no intention of interfering in the internal affairs of Iran, and we have no intention of permitting others to interfere in the internal affairs of Iran. The difficult situation there has been exacerbated by uncontrolled statements made from foreign nations that encourage bloodbaths and violence. This is something that really is deplorable and, I would hope, would cease after this holy season passes.

I think it's good to point out that the Iranian people for 2,500 years, perhaps as long as almost any nation on Earth, have had the ability for stable self-government. There have been changes in the government, yes, sometimes violence, but they have a history of an ability to govern themselves. And because of that and other factors which I've just described, I think the situation in Iran will be resolved successfully.

9

The Shah Falls: Iran Confronts America

In January 1979 the Shah left Iran for what was euphemistically called an extended rest. He never returned. His departure marked the end of a U.S. policy of more than thirty years.

For what proved to be a brief interim, the U.S. looked for a new modus vivendi *with the Iranian authorities. After supporting the short-lived Bakhtiar government, President Carter expressed hope for cooperation with the Ayatollah Khomeini after that dour yet charismatic cleric became the new leader of Iran. Press statements illustrating these stances are to be found in this last chapter.*

As the world now knows well, however, friendly relations with the new Iranian government were not to be. Khomeini claimed that the United States was "the great Satan," whose influence on Iran had corrupted its Islamic institutions. Although Khomeini was not an official of the new Iranian government, he appeared to be the individual with the ultimate power of decision.

Whether Khomeini gave the signal for the seizure of the U.S. hostages, or whether it was the idea of the militant "students" who carried it out, is a question that remains to be settled. Certainly there were times when the militants appeared to be under no one's control, not even Khomeini's, although they always paid him ostentatious deference. In any event, the seizure of the hostages became the axis around which all U.S.-Iranian relations revolved.

In the beginning, President Carter publicly ruled out the use of force to obtain the release of the hostages. He made it clear that the

*United States would not submit to the militants' demands for the return
of the Shah and his wealth to Iran. When the militants, in their turn,
were supported by the Iranian government, President Carter blocked
Iranian assets in the U.S. At the United Nations, the U.S. demanded
sanctions against Iran. Additionally, the U.S. took Iran to the World
Court, where American attorneys obtained a judgment ordering Iran to
release the hostages. None of these measures had any considerable
practical result. Under U.N. sponsorship a group of distinguished
lawyers appeared to have arranged for the release of the hostages, only to
have the plans collapse. One reason for successive failures was the
apparent lack of a real authority with power to act within the structure
of the Iranian government.*

*Frustrated beyond endurance, the United States finally launched a
military strike to rescue the hostages. The attempt failed, partly due to
mechanical failures, partly to planning difficulties, and partly to bad
luck. Statements regarding this attempt are printed in the material
which follows.*

*At this writing the hostages are still in captivity. The shape which
U.S. relations will assume with the new Iran is unknown.*

THE UNITED STATES SEARCHES FOR
A *MODUS VIVENDI*

*The Situation in Iran and Its Implications: Statement
before the Subcommittee on Europe and the Middle East of
the House Committee on International Relations*

*by Harold H. Saunders, Assistant Secretary for Near Eastern
and South Asian Affairs*

January 17, 1979

This hearing provides an opportunity for us to review together the
present situation in Iran and some of its implications for the future of
U.S. policy toward Iran and the Middle East.

I propose to deal with the following questions in this introductory
presentation.

— What have been the interests and role of the United States in
Iran?
— What is the present situation, and how did it arise?
— What are the regional and global implications of these develop-
ments in Iran?
— What is the U.S. posture toward this situation?
— What lies ahead?

In short, I will be developing the following points.

— The United States remains firmly committed—as has every American Administration since World War II—to a free, stable, and independent Iran. Iran's independence is critical in protecting the freedom of other nations in the Middle East. Fifty percent of the petroleum consumed by the free world passes through the Strait of Hormuz on Iran's southern flank.

— Iran, like other nations that have developed rapidly, has experienced fundamental and accelerating change over the past two decades—economic development, widespread social change, and demands for greater popular involvement in shaping the decisions which affect Iran's life and future. In the course of this process of rapid modernization, economic progress has outpaced the development of political institutions. Some Iranians have felt that their traditional roles and religious convictions have been threatened by these developments and by the introduction of an unfamiliar culture. Many are now insisting on a wider sharing of political power as well as economic benefits. This is the crux of the problem in Iran today.

— Our policy over three decades has been to work with Iran, as with other nations undergoing these profound changes, to help it find constructive solutions to the problems it faces, emerge from periods of change with new stability, and preserve its national independence. Our strongly held view is that no outside power should try to dictate Iran's course, exploit instability for its own ends, or seek control of any kind in this area. Each nation should have the freedom to work out its future free from outside interference.

— The entire area of western Asia is characterized by growth and change. Change produces opportunity as well as instability and crisis. The issue is how to channel change along paths leading to stability and strength. Our position in the area is strong. Most of the states there share our objectives for this region—the security and national independence of each state in the area and the opportunity to choose its own ways to build better lives for its people. Because we share those objectives and seek no domination, we believe U.S. help in appropriate ways will be sought in the future as in the past as nations of the area work out their futures. We are in close touch with governments in the region and elsewhere whose interests are also affected by this situation.

American Interests and Role

The interests of the United States in Iran have remained constant over the past generation.

Because of Iran's importance to the security of the gulf region, the future of the Middle East, and the production of oil, we have a strong interest in a free, stable, and independent Iran. We have persistently and actively pursued this objective since World War II.

Working within the limits set by the Government of Iran in areas of common interest, we have helped Iran strengthen itself economically in two ways: (1) We have participated in Iran's modernization, first through development assistance and then through the cooperation of private American firms. (2) American and other Western companies have worked closely in the development of Iran's oil production and marketing, thereby helping to provide the revenues which have been the main engine of Iran's economic development.

As is often the case with governments where authority is highly centralized and where important economic and strategic interests are at stake, our ability to maintain contact with all elements of the society and press effectively and consistently for constructive change has been limited. Where we saw social and political pressures building up within the society, we called attention to them, but the pace of development has been set by the Government and circumstances in Iran.

We have also responded to Iran's requests to help modernize its armed forces, which have played and will continue to play an important role in Iran's defense. Following British withdrawal in 1971 from a special role in the Persian Gulf, we have encouraged cooperation among the states of that region to strengthen security there. In part to compensate for British withdrawal, we expanded our security assistance relationship. The Iranian Armed Forces, in addition to helping neighboring Oman defend against insurgency, have helped protect Western access to oil suppliers.

We have also encouraged Iran's contribution to global economic progress and stability. Until recently Iran has contributed not only by producing oil for the world's energy needs but also by giving substantial aid to other countries, investing in both the developed and developing world and playing a significant role in the world economy.

In international diplomacy, Iran has made numerous positive contributions: peacekeeping in Vietnam and the Middle East, supporting moderate solutions to conflicts in Africa and elsewhere, and working to resolve some of its longstanding disputes with neighbors.

As a consequence of our other interests in Iran, we have an interest also in Iran's internal development and stability. But in any effort to pursue this interest, we must in the future, as we have in the past, respect the rights of Iranians to decide how they shall order their own future.

How the Present Situation Came About

If we are to understand fully the nature of the present situation, we need to examine how it came about. . . .

Confidence and Growth (1963-76).   The economic successes of the "white revolution" heavily overshadowed the absence of a parallel advance in the political system. By 1976 it appeared to most observers of the Iranian scene that Iran's approach to modernization had produced substantial progress. As a result of the reform program, Iran was being transformed into a modern economic power. The future looked bright. Prosperity seemed assured through rapidly increasing oil revenues. By 1976 there was solid achievement, although economic and political development continued to move on separate tracks at very different speeds.

Problems and Pressures (1976-78). The new prosperity did not entirely mask the problems produced by the concentration of political power at the apex of government and the absence of political institutions that could deal with the trauma of modernization. Most prominent among the causes of dissatisfaction were popular resentment of what was seen as widespread corruption, harsh repression, some ineptitude in high places, disregard for the deep religious feelings of the population, imbalances between revenues and expenses, shortcomings in planning and carrying out ambitious projects, rising unemployment in the cities as the construction boom began to subside, insufficient job opportunities for ever larger numbers of graduating students, inequitable distribution of the benefits of development, sacrifice of civilian programs for military procurement, and a high rate of inflation that outstripped wage increases and frustrated expectations for a steadily rising standard of living. These grievances and the absence of political outlets for affecting government policy led moderate secular opposition leaders to make common cause with significant elements of the Muslim clergy.

In response to increasing political ferment and criticism in 1976 and 1977, the government sponsored campaigns against corruption in the public and private sectors, reorganized itself to curb waste and promote efficiency, and gave an official political party a greater role without infringing on royal authority. Moves to improve the human rights situation were directed at eliminating torture and extreme punishments in the prisons and amnestying political prisoners rather than at establishing new political institutions. The government's measures eventually included encouragement of "constructive criticism" to promote citizen participation in government, as well as efforts to slow down the rapid rate of economic growth that had caused severe dislocations in the society. These changes, however, did not satisfy the demands of large numbers of Iranians for a more open political system.

By the end of 1977, Iranian and foreign observers saw these moves as the first results of the official policy of liberalizing Iranian political life that had started in 1976. Those steps, however, did not yet include movement toward basic political change.

By early 1978, widespread disruptions had begun, and sympathy was shown by student demonstrations abroad. By midyear it was clear that a new political dynamic was emerging. Religious figures took the lead in expressing opposition to the government. The Shah publicly stated his intention to pursue liberalization, looking toward free elections. By late August, however, it was apparent that the government had underestimated the depth of dissatisfaction. A new government was installed at that time which promised freedom of activity for legitimate political parties. A few days later it was forced to declare martial law in Tehran and 11 other cities in response to massive demonstrations. By the end of October, strikes and disorders had become widespread. Oil production had dropped dramatically, and the government apparatus was ceasing to function. With massive rioting in early November, the crisis had become fullblown, and a military government was installed.

Today.   The situation in Iran as we see it at this moment consists of the following elements. Widespread strikes and demonstrations have brought the Iranian economy to a near halt. Many people, at least in the main cities, are not working and are suffering shortages of key commodities. The banking system has not been functioning, and petroleum production does not meet domestic needs. Activist religious leaders and many members of the political opposition have been pressing for the Shah's immediate departure from Iran or for his abdication. The Shah has left Iran on vacation. A representative Regency Council has been named to perform its constitutional functions in the absence of the Shah. Prime Minister Bakhtiar's new government faces the tasks of restoring normal life in the country and reconciling political elements that have opposed each other.

In short, Iran has been through a decade and a half of rapid growth and social change while its political institutions have not evolved commensurately. The people most affected by change are now demanding a greater role in determining Iran's future but have not yet found orderly ways of expressing their views on Iran's future course and shaping their own destiny.

Why an Explosion Now?   With hindsight, the story appears deceptively clear and simple, but it is not so simple. Some analysts, both in and out of government, have pointed over the years to various points of weakness in the Iranian economic, social, and political systems. By mid-1976, just as the leadership in Iran began to react to growing discontent, analysts in Washington were pointing out that Iran's rapid economic growth had not produced political participation to match and that the government would find it necessary to share political power more broadly.

Since 1976 a number of developments have reinforced each other to deepen existing dissatisfactions and to accelerate the crisis in unpredictable ways. Some of those issues were stimulated by the very success of the economic modernization itself. An economic downturn with sharply increased unemployment and inflation added to discontent as well as to a pool of unemployed who no longer had a stake in existing economic activity.

While the Iranian Government was taking certain steps to allow freer expression of criticism and to improve its performance in assuring human rights, basic grievances remained. In this context, massive anti-government demonstrations protesting aspects of the Shah's program took place in early 1978, the beginning of the cycle of action and counteraction that has characterized the Iranian scene since then.

The Issues Ahead. The main issue for the Iranian Government is to end the bloodshed and restore order so a new national consensus can be forged on how Iran should be governed and what its priorities at home and abroad should be. The immediate challenge is for the Regency Council and the new civilian government to win enough popular support so that the violence can be ended and normal economic activity can be restored. In addition to ending the suffering which people have experienced in recent months, it is essential to create an environment for rational deliberations on a long-term political solution for Iran's problems.

In a country as complex as Iran, quick solutions are not to be expected. In a country which has suffered so much violence, there will be no painless answers. Domestic peace and probably considerable time will be needed for the Iranian people to work out a new consensus on their political future. It is important that this process be orderly. We cannot predict what direction Iran will choose, but Iranians alone must make the decision.

Regional Implications

The question most frequently posed about the implications of the current crisis in Iran is: Do we see the instability in Iran along with recent developments in Afghanistan, North and South Yemen, the Horn of Africa as pieces in a pattern of instability which will change the political orientation of the strategic Middle East? Four points need to be stated.

First, we, of course, recognize that fundamental changes are taking place across this area of western Asia and northeastern Africa—economic modernization, social change, a revival of religion, resurgent nationalism, demands for broader popular participation in the political process. These changes are generated by forces within each country. We must differentiate among them and resist the impulse to oversimplify. Economic, social, and political development are complex processes which we still do not fully understand. Our policy in the future as in the past 30 years will be to work as we can with the countries undergoing these changes to help them find constructive solutions and to emerge from periods of change with new stability. As long as these nations are genuinely independent and free to pursue their own policies without intimidation, this will contribute to the kind of world which is the goal of the United States.

Second, instability in any country in a strategic area becomes a factor in global politics. We are in close touch with our friends and allies in the Middle East and elsewhere and share their concern that the solution of the problems in Iran not increase the danger to their own independence. We will continue to work with all of them to minimize that danger. We will continue to make clear our view that we share with them the objectives of assuring the stability, the security, and the national independence of each nation in the area. We believe our common purpose will provide the basis for further close cooperation.

Third, our position in this strategically important area will remain strong over the long run as long as most of the countries there are allowed to pursue their own paths to development and progress free from outside interference. Our respect for diversity and pluralism, our encouragement of human freedoms and liberties, the appeal of Western economic and technological strength, and our dedication to democratic principles all evoke a strong resonance among the peoples and nations throughout the area. They also know that we are prepared to support their own efforts to strengthen their defensive capabilities without seeking a special position for ourselves that they do not want.

Fourth, the changes we are witnessing across this area of western Asia and northeastern Africa contain the seeds of progress as well as the causes of crisis. Some parts of this area are among the fastest growing and resource-rich nations of the world. Some are among the most traditional and the poorest. The challenge we and our friends face is how to seize the opportunity to channel change toward constructive results—not simply to react to it as an unwelcome source of instability and conflict. In saying this, we do not minimize the dangers for American interests, but we want also to keep our sights on what will be the interests of the people in this area.

U.S. Policy

U.S. policy toward Iran has been based on three consistent principles as events there have evolved over the past several months.

— We have repeatedly made it clear that decisions affecting the future of Iran and the relationship between the Iranian people and their government are decisions which must be made in Iran by Iranians. We seek no role in deciding those questions, and we consider any external influence improper.

— The U.S. Government has worked within the institutional framework of Iran under its Constitution with the duly established authorities of Iran as specified in the Iranian Constitution. There are constitutional provisions for change, and we support the decisions of the Iranian Government wherever and however we can appropriately be helpful.

— We have supported Iran's independence. We have taken the position that no outside power should exploit instability in Iran—or any other country—for its own advantage. The overriding American objective for Iran is simply that it should have the freedom to work out its own future free from such interference.

These principles have been applied consistently throughout the last year of turmoil in Iran, and they will continue to be our guidelines in the future.

Within the general context of those principles we have pursued these key objectives.

First, we hope to see the end of bloodshed, so the people of Iran can return to normal life. Only in such circumstances can there be rational discussion of a political solution to Iran's current problems which will restore stability there. We will encourage all parties to seek political ends by peaceful means.

Second, we want to maintain a close and friendly relationship with an independent, stable, and secure Iran. We believe the interests of Iran and of the United States are closely intertwined, and we seek an environment of mutual respect and positive cooperation. We believe this will serve the interests of Iran, of the United States, and of the free world.

Third, we seek a stable and prosperous Iran which can play its rightful role in the region and the international community. We are prepared to help Iran—on the technical level, on the governmental level, and on the diplomatic level—to restore its productivity and to regain the international confidence it has earned over the past decade. The resumption of major oil exports will be important both to the economy of Iran and to the economy of the world.

We believe that these objectives serve not only the interests of our own country but also the interests of the Iranian people. We believe they offer a practical basis for cooperation.

What Lies Ahead?

Iran is in the midst of a major social crisis. We have no illusions that this process will be resolved easily, and it would serve no purpose for us to speculate on future twists and turns of events.

The American people and the people of Iran share basic agreement on four fundamental values.

— We both have strong religious heritages. The people of both countries believe in the importance of a life that is guided by moral principles. We believe those principles must guide a government that is truly just.

— We share a belief in the right of the people to express themselves politically through institutions constituted by them. We both believe that it is for the Iranian people to decide how they will govern themselves, just as it is for the American people to choose their own government.

— Both of us believe in the use of our national wealth for the betterment of our people. The United States remains willing to help Iran develop the potential of the country.

— Both Americans and Iranians want to see an Iran that is truly independent. We have no aspiration to dictate the policies of the Iranian government.

On the basis of these shared views and our common interests, we will make every effort to assure a continued close relationship between the United States and Iran.

In looking to the future, the United States will continue to work with the leaders of Iran in their effort to consolidate the civilian government with popular support for restoring order and normal life and building a sound political foundation for Iran's continued progress and independence.

Official United States Press Statements

Secretary of State Vance News Conference

[EXCERPTS]

January 11, 1979

Before taking questions, I would like to say a few words about our approach to the situation in Iran. The United States has a strong and continuing interest in the free, stable, and independent Iran in this strategic region. This is a policy we have consistently and actively pursued over the past generation.

In this recent crisis, we have encouraged the restoration of order so that the bloodshed would end and the people of Iran could return to normal life. Only in such circumstances can there be rational discussion of a political solution to Iran's current problems.

It has been our objective throughout this current crisis to insure the maximum of stability in a time of change by preserving the institutional framework of Iran under its Constitution. The Shah has said that he plans to leave Iran on vacation. That has been his decision, worked out with his Iranian colleagues. The Shah remains the constitutional head of state, and we continue to work with him in that capacity.

The Shah has said that when he leaves, he will do so in the way prescribed by the Iranian Constitution by appointing a Regency Council to serve in his absence. At the same time, a new civilian government under Prime Minister [Shapour] Bakhtiar has been named. We believe that the new government should be given every chance to reconcile the differences in Iran and find a peaceful political solution.

Iran's Armed Forces remain essential to the security and independence of Iran and as a necessary compliment to a legitimate civilian government. We have urged that everything be done to insure their integrity and their support by the people of Iran.

We have urged that leaders of all elements in Iran find ways of working out together a peaceful solution to the present problems. The decisions on Iran's future must be made by the Iranians themselves. No outside government should seek to interfere. We hope for a return to peaceful conditions and a functioning economy that will make possible an orderly and constructive solution of Iran's problems.

Q: What—apart from the statement you have just made—is the United States prepared to do to insure that a civilian government will be able to survive in Iran?

Secretary Vance: We have indicated to the Prime Minister that we will cooperate with him and with his government, and that we will keep very closely in touch with him so that we may be helpful wherever we can.

Q: I noticed that in your opening statement on Iran, sir, you said that the United States has a strong and continuing interest in Iran. In a recent interview in The New York Times, *Dr. Brzezinski, I believe, described it as a vital American interest. Perhaps this is just semantics, but do you believe that Iran is a vital interest of the United States?*

Secretary Vance: I think it is very clear that we have vital interests in the region. I would point out that the oil which comes through the Strait of Hormuz which, as you know, is on the southern Iranian border, comprises about 50% of the oil which goes to the free world. Our trade with Iran and Saudi Arabia over this past year amounted to some $7 billion, a very substantial amount. And obviously this is very important in a period in which we have balance-of-payments problems and we have to increase our exports.

It is also clear that what happens in Iran is being closely followed by others in the Middle East, and that includes those nations which are involved in the Arab-Israeli conflict; so, therefore, it is very clear that our interests in Iran and in the region are vital interests.

Q: Do you see any possibility of American military involvement in Iran as a result of the need to protect those vital interests?

Secretary Vance: I do not see any need for American military involvement. With respect to the vital interests, we are following the situation carefully. We are in constant communication with the many friendly neighbors and allies that we have who are also following, on a daily basis, the tragic events that have unfolded in Iran; and we will continue to do so.

Presidential News Conference

[EXCERPT]

January 17, 1979

Q: What will the posture of our government be now toward the various contending factions in Iran that even continue to vie for power over there?

President Carter: We have very important relationships with Iran—past, present, and I hope in the future. And I expect in the future. They have been good allies of ours and I expect this to continue in the future.

In accordance with the provisions of the Iranian Constitution, a change in government has now been accomplished. Under Mr. Bakhtiar, whose government we do support; the Majlis, the lower house of Parliament; and the upper house, the Senate, have approved his government and his Cabinet.

We have encouraged to the limited extent of our own ability the public support for the Bakhtiar government, for the restoration of stability, for an end of bloodshed and for the return of normal life in Iran.

As you know, the Shah has left Iran [on January 16, 1979]; he says for a vacation. How long he will be out of Iran, we have no way to determine. Future events and his own desires will determine that. He's now in Egypt, and he will later come to our own country. But we would anticipate and would certainly hope that our good relationships with Iran will continue in the future.

Q: A month ago, at a news conference, you said the Shah would maintain power. How could you be so wrong and is it typical of our intelligence elsewhere in the world? And are you in touch with Khomeini in case he winds up at the top of the heap?

President Carter: It is impossible for anyone to anticipate all future political events. And I think that the rapid change of affairs in Iran has not been predicted by anyone so far as I know.

Our intelligence is the best we can devise. We share intelligence data and diplomatic information on a routine basis with other nations. And this is a constant process whenever a problem arises in a country throughout the world. I have confidence in the Iranian people to restore a stable government and to restore their economic circumstances for the future.

No, we have not communicated directly with Mr. Khomeini. Our views have been expressed publicly that he support stability and an end to bloodshed in Iran. And no matter what his deep religious convictions might be—and I don't doubt their sincerity—that he permit the government that has now been established by the legal authorities in Iran and under the constitution to have a chance to succeed. We do know that the

Iranian military and many of the religious and political opponents to the Shah have given their pledge of support to the Bakhtiar government. And that's our hope.

And I would like to add one other thing. We have no intention, neither ability nor desire, to interfere in the internal affairs of Iran, and we certainly have no intention of permitting other nations to interfere in the internal affairs of Iran.

Q: If we had had better intelligence in Iran, is there anything that we could have done to save the Shah? And there's a second part to that question. You just referred to Iran as allies. Would you authorize new weapons shipments to the Bakhtiar regime?

President Carter: Even if we had been able to anticipate events that were going to take place in Iran or other countries, obviously our ability to determine those events is very limited. The Shah, his advisers, great military capabilities, police, and others, couldn't completely prevent rioting and disturbances in Iran.

Certainly we have no desire nor ability to intrude massive forces into Iran or any other country to determine the outcome of domestic political issues. This is something that we have no intention of ever doing in another country. We've tried this once in Vietnam. It didn't work well, as you well know.

We have some existing contracts for delivery of weapons to Iran since sometimes the deliveries take as long as five years after the orders are placed. Our foreign military sales policy is now being continued. We have no way to know what the attitude of the Bakhtiar government is. We've not discussed this with them.

After the Iranian Government is stable, after it assuages the present disturbances in Iran, then I'm sure they'll let us know how they want to carry out future military needs of their own country. It is important to Iran, for their own security and for the independence of the people of Iran, that a strong and stable military be maintained, and I believe that all the leaders of Iran, whom I have heard discuss this matter, agree with the statement that I've just made.

Q: There is a suggestion that if Iranian oil supplies do not begin flowing again, perhaps within two months, there may be a shortage and perhaps a price increase for us. Does our intelligence indicate that might happen, or is there such a prospect as you see it?

President Carter: We derive about 5% of our oil supplies from Iran in recent months—much less than many other countries, as you know, who are more heavily dependent on Iranian oil. I think an extended interruption of Iranian oil shipments would certainly create increasingly severe shortages on the international market.

So far, other oil-producing nations have moved to replace the lost Iranian oil supplies. If this should continue, it would just reemphasize the basic commitment that our nation has tried to carry out in the last two years. That is, to have a predictable energy policy to reduce consumption of energy in toto, certainly to reduce dependence on foreign oil and to eliminate waste of oil.

I don't think there's any doubt that we can cut back consumption of oil by 5% without seriously damaging our own economy. And I would hope that all Americans who listen to my voice now would do everything possible within their own capabilities to cut down on the use of oil and the waste of all energy supplies.

I think that this restoration of Iranian oil shipments is a desire by all the religious and political leaders in Iran who have an influence over the future. We have seen, since the OPEC price increases, even before the Iranian supplies were interrupted, some shortage of spot shipments of oil.

The present price of oil even with increased production from other suppliers is now slightly above the established OPEC price. But our hope is that oil prices will go down at least to some degree as Iranian supplies are reintroduced.

Presidential News Conference

[EXCERPT]

February 27, 1979

Q: Mr. President, what is our Government doing, if anything, to try and influence the new Iranian Government to increase production, keep prices down and, generally, how would you describe the relationship between our Government and the Khomeini government?

President Carter: The Khomeini government has made it clear ever since it came into power, through our direct negotiations with Prime Minister Bazargan and our Ambassador and through their emissaries who have even today talked to Secretary Vance, that they desire a close-working and friendly relationship with the United States.

They have also announced that oil production in Iran will be increased, and that very shortly exports will be recommenced. And my own assessment is that they have strong intentions to carry out both these goals and that they are capable of doing so.

Q: Mr. President, there is, or there appears to be starting a public debate on the question, "Who lost Iran?" I noticed that former Secretary Kissinger was suggesting that your administration should bear some responsibility; former Under Secretary of State George Ball suggested that the Nixon-Kissinger administration did much to destabilize Iran with their billions in sophisticated military hardware. My question was, I suppose, do you agree with Ball? Who lost Iran, or was Iran ours to lose in the first place?

President Carter: Well, it's obvious that Iran was not ours to lose in the first place. We don't own Iran, and we have never had any intention nor ability to control the internal affairs of Iran. For more than 2,000 years, the people in the Iran area, the Persians and others, have established their own government. They've had ups and downs, as have we. I think it's obvious that the present government in Iran, as I just answered, would like to have good relationships with us. I don't know of anything we could have done to prevent the very complicated social and religious and political interrelationships from occurring in Iran in the change of government. And we'll just have to make the best of the change.

But, as I say, we cannot freeze the status quo in a country when it's very friendly to us. When the change is made by the people who live there, we do the best we can to protect American interests by forming new alliances, new friendships, new interrelationships, new trade relationships, new security relationships, perhaps, in the future, with the new government, and that's the best we can do.

But to try to lay blame on someone in the United States for a new government having been established in Iran, I think, is just a waste of time and avoids a basic issue that this was a decision to be made and which was made by the Iranian people themselves.

President Carter's Address upon Receiving an Honorary Doctor of Engineering Degree from the Georgia Institute of Technology

[EXCERPT]

February 20, 1979

As I speak to you today, the country of Iran—with which we have had close relations for the last 30 years—is in revolution. It has been our hope that Iran could modernize without deep internal conflicts, and we sought to encourage that effort by supporting its government, by urging internal change toward progress and democracy, and by helping to provide a background of regional stability.

The revolution in Iran is a product of deep social, political, religious, and economic factors growing out of the history of Iran itself. Those who argue that the United States should or could intervene directly to thwart these events are wrong about the realities of Iran. So, too, are those who spout propaganda that protecting our own citizens is tantamount to direct intervention.

We have not and we will not intervene in Iran, yet the future of Iran continues to be of deep concern to us and to our friends and allies. It is an important nation in a critical part of the world; an immediate neighbor of the Soviet Union; a major oil producer that also sits beside the principal artery for most of the world's trade in oil. And it is still a significant potential force for stability and progress in the region.

Iran is a proud nation with a long history—more than 2,000 years—of struggle to establish and to guarantee its own freedom. The independence of Iran is also in our own vital interest and in the interest of our closest allies, and we will support the independence of Iran.

Out of today's turmoil, it is our hope that these troubled people will create a stable government which can meet the needs of the Iranian people and which can enable that great nation not only to remain independent but to regain its internal strength and balance.

We are prepared to support that effort as appropriate and to work with the Iranian Government and the people as a nation, which shares common interests and common aspirations with us.

But just as we respect Iran's independence and integrity, other nations must do so as well. If others interfere, directly or indirectly, they are on notice that this will have serious consequences and will affect our broader relationships with them.

EMBASSY SEIZURE AND HOSTAGE CRISIS

White House Statement:* The American Hostages in Iran

November 9, 1979

The seizure of more than 60 Americans in our embassy in Tehran has provoked strong feelings here at home. There is outrage. There is frustration. And there is deep anger.

There is also pride in the courage of those who are in danger and sympathy for them and for their families. But the most important concern for all Americans at this moment is safety of our fellow citizens held in Tehran.

The President shares these feelings. He is pursuing every possible avenue in a situation that is extremely volatile and difficult. His efforts involve many countries and individuals. Many of these efforts must of necessity be conducted without publicity, and all require the calmest possible atmosphere.

The President knows that no matter how deeply we may feel, none of us would want to do anything that would worsen the danger in which our fellow Americans have been placed.

---

* Press Secretary Jody Powell read this statement to reporters assembled in the Briefing Room at the White House. The President had met with the members of the families at the State Department.

He calls on all Americans, public officials and private citizens alike, to exercise restraint, and to keep the safety of their countrymen uppermost in their minds and hearts. Members of the families of the American hostages with whom the President met this morning have asked to join with him in this appeal. The President expects every American to refrain from any action that might increase the danger to the American hostages in Tehran.

Executive Order 12170: Freezing Iranian Government Assets in America*

November 14, 1979

Pursuant to the authority vested in me as President by the Constitution and laws of the United States including the International Emergency Economic Powers Act, 50 U.S.C.A. sec. 1701 et seq., the National Emergencies Act, 50 U.S.C. sec. 1601 et seq., and 3 U.S.C. sec. 301,

I, JIMMY CARTER, President of the United States, find that the situation in Iran constitutes an unusual and extraordinary threat to the national security, foreign policy and economy of the United States and hereby declare a national emergency to deal with that threat.

I hereby order blocked all property and interests in property of the Government of Iran, its instrumentalities and controlled entities and the Central Bank of Iran which are or become subject to the jurisdiction of the United States or which are in or come within the possession or control of persons subject to the jurisdiction of the United States.

The Secretary of the Treasury is authorized to employ all powers granted to me by the International Emergency Economic Powers Act to carry out the provisions of this order.

This order is effective immediately and shall be transmitted to the Congress and published in the Federal Register.

Presidential News Conference on Iran

[EXCERPTS]

November 28, 1979

For the last 24 days our nation's concern has been focused on our fellow Americans being held hostage in Iran. We have welcomed some

---

* Other actions taken by the President regarding the Iranian crisis included the following: Proclamation 4702 (44 F.R. 65581) was issued on November 12, 1979 prohibiting oil from Iran from entering the United States. On November 26, 1979, the President issued Executive Order 12172 (44 F.R. 67947) which delegated authority conferred upon him by 8 USC 1185 (travel control of citizens and aliens during war or national emergency) to the Secretary of State and the Attorney General with respect to Iranians holding non-immigrant visas.

of them home to their families and their friends. But we will not rest nor deviate from our efforts until all have been freed from their imprisonment and their abuse. We hold the Government of Iran fully responsible for the well-being and the safe return of every single person.

I want the American people to understand the situation as much as possible, but there may be some questions tonight which I cannot answer fully because of my concern for the well-being of the hostages.

First of all, I would like to say that I am proud of this great nation, and I want to thank all Americans for their prayers, their courage, their persistence, their strong support and patience. During these past days our national will, our courage, and our maturity have all been severely tested and history will show that the people of the United States have met every test.

In the days to come our determination may be even more sorely tried but we will continue to defend the security, the honor, and the freedom of Americans everywhere. This nation will never yield to blackmail.

For all Americans our constant concern is the well-being and the safety of our fellow citizens who are being held illegally and irresponsibly hostage in Iran. The actions of Iran have shocked the civilized world. For a government to applaud mob violence and terrorism, for a government actually to support and in effect participate in the taking and the holding of hostages is unprecedented in human history.

This violates not only the most fundamental precepts of international law but the common ethical and religious heritage of humanity. There is no recognized religious faith on Earth which condones kidnapping. There is no recognized religious faith on Earth which condones blackmail. There is certainly no religious faith on Earth which condones the sustained abuse of innocent people.

We are deeply concerned about the inhuman and degrading conditions imposed on the hostages. From every corner of the world nations and people have voiced their strong revulsion and condemnation of Iran, and have joined us in calling for the release of the hostages.

Last night a statement of support was released and was issued by the President of the U.N. General Assembly, the Security Council, on behalf of all of its members. We expect a further Security Council meeting on Saturday night, at which more firm and official action may be taken to help in obtaining the release of the American hostages.

Any claims raised by government officials of Iran will ring hollow while they keep innocent people bound and abused and threatened. We hope that this exercise of diplomacy and international law will bring a peaceful solution, because a peaceful solution is preferable to the other remedies available to the United States.

At the same time, we pursue such a solution with grim determination. The Government of Iran must recognize the gravity of the situation which it has itself created, and the grave consequences which will result if harm comes to any of the hostages.

I want the American people to know, and I want the world to know, that we will persist in our efforts, through every means available, until every single American has been freed. . . .

I will be glad to answer questions.

Q: The Ayatollah Khomeini said the other day, and I am using his words, that he doesn't believe you have the guts to use military force. He puts no credibility in our military deterrent. I am wondering how do we get out of this mess in Iran and still retain credibility with our allies and with our adversaries overseas?

President Carter: We have the full support of our allies, and in this particular instance we have no adversaries overseas. There is no civilized country on Earth which has not condemned the seizure and holding of hostages by Iran. It would not be advisable for me to explore publicly all of the options open to our country.

As I said earlier, I am determined to do the best I can through diplomatic means and through peaceful means to insure the safety of our hostages and their release. Other actions which I might decide to take would come in the future after those peaceful means have been exhausted. But I believe that the growing condemnation of the world community on Iran will have a beneficial effect.

Q: Why did you reverse your policy and permit the Shah to come into this country when, one, medical treatment was available elsewhere; two, you had been warned by our Chargé that the Americans might be endangered in Tehran; and three, the Bazargan government was so shaky that it was questionable whether he could deliver on the promise to protect our Embassy, and, last of all, in view of the consequences do you regret the decision?

President Carter: No, the decision that I made personally and without pressure from anyone to carry out the principles of our country, to provide for the means of giving the Shah necessary medical assistance to save his life, was proper. At the same time we notified the Government of Iran. We were assured by the Prime Minister and the Foreign Minister that our Embassy would be protected, and it was protected for several days in spite of threats from outside.

Then peremptorily, after Khomeini made an aggravating speech to the crowds in the street and withdrew protection from the Embassy, it was attacked successfully. The Embassy was protected by our people for the length of time possible without help from the host government. No Embassy on Earth is a fortress that can withstand constant attacks by a mob unless a host government comes to the rescue of the people within the Embassy.

But I took the right decision. I have no regrets about it nor apologies to make because it did help to save a man's life and it was compatible with the principles of our country.

Q: What role did the former Secretary play in your decision to permit the Shah to enter the country?

President Carter: None. I did not hear at all from the Secretary, former Secretary Kissinger, nor did he contact Secretary Vance at any time during the days when we were deciding that the Shah should come into the United States for medical care to save his life. In previous weeks and months, since the Shah was deposed, Secretary Kissinger and many others let it be known that they thought that we should provide a haven for the Shah. But Secretary Kissinger played no role in my decision to permit the Shah to come in for medical treatment.

Q: Speaking of the Shah, if he is well enough to travel, would you like him to leave the country?

President Carter: That is a decision to be made by the Shah, and by his medical advisers. When he decided to come to our country, with my permission, I was informed then, and I have been informed since, that as soon as his medical treatment was successfully completed, that his intention was to leave. I have not encouraged him to leave. He was free to come here for medical treatment, and he will leave on his own volition.

Q: There is a feeling of hostility throughout the country toward Iran, because of the hostages. Senator Long said that the taking of our Embassy in Iran, in his words, is an act of war. There are rumors, since denied, that our Navy has been called up for service. I ask you, as our Commander in Chief, is war possible, is war thinkable?

President Carter: It would be a mistake for the people of our country to have aroused within them hatred toward anyone; not against the people of Iran and certainly not against Iranians who may be in our country as our guests. We certainly do not want to be guilty of the same violation of human decency and basic human principles that have proven so embarrassing to many of the Iranian citizens themselves.

We obviously prefer to see our hostages protected and released completely through peaceful means. That is my deepest commitment, and that will be my goal. The United States has other options available to it which will be considered, depending upon the circumstances. But I think it would not be well-advised for me to speak of those specifically tonight.

Q: Serious charges have been placed against the Shah concerning the repression of his own people and the misappropriation of his nation's funds. Is there an appropriate vehicle to investigate those charges and do you foresee a time when you would direct your Administration to assist in that investigation?

President Carter: I don't know of any international forum within which charges have ever been brought against a deposed leader who has left his country. There have been instances of changing governments down through the centuries in history, and I don't know of any instance where such a leader who left his country after his government fell has been tried in an international court or in an international forum.

This is a matter that can be pursued. It should be pursued under international law, and if there is a claim against the Shah's financial holdings there is nothing to prevent other parties from going into the courts in accordance with a law of a nation or internationally and seeking a redress of grievances which they claim.

But as I said earlier, I don't think there is any forum that will listen to the Iranians make any sort of claim, justified or not, as long as they hold against their will and abuse the hostages in complete contravention to every international law and every precept or every commitment or principle of humankind.

United States Ambassador Donald McHenry's Statement on Iran to the United Nations Security Council

December 1, 1979

Twenty-seven days ago, 63 Americans as well as personnel of other nationalities were seized when an armed, disciplined group of demonstrators invaded the U.S. Embassy in Tehran. Eighteen of those captured have been released. At least 50 Americans remain captive.

As with diplomats everywhere, the individuals who were taken hostage are entitled to the protection of the Government of Iran by the most solemn commitment nations can give—the sovereign pledge of governments by treaty and international obligation.

Governments retain the right to require that foreign diplomatic personnel leave their soil. But every standard of international behavior, whether established by practice, by ethics, by treaty, or by common humanity supports the principle that the personnel of a diplomatic mission and diplomatic property are inviolate. Even in the darkest moments of relationships between countries, the security and well-being of diplomatic personnel have been respected.

Iran asks that its grievances be heard and acted upon. Yet Iran, and the authorities who speak for it, are violating the most basic obligation of nations. They hold hostage the very people who facilitate those communications that can resolve differences and lead to understanding and agreement among nations.

None of us, whatever our differences on other issues, can ignore the implications for all of us of this event.

Nor can the world ignore that these diplomatic representatives are being held under degrading conditions. They are threatened, kept

bound, isolated, not allowed to speak, denied mail. Even their where-
abouts are uncertain. All of us at this table are also diplomatic representatives of our countries, charged with the same duties and protected
by the same laws and rules of conduct as those now held captive in
Tehran. It is for all of us to speak up to demand their release and to insist
upon basic conditions of humanity for their care pending that release,
including daily visitation by impartial observers.

Many members of the United Nations, including some members of
this Council, have had ambassadors murdered, diplomatic personnel
injured, embassy facilities destroyed. On each occasion the delicate
framework of our international community has been harmed, but
efforts were made to repair the wounds. The situation in Tehran has a
feature unlike other assaults on the diplomatic ties that bind our world.
In Iran, the government itself defends the violence which holds diplomats hostage. Such a position is intolerable.

The United States insists that its diplomatic personnel be released
and its diplomatic premises restored. These are not negotiable matters.
The United States will hold the authorities in Iran fully responsible for
the safety of the Americans held captive.

I speak today for hostages who are endangered by the frenzy and
uncertainty of events, by the inhumane conditions under which they are
held, and by the threat of the authorities in Iran to compound unjust
acts through trials.

Around the world, nations of East and West, North and South, in
individual and collective statements, have expressed their opposition to
this violation of international law and called for the immediate release
of the hostages. We express our appreciation for this overwhelming
expression of international concern and support in behalf of principles
that lie at the heart of civilized international behavior.

In this spirit, the President of the Security Council, speaking for the
members of this body, has twice urgently appealed for the release of the
hostages. The President of the General Assembly has twice spoken
eloquently in support of this plea. The Secretary General of the United
Nations has worked unceasingly to resolve this crisis.

There has not been a satisfactory response and the hostages are still
not free. We gather here to determine what more can be done.

None of us is deaf to the passionate voices that speak of injustice,
that cry out against past wrongs and that ask for understanding. There
is not a single grievance alleged or spoken in this situation that could
not be heard in an appropriate forum.

In addition, as we have said from the beginning, the United States
remains ready, upon the release of the hostages, to discuss with the
Iranian authorities the differences which exist between us and to seek
their resolution.

But no country can call for justice while at the same time denying it to the defenseless. No country can breach the most fundamental rules of the community of nations and at the same time expect that community to be helpful in the problems which it perceives for itself. In the simplest terms, no country can break and ignore the law while seeking its benefits.

What is it that the world can agree upon if not the protection and respect for those whom we appoint to represent our sovereignty and resolve our differences?

How tragic for Iran, how tragic for the world that threats to peace are being driven to a new crescendo. The most powerful voices in Iran are encouraging violence in neighboring countries and condoning bloodshed rather than condemning it. In addition, totally unfounded charges which can only inflame the situation are being made against the United States with respect to the current crisis.

The United States in all the years of its history has had as a fundamental principle the freedom of all people to worship as they choose. Out of this history and long association, we honor and respect the leaders and the nation of Islam.

The principle of noninterference in the internal affairs of other nations is both a tenet of the United Nations and of the foreign policy of the United States, and that includes, of course, respect for the territorial integrity, political independence, and sovereignty of Iran. We respect the right of the people of Iran to determine their own future through institutions of their own choosing. All of us must accept their decisions.

The President of the United States, speaking for a unified and determined nation, has made it clear that we are seeking a peaceful resolution to this conflict so that the wounds of the past can be healed. In this spirit, the United States has turned to the Security Council and the Secretary General in the search for a peaceful solution. In this spirit, the United States has begun proceedings in the International Court of Justice.

There is in the United States a unity of purpose, a disciplined sensitivity to the needs of peace, a determination to search out all peaceful means to bring this dispute to a just conclusion, and also a determination to do what must be done to protect our fellow citizens and the rule of law. That unity of purpose is shared by all Americans. But make no mistake. Beneath that discipline is a seething anger which Americans properly feel as they witness on daily television new threats and outrages against their fellow citizens.

The hostages must be freed.

United States Initiates Action Against Iran in
International Court of Justice

State Department Press Release   *November 29, 1979*

The United States today took its case against Iran to the International Court of Justice. In an action filed with the Court in The Hague, the United States charges that the Government of Iran has violated fundamental principles of international law in not protecting the U.S. Embassy in Tehran, in supporting the actions of those holding the American hostages, and in threatening to subject the hostages to trial.

In particular, the United States charges Iran has violated the 1961 Vienna Convention on Diplomatic Relations, the 1963 Vienna Convention on Consular Relations, the 1973 Convention on the Prevention and Punishment of Crimes against Diplomats, the 1955 U.S.-Iran Treaty of Amity, and the Charter of the United Nations.

The United States will seek an urgent hearing before the Court and has requested the Court to issue forthwith a preliminary order directing Iran to secure the release of the hostages and to ensure their safety.

The United States' Application to the Court, its Request for Interim Measures of Protection, and a letter from Secretary of State Vance to the President of the Court are available at the press office. The papers were filed by the Legal Adviser of the Department of State, Mr. Roberts B. Owen, who will represent the United States in the action.

The International Court of Justice is the principal judicial organ of the United Nations and is composed of fifteen judges elected by the U.N. General Assembly and Security Council.

A Description of the Court

The International Court of Justice (ICJ) is the principal judicial organ of the United Nations. It was created by the U.N. Charter in 1945 as the successor to the Permanent Court of International Justice. The Statute of the ICJ forms an integral part of the U.N. Charter. The Court's principal functions are to decide such cases as are submitted to it by states and to give advisory opinions on legal questions at the request of intergovernmental bodies authorized pursuant to the Statute of the Court and the U.N. Charter.

The Court is composed of 15 judges, no two of whom may be nationals of the same State, elected by the U.N. General Assembly and the Security Council, voting independently. The electors are mandated to bear in mind the qualifications of the individual candidates and the need for the Court as a whole to represent the main forms of civilization and the principal legal systems of the world. Members of the Court are elected for nine years, one-third of the total number of judges being elected every three years.

The membership of the International Court of Justice at the present time is as follows: President Sir Humphrey Waldock (United King-

dom); Vice-President Taslim Olawale Elias (Nigeria); and Judges
Manfred Lachs (Poland), Isaac Forster (Senegal), Andre Gros (France),
Richard R. Baxter (United States of America), P.D. Morozov (Union of
Soviet Socialist Republics), Jose Sette Camara (Brazil), Jose Maria Ruda
(Argentina), Nagendra Singh (India), Abdullah Ali El-Erian (Egypt),
Hermann Mosler (Federal Republic of Germany), Shigeru Oda (Japan),
Salah El Dine Tarazi (Syrian Arab Republic) and Robert Ago (Italy).

The Case Against Iran Presented by United States Attorney General Benjamin R. Civiletti before the International Court of Justice

December 10, 1979

Mr. President, [Sir Humphrey Waldock of the U.K.] and distinguished members of the Court, my name is Benjamin R. Civiletti. I
appear today as Attorney General of the United States of America and
advocate in support of its request for provisional measures of protection
from illegal acts of the Government of Iran. I feel privileged to appear
on behalf of my government. I should also say that the United States is
grateful to the Court for providing a hearing at this time.

If I may be permitted a personal introduction. I have spent my
working life as a trial lawyer in the United States. I have been an
advocate both for the government and for those who oppose the government, in both civil and criminal suits. Anyone who has been a trial
advocate in any country would approach this Court with respect and
awe. In a real sense this Court represents the highest legal aspiration of
civilized man.

Yet I find myself addressing this Court with awe but with restrained
anger. More than 50 of my countrymen are held prisoners, in peril of
their lives and suffering even as I speak. This imprisonment and this
suffering are illegal and inhuman. It takes no advocate to bring this
cause to you. The facts are known worldwide, and every citizen of the
world—trained in the law or not—knows the conduct to be criminal.

I come to this Court, my government comes to this Court, not so
that yet another body will reiterate the obvious fact that what we are
witnessing in Iran is illegal. The United States comes here so that this
tribunal may demonstrate that international law may not be tossed
aside, that the international fabric of civility may not be rent with
impunity.

My government asks this Court to take the most vigorous and the
speediest action it can, not to settle a minor boundary dispute, not to
give to one national treasury from another, but to save lives and set
human beings free. This is what people everywhere—not just monarchs
and presidents, not just lawyers and jurists—expect of what a judge in
my nation called the "omnipresence" that we know to be the law.

If I come to you with anger, I also come to you with urgency. We who speak the sober language of jurisprudence say the U.S. Government is seeking the "indication of provisional measures." What we are asking this Court for is the quickest possible action to end a barbaric captivity and to save human lives.

For the first time in modern diplomatic history, a state has not only acquiesced in, but participated in and is seeking political advantage from the illegal seizure and imprisonment of the diplomatic personnel of another state. It even threatens to put these diplomatic personnel on trial. If our international institutions, including this Court, should even appear to condone or tolerate the flagrant violations of customary international law, state practice, and explicit treaty commitments that are involved here, the result will be a serious blow not only to the safety of the American diplomatic persons now in captivity in Tehran, but to the rule of law within the international community.

To allow the illegal detention and trial of U.S. diplomatic personnel and other citizens to go forward during the pendency of this case would be to encourage other governments and individuals to believe that they may, with impunity, seize any Embassy and any diplomatic agent, or indeed any other hostage, anywhere in the world. Such conduct cannot be tolerated; every civilized government recognizes that. We therefore submit that this Court has a clear obligation to take every action to bring this conduct to an immediate end.

We shall discuss the simple, clear issues presented in the following order. I shall review the applicable basic principles of international law which bind both Iran and the United States, not only under customary international law but also under four treaties to which both states are parties. These treaties are directly in point. Mr. Owen will then briefly summarize the facts to demonstrate to the Court that the Government of Iran has committed, is committing—and is proposing to commit— clear, flagrant violations of these principles of international law.

We will next demonstrate that the Court has jurisdiction over this dispute and the authority to indicate the provisional measures requested by the United States. Finally, we shall explain why, on the basis of article 41 of the Court's statute, an indication of interim measures is urgently needed and amply justified.

The international legal standards involved here are of ancient origin. They have evolved over centuries of state practice, and in recent years have been codified in a series of international agreements. It is on four of those agreements that the Government of the United States relies here.

Vienna Convention on Diplomatic Relations

Since the subject of this proceeding is focused largely on the status and immunities of diplomatic agents, I shall refer at the outset to the 1961 Vienna Convention on Diplomatic Relations. The purpose of that convention, to which both the United States and Iran are parties, was to codify a fundamental, firmly established rule of international law—that the immunity and inviolability of Embassies and diplomats must be absolutely respected and that in no circumstances may a state engage in the type of conduct that is involved here.

The first relevant provision of the Vienna Convention on Diplomatic Relations is article 22, relating to the physical premises of an Embassy or mission. The words of article 22 are clear:

"1. The premises of the mission shall be inviolable. The agents of the receiving State may not enter them, except with the consent of the head of the mission.

2. The receiving State is under a special duty to take all appropriate steps to protect the premises of the mission against any intrusion or damage and to prevent any disturbance of the peace of the mission or impairment of its dignity.

3. The premises of the mission, their furnishings and other property thereon and the means of transport of the mission shall be immune from search, requisition, attachment or execution."

As to the personnel of such a diplomatic mission, article 29 of the convention goes on to provide that every diplomatic agent "shall be inviolable" and that he shall be free from "any form of arrest and detention." The language is unqualified: It prohibits any form of arrest or detention, regardless of any grievance which the host state may suppose that it has against a particular diplomat. There is a remedy available against a diplomat who a state believes has engaged in improper conduct—to require him to leave the country. But the Vienna convention excludes any form of physical arrest or detention for the purpose of prosecution or for any other reason.

The convention reemphasizes the principle of diplomatic inviolability in several different ways. Article 29 requires the receiving state to prevent any attack upon the person, freedom, or dignity of a diplomatic agent. Article 31 requires that each such agent enjoy unqualified "immunity from the criminal jurisdiction of the receiving State." There is no exception; no matter what the cause, the receiving state is precluded from allowing the criminal prosecution of a diplomatic agent. In the last few days, as we will explain later in our argument, this absolute immunity from criminal prosecution has taken on an overwhelming importance.

Article 37 of the convention extends the same absolute inviolability and absolute immunity from assault and from criminal trial to the administrative and technical staff of an Embassy. All but two of the more than 50 Americans currently being held hostage in Tehran are either diplomatic agents or Embassy administrative and technical staff, some of whom also perform consular functions.

Other immunities and privileges pertinent to this case are found in articles 24, 25, 26, 27, 44, 45, and 47 of the Vienna Convention on Diplomatic Relations. Among these are the inviolability of the archives and documents of the mission, the right of diplomatic agents and staff to communicate freely for official purposes, and the right to depart from the receiving state at any time they wish.

Over the hundreds of years that these principles have been recognized and honored throughout the international community, there have been occasions when a particular state has felt dissatisfied or aggrieved by the conduct of a diplomatic agent of another state or his government; and Iran is claiming some such grievances now. For hundreds of years, however, states have uniformly recognized that the only lawful course open to them is to declare the diplomatic agent *persona non grata*. When a state declares a diplomatic agent *persona non grata*, his government must withdraw him or suffer the eventual termination of his diplomatic status.

These uniformly recognized principles have been codified in article 9 of the Vienna convention. Under that treaty, a receiving state can in effect expel an objectionable diplomat—but under no circumstances may a state imprison an emissary or put him on trial. In diplomatic history and practice there is no precedent or justification for the seizure of a diplomat, let alone an entire diplomatic mission. There is also no precedent or justification of the imprisonment and trial of such persons in an attempt to coerce capitulation to certain demands. It is difficult to think of a more obvious, more flagrant violation of international law.

Vienna Convention on Consular Relations

Both Iran and the United States are also parties to the second international convention on which the United States relies in this proceeding—the 1963 Vienna Convention on Consular Relations. This convention reflects many of the same principles I have just described. Under the consular convention every state party, including Iran, has an international legal obligation to protect the consular facilities and members of the consular posts of every other state party.

Of course, when personnel of a diplomatic mission are providing consular services, they are entitled to the full protection afforded by the Vienna Convention on Diplomatic Relations. The convention on consular relations also requires the receiving state to permit another state party's consular officers to communicate with and have access to their nationals. This right is manifestly violated when the consular officers are themselves held incommunicado by force.

New York Convention

Apart from these two Vienna conventions, the United States and Iran also are parties to the New York Convention on the Prevention and Punishment of Crimes Against Internationally Protected Persons, Including Diplomatic Agents. One of the essential premises of the New York convention is stated in its preamble. It is that crimes against such internationally protected persons, including diplomatic agents, are "a

serious threat to the maintenance of normal international relations"
and "a matter of grave concern to the international community."

The convention defines a number of types of conduct as constituting crimes within its scope. Under article 2 it is a criminal act to
participate as an accomplice in an attack on the person or liberty of an
internationally protected person or in a violent attack on official premises. Under article 4 of the convention, every state party, including Iran,
is required to cooperate to prevent such crimes. Under article 7, every
state party must take steps to see that those responsible for such crimes
are prosecuted. The Government of Iran has violated every one of these
provisions in the plainest way.

All three of the treaties I have discussed were drafted by the U.N.
International Law Commission. They were adopted by conferences of
plenipotentiaries or by the U.N. General Assembly—and thus by the
vast majority of the states of the world. They have been so widely ratified
as to demonstrate that they reflect universally recognized rules of international law.

Bilateral Treaty of Amity

Finally, the United States relies in this case upon a bilateral treaty—
the 1955 Treaty of Amity, Economic Relations, and Consular Rights
between the United States and Iran. This treaty is in a sense even broader
than the three multilateral conventions to which I have previously
referred. Under article 2, paragraph 4, of the treaty of amity, each party
has a legal obligation to insure that within its territory the nationals of
the other party shall receive "the most constant protection and security."

In addition, article 2 provides that, if any U.S. national is in custody
in Iran, Iran must in every respect accord him "reasonable and humane
treatment." Under articles 2 and 19 any such national is entitled to
communicate with his own government and avail himself of the services
of his consular officials. Article 13 requires that the consular officers and
employees themselves be accorded the privileges and immunities accorded by general international usage and that they be treated in a fashion no less favorable than similar officers and employees of any third
country.

That completes my brief summary of the principles of international law that underlie the application of the United States. I could go
on to discuss the provisions of article 2, paragraphs 3 and 4, of the
Charter of the United Nations, under which Iran and all other U.N.
members are obligated to settle their disputes by peaceful means and to
refrain in their international relations from the threat or use of force.
But the United States believes that the three multilateral conventions
and the 1955 bilateral treaty provide as clear a legal predicate as can be
rationally required for its request for an indication of provisional
measures.

*White House Briefing for Members of Congress on the Situation
in Iran and Soviet Invasion of Afghanistan*

[EXCERPTS]

January 8, 1980

. . . I don't recall in history a time, at least in modern history, when our Nation was at peace that it was so deeply concerned as it has been the last two months since American hostages were kidnapped in our own Embassy in Tehran on November 4. I need not go into the details on that incident, because you're thoroughly familiar with it. But I will outline very quickly the basic principles that have guided me the last two months, and then at the end of my brief comments, I'll be glad to have questions from any of you.

This has not been a good two months. It's been a time of strain and trial. It's been a time of initimate negotiations with many foreign leaders, trying to accomplish the basic goals that we have followed since the beginning of this confrontation with the terrorists or kidnappers in Tehran.

Our first commitment has been to protect the interests of our Nation, the long-run, long-range interests; secondly, to do what we can to ensure the lives and the safety of the American hostages, our 50 fellow countrymen; third, to secure through diplomatic means, using every possible channel, their release—unharmed, if God be willing; fourth, to avoid bloodshed, which would very likely lead to the death of our hostages; and fifth and most difficult, to maintain support for the American position by the vast majority of nations on Earth. This has not been an easy last task, because historically in the United Nations and other international fora, our country has not been a favorite, because we are powerful and a super power and because there is jealousy and animosity at times and distrust toward us.

We've now had four votes in the Security Council, as you know. We've not yet experienced a negative vote. On the last vote to set a deadline for the imposition of sanctions and to call the Secretary-General's trip to Iran, there were four abstentions—the Soviet Union and their puppet, Czechoslovakia, and two small Moslem nations, Bangladesh and Kuwait. The other 11 nations voted to send the Secretary-General to Iran for a last effort to negotiate the release of the hostages, at the end of which time the Security Council would come back and take action on possible economic sanctions.

In the International Court of Justice, the vote was 15 to 0, unanimous vote.

So far then, we have accomplished all the goals that we set for ourselves except the release of the hostages, and we are still exploring every possible avenue for that release.

The most difficult part of the Iranian question is that there's no government entity with whom we can communicate or negotiate or register a complaint or a request. When the Secretary-General went over to Iran, he came back and reported the same thing that we had already known, and that is that the most powerful single political entity in Iran consists of the international terrorists or the kidnappers who are holding our hostages. Whenever there has been a showdown concerning the hostages between Khomeini or the Revolutionary Council versus the terrorists, the terrorists have always prevailed.

We don't know what will happen in the future, but I think you possibly recognize that this small group of people—who may originally have comprised some students, but who are not students and should not be referred to as students—have achieved, with the holding of American hostages, a great and significant political influence in Iran. They don't necessarily have as one of their prime interests the integrity of Iran as a nation or the well-being of the Iranian people or even the security of the country within which they live. And so there is no legitimate political bargaining leverage that can be exerted on them, and there is no entity there with whom one can negotiate.

They know that the consequences to Iran will be quite severe if our hostages are injured or killed, and I think only the presence of a very strong military force in the Arabian Sea has deterred them so far from taking action that would have been even more abhorrent to the rest of the world. That problem persists. It's an ever-present consideration of mine and yours. And I'm determined that this country will not forget for a moment those hostages. And the last hostage there is just as important to me as the first one.

Our country is remarkably unified. I've had strong support, which I deeply appreciate, and the American people have been surprisingly patient, which, as you know, is not a characteristic of Americans. But I think most people who've studied the situation, who've looked at the map, who've seen where the Embassy is located within Tehran, can see that a strike force or a military action that might be oriented toward the release of the hostages would almost certainly end in failure and almost certainly end in the death of the hostages.

They are being held in small groups, two or perhaps three in a group, with heavily armed militants constantly guarding them and the hostages constantly being tied, with their hands bound at all times.

We'll continue to persist. Our next step will be in the United Nations to have sanctions imposed against Iran. I cannot predict to you that the imposition of those sanctions, if we get the nine requisite votes, will cause an early release of the hostages. We pray that something will happen and that eventually Iran will recognize that the threat to them is not from the United States, but even more vividly from the Soviet Union, who have, on Christmas Eve, invaded Afghanistan. . . .

Because of the Iranian question, we have greatly built up our naval forces in the northern China Sea or in the Arabian Sea. Those will be maintained at a higher level than they have been in the past. And as you know, there has been a marshaling of worldwide public opinion, not only in the condemnation of the Iranian terrorists who hold our hostages but also against the Soviet Union for their unprecedented invasion of Afghanistan in this recent few weeks. . . .

United States Seeks United Nations Sanctions Against Iran: Statement to the United Nations Security Council

January 13, 1980

Ambassador McHenry

For the third time in the last six weeks, this Council meets to consider a dangerous violation of the principle of diplomatic inviolability—one that, in the words of the Secretary General, poses a serious threat to international peace and security.

After 70 days, the 50 personnel at the American Embassy, who were taken hostage by a lawless mob in Tehran, are still prisoners. We have yet to have a statement of opposition to their imprisonment from the Iranian authorities.

Those few outsiders who have seen the hostages briefly, during carefully orchestrated visits, report that the hostages are isolated, psychologically abused, and afforded an inadequate diet, despite assurances to the contrary. Some have suffered the humiliation of forced participation in propaganda broadcasts. Neutral observers are not permitted to visit them regularly to assess their condition or to minister to their needs. Even the Secretary General of the United Nations, the emissary of the world community, was barred from seeing the hostages.

The past two months have been marked by repeated calls for the release of the hostages from nearly every member of the international community. The Secretary General and many members of this Organization have devoted tireless efforts to promote a peaceful resolution of the present crisis. The broad international support we have received in our efforts to secure the release of the hostages has given encouragement to the American people in this difficult and trying period. On their behalf, I thank all who have worked so hard.

It might be useful to recall the measured steps which have brought us to the current situation.

On two separate occasions during November, the President of the Security Council, expressing the will of the members of the Council, appealed to Iran to release the hostages. But the hostages were not freed.

On December 4 of last year, this Council, by unanimous vote, urgently called on the Government of Iran to release immediately the personnel of the American Embassy who were being held in Tehran, to provide them with protection, and to allow them to leave Iran. Still the hostages were not freed.

On December 15, the International Court of Justice gave the authority of the world's highest tribunal on international legal matters to the position set forth in the Council's resolution. The Court noted that ". . . there is no more fundamental prerequisite for the conduct of relations between States than the inviolability of diplomatic envoys and embassies. . . ." The Court ordered the Government of Iran to release the hostages immediately and to restore possession of the U.S. Embassy in Tehran to American authorities. Still the hostages were not freed.

On December 31, this Council, without dissent, adopted Resolution 461, in which it deplored the continued detention of the hostages as contrary to the order of the International Court and its own prior resolution and urgently called once again on the Government of Iran to release immediately all U.S. nationals being held as hostages. In that resolution, the Council decided that it would adopt effective measures under articles 39 and 41 of the U.N. Charter in the event that Iran did not comply with its mandate. And still the hostages have not been freed.

Five times the world community, acting through the fully constituted organs of the United Nations, has pleaded with the Government and people of Iran to conform to the precepts of international law and release the hostages. Five times our collective plea has fallen on deaf ears.

The International Court and the court of world opinion have demanded that Iran release the hostages in accordance with both the accepted norms of international behavior and its treaty obligations. Yet Iran continues to imprison diplomatic personnel as part of a campaign of terrorism and political blackmail by elements in Iran who have the support of Iranian authorities.

Resolution 461 is a decision of the Security Council adopted under chapter VII of the Charter. The operative language of that resolution, including the Council's decision to adopt effective measures under articles 39 and 41 of the Charter in the event of noncompliance with the resolution, continues in full force. Under article 25 and article 2, paragraph 2, of the Charter, all members of the United Nations are obliged to accept that decision and to carry out its mandate.

Clearly Iran has not complied with the resolution and freed the hostages. The time has, therefore, come for the Security Council to adopt the effective measures against Iran under articles 39 and 41 of the U.N. Charter that are required by paragraph 7 of Resolution 461.

The members of the Council have before them the measures that my government proposes. Admittedly, they should not be taken lightly. But after two months of restraint by the American people and the world community, during which we have explored every possible avenue for a solution, we have failed to secure the release of the hostages and to restore the rule of international law.

Our deliberations this weekend exemplify the patience and good faith with which we have sought to resolve this crisis. The Council was originally scheduled to vote on these measures last Friday, January 11. In the hours before the meeting, various suggestions and reports from voices purporting to speak for Iran led some to believe progress toward release of the hostages was possible. They believed further clarification of Iran's position was necessary before proceeding to vote on sanctions.

Reluctantly the United States agreed to delay the vote—not because we saw any evidence of movement toward a solution but because we were, and are, prepared to explore every proposal that holds any realistic prospect of securing the release of the hostages. The Secretary General then sent an urgent message to Tehran, seeking clarification of the unwritten proposal which some thought they had heard Friday afternoon.

Last night the Secretary General received a letter, but the letter did not respond to the Secretary General's message. The letter does not mention the existence of the hostages or acknowledge the world's concern and responsibility for them. Even the most dexterous among us have had difficulty finding a clue in the letter that could encourage responsible governments to delay the vote on sanctions any longer.

The most that can be said for the letter is that, for the first time since last November, when Mr. Bani-Sadr resigned as Foreign Minister, Iran has sent a written message to the United Nations. Even so, Iran has now explicitly refused to abide by any pronouncements from the United Nations with which it does not agree—including, obviously, the demand for the immediate release of the hostages contained in Resolution 461.

We delayed Friday's vote in order to explore any possible hope represented by Friday's suggestions and by this letter. To have gone ahead without doing so would have been irresponsible. But our efforts at clarification have come to a frustrating end. It would be even more irresponsible for us to delay any longer in discharging our obligations under Resolution 461 and the Charter. Clearly the time to take effective measures has come.

When Secretary of State Vance addressed this Council on December 29, he said that: "As long as Iran remains indifferent to the voices of reason and mercy that have been raised from every corner of the world, as long as it refuses to recognize the common rules of international behavior, it must accept the consequences of its deliberate actions." The sanctions we propose will serve to demonstrate that Iran's continued defiance of international law will result in its increased isolation from the world community.

While the proposed sanctions constitute a meaningful and significant expression of the world's condemnation, they are yet a temperate response to Iranian intemperance. To adopt measures less stringent than those proposed in the resolution before the Council would be tantamount to adopting no measures at all. And to adopt no measures at all would both violate the binding mandate of paragraph 6 of Resolution 461 and constitute an abdication of our obligation to search for peaceful resolutions to international disputes and uphold the fundamental principles of international law.

Some have urged that we not pursue sanctions because they may not result in the immediate release of the hostages and may even harden Iranian intransigence.

We hope that sanctions will strengthen the voices of those in Iran who argue that the holding of diplomatic hostages is wrong and will result in Iran's increased isolation from the international community.

Failure to impose sanctions will confirm the belief of those in Iran who feel that they can act with impunity. The effort of our failure will, thus, be measured in a lessening of this Council's ability to deal effectively with international crises.

Others have urged that the Council set aside the question of sanctions in order to focus the world's attention on Soviet aggression in Afghanistan.

But Soviet aggression in Afghanistan does not reduce our concern over the situation in Iran. On the contrary, it should heighten Iran's concern for its future as an independent nation. It should bring Iranians to a realization that they must rebuild their country quickly and prepare to defend their borders. It should make Iran aware of the danger posed by its isolation from the rest of the world community.

Once sanctions have been imposed, the key to ending this crisis and restoring its status as a fully participating member of the international community will lie with Iran. It has only to free the hostages and provide them with safe conduct until they can leave for home, and the sanctions will automatically expire. Iran can even avoid imposition of the sanctions altogether by releasing the hostages before the members of the United Nations complete the process of taking the necessary steps under their constitutions and laws to implement sanctions. Nothing will prejudice Iran's right to seek redress of its grievances, whether against the United States or its former rulers, in an appropriate international forum.

I remind the Council that this is not a bilateral quarrel but a confrontation between Iran and the entire international community. The continued viability of cherished and heretofore universally observed principles of international law is at stake. As the distinguished delegate from Nigeria, who served so ably on this Council during prior debates, said last month, diplomatic immunities and inviolability are so much a part of international law and custom that all nations that rely on and respect law have an obligation to defend them.

The members of this Council must now do what we can do, in the words of Secretary Vance, ". . . demonstrate that the rule of law has meaning and that our machinery of peace has practical relevance."

We must do what we can under the Charter to defuse this most serious threat to peace and world order. That is the object and purpose of the collective security system. We must show Iran that the world is determined to see the hostages freed.

Draft Resolution

The Security Council,

. . . Acting in accordance with articles 39 and 41 of the Charter of the United Nations,

1. Urgently calls, once again, on the Government of the Islamic Republic of Iran to release immediately all persons of United States nationality being held as hostages in Iran, to provide them protection and to allow them to leave the country;

2. Decides that, until such time as the hostages are released and have safely departed from Iran, all States Members of the United Nations:

(a) Shall prevent the sale or supply, by their nationals or from their territories, whether or not originating in their territories, to or destined for Iranian governmental entities in Iran or any other person or body in Iran, or to or destined for any other person or body for the purposes of any enterprise carried on in Iran, of all items, commodities, or products, except food, medicine, and supplies intended strictly for medical purposes;

(b) Shall prevent the shipment by vessel, aircraft, railway, or other land transport of their registration or owned by or under charter to their nationals, or the carriage whether or not in bond by land transport facilities across their territories of any of the items, commodities, and products covered by subparagraph (a) which are consigned to or destined for Iranian governmental entities or any person or body in Iran, or to any enterprise carried on in Iran;

(c) Shall not make available to Iranian authorities or to any person in Iran or to any enterprise controlled by any Iranian governmental entity any new credits or loans; shall not, with respect to such persons or enterprises, make available any new deposit facilities or allow substantial increases in existing non-dollar deposits or allow more favourable terms of payment than customarily used in international commercial transactions; and shall act in a businesslike manner in exercising any rights when payments due on existing credits or loans are not made on time and shall require any persons or entities within their jurisdiction to do likewise;

(d) Shall prevent the shipment from their territories on vessels or aircraft registered in Iran of products and commodities covered by subparagraph (a) above;

(e) Shall reduce to a minimum the personnel of Iranian diplomatic missions accredited to them;

(f) Shall prevent their nationals, or firms located in their territories, from engaging in new service contracts in support of industrial projects in Iran, other than those concerned with medical care;

(g) Shall prevent their nationals or any person or body in their territories from engaging in any activity which evades or has the purpose of evading any of the decisions set out in this resolution;

3. Decides that all States Members of the United Nations shall give effect forthwith to the decisions set out in operative paragraph 2 of this resolution notwithstanding any contract entered into or license granted before the date of this resolution;

4. Calls upon all States Members of the United Nations to carry out these decisions of the Security Council in accordance with article 25 of the Charter;

5. Urges, having regard to the principles stated in article 2 of the Charter, States not members of the United Nations to act in accordance with the provisions of the present resolution;

6. Calls upon all other United Nations bodies and the Specialized Agencies of the United Nations and their Members to conform their relations with Iran to the terms of this resolution;

7. Calls upon all States Members of the United Nations, and in particular those with primary responsibility under the Charter for the maintenance of international peace and security, to assist effectively in the implementation of the measures called for by the present resolution;

8. Calls upon all States Members of the United Nations or of the Specialized Agencies to report to the Secretary General by 1 February 1980, on measures taken to implement the present resolution;

9. Requests the Secretary General to report to the Council on the progress of the implementation of the present resolution, the first report to be submitted not later than 1 March 1980.

Vote on Draft Resolution, January 13, 1980

For: France, Jamaica, Niger, Norway, Philippines, Portugal, Tunisia, United Kingdom, United States, Zambia.
Against: German Democratic Republic, U.S.S.R.
Abstain: Bangladesh, Mexico.
Not participating: China.

Ambassador McHenry

The Security Council has now completed its effort to discharge the legally binding obligation imposed on it by the passage of Resolution 461/79 and to adopt effective measures against Iran under articles 39 and 41 of the U.N. Charter. It has been prevented from doing so by the negative vote of the Soviet Union. Written by Lewis Carroll as pages out of Alice in Wonderland, the light becomes darkness. The victim becomes the criminal. Commitment to international law becoms a defense of anarchy. How extraordinary to hear from a nation that has just sent its armies and gauleiters into Afghanistan to describe our efforts to seek the freedom of 50 of our citizens held hostage by armed terrorists as interference in "the internal affairs" of Iran.

The Soviet vote is a cynical and irresponsible exercise of its veto power. The motive behind it is transparent. The Soviets hope that, by blocking sanctions, they can divert attention from their subjugation of Afghanistan and curry favor with the Government and people of Iran, who are among those most directly affected by the Afghan invasion.

But the Soviets hope in vain. The nations of the world, viewing this veto in tandem with the Soviet invasion of Afghanistan, cannot fail to note that Soviet tributes to the primacy of international law are purely rhetorical and that Soviet policy only conforms to international norms on a selective and self-serving basis.

And in Iran, even though chaos seems to reign, it should be apparent that the Soviet veto is an act of political expediency designed to buy Iranian silence on Afghanistan and Soviet advantage in the region.

By Resolution 461, the Council undertook a binding obligation to adopt effective measures under article 25 of the Charter; all member states are obliged to respect the provisions of Resolution 461. A Soviet veto now attempts to block the membership from fulfilling that obligation.

The question then arises: what a member, bound by Resolution 461, and acting in good faith, pursuant to its obligations under article 2, paragraph 2 of the Charter, should do to implement it.

Most obviously, Iran remains bound immediately to release the hostages pursuant to Resolution 461. But in addition to that paramount obligation, the membership of the United Nations at large remains obliged to review the situation and the event of Iran's noncompliance with it—an event which has come to pass—to take effective measures consistent with the Charter to carry out that resolution.

My government has already instituted measures designed to exert economic pressure on Iran, as envisaged in the vetoed resolution. These measures will be applied firmly and vigorously until the hostages have been released. We urge all other members of the United Nations to join with us in the application of meaningful measures against the continued holding of the hostages in defiance of international law. Only thus will we demonstrate to Iran that their lawless actions are viewed with disfavor by all nations. The United States will, of course, welcome and cooperate with the continued good offices of the Secretary General and all members of the world community in seeking a solution to the present crisis. We sincerely hope that, despite the Soviet veto, our efforts will lead to the return of the hostages and the return to the rule of law in international affairs.

Presidential Message to the Congress Reporting on Further
Prohibitions on Transactions with Iran and
Transmitting Executive Order

April 17, 1980

To THE CONGRESS OF THE UNITED STATES: Pursuant to section 204(b) of the International Emergency Economic Powers Act, 50 U.S.C. 1703, I hereby report to the Congress that I have today declared a further national emergency and exercised the authority granted by this Act to impose further prohibitions on transactions with Iran.

I am enclosing a copy of an Executive Order I have issued today making this declaration and exercising these authorities pursuant to 50 U.S.C. 1641(b).

1. The circumstances necessitating the exercise of this authority are the continuing events in Iran, including the actions and omissions of the Government of Iran in violation of its obligations under international law, which caused me to declare a national emergency on November 14, 1979, and to take the action set forth in Executive Order No. 12170 of November 14, 1979, and Executive Order No. 12205 of April 7, 1980, and the additional unusual and extraordinary threat to the national security, foreign policy and economy of the United States created by events subsequent to November 14, 1979, in Iran and neighboring countries, including the Soviet invasion of Afghanistan.

2. The events in Iran and neighboring countries threaten the strategic and vital interests of the United States. The occupation of the United States Embassy in Tehran and the taking and holding of American citizens hostage there and the Soviet occupation of Afghanistan are flagrant violations of the international order upon which the security of all nations and international peace are based. Such actions in a region of such vital importance to the United States, and most of the world, constitute a grave threat to the national security, foreign policy and economy of the United States.

3. For these reasons, I find it necessary to prohibit the following:

(a) Effective immediately, the direct or indirect import from Iran into the United States of Iranian goods or services, other than materials imported for news publication or news broadcast dissemination.

(b) Effective immediately, any transaction with a foreign person or foreign entity by any citizen or permanent resident of the United States relating to that person's travel to Iran after today. (I am simultaneously authorizing the Secretary of State to institute passport and departure controls to restrict travel to Iran by citizens and permanent residents of the United States.)

(c) Effective seven days from today, the payment by or on behalf of any citizen or permanent resident of the United States who is within Iran of any expenses for transactions within Iran.

The prohibitions in paragraphs (b) and (c) will not apply to a person who is also a citizen of Iran or a journalist or other person who is regularly employed by a news gathering or transmitting organization and who travels to Iran or is within Iran for the purpose of gathering or transmitting news, making news or documentary films, or similar activities.

4. Effective immediately, I have also amended Executive Order No. 12205 to prohibit payments, transfers of credit or other transfers of funds or other property or interests therein to any person in Iran, except for purposes of family remittances. This prohibition also does not apply to news gathering activities.

5. I have also directed the Secretary of the Treasury, effective fourteen days from today, to revoke existing licenses for transactions by persons subject to the jurisdiction of the United States with Iran Air, the National Iranian Oil Company, and the National Iranian Gas Company previously issued pursuant to regulations under Executive Order No. 12170 or Executive Order No. 12205. This will have the effect of closing down the offices in the United States of those entities.

6. In addition, I have ordered that all undelivered military equipment and spare parts purchased by Iran through the Department of Defense under the Arms Export Control Act now be distributed to our own Armed Forces or transferred to other buyers. The delivery of these defense articles was suspended in November 1979, and they are presently in storage or in the procurement pipeline.

7. This action is taken with respect to Iran and its nationals for the reasons described in this report.

JIMMY CARTER

United States Measures to Further Isolate Iran: Statement before the Subcommittees on International Economic Policy and Trade and on Europe and the Middle East of the House Committee on Foreign Affairs

by Peter Constable, Deputy Assistant Secretary for Near Eastern and South Asian Affairs

May 8, 1980

I welcome this opportunity to discuss with you the measures we have taken under the International Emergency Economic Powers Act. Let me begin by setting the crisis—and our efforts to resolve it—in perspective.

As you know, on November 4, 1979, a mob overran our Embassy compound in Tehran. Militant students occupied the Embassy and announced that our personnel would be held until we returned the Shah to Iran. We had early assurances from officials of Prime Minister Bazargan's government that the hostages would be released. But Ayatollah

Khomeini and prominent clerical leaders announced shortly thereafter their support for the student militants. Our Chargé in Tehran, Bruce Laingen, who was at the Foreign Ministry when the takeover occurred, was not permitted to discuss the release of our people with Prime Minister Bazargan. Then, on November 6, Bazargan himself resigned—apparently in protest against the militants' actions.

A presidential mission headed by former Attorney General Ramsey Clark was sent to Iran, but before the delegation could reach Tehran, Ayatollah Khomeini forbade any Iranian contact with it. Then the newly appointed "overseer" at the Iranian Foreign Ministry, Abdol Bani-Sadr, announced on November 12 that before the hostages could be released the United States would have to:

— Admit that the property and the fortune of the Shah were stolen;
— Promise to refrain from further intervention in Iranian affairs; and
— Extradite the Shah to Iran for trial.

Four early developments in the crisis—Khomeini's support for the terrorism of the militant students, the collapse of the relatively moderate Bazargan government, the unacceptable conditions announced by Bani-Sadr, and Khomeini's orders against any Iranian contact with the U.S. Government—provided convincing evidence that the Iranian authorities had in effect assumed responsibility for the seizure of the Embassy and the hostages and were unwilling or unable to bring about their immediate release.

In view of these conclusions the President undertook a series of actions to demonstrate that the Iranian actions were unacceptable and that we were determined to press Iran for the early release of the hostages. A number of these steps involved diplomatic initiatives worldwide through bilateral contacts with other governments and multilaterally in the United Nations. The President also ordered a series of unilateral economic actions which are detailed below.

On November 12 the President directed a ban on U.S. purchases of Iranian oil under provisions of the Trade Expansion Act. He did so to make clear that our energy needs would not influence our response to the hostage crisis and that the United States would not be blackmailed on the basis of our oil import requirements. The United States then learned that Iran was about to order all Iranian funds moved out of the United States. This jeopardized billions of dollars in potential U.S. claims—both public and private—against those assets and threatened disruption of the international financial system.

The President moved quickly to respond to Iran's violation of international law and to protect the interests of U.S. citizens by preventing the movement of the Iranian funds. In order to do so, the President invoked the provisions of the International Emergency Economic Powers Act. His decision reflected a finding that the situation in Iran then—as now—constitutes "an unusual and extraordinary threat to the national security, foreign policy, and economy of the United States." The act permits the President under certain circumstances to:

. . . investigate, regulate, direct and compel, nullify, void, prevent or prohibit, any acquisition, holding, withholding, use, transfer, withdrawal, transportation, importation or exportation of, or dealing in, or exercising any right, power, or privilege with respect to, or transactions involving, any property in which any foreign country or a national thereof has any interest.

By Executive order 12170 of November 14, 1979, which declared a national emergency with respect to Iran, the President ordered the blocking of Iranian Government assets, and delegated the power to implement the order to the Secretary of the Treasury. This order blocked in excess of $8 billion in this country and abroad.

These presidential actions under the International Emergency Economic Powers Act—and others that followed—have been implemented by the Department of the Treasury through the adoption and amendment of Iranian assets control regulations. Treasury adopted the initial Iranian assets control regulations on November 14, 1979, to implement Executive order 12170 by blocking Iranian assets, and it has amended those regulations from time to time since then.

Our intent was to impress on the Iranians that by continuing to hold the hostages they risked increasing international pressure and increasing direct costs to Iran. At the same time, we continued to pursue every peaceful means available to us to bring this ordeal to an honorable conclusion. Through our efforts in the United Nations, the International Court of Justice, and elsewhere, we aimed at underscoring the growing isolation Iran faces in the international community by its continued gross violation of international law and conduct between civilized nations.

As you will recall, the U.N. Security Council on December 4 called unanimously for the release of the hostages, and on January 13 ten members approved economic sanctions against Iran in a resolution which was vetoed by the Soviet Union. The International Court of Justice also ruled unanimously that Iran must release the hostages and declared the inviolability of diplomatic envoys a fundamental basis of relations between states.

Despite our approaches and those of other nations, divisions within Iran prevented any real progress at this time toward a resolution of the crisis or indeed any dialogue with Iranian authorities.

Later, however, after Bani-Sadr was elected President on January 28—though not permitted to form a government pending election of a new parliament—opportunities appeared to open for diplomacy. We pursued them seriously through the U.N. Secretary General and a variety of intermediaries. We held back temporarily our efforts to press for further international sanctions to give these prospects every opportunity to succeed. But these efforts finally broke down because differences between secular and clerical factions in Iran prevented the Iranian authorities from honoring their promises. The President then moved promptly on April 7 to impose new measures to increase the price the Iranians will pay so long as they deny our people their freedom. Additional unilateral sanctions were also announced on April 17.

— Executive order 12205 of April 7, 1980, prohibited most exports to Iran and imposed prohibitions on financial dealings with Iran.

— Executive order 12211 of April 17, 1980, imposed additional prohibitions on financial transfers to persons or entities in Iran, imports from Iran, and transactions relating to travel to Iran. It also ordered restrictions on travel to Iran under the Immigration and Nationality Act.

As we consider the present situation in Iran, we should have no illusions about the difficulties ahead. We are dealing with a government in Iran that has few of the attributes we expect of national authorities. Iran is a country torn apart by continuing revolutionary turmoil. Our people are hostage not only to the militants but to internal power struggles and rivalries. And we are dealing with a nation that faces not only the threat of internal disintegration but external threats to its independence and territorial integrity from nations on its borders.

We will continue to take such steps as may be necessary and feasible to secure the safe release of the hostages. We will continue to move forward with strong and collective economic and political sanctions to convince the Iranians that it is in their own self-interest to bring an end to the hostage situation. The nine members of the European Community, and other friends and allies, have reaffirmed their support for severe sanctions against Iran. The sanctions contemplated accord, in most cases, with the U.N. Security Council resolution of January 13. Some governments are now seeking legislation to enable them to join this effort. I am confident that the measures they have agreed to as necessary—political steps followed by economic sanctions—will be put into effect as promised.

However, these measures will take time to have an effect. We must have patience as well as determination. It was and is a reality that these pressures are not likely to produce a quick result. Nonetheless, strong, clear, effective international pressures are more important now than ever before to drive home to the Iranians that their present course can only bring growing hardship for their people and continuing damage to their hopes to consolidate their revolution by building a strong, stable, unified, and independent Iran.

We will continue to hold the Iranian authorities fully responsible for the safety and well-being of our people. If our people have indeed been dispersed from the Embassy compound, the responsibility the Iranian authorities have assumed for their safety becomes all the more important.

We will also make every effort to bring home to the Iranian people that the threat to their revolution does not come from the United States; it comes from this crisis. We would like to see a stable and prosperous Iran. If this matter is resolved shortly and without harm to our people, the way will be open to develop a relationship that serves our mutual interests. Clearly, it is not possible to do so as long as our people are endangered and imprisoned illegally.

The measures we have taken under the International Emergency Economic Powers Act were clearly necessary to respond to an "unusual and extraordinary threat." Any decisions which the President may take on additional steps in the months ahead will also be made in conformity with the authority granted by this act.

President Carter's Statement to the Nation on the Hostage Rescue Attempt in Iran

April 25, 1980

Late yesterday, I cancelled a carefully planned operation which was underway in Iran to position our rescue team for later withdrawal of American hostages who've been held captive there since November fourth.

Equipment failure in the rescue helicopters made it necessary to end the mission. As our team was withdrawing, after my order to do so, two of our American aircraft collided on the ground following a refueling operation in a remote desert location in Iran. Other information about this rescue mission will be made available to the American people when it is appropriate to do so.

There was no fighting; there was no combat. But to my deep regret, eight of the crewmen of the two aircraft which collided were killed, and several other Americans were hurt in the accident.

Our people were immediately airlifted from Iran. Those who were injured have gotten medical treatment, and all of them are expected to recover.

No knowledge of this operation by any Iranian officials or authorities was evident to us until several hours after all Americans were withdrawn from Iran.

Our rescue team knew, and I knew, that the operation was certain to be difficult and it was certain to be dangerous. We were all convinced that if and when the rescue operation had been commenced that it had an excellent chance of success. They were all volunteers; they were all highly trained. I met with their leaders before they went on this operation. They knew then what hopes of mine and of all Americans they carried with them.

To the families of those who died and who were wounded, I want to express the admiration I feel for the courage of their loved ones and the sorrow that I feel personally for their sacrifice.

The mission on which they were embarked was a humanitarian mission. It was not directed against Iran; it was not directed against the people of Iran. It was not undertaken with any feeling of hostility toward Iran or its people. It has caused no Iranian casualties.

Planning for this rescue effort began shortly after our Embassy was seized. But, for a number of reasons, I waited until now to put those rescue plans into effect. To be feasible, this complex operation had to be the product of intensive planning and intensive training and repeated rehearsal.

However, a resolution of this crisis through negotiations and with voluntary action on the part of the Iranian officials was obviously then, has been, and will be preferable.

This rescue attempt had to await my judgment that the Iranian authorities could not or would not resolve this crisis on their own initiative. With the steady unraveling of authority in Iran and the mounting dangers that were posed to the safety of the hostages themselves and the growing realization that their early release was highly unlikely, I made a decision to commence the rescue operations plans.

This attempt became a necessity and a duty. The readiness of our team to undertake the rescue made it completely practicable. Accordingly, I made the decision to set our long-developed plans into operation. I ordered this rescue mission prepared in order to safeguard American lives, to protect America's national interests, and to reduce the tensions in the world that have been caused among many nations as this crisis has continued. It was my decision to attempt the rescue operation. It was my decision to cancel it when problems developed in the placement of our rescue team for a future rescue operation. The responsibility is fully my own.

In the aftermath of the attempt, we continue to hold the Government of Iran responsible for the safety and for the early release of the American hostages who have been held so long.

The United States remains determined to bring about their safe release at the earliest date possible. As President, I know that our entire nation feels the deep gratitude I feel for the brave men who were prepared to rescue their fellow Americans from captivity. And, as President, I also know that the nation shares not only my disappointment that the rescue effort could not be mounted because of mechanical difficulties but also my determination to persevere and to bring all of our hostages home to freedom.

We have been disappointed before. We will not give up in our efforts. Throughout this extraordinarily difficult period, we have pursued and will continue to pursue every possible avenue to secure the release of the hostages. In these efforts, the support of the American people and of our friends throughout the world has been a most crucial element. That support of other nations is even more important now. We will seek to continue, along with other nations and with the officials of Iran, a prompt resolution of the crisis without any loss of life and through peaceful and diplomatic means.

President Carter's Letter to the Speaker of the House and the President Pro Tempore of the Senate Reporting on the Failed Rescue Operation

April 26, 1980

DEAR MR. SPEAKER: Because of my desire that Congress be informed on this matter and consistent with the reporting provisions of the War Powers Resolution of 1973 (Public Law 93-148), I submit this report.

On April 24, 1980, elements of the United States Armed Forces under my direction commenced the positioning stage of a rescue operation which was designed, if the subsequent stages had been executed, to effect the rescue of the American hostages who have been held captive in Iran since November 4, 1979, in clear violation of international law and the norms of civilized conduct among nations. The subsequent phases of the operation were not executed. Instead, for the reasons described below, all these elements were withdrawn from Iran and no hostilities occurred.

The sole objective of the operation that actually occurred was to position the rescue team for the subsequent effort to withdraw the American hostages. The rescue team was under my overall command and control and required my approval before executing the subsequent phases of the operation designed to effect the rescue itself. No such approval was requested or given because, as described below, the mission was aborted.

Beginning approximately 10:30 a.m. EST on April 24, six U.S. C-130 transport aircraft and eight RH-53 helicopters entered Iran airspace. Their crews were not equipped for combat. Some of the C-130 aircraft carried a force of approximately 90 members of the rescue team equipped for combat, plus various support personnel.

From approximately 2:00 to 4:00 p.m. EST the six transports and six of the eight helicopters landed at a remote desert site in Iran approximately 200 miles from Tehran where they disembarked the rescue team, commenced refueling operations and began to prepare for the subsequent phases.

During the flight to the remote desert site, two of the eight helicopters developed operating difficulties. One was forced to return to the carrier *Nimitz*; the second was forced to land in the desert, but its crew was taken aboard another of the helicopters and proceeded on to the landing site. Of the six helicopters which landed at the remote desert site, one developed a serious hydraulic problem and was unable to continue with the mission. The operational plans called for a minimum of six helicopters in good operational condition able to proceed from the desert site. Eight helicopters had been included in the force to provide sufficient redundancy without imposing excessive strains on the refueling and exit requirements of the operation. When the number of helicopters available to continue dropped to five, it was determined that the operation could not proceed as planned. Therefore, on the recommendation of the force commander and my military advisers, I decided to cancel the mission and ordered the United States Armed Forces involved to return from Iran.

During the process of withdrawal, one of the helicopters accidentally collided with one the C-130 aircraft, which was preparing to take off, resulting in the death of eight personnel and the injury of several others. At this point, the decision was made to load all surviving personnel aboard the remaining C-130 aircraft and to abandon the remaining helicopters at the landing site. Altogether, the United States Armed Forces remained on the ground for a total of approximately three hours. The five remaining aircraft took off about 5:45 p.m. EST and departed from Iran airspace without further incident at about 8:00 p.m. EST on April 24. No United States Armed Forces remain in Iran.

The remote desert area was selected to conceal this phase of the mission from discovery. At no time during the temporary presence of United States Armed Forces in Iran did they encounter Iranian forces of any type. We believe, in fact, that no Iranian military forces were in the desert area, and that the Iranian forces were unaware of the presence of United States Armed Forces until after their departure from Iran. As planned, no hostilities occurred during this phase of the mission—the only phase that was executed.

At one point during the period in which United States Armed Forces elements were on the ground at the desert landing site a bus containing forty-four Iranian civilians happened to pass along a nearby road. The bus was stopped and then disabled. Its occupants were detained by United States Armed Forces until their departure, and then released unharmed. One truck closely followed by a second vehicle also passed by while United States Armed Forces elements were on the ground. These elements stopped the truck by a shot into its headlights. The driver ran to the second vehicle which then escaped across the desert. Neither of these incidents affected the subsequent decision to terminate the mission. . . .

Sincerely,

JIMMY CARTER

Sources of Documents

The following abbreviations are used frequently in this list of sources:

Bevans refers to *Treaties and Other International Agreements of the United States of America, 1776-1949,* compiled by Charles I. Bevans in 12 volumes (Washington, D.C.: U.S. Department of State, 1968-1974). This collection contains treaties and agreements through 1949.

UST refers to *United States Treaties and Other International Agreements,* compiled by the U.S. Department of State in 29 volumes to date (Washington, D.C.: Government Printing Office, 1950-date). This collection contains treaties and agreements from 1950 to date.

Foreign Relations refers to *Foreign Relations of the United States,* prepared by the U.S. Department of State (Washington, D.C.: Government Printing Office) and presently covering 1861-1950.

Foreign Policy refers to *American Foreign Policy: Current Documents,* prepared by the U.S. Department of State (Washington, D.C.: Government Printing Office). The years 1941-1949 are covered by a single volume entitled *A Decade of American Foreign Policy: Basic Documents, 1941-1949.* The years 1950-1955 are covered by two volumes entitled *American Foreign Policy: Basic Documents, 1950-1955.*

The various *Presidential Papers* are cited by name and year and refer to *Public Papers of the Presidents of the United States* (Washington, D.C.: Government Printing Office). However, *Weekly Compilation: Carter* refers to *Weekly Compilation of Presidential Documents,* prepared by the Office of the Federal Register, (Washington, D.C.: Government Printing Office).

Previously unprinted documents (most of which have been declassified in the past few years) are marked by an asterisk (*). These documents are cited according to U.S. National Archives files and are cross-referenced to more accessible microform collections. For additional information about *Declassified Documents* (referred to as *Declas. Docs.*), contact Carrollton Press (1911 Fort Myer Drive, Arlington, VA 22209). For more information about UPA's publications (*Documents of the National Security Council, 1947-1977; Records of the Joint Chiefs of Staff; OSS/State Department Intelligence and Research Reports;* and many other collections), contact University Publications of America (44 North Market Street, Frederick, MD 21701).

Chapter 1
A PERIPHERAL RELATIONSHIP: 1856-WORLD WAR II
[pp. 1-74]

Treaty of Friendship and Commerce (1856)
8 *Bevans* 1254.

Early Diplomatic Communications
Foreign Relations, 1901, pp. 424-26.

Shuster Mission
Foreign Relations, 1911, pp. 679-86.

United States Attitude toward Persian National Aspirations
Foreign Relations, 1918, Supplement 1, Part 1, pp. 895-97, 900-2, 912-14.

Postwar Relief to Persia
Foreign Relations, 1918, Supplement 2, pp. 563-71.

United States Protests British Postwar Anglo-Persian Agreement
Foreign Relations, 1919, Vol. II, pp. 700, 707-11, 714-17.

Renewed Persian Overtures for American Advisers
Foreign Relations, 1921, Vol. II, pp. 633-35, 638-40.

1st Millspaugh Mission, 1922-1927
Foreign Relations, 1927, Vol. III, pp. 527, 531-43, 547-51, 554.

Negotiations for Oil Concessions in Persia
Foreign Relations, 1924, Vol. II, pp. 541-45, 548-51.

Consultations on Restriction of the Opium Trade
Foreign Relations, 1924, Vol. I, pp. 99-100, 584-88, 590-91, 684-85.

United States Recognition of Change in Persian Dynasty
Foreign Relations, 1925, Vol. II, pp. 678-82.

Treaty Regulating Commercial Relations between the United States and Persia
8 *Bevans* 1263.

Iran Protests American Press Treatment and Withdraws Representatives

Foreign Relations, 1936, Vol. III, pp. 350-55, 358, 361, 363-64, 367-75.

Chapter 2
THE IMPACT OF WORLD WAR II
[pp. 75-144]

United States Attitude toward the Tripartite Agreement between Great Britain, the Soviet Union, and Iran

Foreign Relations, 1941, Vol. III, pp. 406-7, 418-22, 446-47; 1942, Vol. IV, pp. 268-69, 273-75.

United States Concern over Iranian Food Shortages

Foreign Relations, 1942, Vol. IV, pp. 120-23, 155-57.

*Hull to JCS, 11/19/42. U.S. Archives, JCS File 218.

United States Extension of Lend-Lease Aid to Iran

Foreign Relations, 1942, Vol. IV, pp. 289-90, 295, 297-98.

Wartime Politics

Foreign Relations, 1943, Vol. IV, pp. 331-36, 338-43, 351-60, 377-79, 386-88, 408-10, 426-27.

United States Wartime Missions to Iran

Foreign Relations, 1942, Vol. IV, pp. 232-33, 242-43, 258-59; 1943, Vol. IV, pp. 517-23, 532-33, 551, 556; 1944, Vol. V, pp. 397-99, 402-3, 407-8, 434.

*OSS Report on Millspaugh. U.S. Archives, OSS File 59, R&A Report No. 2597; also UPA's *OSS/State Department Intelligence and Research Reports, The Middle East.*

Foreign Relations, 1945, Vol. VIII, pp. 538-39.

U.S.-Iranian Gendarmerie Agreement. 8 *Bevans* 1285.

United States Wartime Presence in Iran
Stationing of United States Noncombat Troops in Iran

Foreign Relations, 1942, Vol. IV, pp. 315-17; 1943, Vol. IV, pp. 456-57; 1944, Vol. V, pp. 372-73.

Iranian Charges concerning Misconduct of American Troops in Iran

Foreign Relations, 1943, Vol. IV, pp. 487-88, 490-91, 496-500.

United States Concern with Internal Communist Movement in Iran

*CIA Report on Tudeh Party. CIA Office of Reports and Estimates; also
Declas. Docs. (79) 12A.

Aid Discussions during the Shah's Visit to the United States

Foreign Relations, 1949, Vol. VI, pp. 569-74, 585-88.

Truman-Shah Joint Statement. *Truman Papers,* 1949, pp. 590-92.

**Mutual Defense Assistance Agreement between the
United States and Iran**

1 *UST* 420.

State Department Announcement of Point Four Project in Iran

Department of State Bulletin, 10/30/50, p. 703.

CHAPTER 4

THE NATIONALIST GROUNDSWELL
[PP. 213-63]

The Anglo-Iranian Oil Dispute

State Department Statement; Aide-Memoire from U.S. Ambassador;
Harriman Observations; and Truman-Churchill Settlement Proposal. *Foreign Policy,* 1950-1955, Vol. II, pp. 2261-70.

Truman-Mossadegh Exchange. *Truman Papers,* 1951, pp. 381-83.

*JCS Memo to Secretary of Defense. U.S. Archives, JCS File 218; also
UPA's *Records of the JCS, Part 2, The Middle East.*

*CIA Estimate of the Crisis. Harry S Truman Library, Papers of Harry
S Truman, President's Secretary's File; also *Declas. Docs.* (77) 271A.

State Department on Purchase of Iranian Oil. *Department of State
Bulletin,* 12/15/52, p. 946.

Mossadegh-Eisenhower Exchange, January 1953. *Department of State
Bulletin,* 7/20/53, pp. 76-77.

Mossadegh-Eisenhower Exchange, May-June 1953. *Eisenhower Papers,*
1953, pp. 482-86.

Eisenhower-Shah Exchange, August 1954. *Eisenhower Papers,* 1954,
pp. 688-89.

Military Relations in the Early 1950s

*JCS Memo for Secretary of Defense on ARMISH. U.S. Archives, JCS
File 218; also UPA's *Records of the JCS, Part 2, The Middle East.*

*JCS Memo for Secretary of Defense on MAAG. U.S. Archives, JCS File
218; also UPA's *Records of the JCS, Part 2, The Middle East.*

*JCS Memo for Secretary of Defense on Suspension of Military Assistance to Iran. U.S. Archives, JCS File 218; also UPA's *Records of the JCS, Part 2, The Middle East.*

*JCS Report on Military Courses of Action regarding Iran. U.S. Archives, JCS File 218; also UPA's *Records of the JCS, Part 2, The Middle East.*

American Technical and Economic Aid

Announcement of Point Four Expansion. *Department of State Bulletin*, 2/11/52, pp. 217-18.

Point Four Agreement Concluded. *Department of State Bulletin*, 4/28/52, pp. 533-4.

Point Four Aid for Iranian Land Distribution. *Department of State Bulletin*, 10/6/52, pp. 535-37.

The Downfall and Return of the Shah

Dulles Statement on Communists in Iran. *Department of State Bulletin*, 8/10/53, p. 178.

Henderson Conveyance of Eisenhower Congratulations to Shah and Announcement of FOA Aid to Iran; Henderson-Zahedi Exchange. *Department of State Bulletin*, 9/14/53, pp. 349-50.

Zahedi-Eisenhower Exchange. *Eisenhower Papers*, 1953, pp. 579-81.

Agreement Extending U.S. Relief Supplies to Iran. 4 *UST* 2809.

Dulles Statement upon Receiving New Iranian Ambassador. *Department of State Bulletin*, 11/2/53, p. 590.

*Excerpt from Eisenhower Speech. Dwight D. Eisenhower Library, Papers as President of the U.S., 1953-61, International File, Box 19; also *Declas. Docs.* (78) 313D.

Byroade, "The Present Situation in Iran." *Department of State Bulletin*, 12/28/53, pp. 894-96.

CHAPTER 5
CONSOLIDATING THE RELATIONSHIP
[PP. 264-312]

Growing United States Strategic Interests in Iran

*NSC Report on U.S. Policy toward Iran. U.S. Archives, National Security Council File 115; also UPA's *Documents of the NSC, 1947-1977.*

*JCS Memo for Secretary of Defense on the MDA Program. U.S. Archives, JCS File 218; also *Declas. Docs.* (78) 365A.

*JCS Memo on Military Objectives for Iran. U.S. Archives, JCS File 401/105.

*ARMISH Chief Report on Meeting the Shah. U.S. Archives, JCS File 218.

*State Department OIR Report on Iranian Foreign Policy. U.S. Archives, OIR File 59, Report No. 7038; also UPA's *OSS/State Department Intelligence and Research Reports, Middle East Supplement.*

Economic and Diplomatic Relations Solidify as United States Economic and Technical Assistance Continues

Announcement of FOA Loans to Iran. *Department of State Bulletin,* 11/54, p. 776.

Description of FOA Loan to Iran. *Department of State Bulletin,* 4/25/55, p. 696.

Treaty of Amity, Economic Relations, and Consular Rights. 8 *UST* 899.

Agreement on Cooperation for Civil Uses of Atomic Energy. 10 *UST* 733.

Conclusions of House Foreign Operations Subcommittee. *Congressional Record,* Vol. 103, pp. 1032-33.

Reece Dissent from House Subcommittee Conclusions. *Congressional Record,* Vol. 103, pp. 1205-6.

GAO Examination of U.S. Aid to Iran. Printed General Accounting Office Report, June 1961.

CENTO and the Eisenhower Doctrine

Communiqué on Richards Mission. *Foreign Policy,* 1957, pp. 838-39.

Multilateral Declaration Respecting the Baghdad Pact, 1958. 9 *UST* 1077.

Agreement on Defense Cooperation, 1959. 10 *UST* 314.

Documents Pertaining to Eisenhower Visit to Iran. *Eisenhower Papers,* 1959, pp. 849-55.

Eisenhower Statement on Soviet Threat to Iranian Security. *Foreign Policy,* 1959, pp. 1065-66.

Chapter 6
RECONSIDERATION AND REAFFIRMATION
[pp. 313-74]

Rethinking Support of the Shah

State Department Denial of Policy Change. *Department of State Bulletin,* 2/8/60, p. 201.

*State Department Report on Internal Politics in Iran. John F. Kennedy Library, National Security File (Iran); also *Declas. Docs.* (78) 80D.

*State Department Report on Iranian Middle Classes. Report of John Bowling, Director of Greek, Turkish, and Iranian Affairs (3/20/61); also *Declas. Docs.* (78) 81A.

*State Department Report on Discussion with Ambassador Zahedi. *Declas. Docs.* (78) 81B.

*CIA Report on Iran's Foreign Relations. CIA National Intelligence Estimate; also *Declas. Docs.* (78) 15B.

Kennedy-Shah Joint Statement. *Kennedy Papers*, 1962, p. 327.

The United States Stresses Economic Development over Military Build-up

Agricultural Commodities Agreement. 11 *UST* 1944.

Agreement Establishing Peace Corps in Iran. 22 *UST* 434.

*Holmes Message on Bowles's Visit to Iran. John F. Kennedy Library, President's Office File, Staff Memoranda, Chester Bowles, Box 62; also *Declas. Docs.* (Retro.) 618A.

McNamara Testimony to Senate Subcommittee. *Foreign Policy*, 1964, pp. 680-81.

The White Revolution: United States Response and Concerns

*Holmes Message to Secretary of State on U.S. Options. John F. Kennedy Library, National Security File (NSC), NSAM 228, Box 340; also *Declas. Docs.* (77) 62B.

*NSC Report on U.S. Strategy regarding White Revolution. John F. Kennedy Library, National Security File (NSC), Box 340; also *Declas. Docs.* (76) 43A.

Mutual Congratulations on Iranian Economic Progress

Documents Pertaining to Johnson-Shah Meeting. *Department of State Bulletin*, 9/18/67, pp. 358-62.

Closing Successful AID Program to Iran. *Department of State Bulletin*, 12/18/67, pp. 825-27.

Documents on Nixon-Shah Meeting. *Department of State Bulletin*, 11/10/69, pp. 399-400.

Excerpt on U.S. Foreign Policy. *U.S. Foreign Policy, 1969-70: A Report of the Secretary of State*, 1971.

CHAPTER 7

HIGH TIDE

[PP. 375-434]

Narcotics Restriction

Nixon-Shah Communiqué, 1972. *Nixon Papers*, 1972, pp. 651-652.

*State Department OIR Report on Attempts to Control Opium in Iran. U.S. Archives, OSS File 59, OIR Report No. 5343; also UPA's *OSS/ State Department Intelligence and Research Reports, Middle East Supplement.*

Economic, Technical, and Military Ties Intensified

Remote Sensing Agreement. 26 *UST* 2936.

Communiqué Announcing Formation of U.S.-Iran Joint Commission. *Department of State Bulletin*, 11/25/74, pp. 729-30.

Kissinger-Ansary Remarks at 1975 Meeting of U.S.-Iran Joint Commission. *Department of State Bulletin*, 3/31/75, pp. 402-4.

Technical Cooperation Agreement. 27 *UST* 975.

Memorandum of Understanding on U.S. Assistance for Civil Emergency Preparedness. 26 *UST* 3031.

Ansary Statement and Joint Communiqué of U.S.-Iranian Joint Commission. *Department of State Bulletin*, 9/6/76, pp. 307-16.

Carte Blanche on Arms Sales

State Department (Sisco) Statement before House Subcommittee. *Department of State Bulletin*, 7/14/75, p. 76

Kissinger Statement at U.S.-Iran Joint Committee. *Department of State Bulletin*, 9/6/76, pp. 305-7.

State Department (Habib) Testimony before House Subcommittee. *Department of State Bulletin*, 10/11/76, pp. 447-48.

Department of Defense Chronology on Sales of F-14s to Iran. *Multinational Corporations and U.S. Foreign Policy: Gruman Sale of F-14s to Iran*, Hearings before Senate Subcommittee on Multinational Corporations, 9/10/76, pp. 80-81.

Senate Report on U.S. Arms Sales to Iran. *U.S. Military Sales to Iran*, a Staff Report to the Senate Subcommittee on Foreign Assistance, July 1976.

Iran in OPEC

Kissinger-Ansary News Conference. *Department of State Bulletin*, 11/25/74, pp. 726-29.

Kissinger-Shah News Conference. *Department of State Bulletin*, 3/10/75, pp. 293-95.

Tremors on the Human Rights Issue

State Department (Atherton) Testimony before House Subcommittee. *Department of State Bulletin*, 10/4/76, pp. 433-36.

State Department Report to Congress on Human Rights in Iran. *Human Rights and U.S. Policy: Argentina, Haiti, Indonesia, Iran, Peru, and the Philippines*, a Report to the House Committee on International Relations by the Department of State, 12/31/76, pp. 18-22.

Chapter 8
PRELUDE TO REVOLUTION
[PP. 435-64]

Close Cooperation Continues

Agreement on Exchange of Atomic Energy Information. 29 *UST* 1053.

State Department Testimony on AWACS Sales to Iran. *Sale of Airborne Warning and Control System (AWACS) Aircraft to Iran*, Hearings before the House Subcommittee on International Security, 7/29/77, pp. 5-7.

Statement at Carter-Shah Meeting. *Department of State Bulletin*, 12/26/77, pp. 907-8.

Communiqué of the U.S.-Iran Joint Commission. *Department of State Bulletin*, 4/78, pp. 48-49.

Human Rights to the Fore

State Department (Naas) Testimony before House Subcommittee. *Department of State Bulletin*, 12/19/77, pp. 894-96.

State Department Report on Human Rights in Iran. *Country Reports on Human Rights Practices*, a Report to the House Committee on International Relations, 2/3/78, pp. 351-60.

The United States Reacts to Iranian Unrest

Presidential News Conference. *Department of State Bulletin*, 11/78, p. 12.

Secretary of State Vance's News Conference. *Department of State Bulletin*, 12/78, p. 18.

Presidential Interview with Bill Moyers. *Department of State Bulletin*, 12/78, p. 15.

Presidential Question-and-Answer Session. *Carter Papers*, 1978, Vol. II, pp. 2171-73.

Presidential News Conference. *Carter Papers*, 1978, Vol. II, p. 2226.

CHAPTER 9
THE SHAH FALLS: IRAN CONFRONTS AMERICA
[PP. 465-511]

The United States Searches for a *Modus Vivendi*

State Department Statement on Situation in Iran (Saunders). *Department of State Bulletin*, 2/79, pp. 45-48.

Official Press Releases. *Department of State Bulletin*, 2/79, pp. 3, 7-8; and *Weekly Compilation: Carter*, 2/27/79, pp. 351-52.

Excerpt from Carter Address at Georgia Tech. *Department of State Bulletin*, 3/79, pp. 21-22.

Embassy Seizure and Hostage Crisis

White House Statement, 11/9/79. *Weekly Compilation: Carter*, 11/9/79, pp. 2101-2.

Executive Order Freezing Iranian Assets. 44 *Federal Register* 65729, November 14, 1979.

Presidential News Conference on Iran. Department of State, Bureau of Public Affairs, Current Policy Release No. 115, 1979.

McHenry Statement to the U.N. Department of State, Bureau of Public Affairs, Current Policy Release No. 116, 1979.

State Department Announcement of U.S. Action to World Court. Department of State, Bureau of Public Affairs, Selected Documents No. 114, 1979.

Civiletti Oral Argument to World Court. Department of State, Bureau of Public Affairs, Current Policy Release No. 118, 1979.

White House Congressional Briefing. *Weekly Compilation: Carter*, 1/8/80, pp. 39-43.

McHenry Resolution Seeking U.N. Sanctions and Reproval of Soviet Veto. Department of State, Bureau of Public Affairs, Current Policy Release No. 126, 1980.

State Department Statement on U.S. Measures to Isolate Iran. Department of State, Bureau of Public Affairs, Current Policy Release No. 179, 1980.

Carter Message to Congress on U.S. Sanctions. *Weekly Compilation: Carter*, 4/17/80, pp. 716-17.

Carter Statement to Nation on Rescue Attempt. Department of State, Bureau of Public Affairs, Current Policy Release No. 170, 1980.

Carter Letter to Congressional Leaders on Rescue Attempt. *Weekly Compilation: Carter*, 4/26/80, pp. 777-79.

Index